Introduction to Contemporary Social Theory

In this comprehensive, stylish and accessible introduction to contemporary social theory, Anthony Elliott and Charles Lemert examine the major theoretical traditions from the Frankfurt School to globalization and beyond. The book's wide range sets new standards for introductory textbooks – social theorists discussed include Theodor Adorno, Herbert Marcuse, Michel Foucault, Jacques Lacan, Jacques Derrida, Anthony Giddens, Pierre Bourdieu, Julia Kristeva, Jürgen Habermas, Judith Butler, Slavoj Žižek, Manuel Castells, Ulrich Beck, Zygmunt Bauman, Giorgio Agamben and Manuel DeLanda.

Extensively developed to take into account significant recent developments in American social theory, the book offers chapters on American pragmatism, structural functionalism, ethnomethodology, black feminist thought and world-systems theory. American traditions of social theory are brought powerfully to life in treatments of intellectuals ranging from Charles Sanders Peirce and William James to Robert K. Merton, David Riesman to Alvin Gouldner, and Patricia Hill Collins to Charles Tilly and Immanuel Wallerstein.

Introduction to Contemporary Social Theory combines lively exposition and clarity with reflective social critique and original insights, and is a superb textbook with which to navigate the twists and turns of contemporary social theory as taught in the disciplines of sociology, politics, history, cultural studies and many more.

Anthony Elliott is Director of the Hawke Research Institute, where he is Research Professor of Sociology at the University of South Australia. His recent books include *Mobile Lives* (2010, with John Urry), *On Society* (2012, with Bryan Turner), *Concepts of the Self* (2013) and *Reinvention* (2013).

Charles Lemert is University Professor and Andrus Professor of Social Theory Emeritus, Wesleyan University; and Senior Fellow, Center for Comparative Research, Yale University. His recent books include *Why Niebuhr Matters* (2013), *Social Theory: The Multicultural, Global, and Classical Readings* (ed., 2013, fifth edition), *Uncertain Worlds: World-Systems Analysis in Changing Times* (with Immanuel Wallerstein and Carlos Aguirre Rojas, 2013).

Once again, Elliott and Lemert have written an exceedingly intelligent, generously interdisciplinary, and politically relevant social theory textbook. From its first story to its last question for further study, *Introduction to Contemporary Social Theory* is a lucid invitation to the critical study of social theory from two of the field's most eloquent and distinguished scholars.

Avery Gordon, Professor of Sociology at the University of California, Santa Barbara

Introduction to Contemporary Social Theory

Anthony Elliott and Charles Lemert

Routledge
Taylor & Francis Group

NEW YORK AND LONDON

First published 2014
by Routledge
711 Third Avenue, New York, NY 10017

And by Routledge
2 Park Square, Milton Park, Abingdon, Oxon OX14 4RN

Routledge is an imprint of the Taylor & Francis Group, an informa business

British Library Cataloguing in Publication Data
A catalogue record for this book is available from the British Library

Library of Congress Cataloging in Publication Data
A catalog record for this book has been requested

ISBN: 978–0–415–52572–5 (hbk)
ISBN: 978–0–415–52573–2 (pbk)
ISBN: 978–0–203–10186–5 (ebk)

Typeset in Scala Sans
by RefineCatch Limited, Bungay, Suffolk

MIX
Paper from
responsible sources
FSC
www.fsc.org   FSC® C013056

Printed and bound in Great Britain by
TJ International Ltd, Padstow, Cornwall

For Niamh
and Julian and Caroline Lemert

Contents

Preface and Acknowledgments

There are few areas of academic inquiry as diverse, multidisciplinary and politically important as social theory. In writing this book, we have sought to develop a readable, comprehensive and critical introduction to the field of contemporary social theory. This, in itself, might be considered something of a tall order – given that social theory now manages to scoop up everything from self-identity, sexuality and signifiers to gender, and governance. In seeking to provide a reasonably comprehensive account of contemporary social theory, we have tried to cover most of the major traditions of thought – from the Frankfurt School to postmodernism, from structuralism to post-feminism – along with overviews of many recent cutting edge developments. As such, the book includes detailed discussions of globalization and the global electronic economy, postmodernism, the rise of networks, the impacts of climate change – amongst other new topics of key importance.

At the outset, this is perhaps the place to briefly comment on recent developments in social theory which have influenced the cast of this book. Social theory emerged in the context of the European Enlightenment, and has for the most part remained a largely continental affair in its traffic with fundamental questions about the social dynamics of our lives and of our lives in the age of modernity. If contemporary social theory represents, among other things, a kind of academic shorthand for the intellectual contributions of, among others, Michel Foucault, Jacques Lacan, Jacques Derrida, Julia Kristeva, Jean Baudrillard and Luce Irigaray, this says something about not only the richness, diversity and esotericism of social theory itself, but also the ambitious critique it has developed of our current ways of life. Contemporary social theory, as we argue throughout this book, is a kind of doubled enterprise: a resourceful, high-powered and interdisciplinary project of the social sciences and humanities on the one hand, and an urgent critique of ideological thought and the discourses of reason, freedom, truth, subjectivity, culture and politics on the other. At its best – and our argument is that the best is to be found in the writings of Charles Sanders Pierce, Herbert Marcuse, Jürgen Habermas, Talcott Parsons, Pierre Bourdieu, Anthony Giddens, Judith Butler, Zygmunt Bauman, Immanuel Wallerstein, Giorgio Agamben, Patricia Hill Collins and Donna Haraway, among many others – contemporary social theory provides a sophisticated, scintillating critique of the arrogance of power as well as engaging the future of progressive politics.

We should like to thank various people and institutions that have assisted in the preparation of, or otherwise influenced, this book. Gerhard Boomgaarden at Routledge has played a critical role in shaping this book and we are grateful for the many ways in which he has assisted in its preparation. It was his idea to build upon an earlier edition of this book written by Anthony Elliott, and for Elliott to work (once again) with Charles Lemert for an edition that included alongside the European theorists representatives of the long and strong American expressions of social theory. This work represents the latest of a good many collaborations going back, now, over a good decade of growing common interests and friendship that, the oddity of our age differences aside, seems more as if it has always been there.

Much of the writing and preparation of the book was undertaken at the Hawke Research Institute at the University of South Australia. Eric Hsu, project manager of the second edition, assisted us throughout with admirable efficiency. We are very grateful for his labours and dedication. We should also like to thank Adam Henderson and Dan Torode for their splendidly scrupulous research and editing of the manuscript. Also at the Hawke we would like to thank: Jennifer Rutherford, David Radford, Daniel Chaffee, Maureen Cotton, Phoebe Smith and Lynette Copus. Finally, at Routledge, I would like to thank Emily Briggs. For better or worse, Charles Lemert did all his writing pretty much on his own in New Haven, where he enjoyed the stimulation of Yale students and faculty nearly as much as the long stretches of solitude that led to his rereading and meditation on American thinkers he has known, one way or another, over his adult life.

Charles, personally, wishes to acknowledge the basic fact of most acknowledgments – that of thanking those too numerous to mention who contributed at a remove. In truth we know very well who they are while failing to identify them in favor of long sentimental comments on the minimal contributions (if that) of life partners and children. He therefore adds the following, in the singular first person: Writing the chapters on

American social theory brought back my debt to Talcott Parsons, my first teacher in social theory. Parsons's course at Harvard on American Social Structure was easily the best, clearest, and most brilliant course I ever took, setting a standard to which I have since aspired without success. Chuck Tilly, a tireless worker, was also a very thoughtful and generous man. He was kind to me when others were not and when he was not required to say a word. Al Gouldner was a notoriously difficult person but to me he was in his way tender-hearted, as to many others in what he called the Theory and Society community of then younger people. Jeff Alexander, more than anyone else, was largely responsible for bringing me back into the field after years of divorce, change, and foolishness as an administrator had all but ruined my scholarly prospects. Immanuel Wallerstein remains the model of who I would like to be when and if I grow up. Long after he must, Immanuel is at the desk, when not in flight, plowing ahead as he puts it. Still, he finds time for social occasions at which he is funnily sly and openhearted. My only regret in the whole thing is that I discovered Charles Sanders Peirce so late in life. Had I read him earlier I would have saved a lot of time at the risk of having nothing to say.

Finally, Anthony would like to thank Nicola Geraghty, again, for her support and for the many ways in which she has contributed to the book. He also thanks Caoimhe and Oscar Elliott. The book is dedicated to Niamh Elliott, the newest budding social theorist of the Elliott family, and proof (if it were needed) that the child's instinctive curiosity (as Freud argued) is disabling to the established adult world and thus a suggestive model for critical social theory. Charles, in turn, offers a dedication to Julian and Caroline Lemert, who have no idea that I write books like this, or even what they mean. Yet, they are lovely children like Niamh. Together, they and their global peers are the hope of the world we and our peers in the field try to figure out.

Anthony Elliott, Adelaide
Charles Lemert, New Haven

chapter 1

The Textures of Society

Natalie is a 26-year-old fashion designer living and working in London. Her design studio is located at Notting Hill Gate, where she spends part of her working week; for the rest of the week, she is regularly in Paris – attending to the business details of her fledgling fashion company. The routine air travel between London and Paris is something that now seems 'normal' to Natalie, after four years of flitting between cities. But the travel she undertakes to see her boyfriend Ross, who relocated to Finland last year, is more difficult for her to schedule. It is not the travel itself she finds difficult; rather it is finding the time to travel. Time is a resource that for Natalie is in short supply.

Natalie, a daughter of Taiwanese immigrants to America, grew up in Brooklyn – where her parents still live. Her father worked as a waiter, and her mother worked long hours in a dry-cleaning store. Natalie's life has been remarkably different to that of her parents – largely the result of her parents' efforts to get a good college education for their only daughter. She keeps in regular touch through phone calls; she has also recently purchased a computer for her parents, to 'keep close' through email. In communication as they are, Natalie misses direct contact with her parents, and often feels worried that she lives so far away from them. These anxieties have been tempered somewhat of late, however, as Natalie is planning a holiday to the US. In addition to seeing her parents, she has also scheduled to meet Ross in Brooklyn – to introduce him to her family.

What might Natalie's life have to tell us about the world today? What might her professional and private life reflect about the changing direction of society? To begin with, it seems evident that Natalie lives a life – like many throughout the expensive cities of the West – which requires ongoing communication and travel across large distances. Natalie's professional success, as well as her private life, depends upon the routine use of systems of transportation (motorways, rail, air) as well as new communication technologies. Yet if technological innovation lies at the core of how Natalie traverses the large distances she has to cover in terms of travel and communication, these social developments are less evident in the lives of her parents – who rarely ever leave Brooklyn. Still, Natalie's parents travel in a kind of 'virtual' way – making use of email communication. Equally significantly, they traverse the different cultures and social landscapes of which they are part, or to which their lives connect – Taiwanese, American, British.

If we seek to broaden out these points, we might say that Natalie's life reflects the dynamic changes occurring within social, cultural and economic life today, and on a global scale. Think, for example, of how her use of new information technologies reflects the social changes now affecting how people and places interweave. There are today more than two and a half billion users of the Internet worldwide, to which Natalie's parents are merely some of the latest users. Or think about Natalie's carbon footprint across the globe, as she routinely travels between the UK and Europe, as well as across the Atlantic oceans. There are today more than nine hundred million international air flights undertaken each year, a figure predicted to pass one billion in the near future. If these statistics are suggestive of the increasingly complex 'border crossings' (at once geopolitical, communicational and virtual) lived by young women like Natalie in the expensive cities of the West, there are also other human migrations that predominate in our own era of globalization which receive less media attention, but which most certainly disturb. These are not the kinds of travel either Natalie or her parents undertake, but are certainly of fundamental significance to the textures of world society today. It has been estimated by Robert Neuwirth, for example, that 70 million people each year leave rural villages for the promises of distant cities. These promises remain, for most, forever out of reach; living without the rights of place or citizenship, there are many tens of millions of refugees and asylum-seekers today roaming the globe, experiencing the social humiliation and bodily degradation that the Italian social theorist Giorgio Agamben calls 'bare life.' The notion of bare life might well be apt to describe the plight of illegal immigrant workers scrambling to earn a few dollars or displaced peoples living on the margins, yet it might equally serve to capture the political mood of a world in which three billion of its inhabitants receive the same total income as the richest three hundred individuals.

To raise the question of the 'textures' of society is thus to consider social trends that are intensely worrying on the one hand, as well as those of the most extraordinary potential on the other. However much Natalie might be aware of the global realities of bare life – of peoples living on the margins; of peoples dispossessed, displaced and humiliated – it seems unlikely that she could end up in any such situation herself. For the society to which she belongs is well insulated from too great an awareness of the shocking trends of enforced human migrations in these early years of the twenty-first century. The society to which she belongs, we might suppose, is that of the West – with its mesmerizing information networks, its dazzling digital technologies and its seductive consumer culture. But if we stop and pause for a moment, the question remains: to which society does Natalie actually belong? She was raised in the USA. Yet her family immigrated to America from Taiwan when she an infant. She now lives in London, but works regularly in Paris. And her boyfriend is based in Helsinki. To which society does she belong?

What is society?

One answer to the question 'to which society does Natalie belong?' derives from common-sense: she belongs where she lives, her homeland, her nation. In social theory as in everyday life, this answer emphasizes that social life must be constructed within the province of the nation and its assured rights of belonging – the entitlements and duties of citizenship. On this view, Natalie is an American citizen, one who now lives and works in the UK, and who holds a permanent British visa. Talk about the connections between nations and societies in the social sciences tends to be fairly general, and yet it remains the case that nations have been regarded as providing societal homes for a remarkably long historical period. Nations, of course, have many different powers and forms at any given historical time, but one reason why they might no longer provide a good enough societal home in our age of intensive globalization is that people are *on the move* as never before. Just think of Natalie's existence. As noted, she grew up in Brooklyn and now lives in the UK. But she spends part of every week in France, and many weekends in Finland. In which national homeland that we call 'society' does she *belong*? Still further, we might also wonder, how does her multidimensional experience of nations and the world actually affect both her experience and conception of society?

Perhaps a better answer to the question then of 'to which society does Natalie belong?' is that of the *globe*. Globalization is an answer to this question when, like Natalie, we universalize the daily operations of our lives, compressing the dimensions of time and space through new technological innovations in such fields as travel and communications. On this view, Natalie emerges as a 'global citizen,' one with a cosmopolitan appreciation of the complexities of living in an age of transnationalism, and thus becomes defined as *one at home* wherever she happens to find herself. A citizen, in other words, of *global society*. But whether it is meaningful to speak of global society in the same manner in which we might speak of national society is a contentious issue – as we will see in the discussion of globalization in Chapter 15. For whilst there is a very specific sense in which we might say that Natalie is a citizen of America or the UK, in what sense is she actually a citizen of the globe? To define society in purely national terms is to circumscribe its operations in terms of, say, territories, boundaries and geopolitical spaces. To define society beyond the terrain of the nation seems to open the textures of human belonging and association in ways which appear to have no limit, pushing the boundaries of social and political understanding to the edge. In one sense, this might be described as a core and intractable problem of our time – a problem that preoccupies social theorists, but one that also arises at the center of public political debate today.

These considerations bring us to the heart of a core issue in contemporary social theory – namely, the nature of society. There is, to date, no single adequate definition of society in social theory – and indeed one objective of this book is to trace the various definitions of society that have emerged in social theory during the course of the twentieth century and into the early 2000s. To indicate the range of meanings attached to the notion of society that we will encounter throughout this book, consider the following random list of definitions currently emanating in social theory:

1 the institutionalization of unequal power relations and domination;
2 the conjuncture of reason and repression;

3   the structuring of social institutions and social interactions;
4   the process whereby linguistic structures are converted to social regulation;
5   the social forms in which signifiers and signifieds are interwoven;
6   forms of thought structured by social differences;
7   ideas and ideologies governed by patriarchy, promoting unequal relations between the sexes;
8   the gendered process of encoding sexual signs and human bodies in social life;
9   systematically distorted communication;
10 reflexively orientated social practices;
11 liquidity;
12 the networks or flows in which self-reflective social actors organize their daily activities;
13 the globalization of the social, involving an interweaving of global and local happenings.

There are a number of points that might be noted about this list of definitions. For one thing, some of these definitions view society positively, others negatively, and some are clearly ambiguous. The more positive of these definitions see society as an indispensable medium for the production of social relations, emphasizing the benefits of interpersonal relationships and the potential gains from intercultural communication. In this sense, society is viewed in a largely technical way, as a process that facilitates not only the constitution of identity and elaboration of forms of thought, but also the reproduction across time and across space of social interactions (think, for example, of family life across generations) and of social institutions (think, for example, of schools, hospitals or prisons). Some of these definitions, however, view society pejoratively – as the inculcation of false beliefs or ideology – and thus emphasize the role of economic and political forces in various forms of human exploitation.

Another point is that this list of definitions carries a range of implications for understanding the world in which we live: not just in academic terms but for everyday life too. Some formulations identify profoundly transformative processes, such that the very existence of a thing known as 'society' appears as either an illusion or an unnecessary hangover from classical social theory. This is a fertile line of social inquiry which emerges out of structuralist social theory, in which society is recast as a language or linguistic process, and runs through in our own time to postmodernism and other forms of critical social thought. A number of conceptual approaches in this respect, from post-structuralism and postmodernism to globalization studies, suggest that the social sciences must radically rethink their subject matter – as a world of 'bounded' societies no longer exists, if indeed it ever once did. Other traditions of thought are much more cautious. Some argue that the so-called 'openness' of the social has been exaggerated: society, according to some critics, is alive and well, and it is only in the writings of obscure social theorists (particularly the French) that the notion recedes into the shadows.

Society and social theory

As it happens, Natalie often thinks about 'society' – or, at least, those societies through which she regularly passes and moves. She has an especially powerful sense of the breadth and speed of social change currently sweeping the globe. She believes, for example, that no single force – neither governments nor corporations – is in control of the global economy. She thinks the idea that the nation-state can manage capitalism has been exposed as fatally flawed. Consequently, she is concerned that the welfare state – an institution she has grown to admire whilst living in the UK, but which was pretty much unknown to her whilst growing up in America – will not be able to meet the demands placed upon it by citizens, especially the growing numbers of elderly people. But there are other anxieties too, perhaps deeper ones, that Natalie has about the future of society. She feels that the entire globe is in a 'state of emergency.' There are tremendous new risks; terrorism, and particularly the threat of high technology nuclear terror, convinces Natalie that the world in which she grew up is gone, and gone for good. Other high risks of today's world that she mentions include global warming and environmental destruction: she worries, for example, about her own carbon footprint and its consequences for the world of tomorrow. And yet she still identifies other social trends as more promising for her future, and the future of the next generation. Her life today she describes as a constantly shifting terrain of exciting experiences. As she moves between cities and countries, her professional and personal life brings her into regular contact with people who think differently, and live quite different lives, from her. She embraces this social complexity, and welcomes moves towards increased cultural diversity and cosmopolitan living.

Natalie's instinctive sense that the world in which she lives is changing fast, mirrors contemporary intellectual assessments of the human condition in the present age. What the 'deep drivers' of society are, and whether they are in point of fact new, are the focus of intense controversy in social theory. I discuss many of the most significant assessments of society – of the complex ways in which we now live – throughout this book. Some of these social theories, as we will see, seek to develop a 'structural method' which holds that social structures – such as the economy or bureaucracy – operate in ways invisible to the naked eye; such a method has been extended by various contemporary analysts of society to encompass, among others, social processes, organizational life, institutional transformations and global networks. Other social theorists have developed more culturalist perspectives – concerned with, among other topics, the body, desire, the unconscious, sexuality and gender – to comprehend the novel global circumstances in which we now find ourselves.

New times demand fresh thinking. Tracing the rise of contemporary social theory from the 1920s to the present day, this book explores how ground-breaking theoretical and sociological concerns have brought topics like selfhood, power, domination, sexuality and gender to the forefront of intellectual and public political debate over recent years. In reviewing developments in social theory, my aim is to introduce readers to some of the most challenging perspectives, and surprising innovations, on the multidimensional aspects of contemporary social processes. Social theorists of a wide variety of perspectives agree – even if they agree on little else – that we live in new worlds of social and cultural organization. To capture the spirit of these new times, a vast array of terms and terminology has been developed. What must urgently be engaged with, according to Theodor Adorno, are the institutional transformations associated with 'the totally administered society,' whereas for Herbert Marcuse the core of our social pathologies stems from 'surplus repression.' Jürgen Habermas speaks by contrast of 'systematically distorted communication' warping contemporary societies, and Axel Honneth widens this focus on communication to encompass problems of recognition and disrespect. If communication and culture brook large in some recent analyses, then structuralist, poststructuralist and deconstructive theories focus attention on the relation between language and social realities in startling new ways. The French semiologist Ferdinand de Saussure's proclamation that we must analyze 'the life of signs in society' has served to establish signifiers, sexualities and simulations as legitimate objects of study in contemporary social theory. The pioneering works of Roland Barthes, Jacques Lacan, Michel Foucault, Louis Althusser, and Jacques Derrida on the intricate entwinement of signs and society call attention to the fundamental importance of languages, discourses and codes in everyday life.

Some of the new social theories, by contrast, seek to anchor their preoccupations in less cultural and more institutional concerns. Anthony Giddens speaks of the current age as one of 'reflexive modernization.' Ulrich Beck writes of 'risk society.' Zygmunt Bauman of 'liquid modernity.' Manual Castells of 'the network society.' Fredric Jameson of 'late capitalism.' All of these social theories, in very different ways, attempt to account for changes in social conditions and institutional life associated with modernity. They represent powerful approaches for thinking about the rise of new information technologies and the current world economy, among others, in these early years of the twenty-first century. Then there are other, perhaps more familiar, attempts to theorize what is truly new today. The term 'globalization' has been social theory's most famed recent reply to the complexities of people's lives today. The adventures of the concept of globalization range all the way from the emergence of transnational financial economies to global satellite communications. Again, social theorists have invented new terms to capture, and indeed define, our new global times – just to mention a few that we will review in this book: 'global transformations' (David Held), 'borderless world' (Kenichi Ohmae) and 'glocalization' (Roland Robertson).

Coping with climate change: Anthony Giddens

Like Natalie, many people today worry about climate change. Some worry in largely abstract terms, feeling that global warming might one day, and probably only many years from now, impact negatively upon their lives. Others worry more about how their daily actions are contributing to the spread of high-carbon societies. Natalie is one such person who worries about the here-and-now of climate change. She is troubled by what she regards as the unthinking actions of people living high-carbon lifestyles. She acknowledges that she travels a great deal for work. But still she thinks that people, in their daily actions, can make a difference in trying to reverse climate change.

The British social theorist, Anthony Giddens, whose work we will examine in subsequent chapters, has studied climate change with an eye firmly on the concerns and troubles of everyday life. He tackles head-on, for example, the thorny topic of SUVs and asks bluntly: 'Why does anyone, anyone at all, for even a single day longer, continue to drive an SUV?' If you happen to drive such a gas guzzler, you needn't feel victimized; Giddens describes SUVs as a metaphor for life in the fast, polished cities of the West. 'We are all,' he writes, 'SUV drivers.' This would be difficult news for Natalie to accept, but it is worth considering further what Giddens means in this connection.

Giddens argues that, at present, 'we have no politics of climate change.' Climate change for Giddens suggests that the world urgently needs political innovations, beyond the confines of orthodox politics, and ones capable of addressing the global risks of greenhouse gas emissions. 'We must create,' writes Giddens, 'a positive model of a low-carbon future.'

Blending the dangers of global warming with possibilities for new low-carbon technologies and utopian strands of cosmopolitan politics, Giddens emerges at various points in *The Politics of Climate Change* as a full-blooded optimist. Certainly, he isn't one to shy away from humor or irony in order to find better motivations for women and men to confront climate change in their daily lives. His vision is one emphasizing 'climate change positives.' As he says, Martin Luther King didn't stir people to action by proclaiming 'I have a nightmare!'

All political tracts on climate change are timely, but some are more timely than others. Whilst political analyses of climate change have taken different forms, the large bulk have emphasized that globally catastrophic processes are at work. From one angle, this is hardly surprising. As global temperatures in the twenty-first century are expected by the international scientific community to rise by four to seven degrees Celsius, rather than the previously predicted two to three, it is increasingly evident to many that we are fast approaching the end of the world as we know it.

In this powerful statement against doomsday thinking and catastrophism, Giddens's captivating study of climate change attempts to bring the debate squarely back to politics, not least with both concrete policy proposals and an energizing utopian vision. As Giddens advocates:

> Season policy with a dash of utopian thinking. Why? Because, however it happens, we are working our way towards a form of society that eventually will be quite different from the one in which we live today. We have to chance our arm.'
>
> (2009: 13)

The problem with trying to clarify, as well as classify, the dangers we face as a result of the warming of the earth's climate is that it is almost impossible not to lapse into abstract claims about the future. In *The Politics of Climate Change*, the author calls this 'Giddens's paradox.' The theorem of Giddens's paradox is stated thus:

> since the dangers posed by global warming aren't tangible, immediate or visible in the course of day-to-day life, however awesome

they appear, many will sit on their hands and do nothing of a concrete nature about them. Yet waiting until they become visible and acute before being stirred to serious action will, by definition, be too late.

And this, says Giddens, accounts for why people continue to drive SUVs: climate change is relegated to the back of the mind, as the future is discounted.

Giddens's work covers a remarkably wide spectrum of political issues stemming from climate change, which he treats with lucidity and learning, while all the time reflecting on the possibilities for a low-carbon future. From analysis of the world's fossil fuel resources and the peaking of oil to careful appraisal of the vast literature on climate change technologies, and from critical dissection of the pros and cons of carbon taxes and rationing to the geopolitics of global warming, Giddens brings a sociological sharpness and radical political edge to the climate change debate that has all too often been lacking from many recent critiques.

Giddens's progressive political sensibilities are especially evident when discussing the complex relations between climate change, global inequal-ities and energy security. He underscores that developing countries, and the poorest people who inhabit them, are especially vulnerable to climate change and that the world community should recognize a 'development imperative' for those living in extreme poverty. As he writes:

> The poorer nations have contributed only marginally to global warming; they must have the chance to develop, even if such a process raises emissions, for a period quite steeply. Development is imperative not simply for moral reasons. The consequences of climate change will worsen the enormous tensions that already derive from global inequalities, with implications for the world as a whole. Through technology transfer and other means, it should be possible for the developing countries to avoid a wholesale recapitu-lation of the path followed earlier by the industrial ones, but essen-tially a bargain between the more and less developed parts of the world has to be struck.
>
> (2009: 9)

Such is the academic and political interest in Giddens's ideas that *The Politics of Climate Change* has quickly become a major publishing event in its own right. The book has been endorsed by Bill Clinton, who describes it as a 'landmark study.' Martin Rees, president of the Royal Society, also rates the book highly. When the book was launched in London, various political heavyweights – from Tony Blair to the Norwegian Foreign Minister Jonas Gahr Store – praised Giddens's efforts to think about climate change anew.

From one angle, Giddens's *The Politics of Climate Change* is the mirror opposite of, say, Al Gore's *An Inconvenient Truth: The Planetary Emergency of Global Warming and What We Can Do About It* (2006). Whereas Gore talks of impending disasters, Giddens speaks of political and business revolutions. Whereas Gore seeks to scare people into action, Giddens wants to motivate them through emphasizing opportunities. For Giddens, the switch to low-carbon technologies opens the way to new business opportunities, ambitious public–private partnerships, Copenhagen-style transnational agreements and large-scale government planning.

What do you think of Giddens's contribution to the climate change debate? Does framing the argument within everyday life make a difference?

Key themes in contemporary social theory

Introduction to Contemporary Social Theory is organized around a number of key themes, to which we will turn at various points throughout the chapters that follow. The first key theme is that of *the relation between the individual and society*, or between human action and social structure. This is perhaps one of the most vexing issues in social theory. Most of the social theorists we examine throughout this book, from Theodor Adorno, Hebert Marcuse, Roland Barthes and Michel Foucault to a variety of contemporary authors including Anthony Giddens, Ulrich Beck, Julia Kristeva and Judith Butler, resolve this issue either by emphasizing the agency of individuals or the power of social structures – or, indeed, through a conceptual combination of these opposing orientations. Which side you take up in this debate depends on whether or not you favor the idea of individuals-first, or society-first, in understanding how practical social life comes about and is sustained throughout history. For those sympathetic to the idea that it is the agency of individuals that creates patterned social life, the systematic study of the reasons, motives, beliefs, emotions and desires of people is regarded as the most appropriate way in which to develop critical social analysis. Understanding what motivates individual human interests, and particularly the complex ways in which individual actions lead over time to collective social habits, is essential from this standpoint if social theory is to adequately engage with the society in which we live and the fundamental conflicts in values, ethics and morality of our own time. A response that focuses on social structure, by contrast, refuses the emphasis on the agency of individuals and instead concentrates on the institutions or organizations of modern societies as the key ingredient of social explanation. On this approach, it is mistaken to believe that people are the source of the common will. Rather, it is social institutions – from the impact of families, schools and prisons to capitalist organizations and large-scale bureaucracies – which ensure that individual practices conform to collective ones. One reason why society-first explanations of social life hold great appeal is that we live in a society where a great many people have to undertake activities that they would prefer not to do – such as holding down a dull job, tidying up one's bedroom when angry parents insist, or looking after a sick relative. Understanding how structures determine our individual actions – in the above cases, as a result of the powerful structures of economics, socialization or morality – is vital for grasping how power operates and how unequal social relations are sustained in modern societies.

Whenever one is pondering the dynamics of social relations, it is always useful to raise the question of the relation between agency and structure. Is society reproduced by the impersonal structures of politics, culture and the economy as these forces press down on the activities of individual agents, or is it rather the variety of choices and decisions that individuals make in their daily lives that makes up social structures? Throughout this book, we will consider various judgments of social theorists on this issue – from those critical of the individualistic bent of a soft subjectivism to those wary of a steel-hard objectivism. My own view is that both individuals-first and society-first standpoints have their uses, and much simply depends on the social practices under examination as to which is the most appropriate approach to adopt. If one wishes to understand an individual's response to a particular film, absorption in popular music, or love of a book, then it no doubt makes sense to consider those theoretical approaches – from psychoanalysis to post-feminism to postmodernism – that adopt strands of the individuals-first case. If one wishes to study, by contrast, political voting systems or the economic trading patterns of multinational companies then an emphasis on how structures shape activities is understandable enough. As will become evident throughout this book, this contrast as I have drawn it here is overstated – and certainly part of the current debate in social theory is that social theory cannot adequately engage with social life by focusing only on structures (which thereby liquidates individuals) or only on individual agents (which thereby downgrades the impact of social systems upon individuals). One way out of this impasse, as examined in Chapter 5 when we turn to the contributions of Anthony Giddens and Pierre Bourdieu, is to blend the two opposing approaches – examining how action is structured in everyday life, and how the structured features of action are thus reproduced in modern societies.

A second, related theme of the book is that of *the degree of consensus or conflict in modern societies*. This concerns the debate in social theory about the hold of values or norms which are dominant in society. Such values or norms, according to some social theorists, may effectively unify societies – such that individuals come to agree with one another in either open or tacit ways. From the import of early socialization in the family and at school through to the propagation of dominant values or norms in communications media, the idea is that the reproduction and legitimacy of the social order is sustained through such mechanisms for the transmission of unifying beliefs and values. To say that society is a successfully achieved unity is to say that we live in a world where people are effectively drawn into the bigger social forces surrounding them, such that individuals come to imbibe the expectations that others have of them and the norms that cultural life lays down for them. There is no need for students of society to assume, however, that such an internalization of the dominant values of society involves the full consciousness or understanding of human agents. After all, many people's experience of the world, especially today, is that of increasing social complexity, cultural diversity and political conflict. Accordingly, sensitivity to the diversity of society and the subtleties of culture is necessary to ensure that social theory does not over-simplify the mixed, ambiguous experience that individuals have of their own identities and of the wider social world.

In examining issues surrounding consensus and conflict in modern societies, we will explore various social theories throughout this book in terms of what they have to say about the reproduction of social formations and the transformation of culture. Some analysts of social theory argue that the unity of society is to be sought in the economic contradictions of capitalism; members of the Frankfurt School, for example, discern in the blending of rationalization and repression that operates in modern culture a unity that they term the 'totally administered society.' Some analysts, by contrast, contend that the unity of society is to be found elsewhere. For some social theorists, we cannot conceive of social relations apart from how people talk about them, which means focusing on language. In this linguistic turn of social theory, which we will focus on in detail in Chapters 5, 6 and 7, how we see the world around us and ourselves is constituted in and through language. On this view, it is language which unifies society – even if, as we will see, this 'unity' is illusory to its roots. Still other critics question whether social order presupposes some kind of consensus. This questioning of the so-called unity of society takes a number of forms. One approach is to suggest that social reproduction involves less an explicit than practical consensus: in the work of Pierre Bourdieu, for example, the unity of society arises from a 'cultural unconscious' which gears individual practices to objective social conditions. Another approach underscores the dispersal or fragmentation of social formations. Such a fragmentation of beliefs, values and norms, it is argued, serves not to produce opposition to the current social order but the reproduction of society as a dispersed, postmodern or liquid orchestration.

A third theme is that of *change*, or social transformation. We live today in an era of enormous social change. Globalization, new information technologies, the seemingly unstoppable growth of consumerism, the techno-industrialization of war: such transformations are taking place not only in modern institutions but also within the very textures of everyday life. Contemporary social theory has been concerned to assess the pace of change occurring in our lives today, as well as to critique the large-scale institutional forces driving such social change. Some theorists of modern societies put an emphasis on capitalist transformations in explaining the emergence of a new – post-industrial, post-Fordist or postmodern – economy. The shift away from industrial production (of factories and large-scale assembly plants) in the West during the 1980s and 1990s, and the subsequent outsourcing of manufacture to low-wage economies in developing countries, is considered key by many social theorists to transformations in the whole capitalist system. For other social theorists, the economy has now become effectively cultural – in the sense that industrial manufacture has been traded throughout the West for a wholesale move into the service, communications and finance sectors. Still, other critics see more cultural or institutional factors as central to explaining the recent changes. The establishment of commercial satellites above the earth during the 1970s, facilitating in time the spread of instantaneous communication through, say, the Internet, is at the heart of the communications revolution that has redefined our age. Or, the crisis in scientific or expert knowledge during the final decades of the twentieth century has been viewed by some as heralding new cultural attitudes – loosely called 'postmodern' – towards society, culture, the arts and lifestyle issues. In all of these standpoints, change or social transformation is essential and this theme will provide a framework for the review of social theories offered within the chapters that follow.

A fourth theme concerns *gender issues*. Social theory has long engaged with feminism, particularly the feminist argument that women's personal troubles should in fact be seen as broader social and political troubles that arise from living in male-dominated societies. Classical social theory by no means sidelined issues of gender and sexuality, although much of the analysis it offered was woefully insufficient. Contemporary social theory, by

the textures of society

contrast, has directly engaged with the social, political, psychological and cultural inequalities between men and women – and in many cases has played a direct role in the women's movement and its search for social justice. Chapter 12 specifically explores developments in both feminist and post-feminist social theory, concentrating in particular upon the gendering of feelings, desires, behaviors and social roles in modern societies. Nancy Chodorow, Jessica Benjamin, Jane Flax, Julia Kristeva, Luce Irigaray and Judith Butler are arguably the central voices in feminist and post-feminist social theory and they have brought to prominence the complex ways in which sexual desire is entangled with broader questions of pleasure and power, with the politics of the body, and the reproduction of individual and collective identities. Issues of gender and sexuality, as feminist and post-feminist analysis highlights, must be urgently engaged with in social theory, and accordingly the chapters that follow regularly return to this most vital matter.

A final theme concerns the relation between the *social* and the *emotional*, between our *public and private worlds*. Contemporary social theory powerfully questions many of the oppositions in both mainstream social science and broader public life governing the relationship between public and private life. Instead of viewing, say, tumultuous political events or the forces of globalization as outside happenings in society, there are various traditions of social theory which critically examine the complex ways in which social, cultural and political processes come to be anchored, regulated and lived at the levels of identity and emotional life. In fact, the ways in which public life organizes the private domain, whilst in turn being reshaped by the emotional responses and reactions of individuals, has bulked large in many traditions of recent social theory. Theodor Adorno, Herbert Marcuse, Jacques Lacan, Roland Barthes, Anthony Giddens, Julia Kristeva, Luce Irigaray and Judith Butler have all explored, in very different ways, the meshing of the social and the erotic, the symbolic and the unconscious, cultural conditions and lived experience, the global and the local. As a result, questions of identity, desire and emotion have certainly emerged as fundamental concerns in social theory. And consequently, throughout this book, I emphasize that to critically study a social situation means analyzing it at both the cultural and personal levels – looking at how the public and private interlock.

Further questions

1   What do you think your own life reflects about our fast changing world?

2   What do you understand by the notion of society?

3   If you think of key social institutions – for example, schools, hospitals, prisons and government – what role do they play in society?

4   To what extent is participation in various social institutions consensual or coercive?

5   We live in a world of radical change: do you agree?

Further reading

This chapter covers a broad sweep of introductory concerns in social theory, but the following books should provide useful discussions for further consideration.

Some of the main arguments and issues in relation to how the self navigates the social world can be found in Anthony Elliott, *Concepts of the Self*, 2nd edition, Cambridge: Polity Press, 2007. For the more adventurous reader, you should try Erving Goffman's sociology of everyday life. The best overview of Goffman is Charles Lemert and Ann Branaman (eds), *The Goffman Reader*, Blackwell, 1997. See also Ann Branaman, *Self and Society*, Cambridge, Mass: Blackwell, 2000, and Anthony Elliott, *Subject To Ourselves*, 2nd edition, Paradigm Publishers, 2004.

Finally, in discussing Natalie's life and experience of the world I have drawn from various works of social theory – either explicitly or implicitly – on current social trends as well as the likely future texture of society. For social theories of current social trends in these early years of the twenty-first century see, amongst others, Anthony Giddens, *Runaway World*, Profile Books, 1999; Terry Eagleton, *After Theory*, Allen Lane, 2003; and, John Urry, *Mobilities*, Cambridge: Polity Press, 2007. For a disturbing portrait of the more tragic textures of the contemporary era see Giorgio Agamben, *Homo Sacer: Sovereign Power and Bare Life*, Stanford University Press, 1998.

the textures of society

chapter 2

The Contemporary Relevance of the Classics

Contents

In the previous chapter we began by looking at the life of Natalie, a young woman living a frenetic lifestyle rooted in the twenty-first century. In many respects, Natalie is of her time and lives for her times. Her world-view is largely cosmopolitan, her orientations are ultra-modern, she is geared to the new economy and its culture of fast communication and fast travel, and in many respects Natalie lives a life which fits hand in glove with the short-term frame of reference promoted by our world of intensive globalization. But Natalie lives not only in the moment. Traces of the past – of traditional ways of doing things, of inherited customs and habits – continue to shape her daily life and influence her sense of personal identity. This is especially evident in terms of values, of Natalie's moral commitments and ethical orientations. When speaking of herself – either to friends or family, or indeed to herself (when reflecting on where life is leading) – Natalie is only too aware of the sway of her parents. She is deeply aware of the worlds of their social living, of the times and troubles her parents have experienced, and of how these experiences have been 'handed down' to her. Sometimes Natalie thinks of her sense of personal identity as deeply divided. This sense of division hinges on what Natalie regards as her experimental self (all the risks she takes in negotiating the complex terrain of the brave new global age) on the one hand, and her inherited self (the social and cultural deposits made by her parents and their world-views) on the other.

Still, we might ask, what is this to do with social theory? And what might it have to do with the origins of social theory – the 'classics' of social thought? To say that Natalie is aware of the influence of the past on how she lives in the present is to say that there are certain conceptual assumptions, precepts and ideas – all of which stretch back into previous decades and indeed previous centuries – influencing and reshaping the social realities all around us. To define the past in purely historical terms is thus to neglect how the past orders and regulates the present. In fact, some contemporary social analysts contend that the past 'haunts' the present, leaping out at us from the dark, erupting from the buried repressions of both individuals and cultures. To think about social life in this way – the ongoing pressure of the past upon the present – is to think *with* and *through* the twists and turns of classical social thought and the complexities of modern reason and knowledge. The legacy of classical social thought is indeed evident in Natalie's life, in how she lives her life and thinks about her personal identity and the wider society, in many ways. For example, Natalie says of herself that she has a strong work ethic. In this we find the traces of Weberian social theory, which as we will see charts connections between religion, and especially the Protestant ethic, and the rise of the modern industrial order. So too, Natalie says she worries about growing disparities between rich and poor, and especially the exploitation of poor, displaced and marginalized peoples. In this we find the influence of Marxist social thought and the class contradictions and exploitations of capitalism. Natalie thus also worries about the moral state of society, and in this focus on ethics there are aspects of her thinking influenced by Durkheimian social theory. And when especially troubled by all of these social forces, Natalie sometimes reflects on the deeper emotional tensions and torments of human life – the turmoil of pain, at both an individual and societal level, as captured in aspects of Freudian social thought.

This is not to say, and this qualification is crucial, that Natalie has necessarily read or engaged with any of these classical traditions of social thought. Part of the argument of this book is that the influence of social theory – certainly contemporary, but also classical – is practical as much as conceptual. Social theory, in this sense, might be said to inform our practical competence; it provides for an orientation towards, and indeed facilitates, the wider social world. In this chapter, we will thus turn our attention to the contemporary relevance of classical social theory. But we will do this in a rather unconventional way – working backwards, as it were. We will begin, in each instance of the four areas of classical social theory set out here, by looking at some current work in the social sciences and humanities seeking to address the major issues of our times. In so doing, we will trace the way contemporary ideas about society often contain reference to, and indeed draw from, classical thinking about the realities of social life.

The contradictions of modernity: Marx

Social life is often described as both freedom and constraint, or possibility and limitation. The capacity to do as one pleases, indeed to experience the new and the different, is seen as a hallmark of modern freedom. And we live in an era in which such creative experience has been dramatically extended for many people, thanks to the explosion of consumer choice arising from the globalization of markets and economies. People desire freedom to choose; as though there is no choice but to choose. But consumer freedom, like many other kinds of freedom in the contemporary era, is also essentially a form of constraint, our pathways of choice pre-shaped or predetermined by the consumer industries. We desire freedom, and freedom reminds us of what is most alive and exciting about human experience. And yet, seemingly all too often, such freedom turns into its opposite – leaving individuals feeling empty, manipulated or distanced from themselves and others.

One of the more obvious things that distinguishes the contemporary age from societies of yesteryear is the exacerbation, or acceleration, of such blendings of freedom and constraint. Life for millions of people in the rich North is life lived increasingly at the edges of freedom, innovation and self-invention. Today, people live lives that are remarkably experimental – at the levels of private life (including family, sex, gender and intimacy) as well as professional careers (in companies, institutions and organizations). And yet experiments do not always work out as we intend. Where there are thrills, there are also spills. If contemporary women and men experiment with freedom in ways previously unimaginable, they also face risks, dangers and hazards that previous generations have never confronted. From this angle, the joys of digital life or the possibilities opened by cosmetic surgical culture jostle uneasily with the cataclysmic dangers of global warming or the risks of worldwide financial crises.

Modernity is an answer to the question of what happens when there is a contrast with tradition. The culture of modernity – being intensely diverse and fragmented – involves particular ways of living which press beyond tradition, custom or habit. It is not that traditions are no longer relevant to social life, but rather that traditions are no longer as durable, solid or fixed as once thought. Today there are myriad combinations of the modern and the traditional in how people live their everyday lives. This, in itself, captures something of the restless dynamics of modern society – its fracturing rhythms and dislocating developments. One fascinating attempt to better grasp the contradictions of modern societies is Marshall Berman's celebrated book, *All That Is Solid Melts into Air*. According to Berman, modern capitalist societies are simultaneously fragmented and unifying, freeing and oppressive. Contemporary urban living, he suggests, produces unique blends of personal isolation and loneliness on the one hand and intense social proximity and cultural interconnectedness on the other. The very personal, social and cultural dislocations which modernity brings into existence, such as isolation and the loss of social connection, paradoxically serve to create a new and instantaneous world of cultural possibilities and pleasures. As Berman writes:

> To be modern is to find ourselves in an environment that promises us adventure, power, joy, growth, transformation of ourselves and the world – and, at the same time, that threatens to destroy everything we have, everything we know, everything we are. Modern environments and experiences cut across all boundaries of geography and ethnicity, of class and nationality, of religion and ideology: in this sense, modernity can be said to unite all mankind. But it is a paradoxical unity, a unity of disunity: it pours us all into a maelstrom of perpetual disintegration and renewal, of struggle and contradiction, of ambiguity and anguish.
>
> (1983: 15)

Modernity, according to Berman, is a double-edged phenomenon. Instead of assigning persons to pre-ordained social roles, as in pre-modern cultures, modernity propels people into a creative and dynamic making of self-making and the fashioning of life-styles according to personal preference. Such a transformation in the social fabric leads to vastly greater opportunities concerning freedom and autonomy. But the modern way of life also has a darker side. Attempts to legislate rational order this century have regularly been at the cost of destroying individual particularity and human life. In the wake of Nazism, the Holocaust, Hiroshima, Stalinism and other social-historical catastrophes this century, the veil of illusions which underpin the moral and political practice of modernity has been lifted for all to see.

Central to modernity is the abandonment of any fixed social status and rigid hierarchy of power relations. This dissolution of communal traditions and customs, says Berman, carries major implications for the individual self, and especially the expression of personal identity. In brief, modernity opens up spaces for continuous individualization; it opens up positive possibilities for self-modification in regard to our emotions, desires, needs, and capabilities. In so doing, anxiety comes to replace the sureties of tradition and of habit. This is an anxiety that is at once deeply disturbing and exhilarating, an anxiety that frames the freedom of the self in its dealings with the social world. The premodern world, the ordered world of role-hierarchy and local tradition, has dissolved, leaving uncertainty and ambiguity. Seen from this angle, modernity is about the celebration of dynamism, an ever-expanding acceleration of personal and cultural life. This acceleration is expressed as a multiplication of the possibilities of the self on the one hand, and of self-dislocation by global social processes on the other. Construction and deconstruction, assembly and disassembly: these processes interweave in contemporary societies in a manner which has become self-propelling.

At the core of Berman's analysis of modernity lies the work of Karl Marx. Indeed, the title of Berman's book – which conjures up the melting of the solidity of traditional ways of doing things – derives from *The Manifesto of the Communist Party* (1848), in which Marx and his co-author Friedrich Engels wrote: 'All that is solid melts into air, all that is holy is profaned and man is at last compelled to face with sober senses, his real conditions of life, and his relations with his kind.' According to Marx as well as authors influenced by Marxism, social bonds are determined to their roots by structured inequalities, or class conflict. In this portrait, society is fundamentally split, torn and divided. The modern world after Marx is *schizoid* to its roots. This is a world continuously dynamic at the level of productive industrial forces, and endlessly restless in its search for profits. Yet if capitalism unleashes human creative powers and fosters material growth for some in society, it condemns the bulk of humanity to a degraded, wretched life. 'More than any other mode of production,' writes Marx (see Cohen 1978: 25), 'capitalism squanders human lives, or living labor, and not only flesh and blood, but also nerve and brain.' Capitalism, simply, generates the brutalization of society through its ongoing revolution of economic life. These internal dynamics of the capitalist system produce, in turn, the most tragic social contradictions – namely, the polarization of rich and poor. It is for this reason, said Marx, that we have to free ourselves from capitalism by restoring to society the realization of human powers through communism. For Marx, the anticipated communist society was one in which the active shaping of history involved a more stable, ordered, free and equal world.

The bourgeoisie, wherever it has got the upper hand, has put an end to all feudal, patriarchal, idyllic relations. It has pitilessly torn asunder the motley feudal ties that bound man (sic) to his 'natural superiors,' and has left remaining no other nexus between man and man than naked self-interest, than callous 'cash-payment.' It has drowned the most heavenly ecstasies of religious fervor, of chivalrous enthusiasm, of philistine sentimentalism, in the icy water of egotistical calculation. It has resolved personal worth into exchange value, and in the place of the numberless indefeasible chartered freedoms, has set up that single, unconscionable freedom – Free Trade. In one word, for exploitation, veiled by religious and political illusions, it has substituted naked, shameless, direct, brutal exploitation.

The Bourgeoisie cannot exist without constantly revolutionizing the instruments of production, and thereby the relations of production, and with them the whole relations of society. Conservation of the old modes of production in unaltered form, was, on the contrary, the first condition of existence for all earlier industrial classes.

Constant revolutionizing of production, uninterrupted disturbance of all social conditions, everlasting uncertainty and agitation distinguish the bourgeois epoch from all earlier ones. All fixed, fast-frozen relations, with their train of ancient and venerable prejudices and opinions, are swept away, all newly-formed ones become antiquated before they can ossify. All that is solid melts into air, all that is holy is profaned, and man is at last compelled to face with sober senses, his real conditions of life, and his relations with his kind.

Karl Marx and Friedrich Engels (2008 [1848]) *The Manifesto of the Communist Party,* translated by Samuel Moore. London: Pluto Press, pages 37–8.

The 'structural method' in social theory had been born with Marx. What this means, in brief, is that Marx's theory of modern societies was an account of all societies as structured by class conflict. Such conflict is itself momentous, and indeed for Marx contradiction is conceptualized as built into the very fabric of the social structure. What was radical in Marx's structural approach was that he developed a method for thinking about – that is, providing a critique of – modern society and its curious inversions between people and their material conditions of existence. No one has ever actually clapped eyes on the entirety of a social structure, and in this sense 'society' is somewhat akin to 'God': it is discernible primarily through its effects and impacts upon the lives of ordinary people. But whilst social structures might be invisible to us mere mortals living life on the ground, Marx's structural method of critique offered a way of capturing the contradictions of modern societies. 'Class' might be a slippery term, but through the critique of capitalism Marx insisted that this economic system produced devastating political consequences – the most notable of these being a fragmented society, in which people became increasingly 'alienated' from the goods and commodities made through their own labors. Capitalism generates what Marx termed 'commodity fetishism,' where people are not only drearily disconnected from their own creative powers of self-making but also, and mystifyingly, deadened to the human element of social life. Under capitalism, relations between people for Marx take on 'the fantastic form of a relation between things.' Disconnected people, haunted by dead social things.

In the social production which men carry on they enter into definite relations that are indispensable and independent of their will; these relations of production correspond to a definite stage of development of their material powers of production. The sum total of these relations of production constitutes the economic structure of society – the real foundation, on which rise the legal and political superstructures and to which correspond definite forms of social consciousness. The mode of production in material life determines the general character of the social, political and spiritual processes of life. It is not the consciousness of man that determines their existence, but, on the contrary, their social existence determines their consciousness.

Karl Marx (1911 [1859]) *A Contribution to the Critique of Political Economy*, translated by N.I. Stone. Chicago: Charles H. Kerr & Co., pages 11–12.

Modernity as iron cage: Weber

The contemporary era is one dominated by speed. Fast production, fast consumption, fast credit, fast relationships and fast travel are just some of the key areas of life dominated by the principle of ever-advancing social acceleration. Indeed a faith in speed, acceleration, pace, swiftness and rapidity lies at the core of the advanced capitalist world. This twenty-first century world is one of just-in-time deliveries, short-term contracts, rapid corporate remodelings, overnight shifts of capital investment, and super-fast identity makeovers and body downsizings. Not surprisingly, a fast world requires fast action: the ever-changing demands of our high-speed society require women and men capable of living and working at a break-neck pace, and it is against this accelerated backdrop of people feeling 'time-poor' that we might grasp the phenomenal rise of fast food. Kentucky Fried Chicken, Pizza Hut, Burger King, Wendy's, Taco Bell, Starbucks: these are global icons of the fast food industry, and have transformed not only food production across the globe but also people's attitudes to what they eat and how they think about food. Indeed, Eric Schlosser's best-selling *Fast Food Nation* (2003) makes the argument that the fast food industry – through its acceleration, consolidation and homogenization of food manu-facturing – has transformed the diet, economy and workforce of nations the world over, often in very disturbing and destructive ways. Schlosser argues that the world of fast food has brought with it an epidemic of obesity, destructive methods of food production throughout the world, and a gulf between CEO pay and temporary-only contract staff wages that is shock-ingly wide.

When it comes to fast food, McDonald's remains the best-known global brand in the industry. Today there are more than 33,000 McDonald's restaurants worldwide, based in 118 countries. This has led American sociologist George Ritzer to speak of the McDonaldization of society. McDonaldization, as defined by Ritzer, is 'the process by which the princi-ples of the fast-food restaurant are coming to dominate more and more sectors of American society as well as the rest of the world' (1993: 1). In stressing the spread of fast food to the rest of the world, Ritzer means to say 'globalization.' What we are witnessing today, through the process of McDonaldization, is a globalization of American fast food culture. McDonaldization for Ritzer is an application of Fordist manufacturing methods and scientific management techniques to the mass production of food – delivered fast to the consumer, for immediate consumption. McDonaldization as a process, however, outstrips the terrain of fast food: this is a process of sweeping reach. According to Ritzer, McDonaldization captures the corporate operations and management rhythms of many other types of business – from Toys "Я" Us to Barnes and Noble to Wal-Mart.

What are the central defining aspects of McDonaldization? Ritzer iden-tifies four dimensions: (1) efficiency; (2) calculability: (3) predictability: and, (4) control. At its starkest, McDonaldization is a process geared towards regulatory control, standardization and the administered ordering of consumption processes. We are talking, in short, about the framing of a society without disruption. The smooth, regulated world of McDonald's is a life without surprises: whether you are in Tokyo or Tehran, Melbourne or Memphis, an order for a Big Mac will get you . . . well, a Big Mac!

Informing Ritzer's account of the McDonaldization of society lies the work of classical sociologist Max Weber, and specifically what Weber called the problem of 'rationalization.' For Weber, bureaucracy was at once the prime propeller and problem of modern society. Writing at the turn of the nineteenth century, Weber was as much preoccupied with the threats to humanity presented by modern industrial society as was Marx, but he addressed these threats differently. He did not, for example, focus on the exploitative practices of the capitalist factory system. His analytical concern was, rather, the spread of bureaucracy – from businesses to governments to the wider civil society. In the relentless bureaucratic search for efficiency, according to Weber, a process of rationalization had been unleashed which produced ever-heightening levels of social regulation, political measurement and cultural order. In education, schools had become increasingly standardized in terms of the teaching curriculum. In law and medicine, the development of professions had brought highly regulated knowledge experts, which in turn limited ad hoc decision-making. In society, the state – via police and the army – dominated by means of the control of violence. Indeed for Weber, unlike Marx, the military was far more consequential than the market for understanding the dynamics of society.

This bureaucratic recasting of society, according to Weber, affected not only businesses and governments but also groups and, crucially, individuals. In the rationalization of bureaucracy, particularly in the measurement, regulation and control of social processes, militarization penetrated deeply into the individual realm. Indeed, Weber's view of bureaucracy casts light on how rationalization organizes the view that an individual has of herself, and of the kind of conduct which is considered appropriate for living in an increasingly administered and regulated world. Weber's focus was thus more internal than external, concentrating on how individual attitudes come to be shaped by the drab, passionless world of bureaucratic routine. The portrait of modern society he bequeathed social theory is that of the 'iron cage' – where people may retain some semblance of authenticity (a kind of pseudo-individualism), but are, in fact, trapped in the 'steel-hard' cage of rational-legal administration. Note again the historical moment of this portrait of society: Weber was writing in the final years of the nineteenth and early years of the twentieth centuries. This is highly significant, since the emergence of industrial capitalism – with its manufacturing factories – was indeed the arrival of a world built out of iron and steel. These manufacturing factories and their associated mechanistic-based routines were the material onto which the bureaucratic impulse – training, measuring, regulating, administering – played its significant role. And indeed this portrait of society has been tremendously influential – for example, literary works such as George Orwell's *1984* implicitly reference the Weberian model of society as fixed, administered and rationalized.

The Puritan wanted to work in a calling; we are forced to do so. For when asceticism was carried out of monastic cells into everyday life, and began to dominate worldly morality, it did its part in building the tremendous cosmos of the modern economic order. This order is now bound to the technical and economic conditions of machine production which to-day determine the lives of all the individuals who are born into this mechanism, not only those directly concerned with economic acquisition, with irresistible force. Perhaps it will so determine them until the last tonne of fossilized coal is burnt. In Baxter's view the care for external goods should only lie on the shoulders of the 'saint like a light cloak, which can be thrown aside at any moment.' But fate has decreed that the cloak should become an iron cage.

No one knows who will live in this cage in the future, or whether at the end of this tremendous development, entirely new prophets will arise, or there will be a great rebirth of old ideas or ideals, or, if neither, mechanized petrification, embellished with a sort of convulsive self-importance. For the fast stage of this cultural development, it might well truly be said: 'Specialists without spirit, sensualists without heart; this nullity imagines that it has attained a level of civilization never before achieved.'

Max Weber (1976 [1930]) *The Protestant Ethic and the Spirit of Capitalism*, translated by Talcott Parsons. London: George Allen & Unwin Ltd, pages 181–2.

Bureaucratic rationalization for Weber goes all the way down, right into the very impulses and attitudes of women and men. But how so? In his best-known work, *The Protestant Ethic and the Spirit of Capitalism*, Weber argued that the modern capitalist order required a certain kind of individual – one who was willing to work hard, one capable of sacrifice and discipline. Such a description points to the capitalist entrepreneur, but significantly Weber traced the origins of such individualism back to religion. Specifically, he contended that the primary source of the new spirit of entrepreneurial individualism was in the arcane doctrines of sixteenth-century Calvinism. What made the capitalist society work so well, in short, was its 'work ethic,' by which Weber means to draw attention to the impact of the 'Protestant Ethic.' For this work ethic arose in the context of puritan religious thinking, but transformed over the years of the eighteenth and nineteenth centuries into the widespread ethic of a new entrepreneurial individualism of modern industrialism. In contrast to Marx's materialist emphasis on capital and labor, Weber put the emphasis on culture. The culture of a hard work ethic had become an inner drive, indeed a cultural obsession. For Weber, this cultural orientation produced many of the *goods* of the modern industrial order; but these *goods* were outweighed by the *bads* of a work ethic which had become, literally, a pathological compulsion.

> When those subject to bureaucratic control seek to escape the influence of the existing bureaucratic apparatus, this is normally possible only by creating an organization of their own which is equally subject to bureaucratization. Similarly the existing bureaucratic apparatus is driven to continue functioning by the most powerful interests which are material and objective, but also ideal in character. Without it, a society like our own – with its separation of officials, employees and workers from the ownership of the means of administration, and its dependence on discipline and technical training – could no longer function. The only exception would be those groups, such as the peasantry, who still had possession of their own means of subsistence. Even in the case of revolution by force or of occupation by an enemy, the bureaucratic machinery will normally continue to function just as it had for the previous legal government.
>
> Max Weber (1978 [1956]) *Economy and Society: An Outline of Interpretive Sociology, Volume I*, Berkeley, CA; University of California Press, page 224.

Modernity as moral bonds: Durkheim

One of the more interesting paradoxes about modern societies is how the search for individualism and personal freedom intersects with, and routinely dislodges, the expectations and obligations of moral bonds. There are, we might say, two projects in the modern search for solutions to social problems and cultural conflicts. The first project is personal well-being, individual self-expression and autonomy. The second project concerns the bonds of morality – that is, the forms of social trust, reciprocity and networks that facilitate civic actions and ethical engagement. This, one might think, represents dualistic thinking, but this is not necessarily the case. Individualism on the one hand, and moral bonds on the other, are not necessarily at loggerheads. Indeed, it is often argued that strong individualism cannot be genuinely achieved without moral bonds. This is the idea that nothing seems to make our lives more exciting, experimental or freeing as the bonds of reciprocity and the pleasures of civic engagement.

And yet one of the striking things about modern societies in the twenty-first century is just how apparently hedonistic and dislocating they can be. Or, another way of putting this point, how much does the free reign of rampant individualism in contemporary societies appear to weaken the norms of trust, tradition and moral reciprocity? Certainly, there has been no shortage of critics – both radicals and conservatives – concerned to tease out cultural contradictions stemming from the dominance of individualism and its undercutting of moral bonds. The American sociologist, Daniel Bell, has argued that people increasingly think only of their own private satisfactions and personal pursuits, which in turn weakens the spirit of active citizenship. Looking at how the age of secular Puritanism transmuted into the age of consumerist pleasure-seeking, Bell considers the rise of multinationals and huge business conglomerates especially consequential. Likewise, Richard Sennett, in *The Fall of Public Man* (1978), traces the dominance of notions of self-fulfillment, sensual gratification and self-absorption at the expense of moral bonds. From a quite different perspective, the critic Allan Bloom has attacked what he terms our 'culture of moral relativism'. People today, writes Bloom, are 'spiritually unclad, unconnected, isolated, with no inherited or unconditional connection with anything or anyone'. And sociologist, Robert Bellah, in an award-winning book *Habits of the Heart*, casts Americans as trapped in a language of isolating individualism, a language that disrupts possibilities for genuine personal growth, ongoing commitments to others and involvement in public affairs.

Perhaps the most influential work which underscores the erosion of moral bonds as a result of a culture of rampant individualism is Robert D. Putnam's *Bowling Alone – The Collapse and Revival of American Community*. According to Putnam, the crisis of modern society is that of broken bonds and deteriorating democracy. He uses the metaphor of 'bowling' to capture recent social changes through which individuals are more and more disconnected from family life, friends, colleagues, neighbors and the social system itself. The metaphor of bowling is crucial. Whereas people once bowled in league teams, during their leisure time after work, now they bowl alone, as solitary entertainment. Putnam thus contrasts the communal character of yesteryear with the impersonality of today's world. Disconnected individualism replaces civic engagement, commercialized competition rules over co-operative community, and transactional encounters replace genuine relationships: these are the oppositions through which Putnam seeks to capture the decline of moral bonds.

Putnam's diagnosis of modernity has been widely applauded as a provocative reflection on the consequences of unchecked individualism. Some critics have found Putnam's picture of modern society disturbing. Other critics have found that Putnam romanticizes the past, leaving a distorted account of present-day society. But I want to leave aside such appraisal for the moment, and instead concentrate on how Putnam's *Bowling Alone* embodies aspects of classical social theory. Putnam's ideas about the decline of moral bonds have their roots arguably in the work of the nineteenth-century sociologist, Emile Durkheim, who sought to show that a complex moral web of social interactions underpin the fabric of modern individualism. Durkheim's ideas arose in the context of the emergence of industrial society, and the moral and social conflicts such a society promoted. In the hands of Putnam, Durkheim's reflections on moral contradictions are recast to fit with the dilemmas of the present-day world.

Perhaps more clearly than either Marx or Weber, Durkheim saw the significance of morality in modern social development. There must be a moral bond for society to exist at all according to Durkheim, and it is from that angle that the moral framework can be considered at the root of both individualism and social relations. In *Elementary Forms of the Religious Life* (1912), Durkheim invoked the term *conscience collective* to show that whenever we think, we think collectively. Conflict for Durkheim arises as a result of society's failure to provide moral bonds. Conflict, *pace* Marx, is not simply the result of class divisions; it rather concerns the moral ethic of society itself, and its failure to guide the actions of individuals. To study society after Durkheim means grasping moral bonds as intricately interwoven with the fine gradations and subtle nuances of our shared social experiences. In the end, the world is known through the social categories of our shared lives. The dilemma in our own time of intensive individualism, according to Durkheim's standpoint, is how to struggle to retain contact with the common aspects of social life. Durkheim's belief that social cohesion depends upon moral bonds, which in turn is bound up with independent and interdependent individuals, was a response to a dichotomous understanding of social change that dominated much social thinking of his era. This was an understanding that contrasted 'traditional' with 'modern' societies. A central figure in this connection was the German sociologist, Ferdinand Tonnies, who contrasted *Gemeinschaft* (community) with *Gesellschaft* (society). Society for Tonnies can be equated with moral indifference, hostility and cool market relationships. According to Tonnies, instrumental, impersonal relationships of large-scale modern societies have replaced traditional, hierarchal relationships of small-scale communities. This was not a view that Durkheim accepted, however. For Durkheim, society is not impersonal and mechanical. On the contrary, society is constitutive of moral individualism and integrative of social relations. Just as Tonnies believed that modern, large-scale societies are characterized by mechanical social relations and a kind of utilitarian individualism, so Durkheim held, inversely, that modern societies are generative of unifying forms of solidarity and advanced forms of moral individualism. Durkheim was suspicious of Tonnies's conviction that only life in small societies can be morally sustaining.

In the shift from mechanical, pre-modern societies to organic, modern societies, individuals find themselves functionally separated members of the whole; however, the expansion of the division of labor, stimulated by the progress of industrial life, also renders individuals, paradoxically, increasingly interdependent. If the industrial world divides people from each other and promotes social differences, it also oversees the regulation of a new morally cohesive code and its further development. Moral regulation and refinement may be an ongoing exercise in adjustment to the independent power of social facts, but this need not imply a denial of agency and will in social action. If we are independent beings, free to develop individual sources of action, we are also part of a complex *conscience* on which our sense of morality and ethics goes to work. If, morally, modern individuals increasingly act as self-cultivators – as free and rational subjects – then a loss of social cohesion perpetually looms – and society hovers on the brink of an anomic condition. But freedom is not necessarily an obstacle to the realization of collective values and hopes, since organic solidarity in Durkheim's view promotes interpersonal dependence connected to external events. And it is precisely this ambiguous or doubled dimension of modern society that critics of Durkheim overlook in making the charge that his theory of the social denies the individual subject and can accommodate no conception of agency. Agency and individualism are, in fact, for Durkheim, involved at the deepest level of structure, with complex interaction between objective and subjective worlds.

[A] society is not made up merely of the mass of individuals who compose it, the ground which they occupy, the things which they use and the movements which they perform, but above all is the idea which it forms of itself. It is undoubtedly true that it hesitates over the manner in which it ought to conceive itself; it feels itself drawn in divergent directions. But these conflicts which break forth are not between the ideal and reality, but between two different ideals, that of yesterday and that of to-day, that which has the authority of tradition and that which has the hope of the future. There is surely a place for investigating whence these ideals evolve; but whatever solution may be given to this problem, it still remains that all passes in the world of the ideal.

the contemporary relevance of the classics

> Thus the collective ideal. . .is far from being due to a vague innate power of the individual, but it is rather at the school of collective life that the individual has learned to idealize. It is in assimilating the ideals elaborated by society that he (*sic*) has become capable of conceiving the ideal. It is society which, by leading him within the sphere of action, has made him acquire the need of raising himself above the world of experience and has at the same time furnished him with the means of conceiving another.
>
> Emile Durkheim (1965 [1912]) *The Elementary Forms of the Religious Life*, translated by Joseph Ward Swain. New York: The Free Press, pages 470–1.

How might these abstract concepts from classical social theory relate to the analysis of present-day societies? There are good reasons to defend Durkheim's relevance in contemporary social theory. As we have seen, Durkheim saw modern society as descending into anomie, and the signs of moral decay were indicated by the failure of societies to provide a regulating ethic to moderate the actions of individuals in terms of the maintenance of social order. The late twentieth and early twenty-first century suggests that such tendencies have accelerated, and indeed Putnam's analysis of the fragmentation of moral bonds is dependent on Durkheim's analysis – even though the latter's influence is not explicitly acknowledged. Today's economic and social changes are profound, and it is certainly arguable that globalization, neo-liberalism and the widespread deregulation of markets have significantly weakened the power of moral bonds in ordinary people's lives.

But it would be mistaken to suppose that the twenty-first century represents merely a new page of moral decay. It seems more likely, and arguably more in keeping with Durkheim's social theory, that individuals are always going to have ongoing conflicts and crises in their moral encounters, both at the levels of actual working and civic life as well as the private domain. It is one of Durkheim's many original theoretical moves to question the notion that tradition and social forms of the past are necessarily to be celebrated. In a striking sociological interpretation, modernity for Durkheim turns the tables on mechanical social relations of the past, reconstituting a more expansive experience of community which is specific to large-scale, modern societies. In bridging the gap between society and community in this way, Durkheim is able to identify new forms of solidarity which are specific to modernity – that which he sees as the upshot of a socially developed division of labor and operationalized through what he termed the 'conscience collective,' the collective conscience or consciousness.

Durkheim could not have predicted the passing of industrial society as a result of the advent of globalization. But his analysis of how civil society can flourish through the spread of associations and networks of trust remains influential. From this angle, the moral bond plays a key role in the development of individualism at the same time that the culture of individualism provides important resources for the increasing complexity of society.

Trauma, tragedy and Thanatos: Freud

Few topics can be as painful to contemplate as the strategies of avoidance we use to shield ourselves from administered atrocities – torture, political massacres, genocides. From the shadows cast by Auschwitz to more recent terrors in Bosnia, Rwanda, Chechnya, Kosovo, Baghdad and Gaza, the apparent indifference of western publics to mass suffering is shocking, disturbing, haunting. As images of atrocity and disaster rain down on us from everywhere, it is as if knowledge of the politics of trauma and tragedy threatens to incapacitate us intellectually and drain us emotionally. Blocking out, shutting off, not wanting to know; fear of disturbing knowledge has become perhaps the condition of our times. Might the supposed indifference of western publics to mass suffering stem from a sense of resigned fatalism? Or, perhaps, compassion fatigue? Not necessarily according to sociologist, Stanley Cohen, since expressions of denial are complex psycho-political phenomena, neither simply 'natural' nor 'static.'

In *States of Denial: Knowing about Atrocities and Suffering* (2001), Cohen investigates our culture of denial and considers afresh how unsettling experiences of violence, aggression and pain are displaced through various modes of avoidance. Cohen is out to show that the personal and political ways in which uncomfortable realities are avoided, and often evaded, are socially and historically deeply layered. When we deny, says Cohen, we use unconscious defense mechanisms to protect ourselves, at both the individual and social or organizational level. While noting that some switching off is necessary in order to retain our sanity, Cohen argues that the inability to be continually 'facing' or 'living with' unpleasant truths can lead to wholesale pathology, in the form of alienated individuals and remote communities. Such wholesale denial is, in turn, connected to a refusal to face the traumas of self-destruction, violence and aggression – key constituents of all human existence.

Violence is a drive central to our species' being. This applies not only to the destruction of others, but also the annihilation of ourselves. The traumatic tribulations of a primary terror are inseparable from the social and political dynamics of the contemporary age, making vivid the ethical complexities and moral uncertainties of our cultural predicament. To convert the whole world into tragedy may seem like too unqualified a gesture, but it is possible to hold in mind both the enabling and constraining aspects of human aggression and destruction. Indeed, this is exactly Terry Eagleton's aim in *Sweet Violence* (2003), where he argues that both traditionalist and radical conceptions of tragedy in the humanities and the wider public sphere turn on a number of key distinctions – between fate and chance, the noble and the ignoble, blindness and insight. Rejecting the assumption that tragedy is one thing and ordinary life another, Eagleton focuses squarely on the everyday, the habitual and common culture. He contends, provocatively, that our age inaugurates a democratization of tragedy. On this view, the idea of the tragic did not die in the twentieth century; rather, it mutated into modernism.

Taking aim at advocates of the death of tragedy thesis, Eagleton seeks to underscore the power of violence, aggression, destruction and the demonic in cultural affairs. As he contends,

> absolutely anybody can now be a tragic figure. Tragedy did not vanish because there were no more great men. It did not expire with the last absolutist monarch. On the contrary, since under democracy each one of us is to be incommensurably cherished, it has been multiplied far beyond antique imagining.
>
> (2003b: 94)

The idea that tragedy is intrinsically ennobling and estimable is, according to Eagleton, only possible to the extent that one denies that history has been awash with warfare, starvation, disease, poverty and political terror. For Eagleton, it is modernism that lends our tragic impulse a new lease of life, not only in the form of art, but also in world-views and real-life events. In one stroke, Eagleton thus widens the whole discourse on tragedy – from Aeschylus to American imperialism, from Goethe to global inequalities, from Shakespeare to suffering – and suggestively extends the political stakes of the idea of the tragic.

If tragedy is still widely regarded today as the most profound of all literary and cultural forms, it is because it speaks to the destructive self-mutilation at the very root of civilization. In Eagleton's delving into the contradictions of this historical psychodrama, desire looms large. The paradox is that society is locked into tragic battle with the very destructive forces that the modern age of Enlightenment seeks to transcend. In a perverse irony, society at once underwrites and undercuts aggression. Death, destruction and the demonic – all lurking within our aggressivity – have an imposing centrality to the lives we share in common. 'Death and self-destruction,' writes Eagleton, 'is a tendency implacably hostile to history which generates historical time. What impels us forward, perversely, is an instinct to travel backward to Eden' (2003b: 248).

How might we best understand this shifting focus in much present-day social theory from denial to destruction? One possible answer is by turning to psychoanalysis, and the claims of its founder Sigmund Freud. For Freud's provocative challenge to social theory consists in the radical claim that the malaise of repression, anxiety and self-destruction are the emotional costs we pay for social order. In respect of Cohen's arguments concerning cultures of denial, the Freudian response focuses on the concept of repression. In respect of Eagleton's arguments concerning violence, the Freudian response focuses on a drive for death which is at the core of selfhood. Let us briefly turn to consider these aspects of Freud's corpus.

Unlike Marx, Weber and Durkheim, Freud was not a social theorist. But the legacy of his work has had a profound impact upon social theory – as we will see in subsequent chapters of this book. From his clinical work with patients suffering emotional torment, Freud theorized that there are various longings, desires and fantasies which come into conflict with the order of social life. Desire, longing and passion often conflict with the rules and regulations of modern social order. In order to grasp how individuals cope with these emotional pressures, Freud coined the term 'repression.' The notion of repression captures aspects of what Cohen is seeking to elucidate when he talks about cultures of denial, but it involves still more. Modern society, says Freud, is repressive. Society imposes severe demands and restrictions upon individuals, some of which can produce intense emotional suffering and misery. But it is precisely from the realm of suffering that Freud discerns resistance. Too much repression, says Freud, leads women and men to intense rage and destruction. At this point, the pressure of desire – which, as we will see in later chapters, Freud conceptualizes in terms of the unconscious – can release the 'mental dams' of sexual repression with far-reaching personal, social, cultural and political consequences.

Scandalously, the cornerstone of Freud's theory of modern discontents is the notion of the 'death drive.' In *Civilization and its Discontents* (1930), Freud outlines a conception of the 'death drive' as forever organizing disabling repressions at the center of social and cultural life. By the death drive Freud understands a will to negation, of self-destructiveness or primary aggression. Human misery and oppression are not the only outcomes of sexual repression – an idea put forward by Freud in some of his earliest writings on society and culture. In his writings of the 1930s, Freud comes to equate culture with the urge for, and repressive constraints upon, self-destructiveness. Civilization protects against the aggressive demands of the death drive. 'The main renunciation culture demands of the individual,' writes Paul Ricoeur (1970: 307) of Freud's interpretation of culture, 'is the renunciation not of desire as such but of aggressiveness.'

As a result, Freud is able at one stroke to rewrite the problem of self and society as a contest between love and hate, or between life and death. Love involves the flowering of civilized co-belonging. Hatred, aggression and the death drive are forces that threaten to tear culture apart. The Freud of *Civilization and Its Discontents* (1930: 59) unfolds love and hate, Eros and Thanatos (Greek words for 'love' and 'death,' respectively), in the following way:

> [C]ivilization is a process in the service of Eros, whose purpose is to combine single human individuals, and after that families, then races, peoples and nations, into one great unity . . . These collections of men are libidinally bound to one another. Necessity alone, the advantages of work in common, will not hold them together. But man's natural aggressive instinct, the hostility of each against all and of all against each, opposes this program of civilization. The aggressive instinct is the derivative and main representative of the death drive which we have found alongside of Eros and which shares world-dominion with it.

The pathological compulsions of everyday life are rooted in a repressive structuring of love and hatred – the very terrain of Eagleton's interpretation of 'sweet violence.' Note that Freud, in introducing the notion of the death drive, still remains faithful to his earlier view that the reproduction of society depends upon sexual repression; but in his late sociological vision, sexual repression becomes integrated into a deathly self-preservation, organized as a destructive assault on the human body, on others, and on nature. Freud particularly had in mind the highly authoritarian European societies before the First World War that sent thousands of young men to their deaths in 1914. But he also became acutely aware of the psychopathologies of fascism, racism and anti-Semitism in the 1920s and 1930s – which, for him, represented a kind of breakdown of civilization. This breakdown resulted from a degeneration of sexual repression into a will to exterminate the alien and disorderly. In today's world, it arguably finds expression in the phenomenon of 'ethnic cleansing,' as well as homophobia and 'moral panics' about people perceived as deviant.

Freud's writings on the fate of the self in contemporary culture have strongly influenced debates in critical theory – from the Frankfurt School approaches of Marcuse and Adorno to the contemporary approaches of Jürgen Habermas and Axel Honneth. The question of the subjective seeds of social and political transformation are thus at the heart of Freud's contribution to social theory.

The fateful question for the human species seems to me to be whether and to what extent their cultural development will succeed in mastering the disturbance of their communal life by the human instinct of aggression and self-destruction. It may be that in this respect precisely the present time deserves a special interest. Men have gained control over the forces of nature to such an extent that with their help they would have no difficulty in exterminating one another to the last man. They know this, and hence comes a large part of their current unrest, their unhappiness and their mood of anxiety. And now it is to be expected that the other of the two 'Heavenly Powers,' eternal Eros, will make an effort to assert himself in the struggle with his equally immortal adversary. But who can foresee with what success and with what result?

Sigmund Freud (1973 [1930]) *Civilization and its Discontents*, translated by Joan Riviere. London: The Hogarth Press, page 82.

Summary points

1   Marshall Berman, in his influential book *All That Is Solid Melts Into Air*, characterizes the experience of modernity as contradictory; individuals have unprecedented freedom to creatively explore new experiences and identities, on the one hand, but are subject to unparalleled levels of uncertainty and ambiguity, on the other.

2   Berman's argument is centered on Marx's understanding of the processes inherent in the transition from traditional feudal society into industrial capitalist society. Transformations in the means of production result in the transformation of the society built around them, according to Marx, and with the emergence of new modes the traditional forms of identity and hierarchy are overridden by new forms that mirror the uncertainty and constant reinvention of industrial production.

3   George Ritzer has argued that the system of McDonaldization – a model centered around efficiency, calculability, predictability and control – has introduced a fast food logic that has come to dominate experiences of consumption and even alter the fabric of society.

4   The previous point draws on the 'iron cage' of rationality that Max Weber envisioned at the turn of the twentieth century. Weber saw

that the rationally administrative logic that had come to dominate industry, the military and particularly government bureaucracy was increasingly penetrating the inner life of the individual, recasting them as cogs in an administered industrial mechanism and denying authentic freedom.

5 In *Bowling Alone: The Collapse and Revival of American Community*, Robert Putnam claims that American society has seen a loss in civic participation and decreased moral bonds since the 1950s. The metaphor of bowling, now a lone activity where it was once a club sport, signifies for Putnam a general trend towards individualism and away from cooperation and communalism

6 Putnam's concern with decreased moral bonds ultimately reflects the conception of society presented by Emile Durkheim. Durkheim's book *The Elementary Forms of Religious Life*, argued that the individualism of 'organic' industrial society, brought about by an increased division of labor, actually underpinned a strong network of moral bonds and interdependence, through the promotion of a collective conscience. Nevertheless, Durkheim argued that the increased power of self-regulation endangered the moral fabric of society and threatened a state of anomie.

7 Many contemporary sociologists are critical of modern society's ability to avoid engagement with violence and death, in spite of the endemic presence of both in the contemporary era. Stanley Cohen links this process to the unconscious defense mechanisms that protect the psyche from trauma, but argues that a culture of continual denial can result in a pathological society. For Terry Eagleton, this denial is linked to a democratization of the cultural narrative of tragedy within the discourse of modernity; an attempt to engage with the aggression and violence inherent in the fabric of civilization.

8 The idea that violent and self-destructive aggression lies at the core of civilization has its roots in the dynamic of the erotic and death instincts set out in Sigmund Freud's *Civilization and its Discontents*. Freud claimed that the aggressive death instinct, Thanatos, represents the greatest threat to social life, which Eros, the life instinct, serves to promote. For Freud, the demands of modern life require intense repression of both Eros and Thanatos, which leads to anxiety and unhappiness and, given sufficient repression, outbreaks of pathological violence.

Further questions

1   What do you think of Marx's claim that modern life involves the stripping away of tradition? Do you agree?

2   Can you think of an example from your life where freedom, and having to live with the consequences, made you feel uncertain or anxious?

3   Have you experienced McDonaldization in your day-to-day life, particularly outside of the fast food restaurant?

4   Weber was pessimistic that society could ever break out of the logic of bureaucratic administration. Do you think that we are still trapped in the 'iron cage'?

5   How do individuals acquire moral values in contemporary society?

6   Do you think that our society is moral, or anomic?

7   'The main renunciation culture demands of the individual is. . . of aggressiveness.' Discuss.

Further reading

Marshall Berman

All That is Solid Melts Into Air: The Experience of Modernity (London: Verso, 1983)

Karl Marx

(with Friedrich Engels) The Manifesto of the Communist Party, Trans. Samuel Moore (London: Pluto Press, 2008)
A Contribution to the Critique of Political Economy, translated by N. I. Stone (Chicago: Charles H. Kerr & Co., 1911)

George Ritzer

The McDonaldization of Society: An Investigation Into the Changing Character of Contemporary Social Life (Thousand Oaks: Pine Forge Press, 1993)

Max Weber

The Protestant Ethic and the Spirit of Capitalism translated by Talcott Parsons (London: George Allen & Unwin Ltd, 1976)

Economy and Society An Outline of Interpretative Sociology, Volume I (Berkeley, CA; University of California Press, 1978)

Robert Putnam

Bowling Alone: The Collapse and Revival of American Community (New York: Simon & Schuster, 2000)

Emile Durkheim

The Elementary Forms of the Religious Life, translated by Joseph Ward Swain (New York: The Free Press, 1965)

Stanley Cohen

States of Denial: Knowing About Atrocities and Suffering (Cambridge, UK: Polity Press, 2001)

Terry Eagleton

Sweet Violence: The Idea of the Tragic (Oxford, UK: Blackwell, 2003)

Sigmund Freud

Civilization and its Discontents, translated by Joan Riviere (London: The Hogarth Press, 1973)

chapter 3

The Frankfurt School

Contents

Marxism, of all the classical sociological traditions, arguably provides the most scintillating storyline regarding the ongoing, frantic expansion of capitalism. 'The bourgeoisie,' wrote Marx, 'has through its exploitation of the world market given a cosmopolitan character to production and consumption in every country.' From San Francisco to Sydney, New York to New Delhi: anyone shopping in a downtown mall, surveying flashy designer goods and hi-tech products flown in from China, Taiwan or India, would most likely agree with Marx's assessment. What happens to people under capitalism for Marx is an extravagant inflation of sensory life and human desire, creating a sort of permanent revolution across society in which pleasure depends upon the continual accumulation of more and more things. People, simply, want newer and newer experiences. One can argue about whether designer jeans, mobile phones or iPods really constitute an advance in societal well-being, but the essential point from a Marxist perspective is that such consumption has today become perversely self-constituting, self-breeding, self-referential.

Next to watching TV, shopping is now the most popular leisure pursuit the world over. Think about that for a moment. Today, more and more people define their lives in terms of what they buy and what they own, and arguably more so than in terms of what they think or what they do for a living. In the new consumer society of the twenty-first century, individuals consume not only material goods but various seductive products and services targeted to the insatiable wants of mass society. Shopping in today's free-floating consumer landscape – in which shops, services and internet sites are open around the clock – individuals go about trying to quench their insatiable wants in societies where there just seem to be not enough hours in the day. From online shopping on Amazon.com to Rolex watches, from figure-hugging Calvin Klein jeans to the ultra-fashion sportswear of Nike, from age-reversing cosmetics and creams to the designer clothes of Armani or Versace: the near-universal pursuit of shopping in the West has established itself as fundamental to experiences of personal liberty and human freedom.

The ascendancy of universal consumerism is a remarkable phenomenon. It has, for one thing, transformed modern societies away from industrial production (that having been 'outsourced' to other developing countries) and towards the post-industrial consumption of products, services and brands. It has also helped fashion a new set of social attitudes in which shopping has become redefined as an end in itself. Unlike Sigmund Freud's psychoanalytic description of society as a trade-off in which people sacrifice happiness for security, today's consumer society is all about instant self-gratification and pleasure. The freedom to consume, or so runs the global laissez-faire doctrine, is essential to how contemporary women and men consume freedom.

Yet there are powerful reasons to question the supposed liberty which arises from our culture of consumerism. Do so-called lifestyle statements – Apple iPods, Gucci watches, Mont Blanc pens – really satisfy our deeper personal strivings, or are they just a further stimulus to a society that cannot stop desiring to desire? How many online shoppers find that they really have more quality time available in their lives – for family, friends or meaningful pursuits? How many parents avoid spending time with their children as a result of our culture of shopping? And do today's consumer industries – from travel agencies selling pre-packaged holidays to IKEA-inspired firms selling pre-packaged living – promote new freedoms or new insecurities?

One influential contribution to thinking about the societal consequences of advanced capitalism, and especially tracking the contours of the cultural and consumer industries that people must now navigate, is that of the Frankfurt School. Central to the parameters of Frankfurt School social theory is Theodor Adorno's vision of the 'administered society' and Herbert Marcuse's thesis of the 'one-dimensional society' in which individuals suffer from 'surplus-repression.' The work of Adorno and Marcuse is incorrigibly interdisciplinary (involving certain traditions of classical social theory, and especially Freudian psychoanalysis), purveying a view of society that may well be unrecognizable to many contemporary men and women who inhabit the fast-paced, consumer-orientated societies of today. Yet, as two of the most important German intellectuals of the twentieth century, their writings – and indeed the work of the Frankfurt School as a whole – is of profound importance for engaging not only with recent world history, but with the impacts of large-scale societal processes upon individuals and their private worlds.

The Frankfurt School, as it came to be called, was formed in the decade prior to the Nazi reign of terror in Germany, and, not surprisingly, many of its leading theorists conducted numerous studies seeking to grasp the wave of political irrationalism and totalitarianism sweeping Western Europe. In a daring theoretical move, the School brought Freudian categories to bear upon the sociological analysis of everyday life, in order to fathom the myriad ways that political power imprints itself upon the internal world of human subjects and, more specifically, to critically examine the obscene, meaningless kind of evil that Hitler had actually unleashed. Of the School's attempts to fathom the psychopathologies of fascism, the writings of Adorno, Marcuse and Fromm particularly stand out; each of these authors, in quite different ways, drew upon Freudian categories to figure out the core dynamics and pathologies of post-liberal rationality, culture and politics, and also to trace the sociological deadlocks of modernity itself. The result was a dramatic underscoring of both the political dimensions of psychoanalysis and also the psychodynamic elements of public political life.

the frankfurt school

Horkheimer and Adorno: *Dialectic of Enlightenment*

While in exile in the United States, Adorno and Max Horkheimer wrote *Dialectic of Enlightenment* (1944) – a brilliant work of social theory that sought to grasp the dark side of the modern age. Written with remarkable philosophical range and sociological insight, the task Adorno and Horkheimer set for themselves was spelt out thus: 'The discovery of why mankind, instead of entering into a truly human condition, is sinking into a new kind of barbarism.' The hell to which the authors referred was the political nightmare they had left behind in Germany – the fascism of the Third Reich. But such was the increasingly comprehensive sweep of instrumental reason throughout modern societies that Horkheimer and Adorno also found signs or symptoms of fascist domination in liberal democracies too, especially America. In fact, the American entertainment industry – from jazz to Hollywood – was a fundamental part of this process of commercialized brain-washing, and thus indicative of the rise and domination of fascist ideology. The idea that enlightenment and domination are intricately interwoven lies at the core of *Dialectic of Enlightenment*, and is fundamental to the comprehensive sociological diagnosis of modernity that Horkheimer and Adorno expounded.

Reason is, of course, essential to human existence. With Horkheimer and Adorno's critical theory, however, the philosophy of the Enlightenment and instrumental reason are revealed as having capsized into a form of sickness. Reason at its extreme limit, transformed into a mirror-image of the very madness it seeks to repress, is explored by Horkheimer and Adorno with reference to various definitions of the term 'enlightenment.' One key definition is associated with the variety of political and intellectual currents which shaped social upheavals in Europe, from the great French Revolution of the eighteenth century to the Russian Revolution in the early decades of the twentieth century. This is the revolutionary idea of enlightenment as rationalist, republican and universal in scope. Another key definition springs from modern science, especially the age of discoveries and transformations occurring in science as a result of technological innovations such as the telescope, microscope, compass and clocks. In examining these versions of enlightenment reason, Horkheimer and Adorno observe a general shift in people's attitudes towards their own lives, towards the lives of others and in the external world. Whereas traditional societies turned to mythology in governing human affairs, modern societies greeted the force of human reason as decisive. Such an emancipatory notion of enlightenment was essential, for both liberals and conservatives, to the supposed erosion of mythology – facilitative of contemporary developments in science, technology and the economy.

This modern idea – that reason destroys myth – is however nothing but sheer illusion, according to Horkheimer and Adorno. On the contrary, enlightenment and myth are closely allied. This means, however, that there is a secret complicity between what founds enlightenment – reason – and that which it seeks to overcome – namely myth. On this view, the rational becomes more and more entangled in myth, as the social order comes to define itself as enlightened. 'In the most general sense of progressive thought,' write Horkheimer and Adorno, 'the Enlightenment has always aimed at liberating man from fear and establishing their sovereignty. Yet the fully enlightened earth radiates disaster triumphant.' From fascism in Europe to commercialized mass culture in the United States, the Enlightenment's promise of freedom had produced disastrous social consequences on both sides of the Atlantic.

'Enlightenment,' write the authors of *Dialectic of Enlightenment*, 'is totalitarian.' From the rise of National Socialism in Germany to the culture industry in America, from Hitler's annihilation of European Jews to the unparalleled destruction of modern technological warfare: enlightenment reason has failed the West and indeed humanity as a whole. At the core of this sceptical, indeed bleak, assessment of the modern age is the concept of domination. Whilst Horkheimer and Adorno do not define domination with any degree of sociological precision, it seems clear that they seek to underscore the power of instrumental, technological and scientific reason in the establishment of domination over the self, over one's inner nature and over external nature and society.

The enslavement to nature of people today cannot be separated from social progress. The increase in economic productivity which creates the conditions for a more just world also affords the technical apparatus and the social groups controlling it a disproportionate advantage over the rest of the population. The individual is entirely nullified in face of the economic powers. These powers are taking society's domination over nature to unimagined heights. While individuals are vanishing before the apparatus they serve, they are provided for by that apparatus and better than ever before. In the unjust state of society the powerlessness and pliability of the masses increase with the quantity of goods allocated to them. The materially considerable and socially paltry rise in the standard of living of the lower classes is reflected in the hypocritical propagation of intellect. Intellect's true concern is a negation of reification. It must perish when it is solidified into a cultural asset and handed out for consumption purposes. The flood of precise information and brand-new amusements make people smarter and more stupid at once.

Max Horkheimer and Theodor Adorno (2002 [1944]) *Dialectic of Enlightenment: Philosophical Fragments*. Edited by Gunzelin Schmid Noerr and translated by Edmund Jephcott. Stanford CA: Stanford University Press, page xvii.

By dominating nature, argue Horkheimer and Adorno, society and social relations are secured, while individual identity is transformed from blind instinct to reflective consciousness of the self. This is, in effect, a shift from nature to culture. But in a tragic irony, the violence which wrested society out of nature turns back upon itself, mutilating identities and robbing people of possibilities for happiness and freedom. That is to say, the aggression, rage and violence which were initially necessary to protect the social order from the ravages of nature do not magically disappear once culture and political life are constituted. On the contrary, violence is written into the very fabric of social order; aggression strikes at the heart of every attempt by social actors to change the world, no matter how noble or high-minded their intentions might be. This means that the unstoppable urge to 'administer' society through the application of rationalist blueprints is always dangerously in excess of necessity. There is something delusional about the desire for reason: it is delusional because reason conceals a mind-shattering repression which is, in fact, the exact opposite of autonomy. One symptom of this disease of enlightenment is fascism, especially anti-Semitism. Hatred of Jews, contend Adorno and Horkheimer, is a projection of modern society's ferocious inner compulsion onto a marginalized group. Yet anti-Semitism is not the only symptom of the frightful excess of enlightenment reason, which is why domination in our own era runs all the way from the destruction of nature to the colonization of developing nations.

Freudian revolution: the uses of psychoanalysis

One of the most distinctive features of the development of critical theory undertaken by the Frankfurt School was its use of Freudian psychoanalysis for the study of identity, politics, culture and ideology. Almost all of Freud's central discoveries – the unconscious, sexual repression, the Oedipus complex, and the like – were deployed by key Frankfurt School theorists to reconsider the relation between selfhood and society, the family and social-ization, ideology and political domination. In an essay 'Sociology and Psychology,' for example, Adorno defended the importance of Freud to social theory. He argued that psychoanalysis is valuable because it explored in detail the processes of identity formation in the late nineteenth and early twentieth centuries, and to that extent could be marshaled in the service of critical theory for the development of a critique of identity. Paradoxically, however, psychoanalysis is at its most radical when its concepts are pushed to breaking point – as with some of the wilder 'arm-chair' conjectures of Freud. 'In psychoanalysis,' Adorno wrote in *Minima Moralia*, 'nothing is true except the exaggerations.' What Adorno meant by this remark, it seems, is that the more outrageous features of Freud's work – the fictions of psychoanalysis, if you will – actually contain key insights into the contemporary social and political world. From this angle, Freud's theory of, say, castration anxiety (a theory which, as a universal condition, has been rejected even within psychoanalytic circles) can be recast as an appropriate *metaphor* for the destructive and brutal nature of social relationships promoted in an age of advanced capitalism. As Martin Jay (1984: 90) observes, what 'drew Adorno to the early Freud was the way in which his theory unflinchingly registered the traumas of contemporary existence. Telling the harsh truth was itself a kind of resistance to the acceptance of those traumas as inevitable.'

Marcuse's use of Freud in critical theory to understand modern society parallels some of the perspectives advanced by Adorno, but his writings were far more influential. Like Adorno, Marcuse focuses on the early 'biological' Freud, or what is termed 'drive theory.' Whilst this reliance on the traditional Freudian vocabulary of repressed drives and sexual energies is unfashionable today, and ultimately accounts for certain limitations in Marcuse's critical theory of society, it is also provides the conceptual context for many of his most important insights into how modern societies penetrate the internal landscape of identities in a profoundly repressive fashion. Both Marcuse and Adorno were, for example, deeply suspicious of American ego-psychology, a rewriting of Freudian theory away from its traditional focus on the split and fractured nature of the individual self and towards integration. Such a reading of Freud, argued Marcuse, robbed psychoanalysis of its revolutionary potential. Rather than graft society onto psychoanalysis, Marcuse sought to unfold psychoanalysis from the inside, in order to reveal its inherently critical edge. Unlike Adorno, however, Marcuse argues that the undoing of sexual repression opens the possibility for a radical transformation of identity, society and culture.

What has been of incomparable value, however, is the School's analysis of why human subjects, apparently without resistance, submit to the dominant ideologies of late capitalism. The general explanatory model developed by the Frankfurt School to study the socio-psychological dimension of the relation between the individual and culture has received considerable attention in social theory.

Fromm: fear of freedom

Fromm, who had been practicing as an analyst since 1926 and was a member of the Frankfurt Psychoanalytic Institute, sought in his early studies to integrate Freud's theory of the unconscious with Marxist sociology. Influenced by Wilhelm Reich's book *Character Analysis* (1972 [1933]), which connected society to the functioning of the unconscious, Fromm became preoccupied with the themes of sexuality and repression, as well as the mediating influence of the family between the economy and the individual. According to Fromm, Freudian psychoanalysis must supplement Marxism in order to grasp how social structures influence, indeed shape, the inner dimensions of personal life. Fromm's analysis of repression, however, differed substantially from that worked out by Reich. In Fromm's view, Reich had been unable to develop an adequate theory of society because he had reduced Freud's theory of sexuality to the level of individual psychology. Yet Freudian psychoanalysis, Fromm maintained, was fundamentally a 'social psychology.' For Fromm, the individual must be understood in his or her relation to others.

The social system, in Fromm's reinterpretation of Freud, shapes people's lives to fit the economic and cultural context of the historical age. Feudal society produced individuals adapted to the roles of serfs and lords; market capitalism produced individuals as capitalists and workers; and advanced monopoly capitalism churns out people as, first and foremost, consumers. Fromm describes this as the production of 'socially necessary character types.' Society goes to work, in effect, on individuals, ordering the psyche along pre-set social pathways, projecting social values and attitudes into the deepest recesses of the self. The result, says Fromm, is people 'wanting to act as they have to act.'

For Fromm, as for Freud, the family plays a key role in the emergence of repression. The winning of parental love entails the repression or denial of inner selfhood, and the adaptation to socially prescribed patterns of behavior. As Fromm puts this: 'The family is the medium through which the society or the social class stamps its specific structure on the child, and hence on the adult. *The family is the psychological agency of society*' (Fromm 1985 [1932]: 483). The family is an institution that implants external, social contradictions at the heart of personal life, sustains economic conditions as ideology, and shapes perceptions of the self as submissive, self-effacing and powerless. The central thread of Fromm's argument is that the destructive effects of late capitalism are not only centered on economic mechanisms and institutions, but involve the anchoring of domination within the inner life and psychodynamic struggles of each individual. If society, in Fromm's eyes, is a matter of sexual repression, libidinal renunciation, and pathologies of self, then it is really not all that far from the general tenets of classical Freudianism. In arguing that social and political relations affect self-identity in different and changing ways, Fromm enriches Freud's account of repression. Fromm's later writings, however, change direction quite dramatically. Increasingly skeptical of Freud's dualistic theory of the life and death drives (see subsequent discussion of Freud later in this chapter), he argued that classical Freudianism could not adequately grasp the importance of interpersonal relationships. In particular, Fromm rejected Freud's notion of the death drive, arguing that it only served to legitimate the increasingly destructive and aggressive tendencies of modern societies.

Significantly, Fromm also became influenced by neo-Freudian analysts – such as Harry Stack Sullivan and Karen Homey – who stressed larger social and cultural factors in the constitution of selfhood. This emphasis on cultural contributions to identity-formation was underscored in some of Fromm's major books, notably *Escape from Freedom* (1941) and *The Sane Society* (1955). These books put the argument for an essential 'nature of man', a nature repressed and distorted by capitalist patterns of domination.

In *The Sane Society* (1955), Fromm examines modern society in terms of the pathologies it inflicts upon selfhood, considering the extent to which the pressures of social life deform intimate relationships. In particular, he argues that Freud underemphasized social and cultural relations, and also the general impact of culture upon human needs. Selfhood, says Fromm, is best understood in terms of interpersonal processes. From this angle, psychical life is composed of emotional configurations derived from relations between self and others. For Fromm, self-organization, though influenced by unconscious drives and passion, is reflexively organized through 'awareness, reason and imagination.' Fromm's theory of selfhood can be stated in five theses:

1   *Relatedness vs. narcissism* The human condition is rooted in an essential need for relatedness – a thesis from which Fromm challenges Freud's so-called solitary individual. The need for relatedness is not instinctual, but arises from the separation with nature. The flourishing of intimacy depends upon creative social relations. Without such relations the self is impoverished, as in pathological narcissism.

2   *Transcendence-creativeness vs. destructiveness* Against the backdrop of our biological needs, personal and social creativity unfold in both positive and negative forms. Creation and destruction, Fromm argues, 'are both answers to the same need for transcendence, and the will to destroy must rise when the will to create cannot be satisfied.'

3   *Rootedness – brotherliness vs. incest* Mature social life, Fromm argues, depends upon an interplay of masculine and feminine values. Against what he considers the masculinist bent of Freud's work, Fromm

contends that the potential of the self depends upon the integration of feminine qualities (such as care and nurturing) into the masculine realm of reason. But for this very reason, feminine qualities are considered dangerous in modern society since they threaten incorporation back into a 'state of nature.'

4   *Sense of identity – individuality vs. herd conformity* The search for self-identity is intrinsic to the human condition, and modern societies play an essential role in structuring socio-economic possibilities for self-organization. The repressive transformation of this need, he argues, produces authoritarian ideologies such as fascism and anti-Semitism.

5   *The need for a frame of orientation and devotion – reason vs. irrationality* The need for emotional connection with the world is a precondition for human autonomy. Without emotional connection, the individual is drained of ego-strength.

The central feature of Fromm's work then is that helplessness or isolation are key building blocks in relations between the self and other people. In this respect, intimate relationships can be either progressive or regressive. Progressive relations with other people involve emotional qualities of care, empathy and love. The pain of individual isolation must be confronted and accepted in order for healthy interpersonal relations to develop. By contrast, a regressive involvement with other people is caused by denying individual separateness. In this mode of functioning, inner pain and emptiness are sidestepped by a neurotic immersion in infantile illusions. An endless menu of regressive fantasies is offered by mass consumer culture in this connection, fantasies which produce narcissistic pathology and related disturbances. The key feature in this neurotic, regressive zoning of the self is that other people are used instrumentally in order to bolster self-identity, and thus to avoid inner emptiness and isolation. Here Fromm's standpoint converges on a crucial object relational distinction between self-development and self-distortion – as in Fairbairn's formulation of good and bad object relations, or Winnicott's account of the true self and the false self. However, Fromm proposes a more open psychoanalytic theory of the self by directly linking interpersonal relations and social context. The core of his argument is that problems of self, which link with social relationship pathologies, have their roots in already-existing patterns of cultural domination. Because the spheres of economic, political and cultural life are shot through with the sadistic satisfactions of power and domination, regressive self-solutions are reproduced in the individual domain.

Given that contemporary social arrangements so violently deform and warp self-constitution, is there anything that can be done to reverse this pathological state of affairs? Can human beings create, and sustain, any kind of meaningful liberation? Fromm believes that they can. Surprisingly, given the pessimistic tone of the foregoing analysis, Fromm contends that it is still possible to face the painful realities of life in a mature and rational way. To do this, Fromm argues, it is vital for the self to *disengage* from the corrupting influences of the contemporary epoch. To live authentically means fashioning a creative and responsive selfhood, a self that can productively engage in intimacy and mutuality. Such a capacity, he contends, depends on coming to terms with individual separation and aloneness – realities that are usually experienced as isolation or emptiness in modern culture. A shorthand way of describing this is that Fromm is encouraging a more reflexive involvement with the self. But what then of social conflict? In this context, Fromm attempts to develop a moral dimension as an energizing vision for emancipation. The more that human subjects reclaim the possibility of authentic existence through introspection and self-reflection, the more a social order based on mutual respect and autonomous activity will develop.

Although Fromm's early studies on the integration of individuals into capitalism was broadly accepted by other members of the Frankfurt School, his subsequent, more sociological diagnosis of an essential human nature twisted out of shape by capitalism was strongly rejected. Marcuse, for example, charged Fromm (and other neo-Freudian revisionists) with undoing the critical force of Freud's most important ideas, such as the unconscious, repression and infantile sexuality. According to Marcuse, Fromm's revisionism underwrites the smooth functioning of the ego only by displacing the dislocating nature of the unconscious. Marcuse (1956: 240–1) sums up the central point in the following way:

> Whereas Freud, focusing on the vicissitudes of the primary drives, discovered society in the most concealed layer of the genus and individual man, the revisionists, aiming at the reified, ready-made form rather than at the origin of the societal institutions and relations, fail to comprehend what these institutions and relations have done to the personality that they are supposed to fulfil.

Fromm's attempt to add sociological factors to psychoanalysis, says Marcuse, results in a false political optimism as well as a liquidation of what is truly revolutionary in Freud: the discovery of the repressed unconscious.

Fromm's writings rank among the most important post-Freudian mappings of the relations between self and society. Indeed, his model has had a major influence upon the reception of psychoanalysis into social and cultural theory. There are, however, the important problems with humanistic psychoanalysis. It has been argued, for example, that his account of self-constitution and the social process leads to a form of sociological reductionism. What is meant by this charge is that Fromm reduces the complex, contradictory relations between self and society to a dull, mechanical reproduction of pre-existing social values. The subject is repressively constituted through certain agencies of socialization, which stamp the prescriptive values of society into the human soul and thereby deform the essential needs of the self. In this critique, Fromm presents an account of self-constitution that eliminates the profound role of unconscious imagination, and leaves unexamined the diverse human possibilities for agency, creativity, critical reflection and transformation. He reduces Freud's notion of the unconscious to a deterministic conception of individual malleability. The limitations of such an approach are plain. The ambivalence that Freud locates between self and society – the tension between psychical and social reality – is obliterated. Although wanting to compensate for Freud's focus on unconscious drives, Fromm's cultural analysis proceeds too far in the other direction – sociologizing psychical reality out of existence. Ironically, then, it is the *post*-Freudian Erich Fromm that ultimately speaks up for a *pre*-Freudian conception of the 'total personality.'

A related criticism is that Fromm evaluates society against some 'human essence' of a non-cultural kind. It is as if Fromm, having diagnosed modern selfhood as thoroughly ideological, has to safeguard some resistant kernel of the human condition in order to articulate an emancipatory claim at all. Rationality, individualism, transcendence: these ideals may be absent from modern society, but they underlie all human experience and will potentially transform the social world. But in arguing that there is a trans-historical, universal 'human condition,' Fromm seems blind to the fact that ideals such as rationality and self-mastery are often quite explicitly oppressive. Many contemporary world problems – global warming, the risk of massively destructive warfare, the exploitation and pollution of nature – are intimately bound up with the expansion of Western rationality and mastery. As one commentator puts it: 'Fromm revives all the time-honored values of idealist ethics as if nobody had ever demonstrated their conformist and repressive features' (Marcuse 1956: 258). Significantly, the ideals which Fromm stresses are also those of a male-dominated realm. Little is said about gender or the repression of female sexuality in Fromm's work. His humanistic psychoanalysis, and its underwriting of the 'essential needs of mankind' thus reproduces at a theoretical level masculinist or omnipotent self-control. Seen in this light, the inadequacy of Fromm's belief that authentic living is possible through social disengagement becomes evident: to turn inward in the hope of discovering authentic existence represents not a 'radical endeavor' but rather an illusory wish to overcome domination and suffering by escaping society.

Adorno: *The Authoritarian Personality*, anti-Semitism and the psychodynamics of modernity

Like Fromm, Adorno thought it important to study pathologies of culture – especially fascism – both sociologically and psychologically. For Adorno, investigating the role of irrational authoritarianism in the rise of fascism and anti-Semitism throughout Europe during the Second World War was of the utmost political importance. But so, too, was studying whether such evil could ever firmly take root in the United States. To that end, Adorno joined with Else Frenkel-Brunswik, Daniel J. Levison and R. Nevitt Sanford in the late 1940s to conduct a large-scale analysis of the 'potentially fascistic individual.' The result was one of Adorno's best known books, *The Authoritarian Personality* (1950).

In contributing to *The Authoritarian Personality*, Adorno was arguably seeking to find empirical confirmation for the social theory of domination he developed with Horkheimer in *The Dialectic of Enlightenment*. Again, Freudian psychoanalysis loomed large. Adorno found in fascist leaders, fascist regimes and fascist propaganda the psychodynamic logic of the 'sado-masochistic character' – of identities split between the bloodthirsty desire to denigrate and destroy outgroups on the one hand, and a submissive orientation to social authority on the other. Yet this was far from any simple-minded Freudianism. Like Fromm and Marcuse, Adorno sought to discern how the repressed unconscious shaped, and yet was itself shaped by, social and political conditions. 'The political, economic and social convictions of an individual,' wrote the authors of *The Authoritarian Personality*, 'often form a broad and coherent pattern, as if bound together by a 'mentality' or 'spirit,' and that this pattern is an expression of deep-lying trends in his personality.'

For our purposes, there are three key elements in Adorno's thesis of irrational authoritarianism spreading throughout modern societies. Succinctly put, these are (1) the thesis of the 'end of the individual'; (2) the triumph of the unconscious over consciousness of self; and, (3) the murderous rage associated with fascist tendencies or authoritarian identities. Let us briefly consider each of these points in turn.

Adorno's account of the rise of irrational authoritarianism proceeds from the insight that there has been a major shift in how society constitutes the individual. He contends that today, throughout the West, we witness the 'end of the individual.' Contemporary society overpowers the individual through a standardized, monotonous mass culture, leaving little room for authentic individualism. Instead, society produces authoritarian social character types. These claims are advanced by Adorno through an interpretation of Freudian psychoanalysis as revealing large-scale historical shifts in identity-formation. From this angle, Freud's theory of the Oedipus complex – the psychosexual drama involving the small infant's emotional dealings with its mother's love and father's authority – maps the realization of mature identities in the age of bourgeois capitalism. Throughout the liberal phase of capitalism, according to Adorno, the child's emerging sense of identity was dramatized through resistance to, and internalization of, the authority of the Oedipal father. The new world of administered capitalism, however, changes all that. In late modern society, massive changes in the economy directly serve to undermine the father's authority within the nuclear family. As businesses become corporate, and as jobs shrink or disappear at an unprecedented pace, men as fathers suffer a loss in economic and social standing. A father who becomes unemployed suffers new kinds of insecurity – not just economic, but emotional and social. One significant consequence of these changes from liberal capitalism to the administered society is that the child aspires less and less to be like its father, according to Adorno. In post-liberal societies, therefore, changes in family life mean that the father no longer functions as an agency of social repression. Instead, individuals are increasingly brought under the sway of the logic of techno-rationality itself, as registered in and through the rise of the culture industries. As Adorno summarized these historical developments in identity-constitution: 'The pre-bourgeois world does not yet know psychology, the oversocialised knows it no longer'. Repressive desublimation functions in Frankfurt School sociology as that psychic process which links what Adorno called the 'post-psychological individual' to the historical emergence of fascism and totalitarian societies.

These psychological and historical shifts in identity-formation lead to the second aspect of Adorno's account of authoritarian irrationalism, namely the individual's susceptibility to fascist ideologies. In 'Freudian theory and the pattern of Fascist propaganda,' written in 1951, Adorno argues that Freud's work on group psychology foresaw the rise of fascist movements, and that psychoanalysis provides a powerful explanation of the relation between leaders and followers. The psychological mechanisms uncovered by Freud's analyses of group processes are vitally significant to critical theory, Adorno argues, since they draw attention to the ways in which individuals yield to political manipulation by external, social agencies. For Adorno, as for Freud, the individual, when in a large group, is likely to identify less with its own 'ego-ideals' and more with impersonal 'group ideals.' This identification with the group involves the undoing of various repressions at the level of the individual, and Adorno argues that fascist propaganda transposes aggression into hatred of the outgroup – in short, racism. With reference to the theme of the 'end of the individual,' Adorno contends that fascist leaders become the guarantor of the social bond to the extent that fathers no longer represent a superior social authority. This is a complex psychoanalytic point, but broadly speaking

Adorno underscores that fascist leaders rarely present themselves as traditional figures of authority. The fascist leader is more likely to model himself in the style of an elder brother, as one who challenges traditional forms of patriarchal authority. Hitler as Fuhrer was just such a fascist leader, says Adorno: less a patriarchal president than an elder brother, the 'great little man.' 'Hitler,' wrote Adorno, 'posed as a composite of King Kong and the suburban barber.' This complex combination of power and personalism spoke to the Nazi movement's followers in a profound way, and ultimately resulted in masses hell-bent on violence. Adorno interprets such mobilizations of fascist, and especially anti-Semitic, aggression as suggestive of key changes in structures of personal subjectivity in modern societies as a whole. Indeed, he (1951: 136) writes of individuals today as 'postpsychological de-individualized social atoms.'

> The individual owes his crystallization to the form of political economy, particularly to those of the urban market. Even as the opponent of the pressure of socialization he remains the latter's most particular product and likeness... Socially, the absolute status granted to the individual marks the transition from the universal mediation of social relation – a mediation which, as exchange, always also requires curtailment of the particular interests realized through it – to direct domination, where power is seized by the strongest. Through this dissolution of all the mediating elements within the individual himself, by virtue of which he was, in spite of everything, also part of a social subject, he regresses, impoverished and coarsened, to the state of a mere social object... If today the trace of humanity seems to persist only in the individual in his decline, it admonishes us to make an end of the fatality which individualizes men, only to break them completely in their isolation.
>
> Theodor Adorno (1974 [1951]) *Minima Moralia: Reflections from Damaged Life*. Translated by E. F. N. Jephcott. London: NLB, pages 148–50.

It is obvious from all this that the individual subject, dominated by archaic unconscious impulses, languishes in the grip of an insanely powerful social order. What this period of Adorno's work represents, in fact, is psychoanalytic criticism transfigured by social theory. This is social theory as a more individually focused and less dispassionate enterprise, and which is thus able to harness the unconscious aspects of human activity to social research. Adorno's version of critical theory consists in generalizing beyond an image of the bureaucratized, administered world of advanced capitalism to consider how such alienated forms of consciousness become deeply implanted at the level of personal identity itself. This takes us to his final point concerning irrational authoritarianism – namely, that fascist ideology is a core mechanism for the seamless monolith of contemporary social processes. In *The Authoritarian Personality*, Adorno and his co-authors sought to identify how an all-pervasive social authority is internalized by women and men in what they called the F scale – designed as a measurement of fascist potential. Through over two hundred questionnaires and detailed psycho-analytic profiles, Adorno and his colleagues explored such topics as their respondents' early childhoods, family relationships and wider political 'world-views.' The F scale sought to measure implicit 'prefascist tendencies' towards anti-Semitism, ethnocentrism and political and economic conservatism. To clarify the personal dimensions of fascist ideology, *The Authoritarian Personality* identified nine emotional traits of interviewees who were judged to be high as regards possible authoritarian tendencies:

1   *Conventionalism*: A rigid adherence to middle-class values and inflexible attitudes to others.
2   *Authoritarian Submission*: An uncritical, submissive orientation to figures of authority.
3   *Authoritarian Aggression*: A tendency to actively search out people who transgress conventional values, with the desire to see them punished.
4   *Anti-Intraception*: Rejection of imagination, creativity or the emotionally-minded.
5   *Stereotype and Superstition*: Belief in the mystical determinants of fate, as well as ordering of the world through rigid stereotypes.
6   *Power and Toughness*: An exaggerated assertion of strength, coupled to a preoccupation with dichotomies – dominance/submission, strong/weak, leader/follower.
7   *Destructiveness and Cynicism*: Generalized hostility and even hatred of the human condition.
8   *Projectivity*: The projection of unwanted emotional aspects of the self onto others.
9   *Sex*: An exaggerated concern with the sexual activities of others.

Whilst Adorno and his colleagues did not discuss in any detail how widespread the authoritarian personality might be in conditions of advanced capitalism, the study did suggest that this syndrome is especially characteristic of the lower middle-classes in Europe. The conclusion of the book is that the authoritarian suffers from ego weakness, idealizes social authority, submits in the face of powerful social forces, and demonstrates propensities for racial prejudice and ethnic hatred.

The Authoritarian Personality has been criticized as an attempt to reduce the complex social phenomenon of authoritarianism to the level of individual psychology. If, indeed, Adorno and his colleagues had meant to show that every social formation with authoritarian or fascist potential could be explained away through reference to childhood experiences or stereotypical character traits, then the criticism of 'psycho-babble' could reasonably apply. However, such criticism is surely wide of the mark. For Adorno in particular, transformations in identity-formation – and especially pathologies of the self – are inscribed in the very structures of social life, while the analysis of personality traits in relation to authority, and particularly anti-Semitism, can only be adequately undertaken with sociological reference to major changes in the family, culture and the economy. What is pathological about authoritarianism for Adorno is traced not only to disturbances of the psyche, but to general developments in the nature of rationality. Whether Adorno's social theory will do as an explanation of *social pathologies* is, however, perhaps more questionable. His general theoretical and political conclusions, for one thing, would appear to render individuals mere ciphers of the wider society. This is problematic because, if an unconscious authoritarian submission exerts its hold everywhere, then this must presumably extend to the realm of critical social theory itself; what is striking about the more pessimistic elements of Adorno's cultural diagnosis, in other words, is that logically it would appear impossible for the Frankfurt School to have unearthed the thesis of the 'end of the individual' in the first place. Adorno does indeed speak of personal autonomy as essential to the flowering of democracy, but the global tone of his pessimistic, social theory overrides such occasional contrasts to the dominance of authoritarian identities. And even within the sociological terms of the 'Dialectic of Enlightenment,' it seems likely that Adorno overestimated the degree of cultural cohesion operating within modern societies. To that extent, as Terry Eagleton (1990: 47) comments, Adorno judged the contemporary social order 'as it would *wish* to appear.'

Written in the stars: Adorno on astrology

What's in a star forecast? For many people, reading a magazine astrology column is merely a source of amusement. But not so, says Theodor Adorno, who sees in such commodified mass culture something far more sinister and disabling. For Adorno, the newspaper or magazine astrology column follows the social logics of the American entertainment industry – from TV soaps to Hollywood movies. Instead of the differentiated elements of selfhood on the one hand and culture on the other, astrology collapses the former into the latter, promoting conventional and contended attitudes in the process. Unable to accommodate social contradictions without commodifying them, newspaper and magazine astrology columns offer stereotypical scenes to remind us of the *dependency* of our social existence in the administered world of late capitalism.

In the early 1950s, during a return visit to the United States from Germany, Adorno undertook a study of an astrology column in the *Los Angeles Times*. The result was 'The Stars Down to Earth.' According to Adorno, Caroll Righter's 'Astrological Forecasts' column in the *Los Angeles Times* promoted attitudes of fatalism. This is the attitude that, whilst we live in a threatening world where things are out of control, it is nonetheless a world where things are likely to turn out for the best in the long run. As Adorno (1994: 56–57) develops this point:

> The semi-rationality of 'everything will be fine' is based on the fact that modern American society in spite of all its conflicts and difficulties succeeds in reproducing the life of those whom it embraces. There is some dim awareness that the concept of the forgotten man is outdated. The column feeds on this awareness by teaching the readers not to be afraid of being weak. They are reassured that all their problems will solve themselves even if they feel that they themselves are unable to solve them. They are made to understand – and in a way rightly – that the very same powers by which they are threatened, the anonymous totality of the social process, are also those which will somehow take care of them.

What, in your view, does the regular newspaper or magazine astrology column tell us about the nature of modern societies? Is Adorno's thesis of psychological dependency and social conformism still relevant to today's global realities?

Marcuse: Eros, or one-dimensional futures?

For Marxist social theorist Herbert Marcuse, one-time member of the Frankfurt School and close colleague of Horkheimer and Adorno, this deranged logic of capitalism is, among other things, imposed through the culture industries of advertising, marketing and entertainment. Capitalism for Marcuse operates on a deeply unconscious level, a realm of chimerical fantasy in which sexuality is paradoxically stripped of erotic aura and transferred to the selling of things – both products and people. Marcuse calls this insidious process 'repressive desublimation.' The power of capitalism is that we are all embroiled in a social landscape of commodities and wages, prices and profits. Gradually but unstoppably, people in such a world come to feel personally content only when their appetites and desires are dictated by the emotional system in advance, by socially controlled desublimation.

Marcuse was in broad agreement with Horkheimer and Adorno as regards the thesis of a 'decline of the individual.' Having departed Germany when Hitler came to power, Marcuse joined with his Frankfurt School colleagues in the United States and, throughout the late 1930s and 1940s, worked on a series of research projects investigating transformations of state and monopoly capitalism, the dynamics of mass communication and popular culture, social dislocation, racism, anti-Semitism and other forms of authoritarianism. According to Marcuse, modern culture is repressive, often tyrannically so. However, the transformation of society remains the key to utopian thinking, critical theory and progressive politics. In an early book, *Reason and Revolution* (1941), Marcuse speaks up for the progressive side of utopian thinking. Yet he takes to task those Marxists who argued either that socialism was an inevitable outcome of history, or that workers were the revolutionary agent of social change. Such standpoints for Marcuse were far too simple. The collapse of the Russian revolution into Soviet Marxism, the failure of various working-class movements and the decline of political dissidence as a result of the rise of mass communications and popular culture were all for Marcuse signs that there could be no privileged agents in the transformation of social life. That this is the case is not necessarily bad news for progressive politics, however. Just because political developments had not unfolded in the manner predicted by orthodox Marxism did not mean that social change was either unjustified or unlikely. A non-repressive society for Marcuse always remained a theoretical and political possibility, and in attempting to address these problems he opened new perspectives in critical social theory by turning to Freud and psychoanalysis.

It is against this political and intellectual backdrop that Marcuse's seminal *Eros and Civilization* (1956) should be contextualized, as a work that was at once resolutely critical of existing capitalist societies and profoundly utopian in its defense of the possibilities for radical social change. Repression is Marcuse's theme from beginning to end in *Eros and Civilization*, and in particular the Freudian insight that the renunciation of emotional energy and sensuality is always filtered through both historical and trans-historical forces. People suffer from too much repression in contemporary society, says Marcuse. The contradictions of capitalism, he argues, pass all the way down into the deepest textures of lived experience and personal subjectivity. Capitalist processes of technological mechanization and standardization have become inscribed within the inner fabric of identity, particularly as a result of the oppressive, dull labor to which people are subjected. Here Marcuse's ideological target was the cultural conformity of middle America, of faceless bureaucrats coping with the crushing repetitions demanded by the workplace and of middle-class housewives bored with their lives at home in the suburbs. Something was deeply amiss. America in the 1950s was easily the wealthiest and most industrially advanced society on earth, and yet such economic prosperity seemed to run directly counter to the constrained and constraining lives that people experienced, most especially in terms of emotional literacy and interpersonal relationships. Repression, for Marcuse as for Freud, was vital in converting nature into culture, and he interpreted the classical psychoanalytic account of the Oedipus complex as a kind of social parable regarding sexual and social reproduction. According to Marcuse, however, the torments and repressions of contemporary women and men are not quite the same as those of Freud's era. In his view, repression has become heightened, with particularly excessive restrictions placed on sensuality and eroticism, in a world organized around prices and profits, money and monopolistic corporations.

How to explain this? Marcuse presented much of his historical analysis in the language of Freud, but throughout *Eros and Civilization* he sought to contextualize psychoanalytic insights within the broader Marxist tradition of critical theory. In contemporary societies, the unconscious is denied true expression as a result of the reproduction of capitalist profit and exploitation. In Marcuse's view, however, Freud's interpretation of the conflict between repressed desire and social order was ahistorical, which in turn renders a picture of social repression the same in all possible worlds. To recapture this potential historical dimension of psychoanalysis, Marcuse distinguished between two kinds of repression: 'basic repression' and 'surplus repression.' Basic repression refers to the minimum level of sexual renunciation for facing social life and the tasks of culture. Marcuse contends that a certain amount of repression is always necessary for effective socialization and social order. Surplus repression, by contrast, refers to the intensification of self-restraint generated by capitalist exploitation and asymmetrical relations of power. Marcuse gives as an example of this repressive surplus the conjugal family, in which the conventional sexual norms of patriarchy are strictly enforced in the interests of maintaining existing values and society. The repression this surplus generates is not necessarily understood very well by individuals in terms of its emotional damage. According to Marcuse, repression becomes surplus to requirements as a result of the 'performance principle,' a culturally specific form of sexual and social demands instituted by the economic order of capitalism. According to Marcuse, the capitalist performance principle recasts repression as surplus in several key ways. The performance principle causes human beings to face one another as 'things' or 'objects,' replaces general eroticism with genital sexuality, and fashions a disciplining of the human body (what Marcuse calls 'repressive desublimation') so as to prevent repressed desire from interfering with capitalist exchange values.

In a subsequent book, *One-Dimensional Man* (1964), Marcuse takes the analysis of the forces of domination to extreme lengths. In the course of the twentieth century, says Marcuse, our personal and social lives are constantly being pulled in two directions at the same time. Arguably, with the advent of advanced industrial society, people's encounter with culture becomes more individuated, complex and subtle. Yet on another level, this potential cultural and aesthetic liberation within advanced capitalism has been thoroughly stunted. Advanced capitalism has brought little more than domestic appliances, Hollywood movies and packaged holidays into the reach of many people in the West. In this age of mass consumerism and popular culture, according to Marcuse, a new social order has emerged that sharply curtails individuality, dissent and opposition. Advanced capitalism generates a one-dimensional society based on 'false' consumer needs, and increasingly integrates individuals into the smooth running of a mass system of domination and social inequality. In Marcuse's view, the most striking feature of the modern world is conformity. Contemporary forms of repression and domination are suffocating, and it is against this backdrop that Marcuse raises the issue of how society might confront the systematic erosion of critical thinking, dissent and opposition to capitalism and industrial management. 'How,' writes Marcuse, 'can the administered individuals – who have made their mutilation into their own liberties and satisfactions . . . liberate themselves from themselves as well as from their masters? How is it even thinking that the vicious circle be broken?'

The desublimation rampant in advanced industrial society reveals its truly conformist function. This liberation of sexuality (and of aggressiveness) frees the instinctual drives from much of the unhappiness and discontent that elucidate the repressive power of the established universe of satisfaction. To be sure, there is pervasive unhappiness, and the happy consciousness is shaky enough – a thin surface over fear, frustration and disgust. This unhappiness lends itself easily to political mobilization; without room for conscious development, it may become the instinctual reservoir for a new fascist way of life and death. But there are many ways in which the unhappiness beneath the happy consciousness may be turned into a source of strength and cohesion for the social order. The conflicts of the unhappy now seem far more amenable to cure than those which made for Freud's 'discontent in civilization,' and they seem more adequately defined in terms of the 'neurotic personality of our time' than in terms of the eternal struggle between Eros and Thanatos.

Herbert Marcuse (1964) *One-Dimensional Man*. Boston: Beacon Press, pages 76–7.

What, then, of the possibilities for change? Marcuse differs sharply from Freud as regards the nature of emancipation. Marcuse contends that the performance principle, ironically, generates the cultural conditions necessary for a radical transformation of society. What promises an end to surplus repression are the industrial-technological advancements of late capitalism itself. For Marcuse, the material affluence generated by Western capitalist industrialization and techno-science opens the way for an unraveling of sexual repression. The overcoming of cultural domination will release repressed unconscious forces, permitting the reconnection of sexual drives and fantasy to the social network. Such a reconciliation between culture and the unconscious will usher in a new, sensuous reality – a reality Marcuse calls 'libidinal rationality.' Libidinal rationality, though abstract as a concept, involves a radical reversal of surplus repression. Liberation from this surplus will facilitate a general eroticism, not only of the body, but of nature and cultural organization. Yet Marcuse's grounding of social theory in psychoanalysis stresses that emancipation requires more than just sexual freedom. It demands an integration of sexuality and love into transformed social, institutional life.

How are we to understand this notion of libidinal rationality? Is it just some emancipatory dream of the Frankfurt School theorist Herbert Marcuse, or does it unearth certain psychical tendencies that point towards an alternative social condition? As a resexualizing of social life, libidinal rationality can be interpreted as an encouragement of emotional communication and intimacy. Fantasy occupies a special place in this context, Marcuse says, since desire contains a repressed truth value. As he puts this:

> Imagination envisions the reconciliation of the individual with the whole, of desire with realization, of happiness with reason. While this harmony has been removed into utopia by the established reality principle, fantasy insists that it must and can become real, that behind the illusion lies knowledge.
>
> (1956)

Fantasy is itself a longing for reconciliation – between pleasure and rationality, desire and reality. For Marcuse, this recovery of unconscious desire will facilitate the resexualization of the human body, thus creating harmonious social relations. Against the repressive structuring of 'sex' under the performance principle, the release of fantasy will eroticize all aspects of society, allowing for a spontaneous and playful relation to life.

Criticisms of Marcuse

There remain many unresolved difficulties in Marcuse's work. Among these it is important to mention deficiencies in his approach to human agency, particularly his long-standing emphasis upon the concept of the repressed unconscious as the key to social transformation; the limitations of his analysis of contemporary societies, especially as regards the critique of domination and exploitation; and a series of problems to do with human needs, meanings, ethics and justice. Let me briefly address these three criticisms in turn.

Firstly, in an age of media sound-bites, spin and seduction, Marcuse's ironic concept of 'repressive desublimation' serves as a powerful tool with which to grasp how apparent forms of sexual liberalization actually serve to promote heightened repression. Marcuse's argument is that the glossy commercialization of sexuality we see everywhere in the West today confines human desire, eroticism and intimacy to only a partial and restrictive understanding of sexuality. In this view, the sex industry in all its guises, from porno movies to lap-dancing clubs, serves to dull human sexuality and instead promotes conventional behavior and values. Yet if such a viewpoint offers a powerful critique of the repressive contradictions of capitalism and mass culture, it nonetheless remains certainly vulnerable to charges of oversimplifying both the psychoanalytic understanding of emotional life as well as the complex, contradictory relations between self and society. Many would now agree, for example, that Marcuse's conceptualization of surplus repression is wanting. His recasting of repression as surplus in order to capture aspects of the dismantling of emotional contradictions fostered by one-dimensional mass culture, whilst provocative, ultimately gives rise to a top-heavy version of cultural domination, where society stands over and above the individual agent. The problem with this is that it overlooks the fact that the psyche is shot through with unconscious conflict, which in Freudian terms is one important reason why selfhood can never be serenely inserted into social relations without tensions and contradictions. A related difficulty stemming from Marcuse's wall-to-wall image of surplus repression is that he is subsequently forced to round the individual subject back upon itself in order to find an escape route from the contemporary performance principle. The way forward is through the unconscious – which, somehow, is beyond the scope of social domination, and thus prefigurative of an alternative society. Despite this stress on alternative political visions, however, Marcuse has remarkably little to say about new forms of intimacy, interpersonal relationships or cultural association. His utopianism rather focuses on the overcoming of sexual repression. Yet such a vision of liberation is highly questionable. A mechanistic conception of the repressed unconscious, and not people, is key to Marcuse's view of social transformation. Human agency is reduced to domination, while the repressed unconscious is linked to emancipation. But this gives rise to a thorny political issue: if the individual subject is obsolescent and repression complete, who would be in a position to transform, or even to know, the truth of the unconscious? Who, exactly, would be capable of sustaining a liberation known as 'libidinal rationality'? Marcuse's focus upon unconscious potentialities, although valuable in some respects, actually mirrors an individualist culture which forecloses issues about social bonds and cultural association. Significantly, Marcuse's argument in favor of the liberation of repressed drives also smacks of essentialism. This argument recalls a *pre*-Freudian view of human passion as somehow natural and timeless, outside and beyond the reach of the social structure. The view that the repressed unconscious, or fantasy itself, will only gain expression in the non-repressive society falls to see that fantasy structures are already bound up with institutional life. Such a view fails to recognize that the 'truth of the unconscious' is already interconnected with embattled human relationships, violent gender tensions and ideological conflict.

Secondly, there have been a number of sharp criticisms made of Marcuse's analysis of the nature of modern societies, particularly his account of advanced capitalism. It is important to be quite specific about the limitations of Marcuse's social theory in this respect, as there are contradictory elements in his analysis of modern societies and it is my view that he did not manage to reconcile these elements successfully. Now the bleak critique of advanced capitalism that Marcuse outlined in *One-Dimensional Man* stands in blunt opposition to his optimistic analysis of the potentialities for radical social transformation in *Eros and Civilization*. Some critics have put this discrepancy down to Marcuse's heavy concentration upon the American postwar boom in the former book, while other critics have noted his implicit indebtedness to German Romanticism in the latter book. Whatever the exact division between these optimistic and pessimistic threads in his thinking, however, it is clear that the idea of an emergent stabilization of capitalism played an important role throughout the bulk of his writings. But there are good reasons to object to Marcuse's outline of such trends of social development. For one thing, in focusing too exclusively on the containment of the contradictions and crisis-tendencies of advanced capitalism, Marcuse seemed to assume that cultural conformity plays a central role in the reproduction of modern societies. But such consequences are not borne out by recent sociological research, which rather indicates that social reproduction can be an unintended consequence of the rejection of the values and norms promoted by popular culture and the mass media. For another, in overemphasizing the intensification of technological rationality in our own time and its capacity to integrate culture, society and personhood into a closed, harmonious system, Marcuse's social theory remains unable to account for what prompted the widespread social revolt of the 1960s – notwithstanding his close association with various aspects of these revolts. And his social theory is equally lacking in critical edge if forced to confront, say, the recent war on terrorism or the global economic crisis of the early twenty-first century. Nowhere did Marcuse adequately confront the potential explosive disequilibrium of global capitalist markets, nor the massive development of militarization on the part of the world's superpowers.

Finally, some critics have lampooned Marcuse's radical politics and vision of utopia. Marcuse's social theory addresses what the transformation of libido would mean at the level of the whole society, as the notion of 'libidinal rationality' tries to clarify what counts as creative, sensuous reason between individuals, groups and nations. For some of its critics, however, the very idea of an eroticized reason is a contradiction in terms, since rationality and the passions remain stubbornly particular and are separate domains. Reason is universal, emotion is particular. This contradiction, however, is only apparent – and for reasons which Marcuse's writings actually make clear. When social rationalization is pressed beyond all reason, it flips over into surplus repression; and one name for such pathology is 'repressive desublimation.' The problem is not that reason and emotion are separated, but that a deformed, perverse version of the latter has come to exert the upper hand over the former. Historically speaking, however, social conditions now offer the slim possibility of eliminating surplus repression. What social theory needs to engage, in Marcuse's own terms, is a 'new rationality of gratification.' This position, however, still gives rise to the dilemma of how people could ever determine that a form of rationality was sufficiently aesthetic, concerned with creativity, fulfillment, pleasure. As David Held writes of this problem, 'one cannot simply appeal, as Marcuse does, to instincts to settle questions about real wants; for wants cannot be articulated independently of the circumstances of their development and of the way in which they are conceived.' Marcuse may indeed be correct, following Freud, in locating reason or rationality in unconscious desire. But even if this reason is an outcrop of desire, social theory still demands a language for grappling with how individual needs and potentials are constituted, conceived and recognized between social actors. This is not to take issue with Marcuse's vision of freedom in terms of the 'rationality of gratification,' but it is to raise questions about how concrete history bears on the deliberation of the actual needs and desires of individual human beings. Such questions necessarily involve a shift away from the rather solitary Freudian language of individual drives, desires and repressions and toward a more interpersonal language of communication, discourse and symbolic exchange.

Summary points

1   The Frankfurt School – or first generation of critical theorists – refers to the work of leading German neo-Marxist intellectuals who transcended orthodox Marxism through an interdisciplinary integration of sociology, economics, politics and psychoanalysis. The contribution to social theory of the Frankfurt School remains one of the most important of the twentieth century, and critical theory in particular caught the imagination of intellectuals and new social movements in the 1960s and 1970s.

2   The Frankfurt School, in numerous theoretical projects, was concerned above all with the 'dark side' of the modern age, and traced various social pathologies back to general developments in the nature of reason, rationality and the Enlightenment.

3   Reason, according to the Frankfurt School, has become inherently pathological. In Horkheimer and Adorno's *Dialectic of Enlightenment*, society – in securing its own survival through the domination of nature – secretly mutilates itself and destroys the opportunity for freedom. Reason today is automatically transformed into instrumental rationality, and simply to act as an individual subject is to denigrate and destroy.

4   Utilizing Freudian psychoanalysis, the Frankfurt School undertook various investigations of the psychodynamics of identity, politics, culture and ideology. In Fromm's work, psychoanalysis is used to focus on the family as mediator between self and society. In Adorno, Freud is utilized to analyze fascism, anti-Semitism and authoritarian irrationalism. In Marcuse, Freudian psychoanalysis is read 'against the grain' to develop a general social theory of modern societies.

5   The arrival of the administered world of advanced capitalism, according to Adorno and Marcuse, means that the role of the patriarchal family is undermined in identity-formation.

6   The totally administered society eliminates the requirement for adaptive citizens with a measure of autonomy, one result of which is heightened levels of repression. As a result, society extends its domination over the personal domain through increasing levels of control over the individual's unconscious. This societal manipulation produces what Adorno terms the 'boundlessly elastic, subjectless subject.'

7   In Marcuse's work, modern societies are portrayed as increasingly 'one-dimensional' in scope. This gives rise to an oppressive existence for many, in which people suffer from crippling levels of 'surplus

repression' and are traumatized by the harsh economic imperatives of the capitalist 'performance principle.'

8   For Marcuse, all sociality contains a utopian possibility. Even the most repressive social regimes cannot shut off the radical imagination. A revitalized society for Marcuse is one in which 'libidinal rationality' will flower, permitting reconciliations between reason and desire, intimacy and sexuality.

9   One key criticism is that critical theory betrays an overreaction to fascism. The sociological and political claims of Adorno and Marcuse especially tend to elide some of core institutional differences between liberal capitalism and fascist regimes.

Further questions

1   Contemporary western cultures are obsessed with consumption. Do you agree?

2   The bureaucratic administration of society turns reason into its opposite. Evaluate this claim.

3   Why is the Freudian psyche important for social critique?

4   In our age of global terrorism, do people fear freedom?

5   The Frankfurt School sees repression as central to political domination. In our supposed age of liberal, anything goes society, how does an analysis of repression contribute to cultural critique?

Further reading

Frankfurt School

(edited by Andrew Arato and Eike Gebhardt) *Essential Frankfurt School Reader* (New York: Continuum, 1982)

Theodor Adorno

(with Max Horkheimer) *Dialectic of Enlightenment: Philosophical Fragments*. Trans. Edmunt Jephcott (Stanford: Stanford University Press, 2002)

(with co authors) *The Authoritarian Personality* (New York: Harper and Row, 1950)

Minima Moralia (London: NLB, 1974)
Negative Dialectics. Translated by E.B. Ashton (London: Routledge, 1973)
The Culture Industry (London: Routledge, 2001)

Erich Fromm

Escape From Freedom (New York: Farrar & Rinehart, 1941)
The Sane Society (New York: Rinehart, 1955)
The Anatomy of Human Destructiveness (Holt Paperbacks, 1992)
The Art of Loving (Allen & Unwin, 1957)

Herbert Marcuse

Eros and Civilization (Boston: Beacon Press, 1955)
One-Dimensional Man (Boston: Beacon Press, 1964)
The Aesthetic Dimensions (Boston: Beacon Press, 1978)

chapter 4

American Pragmatisms

Contents

Pragmatism is the one enduring tradition of social and philosophical thought to have begun uniquely in America. Since Charles Sanders Peirce first sketched the idea of pragmatism in 1878, it has come to influence thinkers around the world. Thus, when attempting to understand pragmatism, the first fact to consider is its association with the down-to-earth, action-oriented values many consider the dominant cultural ethic in the United States. Of course, generalities of this sort leave out the fine-grained details; no single set of values or ideas can be simply American or German or French or whatever. Yet, it remains that social theories are always rooted in historical circumstance and, therefore, reflect something of the social experiences of a given culture. Still, social theories would not endure beyond the time of their origins were they not able at least to call attention to some set of truths that transcend a locale or a time.

Pragmatism entered American life at a crucial but bitter moment in the nation's history – the years just following its Civil War (1861–1865). That war was violent beyond belief. Some 600,000 on both sides died in battle or from disease. The civil conflict threatened the very idea of the *United* States as a union of diverse states with a common purpose. When it was all over in 1865, the nation was awash in blood that carried away many of the cultural and even scientific traditions that had emerged since its War of Independence (1775–1783).

From the revolution of the 1770s until the Civil War of the 1860s, the new American society struggled to establish itself as an independent nation with its own political system, a free economy among others in the Atlantic system of world trade, and its own distinctive culture. The dissidents and economic refugees coming to the New World had to detach themselves from the past from which their European ancestors had fled but to which they remained connected. As a result, long after its political system was well established, America had yet to find its unique cultural voice.

It is commonly said that the American declaration of *cultural* independence was a speech given at Harvard in 1837 by Ralph Waldo Emerson. In his 'The American Scholar' oration, Emerson proclaimed the necessity for the scholar to take his place among the practical men who were building the towns and cultivating the farms. The time had come, he said, for America to make room for Man Thinking. The American Scholar would not however be a recluse or a mere speculator. She too (and Emerson meant women as well as men) would be engaged in public life, as he was. 'Action is with the scholar subordinate,' he said, 'but it is essential.' The day after Emerson's August 31, 1837 proclamation at Harvard, he met in Boston with a group of intellectuals to form what some called the Transcendental Club (Richardson, 1995: 266–70). Members of the Transcendental Club shared the common purpose of rethinking European philosophies in ways consistent with American cultural independence.

Forty-five years later, in 1872, just across the river from Emerson's club in Boston, another club was loosely organized in Cambridge, Massachusetts. Its members were a good generation younger than Emerson. They had all lived through the Civil War – several as combatants, all as veterans of America's soul-wrenching internal war over slavery. Some called this the Metaphysical Club (Menand, 2001: 201–32). Its members included Charles Sanders Peirce and William James, acknowledged founders of pragmatism. Though its name suggests a reversion to classically European philosophies, the Metaphysical Club was a haven for ideas that were even more practical than Emerson's. Some years later, in *Pragmatism: A New Name for Some Old Ways of Thinking* (1907), William James would popularize and explain the pragmatic method: 'To develop a thought's meaning, we need only determine what conduct it is fitted to produce: that conduct is its sole significance.'

On the surface, Emerson's club in 1837 and James's in 1872 would seem to have shared a commitment to the importance of action in social and philosophical thought. They did, but, more deeply; pragmatism differed sharply from Emerson's American transcendentalism by bringing action and its relations to thought and language to the forefront of the new method. To be sure, Peirce and James, like Emerson, were highly sophisticated philosophers (as the names of their clubs remind us). But the early pragmatists were philosophers with a fresh agenda in which the consequences of ideas for social and practical life were essential *and* primary. The writings of social theorists in the pragmatist tradition are not always clear and succinct to the practical mind. Still, in this tradition one can see the background influence of the practical experiences of the American nation – a society committed to building a state self-consciously different from that which it rebelled against, in spite of the many social, political and ideological challenges it faced in the century since the War of Independence. Such a project requires attention to practical realities. It may not always succeed, as today we realize that the American experiment has failed in many ways. Yet, whatever is good, or even acceptable, about the nation's institutions and its culture is owed largely to its famous willingness to solve, or try to solve, the world's problems. Pragmatist social theories are decidedly not as simple as this easy slogan, but they are related to this quality of American history.

The reader may find it strange in a book on *contemporary* social theory to begin a chapter with allusions to nineteenth-century intellectual movements; and then, to discuss William James and Charles Sanders Peirce, writers who died early in the twentieth century. Social theory in North America, unlike its counterparts in Europe, was late to develop for several reasons. As recently as the mid-twentieth century, American culture as a whole was still very young – agile in many ways but slow to disentangle itself from Europe's. When Americans began to assert themselves as independent thinkers, they had to rely on the European ideas in which they had been schooled. Emerson's Transcendental Club, for example, was named after the key term in German idealism of Immanuel Kant (1724–1804), the great eighteenth-century Enlightenment philosopher. Furthermore, until late in the nineteenth century, the United States lacked anything like the university system it has today. William James, as a child, attended European schools and, later, as a distinguished Harvard professor, visited Europe often to study the latest scientific and philosophical methods. Harvard, in James's student days, was just emerging from the small, parochial school of Emerson's day. Less obviously, it could be said that 'theory' did not move the American heart or head as 'theory' today still does not. After the Civil War, the business and industrial sectors matured (if that is the word) much more quickly than, even, America's political system and, certainly, than its scientific and intellectual institutions.

It was, thus, only in the mid-twentieth century that a growing number of Americans began to read European social theories as distinct from Europe's classical philosophical literatures. Until then, American social thinkers were more likely to have been psychologists or philosophers. American sociology, for example, first prominently institutionalized at the University of Chicago in 1892, was a field for researchers who worked on empirical problems arising from the welter of ethnic and racial differences of the immigrant populations whose labor drove the burgeoning industrial United States. It was not until the world-wide revolts of the 1960s that American culture began to explore theory as a way of understanding the world. Theory can be obscure, but one thing it does better than the collecting of data is to demand a deeper and broader intellectual attitude. Only when the cultural and global political crises of the 1960s proved unyielding to sheer empirical science did the founding traditions of pragmatism begin to influence social theory in the United States: James, Peirce, and the theorists that followed them, in different ways and to differing degrees, influenced 'contemporary' to American social thinking at the time of its tardy but most robust growth after the 1960s.

William James: experience and the social self

William James did not invent pragmatism. Peirce did. James himself was generous enough to say so in 1907 in *Pragmatism: A New Name for Old Ways of Thinking*. William James was the one who popularized the new method which, as things turned out, was far more than just a 'new name' for traditional ideas. The genius of the popularizer, is to be able to link the new with the familiar. *Pragmatism* did just that by challenging two prevailing schools of nineteenth-century epistemology, the philosophical theory of knowledge. These were on the one hand, *rationalism*, which holds that knowing begins with principles, of which the most famous was then Immanuel Kant's philosophy that we can never know things in themselves.

Knowledge, Kant argued, begins with mental categories; hence the name rationalism. On the other hand, there was *empiricism,* for which knowing begins with observation or sense experience of the real world, popularized by the works of John Locke and David Hume, the leaders of the English and Scottish Enlightenment. William James cleverly situated pragmatism as a third way between the two schools of modern scientific philosophy.

In 1907, William James, writing ever more simply of ideas that Peirce first spoke of some twenty years before, began with the bold statement that truth is nothing more, nothing less, than an idea that works:

> *True ideas are those that we can assimilate, validate, corroborate, and verify. False ideas are those that we can not.* That is the practical difference it makes for us to have true ideas; that, therefore, is the meaning of truth, for it is all that truth is known-as . . . . The truth of an idea is not a stagnant property inherent in it. Truth *happens* to an idea. It *becomes* true, is *made* true by events.

(2000: 88)

So when James spoke of verifying and validating an idea he was not referring to the pure logical procedure. He was referring instead to ideas that were tools for making sense of human experience, without falling into either the rationalist or the empiricist camps of principles imposed deductively or induced from evidence. Experience was, in effect, a primary, generative aspect of human life.

Pragmatism asks its usual question. 'Grant an idea or belief to be true,' it says, 'what concrete difference will its being true make in anyone's life? How will the truth be realized? What experiences will be different from those which one would obtain if the belief were false? What, in short, is the truth's cash-value in experiential terms?' The moment pragmatism asks this question, it sees the answer. True ideas are those that we can assimilate, validate, corroborate, and verify. False ideas are those we cannot. That is the practical difference it makes to us to have true ideas; that therefore is the meaning of truth, for it is all that truth is known as.

William James (1907) *Pragmatism: A New Name for Some Old Ways of Thinking.* Oxford (UK): Longmans, page 97.

In our day, still early in the twentieth-first century, many theorists who are familiar with twentieth century debates over logical or empirical positivisms and analytic philosophies would say that James's pragmatism was a sincere but insufficient response to nineteenth-century debates. Indeed, one need not be a latter day empiricist or rationalist to find James's theory of truth not up to the demands of social theory in our time. Beyond this, where James does come down to us in still powerful ways is by what is known, because of him, as the idea of the social self.

James actually started out in medicine, then turned to biology and physiology – fields then as now not obviously associated with the Self concept. In 1876, however, James abruptly changed his teaching program at Harvard to include what was then called physiological psychology. It would be a good while before his first major publication in this new field. Finally in 1890, when he was already 48 years old, he published his first major book, *Principles of Psychology*, which earned James the reputation for being a founder of modern psychology. This sprawling textbook of nearly 1,300 pages is little read today – except for its still famous Chapter 10, 'The Consciousness of Self.' The enduring value of this single chapter is that it invented the key dynamic terms for understanding the Self in ways that wrenched this modern concept out of its association with the ancient idea of a Soul, in particular by its often quoted lines:

> *A man has as many social selves as there are individuals who recognize him and carry an image of him in their mind.* To wound any one of these his images is to wound him. But as the individuals who carry about the images fall naturally into classes, we may practically say that he has as many different social selves as there are distinct groups of persons about whose opinion he cares.
>
> (1981: 281–2)

Today, we know very well that who we are is a consequence of very many social influences, a good many of which – parents, siblings, friends, lovers, teachers – are so powerful that they become who we think ourselves to be. To have a self is to contend with these many social selves, a trick we perform not quite consciously until they come into conflict with each other. Generally speaking, however, what James was taking seriously in 1890 was a new kind of practical dilemma faced by generations of people having to adjust to the psychological stimuli that came from living in crowded, largely impersonal, cities. James himself was by no means a sociologist; the theory of the social self was only part of the practical matters he meant to account for in his formal psychology. But it would be this practical sociological sensibility that would lead, in time, to his influence on subsequent social theorists.

James's self was made up four elements. The *social Self* was one, of course. The others were the *material Self* (roughly, the bodily and personal extensions of the Self into its external worlds such as his family, home, and properties), the *spiritual Self* (or, the Self of selves, a kind of residual aspect of the idea of a Soul), and the *pure Ego*. Curiously, for a thinker of such supreme philosophical abilities, James failed to integrate the four parts. This may be because two of the elements (the material and spiritual selves) were more descriptive than dynamic. There can be no question that we identify with the material features of our life worlds; nor can there be doubt that we experience the many social selves we contend with as somehow part of a whole.

Key to James's psychological pragmatism was the notion that, though the Self is cognitive, it is also deeply infused with feeling. The mind is never simply an instrument for thinking. We not only have Self-feelings, but these feelings and their attendant thoughts prompt actions of Self-seeking and Self-survival. Yet, when all is said and done, what one feels, thinks, and does must issue from some practical sense of sameness. This is where the Pure Ego, or sense of personal identity, comes in. Consciousness of Self entails a sense of the integrity of the Consciousness. Hence, the second most famous line in James's theory of Self:

> The sense of personality identity is . . . the sense of sameness perceived *by* thought and predicated of things *thought-about*. These things are a present self and a self of yesterday. The thought not only thinks them both, but thinks they are identical. The psychologist looking-on and playing the critic, might prove the thought wrong, and show there is no real identity. In either case the personal identity would not exist as a *fact*; but it would exist as a *feeling* all the same; and the consciousness of it by the thought would still be there and the psychologist would still have to analyze . . . [the practical question whether] *I am the same self that I was yesterday.*
>
> (1981: 315–16)

Consciousness itself is consciousness of an integrated whole. It is in effect impossible to be conscious of an inchoate welter of differences. However many social selves we may have (and they can be very many indeed), we cannot be conscious of them all at once. Even the multiple personality syndrome requires the loss of one self to enter another. The puzzle inherent to the pragmatics of the thinking, acting, feeling Self is: how does an individual maintain her individuality against the powers of the social environment?

Here is the dynamic element at the heart of James's theory of self. Social differences come up against the practical reality that the individual thinks he is One. Social Self and Pure Ego are at unrelenting odds with each other – at least in the realm of practical experience. In fact in a number of places James speaks of the Self as divided (1981: 295–302). It would not be long before this concept would be taken up and essentially remade by social theorists. Yet, though others after James would try, none could quite solve the conflict he identified between the inherent parts of the Self.

Pragmatism and Darwin's *The Origin of the Species*

By situating pragmatism between empiricism and rationalism, James was influenced by the controversial findings of Charles Darwin (1809–1882). Darwin was not by any means a pragmatist by name; but in effect he was at least a precursor. It is clear that, in one sense, Darwin was an empiricist. His 1859 book, *The Origin of the Species*, was the fruit of his 1831 scientific voyage of the HMS *Beagle*, during which he collected specimens of different species from around the world. He worked with evidence garnered from the plants and animals he saw, collected, and shipped back to England. Yet, Darwin took nearly thirty years back home in England studying and thinking about his collection before he would publish his findings. Why so long? Simply put: because he wanted to get the principle right. He knew that his science would challenge old ways of thinking about human nature, religion, natural history, and about science itself. Induction for Darwin was not enough; yet neither was sheer deduction. He did not start with the idea any more than he allowed the empirical evidence from his voyage to rush him to a conclusion. Ultimately, the conclusion required an entirely new method that at the time had no name at all.

Darwin's question was: why are there regional differences in the kind and number of natural species? His answer was: *chance variation*. Living forms 'evolve' and new and differing species arise because of the 'survival of the fittest.' Different times and places threaten living organisms differently. The organisms best suited to overcome these challenges live on, the others die out. Cockroaches are still with us because, to our disgust, they manage to survive even in modern cities. Dinosaurs are gone because they were too big to hide under dank rocks when the earth was barren. This, in the attitude assumed by pragmatism, neither induced facts nor claims deduced from principles is sufficient. Cockroaches do better in cities than dinosaurs, if only because they have figured out that they are able to feed on all kinds of nasty little things. Pragmatism, the philosophy, thinks like cockroaches in the sense that it takes chance seriously and adapts to realities. Its standard is not truthful principles or sheer evidence but *how do things work?*

The foundations of pragmatist social theory today

By 1910, when James died, pragmatism had secured a foothold in American intellectual culture. Actually, if one could speak this way, it would be better to say that it secured two footholds, different, distinct, but ultimately compatible. Both of them came, in time, to begin to solve James's dilemma of the contradictory experience of the modern Self as both social and individual. All-too-simply put, the two footholds, so to speak, were, first, a deep reconsideration of the role of language and meaning in human life; and, the other, roughly put, was primarily a fusion of social ethics, educational theory, and democratic politics. Put more simply still: the two were theories of *meaning* (what today we would call culture) and theories of *democratic values*. The two can best be visualized as lines of theory that began separately and in different periods of late nineteenth- and early twentieth-century American thought. The one (what I am calling the meaning theory) lay fallow for decades until late twentieth-century social theory, when it reemerged as a large number of debates over the role of language as a key to understanding culture and social behavior. At about the same time, the blossoming meaning line became entangled above ground with branches of social theories of democratic values associated with pragmatism (which after the 1930s had itself fallen dormant). Yet, in spite of their various divergences and disappearances, aspects of each line had shown an affinity for each other even before they blossomed late in the twentieth century. This, then, is the story of the strange, almost rhizomatic, root system that connected James and Peirce, then James with John Dewey, then Dewey with George Herbert Mead, then later Mead and Peirce with Jürgen Habermas and, strangest of all, Dewey and analytic philosophy with Richard Rorty. Admittedly, this is a complicated way of introducing the development of contemporary pragmatist theory which even now is contemporary only to the degree that it continues to draw on its own classical sources.

Charles Sanders Peirce: semiotics and the unity of ego

Charles Sanders Peirce, unlike his friend William James, was never a celebrity; nor was he, it seems, even capable of popularizing of his ideas. In fact, the unsurpassed genius of his writings was so far beyond even the next most intelligent of his peers that many would say, as James himself once did, that they understood nothing of what he was saying but they took pleasure in listening to him say it. Peirce was, in effect, a philosophical wizard (Menand 2002: 153) whose thoughts few others, then or now, can grasp. He was a kind of magician of pure philosophical inventiveness.

The very complexity of Peirce's ideas may well be the reason behind the strange fact that a writer whose first works appeared nearly a century-and-a-half ago is justly considered a *contemporary* social theorist. Hard thoughts take time to sink in. Plus, they sink in only when the times themselves are right. One way to illustrate this fact of the life of ideas, is with reference to William James's important but unresolved theory of the Self. When James clarified the importance of the social self in the mental life of an individual he was, in effect, taking into account an important social fact that could no longer be avoided late in the nineteenth century. The fact was that in the industrializing and urbanizing early modern world, there were few who experienced themselves free from hitherto unthinkably powerful social forces. The individual ego, in other words, was by then understood to be caught in tensions with the ever-present social forces that pressed in through the social self. Not even those who, like James, lived relatively cloistered lives in towns like Cambridge, could deny this fact. Yet, as we've seen, James could not resolve the tension. One of the reasons he could not was that social thought and psychology, like most late nineteenth-century habits of thought were, as we say today, strictly binary. Binary, in the sense, that almost everything considered a legitimate concept came in twos – subjects/objects, actions/structures, private/public, women/men, and so on, endlessly. Thus it was for James and others that the idea of *the* Self was necessarily one member of a couplet – self/society or I/me, and the like.

Still how could it be that Peirce re-enters the picture so much later in social time, at the end of the twentieth century and still now early in the twenty-first? One answer is the very idea of the individual self as it has been subjected to an ever greater number of social, visual, and informational pressures, thus complicating further the inscrutable relations among social things.

This is where Peirce comes in. He is an acknowledged inventor not only of pragmatism but also of semiotics, the theory of signs and meanings. Others in Peirce's day worked on the development of a general theory of signs, or semiotics (and sometimes called semiology). The most important of these parallel sources on the subject was going back to Peirce's contemporary, the Swiss linguist, Ferdinand de Saussure (1857–1913). Saussure's theory of language, of which a more detailed discussion can be found in the following chapter, is built upon the arbitrary relationship between the linguistic 'sign' and the 'signified,' the meaning that it refers to. You can see, perhaps with a little difficulty, that this is a strict binary theory. Saussure's theory of signs, however, had an enormous influence, beginning in the 1960s in large part because it provided, in effect, a model for the puzzling relation that James himself dealt with – how does the individual 'communicate' with the 'social.' For James the 'social' was the social self. For Saussure, the 'social' was the social structures of language which is why it became an important source for twentieth-century structuralisms.

Saussure's scheme, being binary, fails at a crucial point. How does the ongoing communication, or conversation, work? It is one thing to explain that meaningful signs depend on a social contract among those who live in the sign- or language-community. But quite another is to explain, beyond a simple binary communication, how meanings move forward in practical life from one meaningful sign to another. Peirce provides an answer and one entirely distinct from Saussure's theory.

Peirce's pragmatism, as it developed over the years, came to be the core of his general philosophy. He had gone so far, for example, as to say that 'logic, in its general sense, is ... only another name for *semiotic*' (1960a: 134). Already, from this scant line, you can see that he considered thought itself as the fundamental semiotic of mind — that reasonable thought is itself a signifying process. This goes farther beyond (or one might say, deeper than) Saussure's concept and especially in the way that Peirce challenged the fundamental binarism of modern social thought for which he substituted a doctrine of thirds. Thinking and meaning, as well as action, are triadic:

> The action of a sign calls for a little closer attention. Let me remind you of the distinction referred to above between dynamical, or dyadic, action; and intelligent, or triadic action. An event, A, may, by brute force, produce an event, B; and then the event, B, may in its turn produce a third event, C. The fact that the event, C, is about to be produced by B has no influence at all upon the production of B by A. It is impossible that it should, since the action of B in producing C is a contingent future event at the time B is produced.
>
> (1960b: 323)

Hence, Peirce developed his theory of the sign as comprising three elements (strictly speaking, the association between three actions) – sign, object, interpretant. The three have, thus, as he states, the effect of signifying 'by means of another mental sign' which, he adds ironically, is not purely and simply 'mental' in the sense of being ideal as opposed to real.

Suppose, for example, an officer of a squad or a company of infantry gives the word of command 'Ground arms!' The order is, of course, a sign. That thing which causes a sign is called the *object* (according to the usage of speech, the 'real,' but more accurately, the *existent* object) represented by the sign: the sign is determined to some species of correspondence to that object. In the present case, the object the command represents is the will of the officer that the butts of the muskets be brought down to the ground. Nevertheless, the action of his will upon the sign is not simply dyadic; for if he thought the soldiers were deaf mutes, or did not know a word of English, or were raw recruits utterly undrilled, or were indisposed to obedience, his will probably would not produce the word of command. However, although this condition is most usually fulfilled, it is not essential to the action of the sign. . . . In [this case] however, a mental representation of the index is called the *immediate object* of the sign; and this object does triadically produce the intended, or proper, effect of the sign strictly by means of another mental sign. . . . For the proper significant outcome of a sign, I propose the name, the *interpretant* of the sign. The example of the imperative command shows that it need not necessarily be of a mental mode of being.

Charles Sanders Peirce (1960) *The Collected Papers of Charles Sanders Peirce Vol V: Pragmatism and Pragmaticism.* Cambridge, MA: The Belknap Press of Harvard University Press, pages 324–5.

In respect to his pragmatism, Peirce's claim that thinking is a semiotic of signs breaks open the confining binary idea that, most generally, the thinking subject thinks about external objects or, more generally, that the acting subject acts against in relation to structured objective realities. Instead, the practical actions themselves – whether of thinking, communicating, or acting – are simultaneously inside and outside the individual concept, sign, or action. Admittedly, Peirce's words are heavy with abstraction, but the idea that all events occur in threes, in which a first or original event intends to produce a second or, let us say, an outcome. Yet, there can be no outcome (no final result of the sign) unless there is an interpretant in the pragmatic relations. The interpretant is thus not an abstract concept but the significant action, an action that signifies by becoming the object of the sign.

Behind Peirce's idea of logic as sign-making stands the single most important of his principles that influenced James's pragmatism. Like James, but even more so, Peirce took Darwin's scientific method of chance variation as the key to modern science. Truth is not a fixed idea, he thought, but a fixed belief. Events happen and we, like the cockroaches, react to the events. It is entirely a matter of chance that we encounter certain events – which is to say, they are neither imprinted in the nature of things, nor are they purely of an individual's making. Indeed, Peirce argued, events are experienced as chance occurrences to which we respond – and we respond not by thinking but by actions. An event is thus a sign that leads to any object or action. In time, we come to understand the signs we encounter in the field of action and we act in accordance with them; when we do, we form a belief – which is the interpretant of ordinary practical signs and the objects they generate in action. Eventually these beliefs are sedimented as habits. And here is the crux of James's pragmatism and, for all intents, the key to pragmatism itself.

Surprisingly, Peirce also had a theory of what James called the self. In effect that theory was that the self's consciousness of itself is the elemental form of meaning making, or as he put it, logic. In fact, all consciousness is, practically speaking, a general idea that depends on a prior sense of a person being an ego.

> The consciousness of a general idea has a certain 'unity of ego,' in it, which is identical when it passes from one mind to another. It is, therefore, quite analogous to a person; and, indeed, a person is only a particular kind of general idea.
>
> (1892: 22)

This way of explaining the self is not by any means as clear as James's I/Me concept but, then again, it may be more accurate. One of the problems with, as we shall see, most pragmatist theories of the self is that they cannot provide a strong point of integration between individual experience and social forces. Peirce's original semiotic of the self and meaning may not be a fully developed alternative. Yet his triadic theory of meanings, logics, and actions does open a new line of inquiry.

The Progressive Era: John Dewey and Jane Addams

The Progressive Era in the United States was roughly from the 1890s through to the 1920s, when the new nation ripened just to the point of political and economic maturity. The most notorious aspect of the era was the emergence of the country as a global economic power riding on the rapid, post-Civil War development of railroads, industrial manufacturing, oil production and, somewhat later, mass production of automobiles. Even the economic downturn of 1893, usually taken as the end of the Gilded Age, did not reverse the astonishing growth of wealth, nor the terrible inequalities that fell upon the poor and the nascent working classes. The great bosses of industry accumulated wealth beyond what was then imaginable. Many of them, like John D. Rockefeller, Andrew Carnegie and Cornelius Vanderbilt, were also philanthropists, as were others to a lesser degree. But still others, like George Pullman and, later, Henry Ford were, more than most, exploiters of the workers who helped them accumulate their wealth.

As Mark Twain's 1873 novel, *The Gilded Age*, identified the greed of this era, other muckraking novels, like Upton Sinclair's 1906 *The Jungle*, described the corruption of the new industrial age in the United States. The Progressive Era that came into being in the 1890s was a many-sided reform movement, ranging from woman's suffrage and educational reform and the Social Gospel and Settlement House movements to prohibition and political attacks on corporate and political corruption as well as the still young trade union movement. If there was a key principle of the Progressive Era, it was that change by reformation of the political and economic structures is possible. If, in time, prohibition and aggressive trade unions came to be seen as the outlying extremes of the Progressive Era, in the period from the 1890s to the 1920s democratic values of fairness and cooperation were salient. And none better represented these ideals than two Chicago friends, the Settlement House leader, Jane Addams, founder of Hull House, and John Dewey, founder of the Laboratory School of the University of Chicago and the foremost proponent of liberal, democratic reform in education.

Though Addams and Dewey were reformers in the Progressive Era, in time each, differently, developed more radical ideas about methods of democratic change. Addams was an activist, Dewey a philosopher and, after James and Peirce, a founder of modern pragmatism. Yet, at a crucial moment in American history they engaged with each other to important effect. That moment was the Pullman Strike of 1894. George Pullman had made his wealth by the design, construction, and operation of Pullman cars which provided luxurious rail travel to the wealthy. Pullman, Illinois, was the company town he built to house his workers, at rents he fixed without option to purchase. The economic downturn of 1893 cut into his profits, which led Pullman to cut back wages to his workers, but without reducing the rental rate for their housing. The strike became a national cause célèbre. Among liberals who sympathized with the plight of the workers there arose the first major national debate over the conflict between labor and capital in the American democracy, a debate that was already well underway in Europe.

In an evening's discussion at Hull House in 1894, Addams and Dewey debated the moral grounds of proper attitudes toward the strike. What was to be done when major institutional sectors like labor and capital came into conflict? Addams's idea was that the conflict fractured the unity of democratic society and that direct action that aggravated the conflict must be avoided at all costs. Dewey, then still under the saw of the Hegelian dialectic, held that structural antagonism would lead to change for the better, a new democratic synthesis. But, that night, after he left Addams, Dewey struggled with his position and by morning came to the conclusion that she was right and he was wrong. In that moment of their accord, the Progressive ideal and pragmatism were joined. They would remain friends ever after, even as their respective philosophies changed in accord with the wars and economic disasters of the twentieth century. Years later, in reflecting on the Strike of 1894, Addams wrote:

> To touch to vibrating response the noble fiber in each man, to pull these many fibers, fragile, impalpable and constantly breaking, as are into impulse, to develop that mere impulse through its feeble and tentative stages into action, is no easy task, but . . . progress is impossible without it.
>
> (2002: 176)

This was precisely the philosophy that Addams built into Hull House and which served the noble instincts of marginalized immigrant people by affirming their dignity through education and humanitarian programs. Hull House, which continued her work from its founding in 1899 until its closing in 2012, was never a philanthropic program that condescended to its people but one that showed democratic respect for their nobility.

Addams, strictly speaking, was more a progressive activist than a philosophical pragmatist. Yet her relations with Dewey indicated the extent to which the leading public figures of early twentieth-century America would at close or distant remove find encouragement in a national movement that meant to advance the causes of democratic society against the ravages of economic greed and social discord. Louis Menand, for example, commenting on the importance of these historical circumstances to pragmatism said: 'Everything James and Dewey wrote as pragmatists boils down to a single claim: people are the agents of their own destinies.' (2001: 371) In Dewey's case, nothing more strongly exemplified his progressive pragmatism than his commitment to education – a commitment that was every bit as much an activism, like Addams's work at Hull House, as an informed philosophy. As she developed Hull House, Dewey developed the Laboratory School at the University of Chicago in which he developed his philosophy of education that, in his view, was at the heart of modern democracy – a philosophy he carried forth later in his writings as well as his teaching at Teachers College, Columbia University:

> A democracy is more than a form of government; it is primarily a mode of associated living, of conjoint communicated experience. The extension in space of the number of individuals who participate in an interest

so that each has to refer his own action to that of others, and to consider the action of others to give point and direction to his own, is equivalent to the breaking down of barriers of class, race, and national territory which kept men from perceiving the full import of their activity. These numerous and more varied points of contact . . . secure a liberation of powers which remain suppressed as long as the incitations to action are partial, as they must be in a group which in its exclusiveness shuts out many interests.

(1916: 101)

Education, thus, is a primary social function of a democratic society and the school 'coordinates within the disposition of each individual the diverse influences of the various social environments into which he enters' (1916: 26). The work of the school, in his mind, cannot be exclusively the direct inculcation of beliefs and knowledge. Schools must coordinate among children the experiences of society, and especially those arising from social conflicts and differences. As with Peirce and James, once again experience is at the heart of the pragmatic philosophy which, for Dewey, was the foundational philosophical principle in a democratic society.

Even with his best thought, a man's proposed course of action may be defeated. But in as far as his act is truly a manifestation of intelligent choice, he learns something: – as in a scientific experiment, an inquirer may learn through his experimentation, his intelligently directed action, quite as much, or even more, from a failure, than from a success. He finds out at least a little as to what was the matter with his prior choice. He can choose better and *do* better next time; 'better choice' meaning a more reflective one, and 'better doing' meaning one better coordinated with the conditions that are involved in realizing his purpose. Such control or power is never complete; luck or fortune, the propitious support of circumstances not foreseeable is always involved. But at least such a person forms the habit of choosing and acting with conscious regard to the grain of circumstance, the run of affairs. And what is more to the point, such a man becomes able to turn frustration and failure to account in his further choices and purposes.

John Dewey (1993) 'Philosophies of freedom,' in D. Morris and I. Shapiro (Eds), *John Dewey: The Political Writings*. Cambridge: Hackett, pages 133–4.

Dewey's philosophical writings, both technical and applied, are voluminous. In his time, which lasted through the better part of the first half of the twentieth century, he was one of the nation's most famous and respected public intellectuals, as Addams had also been earlier that century. From writings like *Democracy and Education* in 1916 to his later years, Dewey changed in many ways but he never abandoned his faith in democracy. In 1939, in 'Creative Democracy,' he wrote that democracy is 'the sole way of living which believes wholeheartedly in the process of experience as an end and as means.' Today this principle, like Addams's opposition to social conflict, may seem naïve and ill-suited to more complexly structured democratic societies in which experiences are disjointed and artificially at odds. Still, Dewey's influence on pragmatist social theory has had an enduring effect on subsequent, truly contemporary, schools of social theory, the first of which derived from Dewey's close friend in early life, George Herbert Mead.

George Herbert Mead: mind, self and society

George Herbert Mead was with Dewey at the University of Michigan where they entered into an enduring friendship that was both personal and intellectual. In 1894 they both moved to the Philosophy Department at the University of Chicago where Mead remained until his death in 1931.

Where Dewey was very much a public figure, Mead was not. Yet, they shared important philosophical values, already apparent in the academic articles each wrote early in the Chicago years. Dewey's bore the ominous title, 'The Reflex Arc in Psychology' (1896), while Mead's was called, just as abstractly, 'The Definition of the Psychical' (1903). Though neither article is read seriously today, except for their historical importance, they share two striking features in common. Both are hyper-academic studies of then-prevailing concepts in the field of psychology. In a subtle and authoritative review of the literature on the relation between a neural stimulus and a cognitive reflex, Dewey argued that the reflex is always and necessarily indistinguishable from the stimulus – that, in effect, there is no arc in time between the two. This was a crucial idea for his brand of pragmatism because it amounted to the deeper conclusion that action is not first and foremost mental or cognitive. More generally, Dewey held that thoughts or ideas are rooted not in the mind but in the experience of action.

Mead, in his 1903 article, just as authoritatively reviewed the scientific literature defining the 'psychical' (roughly, mental process or mind):

> The image is the suggested object-stimulus, adapting itself to the conditions involved in the problem. It interprets the conditions as the predicate interprets the subject. But neither the subject nor the predicate is there in fixed form, but are present in the process of formation.

The value and content of the conditions is continually changing as the meaning of the problem develops, and this meaning grows as it recognizes and accepts the conditions that face it. It is evident in this that in this state of reflection it is impossible to present the elements out of which the new world is to be built up in advance.

(1903: 112)

In a comparison to Dewey's concept of the primacy of experience, one sees not only their common thinking, but also the ways, early in their careers, both shared an attitude that Peirce had already announced and James was soon to publicize – that thinking begins not in the mind but in experience.

With Mead, in particular, pragmatism's thread of language and signification as a source of meaning, first identified by Peirce, re-enters the story of contemporary pragmatism. Mead's best known book is *Mind, Self, and Society*, which was published on the basis of student notes edited by Charles Morris after Mead's death in 1931. Oddly, it was Morris himself who exaggerated Mead's way of thinking as social behaviorism – a mistake partly excused by the fact that behaviorism as we know it today was just then distinguishing itself as a formal method distinct from other nineteenth-century psychologies. In fact, Mead does not abandon his earlier principle that it is experience that unifies thought and action. What he adds in his later work is the role of symbols and language:

Only in terms of gestures as significant symbols is the existence of mind or intelligence possible; for only in terms of gestures which are significant symbols can thinking – which is simply the internalization or implicit conversation of the individual with himself by means of such gestures – take place. . . . [The] genesis of existence of mind or consciousness – namely, the taking of the attitude of the other toward oneself, or toward one's own behavior – also necessarily involves the genesis and existence at the same time of significant symbols, or significant gestures.

(1934: 47–8)

Here, Mead, discussing the mind, sets the role of language and signs straight at the center.

Though Mead was always a philosopher and, at best, a social psychologist, what made Mead's use of meaningful gestures and significant symbols so valuable to sociologists and social theorists was how he understood them as the integrating and dynamic elements of the two sides of the consciousness of experience – the attitude toward oneself and the attitudes others take toward oneself. And here we encounter, once again, William James's dilemma of self-consciousness: how does one maintain a sense of personal identity while also contending with the realities of social selves? Where James kept the identity/pluralist aspect of self separate, Mead's theory illustrated how in experience they are kept together. Thus, and famously, Mead re-configured James's original description of the 'I' and the 'Me' in self-consciousness:

> The 'I,' then, in this relation of the 'I' and the 'me,' is something that is, so to speak, responding to a social situation which is within the experience of the individual. It is the answer which the individual makes to the attitude which others take toward him when he assumes an attitude toward them. Now the attitudes he is taking toward them are present in his own experience, but his response to them will contain a novel element. The 'I' gives the sense of freedom, of initiative. The situation is there for us to act in a self-conscious fashion. . . . Such is the basis for the fact that the 'I' does not appear in the same sense in experience as does the 'me.' The self is essentially a social process going on with these two distinguishable phases.
>
> (1934: 177–178)

Still one could ask, as many have: what holds the two phases, or the two aspects, of self together? And what becomes of his earlier idea of the unity of experience and thought?

What does Mead mean, thus, in the most oft-quoted of all his lines – that 'the "I" of this moment is present in the "me" of the next' (1934: 174)? The key is the subtle interjection of the word 'present' as if to suggest that the 'I' and the 'me' are always ever-present one to another. Still, how does this work? And here is where his implicit semiotics comes in. The I/Me relation is a symbolic dialogue in which the 'Me' presents the social situation to the 'I' which, in that instant, to use Peirce's term, interprets the experience. Though Mead had little of interest to say about Peirce, it is hard to miss the notion that symbolic meanings, even gestures, are the interpretants that, in effect, hold together the straining parts of self-consciousness while, also, carrying forward the self itself. He could very well have said, after Peirce's triadic scheme, that the interpretant of this moment is present in the meaning of the next.

This is no more than a sampling of Mead's remarkably systematic social theory of the mind–self–society relations. Among the many other details of his social theory is a clear, if sparsely, worked-through developmental theory of the human social self as a meaning maker. He argued that even lower, pre-human, animals have a sort of self-consciousness insofar as they engage in a communication of gestures – high-pitched sounds, chemical trails, urine markings, and the like. In this, the human infant is still animal-like in that she will use gestures such as cooing or crying to

american pragmatisms

communicate pleasure or need. In the meantime, the infant is at once taking in the maternal object and engaging in a crude conversation of gestures that in time shapes her into what humans rather arrogantly consider a *human* being.

Mead in the Self section of *Mind, Self, and Society* notably distinguishes between the play and game stages of childhood development. A child's play is often no more than taking the role of another, often an imaginary one – a doll becomes the 'child' as the actual child becomes the 'mother' just as, in other instances, a phantom friend becomes part of her ongoing conversation in which she plays out feelings or fantasies. This is the phase in which self-consciousness ripens. The play stage is necessary for development, but it is insufficient for full social participation. Try to teach a group of four-year-olds how to play football and you will have a strange set of random runnings about. At best they may be able in time to manage hide-and-seek, which still involves a degree of pretending. Social activity is possible only when the child enters the game stage, which demands that all in the game know the rules of the game but, thereby, understand what each player is meant to do. In football you cannot score, or even know that scoring is what you are meant to do, unless you understand the basic rules of the game – that no one can use his hands in moving the ball, that there is a difference between offense and defense, that a goalie is particularly responsible for stopping your kicks or headers from entering the net, and so on. It is the same in social life.

One gets on with others, even strangers, because one has a normal set of expectations as to what others will do under certain social circumstances. Queues for tickets or services don't work unless everyone in the line knows what the others are doing. Where there is a queue, those who try to cut will be told to get in line, often with anger and disgust. Visualizing what others are doing or meant to do involves visualizing what one is meant to do in the same situation. This is the symbolic aspect of social communication – the ability to develop an image of the significant meaning of self and other in the experience at hand. Meaning is what meaning does in ordinary experience. The meanings we encounter become significant when we attach a symbolic interpretant to the action. The chemical trace is an ant's gesture, just as the queuing is the meaningful symbolic sign, applicable in many (not all) cultures, that one who takes his place is a self worthy of inclusion in that little slice of social experience. Ants who wander off on their own will die, as line cutters are usually killed off in the instance of their rule breaking. Knowing the rules and symbolically appreciating (or knowing) the meaning of the actions of all others is the foundation of the self's social ability to be conscious of himself through a dialogue with the attitudes others take toward him. This, Mead called the competence of possessing a sense of the Generalized Other.

What goes on in the game goes on in the life of the child all the time. He is continually taking the attitudes of those about him, especially the roles of those who in some sense control him and on whom he depends. He gets the function of the process in an abstract way at first. It goes over from the play into the game in a real sense. He has to play the game. The morale of the game takes hold of the child more than the larger morale of the whole community. The child passes into the game and the game expresses a social situation in which he can completely enter; its morale may have a greater hold on him than that of the family to which he belongs or the community in which he lives. There are all sorts of social organizations, some of which are fairly lasting, some temporary, into which the child is entering, and he is playing a sort of social game in them. It is a period in which he likes 'to belong,' and he gets into organizations which come into existence and pass out of existence. He becomes a something which can function in the organized whole, and thus tends to determine himself in his relationship with the group to which he belongs. That process is one which is a striking stage in the development of the child's morale. It constitutes him as a self-conscious member of the community to which he belongs.

George Herbert Mead (1934) *Mind, Self and Society*. Chicago: University of Chicago Press, page 160.

There is no question that Mead fleshed out a more sociological idea of the social foundations of self-development based on Peirce and James. For his time, it was a truly impressive feat to clarify the I/Me dialogue as an ever-in-the-present dialogue linking the interior and exterior dimensions of self-consciousness; as was his argument for a generalized other as a necessary embracing idea of the role of the social whole to the individual self. That Mead accomplished so much by recovering the role of signification in meaning-making is itself a tribute to Peirce's original semiotic, but it is also an important contemporary affirmation of what has come to be called the linguistic turn in both philosophy (after Wittgenstein) and social theory (after Lévi-Strauss). What transpired in these two areas, well after Mead was gone, probably would not have moved him. Yet, what remains, in the larger picture of the history of social theory is the importance of his refinement of a working idea of language and sign systems as central to cultural meanings – as, in effect, just how hard it is to get away from the symbolic.

Herbert Blumer: Symbolic Interactionism

To the degree that Mead was not, even metaphorically, a sociologist, Herbert Blumer was. When mortally ill, Mead designated Herbert Blumer, a former graduate student, to take over his course at Chicago in Social Psychology. Over the four decades after Mead's death, Blumer named, and to a considerable degree codified, the single most important sociological tradition to come directly from Mead: Symbolic Interactionism.

It is relatively easy, even on a quick look, to see the influence of Mead on the Symbolic Interactionist tradition. At the same time, it may be easier to miss Blumer's serious attempt to introduce the one sociological element that was missing in Mead and all prior pragmatist thought – a robust theory of hard, enduring, and powerful social structures. It was not until Blumer that a strong theory of what he called 'the obdurate character of the empirical world' came into the tradition. In his foundational text, *Symbolic Interactionism: Perspective and Method* (1969), Blumer says:

> The empirical world can 'talk back' to our pictures of it or assertions about it – talk back in the sense of challenging and resisting, or not bending to, our images and concepts of it. . . . It is this obdurate character of the empirical world – its ability to resist and talk back – that both calls for and justifies empirical science.
>
> (1969: 22)

A true theory of social structures arises on two conditions, both of which Blumer comes close to meeting – first, an attempt to establish an empirical science in the sense of a science that aims to explain reality as such; and second, a sociology in which it is granted that structures that transcend local, practical actions are an essential feature of the empirical study of societal arrangements. One indication of Blumer's effort to convert Mead's pragmatism into an empirical sociology is that he engaged in sociological research on a variety of subjects, including collective behavior, crime and delinquency, and media. A reading especially of his writings from 1931, when he took over Mead's social psychology course at Chicago, to 1969, when he published the *locus classicus* of Symbolic Interactionism, his theoretical work on specifically structural and empirical subjects was the means through which he worked out the general principle of the school of thought he names.

Social theorists insisting on a formal theory of social structures have never been satisfied with Blumer's program, but a general summary of his basic principles in *Symbolic Interactionism* makes it clear that, while he remained faithful to the general terms of Mead's pragmatism, there was always a kind of structural theory struggling to get out from behind the primacy of languages, actions and experiences. Here is a reasonably complete outline of Blumer's general theory of society:

1   Societies comprise human groups, and groups are made up of individuals.
2   Interactions among individuals are never fixed but are formed in the course of human conduct.
3   Symbols are essential to human interaction because they are necessary for individuals to indicate to others the expectations and meanings behind their actions.
4   There are three sets of objects – physical, social, and abstract – as a result, people must be able to understand them all in order to act.
5   Yet, persons are only able to act because they can think of themselves as objects to themselves which allows them to engage in role-taking.
6   Human action is unavoidably social because the individual can only interpret her actions by interpreting the actions of others; thus collective action is, in effect, a process of interpretation.
7   Action, therefore, is not random, but always fitted to the actions of others and this elemental fact is the basis for the formation of institutions (1969:11–20).

It is impossible to read through this list and not to see the main traditions of pragmatism in general, and especially of Mead. Blumer himself was a major figure in the second and most theoretical tradition of what is known as Chicago sociology – after the first founded and enduringly influential department in the United States at the University of Chicago. Among others who worked along the same lines as did Blumer were Everett Hughes and Lloyd Warner, Howard Becker at a later time, and some would add (rather conjecturally) Erving Goffman. At the very least, however one defines the membership list of this line of the Chicago School (of which there were at least two other, differing approaches), no single tradition has done more to support and encourage careful and thoughtful research and thinking about the lives of people in local gatherings.

Pragmatism's limits and prospects: Habermas and Rorty

Today, well outside sociological social theory, there are at least two active lines of the pragmatist tradition at work. One is the latter-day critical theory inspired by Jürgen Habermas. Habermas, whose work we will examine in detail in Chapter 11, had begun late in the 1960s to explore the role of language as a practical, quasi-universal human resource for and topic of what he then called, in *Knowledge and Human Interests* (1987), critical knowledge with an interest in emancipation. Habermas slowly turned to linguistics and speech act theory to study the ideal speech situation (already an important concept in linguistic philosophy) as an inherent aspect of all human dialogue and communication. Ever restless, Habermas soon enough turned to the question asked in a 1979 essay, 'What is universal pragmatics?' As this question suggests, he was by this time at least attuned to the two main strains of American pragmatism – language and democracy.

Still, it is far from clear that even in the use of the term pragmatics Habermas could or should be considered a pragmatist, pure and simple. In either case, the key term that surfaced in Habermas's long transition through language to a critical theory of emancipatory democracy is in the title of his massive, two volume, 1981 manifesto, *The Theory of Communicative Action*. From the point of view of his alleged pragmatism, the most striking essay in the book is the one with which he begins Volume Two, 'The Paradigm Shift in Mead and Durkheim: From Purposive Activity to Communicative Action.' The section on Mead begins, first with the important acknowledgement that 'Mead's theory of communication . . . recommends itself as a point of intersection of the two critical traditions stemming from Peirce' (1989: 3). While he has little directly to say of Peirce (with whom Habermas would have been unlikely to be satisfied) he gives careful attention to Mead, whose work he summarizes as 'the task of capturing the structural features of symbolically mediated communication' (1989: 5). Though Habermas treats Mead at times more as a template than an original of critical theory, there can be no doubt that Habermas's critical social theory of communicative action is, for all intents and purposes, pragmatist in theoretical disposition if not formal allegiance.

Habermas, himself, is one of the world's most accomplished and influential social theorists, and has, very probably, done more that anyone in his lifetime to clarify the cultural grounds of democracy in complex worlds. It makes little difference, thus, whether he should be called a pragmatist. For one, Richard J. Bernstein of the New School, a distinguished theorist in his own right, has not the least reservation on this point as he makes clear in *The Pragmatic Turn* (2010), the single best current work on the varieties of pragmatism. What is important is that quite a number of younger sociologists, many in Europe, are working as sociologists to advance something like a critical pragmatism. Hans Joas, the German sociologist, is author of *Pragmatism and Social Theory* (1993) which in effect re-imports European ideas back into a relation with American social and critical theory. Filipe Carriera da Silva, a Portuguese sociologist, is among other European social thinkers who have taken up the task of interpreting both Mead and Habermas and their respective relations to pragmatism.

The other current line of pragmatist thought is inspired by the American philosopher Richard Rorty (1931–2007) who is widely considered, with John Rawls and a few others, as at the top of a shortlist of greatest American philosophers in recent years. Among his many contributions, Rorty is noted for two important and interrelated ideas, each embedded in a long and rich corpus of writings. One is his devastatingly persuasive dismissal of foundationalism, the idea that mind and knowledge reflect the essential nature of things – an argument alluded to in the title of his revolutionary work, *Philosophy and the Mirror of Nature* (1979). The second of Rorty's striking ideas follows on the first, namely his account of a philosophy that must take the place of essentialism. In *Contingency, Irony, and Solidarity* (1989) Rorty begins with the pragmatist axiom, 'truth cannot be out there' (1989: 5), from which he moves immediately to the startling claim that philosophy without foundations in reality must be replaced by literary criticism! The philosopher, hence, must be not the truth teller but the ironist – a vocation required by the prior claim that if there is no truth out there, all there is is language; and language is contingent in the sense that an ironist must, in effect, tell what truth there might be even though there are no final arguments. A philosopher cannot hope, he says, to demonstrate convincingly that her ideas are right and another's wrong.

What is remarkable about Rorty's ideas is that they are explicitly pragmatist in the formal sense of his robust rejection of epistemological essentialism and his turn to language and the symbolic as the foundation without foundationalism of social life. Just as remarkable is the degree to which his claim that philosophy must be ironic literary criticism has led many to characterize this very liberal, even gentle man, as a radical, even a postmodern one. This characterization is not entirely idle. He was attacking the very core principles of modern culture to the same degree as Habermas, at the same time, was attempting to shore them up.

Needless to say, always implicit in every major pragmatist thinker from James and Dewey to Mead and Blumer to Habermas and Rorty was a commitment to revising and affirming basic democratic beliefs (as Dewey put it) and actions (as Habermas has it). Yet, once the Progressive Era in which James and Dewey worked, and from which Mead benefitted, gave way to economic crisis, war upon war, false post-WWII affluence and mass culture, the principle of democratic communication fell on hard times. Even Blumer's Symbolic Interactionism was not well suited to all that followed after his great book of 1969. In many ways, Habermas, in one way, and Rorty, in another, applied the principles that throve in early pragmatism to the new, late-modern circumstances. Habermas has done so directly by a series of political writings that have made him Germany's, and possibly Europe's, most important public intellectual. Rorty's life was cut short, so who knows what he might have done. Younger pragmatists, like Judith Green, in *Pragmatism and Social*

Hope (2008) extends Rorty's ideas in a serious and compelling way as in *Deep Democracy* (1999) where she applies pragmatist values to questions native to feminism and race theory. Then too, there are the early writings of the gadfly philosopher, Cornell West, who started his intellectual career as a pragmatist much in the vein of Rorty before turning to public and academic commentary on the cultural and political issues of the day.

Whether democracy endures is, to some, an open question. Whether pragmatism will be among the cultural and intellectual resources to that end is also open, of course – but not unreasonable. There can hardly be any question that the single most formidable barrier to democratic culture is the corruption of public language – a corruption due, in the first instance, to the mind-numbing effect of popular culture and media but, no less, to the narrow focus and foolish abstractions of a good many academics who ought be at the fore of this movement. Pragmatism has always been at the advanced guard of progressive thought in America. Whether it can accommodate its principles to the harsh global structures of global realities is what remains to be seen.

Summary points

1   As one of the enduring traditions of social and philosophical thought to have begun uniquely in America, pragmatism is associated with the down-to-earth, action-oriented values many consider the dominant cultural ethic in the United States.

2   William James, the first influential popularizer of pragmatism, developed and justified the method's belief in the primacy of human experience, asserting that the truth is nothing more, nothing less than an idea that works. James sought a middle way between the two prevailing schools of thought on epistemology in the nineteenth century: rationalism and empiricism.

3   James is also known for his theory of the Self, comprising four elements: the social Self, the material Self, the spiritual Self and the pure Ego. Accordingly, James held that the Self was a 'Self-divided.'

4   Charles Sanders Peirce was a precursor and a main influence on James's work on pragmatism. From a pragmatist perspective, Peirce developed a theory of semiotics, one that avoided the binary conceptualization of signification, as set out in the parallel work of Ferdinand Saussure.

5   A prominent application of the pragmatist approach was advocated by the work of James Dewey and Jane Addams during the Progressive Era (1890s–1920s) in America. Dewey, in particular,

sought to exemplify the virtues of the pragmatist approach by focusing on the transformative role of education against the backdrop of democratic practice.

6   George Herbert Mead's brand of pragmatism furthered James's notion that thinking begins not in the mind but in experience, by positing that there are two sides of consciousness of experience – the attitude toward oneself and the attitudes that others take toward oneself. Mead proposed that the Self was an ongoing interplay between these two distinguishable phases.

7   Herbert Blumer was a proponent of Mead's pragmatist-influenced theories. Blumer later used some of these theories to found the prominent sociological tradition known as Symbolic Interactionism. With Symbolic Interactionism, Blumer involved the Pragmatist approach in the study of social structures.

8   Today, there are at least two active lines of the Pragmatist tradition at work. Jürgen Habermas has heavily relied on Mead's conceptual framework to develop his seminal theory of 'communicative action,' which has been vital to his critical understanding of emancipatory democracy. The other current line of pragmatist thought follows American philosopher Richard Rorty who, drawing from pragmatic principles, has offered a powerful critique of the Foundationalist philosophical tradition.

Further questions

1   How did the post-Civil War era contribute to the development of American Pragmatism?

2   What did Charles Saunders Peirce contribute to the new science of semiotics (or semiology) and what justifies a discussion of his ideas in respect to contemporary social thought?

3   How does William James's psychology of the social self suggest his later contributions to pragmatism?

4   What is George Herbert Mead's famous theory of the I/Me dynamic and how does it relate to his ideas on the practical experience of childhood development?

5　Herbert Blumer invented the field of sociology theory called Symbolic Interactionism. What is it and how was it influenced by Mead's pragmatism?

Further reading

William James

Pragmatism: A New Name for Some Old Ways of Thinking (Oxford, UK: Longmans, 1907)
The Meaning of Truth: A Sequel to Pragmatism (London: Longmans, 1909)
The Principles of Psychology (Chicago: Encyclopaedia Britannica, 1952)

Charles Sanders Peirce

(edited by Charles Hartshorne and Paul Weiss) *Collected Papers of Charles Sanders Peirce* (Cambridge: Harvard University Press, 1931–58)
(edited by Charles S. Hardwick, with the assistance of James Cook) *Semiotic and Significs: The Correspondence between Charles S. Peirce and Lady Victoria Welby* (Bloomington: Indiana University Press, 1977)

John Dewey

Art as Experience (New York: Capricorn Books, 1959)
Democracy and Education: An Introduction to the Philosophy of Education. (New York: Free Press, 1966)
Essays in Experimental Logic (New York: Dover, 1953)
How We Think: A Restatement of the Relation of Reflective Thinking to the Educative Process (New York: D. C. Heath and Company, 1933)

Jane Addams

(edited by Anne Firor Scott) *Democracy and Social Ethics* (Cambridge, MA: Belknap Press, 1964)
(edited by Jean Bethke Elshtain) *The Jane Addams Reader* (New York: Basic Books, 2002)
Twenty Years at Hull House (New York: Macmillan, 1964)

George Herbert Mead

Mind, Self and Society (Chicago: University of Chicago Press, 1934)
(edited by Anselm Strauss) *On Social Psychology: Selected Papers.* (Chicago: University of Chicago Press, 1964)

The Philosophy of the Act (Chicago: University of Chicago Press, 1938)
The Philosophy of the Present (Chicago and London: Open Court Publishing
   Company, 1932)

Herbert Blumer

George Herbert Mead and Human Conduct (Oxford: AltaMira, 2004)
Symbolic Interactionism: Perspective and Method (Berkeley: University of
   California Press, 1986)

Jürgen Habermas

Communication and the Evolution of Society (Boston: Beacon Press, 1979)
Knowledge and Human Interests (Cambridge: Polity Press, 1987)
The Theory of Communicative Action (Cambridge: Polity Press, 1991)

Richard Rorty

Consequences of Pragmatism: Essays 1972–1980 (Brighton: Harvester, 1982)
Contingency, Irony, and Solidarity (Cambridge: Cambridge University
   Press, 1989)
Philosophy and the Mirror of Nature (Princeton: Princeton University
   Press, 1979)
Achieving Our Country: Leftist Thought in Twentieth-Century America
   (Cambridge, MA: Harvard University Press, 1998)

Structuralism

Contents

Chris is a commissioning editor at a major New York publishing house, where he has worked for many years. Over this time, he has developed considerable skills in anticipating the kinds of non-fiction books people hunger to read. He has become quite adept, one might say, in *reading the signs* of what the general reading public want. Indeed, picking up on the signs of the book market is how he has got to where he is today. He made his reputation commissioning popular works of history, and in recent years has moved more in the direction of popular culture, celebrity and media. In recent months, he's commissioned books on the rise of reality television, the politics of 'size o' fashions, and several celebrity biographies.

It is almost impossible for Chris to travel around New York, or anywhere else for that matter, without thinking about the reading interests of people. Acutely aware that publishing has come under increasing challenges as a result of the Internet and new digital technologies, Chris nonetheless strives to find the best contemporary writers for his publishing list. He acknowledges that publishing confronts new difficulties in these early years of the twenty-first century, but insists that the *signs* are that people still want to read good books.

Whilst Chris may be gifted in reading the signs of what the general public want to read, like anyone else in our society he also needs certain skills for interpreting messages and information all around him in the general culture. Today, for example, Chris woke to morning television and watched the breakfast news. On the way to work on the subway, he read the morning newspaper, and along the way was confronted by countless advertising promotions and billboards. Walking the streets to his office, he found himself surrounded by branded signs: Starbucks, The Gap, McDonald's, Apple, Victoria's Secret. Then there were the various signs of daily interpersonal interaction, as colleagues at the office go through the morning ritual of greeting each other and enquiring how people are and what they have planned for the day.

Like most people going about their morning routine, Chris doesn't give much attention to the signs that envelop him. Nor does he pay any particular attention to his own use of signs, from nodding to the man at the subway newspaper stand to greeting his secretary in the customary fashion at work. Yet all of these signs – both those encountered and those used by Chris – are fundamental to the business of social life. Signs not only point us in particular directions, and inform us of what is going on around us, they are essential to the very tissue of human communication and everyday life. Perhaps the best way to think about Chris's 'unthinking attitude' to the world of communication in which he dwells, therefore, is that – like everyone else – he experiences signs as existing independently of himself. Signs are just everywhere. This is not to say that there isn't a factor of choice in our use of signs, or language, and the communicative forms we use to express ourselves. But it is to say, and to recognize people's tacit understanding of the fact, that signs exist independently of us. For when people recognize that language and communication are not fully the product of their own intentional activity, then they recognize – even to some minimal degree – the extent to which they are the passive prisoners of signs.

To say that we might be the 'passive prisoners of signs' is to move into territory that social theorists term 'structuralism.' Structuralism flourished in the 1960s as an attempt to apply the insights of linguistics to the study of the impersonal effects of social structures and political systems. As its name suggests, structuralism proceeds from the notion that people live their lives within the context of larger structures – social, cultural, political and historical – and that such structures shape and even determine individual decisions, choices, beliefs and values. Structuralism in general is an attempt to shift away from the humanistic viewpoint that people are self-directing, autonomous agents and to focus instead on the structures which give coherence, regularity and meaning to social interactions. Language is taken as the central model of analysis in structuralism, on the grounds that individual speech – as a universal element of all societies and cultures – would not be possible without an enabling structure to give words meaning. The words that I am writing now, for instance, are able to convey meaning only to the extent to which they accord with the structural rules of language – and structuralism is thus an attempt to interrogate such linguistic rules governing objects, events and interactions in fields beyond language itself. In this chapter, we will look in detail at structuralist social theory, starting with the methods developed in structural linguistics. We will then turn to consider how these methods came to be applied to social analysis in the writings of influential public intellectuals associated with structuralism, principally Roland Barthes and Michel Foucault. Throughout, the aim is to scrutinize the structuralist method for understanding the production of a social world teeming with *signs*.

Saussure and structural linguistics

Not all of us are necessarily as gifted as Chris in reading the signs of professional or business life. But this does not mean that we are not endowed with a capacity to pick up on and read the signs of the endless forms of daily social life. The practical knowledge of how to read the signs of social life are many and varied, ranging from how to read a road map to how to 'handle oneself' at a party or similar social gathering. In any event, how we pick up on the signs around us – using language along the way to communicate with others – has become a core preoccupation of contemporary social theory. One influential viewpoint is that the signs in which we dwell, and the languages we use daily, are given to us – indeed, assigned to us – by this world and its general social structures. This is a viewpoint derived from modern structural linguistics.

Although he was not a social theorist, the founder of structural linguistics, Ferdinand de Saussure (1858–1913), has come to exert a remarkable influence over contemporary social theory – primarily through the traditions of structuralism and post-structuralism. A linguist who worked in both Geneva and Paris on highly technical issues to do with Indo-European languages, Saussure set himself against nineteenth-century linguistics by questioning the view that language functions as a naturalistic representation of things or events in the world. In his work, he attempted to study the systems and structures revealed by language and which are essential to speech and communication. His epoch-making *Course in General Linguistics* (1916), one of the most widely read books in social theory, was published posthumously after a group of his students transcribed and edited Saussure's lecture notes to introductory linguistics. In his *Course*, Saussure advanced five central arguments. These are:

1   The distinction between language (*langue*) and speech (*parole*);
2   The arbitrary character of the sign;
3   The key role of difference in the constitution of meaning;
4   The making of the sign through the bonding of signifier and signified;
5   The division between synchrony and diachrony.

These doctrines, as we will later examine, have come to define the core of structuralist social theory – from the works of Claude Lévi-Strauss to Michel Foucault. In the next chapter, we will consider how a subsequent generation of Parisian intellectuals came to adopt, and then substantially modify, Saussurian linguistics in the development of what was to become post-structuralist social theory. At this point, however, it is worth inquiring into the logic of Saussure's key doctrines in order to better grasp how they came to shape the direction of social theory during the twentieth century.

In Saussure's view, the domain of signs and the realm of language must be approached from the standpoint of society, or the collective, and not the individual. The individual does not just spontaneously create meaning through the free-play of imagination; our language pre-exists us as individuals, and we must assimilate ourselves to its pre-existing forms and rules. This is another way of saying that language is a *social institution*. But if language cannot be divorced from society, then neither should the speech of individuals be isolated from concrete structures of linguistic interaction. Saussure, in point of fact, did not use the term 'structure.' But he did speak of 'system': it is from the systemic character of language (*langue*) that speech (*parole*) is ordered, regularized and reproduced. Our speech does not so much *reflect* our inner world as *instantiate* and *reproduce* discrete spheres of language as system. To put the point differently, language is less something 'within' our minds or selves than something around us in the societal structure – even though, somewhat like God or Santa Claus, language as system is unobservable. No one has ever actually seen, say, the English language: you can read the *Oxford English Dictionary* from cover to cover, but that only involves you in looking at specific words, and not the totality of language. Thus Saussure's purpose, roughly speaking, was to focus analysis on language as a structure – a structure that constitutes us to our very roots.

The individual's receptive and coordinating facilities build up a stock of imprints which turn out to be for all practical purposes the same as the next person's. How must we envisage this social product, so that the language itself can be seen to be clearly distinct from the rest? If we could collect the totality of word patterns stored in all those individuals, we should have the social bond which constitutes their language. It is a fund accumulated by the members of the community through the practice of speech, a grammatical system existing potentially in every brain, or more exactly in the brains of a group of individuals; for the language is never complete in any single individual, but exists perfectly only in the collectivity.

Ferdinand de Saussure (1916) *Course in General Linguistics.* London: Fontana, page 13.

In making this core distinction between *langue* (the abstract structure of language) and *parole* (particular utterances of individual speech), Saussure advanced the thesis of the 'arbitrary character of the sign.' It is sometimes difficult, with Saussure, to know how far to press this anti-rationalist case that our languages do not reflect the real things we see around us in the world. For Saussure expressed various equivocations on this point in the *Course*. What his general argument comes down to, however, is that the relation between language and the object-world is conventional – by which he meant structured by society – thus, *radically arbitrary*. For Saussure, language does not just magically reflect an unchanging world. There is no such thing as a 'fixed language,' one fully locked down and unchangeable. Rather, the world is internally structured along the lines of its languages, by which individuals come to know the social things around them and operate within society. One way that Saussure demonstrated this to be the case was by comparing words across languages. Although the meaning is similar, the sounds conveyed in the pronunciation of 'ox' in English have nothing in common with '*boeuf*' in French or '*ochs*' in German. Likewise, the word 'sister' is not linked in any way to the sounds expressed '*soeur*' in French. Different societies carve up the world through language in different ways. Another equally, if not more, compelling argument he made hinged on discrediting the common-sense view that there is some intrinsic connection between words and the physical objects to which they refer. Consider, for example, the word 'tree.' According to Saussurian linguistics, there is nothing about the linguistic marks – t-r-e-e – which 'fits' or 'captures' the intrinsic properties of actual trees as vegetative things. Again, comparison is useful here: the term in French is '*arbre*.' But, and this is fundamental, there is no intrinsic reason why either term is more or less appropriate to a tree as an object. But if there is no necessary relation between these words and objects, then that leaves the relation as *arbitrary* – which is precisely Saussure's argument. The relations between language and the object-world are ones which we as a society fashion within given social and historical contexts; these relations are not in any sense independent from the systemic character of language, or the ways in which we deploy speech in daily life.

According to Saussure, the key to understanding language is to be found not in any connection between words and the physical objects designated, but in the *arbitrary nature of linguistic signs* that, in turn, depend upon *differential marks*. It may seem, at first, difficult to make sense of this terminology and particular way of thinking about language and its relation to the world. But let us stay a little longer with some of Saussure's terminological innovations, as it is certainly arguable that the world looks remarkably different once one grasps Saussure's principle of the arbitrary nature of linguistic signs. Meaning for Saussure is composed of combinations of 'signifiers,' by which he means sounds and images as well as 'marks' of written text on the one hand, and 'signifieds,' the mental image to which signifiers refer, on the other. Taken together, the signifier and signified make up the linguistic sign as realized in speaking and hearing, or reading and writing. But how, exactly, are such 'signifiers' and 'signifieds' brought into mutual connection? Connections are established, according to Saussure, through the power of difference: 'day' is constituted as a sign in terms of its difference from 'night,' 'black' from 'white,' 'man' from 'woman' and so on. This is a fundamental point in Saussurian linguistics, and he insists in the *Course* that every linguistic sign is inscribed in a structure of difference. 'In language,' says Saussure (1974: 120), 'there are only differences. Even more important: a difference generally implies positive terms between which the difference is set up; but in language there are only differences without positive terms.' This is an insight that has major ramifications for grasping the connections between language and the world: the use of a signifier is part of a linguistic process that involves the negating, denying, or 'forgetting' of other signifiers. 'Hot' only takes on the force of signifying to others by means of its difference to 'cold.' The semiotic power of signs, so to speak, is always differential.

All of this, from the standpoint of Saussurian linguistics, is to do with the internal structure of language. It is *difference* that creates meaning: terms only acquire meaning, continuity and durability in so far as they are differentiated from one another as oppositions within the structure of language as a whole. This, clearly, goes to the heart of questions concerning the systematic character of language on the one side, and the realization and reproduction of speech in daily life on the other. But it is not just the 'internal' dimensions of language that are addressed here, as this is also a theory rich in implications for society and its processes of linguistic and ideological production. Saussure helps make this point clear in his famous discussion of the 'Geneva-to-Paris train.' In conventional language, says Saussure, we would say that the 'same' train leaves Geneva for Paris every day at 8.25 p.m. – even though it is, in fact, the case that the 8.25 p.m. may actually change daily in terms of its carriages, engine and personnel. It is, then, the difference of the Geneva-to-Paris 8.25 p.m. from the 10.05 p.m., say, that singles out the identity of the train. Difference fosters the illusion that this is, always, the 'same' train – separating it out from other trains. And it is such linguistic difference that facilitates purposive social life, providing the fundamental distinctions and oppositions that are indispensable to daily social existence.

But in examining the arbitrary nature of linguistic signs, it was not just the object-world that is carved up through difference. For language is a structure that goes all the way down, penetrating to the roots of identity and everyday life. The principle of difference, as Saussure develops it at any rate, also refers back to the individual speaker or self. If this is so, a signifier is a sound, image or linguistic mark that has the power to pull individuals this way and that, inscribing them within 'majorities' or 'minorities,' 'inclusions' or 'exclusions,' the 'center' or 'periphery.' Saussure himself did not theorize the political forces of language and signs in such a direct fashion, and to that extent we are now pushing ahead of ourselves. But to the degree that Saussure made the point that meaning is an upshot of the differential, decentered forces of language, including the inner workings of lived experience, then it becomes possible to see how this brand of linguistics transformed itself in time as a properly social structuralist theory. Saussure's work has given rise, as I have mentioned, to a fertile strain of social theory, and, as we will subsequently examine, structuralism as a social theory is powerfully concerned with how the inscription of power and domination can be mapped within language and structures of linguistic relation.

The final thread in Saussure's argument concerns *the distinction between synchrony and diachrony.* Saussure looked at the development of language primarily in terms of its synchronic, or static, structures: it was the systematic character of language, rather than any particular modifications of speech by individuals, to which he addressed the project of structural linguistics. To study the structures of language, according to Saussure, means we must abstract fully from the individual articulations of speech. The privilege accorded to synchrony over diachrony, tied as it is to the placing of *langue* over *parole*, has been interpreted by some critics as an erasure of *time* – or, historical change – in structural linguistics. As Terry Eagleton (2008: 96) argues, for example, 'behind this linguistic model lies a definite view of human society: change is disturbance and disequilibrium in an essentially conflict-free system, which will stagger for a moment, regain its balance and take the change in its stride.' Linguistic change for Saussure seems a matter of accident: it happens 'blindly.' Stated thus, however, this is not quite accurate. Saussure did not so much eliminate 'change' – especially the unfolding of historical change through *time* – as recast the idea of how structural transformations occur. It is because a linguistic structure (or, 'social system' for that matter) is only observable in its particular articulations or practices that the notion of time must be related to connections between the whole of a system and its particular elements. Time is thus much more complex than any strict separation between continuity and change. That said, Saussure did emphasize the independence of the synchronic from the diachronic – an emphasis which, among others of Saussure, gives rise to various problems in social theory that we will now turn to consider.

Criticisms of Saussure

The work of Saussure was limited to the field of linguistics, but as we will see his influence has been immense. His *Course in General Linguistics* is widely viewed as inspiring structuralism in contemporary social theory, and indeed Saussurian themes have been extensively (and sometimes laboriously) used to analyze all possible aspects of social life – from eating habits to fashion, from myths to literature and the arts. What perhaps remains most suggestive in Saussure, although as we will see also much debated, is the theorem of the arbitrary character of the sign. Language is not, as with conventional wisdom, the intentional act of a speaker; and 'meaning' is not just the spontaneous expression of 'things' given in the world. For the fact is that meaning is always produced out of difference, the bonding of signifier and signified – which occurs differently in different places and in specific ways. Sociologically speaking, this provides for a fertile understanding of the social dynamics of language since *transformation* is now written in to the relation between language and the material world.

However, critics have raised a number of criticisms of Saussure's theory, of which I want to raise some of the more pressing difficulties here. To begin with, if the production of meaning is radically arbitrary, how does the individual human subject come to navigate its way around the social world at all? Through difference, a bond between signifier and signified is said to be fashioned and meaning produced. But how, exactly, is meaning produced in such an unstable, free-floating linguistic system? Aware of these difficulties, Saussure made it clear that arbitrariness did not mean that speakers were unconstrained in their daily linguistic interactions with others; on the contrary, the speaker has no choice but to follow the rules already established in language. But if this is so it remains difficult then to isolate what is actually arbitrary about signs. The idea that objects are wholly internal to the bonding of the signifiers and signifieds that constitute them leaves obscure the issue of *reference* – of how ideas or concepts refer to objects or events in the social world. According to some critics, part of the difficulty here stems from Saussure's excessive concentration on the signifier/signified relation at the expense of how objects are actually referenced. As Benveniste argues:

> Even though Saussure said that the idea of 'sister' is not connected to the signifier s-o-r, he was not thinking any the less of the *reality* of the notion. When he spoke of the difference between b-o-f and o-k-s, he was referring in spite of himself to the fact that these two terms applied to the same *reality*. Here, then, is the *thing*, expressly excluded at first from the definition of sign, now creeping in by a detour.
>
> (1971: 44)

What is thus missing in Saussurian linguistics is consideration of a third, higher term – what Benveniste calls 'the thing.' By focusing exclusively on the relation between signifier and signified, Saussure was able to unearth the productivity of language in defining and shaping the world, but at the expense of attending to how language actually refers to objects or events in the world.

That social relations do not exist independently of language, and that speech does not so much reflect the world as signify it, are undoubtedly vital insights of Saussurian linguistics. But there are surely limits as to how far we might press the argument that language is pure form, defined wholly internally through difference. For where difference derives from, arguably, is the social context in which language operates. Consider again Saussure's example of the Geneva-to-Paris train. Saussure, as we have seen, seeks to identify the internal composition of signifiers inscribed around the train in terms of defining a distinct identity. To say that the 8.25 p.m. occupies a distinct identity within a timetable of train scheduling by virtue of its difference from other times is one way of understanding how meaning is produced. But this is not the only way of understanding the matter, and arguably Saussure's position is one that at any rate grants privilege to the position of tourist or traveler. As one commentator argues:

> The identity of the 'Geneva-to-Paris train' cannot be specified independently of the context in which the phrase is used; and this context is not the system of differences themselves, as Saussure mentions, but factors relating to their use in practice. Saussure implicitly assumes the practical standpoint of the traveler, or the time-tabling official, in giving the identity of the train; hence the 'same' train may consist of quite distinct engines and carriages on two separate occasions. But these do not count as instances of the 'same' train for a railway repair engineer, or a train-spotter.
>
> (Giddens 1979: 16)

Difference, in short, is *context dependent*: meaning is fashioned in relation to distinctions and oppositions grounded in social practice.

We have seen that Saussure distinguishes between *synchronic* and *diachronic* ways of analyzing language; and we have seen that his version of structural linguistics concentrates on the synchronic – that is, the structural conditions of language – while bracketing off the diachronic, or historical, study of language. However, some critics have rightly objected that we should be dubious of a too hard-and-fast distinction between synchrony and diachrony, or statics and dynamics, in studying processes of change. For the problem that arises, which will become increasingly evident when we turn to consider structuralist social theory, is that to view language as all form and no substance results, ultimately, in the neglect of the social and historical conditions in and through which systems and structures are both produced and modified. That is to say, structuralism has immense difficulties explaining social change or historical transformation. Some critics, such as E. P. Thompson (1978), have gone as far as to argue that structuralism betrays a radically impoverished conception of historical processes, such is its elevation of system statics over and above the creative dynamics of human agency. We need to be careful in assessing this criticism, however, since Saussure himself was at pains to stress that the synchrony/diachrony division was only a methodological one. Thus, the claim 'structuralism fails to recognize that language is constantly undergoing change' is not strictly accurate. It is arguably the case, though, that such a division – even for methodological purposes – means that the production and reproduction of systems and structures cannot be adequately grasped.

The Raw and The Cooked: Lévi-Strauss and structural anthropology

At first sight, no idea might be more removed from the realm of culture and the social than that of nature. Nature, after all, smacks of physical processes unaffected by human activity, and calls to mind the eternal, the timeless and universal. Nothing, it might be thought, could be more natural than nature. And yet, if we think about it for a moment, it is evident that what we experience as natural is rooted ultimately in culture. From biology and physics to the environment and Mother Nature, what we know about the natural is based in turn upon our culturally specific ways of understanding the world. For Claude Lévi-Strauss, the link between the natural and the human is dazzlingly complex. Rejecting as too simplistic the idea that there are natural aspects of culture, or alternatively that culture incorporates nature in all its variations, Lévi-Strauss instead proposes a *structural link* between the natural and cultural which constitutes social relations from end to end.

Lévi-Strauss became one of the most celebrated and fashionable structuralists throughout Europe during the postwar years, applying with beautiful prose the methods of structural linguistics to the anthropological analysis of kinship, primitive classification systems, myth, music, totemism and art. In particular, Lévi-Strauss drew upon Saussure's structural linguistics to examine cultural production as a *system of oppositional relations of difference* that compose social meanings. From this angle, one of his major contributions to social theory was the insight that the products of culture are organized and ordered in much the same way as we imagine the products of nature to be segmented.

In his book, *The Raw and The Cooked* (1964), Lévi-Strauss comments that, in the same manner that all historical societies have spoken languages, so also human societies have processed food, in some fashion or other, through cooking. Cooking may take the form of boiling, roasting, grilling, steaming or frying, but whatever the method the act of cooking itself is a transformational one involving shifts from nature to culture. According to Lévi-Strauss, the cooking of food is, in effect, a form of mediation between nature and society, between heaven and earth, and between life and death. The cooking of food involves the transformation of raw fresh food geared to culture, whereas raw fresh food left to nature is transformed as rotten. To claim, as Lévi-Strauss does, that there is a 'culinary triangle' of foods in human culture everywhere is to claim that various binary oppositions – for example, transformed/normal and cooked/rotten – become internalized in the human mind. As one of Lévi-Strauss's foremost interpreters, Edmund Leach, sums up *The Raw and The Cooked*:

> What Lévi-Strauss is getting at is this. *Animals* just eat food; and food is anything available which their instincts place in the category 'edible.' But *human beings*, once they have been weaned from the mother's breast, have no such instincts. It is the conventions of society which decree what is food and what is not food, and what kinds of food shall be eaten on what occasions. And since the occasions are social occasions there must be some kind of patterned homology between relationships between kinds of food on the one hand and relationships between social occasions on the other.
>
> (1970: 32)

It is important to be clear here as to what Lévi-Strauss is not saying. He is not saying that nature as such does not exist. For example, fresh raw food is essential to life and without it we would die very quickly. Because culture is natural to us, however, it is what we do with foodstuffs (milk, cheese, meat and so on) that constitutes food as a sign-system geared to meaning, symbolism and interpretation. Whether we speak of a Londoner or an Amazonian Indian, according to Lévi-Strauss, food is divided in sub-categories – food-type 1, food-type 2, food-type 3 – which are, in turn, accorded differences through social relations. For example, according to Western conventions, the presentation of oysters at a dinner party usually signals an entrée, just as roast beef is accorded the status of main course and chocolate mousse is suitable for dessert. Why this should be the case, says Lévi-Strauss, arises from forms of symbolism planted deep in the human mind, and structured by powerful binary oppositions – savory/sweet, raw/cooked, nature/culture.

Do you agree with Lévi-Strauss that, if we dig deep through culture, we can find universal laws (structured by binary oppositions) governing the human mind? How relevant do you find Lévi-Strauss's *The Raw and The Cooked* to today's world of fast-food outlets and multicultural cuisines?

Roland Barthes: structuralist semiology and popular culture

The early structuralist, Barthes appears most decisively in *Elements of Semiology*, a book that illustrates the method of structuralism for the critique of culture in our era of mass communications. Quite beyond the austerely technical details that Barthes rehearses in considering Saussurian linguistics and structuralist semiology, his underwriting of the power of deadly structures upon human lives is what led to widespread critical acclaim of *Elements of Semiology*. The first major exercise in what was to become Barthes's structuralist methodology for a new style of cultural research in decoding signs, *Elements* insisted upon the Saussurian insight that meaning is an upshot of oppositions between signs within a linguistic and cultural system. Barthes took Saussure a step further however, and in at least two key respects. Firstly, whilst arguing that Saussurian linguistics uncovers the absent structures of meaning – by stressing the unremitting play of differences in society, the power of unconscious convention, and systematic function – he also considered limitations to the structural critique of meaning. For Barthes, oppositions leave out of account the various social things which do not fit into either of the opposed linguistic categories of Saussurian analysis. To that extent, Saussurian linguistics – if not supplemented with a properly semiological appreciation of the complexity of human experience – runs the risk of downgrading individuality and issues pertaining to individual style. These were matters of considerable importance to Barthes, whose structuralism was always tempered by an appreciation of other theoretical approaches – from sociology to psychoanalysis. But he also extended Saussure in still another respect. *Elements* sets out the method of structuralism for the critique of culture and society, and not simply the functional analysis of language. In Barthes's view, semiology – the study of the signs produced by society – is vital to the critique of capitalist consumerism, of the deep structures that orientate desire for flashy cars, designer clothes and technological gadgets, and which purge the political realm of creativity and alternative possibility.

> ike the linguist who deals only with the phonic substance ; in the same way, ideally, a good corpus of documents on the food system should comprise only one and the same type of document (restaurant menus, for instance). Reality, however, most commonly presents mixed substances; for instance, garments and written language in fashion; images, music and speech in films, etc; it will therefore be necessary to accept heterogeneous corpuses, but to see to it, in that case, that one makes a careful study of the systematic articulation of the substances concerned (and chiefly, that one pays due attention to separating the real from the language which takes it over), that is, that one gives their very heterogeneity a structural interpretation.
>
> Roland Barthes (1967) *Elements of Semiology*. London: Cape, pages 98–9.

If *Elements of Semiology* details the structuralist method and conceptual toolbox for the critique of culture, it is *Mythologies* that uncovers the ideological consequences of popular culture itself. His most famous work as a 'high' structuralist, *Mythologies* finds Barthes analyzing a panorama of 1950s French culture – from wrestling to striptease, advertising to the Tour de France. Derived from journalistic essays he had penned during the early 1950s, *Mythologies* took French intellectual culture by storm, perhaps partly because these little essays seemed an easier way for readers to engage with structuralism, and partly because Barthes's short, witty reflections revealed a structuralist with a radical political agenda. For his aim throughout the book, wrote Barthes, was to decode the function of myths as rendering social reality 'natural'; alarmed at seeing 'Nature and History confused at every turn,' Barthes found in everyday mythologies the making of what is thoroughly cultural seem natural, what he referred to as the ceaseless 'what-goes-without-saying.' In order to uncover how myth converts culture into Nature, Barthes brought to bear a lightly worn-on-the-sleeve structuralism upon popular culture. He found at work within the mythological façade of culture a dramatic series of displacements, substitutions and repetitions of meaning, all of which served to pass off the signs of culture as natural. The structuralist argument that Barthes weaves throughout *Mythologies* is that culture promotes particular meanings only through a concealment of other ideological ones. Wine, steak and fries, for example, are the apparently natural diet of the French – 'an alimentary sign of Frenchness.'

Perhaps the best way to illustrate Barthes's arrestingly original semiological structuralism is by looking in a little more detail at one of his essays in *Mythologies*. In 'The Brain of Einstein,' Barthes reviews the famous scientist's 'body in the library' of popular culture. That is to say, he carefully appraises the complex cultural meanings attributed to Einstein and to natural science. 'Einstein's brain,' writes Barthes (1972: 68), 'is a mythical object: paradoxically, the greatest intelligence of all provides an image of the most up-to-date machine, the man who is too powerful is removed from psychology, and introduced into a world of robots.' What Barthes finds notable about Einstein is how the creativity and innovation of natural science is bracketed off from popular consciousness of his scientific genius; instead, Einstein is reduced to a machine, his scientific labors to 'the mechanical making of sausages.' Still further, the complexity of scientific analysis is reduced in our general culture to the utter simplicity of a singular formula, $E = mc^2$.

> There is a single secret to the world, and this secret is held in one word; the universe is a safe of which humanity seeks the combination: Einstein almost found it, this is the myth of Einstein. . . . The historic

equation $E = mc^2$, by its unexpected simplicity, almost embodies the pure idea of the key, bare, liner, made of one metal, opening with a wholly magical ease a door which had resisted the desperate efforts of centuries.

(Barthes 1972: 69)

The stylish, playful prose of Barthes's writing on Einstein works to occlude the rigors of his structuralist enquiry. For stripped of its elegant writing, Barthes's semiological analysis reveals a series of oppositions which structure the internal relations of meanings attributed to myths that Einstein embodies. Traversing the themes discussed above – from Einstein as the world's 'greatest intelligence' to his insertion into a 'world of robots,' from the 'magic' (as Barthes puts it) of his theory of relativity to his 'mechanical making of sausages,' and from the complexity of his science to the simplicity of the world's secret unlocked in one equation – we could condense this structuralist analysis to a series of binary oppositions. These would presumably include: human/machine; psychology/anti-psychology; magical/mechanical; and, complexity/simplicity. Written in this way, this is obviously not as gripping or eloquent as Barthes's decoding of the myth of Einstein. But my point is to indicate that, notwithstanding Barthes's aesthetic and brilliant style, the core of his structuralist analysis shifts the content of the issue under review to the sidelines in order to concentrate entirely on form. As with Saussure, then, it is the structure of internal relations of the signs under consideration that matters.

Structuralism has sometimes been criticized as apolitical. The criticism is that, with its relentless focus on linguistic units of discourse, structuralism turns away from the historical conditions and actual political struggles of people, substituting an empty formalism. In the light of reading Barthes's *Mythologies*, however, it seems difficult to give much weight to such criticism, such is the penetrating political analysis and ideological engagement of his writing. Famously, Barthes attacked French involvements in Indo-China and Algeria. A key example was his analysis of the cover of an issue of *Paris-Match*, with a photo of a black soldier in uniform saluting the French flag. For Barthes, the magazine cover traded in the mythology of French imperialism. At the time, France was engaged in a prolonged war with Algeria; against the backdrop of the break-up of the French colonial empire, there was considerable debate in France over whether Algeria should be given its independence. The *Paris-Match* cover, said Barthes, tacitly underwrote imperialism. The mythological message of the cover, he wrote, was

that France is a great Empire, that all her sons, without distinction of color, serve faithfully beneath her flag, and that there is no better answer to the detractors of a supposed colonialism, than the zeal of this Negro to serve his supposed oppressors.

In Barthes's view, myth is around to make us feel socially 'ordinary' or 'natural'; criticism remains the difficult theoretical labor of demonstrating why myth is a kind of 'social lie.' To see the world through the prism of myth, for Barthes, is akin to having one's head buried in the sand – as culture palms itself off as nature. In 'Myth Today,' a theoretical overview of the Saussurian model at the conclusion of *Mythologies*, Barthes details the complex ways in which mythological language is at once intimate and alien to us. Deep in the Saussurian mode, Barthes theorizes a 'pyramidal' sign divided between the signifier (the voice or graphic mark) and signified (the representation or concept attached to it). The relation between signifier and signified, for Barthes as for Saussure, is arbitrary – that is to say, socially conventional. Barthes calls this a 'first-order' signifying system in which the proliferation of discourse is contingent – signs are always a matter of historical and cultural convention. Language in this sense, for Barthes, is creative, rich in its multiple associations, and capable of turning back upon its own conventional 'arbitrariness' – for example, when people use irony. By contrast, there is a kind of language which is ideological because it blocks its own relative, artificial status and attempts to pass itself off as transcendent, natural and universal. Barthes calls this a 'second-order semiological system' and the ideological language which corresponds to this system is myth. Mythic speech, according to Barthes, draws upon the first-order system of language in the fashioning of a second-order system which offers up a version of reality 'as it is,' the 'natural' attitude. Agreeing that appreciation of wine is a mark of sophistication, or that wealth creation is intrinsically beneficial, seems the most obvious thing in the world. Nothing could more mythic than the 'most obvious,' according to Barthes – as layers of free-floating 'first-order' signs are gathered up, glued together through repetition, and displaced to the fixed 'second-order' of mythic speech.

Myth hides nothing and flaunts nothing: it distorts; myth is neither a lie nor a confession: it is an inflexion. Placed before the dilemma which I mentioned a moment ago, myth finds a third way out. Threatened with disappearance if it yields to either of the first two types of focusing, it gets out of this tight spot thanks to a compromise – it *is* this compromise. Entrusted with 'glossing over' an intentional concept, myth encounters nothing by betrayal in language, for language can only obliterate the concept if it hides it, or unmask it if

> it formulates it. The elaboration of a second-order semiological system will enable myth to escape this dilemma: driven to having either to unveil or liquidize the concept, it will *naturalize* it.
>
> Roland Barthes (1972) *Mythologies*. New York: Hill and Wang, page 129.

Barthes thus presents what might be called the two faces of language. One is associative, free-flowing, relative, artificial, poetic. This is the 'first-order' realm of language, as captured in Saussurian linguistics. The other is fixed, repetitious, closed. This is the 'second-order' realm of language, and for Barthes the preserve of ideology and mythological speech. It is here – in the structural transformations from 'first' to 'second' order signifying systems – that social theorists can most usefully deploy structuralist methods for the analysis of ideology, myth and popular culture.

Barthes's structuralist-inspired writings have powerfully challenged traditional forms of sociological analysis, and even today works such as *Mythologies* continue to inspire significant work in critical cultural studies. Barthes's semiological method for the decoding of signs has found many supporters – from Susan Sontag to Julia Kristeva – and subsequent authors working in the structuralist tradition have refined and elaborated Barthes's cultural critique. The ongoing relevance of Barthes's structuralist semiology surely lies in its radical account of the conventional 'arbitrariness' of the sign's relationship to society, its painstaking structural lucidity, and its account of social and ideological forms. On the other hand, it is now widely agreed that there are major limitations to Barthes's early structuralism, and indeed Barthes himself was to express serious reservations about the 'scientific pretensions' of his earlier structuralist writings. One limitation, according to some critics, is that the individual appears diminished – determined exclusively by the powers of structure – in Barthes's work. This may be so in one sense, but it would appear to neglect the broader political thrust of Barthes's work. For the structuralist tradition, social analysis cannot adequately proceed from the individual's 'experience' – for that very 'experience' is, in fact, the effect of an impersonal structure. Thus, Barthes's social theory, at its best, steers a middle course between individual subject and social process by examining instead the *system of differences* in which discourse is embedded. And it is here that we find the ongoing political edge in Barthes's work: society reveals itself through the system of differences it produces, ideology reveals itself through the closure of those differences. In myths, in the obviousness of the 'natural,' in pseudo 'common sense', culture seeks to naturalize social reality. But still Barthes's commitment to structures at the expense of identity produces tensions and contradictions – and, at its worst, casts the individual as the passive victim of impersonal processes. 'The excitement of innovative methods and new materials,' writes Rick Rylance (1994: 54) of Barthes, 'contradicts the gloomy scenarios of determinism and limitation.'

Foucault: knowledge, social order and power

Michel Foucault (1926–1984) is perhaps the most influential French intellectual associated with the theoretical current of structuralism. Though he rejected any direct linkage with this tradition of thought, Foucault's early works – such as *The Birth of the Clinic* (1963), *The Order of Things* (1966), and *The Archaeology of Knowledge* (1969) – demonstrate the method of a 'high' structuralist, analyzing the origins of modern medicine, psychiatry and systems of classification in terms of the systemic features of language and discourse. Foucault's own typical habit of energetically attacking the present, as well as all things 'familiar' or 'normal,' is to dig into the past – examining the archives of previous historical epochs. This historical approach informing Foucault's structuralist criticism produced, in time, powerful insights into the systems of power that people make to entrap themselves – as well as pushing the structuralist method to its limit. Foucault's work, that is to say, is concerned in the broadest sense with the gentle wiles of modern reason and knowledge; and his structuralist-inspired social theory reveals the subtle and complex ways in which the rules of social formation shape the lives of individuals.

The early structuralist Foucault details the possibility of a scientific method, labeled either 'archaeology' or 'genealogy,' which can discern unconscious processes of social change. Such an archaeological or genealogical method in the hands of Foucault sought to trace the unthought processes governing the structure of social things; the aim was to reveal 'a positive unconscious of knowledge: a level that eludes the consciousness of the scientist and yet is part of what is scientific.' Foucault sought to do this by applying structuralism to the rules of social formation whereby certain discourses became deeply layered in social life. In *The Order of Things* (1966) and *The Archaeology of Knowledge* (1969), Foucault set about analyzing the production of modern reason and knowledge by 'digging' into the past. At one level, this meant attacking certain taken-for-granted concepts, ideas and structures that have served to legitimize Western knowledge and philosophy – such as the widespread belief in scientific advancement and faith in humanly engineered progress. This he did by working the archives, critically interrogating the ways that the production of knowledge has been shaped and organized over the centuries by bodies of texts, doctrines and discourses. He sought, in effect, to reread the commentaries, authors and disciplines of the human sciences in terms of the rules of language whereby knowledge becomes the ultimate ground of all power. At a deeper level, Foucault's archaeological or genealogical method sought to rise above certain familiar themes dominant in Western thought – such as the privilege accorded to consciousness – to a point where the production of knowledge through the linguistic systems that structure social, political and technological life could be comprehended. As Foucault represents this, archaeological analysis addresses 'the general space of knowledge' and 'the mode of being of things that appear in it.'

In a society such as ours, but basically in any society, there are manifold relations of power which permeate, characterize and constitute the social body, and these relations of power cannot themselves be established, consolidated nor implemented without the production, accumulation, circulation and functioning of a discourse. There can be no possible exercise of power without a certain economy of discourses of truth which operate through and on the basis of this association. We are subjected to the production of truth through power and we cannot exercise power except through the production of truth.

Michel Foucault (1980) 'Two lectures' in C. Gordin (ed) *Power/Knowledge: Selected Interviews and Other Writings, 1972–1977*. New York: Pantheon Books.

According to Foucault, the power of knowledge moves on several levels. Firstly, it is the power of classifying languages – of determining that certain languages will come to have an overarching hold over the organization of discrete aspects of daily life. In *The Order of Things*, Foucault maps the force-fields of the human sciences, from their emergence in the Renaissance to the nineteenth century in the domains of biology, economics and linguistics. Secondly, it is the power of classifying discourse itself, classifying the rules which underpin formations of discourse and their domains of application. Economic discourses, so to speak, construct 'productive individuals' subject to the laws of economics; biology constructs individuals as 'living organisms' subject to laws of nature; and, linguistics locates speaking subjects as governed by structures of signification. Finally, such systems of thought and their classifications govern not only how discourse is produced but the power-relations operating throughout society in general – of which we will consider Foucault's treatment of the relation between power and knowledge in more detail shortly.

In order to better understand how knowledge becomes inscribed in techniques of individuation and objectification, let us now turn to consider

Foucault's famous work on prisons. In his best-selling *Discipline and Punish*, Foucault develops a genealogical history of punishment and prisons and introduces his celebrated concept 'power-knowledge.' The historical problem to which Foucault turns, in effect, concerns the relations of power and knowledge as imprinted on the human body through disciplinary codes and related forms of punishment. Foucault's aim, he writes, is to 'study the metamorphosis of punitive methods on the basis of a political technology of the body in which might be read a common history of power relations.' To see modern judicial punishment and disciplinary codes through the frame of a genealogical history, for Foucault, is a valuable advance on seeing it simply as an ongoing 'humane improvement' over earlier historical forms of punishment. For it allows us to see that the discipline of the body as performed by prisons scoops up various disciplinary codes that originated at different points in history, and which have come to shape the functioning of wider relations of power in schools, military life and organizations. In modern society, says Foucault, individuals are increasingly subject to what he terms 'disciplinary power,' a power that is hidden, monotonous and invisible.

Discipline and Punish asserts that the institutional framework of prisons has its origins in the Panopticon, an organizational proposal for the treatment of offenders put forward by the social philosopher Jeremy Bentham in the nineteenth century. 'Panopticon' was the term Bentham used for a set of proposals he tried to sell to the British government for the retraining of a criminal's mind from irrational law-breaking to rational law-following. The design of Bentham's panoptical prison was circular in shape, with a guard in a central tower looking out onto prisoners' cells. The purpose of the design was to make it impossible for the prisoner to tell if the guard was watching or not, for the tower windows were fitted with a Venetian blind, thus establishing a kind of one-way, total surveillance of prisoners by the prison staff. It was this element of surveillance of central control that Foucault isolated as fundamental to the exercise of power.

Panoptical surveillance takes several forms. One is the direct monitoring of the prisoner's actions at any time. Whether mixing with other inmates or alone in one's cell, there was to be no place of escape from the panoptical gaze. For Foucault this principle was a structure of domination at the heart of the penitentiary, but also in other organizations too. 'Is it surprising,' asks Foucault (1979: 228), 'that prisons resemble factories, schools, barracks, hospitals, which all resemble prisons?' The panoptical prison, it transpired, was everywhere – organizing the practical knowledge of daily life.

A second form of surveillance consists of record keeping, the updating of files, and the development of case histories for the reform of criminals.

Such administrative paperwork is for Foucault not only essential for the operation of prisons, but crucial to the regulation and disciplining of human bodies. As Mark Poster observes:

> The principle of one-way, total surveillance of the subject was extended to the keeping of files. Without a systematic record of the subject's behavior surveillance is incomplete. For the Panoptical machine to have its effect the individual must become a case with a meticulously kept dossier that reflects the history of his deviation from the norm.
>
> (1990: 91)

Foucault thus sees the organizing influence of Panoptical surveillance at work in more and more modern organizations, such as mental asylums, schools, hospitals, and the military and secret services. In contemporary culture, says Foucault, power is imposed upon people through the bureaucratic surveillance of populations, the routine gathering of information and the continual monitoring of daily life; in effect, the modern age is one of 'panopticism,' a society in which individuals are increasingly caught up in systems of power in and through which visibility is a key means of social control. Society for Foucault can be understood as a struggle of discourses in which power relations are shaped, with specific forms of discipline and resistance defining the nature of what it feels like to be alive. Those in positions of power, in order to further their material and symbolic interests, seek to gain control over the policing of discourse – of defining what is acceptable and unacceptable within specific forms of life within society at large. But power, warns Foucault, is never fixed. Power is instead best conceived as a relationship, a mysterious force between individuals, groups and institutions. It is for this reason that Foucault often speaks of a micro-politics of power, by which he means the multifarious submissions and resistances of individuals in their engagement with social and institutional life.

Society and disciplined bodies

An early use of Foucault's ideas for thinking about the relations between self, society and power is that offered by the British sociologist Bryan S. Turner. In a series of books, from *The Body and Society* (1984) to *Regulating Bodies* (1992), Turner (b. 1945) has sought to develop a sophisticated sociological reading of Foucault. Now Foucault was a philosopher and historian, not a sociologist. Yet Turner argues that there is much in Foucault's work that can be drawn upon with profit for developing a sociology of the 'embodied self.' The self has been passed off for too long, says Turner, as peculiarly disembodied; the body is conceptualized in mainstream sociological approaches as a biological constraint upon human agency and social action. However, Turner sees the embodied self as fundamental to social interaction. The body is something we are, we have and we do in daily life; the body is crucial to an individual subject's sense of self, as well as the manner in which the self relates and interacts with others. The relationship between self, body and knowledge, says Turner, is central to Foucault's work and, when sociologically interpreted, provides a valuable model for understanding the changing relations between self and society. The body for Turner connects self-identity, physical self-regulation and sexuality in the context of post-modern city culture. The increasing emphasis on fitness, hygiene, thinness and youthfulness are central planks in the maintenance of self-regulation in relation to consumer capitalism. This political struggle around the body, particularly the commodification of body images, occurs not only in relation to the regulation of self and sexuality, but also through legislative and administrative structures. *In vitro* fertilization programs, abortion, childcare, the medicalization of AIDS as a modern epidemic: it is here that we witness the progressive institutional management, regulation and surveillance of the embodied self in contemporary culture.

In an essay 'The Government of the Body,' Turner extends Foucault's ideas by analyzing the regularization of self, the rationalization of diet and the discipline of the body. Diet, says Turner, is linked to a micro-politics of the human body, since it transfers responsibility for the discipline of the self into the hands of human subjects. The growth of dietetics and social science consolidate the administrative management of food consumption as part of the bio-politics of population, in so far as this involves the regulation of individuals, of health, and of mortality. Analyzing the rise of expert technical knowledge (medicine, dietetics, social science) as interwoven with the political management of populations, Turner argues:

> Dietary tables were typically aimed at forms of consumption which were regarded as 'irrational' threats to health, especially where overconsumption was associated with obesity and alcoholism. These dietary programs were originally addressed to those social groups which were exposed to abundance – the aristocracy, merchants and the professional groups of the London taverns and clubs . . . It was not until the latter part of the nineteenth century that the science of diet became important in the economic management of prisons

and the political management of society. The principles for the efficient government of prisons and asylums were quickly applied to the question of an effective, healthy working class supported on a minimum but adequate calorie intake.

(Bryan S. Turner, *Regulating Bodies: Essays in Medical Sociology*, London: Routledge, 1992, pages 192–3)

Dietetics, with its focus on consumption and the body, led people increasingly to care for themselves according to pre-given administrative rules and regulations; it led people to follow expert information in the management and control of the self.

Turner is refreshingly ambivalent about the wider social and political consequences of the complex interrelationship between self, embodiment and gender. He does not see a single source of social power guiding the government of the body/self. Rather, our growing awareness that the body is socially produced and regulated occurs on many different symbolic levels, from medicine to the fashion industry. Like sexuality and the self, the body is today located within consumer culture as a mark of distinction; bodily appearance and control link to the symbolic representation of identity – as a metaphor of society, as a field for gender differentiation, as a site for racial and ethnic cultures and conflicts. However, the embodied self for Turner is not the passive product of institutional and ideological forces, but rather is integral to the very nature of being and of agency in the routine presenting, interpreting and monitoring of daily life. In contemporary culture there is for Turner a kind of lifting of the care of the self to the second power, with regimens of calorie measurement, jogging, and health clubs the means through which people discipline their bodies. From this perspective the politics of identity is increasingly wrapped around configurations of the body – the fit body, the disciplined body, the body beautiful, body piercing, the body in cyberspace. There is also, of course, the troubled and troubling anorexic body; eating disorders, says Turner, are central self-pathologies of our age. In all of this, however, the body is itself the site of intensified self-management, self-regulation and self-mastery.

The limits of structuralism: Foucault's *History of Sexuality*

During the late 1970s and early 1980s, Foucault moved away from structuralism. Like Barthes, he became increasingly concerned with the limits of structuralist analysis to comprehend the complexities of social transformation and the intricacies of human action and matters pertaining to individual style. But this theoretical move involved less a wholesale break with the core tenets of structuralism than a pushing of structuralist analysis to its limits. This he did in the final part of his academic career through the development of a sweeping, brilliant history of sexuality.

In *The History of Sexuality* (1978) Foucault contends that knowledge about sexuality compels individuals to situate themselves in relation to regimes of the erotic, particularly to what is regulated, forbidden, prohibited. 'Each person,' writes Foucault (1988: 40), 'has the duty to know who he is, that is, to try to know what is happening inside him, to acknowledge faults, to recognize temptations, to locate desires.' In the first volume of *The History of Sexuality*, Foucault sets out to debunk what he calls 'the repressive hypothesis.' According to this hypothesis the healthy expression of sexuality has been censured, smothered and forbidden; at any rate, this is held to be the case in the West. However, Foucault takes issue with this hypothesis, and in fact seeks to undermine the conventional wisdom that sex is repressed. Sex, says Foucault, has not been driven underground in contemporary culture. On the contrary, there has been an ever-widening discussion of sex and sexuality. Sexuality for Foucault is the result of a process of endless monitoring, discussion, classification, ordering, recording and regulation. The medicalization of sexuality, particularly notions of sexual perversion and deviance, has brought into focus the complex interrelationship between desire, sex and power. Questioning the conventional view that power constrains sexual desire, Foucault advances the view that power serves not only to regulate 'sexual taboos' but also to produce sexuality and its pleasures. That is to say, power and sexual pleasure are intricately intertwined.

To demonstrate this Foucault examines Victorian attitudes towards sexuality in the late nineteenth century. Victorianism, writes Foucault, is usually associated with the emergence of prudishness, the silencing of sexuality, and the rationalization of sex within the domestic sphere, the home, the family. Foucault disagrees. He argues that one sees in the advent of the Victorian era the development of sexuality as a secret, as something forbidden or taboo, which then required administration, regulation and policing. For example, doctors, psychiatrists and others catalogued and classified numerous perversions, from which issues about sex became endlessly tracked and monitored with the growth of social medicine, education, criminology and sexology. These discourses about sex and sexuality form part of a broader realm of techniques for the care of the self in society, techniques which Foucault sees as shaping the mind externally.

To understand the rise of techniques for the care of the self, Foucault argues it is necessary to connect the West's prohibition against sex to discourses of sexuality in nineteenth-century scientific disciplines and culture. Foucault's approach to the analysis of the intertwining of sex and power is brought out nicely in the opening chapter of *The History of Sexuality*, where he discusses a medical report about a farmworker, apparently simple-minded, who was arrested and then incarcerated in a clinic for sexual transgressions:

> One day in 1867, a farm hand from the village of Lapcourt . . . obtained a few caresses from a little girl, just as he had done before and seen done by the village urchins around him . . . So he was pointed out by the girl's family to the mayor of the village, reported by the mayor to the gendarmes, led by the gendarmes to the judge, who indicted him and turned him over first to a doctor, then to two other experts who not only wrote their report but also had it published. What is the significant thing about this story? The pettiness of it all; the fact that this everyday occurrence in the life of village sexuality, these inconsequential bucolic pleasures, could become, from a certain time, the object not only of a collective intolerance but of a judicial action, a medical intervention, a careful clinical examination, and an entire theoretical elaboration. The thing to note is that they went so far as to measure the brainpan, study facial bone structure, and inspect for possible signs of degenerescence the anatomy of this personage who up to that moment had been an integral part of village life; that they made him talk; that they questioned him concerning his thoughts, inclinations, habits, sensations, and opinions. And then, acquitting him of any crime, they decided finally to make him into a pure object of medicine and knowledge – an object to be shut away till the end of his life in the hospital at Maréville, but also one to be made known to the world of learning through a detailed analysis.
>
> (1978: 31–2)

For Foucault, the point of this story is that inconsequential pleasures are subjected to the workings of power; he detects in this investigation the emergence of diagnosis, analysis, measurement, classification, and specification of bodies and pleasures; through this investigation state officials and medical specialists attempt to regulate and control pleasures which are, in Foucault's opinion, relatively harmless and innocent.

Foucault sees sex as the focal point of our contemporary cultural fascination with personal identity and the self. By concentrating its gaze more and more on sex, society is able to channel into various discourses a 'regime of truth' in which pathologies and deviations may be read, interpreted, uncovered, disclosed, regulated and restricted. All of this is related to science, as the central discourse which influences many variant actions.

Scientists – in the form of medical experts, psychologists, sexologists and assorted specialists – deploy knowledge in order to distinguish between norm and pathology; moreover, Foucault argues that in analyzing and interpreting human behavior, science creates sex at the same time as it excavates secrets of the self. The case history, the medical report, the scientific treatise, the questionnaire: these are the means by which science establishes a position from which it discloses, and legislates upon, sex and its regimes of truth. Knowledge and power, once again, tangle and interpenetrate.

Foucault's approach to sexuality, power and the self has sometimes been caricatured by his critics – so it is important to be clear about his argument. To begin with, it should be stressed that Foucault is not suggesting that the production of sexuality as a process of regulation and normalization is simply the result of external or societal constraint. Rather, his argument is that, while power may prohibit sex in various forms, it also serves to implicate individuals in multiple self-organizations, by inciting desires, dispositions, needs, practices, activities and transgressions. When an adult watches a talk show about marriage infidelities, for instance, he or she participates in mediated talk about sex – talk which is imbued with highly structured rules and conventions, as well as hierarchies of gender power and social prestige. Similarly, people who read self-help manuals about intimate relationships, and how to handle such relationships, are enveloped in a world of instruction as to the protocols of sexual behavior. Individuals everywhere, for Foucault, are involved at a personal and emotional level with talk about sex, preoccupied with the cultivation of the self in and through sexuality.

What this amounts to saying, in short, is that individuals today willingly monitor and track down, with a view to controlling, their sexual feelings, fantasies, inclinations, dispositions and activities. Modern culture in the West has become obsessed with sex as the truth of identity; deviations from accepted adult sexual norms must be guarded against vigilantly. The lives we live are lived against a preconscious backdrop of self-policing. Foucault discerns this shift to the self-policing of sexuality in relation to the role of confession, particularly the need for self-punishment, in the psychological sciences, but also within intimate relationships and the family. In fact, Foucault tells us we have become a 'confessing society'; a society which, through confession, continually monitors, and checks against, the dangers of sex. He outlines a number of more general historical developments in this respect, but the broad thrust of his argument is as follows. The Roman Catholic confessional, Foucault contends, was a means of regulating the sexuality of its believers; the church was the site in which subjects came to tell the truth about themselves, especially in relation to sexuality, to their priests. When seen from this angle, the confessional can be regarded as the source of the West's preoccupation with sex, particularly in terms of the sanctioned inducement to talk of it. Confession became unhooked from its broad religious framework, however, somewhere in the late eighteenth century and was transformed into a type of investigation or interrogation through the scientific study of sex and the creation of medical discourses about it. Sex became increasingly bound up with networks of knowledge and power, and, in time, a matter for increasing self-policing, self-regulation and self-interrogation. In other words, instead of sex being regulated by external forces, it is much more a matter of attitudinal discipline, which is in turn connected to issues of, say, knowledge and education. Psychotherapy and psychoanalysis, says Foucault, are key instances of such self-policing in the contemporary era. In therapy the individual does not so much feel coerced into confessing about sexual practices and erotic fantasies; rather the information divulged by the patient is treated as the means to freedom, the realization of a liberation from repression.

The publication of Foucault's subsequent volumes on the history of sexuality, *The Use of Pleasure* (1985) and *The Care of the Self* (1986), saw a shift in emphasis away from the modern, Christian world to the classical world, specifically ancient Greek culture. Foucault became interested in the study of Roman morality as a means of undermining the claims to universality of our contemporary system of sexuality in the West. The fundamental difference between classical and Christian sexual moralities, contends Foucault, is that while the latter seeks to regulate sexual behavior through coercion and compulsion, the former promoted sexuality as something to be self-managed and self-mastered: sexual conduct was something to be indulged in or abstained from at appropriate times. The classical world, says Foucault, initiated a concern with 'care of the self,' in which the individual attended to problems of techniques of the self, self-examination and self-stylization. Nowhere was this better demonstrated, according to Foucault, than in the exercise of restrained sexual behavior both within marriage and in extramarital liaisons. With regard to marital relations, what distinguished the ethical husband was not the demonstration of affection towards his wife but rather the self-control with which he conducted himself in relation to sex and pleasure. 'For the husband,' wrote Foucault, 'having sexual relations only with his wife was the most elegant way of exercising control' (1985: 151). For Foucault, the ancient Greek and classical Roman arts of existence demonstrate the intimate connection between self-control and the elegant stylization of sexual conduct: the individual self, in exercising self-restraint and moderation in relation to all sexual conduct, established ethical worthiness and moral authority.

This notion of sexual moderation also pertained to extramarital relations, and Foucault devotes considerable discussion to dissecting the aesthetic values and stylistic criteria governing homosexual conduct in classical Greek society. The Greeks, he argues, did not stigmatize the love felt for a boy by an older man. On the contrary, men were permitted to have love affairs with younger boys; non-marital sex was not considered dangerous or unnatural in the manner in which it is viewed by Western culture, and homosexual bonds did not prevent a man from maintaining heterosexual intimacy and commitment to his wife; the love between boys and adult males was one use of pleasure among others, with different moral rules of conduct and self-stylization. Note that Foucault is not suggesting that the classical age was some golden period in the history of sexuality; for the Greeks, sexuality was at once a source of pleasure and a source of anxiety. Moreover, there were many regulations governing the nature of Greek homosexuality. Older men could engage in homosexual bonds with boys, but not with other, adult men; the relation between adult men and boys was required to be moderate in its display of sexual desire. Indeed self-restraint and sexual abstinence, suggests Foucault, were central to the ethical regime in which the individual carried out sexual acts. Self-control, self-awareness and self-mastery in the realm of sexuality defined the ethical regime of the classical age; appropriate forms of sexual moderation shaped a way of being, of living, of a whole technology of the self.

In discussing an ethics of the self in the classical age, in which the language of pleasures and the eroticization of the body figures prominently, Foucault came very close to revealing aspects about his own private life and sexuality. In his later years, Foucault was openly homosexual. Profoundly troubled by his own sexuality as a young man, Foucault long considered French sexual culture restrictive and intolerant. It was not until the 1970s, when he travelled to lecture at universities in the United States, that Foucault encountered the affirmative sexual politics of the gay and lesbian communities. The assertion of gay identity and culture fascinated him, and he described the emergence of American gay urban areas – such as Christopher Street in New York and the Castro Street area in San Francisco – as 'laboratories of sexual experimentation.' Yet he was also ambivalent about the gay sexual liberation movement, particularly the assumption that gayness formed a common sexual identity. Time and again Foucault debunked the idea of a true self; he was scathing of what he called the 'Californian cult of the self,' in which the deciphering of sexual desire is treated as revealing the essence of a true self. In contrast to those who spoke of liberating a sexual essence, Foucault argued that gayness meant the *invention* of new identities, the extension of pleasure beyond narrow sexual relations to multifarious parts of the body. Such an ethics of the self, Foucault said of gayness, could herald 'a culture which invents ways of relating, types of existence, types of exchanges between individuals that are really new and are neither the same as, nor superimposed on, existing cultural forms' (1982: 39).

Governmentality

During the final years of his life, Foucault conceptualized technologies of the self and their associated practices of coercion, constraint and domination in terms of the idea of 'governmentality.' In a lecture given at the Collège de France in 1978, he explained that governmentality referred to all endeavors involving 'how to govern oneself, how to be governed, how to govern others, by whom the people will accept being governed, how to become the best possible governor (1991: 87). Like the theme of 'care of the self,' governmentality focused largely on the productive transformation of proposals, strategies and technologies for self-conduct. What subsequently emerged in social theory during the 1980s and 1990s, with the so-called school of governmentalities, was a style of critique which revolved on the socio-historical shaping, guiding and directing of conduct of individuals. Indeed one of Foucault's key acolytes summarizes governmentality as capturing 'the ways in which one might be urged and educated to bridle one's own passions, to control one's own instincts, to govern oneself.' (Rose 1999a: 3). Like many postmodern forms of thought, the Foucauldian-inspired school of governmentalities turned out to offer a dark, oftentimes sinister, account of social processes.

Nikolas Rose, a card-carrying Foucauldian, sought to advance investigations of governmentality through a series of influential works, all of which are mostly politically pessimistic in temper. In *Governing the Soul* (1999b) and *Inventing Our Selves* (1996), Rose set out to show how the 'psy' professions (from counseling to psychotherapy), as well as medicine, education, welfare, and the social sciences and humanities, lead individuals into devoting attention to their own self-conduct, thereby implicating the self within oppressive structures that underpin society. For Rose, governmentality is the power of shaping language – seducing people to conform to what is acceptably sayable in day-to-day life. It is the power of authenticating ways of doing things, certificating modes of conduct, and thus inscribing the self in multiple modes of power. As Rose writes of the relation between the self, truth and power:

> [Expert knowledge] enables us to appreciate the role that psychology, psychiatry, and other 'psy' sciences have played within the systems of power within which human subjects have become caught up. The conceptual systems devised within the 'human'

sciences, the languages of analysis and explanations that they have invented, the ways of speaking about human conduct that they constituted, have provided the means whereby human subjectivity and intersubjectivity could enter the calculations of the authorities.

(1999: 7)

For Rose, the growth of 'psy knowledges' connects directly with the government of the self and its increasing regulation. During the course of the twentieth century, in particular, the self became more and more subject to 'psychotherapies of normality' – by which he means to say that psychological knowledge became central in how people related to themselves and others, to ways of understanding personal problems as well as in planning for the future.

Rose's work is a suggestive conjuncture of Foucauldian theory, sociology and psychology – interestingly, Rose trained as a psychologist before he moved under the influence of Foucault. His work is not, however, without its problems. Politically speaking, this is a covertly libertarian account of the self, which distrusts virtually all arenas of social activity and uncritically celebrates the 'minority politics' of resistance to the organized and systematized power of governmentality. Rose inherits Foucault's wariness of all forms of social routine, and in the process fails to consider the cognitive anchors that people require to realize and maintain forms of emotional security in all cultures. At the individual level, Rose's Foucauldianism theorizes processes of personal transformation as the result of discursive forms of governmentality involving scrutiny of self and others. From this angle, the individual is not only free to construct new cultures of the self, but indeed is obliged under the force of governmentalities to do so. The difficulty with this standpoint, however, is that it provides no adequate account of human agency, since the self simply appears as the decentered effect of an analytics of governmentality. At the social level, this kind of analysis is generally too eager to overlook long-term historical trends in its excessive concentration on the 'technological' aspects of governmentality. In short, inadequate attention is given to the active, creative struggles of individuals as they engage with their own social and historical conditions. One key reply to this neglect of social and historical structures in the school of governmentalities has been the rather different doctrine of reflexivity, which – as examined in the previous chapter – displays greater attention to the sociological forms of the relation between self and the individual agent than that offered in its French-inspired counterpart.

Criticisms of Foucault

Notwithstanding its theoretical brilliance, rich historical insight and literary style, Foucault's work has been criticized from many angles. Some have argued, for example, that his early structuralist-inspired writings are too deterministic. In making this charge, critics argue that Foucault's work renders discourse and language as a one-way intrusion of power into the lives of people – such that the workings of society operate 'behind the backs' of actors. Others have claimed that the key notion of 'power-knowledge' is too general, as it fails to illuminate the complex historical factors by which social change comes about. Still others have questioned his later works on sexuality and their debunking of the myth of repression. Yet there are various aspects of Foucault's account of society that are accepted by many; in particular, there are three core in-sights in Foucault's writings which have profoundly influenced contemporary social theory – though each of these insights also contain various limitations of understanding. These concern (1) power; (2) discourse and (3) sexuality.

Firstly, 'disciplinary power' as described by Foucault is a valuable advance on traditional conceptualizations of punishment and social control. His work has made clear the degree to which disciplinary power depends not simply upon the direct supervision of individuals, but crucially upon *indirect forms of surveillance* – from information-keeping to the use of new technologies in observing individuals and groups. Indeed, Foucault's thesis of 'disciplinary power' has powerfully influenced contemporary studies of crime, surveillance and punishment. Yet his approach to surveillance, and in particular power/knowledge or 'bio-power' as he defines it, makes for severe difficulties. It seems mistaken, for example, to treat disciplinary power as representative of power in general within modern societies. Taking Bentham's panopticon as the epitome of disciplinary power, Foucault focuses on the structural forms through which organizations like prisons and asylums fashioned the daily routines of their inmates through the use of administrative mechanisms such as strict time-tabling, continued observation and the keeping of personal records. He argued that such surveillance, and especially the technological devices that are used in ongoing observation, is fundamental not only to prisons and asylums but the general characteristics of modern organizations – from schools to work-place settings. Now certainly prisons and asylums are institutions in which individuals are incarcerated against their will. Such institutions, however, have very clear differences from other modern organizations, such as the school or the workplace, in which individuals spend only part of their day. While it is arguable that workplace and school settings are partly fashioned through the routine bureaucratic monitoring of individuals, it remains the case that disciplinary power is far more fractured and diffuse in such institutions than Foucault recognizes.

Part of the problem in this respect is that power moves in mysterious ways in Foucault's writings. Power in the hands of the early Foucault, as we have seen, is regarded as coextensive with the mushrooming of disciplinary discourses and codes. In this sense, Foucault as high-structuralist focuses on the language of punishment and the codes of discourse. The structuralism is evident in Foucault's claim that there has been a shift away from one discourse of punishment (spectacular, violent, open) to another discourse (disciplinary, covert, monotonous). Following Saussure's structural linguistics, Foucault was interested not in what participants in such organizational settings actually said or did but in the structure that both facilitated and constrained their possible discursive moves – and, even then, with the focus principally on carceral institutions. The neglect of other, less 'total' institutions – such as schools or the workplace – is striking in Foucault, and it is one from which he fails to appreciate the extent to which disciplinary power is routinely contested. Rather than the complexities of social bargaining arising as a central feature of modern organizations, Foucault's focus was, in point of fact, in how the language of discipline shapes the speech and action of individuals. But this approach to language, as we have seen in reviewing Saussure, is one that privileges structure at the expense of individual action, placing a monolithic system over and above the ordinary activities of people. Foucault's disciplinary society denies the agency and knowledgeability of individuals; the emphasis he places on the social organization of power results in an account of human agents as passive bodies.

Arguably, this top-heavy approach to understanding the reach of power is still evident in Foucault's later writings on sexuality – undertaken long after his earlier structuralist studies of prisons and punishment. Yet the assumption that discourse determines the shape of speech and behavior of individuals in matters pertaining to sexuality, intimacy and love is questionable. For one thing, it is surely mistaken to suppose – as Foucault does – that the historical development of public discussion about sex was uniformly or generally self-deceptive. The phenomenon of the medicalization of sexuality – the process by which physicians, sexologists, psychiatrists and scientists make sex a site of objective knowledge – is significant, and primarily (as Foucault suggests) for its regulation of human bodies, desires, pleasures, actions and social relations. These proliferating Victorian discourses concerning sexuality, however, were not as widely available to people, nor were they as commonly discussed and analyzed, as Foucault contends. Medical, scientific and psychiatric journals on sex were primarily consumed by experts in the field; low levels of literacy during the late nineteenth century blocked the wider dissemination and analysis of such texts, and some have argued that even more educated groups were often denied access to this literature. The medicalization of sexuality certainly helped create a new world of knowledge and discourse, but it also functioned to *restrict* sex to expert fields of discussion – which was in turn linked to gender power, of which more shortly. Another way of putting this point is to say that Foucault too readily assumes that individuals were the passive victims of specific technologies (medical, psychotherapeutical, legal and the like) which unleashed their deadly weight through a fixed intrusion of power/knowledge into the lives of individuals.

This brings us, secondly, to the limitations of the notion of 'discourse.' Foucault's concentration upon discourse leads, arguably, to a neglect of the creativity of human action. In Foucault's approach to sexuality it is discourse which produces human experience rather than experience (individual dispositions, emotional desires, personal biographies) producing discourse. The strength of Foucault's position is that he underlines the extent to which individuals, in defining themselves as sexual subjects, become fixed in relation to symbolic discourses and social prohibitions. The making of sexual identities, says Foucault, is always interwoven with a mode of social control. However, the weakness of this standpoint is that it bypasses the complexity of individual agency. Thus Foucault's work often implies a one-way movement of power over and above the individual. This is certainly true, for example, of Foucault's discussion of psychotherapy and psychoanalysis, where he develops a forced account of the links between therapy and confession. His account is forced because, unlike the religious confessional, self-knowledge is seen as inhibited by unconscious blockages in psychoanalysis. This is important for conceptualizing the self because emotional blockages are deeply intertwined with memory, desire and childhood. Frames of experience are at once structured internally, organized in terms of the psycho-sexual development of the individual and, externally, organized by the symbolic textures of society. In analyzing sexuality and the self, Foucault ignores this permeability of internal and external worlds, and downgrades the individual to a mere cipher in the reproduction of the larger social world.

Finally, Foucault says little about gender and the intimacies of love. Sexuality is usually described by Foucault as a realm of androgynous pleasures and sensations; his views concerning sexual self-practices and self-control informed his broader political strategy of desexualization – that is, pressing beyond the repressive confines of gender polarity (male/female, masculinity/femininity, subject/object). However, while Foucault's plea for a redefinition of the body and its pleasures is important, his failure to link the embodied structure of the self to issues of gender polarity and oppression is a significant problem. Certainly many feminists have argued that Foucault's failure to develop a systematic theory of gender leads in turn to significant political difficulties in relation to a feminist appropriation of his work on the self. Certainly, the world of sexuality that he writes about is, for the most part, one in which virile men undertake the exercise of defining themselves as subjects of sexuality. The troubles of sexuality are mastered by men restraining the self, performing desires, maintaining moderation and stylizing pleasures. Foucault's history of sexuality is thus very much in the masculinist tradition of *history*: it is a world *without women*. It is a world in which gender and love have few long-term social influences. The omission is startling.

The foregoing critical comments concerning the notions of power, discourse and sexuality in Foucault's work raise, in turn, issues about the status of autonomy and freedom in social theory. The ethical techniques of the self with which Foucault was concerned in *The History of Sexuality* were those of bodily surfaces, pleasures, sensations. Yet Foucault has relatively little to say about how a new order of bodies and pleasures might produce a transformation in intimate relationships and cultural association. Because Foucault saw individualization as a form of self-imprisonment, and because he viewed the self as shot through with modern technologies of power, he steadfastly refused to consider how individuals might reflect on social practices and, in turn, transform aspects of their lives in the process. The issue of what a better society might look like thus remains unaddressed. Foucault's own answer to this gap in his work was to insist that theory cannot legislate in advance the concrete conditions of social life; to do so, as the history of Marxism shows, is only to court the dangers of political totalitarianism. Rather than prescribing what relationships should be like, Foucault regarded his work as opening a potential space for the individual to experiment with self-definition and self-regulation. Again, however, it is Foucault's failure to discuss the interpersonal, moral and ethical implications of his own studies of sexuality that limits the appeal of his call for a new order of bodies and pleasures.

Summary points

1   Structuralism, derived from the structural linguistics of Saussure, examines the linguistic rules governing objects, events and interactions in fields beyond language itself.
2   According to Saussure, the analysis of meaning involves the distinction between language and speech; the arbitrary character of the sign; difference; the bonding of signifier and signified in the making of signs; the division between synchrony and diachrony.
3   Saussure contends that the key to language is not in any connection between words and objects, but in the arbitrary nature of linguistic signs. It is through difference that meaning is fashioned.

4 There are many criticisms of Saussure's structural linguistics, including that this approach isolates language as a structure from the social environments of language use. This results in a defective account of the creativity of action, and is a limitation carried through in various versions of structuralist social theory.

5 In the work of Barthes, there is an application of structural linguistics to other areas of cultural analysis – from fashion and film to consumption and myths.

6 The preoccupation with the deadly weight of structures in the lives of individuals appears in various guises in structuralist social theory. In Barthes, it is a series of claims concerning the promotion by culture of particular ideological meanings at the expense of other meanings. In Foucault's discussion of prisons and punishment, it is largely a set of historical observations about the objectification of individuals through the impacts of power/knowledge.

Further questions

1 What role do you as a member of society play in creating signs?

2 Explain the relationship between sign, signifier and signified.

3 How are speech and language different?

4 From intimacy to nationalism, how does culture work to promote particular meanings?

5 How does discourse determine identities and individual actions?

Further reading

Ferdinand de Saussure

Course in General Linguistics. Edited by Wade Baskin (Peter Owen, 1960)

Claude Lévi-Strauss

The Elementary Structures of Kinship (Boston: Beacon Press, 1969)
The Raw and The Cooked: Introduction to a Science of Mythology (London: Jonathan Cape, 1970)

Roland Barthes

Elements of Semiology. Trans. Annette Lavers and Colin Smith (Boston, MA: Beacon Press, 1970)

Mythologies. Selected and trans. Annette Lavers (London: Granada, 1973)

Michel Foucault

The Order of Things: An Archaeology of the Human Sciences (New York: Pantheon Books, 1971)

The Archaeology of Knowledge (New York: Pantheon Books, 1972)

Discipline and Punish: The Birth of the Prison (New York: Vintage Books)

The History of Sexuality, Volume 1: An Introduction (New York: Pantheon Books, 1978)

chapter 6

Structures, Functions and Culture

Contents

Talcott Parsons: *The Structure of Social Action*

Talcott Parsons burst on the scene of American social thought in the years just after the publication in 1937 of an astonishing theoretical masterpiece, *The Structure of Social Action*. At the time, he was a young, but rising, notable at Harvard in the earliest years of the Department of Sociology. In 1944, seven years after this book, he had become the leader of the Department and a major figure in American sociology.

The Structure of Social Action was intellectually informed by Parsons's personal experience as a doctoral student at the University of Heidelberg in the 1920s. His European sojourn, which included a period at the London School of Economics, trained him in European traditions of thought as no other major American sociologist of his generation had been. Also, important to note, the book was written and appeared during the Depression of the 1930s. While not even remotely a commentary on then current events, it is evident that this book was a deep reconsideration of nineteenth-century values. The wars and economic crises of 1914–1945 demanded a rethinking of classical values, as they did for most serious social theorists in the inter-war period. Parsons's critical theory was less overtly critical than those in Europe, but it was a deep revision emphasizing the structural effects that limit the autonomy of individual actors.

As the title of Parsons's book suggests, *The Structure of Social Action* aimed to explain social action, by which its author decidedly did not mean 'social action' in the sense of political activism. What, then, did he mean by social action and why is it important? Nothing could be more basic than the question of why people act as they do. If social theory is ultimately about social things, then it must account for social structures. Hence a puzzle: action theory must of course consider how social actions are motivated; at the same time, if the theory is to be robustly social, then it must also examine how actions are limited by structural forces beyond the control of individual actors.

Parsons's theory of *social* action was lodged in an ambitious general theory of all action systems and of how they are *conditioned* (which is to say: enhanced but also limited). He began, thus, with the general idea that action, wherever it appears (which is everywhere), involves a series of environing systems to which all systems, including human societies, must adapt. Of these, the ultimate ones are the physical and biological environments; 'the situation of action includes parts of what is called in common-sense terms the physical environment and the biological organism' (1937: 47). We act, therefore, with and in our bodies against the physical and natural worlds, which are action systems in their own right (ecosystems, for example). In this respect, Parsons in 1937 was way ahead of the times in that he took the larger question of the natural environment with utter seriousness. He was not, however, an environmentalist.

Parsons was nothing if not bold. In a field like sociology, which in America had long been (and still is) strongly empirical, he wrote unflinchingly as a theoretical sociologist. Parsons argued from the start that the common trouble with the whole line of early modern social thought was that, one way or another, it suffered from the 'utilitarian dilemma' that either action is considered 'the active agency of the actor in the choice of ends' or the 'randomness of ends is denied' leaving the outcomes of actions 'assimilated to the conditions of the situation' (1937: 64). Roughly this means that action in society is *either* the rational choice of the free and relatively autonomous individual *or* the effect of means determined by the structural conditions. Either I freely choose a mate, or he is selected for me.

Parsons did not completely reject utilitarian philosophies of action. He retained both their well-known belief in the rationality of human action and also their concept of utility as the adjustment of means to ends. This is evident in Parsons's early summary of the four necessary components of a working action system:

> An 'act' involves logically the following: (1) It implies an agent, an 'actor.' (2) For purposes of definition, the act must have an 'end,' a future state of affairs toward which the action is oriented. (3) It must be initiated in a 'situation' of which the trends of development differ in one or more important respects from the state of affairs to which the action is oriented, the end. The situation is in turn analyzable into two elements: those over which the actor has no control, that is which he cannot alter, or prevent from being altered, in conformity with his end, and those over which he has such control. The former may be termed the 'conditions' of action, the latter the 'means.' Finally (4) there is inherent in the conception of this unit [or unit act], in its analytic uses, a certain mode of relationship between these elements.
>
> (1937: 44)

A rereading of this passage from *Structure of Social Action* will confirm two aspects of Parsons's thinking and writing styles. The ideas are complicated (therefore, sometimes hard to follow), but the style is clear and (in his key word) analytic. In points 3 and 4, Parsons retains the utilitarian terms: means/ends. The actor uses the means she can control rationally to adjust her action toward a goal (or end) that is one of several outcomes possible in a given situation. In other words, the *unit-act* of all social systems is an agent's act which is directed toward an *end* in a particular *situation* which includes *structural* conditions she alone cannot control even with the *means* at her disposal. Together – acts, ends, situations, conditions, means – are the unit-act of social systems.

These four elements described in *Structure of Social Action* served as a foundation for the theoretical work that followed in two important ways. The first is the principle that agents, ends, situations, means, and conditions of action are always in a systemic relation. The second is that action systems are at once analytic and empirical. The two general principles are necessary to each other. Parsons argued that to attribute a system-like quality to actions (of all kinds) is to form a theory of how things work in the real world. *But* the analytic concepts used to describe real action systems are not in themselves *in* or *from* the real world even though they, the analytic concepts, are themselves real, therefore empirically effective. This sounds odd, so what did he mean?

It is not, in the first place, exactly absurd to suggest that we, like all living creatures, live in systems that include conditions we, as actors, cannot control but with which we must contend. Still, structural conditions beyond our control are not completely beyond control. We at least use some of them as means; schools for example. The social conditions involved, for example, in an educational system do not readily yield to the wishes of students, nor even to those of State officials who might want them changed. As a result, most children on their first days of school are overwhelmed by the school environment – just as are immigrants or tourists in foreign places, or workers new to the factories or offices of work life, or a new prisoner facing his first lock-down. School starting, in particular, is the start of life in a previously structured system. When schools work well in a democratic society (as they often do not) their whole purpose is to initiate young children into the wider system of life and work in a given society. In schools, the child knows that something she cannot control is well beyond her but soon she realizes that, whether it is good or bad, it has a systematic quality. Schoolyard complaints reinforce a common sense of, say, the evils of a school. Some of it makes no sense other than it is what it is. In time, students in good enough schools begin to make sense of the school system. Sooner or later, when a pupil is paroled from the school system, the idea dawns that one must deal with the wider social system. The systems of social life and action do not boil down to any one subsystem. Thus social action is always a deploying of acts toward goals using the conditions and means one can master. We learn over time to accept the systems for what they are and to realize that they are many, each conditioning us in different ways.

So however we know or come to know (or think we know) these sorts of things, according to Parsons, what we know are not just the facts of life, so to speak. Facts are always themselves out of the reality they represent. Thus, Parsons thought, empirical facts and theories are always analytic – which is to say, concepts that scientists and human actors of all kinds, including school-going kids, have in order to come to terms with the structured conditions of real world systems. 'Theory,' he said at the beginning of *Structure of Social Action*, 'is an independent variable in the development of science' (1937: 7). Thus, theories are themselves systems of action. This is what, at the end of *Structure of Social Action*, Parsons called his method of analytic realism, which, in his view, allowed for the possibility that theories

structures, functions and culture

are empirical in that they too must be conditioned by the analytically real historical conditions in which they occur (1937: 753).

Though Parsons's theoretical method became controversial, especially when Parsons's influence began to decline in the late 1960s, it remains a compelling attitude toward the problem with which social theories always must contend. As for Parsons himself, the method he described in his first big book in 1937 allowed him to move toward elaborating his systematic theory of social action.

Over the years, Parsons wrote essays on propaganda, family structures, sex roles, medicine, the legal profession, Japan, Russia, race relations, and many others (including of course theoretical issues). Of course, it is not surprising for a sociologist to write on subjects like these. What was unique to Parsons is that he seldom, if ever, engaged directly in empirical research on the topics. He wrote about empirical subjects as though theoretical concepts were themselves more than capable of handling the empirical knowledge available from the work of others or from plain straightforward observation. Still, if in retrospect one grants him the theoretical method he invented, much can be said for the contributions he made to reframing a certain kind of social theory, structural functionalism.

Functionalism, in a word, is the idea that social systems are like organisms of all natural kinds. There are certain functions they *must* perform in order to survive, among them: adjusting to external temperature changes, finding and ingesting food and fluid, distributing digested food throughout the body, expelling bodily waste, and reproducing the species. It is not too hard to see that, even in this elementary example, functional organisms must be structured in a way that allows them to *act* in an *environment* towards the *end* of finding the *means* unto survival. Thus, the four key elements in Parsons's first general theory of action in 1937 were already a kind of structural theory of action that embraced a functionalist idea. It remained for him to work out the nuances of such an idea for *social* systems.

The Social System: Parsons and the AGIL paradigm

By 1951 Parsons offered the first of several systematic textbooks, *The Social System*, one of two big books published that year (the other was a collection of essays, *Toward a General Theory of Action* (1951)). *The Social System* began with an essay that creates the impression of being a redo of his 1937 book, though with a mind-numbing title of its own: 'The Action Frame of Reference and the General Theory of Action Systems; Culture, Personality, and the Place of Social Systems.' As off-putting as this title may be today, the reader soon sees what Parsons means:

Reduced to the simplest possible terms, then, a social system consists in a plurality of individual actors interacting with each other in a situation which has at least a physical or environmental aspect, actors who are motivated in terms of a tendency to the 'optimization of gratification' and whose relation to their situations, including each other, is defined and mediated in terms of a system of culturally structured and shared symbols.

(1951: 3)

Though the basic elements in Parsons's theory were present in *Structure of Social Action*, in *The Social System* the intensely formal nature of his structural theory comes clear. Here too, when the focus is narrowed (if that is the word) to *social* systems; there appears among the system's functional aspects, a strong concept of culture. Over the years since, the social importance of culture would become one of Parsons's most influential contributions.

In 1951, Parsons's *Social System* introduced what came to be called the AGIL paradigm in which culture played a prominent role. Ten years later, after a good many elaborations, the AGIL paradigm would be succinctly summarized in a remarkable essay 'An Outline of the Social System' (1961: pages 30–97). The acronym, AGIL, stands for *Adaptation, Goal Attainment, Integration*, and *Latent Pattern Maintenance*. Again, readers will be forgiven if their first reaction is, 'What the hell?' Parsons was not writing for the weak of heart. Still, as more and more sociologists studied his paradigm, its meaning as a functional theory was apparent.

The AGIL paradigm is, first of all, an original, if obscure, way of formalizing the four basic functions Parsons attributed to all systems of social action (and, in theory, all action systems). *Adaptation*, then, is the function, literally, of adapting to the social system's environments, chiefly the natural world. *Goal Attainment* is the function whereby individuals and groups in the system are motivated to pursue goals. This element could be viewed as the motivational factor in social action. Individuals, themselves systems, must adapt to their environments including the wider society. But, when social systems are well developed, they pursue goals that exceed the simple needs of survival. Not all do; the very poor often live at the most basic subsistence level of life. But, generally, individuals and groups are motivated by more than surviving. They seek certain pleasures in life, for which they need resources: to eat well on special occasions, to go to religious services, to maintain friendships, to play with their children. These, and many others, are goals that require work at hunting or farming or wherever they can generate the material means to support their life's goals beyond mere subsistence.

Yet, when individuals and groups pursue goals in a society, they run into others pursuing their goals who are rivals for the means necessary to get whatever they desire. Some people may want to live in a certain kind of house, but they must compete at work of some kind for the income that makes that goal attainable. And if they earn the money, it sometimes happens that there are real disputes over the price of the home, over whether their kind of people 'belong' on that street, and so forth. When competition verges toward conflict, the social system must provide a function for resolving that conflict. This is where *Integration* comes in. In the face of conflict over goals, there needs to be a way to resolve differences so that the system does not fall into disorder. This is the function of tribal chiefs and shamans, of police and militia, of knights and courts of law, and the similar. So, crudely put, the first three functions are economic (A), political (G) and legal (L).

Of all the four AGIL concepts, surely the most obscure one is *Latent Pattern Maintenance*. In a few words, this rather cumbersome term stands for the structural function of the cultural elements that stand behind (hence, 'latent') ordinary life actions and institutions. In the higher forms of animal life, the brain serves to maintain and regulate the body as a whole, so in society there must be a structure that serves the same function. Though culture is a notoriously over-general concept, it does the work of identifying the shared beliefs, habits, manners, ideals, and ideologies that guide a social system. To put it bluntly, adaptation could be called the most elemental of all social functions, the one that contends with the forces of nature from which individuals are bequeathed their natural instincts and drives and against which social groups must derive their basic needs for survival. The adaptive function, thus, is anything but regulated. Thus, just as adaptation to natural forces is the most primitive drive for social action, and goals are social normal aspirations that must be integrated in the wider societal community, so culture is the mechanism that lends the system a sense of social order created by allegedly common values and the like that stand behind the goals pursued and the integrating laws that regulate competing, goal-seeking actions that derive their raw power from the natural environment.

Today, cultural theory has become one of the most prominent independent aspects of social theory. Parsons was not, however, a cultural theorist in today's terms even though he was the first American sociologist to identify its importance to the social system. 'The structure of cultural meanings,' he said, 'constitutes the ground of any system of action' (1961: 963). With Parsons, nothing was ever simple. He was quick to add that, as important as culture is to a functioning system, cultural systems are systems in their own right, without ever being identical with a social system. One can interpret this to mean that even though all social systems have the same functional (or AGIL) elements, no social system is the same as any other; and one of the reasons this is true is that cultures, obviously, are different from society to society. The US and the UK may have many social features in common, especially their laws and their general economic systems, even many features of their political systems. But it is just as clear that in practical terms British and American cultural habits differ. The British often find Americans weirdly aggressive; as they, to Americans, seem oddly reserved. These may appear to be nothing more than prejudices; sometimes they are, but always they are more. Cultural things, in Parsons's theory, are system features.

Parsons is read more today, if at all, in Europe than in the US. In the revolutionary 1960s, young American sociologists discovered Marxism, against which Parsons seemed just too naïve in respect of the ability of societies to overcome conflict. Fair or not, this is the way history judges even social theorists. Still, while today you will find very few confessing structural functionalists anywhere, the ghosts of Parsons's brilliant thinking lurk about and nowhere more than behind American ideas of cultural theory.

Robert K. Merton: social theory and social structures

Robert K. Merton was young enough to have taken graduate courses with Talcott Parsons at Harvard in the 1930s. In Merton's major book, *Social Theory and Social Structure* (1957 [1949]), he acknowledges his debt to Parsons as his 'teacher and friend, . . . who so early in his career conveyed his enthusiasm for analytic theory to so many' (1957: x). It is a popular myth, however, that he and Parsons formed a kind of partnership to advance functionalist theory. In fact, though Merton wrote at length on functionalism (and was still at Harvard when Parsons's *Structure of Social Action* was published), his doctoral thesis became the book *Science, Technology and Society in Seventeenth Century England* (1938). His thesis advisor was George Sarton, the founder of the history of science. Sarton's influence endured, not only in Merton's founding of the sociology of science, but in the elegant seriousness with which he contributed to the science of sociology.

Yet, as important as Sarton and Parsons were to him, after Merton left Harvard he set off on his own. He differed from Parsons in that he always gave consideration to the importance of original empirical evidence in the formulation of analytic theories. His life-long interest in science studies stood behind his insistence that sociology must be equally rigorous in theory and empirical research, both at once. Merton's friendship at Columbia University with Paul Lazarsfeld, the Viennese mathematician, and founder of Columbia's Bureau of Applied Social Research, set the trend for post-World War II American empirical sociology. Together Parsons at Harvard and the Merton-Lazarsfeld partnership at Columbia taught or otherwise influenced the great majority of American sociologists working outside the Chicago tradition.

Merton's distinctive approach was *middle* range theory which in a sense was a rebuke of analytic theory but also an attempt to insist, against crude empiricism, that theory must inform and guide research in a deep structural way.

> I attempt to focus attention on what might be called *theories of the middle range*: theories intermediate to the minor working hypotheses in abundance during the day-by-routine routines of research, and the all-inclusive speculations comprising a master conceptual scheme from which it is hoped to derive a very large number of empirically observed uniformities of social behavior.
>
> (1957: pages 5–6)

As a result, though Merton published many books and articles, his major work is one of the most unusual books in American social theory – *Social Theory and Social Structure* (first published in 1949, and twice revised and enlarged, in 1957 and 1968). *Social Theory and Social Structure* is a collection of Merton's shorter writings, some of them published first in one of the editions of this book, most of them reworked from edition to edition. There is no better place to see his middle range theory at work. This is evident in the titles of some of the articles: 'Bureaucratic Structure and Personality,' 'Role of the Intellectual in Public Bureaucracy,' 'Theory of Reference Groups,' 'Patterns of Influence: Locals and Cosmopolitans,' 'The Self-Fulfilling Prophecy,' 'Science and Economy in 17th Century England and, notably, his famous article with Paul Lazarsfeld, 'Studies in Radio and Film Propaganda.'

Merton's big book was intended more or less as a textbook – not in the sense of a book for students (though many have read it) but in the sense of a book of scientific texts, each meant to renew or define a working paradigm (the term made famous by another Harvard historian of science, Thomas S. Kuhn). The role of paradigms in science, according to Kuhn's *The Structure of Scientific Revolutions* (1962), is to organize a normal condition of scientific research, always understood as an ongoing practical labor. In time paradigms break down as new knowledge demands a scientific revolution, which in turn leads to a new normal. Darwin and Einstein are examples.

For Merton, functionalism was a revolutionary paradigm in sociology. The lead essay in *Social Theory and Social Structure*, 'Manifest and Latent Functions,' is the definition and defense of a paradigm in the making:

'Functional analysis is at once the most promising and possibly the least codified of contemporary orientations to the problems of sociological interpretation' (1957: 19). Later, in the same article, he adds: 'the first and foremost purpose [of the functionalist] paradigm is to supply a provisional codified guide for adequate and fruitful functional analysis' (1957: 55). Merton's intention in 'Manifest and Latent Functions,' was to develop the history of the term 'function,' the history of functionalism in social science, the postulates of functional analysis, and the working concepts needed to guide functionalist research. All this, and more, is carefully worked through over sixty-five pages, each laden with an astonishing number of references – to the various literatures, many quite outside social science. Thus, before defining the paradigm he comments on its background in Marx, Weber, and Durkheim, but also (a rarity in those days in American sociological theory) Freud. 'I have adapted the terms "manifest" and "latent" from ... Freud (although Francis Bacon had long ago spoken of "latent process" and "latent configuration" in connection with processes which are below the threshold of superficial observation' (1957: 61).

The paradigm itself is:

> The distinction between manifest and latent functions [refers, first] to those objective consequences for a specified unit (person, subgroup, social or cultural system) which contribute to its adjustment or adaptation and were so intended; the second [refers] to unintended or unrecognized consequences of the same order.

Thus, the manifest function of a school system is to educate children, the latent function is turn them into compliant citizens; just as the manifest function of a war is to defend a nation, while the latent function often is to stimulate a nation's war-time economy. In Merton's marvelously fluent writing and thinking functionalism, thus, is middle range but also a general paradigm for structural analysis. Structures may be objective occurrences but they are never limited to the intentions of their actors, who much of the time stumble upon their unintended consequences (1957: 63).

The first appearance of the 'Manifest and Latent Functions' was in 1949, just more than a decade after another classic essay that already contained many of the same ideas. In 1938, one year after Parsons's *Structure of Social Action*, in the *American Sociological Review,* Merton published what may be his most widely read and taught essay, 'Social Structure and Anomie' (1938: 672–682). 'Social Structure and Anomie' made two paradigmatic contributions at once. Even before Parsons worked through the role of culture in his AGIL paradigm, Merton demonstrated not only the structural importance of culture but, also, how that importance turns on the changing relations between cultural and social structures. Merton thus initiated a structuralist movement in American social theory – a movement different from the French structuralism of Claude Lévi-Strauss who at the same time was publishing his earliest writings.

'Social Structure and Anomie' turns on its reinterpretation of Emile Durkheim's original definition of anomie as the social condition in which society fails to provide moral guidance to individuals. Durkheim's idea in *Suicide* (1897) was that when a social bond is weak or lacking, the number of suicides rises as, for example, when bourgeois men commit suicide during an economic crisis. Durkheim's book examined different types of suicide associated with different social causes. Where Merton parted ways with Durkheim was by emphasizing that from culture to culture, and among different groups in a society, the power of culture was always dependent on 'institutional means' that may be unequally available. Anomie – a sense of aimlessness or of not knowing how to behave – becomes acute when cultural goals encounter a deficiency of institutional means. When anomie occurs, he argued, the individual must adapt as best he can. Adaptation is less the goal of dealing with an environment than a practical effort to adjust to a conflict between structures that put the individual in crisis and require her to adapt. Durkheim understood this, and Parsons's theory allowed for it, but Merton worked out the structural relations.

Merton's 'Social Structure and Anomie' is perhaps the clearest instance in contemporary sociology of an attempt to work through an analytic paradigm. The working concepts are *cultural goals* and *institutionalized means* alongside *anomie* and the *modes of adaptation* available. Merton's article takes the American cultural and social structures as his empirical case. In typically thorough fashion, he outlines its central cultural goal as monetary success – in effect, the culture may not demand wealth of its members but it does require *sufficient* monetary success to certify an actor's social worthiness. Put this way, the interpretation gets at an arguable but plausible fact of the American way of life, at least in the long transition period from the rise of an American middle class in the nineteenth century through the emergence of a consumption-oriented culture in from the 1950s on through to the present. But, in 1938, when the United States was still in the throes of the Depression, the fact had a particular poignancy. Many were out of work. Merton's paradigm suggests this was not just an economic problem but also a cultural one. This because the structural correlate to the cultural goal was that monetary success must be achieved by institutionally normal means; namely, a means of gainful employment. Soup kitchens and begging, then and still, are not a normal means even when people have nowhere else to turn.

From this general scheme Merton postulated five modes of adaptation. The first and most normal (or ideal) is *conformity*, where belief in the cultural goal is demonstrated by monetary success attained through a job of one kind or another – what is often called 'honest labor.' This is the ideal state that was shaken by the widespread anomie caused by the economic crisis of the 1930s. While Durkheim jumped all the way from anomie to suicide, Merton proposed that there were other less drastic modes of adaptation; for example, *innovation*. One might believe in the cultural goal but resort to a deviant means that is not institutionally normal. Among these can be begging, but innovation can include holding up a liquor store, smuggling alcohol during prohibition, sex work and drug dealing, white collar crime, and much else. If a mother steals to feed her babies she is breaking the law, but she is also innovating in an attempt to achieve the goal of being a good mother. There are over-the-top instances of innovation – the drug dealing that turns to gang banging, embezzling out of greed, pimping of working girls by enslaving them to drugs. On the other hand, in the case of sex work, stripping may be a short cut to create income but a career in street prostitution is more likely to be a desperate attempt to survive.

Merton's other modes of adaptation were: *ritualism*, where individuals no longer believe in the cultural goal of success but keep digging away at some or another life just because that is what is done in his neighborhood; *retreatism*, where people simply give up on the cultural goals and the normal means, as in the case of drop-outs, vagrants, addicts and others who live a sad existence because they have given up; and *rebellion* in which people seek to build or join a utopian community. Clearly, though, for Merton the two basic modes of adaptation for analytic sociology are *conformity* and *innovation*. The other three are in evidence, but *ritualism* usually yields to generational changes, *retreatism* is a dead end, and *rebellion* almost never leads to a radical change in society.

A superficial survey of the five modes reveals how and why 'Social Structure and Anomie' made such a deep impression on the social theory of deviance. More generally, it stands as a model of social theoretical structuralism that allows for careful empirical study (distribution of crime according the unemployment rates, for instance) but serves also as a dynamic account of how social deviance can be understood as a socially 'normal' outcome in certain cases – an account that goes well beyond the idea of the deviant or criminal personality. Merton's theory locates normal conformity and innovative deviance in the structural tensions between culture and social forms. Like Parsons, Merton was not a cultural theorist; but also like Parsons, his supple use of structural functional analysis contributed importantly to American social theory's ability to understand the social and economic entanglements of culture.

Jeffrey C. Alexander: theoretical logic of cultural sociology

There would be an interlude after the Parsons-Merton era before an overt sociology of culture would again take hold in America. The first major break-through came, not surprisingly, from a cultural anthropologist who had studied at Harvard in the 1950s, Clifford Geertz. Again, the Harvard connection was important. Geertz was there when cultural anthropology was taught as part of Parsons's attempt to reorganize the social sciences into a single integrated program, the Department of Social Relations. The Social Relations experiment (from 1946 to 1972) had its own textbook, *Theories of Society* (1961), which included an entire section representing social theories of culture as a social system. Cultural anthropology was generously represented. Many prominent social scientists were informed by their work in the Harvard program, but Geertz was chief among those who took seriously its functionalism while also moving cultural theory well beyond it. One of his earlier texts, 'Religion as a Cultural System' (1966), was almost orthodox in following the Harvard school. Its paradigm, Geertz said, is 'that sacred symbols function to synthesize a people's ethos' (1973: 89). Not many years later, he published *The Interpretation of Cultures* (1973), which has since become a classic in culture studies, in large part because of the lead article 'Thick Description: Toward an Interpretive Theory of Culture.' Here Geertz opened his thinking to fresh perspectives – strikingly those of Ludwig Wittgenstein and Gilbert Ryle who lead to his then original statement that the 'concept of culture is essentially a semiotic one' and that culture itself is a public and 'an acted document' (1973: 5).

About the same time in the 1970s, Americans began to read the French sociologist Pierre Bourdieu, whose influence led to a movement toward the sociology of culture. Now prominent sociologists Paul DiMaggio at Princeton and Michelle Lamont at Harvard, among many others, started out writing in the spirit of Bourdieu's idea of cultural capital. Since then they have moved beyond Bourdieu, leaving the sociology of culture with a leadership void. By the 1990s, the void began to be filled by the cultural sociology developed by Jeffrey Alexander, then at UCLA, now at Yale.

The difference between 'a sociology of culture' and 'a cultural sociology' may seem trivial. Alexander astutely lent the distinction its energy. Roughly put, the sociology of culture owes its existence to the fact that academic sociology is fond of inventing new subfields according the formula the *sociology of X*, where X stands for any number of possible subjects. The problem here is that, whatever the X might be, the formula tends to reduce the subject to a variable among other variables. Alexander wants to argue that only with a cultural sociology can culture be examined for its distinctive qualities and cultural research be advanced under what he calls a strong program.

It is important to note that Alexander studied with Parsons in his college days at Harvard. Later, at the University of California at Berkeley, he wrote a distinguished 1978 doctoral thesis that would become an undeniably famous four-volume book, *Theoretical Logic in Sociology* (1982). Cynics tried to dismiss Alexander's first book as a kind of latter day remake of Parsons's *Structure of Social Action*. Calmer heads saw it for what it is – a thorough re-examination of the logic of classical and contemporary social theory, including Parsons's, with an eye to developing a theoretical logic for sociology. Alexander's *Theoretical Logic in Sociology* is at least an important reworking of Parsons's analytic realism. Alexander says

> Science proceeds as surely by a generalizing or 'theoretical logic' as it does by the empirical logic of experiment, and the positivist decision to focus on the latter alone must ultimately prove as self-defeating as reading only one side of a column of figures.

(1982: 33)

Like Parsons, Alexander identifies the independent authority of theory; like Parsons at an early stage in his thinking, the younger Alexander is still under the sway of a functionalist model. Yet, in the years following, Alexander would write more critically of Parsons and his position as a proponent of neo-functionalism became less and less easy for him. In 1989, in a collection of essays, *Neofunctionalism and After*, Alexander declared intellectual independence by announcing his shift to a strong program of cultural sociology (1998: 220). By 2003, in *The Meanings of Social Life: A Cultural Sociology*, he pulled together early essays on culture and American civil society that would become the backbone of his major work in cultural sociology, *The Civil Sphere* (2006).

Anybody who has not read *The Civil Sphere* might glance at the title and wonder what a book that appears to be political theory has to do with a social theory of culture. The first answer, not generally well-recognized by Alexander's critics, is that since his Harvard days at the height of the political turmoil of the late 1960s, he has been reflecting seriously on his relation to Marxism and radical politics (2010). Not then, nor since, could Alexander be considered a wildly leftist thinker, but politics in general, and political movements in particular, have long been important considerations to him. Thus, unlike many for whom culture is a thing unto itself, for Alexander when it came time to make his grand theoretical statement of *cultural* sociology, he chose to engage with civil society, normally more a subject associated with theories of democratic society than with the sociology of culture.

Thus it is that Alexander's interpretation of the nature and promise of democratic politics uses the self-same Weberian term that stands behind his cultural sociology. The key word in the title is the civil *sphere*. 'We need,' he says, 'to understand civil society as a sphere that can be analytically independent, empirically differentiated, and morally more universalistic vis-à-vis the state and market and from other social spheres as well' (2006: 31). As Weber did, Alexander understands modern complex societies as comprising a series of spheres related but not joined. Yet, truth be told, it is the cultural sphere that interests him most. Thus in his work it appears as if it were the most salient of them all. In reality, what he seeks to do is to study culture, in the phrase he uses for the civil sphere, as 'analytically independent, empirically differentiated, and morally universalistic' qualities.

In Alexander's best known statement of his strong program in cultural sociology, he acknowledges Geertz as an early resource for 'a theory of culture that has autonomy built into the very fabric of meaning as well as a more robust understanding of social structure and institutional dynamics' (2003: 23). A skeptic, of course, can fairly respond that any such programmatic statement does not a program make. Though Alexander is nothing if not thorough in applying and advancing the desiderata of his cultural sociology, it is not always clear that he is not sometimes straddling important theoretical fences. For example, following the statement just quoted, he makes important reference to the classic Swiss linguist Ferdinand de Saussure, from whom he takes a strong structural theory of culture itself as well as of the nuances of its relation to social meanings. Here is one of the ways Alexander, like few other American social theorists today, reads widely and seriously in European social thought. Saussure, though important to a great deal of European (especially French) social theory, is generally ignored by the Americans even though, as Alexander here states, structural linguistics recognizes 'the autonomy and centrality of meaning but does not develop a hermeneutics of the particular at the expense of a hermeneutics of the universal' (2003: 23). Not one of Alexander's clearer statements, the line illustrates Alexander's method of inventing new forms of cultural theory that overcome the limitations of others. So when he talks about a structural theory of culture that is sensitive to meaning and simultaneously able to interpret the particular and the universal, he means to get around what others (himself included at an earlier time) have called by various names – the micro–macro problem, qualitative versus quantitative methods, subjective actors and objective structures, and such like. The traditional bias among sociologists is that only the qualitative study of micro settings can uncover meanings, while only quantitative data can generalize about macro-settings. While Alexander does not address this issue in so many words (except perhaps in his *Theoretical Logic in Sociology*), his cultural sociology is designed with a broader ambition in mind – to solve or at least consider sociology's most fundamental dilemmas in respect to which his cultural sociology is situated. Some may miss this point, or doubt that he achieves his goal, but there can hardly be any fair doubt that Alexander does much of what others like Bourdieu and Anthony Giddens did more explicitly (for a discussion of these two theorists, see Chapter 9 on Structuration).

That he reaches beyond the regional concepts of mainstream American sociology is to his credit, especially in the surprising use of the Swiss structuralist Saussure. This is both Alexander's genius and his Achilles heel. He takes a strong theory of binaries from Saussure's influential theory that meanings are communicated in speech when speakers express themselves as individuals according to the socially structured rules and contents of their shared language. Speech (*parole*) is the act; language (*langue*) is the structure – a binary required for communicative meanings derived from a socially structured set of possibilities. Alexander does not go so far as to describe Saussure's as a strong program, a designation he seems to allow only for his own cultural sociology. All others, however notable their contributions (Bourdieu, Foucault, Derrida, even Geertz, for examples), are limited by their weak programs, as he understands them. Thus, Alexander's ambition, if not always his proven achievements, is precisely to invent a strong program that, in keeping with his theoretical logic, is at once strong theoretically (a structural idea of meanings) and no less strong empirically (a program of research in which culture, in particular, is at least an autonomous sphere) and, to keep to the litany, 'morally universal.' It is the combination of the three that makes Alexander's strong program truly strong. To this end, no basic technique is more central to his theory than the binaries.

In *The Civil Sphere* the crucial, theoretical Part II is devoted to the introduction, then elaboration, of the binaries Alexander sees as fundamental to the culture of the civil sphere. Thereafter, the remainder of this very long book explores the empirical applications of the theory of the binaries to social movements. The movements he attends to are ones that most obviously engage in (his words) civil repair – the women's movement, the Civil Rights Movement, and (his phrase) the Jewish question. In each case, he is at pains to examine applicable historical detail to the end of demonstrating how in the broadest sense these structural lesions on the body of American civil society have been and can be repaired. The analysis is not always satisfying (for example, a scant few pages address the Black Power phase of the Civil Rights Movement), yet the project is sustained insofar as it is a contribution to a deep revision of the social theory of culture.

Theoretically, the organizing binaries are: the pure and impure aspects of civil discourse, the binary structures of motives, relationships, and institutions, and the civil narratives of good and evil. Alexander is clear that these are at once analytic and real, in the sense that the pollution of the civil sphere is historically powerful and affecting if not ever to be found apart from its binary. The binaries are, he states, 'codes that *appear schematic*' – both at once. Even in the civil sphere as it is lived, they are indisputably at work in the historical development of the contents of public culture

When they are presented in their simple binary forms, these cultural codes appear schematic. In fact, however, they reveal the skeletal structures on which social communities build the familiar stories, the rich narrative forms, that guide their everyday, taken-for-granted political life. The positive side of these structured sets provides the elements for the comforting and inspirational story of a democratic, free, and spontaneously integrated social order, a civil society in an ideal-typical sense. The elements on the negative side of these symbolic sets are also tightly intertwined. They provide the elements for the plethora of taken-for-granted stories that permeate democratic understanding of the negative and repugnant side of community life. Taken together, these negative structures and narratives form the discourse of repression (2006: 60–61). From these words, as from *The Civil Sphere* as a whole, one can reasonably take a sense of respect for Alexander's subtle yet promising idea of what a strong cultural theory might be. After *The Civil Sphere*, he has applied his basic binary technique to a good many current, empirical cases like Egypt's Arab Spring (see *Performative Revolution in Egypt* (2011)) and Barack Obama's political movement, the wars in Iraq and Afghanistan, among other topics (see *Performance and Power* (2011)).

The risk of using a strong binary theory is that of implying an all-too-simple picture of actual historical realities. In one sense, this is the risk of any strong analytic logic. If theoretical, then the empirical correlates can be a distortion of the utterly defiant complexity of social events and patterns. In Alexander's case, one could add that he verges on taking the Saussurian model all too loosely, without situating it in the wider tradition of Francophone theory. For example, he does not allow for the possibility that the schemes of Bourdieu, Derrida or Foucault, among others he dismisses as too weak, may in fact be weak, if that is the word, because history itself is not analytically strong.

Yet, as important as others in the sociology of culture may be, it would be a weak argument to view Alexander's work over so many years as anything short of the best that American sociological social theory has achieved. Geertz (whom he also considers a weak theorist) may have been more nuanced in his field work. Merton (a proponent of strong science) was the more self-conscious paradigm definer. And Parsons (the strongest of all theorists) initiated a more radical departure from his past. But when it comes to structural theories of culture, Alexander is at least in their league. There is room for sharp criticisms of his work. For one, Alexander relies on cultural media as sources of empirical data (especially in the short essay on Egypt) and of secondary cultural reports on histories (of the Civil Rights Movement for example); yet he does not seem to appreciate the extent to which, now, media, notably technomedia, are themselves primary contents of emerging global culture. Manuel Castells, in his multi-volume series on *The Network Society* (2000 and since), has written of information technologies as the new foundational forces in global culture and political economy. Even Anthony Giddens, as Daniel Chaffee of the University of South Australia has shown, has sketched, since *The Constitution of Society* (1984), a theory of radical modernity that opens the way to information technologies. Younger writers, like Sam Han of TK University in Singapore in *Web 2.0* (2011) among other writings, have been among those who have studied technomedia as both an independent cultural dispensation and a transforming feature of global culture. Then too, referring to the new generation of sociologists, there are some like the Italian, Andrea Cossu, in *It Ain't Me Babe: Bob Dylan and the Performance of Authenticity* (2012), who study culture with, if anything, a much better informed semiotic of culture.

What will happen to American structural theories of culture in the future remains to be seen. That its tradition is now long and important can no longer be doubted.

Summary points

1   Structural Functionalism, a theoretical approach that emerged in the United States in the 1930s, examines social acts as goal, or *function*, oriented actions taken within the limits imposed by the environment.

2   Talcott Parsons set out the theoretical framework of structural functionalism in *Structures of Social Action*, taking as his object of study the unit act, comprised of an *actor*, an *end* which the action is supposed to achieve, the *situation* in which the action is carried out, and the *normative orientation* that influences the actor's choice of means.

3   Developing on his model of structural functionalism, Parsons's later works introduce a more formalized understanding of the functions within social action: *Adaptation* to the environment; *Goal Attainment*, or the motivation for action; *Integration* of the varied interests and goals present with the social system; and *Latent Pattern Management*, the cultural elements that govern both the goals and systems of integration.

4   Culture, thus, for Parsons represents a crucial aspect of social action for structural functionalism. Culture influences both the means and the ends of social action but remains an independent variable that differs in each social system.

5   Similar to Parsons's ideas, Robert K. Merton helped to refine and popularize the structural functionalist paradigm. Merton distinguished between *manifest functions*, with explicit, intentional ends, and *latent functions*, whose ends are unintended.

6   Merton's *Social Structure and Anomie* is the classic text of American structural functionalism at work. Developing Durkheim's theory of a social state of normlessness and its catastrophic results, Merton contends that the individual adapts to cultural norms (or lack thereof) through one of five modes: *conformity, innovation, ritualism, retreatism* and *rebellion*.

7   Cultural anthropologist Clifford Geertz was a key theorist in expanding the understanding of culture within structural functionalism, and eventually moving the concept beyond it, by introducing the concepts of 'thick description' and culture as an 'acted document.'

8   The role of culture as a key aspect of social action has been carried forward by Jeffrey C. Alexander. For Alexander, culture is an autonomous force among social structures. This distinction forms the basis of his 'strong program' of cultural sociology.

Further questions

1   Think of an action that you have taken recently. You should not have any problem identifying the actor (you) but can you pinpoint the 'end,' the 'conditions' and the 'means' in this action system? How was the result of this action influenced by the means that you used, and the conditions that you acted within? Did this action have any unintended results?

2   Merton suggested that there were five strategies of adaptation to cultural norms. Can you think of a situation in your own life where you have had to adapt? Which strategy, or strategies, did you use?

3   How does Alexander's 'strong program' of cultural sociology differ from other 'weak' concepts of culture?

4   Social action is embedded in cultural meaning. Do you agree?

Further reading

Talcott Parsons

The Structure of Social Action (The McGraw-Hill Book company, 1937)
The Social System (London: Routledge and Kegan Paul Ltd., 1951)
Toward a General Theory of Action (Harvard University Press, 1951)
Theories of Society: Foundations of Modern Sociological Theory (Free Press of Glencoe, 1961)

Richard Merton

Social Theory and Social Structure (Free Press, 1957)

Clifford Geertz

The Interpretation of Cultures (Basic Books, 1973)

Jeffrey Alexander

Theoretical Logic in Sociology (University of California Press, 1982)
Neofunctionalism and After (Blackwell Publishers, 1998)
The Meanings of Social Life: A Cultural Sociology (Oxford University Press, 2003)
The Civil Sphere (Oxford University Press, 2006)

structures, functions and culture

Post-structuralism

Contents

We left social theory at the end of Chapter 5 in the grip of the 'linguistic turn,' refashioning concepts taken from the study of language and extending these ideas to other aspects of social activity. In the perspective of structuralism, language is form not substance. Words, as the reader will remember, cannot mean their objects. A 'tree' is what it is because it is not 'flee' or 'bee,' and likewise 'bee' is what it is because it is not 'she' or 'he,' and on and on in an endless chain of signification. Suddenly, things look more complex. If a signifier only refers us to another signifier, and if we can never arrive at an ultimate signified, what are we to make of the structuralist insistence that language forms a stable system? How are we to understand the structuralist account of meaning in terms of systemic structures? Is there not a tension between the structuralist emphasis on the differential nature of meaning on the one hand, and the presumption that as speakers or writers we have no choice but to follow patterns of meaning already established in language as a closed system?

To put these questions is to raise doubts about structuralism as a social theory. Such questions go to the heart of the adequacy of the structuralist conceptualization of the sign as a tidy symmetrical unity of signifier and signified. What remains missing in structuralist linguistics is any detailed treatment of how concepts become firmly tied to signifiers, or indeed of what it is that prevents a signified (that is, a concept or idea) from transforming back into another signifier. Think about it for a moment, as the problem is less abstract than it might first appear. If you look up the meaning of a word in a dictionary, all you find are more words, more signifiers. These words too can, in turn, be looked up. But the same issue arises. For, again, the reader is referred to yet more words, more signifiers. All of this would seem to suggest that there is no neat or fixed distinction between signifiers and signifieds.

Jacques Lacan, the French psychoanalyst who has had a major impact upon the development of social theory and whose work I shall examine in this chapter, put the argument that meaning is always somehow suspended, divided and dispersed, a displaced outcrop of the endless productivity and play of signifiers. Lacan developed his exciting method of reading psychoanalysis through the lens of structuralist doctrines, his infamous 'return to Freud,' in the most philosophical and avant-garde of world cities, Paris. Although by training a psychiatrist, Lacan appropriated the ideas of various European thinkers – from Hegel and Husserl to Saussure and Lévi-Strauss – to develop a rigorous form of thought – often very abstract, sometimes seemingly unintelligible – on the psychoanalytical constitution of the human subject, specifically in terms of speech and language. In so doing, and long before his work came to the attention of a wider public, his project was to open knowledge to a world of social differences, to explore and affirm Otherness – particularly its effects upon all identities. In 1957, in a now-famous essay titled 'The Agency of the Letter in the Unconscious or Reason since Freud,' Lacan reflected on the unstable terrain of language and pushed structuralist doctrines to their limit by advancing the view that meaning is never immediately present in the interlocking of signifier and signified. Lacan tells a most simple, yet powerful, story involving a girl and boy and their encounter with the established world of signs, particularly sexual meanings:

> A train arrives at a station. A little boy and a little girl, brother and sister, are seated in a compartment face to face next to the window through which the buildings along the station platform can be seen passing as the train pulls to a stop. 'Look,' says the brother, 'we're at Ladies!'; 'Idiot' replies his sister, 'Can't you see we're at Gentlemen.'

Reading a sign, according to Lacan, cannot be reduced to an imagined unity between one signifier and one signified. For the doors are identical. What, then, distinguishes one toilet door from another? Nothing, says Lacan, but the signifier itself, which enters into, intrudes upon, displaces and derails the signified. The meaning of a sign is a matter of what the sign is not, and so in this instance 'Ladies' is somehow located in a chain of meaning which is traced through with terms that are absent from it, namely 'Gentlemen.' At the same time this play of signifiers enters fully into our sexual and personal lives, locking gender identity into a kind of constant flickering of presence and absence. The 'constant flickering' of signifiers is what most interests Lacan, and is what gives rise to the dispersal and division that marks our identities (sexual, private, public) for the rest of our lives.

Lacan's quite abstract psychoanalytical and philosophical doctrines struck a chord, at first, with Parisian avant-garde intellectuals and artists, and later with a wider public. In underscoring the instabilities of language and the open-ended play of signification, his structuralist-influenced reinterpretation of psychoanalysis struck a chord because, in part, it reflected the growing experiences of dislocation and fracture of many people the world over. As the structuralist 1960s gave way to the post-structuralist 1970s in France, Lacan was to emerge as a celebrity of the cultural Left. Indeed, he became widely hailed as one of the most important European intellectuals of the postwar years, in large part because of his radical insistence on identity and sexuality as decentering, which he in turn linked to a culture that was decentering. In this connection, his intellectual influence was only to be matched by the French philosopher, Jacques Derrida, whose powerful blending of linguistics and post-structuralism in the form of deconstructionism will form the major thread of discussion in the second half of this chapter.

Derrida, like Lacan, is much indebted to Saussure and structuralist linguistics, but he gives a new impetus to social theory in his most exciting and brilliant method of understanding the multivocal and shifting textures of speech and language. The pure productivity of language is Derrida's theme from beginning to end. He puts the argument, which I reproduce here from a 1966 lecture delivered in the United States, that the 'absence of the transcendental signified extends the domain and the play of signification infinitely.' Not, perhaps, the easiest of philosophical statements to grasp for the beginning student. But certainly Derrida makes clear the consequences for social theory of the recognition that there is no harmonious one-to-one set of correspondences between words and objects, or as he puts it the 'absence of the transcendental signified.' The consequence Derrida specifies is, precisely, nothing less than the recognition that meaning is an outcrop of a potentially endless 'play of signification.' This tissue of social differences extends, says Derrida, 'infinitely.' Not only beyond the boundaries of the closed, structuralist system, but infinitely. Elsewhere in the lecture, Derrida implicitly links his argument that the process of difference in language can be traced along a chain of broader cultural and political differences. 'In the absence of a center or origin,' argues Derrida, 'everything becomes discourse.'

What, exactly, is this 'absence of a center'? And how is this 'absence of a center' transformative of social relations into discourse or language? To understand the connections between Derrida's early philosophical thinking and the changed social world to which it paid close attention, it is necessary to recall that the late 1960s was a period of mass political unrest throughout many Western capitals. In 1968, student protests in the United States against the Vietnam War generated considerable public support. These student protests subsequently swept across Europe, and in Paris the student movement forged various alliances with the trade unions and working class. Major social upheaval occurred in Paris in May 1968, when millions of workers went on strike and protestors took to the streets. For a brief period, the French Fifth Republic look gravely threatened, although the police and army in time gained the upper-hand and the French political establishment, under the leadership of General Charles de Gaulle, reasserted social control.

Derrida's post-structuralist recasting of social theory – widely referred to as 'deconstruction' – was at once prefigurative of and reaction to the widespread public discontent which was 1968. Social theory, he argued, should break from the search to identify a center or origin of meanings. For the Center – the West, its belief-systems and its philosophy – was under severe political strain, seeking to respond to, cope with and shore up widespread social protest. His method of deconstruction, as we shall see, was a means of decentering the oppressive search for a political Center, and opened social theory to the ambiguous, conflicting meanings of social differences. Derrida's deconstruction was both a philosophical and political method for continuing the disruptive revolts of 1968 to the cultural and institutional powers of the West. In devoting his philosophical energies to deconstruction, Derrida's social theory proceeded from an unspoken alliance with those individuals and groups – students, workers, women, blacks, marginalized outsiders, former colonial subjects – questioning the political structures of Western power and the ongoing relevance of a principle of the Center. This was politics carried on under a different name, that of deconstruction or post-structuralism. Let us now turn to consider in more detail the detailed theoretical arguments which produced this shift from structuralist to post-structuralist social theory.

Lacan: the mirror stage and imaginary

Like Saussure, Lacan was no social theorist. Yet his influence over contemporary social theory has been profound. That this should be so is, at first sight, hard to figure – not only because of the dense and very difficult conceptual terminology of his work, but because Lacan's central reference point was the founder of psychoanalysis, Sigmund Freud. This was not the first time that Freud was to loom large over social theory. In Chapter 3, I described how for the Frankfurt School the insights of Freud and psychoanalysis are of fundamental relevance for social theory, particularly for grasping how individuals come to submit to unequal social relations based upon political power and domination. It is the writings of Freud himself, rather than those of his followers, which Frankfurt School theorists such as Adorno and Marcuse turned to in refashioning social theory. A similar orientation is to be found in Lacan, who returns to some of Freud's earliest theoretical speculations – particularly his book *The Interpretation of Dreams* (1900) – in formulating a post-structuralist account of how the individual becomes 'other' to itself. By this reference to 'Othering,' Lacan was to draw attention to the split and fractured nature of identity as operationalized through the repressed unconscious.

Like Adorno and Marcuse, Lacan held a negative view of post-Freudian psychoanalysis, particularly the American model of ego-psychology. He argued that ego-psychology represented a flattening of the Freudian revolution. By contrast, Lacan sought to develop a radical language for psychoanalysis, a language adequate to the strange workings of the unconscious. One might better appreciate the metaphors, puns and elliptical nature of his writings if this is borne in mind: Lacan believed that theoretical discourse must reflect the distortions of the unconscious in order to engage with both the practical and poetic textures of who we are as human beings.

When Lacan, early in his career, formulated the outlines of his new social theory based upon a rigorous 'return to Freud,' he focused on the precariousness of the ego and its imaginary lines of engagement with the world. Why? Why *imagination* as the basis upon which to question how individuals come to see themselves, and how individuals understand how other people look at them as actors in the world? Lacan's line of analysis was, in essence, premised on one basic idea: that identity involves a *fundamental division*, one which secures and sets the unconscious life of the subject in the direction of imaginary lures, snares, misrecognitions and misadventures. In perhaps his most influential paper, 'The mirror stage as formative of the function of the I' (1949), he describes a small infant contemplating its image in a mirror. Noting that from the beginnings of life the infant is physically uncoordinated, psychologically fragmented and without any defined sense of center, he asks how it is that the small child becomes centered on the world and on itself. Elaborating upon Freud's argument that the ego is built upon self-love or narcissism, Lacan speaks of an 'imaginary' state in which a degree of unity, wholeness and centeredness occurs. The infant's drafting of a distinction between itself and the outside between the age of six and eighteen months, says Lacan, takes place within the paradoxes and illusions of the visual field, or what he calls the 'mirror stage.' As a metaphorical and structural concept, the mirror provides the subject with relief from the experience of fragmentation by granting an illusory sense of bodily unity through its reflecting surface. Note that Lacan stresses that the image is cast within the field of optics: it is in and through a *reflecting surface* that the subject narcissistically invests its self-image. This contrasts radically with other conceptions of mirroring, such as the work of Cooley (1902) who speaks of a 'looking glass self' that exists in relation to the gaze of others and also the work of D. W. Winnicott (1960) who views the early interchange between self and others as crucial to the founding of a 'true' self.

We only have to understand the mirror stage as an identification, in the full sense that analysis gives to the term: namely, the transformation that takes place in the subject when he assumes an image – whose predestination to this phase-effect is sufficiently indicated by the use, in analytic theory, of the ancient term *imago*.

This jubilant assumption of his specular image by the child at the infant stage, still sunk in his motor incapacity and nursling dependence, would seem to exhibit in an exemplary situation the symbolic matrix in which the I is precipitated in a primordial form, before it is objectified in the

The mirror, for Lacan, is therefore not what it seems; it appears to provide a sense of psychological unity and cohesion, but what it in fact does is distort and deform the self. As Lacan proclaims, the mirror situates the self in a line of *fiction*. The self or ego is created as defensive armor to support the psyche against its otherwise terrifying experience of fragmentation and dread. The capture of the self, or what Lacan terms the 'I,' by the subject's reflection in the mirror is inseparable from a fundamental misrecognition of its own truth. In a word, the mirror *lies*. The reflecting image, because it is outside and other, leads the infant to misrecognize itself: the image yielded up by the mirror looks pleasingly unified and gratifyingly alluring, but the reality is that the mirror is just *image*. The image is not in reality the subject. Still more, Lacan believes that the 'mirror stage' is not something we ever fully pass through or get over in our personal and social lives; it is rather a 'drama' that defines a core aspect of our ongoing experience of ourselves and others in the social world. Television soaps, media advertising, pop music, Hollywood blockbusters: all the signs that circulate in contemporary society are shot through with imaginary investments and distortions. This is not a point that Lacan himself developed in any detail, but it is a line of argument taken up by some of his followers in media studies and social theory. We will turn to consider these developments in Lacanian-inspired post-structuralist theory later in the chapter.

Lacan's reformulation of structuralism: language, symbolic order and the unconscious

Having argued that the ego is a paranoid structure, an agent of misconstruction and misrecognition, Lacan's subsequent work aimed to demonstrate that the subject is also divided through insertion into a symbolic order of speech and language. Through extensive engagement with Saussure's *Course in General Linguistics* (1916) and Lévi-Strauss's *The Elementary Structures of Kinship* (1969), Lacan derived a structuralist-influenced account of the subject in which the concepts of signifier, system, otherness and difference figure prominently. The central essays in which he elaborates this antihumanist or structural-scientific conception of psychoanalysis are 'The field and function of speech and language in psychoanalysis' (1953) and 'The agency of the letter in the unconscious, or reason since Freud' (1957), to which we will now briefly turn.

In setting out his idea that life, both private and public, is dominated by the primacy of language, Lacan drew from and refashioned Saussure's theory of the arbitrary nature of the linguistic sign. The importance that Saussure placed upon the status of oppositions – upon not things themselves but on the relationship between words – appealed to Lacan's psychoanalytic and structuralist sensibilities. Saussure provided Lacan with the means to bridge his theoretical concerns with both symbolic production and the formal organization of desire. He argued in his seminar, following Saussure, that the linguistic sign comprises two parts: the signifier (the acoustic component or linguistic mark) and the signified (the conceptual element). In line with structuralist thought, Lacan argued that the relationship between signifiers and signifieds is arbitrary. However, where Saussure placed the signified over the signifier, Lacan inverts the formula, putting the signified under the signifier, to which he ascribed primacy in the life of the psyche, subject and society. All is determined for Lacan by the movement of signifiers. In fact, the position of each of us as individual subjects is determined by our place in a system of signifiers.

This brings us to the relation between language and the unconscious, a central preoccupation of Lacan. The idea that language might be a product of the unconscious was widespread among many psychoanalysts, and indeed Lacan continually affirmed in his writings and seminars that the importance he placed upon language was in keeping with the spirit of Freud's corpus. However, Lacan's structuralist elaboration of Saussure is, in fact, a radical conceptual departure from the Freudian conception of the unconscious. Whereas Freud sees connections between the psychic systems of unconscious representation (fantasy) and conscious thought (language), Lacan views subjectivity itself as constituted to its roots in language. This linguistification of the unconscious has important ramifications, making of this psychic strata not something which is internal to the subject (as with, say, a bodily heart or kidney), but rather an intersubjective space of communication, with language constantly sinking or fading into the gaps which separate signifier from signifier. The unconscious, writes Lacan, represents 'the sum of the effects of the parole on a subject, at the level where the subject constitutes itself from the effects of the signifier.' (Lacan quoted in Ragland-Sullivan 1986: 106) Or, in Lacan's infamous slogan: 'The unconscious is structured like a language.' (1998b: 48)

If the unconscious is structured like a language, as a chain of signifiers, the apparent stability of the individual's 'mirror image' is alienated twice over. Firstly, the individual is alienated through the mirrored deceptions of the imaginary order, in which the ego is organized into a paranoid structure; secondly, the person is constituted as an *I* in the symbolic order, an order or law indifferent to the desires and emotions of individual subjects. Language is thus the vehicle of speech for the person, but this is an *order* in which the individual is *subjected* to received social meanings, logic and differentiation. It is this conception of the function of the symbol which paves the way for Lacan's incorporation of Lévi-Strauss's structural anthropology. Drawing upon Lévi-Strauss's conception of the unconscious as a symbolic system of underlying relations which order social life, Lacan argues that the rules of matrimonial exchange are founded by a preferential order of kinship which is constitutive of the social system:

> The marriage tie is governed by an order of preference whose law concerning the kinship names is, like language, imperative for the group in its forms, but unconscious in its structure . . . The primordial Law is therefore that which in regulating marriage ties superimposes the kingdom of culture on that of a nature abandoned to the law of mating . . . This law, then, is revealed clearly enough as identical with an order of language. For without kinship nominations, no power is capable of instituting the order of preferences and taboos that bind and weave the yarn of lineage through succeeding generations.
>
> (1953: 66)

This primordial Law to which Lacan refers is the Freudian Oedipus complex, now rewritten in linguistic terms. What Lacan terms *nom-du-père* (name-of-the-father) is the cornerstone of his structural revision of the Oedipus complex. For Lacan, as for Freud, the father intrudes into the imaginary, blissful union of the child/mother dyad in a symbolic capacity, as the representative of the wider cultural network and the social taboo on incest. It is, above all, the *exteriority* of this process which Lacan underlines. Broadly speaking, Lacan is not arguing that each individual father forbids the mother-infant unity. Rather he suggests the 'paternal metaphor' intrudes into the child's narcissistically structured ego to refer her or him to what is outside, to what has the force of the law – namely, language.

After Lacan: Althusser and society as interpellation

Throughout his career Lacan was primarily concerned with clinical issues arising from psychoanalysis, though he did often speculate on broader philosophical and aesthetic matters. He was not much concerned, however, with the social and political applications of psychoanalysis. In order to consider the import of Lacanian psychoanalysis for social theory, we need therefore to briefly look at the writings of one of Lacan's followers, the French Marxist philosopher Louis Althusser. In several essays published during the 1960s, Althusser argued for the importance of Lacanian psychoanalytic theory for understanding how social relations are sustained through ideology. Ideology for Althusser was a concept of major importance for grasping how societal arrangements are sustained and reproduced in the daily lives of people, and especially for addressing the many forms of political domination. In order for production to be possible in any society, according to Althusser, it is necessary to reproduce the conditions of production. That is to say, reproduction depends not only on the forces of production, such as raw materials, buildings and machines, but crucially also on labor-power, which in turn requires individuals with the requisite know-how and training to carry out particular roles and tasks. The central issue in social theory which Althusser seeks to illuminate thus concerns how it is that individuals come to *submit* to the rules of established society.

There are two major theses on ideology put forward in Althusser's writings. The first thesis asserts that ideology both confers a sense of coherent identity and subjects individuals to a particular social position in class society. Althusser's exploration of the ways in which ideology leads individuals to feel 'centered' in relation to society is perhaps best captured by his oft-quoted slogan, 'ideology interpellates individuals as subjects.' This notion of 'interpellation,' whilst the topic of considerable debate in social theory throughout the 1970s, provides a theoretical underpinning for understanding the social processes through which an individual comes to experience a sense of unitary identity. As a structuralist Marxist, Althusser was particularly insistent that individuals have no essential unity, and derive whatever sense of meaning and value they have in their lives from the signs and social practices which go on around them. Ideology in this sense is less a set of well-articulated political ideas or doctrines than deeply resonant unconscious images and associations generated in everyday interaction which lead individuals to feel centered on others and the wider world. Just like the unconscious which structures it, 'ideology is eternal.' To capture this lived tissue of ideological structures, Althusser uses the term 'ideological states apparatuses,' which includes schools, family, the Church, legal systems, political parties, trade unions and the mass media. It is through our day-to-day involvement with such wider social structures, according to Althusser, that ideology does its work, 'hailing' or 'interpellating' the individual as a subject of society. Moreover, the consequences of such interpellations are material, as ideology itself is deeply inscribed in social practices. A terrorist, for example, is not just someone who believes in various fundamentalist doctrines, but rather situates their beliefs in relation to specific extremist practices centered on violence and acts of destruction.

The second thesis proposed by Althusser explores the ideological nature of the individual subject's lived relationship to the world and to itself, and it is here that Lacan's ideas on the imaginary are employed by Althusser to dramatic effect. Seeking to break from the dominant tendency in Marxist thought – derived from various comments in Marx's *The German Ideology* – which casts ideology as a mere 'reflection' of the institutional structures of society, Althusser argues that ideology is not a representation of reality but rather comprises the individual subject's lived relation to their conditions of existence. Borrowing from Lacan, Althusser writes of the 'duplicate mirror-structure of ideology' in which the individual's relation to society parallels the narcissistically encircled space of the imaginary. Like the small infant before a reflecting mirror, jubilantly imagining itself to possess a unitary identity that in reality it lacks, the 'subject of ideology' similarly misrecognizes itself. This misrecognition is, above all, a *self-misrecognition*. As in the case of the luring mirror image, the ideological sphere entraps the individual *as* a subject, although the individual does not comprehend that its subjectivity is thereby produced. From routine social interaction through mass media to party politics, ideology confers an identity upon individuals that in actuality serves as a form of subjection.

To speak in a Marxist language, if it is true that the representation of the real conditions of existence of the individuals occupying the posts of agents of production, exploitation, repression, ideologization and scientific practice, does in the last analysis arise from the relations of production, and from relations deriving from the relations of productions, we can say the following: all ideology represents in its necessarily imaginary distortion not the existing relations of production (and the other relations that derive from them), but above all the (imaginary) relationship of individuals to the relations of production and the

Althusser's writings on ideology received widespread attention throughout
the 1970s, but most critics now agree that there are serious flaws in his
social theory. For one thing, his account assumes that individuals are
serenely subjugated through ideology and just passively adapt to processes
of socialization. But what is lost by Althusser, and no less by his many
followers, is any sense of the politics of ideological struggle. What is lost
is an understanding of the complex, contradictory ways in which people
inculcate dominant forms of ideology and established ways of doing
things as well as how people come to dis-identify with, and in turn
contest, existing societal arrangements. This difficulty with Althusser's
social theory arises in part from his interpretation of Lacanian psychoanalysis, an interpretation which focuses almost exclusively on the
imaginary and the ego. But to view ideology solely in terms of the narcissistic lures of the imaginary is to ignore Lacan's emphasis on both the
symbolic and real orders of psychic life, and particularly their unconscious
contradictions and fissures. These are problems to which we will return
when reviewing problems with Lacanian theory in the next section of this
chapter. For the moment, I simply note that the tendency to present the
human subject as a 'cultural dope' in Althusserian social theory was a key
reason for the fading of influence of this perspective on ideology in the
social sciences.

Žižek: beyond interpellation

Althusser's social theory, deeply influenced as it was by the thinking of
Lacan, was a powerful attempt to demonstrate that social change is
never the simple unfolding of economic or institutional contradictions in
society. Since Althusser's appropriation of Lacan's ideas, social upheaval
must necessarily be seen in terms of an imaginary crisis of human relationships. This may seem a self-evident truth in today's world, in which
ideologies of extreme nationalism, racism, ethnic hatred and xenophobia

proliferate, and yet one might easily underestimate the extent to which mainstream social theory in the English-speaking world for many years by-passed or ignored the volatility and vulnerability of cultural relations and societal arrangements. One influential figure in social theory who has emphasized the deeply unconscious dimension of social antagonisms and cultural traumas, with the implicit aid of Althusser's social theory of ideology, is the Slovenian critic Slavoj Žižek. For Žižek, as for Althusser, ideology implies an imaginary relationship to socio-symbolic forms of class, race and gender. In contrast to Althusser, however, Žižek contends that ideology always outstrips its own social and political forms; it is a realm beyond interpellation or internalization. Ideology, he says, is not something which just magically goes to work on individuals, assigning identities and roles in the act of producing itself. Rather, ideology should be conceived as an over-determined field of passionate attachments. 'The function of ideology,' writes Žižek, 'is not to offer us a point of escape from our reality but to offer us the social reality itself as an escape from some traumatic, real kernel.' (1989: 45)

According to Žižek, politics is that public field of activity that vainly tries to build upon a melancholy loss at the core of desire – those deeply entrenched, threatening passions that people find too painful to acknowledge. In this sense, ideology provides a 'lining' or 'support' to the lack or antagonism which lies at the core of the self. Ideologies of nationalism, racism, or sexism are the very stuff of cultural fantasy – with the result that displaced, unconscious forms of libidinal enjoyment periodically erupt in violent waves of killing and 'ethnic cleansing.' Žižek sees the various eruptions of neo-nationalism and ethnic xenophobia across Europe during the 1990s in precisely these terms. Racism in his sense is an outer displacement of that which people cannot accept within. The projection of what he calls a 'surplus of enjoyment' onto denigrated others, the dumping of distressing and painful affect on socially dehumanized objects of antagonism, lies at the heart of the psychic dimension of political exclusion. This eruption of excess enjoyment, directed at the Other, represents an unbearable kernel of desire. Such excess is alleviated solely through its translation into an ideological symptom. Thus the collapse of Soviet totalitarianism in Eastern Europe unleashed a surplus of fantasy. It involved the projection of pain onto something perceived as strange and Other.

It is possible to criticize Žižek's radicalization of Althusser in various respects. It can be argued, for example, that if loss, lack and absence are ideological anchors for desire, their many forms and changing circumstances would seem more politically differentiated than Žižek recognizes. Žižek sees ideology in terms of a fantasy scenario, the sole purpose of which is to fill-in or cover over painful elements of lack. Yet there is a problem with this view insofar as it tends to flatten out the complex, variable reception of ideological forms by individuals and groups. Žižek sees no significant difference between whether one is in the grip of identity-politics, reading philosophy or classical literature, or watching a TV talk-show host such as Oprah Winfrey. These are all equally to be seen as pieces of ideological fantasy, aimed at effacing the sour taste of lack, gap and antagonism. In this respect, what is lost is the connection between self-identity, ideology and politics. For Žižek tends to pass over the complex ways in which people come to challenge political ideologies, and to treat the very worst and most sinister ideological formations on the same level as other relatively progressive formations. These problems in Žižek can to some degree be traced back to his engagement with Althusser, and in particular the project of using Lacan's ideas to develop a resolutely negative critique of culture. For the Althusserian and Lacanian linkage of the 'subject of the unconscious' to the idea of the arbitrary nature of the sign tends to give an inadequate account of how some political meanings and established ideologies predominate over others in personal and social life. This brings us back to Lacan's essential contribution to social theory, as well as a consideration of problems associated with Lacan's Freud.

Appraisal of Lacan

Lacan's 'return to Freud,' as we have seen, has powerfully influenced the direction and development of social theory. Any theory as complex and difficult as Lacan's post-structuralist rewriting of Freud is, however, inevitably the source of fierce debate. Lacanianism has been enthusiastically applauded and critically attacked on a great number of grounds, and in what follows here I want to briefly consider some of the more important of these points. To begin with, Lacan's account of the imaginary constitution of the ego has served as a corrective balance against other social theories and particularly versions of orthodox social science which place the self at the center of rational action, agency and autonomy. By contrast, Lacan emphasizes that the subject is necessarily alienated from its own history, formed in and through an interpersonal field haunted by otherness, and inserted into a symbolic network which decenters. Equally significant is that in emphasizing that the 'I' is an alienating screen or fiction, a medium of misrecognition which masks the split and fractured nature of unconscious desire, Lacan debunks certain traditional theories of meaning. For such theories, there is a presumption that mind and reality automatically fit together. But not so says Lacan, who not only powerfully questions the view that signs can be explicated in terms of corresponding features of the social world, but raises the issue of whether meaning can ever be immediately present in speech and language. This issue applies not only to meaning but equally importantly to identity itself. For on Lacan's theory of the ego and imaginary, the subject can never be fully present to itself. The self is an illusion, a narcissistic mirage, and every attempt to represent identity is always somehow dispersed, displaced and decentered.

One criticism of Lacan sometimes heard in political circles is that his understanding of culture and social relations is too pessimistic. To say, with Lacan, that we are prisoners of lack, caught within the distortions of the imaginary, and trapped by laws of the symbolic is surely to undermine that sense of resistance and utopianism which is central to the radical political imagination. Whether this is true or not, the variety of contemporary approaches in social theory indebted to Lacan would seem to indicate that a sense of political resignation and cultural pessimism has been important to recent contestations of the established social order. From Althusser to Žižek, Lacan's pessimistic doctrines have been marshaled to assault such notions as Truth, Freedom, Liberty and Meaning. In Lacanian terms, to believe that these terms might hold some absolute value necessarily involves accepting the world as it is. By contrast, Lacanian cultural criticism is out to probe the 'naturalness' of the signs by which women and men live, and in so doing attempts to subvert dominant structures of language. Here it is not too fanciful to detect similarities between Lacanian social theory and the psychoanalytic-influenced social theory of the Frankfurt School, as discussed in Chapter 3. For like Lacan, Frankfurt School theorists such as Adorno and Marcuse drew from Freud to uncover the repressive forces at work in the construction of the self. In contrast to Lacan, however, the recovery of the repressed unconscious for these authors is also said to hold out a promise for autonomous social relations. In Lacanian and post-Lacanian social theory, however, a radically different tack is taken. Lacanian-inspired social theorists such as Althusser and Žižek do not so much evaluate society in terms of psychoanalysis itself, but rather explore the logic of desire (as revealed by the master, Lacan) as an index of society itself. That said, one of the less fortunate legacies of much social theory indebted to Lacan – especially those forms of social theory as represented by Althusser and Žižek – is an impoverished conception of the relation between the self, creativity and autonomy. Let us turn to consider three major limitations of Lacanian-inspired social theory.

Firstly, there are problems with the Lacanian proposition that the imaginary dimension of self-identity is a product or construct of illusions or misrecognitions. Lacan, as we have seen, viewed the imaginary as a *distorting trap*. The mirror constitutes a narcissistic self through consoling images of unity and thus screens out the dismal truth that subjectivity is, in fact, fractured. But the argument that the 'mirror' distorts fails to specify the psychic processes which make any such misrecognition possible. For example, what is it that leads the infant to (mis)recognize itself in its mirror image? How, exactly, does the individual cash in on this conferring of self, however deformed or brittle? Surely for an individual to begin to recognize herself in the 'mirror' she must already possess a more rudimentary sense of self-organization. Cornelius Castoriadis (1997b), an acclaimed European social theorist, has convincingly argued that Lacanianism fails to account for how the 'mirror,' or indeed the other person as a reflecting mirror, is perceived as *real* by the individual. By contrast with Lacanian-orientated social theory, Castoriadis argues that a radical psychoanalytic approach must engage with the capacity of the self to 'gather meaning and to make of it something for him/herself.'

Secondly, and equally serious, is the complaint that Lacan actually suppresses the subversive implications of Freudianism by structuralizing the unconscious and reducing it to a chance play of signifiers. This criticism engages Lacan's reading of structuralist and post-structuralist theory, specifically his claim that the unconscious is co-terminous with language. Many critics – including Paul Ricoeur, Jean-François Lyotard, Julia Kristeva and Jean Laplanche – have argued the Freudian point against Lacan that the unconscious is resistant to ordered syntax. These critics, in focusing on different threads of Lacan's work, rightly argue, in my view, that the unconscious *precedes* language. According to this account, the unconscious – as Freud emphasized throughout his writings – twins meaning and energy, representation and affect. The unconscious may thus intrude upon language, as in slips of the tongue or pen, and yet cannot simply be equated with it. Malcolm Bowie has expressed this well:

> It is our lot as speaking creatures to rediscover muteness from time to time – in rapture, in pain, in physical violence, in the terror of death – and then to feel a lost power of speech flowing back. One may be ready to grant that these seeming suspensions of signifying law are themselves entirely in the gift of the signifier, yet still wish to have them marked off in some way as events of a special kind. A long gaze at the Pacific may be taciturn at one moment and loquacious the next. Language offers us now a retreat from sensuality, now a way of enhancing and manipulating it. Yet to these differences Lacan's theory maintains a principled indifference.
>
> (1991)

The unconscious, for Freud, is completely unaware of contradiction, time, or closure. With Freud, we are the biographers of ourselves but not in the manner of our conscious choosing. Constructing self-identity is a project that emerges out of family, interpersonal and historical narratives, and is thus intricately interwoven with language. And yet our deeper sense of who we are is fashioned beyond the borders of language, as emotions, drives and memories are linked together in the specific ways that people develop as individuals.

To emphasize the pre-linguistic, unconscious character of the self is also to bring into view important social-theoretical considerations concerning Lacan's assimilation of the unconscious with language as a fixed structure. These considerations pertain to the agency of the individual subject. One influential interpretation of Lacan holds that, in presenting a model of desire as disembodied and pre-structured linguistically, the individual subject is effectively stripped of any significant capacity for lasting identity, emotional change or personal autonomy. This complaint is, however, more appropriately leveled at those post-structuralist thinkers that champion the 'death of the subject' instead of Lacan. Rather than celebrating the disappearance of the human subject, Lacan posits a 'subject of the unconscious,' a subject located in the *spacings of language*. Another widespread reading of Lacan is that, in conceptualizing the 'subject of the unconscious' in terms of difference and specifically oppositions that are structured linguistically, no theoretical room is given to practical agency, emotional literacy and the capacity for personal resistance to external social forces. In my view Lacanianism does indeed face a problem in this respect, casting off the most vital questions of self and identity onto an abstract theory of language.

All of this carries particular implications for the account of culture developed in post-Lacanian social theory. For one thing, Lacan's equation of language with cultural domination seriously downplays the importance of power, ideology and social inequalities in the reproduction of institutional life. For writers influenced by Lacan, individuals are transformed into subjects who act in accordance with the symbolic structure of society which is determined in advance. This is obviously a strongly deterministic interpretation of Lacan, but such a reading has powerfully shaped the contours of much contemporary social theory. Whether we turn to Lacan's subsequent explorations of the dislocating force of imaginary, symbolic and real orders, or indeed whether we simply reject Lacanianism altogether and approach the issue of selfhood from an alternative theoretical approach, this deterministic reading of Lacan's work is surely open to dispute. For whilst language certainly pre-exists us as individual subjects, it is surely implausible to suggest – as Lacanian-orientated social theory does – that the symbolic constitution of the human subject is singular, authoritarian and pre-structured in advance. It is crucial to emphasize here that identity is not constituted as 'self-divided' simply because of the insertion of the subject into language. The traumatic divisions and emotional fissures which people experience in today's world are replete with the conditions and consequences of asymmetrical relations of social power. To understand this requires, I argue, a theoretical framework more sensitive to the articulation of identity in relation to social context. This requires attention to the multiple forms in which identity is constituted in deeply unconscious ways, specifically in relation to globalization and multinational capitalism but also to the mass media and new information technologies. It remains the case, of course, that such constructions of the self – at once conscious and unconscious – will be filtered through modes of discourse. And yet the specific criticism here is that Lacan's work fails to consider what the cultural and political determinants of such codes might be.

Finally, these issues involve broader dilemmas relating to knowledge. The Lacanian narrative which we have traced – that the self is narcissistic, the imaginary a specular trap, the law omnipotent, and the symbolic a mask for 'lack' – risks coming undone at the level of social theory. For surely any political project concerned with enhancing freedom must be caught in the same imaginary networks of illusion as the Lacanian account of the self/society nexus? But if this is so, then perhaps the whole Lacanian framework might be deconstructed. For example, how can Lacan's discourse evade the distorting traps of the imaginary domain? Surely Lacan does not seriously believe that the only way of overcoming imaginary distortion is through comic word-play, puns, and irony? In failing to grasp that human subjects are capable of critical self-reflection and self-actualization, the issue of individual and collective autonomy remains repressed in Lacan's work.

Derrida: difference and deconstruction

Lacan's 'return to Freud' might well be seen as another instance of Grand Theory, revolving on such concepts as a universal mirror stage and the symbolic order of language, whereas Jacques Derrida is more concerned with the intricate productivity of chains of signification, as revealed in language in general and writing in particular. To do this, Derrida develops in an early trilogy of books – *Of Grammatology* (1976), *Speech and Phenomena* (1973) and *Writing and Difference* (1978) – first published in 1967 (the year just prior to the student and worker rebellions in France) the concept of *différance*, by which he means the spacing inherent in the system of differences governing discourse. This may at first sound like a continuation of Saussure's theorem that meaning in language is a product of difference, but it is in fact a radicalization of structuralism. This radicalization is to do with a fundamental stress on the never-ending process of difference which *unsettles* signification, and it is this stress which in many ways lies at the heart of the shift from structuralism to post-structuralism. For Derrida, as for Lacan, meaning is always necessarily unstable as it is relayed through an endless chain of signifiers. Yet unlike Lacan, Derrida refuses the philosophical concept of subjectivity in general and rather proposes an ingenious critique of decentering, difference and discourse in *exclusively linguistic terms*. In various forms of social theory, particularly among feminist, queer, post-colonial, and Afro-American critics, Derrida's application of linguistic models in the context of post-structuralism has powerfully influenced the explication of social and cultural phenomena. We will turn to consider these developments in social theory later in the chapter, but first we must briefly consider Derrida's work to see how post-structuralism and linguistics are interrelated.

In discussing Derrida's key ideas, we are considering a form of criticism that has become widely known as *deconstruction*. This is a term which has suffered from various abuses at the hands of sympathizers and critics alike, and indeed Derrida often sought to distance himself from the more purely gestural uses of the term – especially in American deconstructive criticism. According to many critics of Derrida, deconstruction is notable for its belief that meaning is random, truth a fiction, and the human subject a mere metaphor. As we will see, this widespread view of Derrida as a subversive nihilist is in various respects inaccurate. Deconstruction, the philosophical method Derrida promoted, means not destroying Western philosophical ideas, but pushing them to their limits, to the point where their latent contradictions are exposed and criticism can press beyond them. To 'deconstruct' ideas then is to reconstruct and resituate meaning within broader structures and processes. Nevertheless, as Derrida argued, the deconstruction of language must necessarily have recourse to terminological innovation if it is to adequately subvert established categories of meaning. This is one significant reason why Derrida's work seems to many bafflingly opaque, as he deployed various stylistic ironies to question modernity and its distinctive language of a 'metaphysics of presence.' By placing 'under erasure' or drawing an erasing X through the pivotal ideals of Western culture – the primacy of speech over writing, the presumption that meaning is fully transparent or present in communication, the foundational belief in some alternate Center to social affairs – Derrida unearths the endless process of transformation which underlies all signification.

Derrida can be said to have fashioned a whole new style of philosophical writing, and this is nowhere more evident than in his deployment of the neologism '*différance*.' In French, the words *différence* and *différance* sound the same when spoken, but the 'a' in Derrida's idiosyncratic concept cannot be heard. In this distancing from established categories of language through deliberate misspelling, *'différance'* – as Derrida uses the term at any rate – refers to 'the act of deferring.' This is quite a complicated point and I shall return to it in a moment, but here it is important to note that *'différance'* indicates that you will never arrive at a final signified of social differences which is not in itself *deferred*. In emphasizing the *'différance* of difference,' Derrida at once continues and transgresses the tradition of Saussurian linguistics. Meaning, for Derrida as for Saussure, is created by the play of difference in the process of signification. For Derrida as against Saussure, however, signification is always deferred through potentially endless tissues of difference; our communications with ourselves and others can never reach an ultimate destination point or scoop up the idea or object they represent.

Nothing – no present and in-*different* being – thus precedes *différance* and spacing. There is no subject who is agent, author, and master of *différance,* who eventually and empirically would be overtaken by *différance*. Subjectivity – like objectivity – is an effect of *différance*. This is why the *a* of *différance* also recalls that spacing is temporization, the detour and postponement by means of which intuition, perception, consummation – in a word, the relationship to the present, the reference to a present reality, to a *being* – are always *deferred*. Deferred by virtue of the very principle of difference which holds that an element functions and signifies, takes on or conveys meaning, only by referring to another past or future element in an economy of traces. This economic aspect of *différance*, which brings into play a certain not conscious calculation in a field of forces, is inseparable from the more narrowly semiotic aspect of *différance*. It confirms that the subject, and first of all the conscious and speaking subject, depends upon the system of differences and the movement of *différance*, that the subject is not present, nor above all present to itself before *différance*, that the subject is constituted only in being divided from itself, in becoming space, in temporizing, in deferral.

Jacques Derrida (1981a [1972]) *Positions*. Translated by Alan Bass. Chicago: University of Chicago Press, pages 28–9.

In fashioning the term *'différance,'* which he says is 'literally neither a word nor a concept,' Derrida underscores that thought itself necessarily turns slowly (Derrida 1982: 3, 7). Language is not a transparent medium, but an opaque domain of traces or inscriptions whose content and rhetoric must be questioned (to be put, as Derrida says, 'under erasure') and thus resituated in a new register. Here we return to the spatial and temporal dimensions of Derrida's social theory. I say *social theory* because it is Derrida's emphasis on the displaced, deferred aspects of signification which has prized open conventional understandings of the relation between society, culture and history. One of the ways, according to Derrida, that social differences are ignored or repressed is through the act of delay. To differ for Derrida is to defer. Think about it. The present moment, once grasped, has passed. When I hear someone speaking or when I read a sentence, the meaning of what is conveyed is always somehow suspended. Each marking or inscription is shaken up, as it were, by the trace of other signifiers – again and again without end. '*Différance*,' writes Derrida, 'is thus a structure and a movement which can only be grasped in relation to the opposition of present/absent. *Différance* is the systematic play of differences, or traces of differences, of the *spacing* whereby elements are connected to one another' (Derrida 1972, cited in Giddens 1979: 31).

One way in which we might pursue Derrida's ideas on the repressed logic of *différance* in the structuring of a center of meaning in more concrete terms is by reconsidering aspects of self-experience and identity. I might, for example, persuade myself that – as author of this book – I am fully in control of the arguments developed and meanings conveyed, that I am as it were at the center of arranging, explaining and explicating the social theories reviewed in these pages. In some obvious ways, much of this is of course the case; yet there are other powerful forces, at once intra-linguistic and extra-linguistic that function to decenter my authorship. For one thing, since meaning is an endless play of signifiers, it is an illusion for me to believe that I can ever completely get to the nub of Derrida's thinking about deconstruction. Sure, I might use various modish deconstructive terms – *différance*, logocentrism, trace – and yet, on Derrida's account at any rate, these words are themselves always somehow differentiated – dispersed, divided, displaced. The endless circularity of the process of *différance* is thus reproduced and destabilized by the constant transformations of signification itself. Still more, another thing that decenters my authorship of this book is that I am not at the center of my own subjectivity. For Derrida as for Lacan, the conscious self is always decentered in relation to the unconscious. In Derrida, this is less an appeal to some pre-linguistic substratum of the subject than a critical focus on the binary oppositions that situate identity, subjectivity, authorship. Thus the oppositions of self-other, conscious-unconscious and identity-difference are at the core of how discursive practices structure our whole system of thought and experience of ourselves.

Another concrete way of grasping Derrida's argument that meaning is always dispersed, displaced and deferred is by considering the political oppositions of center and periphery in the history of Western colonialism. The West in various political incarnations – the British, the French, the Dutch, amongst others – has historically represented itself as the center of world order. Imperial designs have thus been fashioned through the construction of linguistic, social and political hierarchies – of a Center of civilization, culture and reason on the one hand, and a periphery of barbarism, philistinism and unreason on the other. Constructions of social and political identities have likewise occurred within the organizing linguistic frames of nation, state, race, ethnicity and gender, all of which has served to reinforce an ideology of the West versus the rest. Yet such political hierarchical oppositions are always far from fully secure, as the slow decline of the American imperium in our own times graphically indicates. Deconstruction in such a political context aims to displace political hierarchy, not only by examining how the West depends on its Others to constitute itself as Center, but by tracing the ongoing, deferred significations through which the West as center is decentered by political peripheries.

Rereading psychoanalysis: Derrida's critique of Lacan

Derrida's post-structuralist social theory uses language to call attention to meanings, and in particular sees the process of naming as central to what is named in any classificatory system. The theory or edifice of psychoanalysis in this sense is no different to any other classificatory system from the standpoint of deconstruction, and in fact Derrida engaged at various points throughout his career with the writings of Freud and Lacan – most notably in his book, *Resistances to Psychoanalysis* (1998).

Difference, says Derrida, is always a moment of deferral, a delay in which internal contradictions and conflicts impede the search for the identity of an individual or group, derail the full realization of a structure or center, and displace the final moment in which ideals and illusions might be confronted. Developing a series of close readings of psychoanalytic theory in *Resistances of Psychoanalysis*, Derrida deconstructs Lacan's texts and teachings within the broader frame of post-structural linguistics. He questions, in effect, what people think they might know about Lacanian psychoanalysis by pointing to the complex structures of this body of theory and practice – all of which is only available to us as seminars, tape-recorded archives, texts, transcripts, quotations and slogans. Against this backcloth, Derrida argues that it is impossible to speak of

'Lacan in general – who does not exist'. In developing this viewpoint, Derrida insists on the power of resistance. There is an unavoidable ambiguity, he says, between Lacanian theory and that to which it lays claim – the thought of Lacan. But if resistance is understood as structural limit, not in the psychological but rather rhetorical sense, where exactly does this leave psychoanalysis?

Returning to classical psychoanalytical theory, Derrida finds 'resistance' at the heart of Freud's ideas, including the unconscious, repression and the Oedipus complex. He understands resistance not in the psychoanalytic sense of repression of defense, but rather in terms of a linguistic distortion or failure, of something that resists the identity of author and meaning. In a kind of lifting of psychoanalysis to the second power, Derrida contends that resistance arises from the structure of psychoanalysis itself. In short, Freud's dream machine is, for Derrida, continually on the brink of bringing itself undone.

Derrida contends that psychoanalysis is itself inscribed in an infinite tissue of differences. Freud's legacy is best approached as a product of numerous texts, histories, institutions and processes of inscription. There is no such thing as psychoanalysis in general. Only various theorists, concepts, quotations, teachings, schools and factions, all of which exist as socially structured differences. This seems to me an interesting and useful angle on the place of psychoanalysis as a discourse and practice within our culture. The scope of psychoanalytic theory is extremely wide today, ranging from classical to postmodern approaches in therapeutic settings, and with an equally broad range of theory (object-relational, clinician post-Lacanian) that circulate within the social sciences and the humanities.

However, there are limitations to Derrida's critique of Lacan as well as his deconstructionist recycling of Freud. To say of a particular school of psychoanalysis that its structure arises in and through 'difference' is interesting only up to a point. Why, for example, did Lacanian theory fail for so many years to establish its legitimacy in Anglo-American psychoanalysis? Why, for example, is Slavoj Žižek's reading of Lacan so popular in the academy at the current time, and why is it preferred over Derrida's Freud? Derrida is unable to satisfactorily address these issues, I believe, since they require an examination in depth of the political context in which psychoanalytic theory operates. Derrida himself has hardly been noted for his political and institutional as opposed to his linguistic and discursive critiques.

Appraisal of Derrida

Derrida's writings in particular and deconstruction in general, it is often suggested, have provided a vital stimulus to social theory. Given the experimental, enigmatic qualities of post-structuralist criticism, it is perhaps not surprising that some have viewed this stimulus in a negative light. Very often, though, assessments of Derrida in social theory have been positive. Derrida's debunking of totality and transparency, of uniform linguistic patterns and absolute truth claims, and of grand organizing principles and final solutions have powerfully influenced many if not all post-structuralist sociologies and versions of postmodernist social science. The radical credentials of this deconstructive assault on official or mainstream thought is said by its advocates to stem from attention to the multifarious ways in which language invades meanings, values and all 'naturalized,' ideological forms of experience. The result of this philosophical appreciation of difference has been a new kind of social critique, one in which language is understood to exist on its own terms, self-generative and self-validating in equal measure. Derrida was one of the first French theorists in the aftermath of the political explosion of May 1968 to grasp the extent to which culture and politics revolve on the violent suppression of difference, on the paranoid insistence of exclusive linguistic oppositions: inside/outside, truth/falsity, reality/illusion and good/evil. His deconstructive style, which in a dramatic performative sense enacted the post-structuralist fascination with undecidability, was thus an attempt to give free rein to the ambiguous, open-ended play of signification.

This aesthetics of language, however, is also for many enthusiasts of Derrida's work a *politics of discourse* – and it is here that deconstruction is of most direct relevance to social theory. In so far as Derrida demonstrates that meaning is indeterminate and that language is unstable and ambiguous, he can be seen as speaking up for the dispossessed, the marginal and the voiceless. To the extent that deconstruction is a critical technique opposed to linguistic, social and political closure, it is an attempt to recover – to put back into words – excluded narratives and alternative histories which have been repressed. In more sociological terms, Derrida has provided social theorists with a richly textured battery of terms (*différance*, trace, inscription) for rethinking action in a dynamically open field of social differences. The application of deconstructive techniques to social theory in this way has been successfully deployed to reconstruct and resituate the narratives of people – oppressed women, blacks, gays and subalterns of various kinds – excluded by mainstream political hierarchies and institutional frameworks.

Post-structuralism and post-colonial theory: Bhabha's *The Location of Culture*

Post-structuralism, especially the deconstructive theory advanced by Derrida, has exerted considerable influence over the development of post-colonial analyses of identity, culture, race, gender and the broader struggles of the Third World against the oppressions of our modern age. Harvard University's Homi Bhabha is one of the most influential post-colonial theoreticians of diasporic culture and multiculturalism, and has sought to deconstruct various narratives of nationality that serve to naturalize Third World countries as subordinate to the West.

To do this, Bhabha draws extensively from psychoanalysis – in particular Lacan, but also the post-Lacanian theories of Julia Kristeva (examined in Chapter 12). But it is Jacques Derrida who perhaps most influences his thinking. In *The Location of Culture* (1994), Bhabha argues that racism is never fixed or frozen; race is a 'liminal' category, always in process, shifting, transformational. For Bhabha, colonial identities (for example, the British in India or Africa) are always defined in relation to a marginalized, excluded Other – the colonized or colonial territories. Colonial identity thus both draws upon and represses the black Other; indeed, denigration and denial of the Other is fundamental to the imagined survival of the colonizer. Repression may well be essential to the West's existence, but Bhabha contends that psychic exclusion of the excluded Other never fully succeeds. The repressed unconscious returns to derail Western orderings of power, and this for Bhabha is nowhere more evident than in colonial strategies of 'hybridization' and 'mimicry.' The attempt to imitate, copy or blend racialized identities must necessarily come unstuck according to Bhabha, because colonized subjects are in fact different to those that advance the strategies of colonial power. Against this backdrop, Bhabha situates racial stereotyping in relation to the psychoanalytic notion of repetition. The repetition of racial insults, for example, indicates that the relation between colonizer and colonized is radically ambivalent. The racial slur or denigration is always for Bhabha in danger of coming unstuck, and this is one reason why social actors must work overtime in the making and remaking of relations of domination and submission. This 'ambivalence of colonial rule' enables a capacity for resistance throughout colonized cultures; through performative 'mimicry' of the colonizer, the colonized are able to preserve some hidden or pure aspect of themselves under the sign of an authorized identity. Discussing writers such as Nadine Gordimer and Toni Morrison, Bhabha hunts the 'location of culture' in the marginal, displaced, haunting spaces between Western Enlightenment values and its excluded others.

Bhabha, a product of Elphinstone College, Bombay and Oxford University, has sometimes been rebuked by his critics for preaching the rights of native peoples, migrational groups and marginal cultures from the lofty heights of European post-structuralism. Whatever one makes of this charge of elitism and elitist language, there can be little doubt, in my view, that Bhabha has powerfully engaged psychoanalysis with the rapidly changing social and demographic movements unleashed by the forces of globalization. Moreover, following in the footsteps of Fanon, Bhabha has fashioned a very particular politically informed psychoanalytic critique of post-colonialism, one that deploys concepts of hybridity, liminality and mimicry to challenge neo-colonial forms of political power over the colonized Third World and to deconstruct imaginary constructions of national and cultural identity. He forcefully argues against the colonial tendency to essentialize Third World cultures as homogeneous, the bearers of historically continuous traditions; rather, he suggests relations between First World metropolitan and Third World cultures are constantly changing and evolving, involving creative hybrid interactions of various cultural identities. The theme of equal respect for cultures has emerged in his more recent writings, drawn in part from Derrida's speculations on the centrality of hospitality to justice and freedom.

Notwithstanding the significant impact of deconstruction upon social theory in particular and the social sciences in general, however, there are a number of critical objections that have been made against Derrida's work. Derrida's account of *différance* and the deconstructive technique of close reading this entails, according to some critics, leads social theory to ignore the social and cultural context in which dialogue and debate takes place. The criticism is that deconstruction produces a retreat into linguistic codes. In this sense, a major limitation is that Derrida's approach inherits and compounds Saussure's failure to explicate the *social dimensions* of language and of the arbitrary sign. This is an issue of considerable importance to sociological post-structuralism, as compared with, say, post-structuralist literary criticism, because it concerns those hidden or underlying political variables that shape and structure the ways in which speakers deploy language in specific social situations. Critics have argued, for example, that while deconstruction supposedly excavates processes of signification as productivity, Derrida's work tends to dismiss the issue of reference altogether and instead concentrates on the play of pure differences, of codes themselves. But does not the internal identity of codes, separated by Derrida from any connotation of reference, actually derive from the social and political context in which it is embedded? What shapes the 'identity' of codes if not the social context or the semantic aspects of forms of life in which such codes are expressed?

Related to the foregoing complaint is the charge that Derrida rewrites everything social as linguistic or discursive. This is problematic, some argue, because it reveals deconstruction as elitist. The strong version of this criticism is that deconstruction is little more than a trivial play with words, a kind of embroidered academicism. For such critics, the playful self-irony of deconstruction is itself apolitical. A disengagement with the world of structured social differences is not in my view necessarily implied by Derrida's social theory, although it is the case that deconstruction has been interpreted too crudely at times, especially in the United States. The more moderate version of this critique questions the fruitfulness of approaching social practices as exclusively linguistic. This critique draws attention to the pre-discursive, the non-linguistic, of what cannot be said in language – and powerfully questions whether such fundamental aspects of social life are really best captured through an exclusively linguistic notion of social differences.

Summary points

1   Post-structuralist social theory represents not so much a break with structuralism as a radical extension of its key ideas – especially concerning the notions of difference and the arbitrary nature of the sign.

2   In structuralism, language was treated as a reliable measure for the analysis of other signifying systems. In post-structuralism, the structuralist account of language as a structured system is powerfully critiqued.

3   Post-structuralist social theory questions the structuralist prioritization accorded to signified over signifiers in the constitution of meaning. In Lacan, this is part of an attempt to link the insights of Saussure and Freud, giving priority to the signifier over the signified. In Derrida, it is part of a reversal of the priority usually given to speaking over writing; writing for Derrida is the best illustration of difference.

4   In Lacan's post-structuralist reading of Freud, the individual subject emerges as radically split between the narcissistic illusions of the ego and the repressed desires of the unconscious. This further

involves a series of claims that the unconscious exemplifies certain features of language as a systematic structure.

5   In Derrida's critique of the Saussurian version of difference, a temporal element is introduced into the critique of meaning: to differ is to defer.

6   There have been many criticisms made of post-structuralist social theory, including that it represents a further 'retreat into the code' initiated by Saussure's structural linguistics. This is problematic for social theorists as post-structuralism – notwithstanding its radical insights into cultural difference and decentered identities – has generally failed to generate an adequate account of reference, that is the *reality* of social things.

Further questions

1   What is problematic for identity about the image a mirror reflects back?

2   Is Lacan's mirror stage helpful for a critique of contemporary popular culture – pop music, television soaps, the Internet?

3   Can words ever adequately represent your desires?

4   Fundamentalist ideologies – racism, nationalism, xenophobia – are all-embracing and all-consuming. For people in the grip of such ideologies, what are they seeking to escape?

5   According to Derrida, the deferral and spacing of language is essential to the generation of meaning. But beyond language, what role might social context play?

6   Thinking of current examples, how do you see the politics of difference at play in the recovery of excluded narratives and histories of individuals and groups?

Further reading

Jacques Lacan

Ecrits: A Selection (London: Tavistock Press, 1977)
The Four Fundamental Concepts of Psychoanalysis (Harmondsworth: Penguin, 1979)

The Seminar of Jacques Lacan, Vol. 1: Freud's Paper on Technique 1953–54 (Cambridge: Cambridge University Press, 1988)

The Seminar of Jacques Lacan, Vol. 2: The Ego in Freud's Theory and in the Technique of Psychoanalysis 1954–55 (Cambridge: Cambridge University Press, 1998a)

The Ethics of Psychoanalysis 1959–60: The Seminar of Jacques Lacan (London: Routledge, 1992)

Jacques Derrida

Of Grammatology (Baltimore, MD: Johns Hopkins University Press, 1976)

Writings and Difference (London: Routledge, 1978)

Dissemination (London: Athlone Press, 1981b)

Margins of Philosophy (Brighton: Harvester-Wheatsheaf, 1982)

Resistances of Psychoanalysis (Stanford, California: Stanford University Press, 1988)

chapter 8

The Interaction Order

One summer night, in Santa Maria, Brazil, 233 young people died in a night-club fire. They were crushed by the chaos of party goers trying to flee the club. The sole exit was blocked by bouncers who, unaware of the fire, thought they were fleeing without settling their accounts. In a matter of seconds, it was too late. A night of pleasure turned deadly. Lives were lost. As horrifying as social disasters are, in an odd way they can be said to be orderly. The kids at the club were having normal fun. The bouncers were doing, as best they could tell, what they were paid to do. Even the club owners who made their profits by neglecting safety measures were doing what those who make their money off kids do – cutting corners in a systematic way.

The interactions we have in our lives with others are orderly in many ways – most of them good enough for life to go on even when what order there may be is illicit. We interact with others all the time. You might say that we interact with pets and other animals. Some people have relations of a kind with flowers, trees or potted plants. Whatever may be the subject of an interaction, what transpires is usually, if not always, orderly. Interaction is the most fundamental aspect of any social order. Individuals in a given society obviously *interact* with some degree of regularity. Without the interaction there would not be anything like social *order*.

Yet, in American social theory at mid-twentieth century there came into play the idea of *the interaction order*. The definite article, *the*, signals something more concrete conceptually than the general idea of social order pure and simple. Still, what *the* or *an* interaction order might be has not been self-evident in the history of social theory. Among early modern social philosophers like Hobbes and Rousseau social order was understood to depend on a social contract, but there was no such thing as a theory of interaction order. Nothing like the concept appears in Durkheim and Weber, or Marx and Freud. The pragmatist idea of Symbolic Interaction bears a strong resemblance, but is still not the same thing. Attempts to trace the lineage of an idea by reference to analogies with prior concepts is a risky business. It can be done, and is, but the interaction order demands respect for what it is.

The deep background of the concept owes to the early culture of the University of Chicago. Since its founding in 1892, the University meant to distinguish itself as independent of European traditions. Its encouragement of philosophical pragmatism and, in sociology, of ethnographic field work were prime examples. Even now, the University of Chicago website claims as its foundational purpose the ideal of its first president, William Rainey Harper, 'to establish a modern research university combining an English-style undergraduate college and a German-style graduate research institute.' At that time, late in the nineteenth century, in the United States there were but two serious graduate research schools (Clark and Johns Hopkins) and a number of vaguely English small colleges like Harvard and Yale, but nothing like Harper's grand idea.

The University of Chicago venture to build a unique, world-class institution out of nothing was a typically American conceit. Yet in the 1890s, no American city was a better place for such an enterprise. Chicago was the new industrial and railroad capital, energized by immigrant workers and their families, reinventing itself architecturally after the fire of 1871, and, in historian William Cronon's phrase, nature's metropolis – the city at the heart of America's cultural geography. Chicago, then, was a natural laboratory for a field such as sociology, as it was for John Dewey's theories of democratic education, and for Jane Addams's settlement house work with the poor. The interaction order was there before the concept.

Altogether, Chicago's spiritual and social qualities conspired to introduce social thought to a different idea of what social interaction was and, in particular, how interactions are embedded in settings each in some ways different from the others. In time, *the* interaction order came to refer to social interactions in a given setting. The 'the' came to refer to the fact that, whatever the differences between and among settings, for an encompassing society to be orderly, there must be interaction mechanisms at work from setting to setting.

David Riesman: conformity and the American character

David Riesman was an accidental sociologist. Professionally he was a lawyer, graduate of Harvard Law School, one-time clerk to Supreme Court Justice, Louis Brandeis, and law school professor. It is social theory's good fortune that, after World War II, he became interested in questions of individual and social character. By 1949, he was invited to teach social science in the University of Chicago's still free-wheeling but serious college program. The following year, 1950, he published (with the assistance of Nathan Glazer and Reuel Denney) *The Lonely Crowd: A Study of the Changing American Character*. The book immediately became a best-seller, read by an American public eager to understand changes in their national culture. Since 1950, 1.5 million copies have been sold. No other sociological book in the contemporary period has even approached this figure. It sells still today and is taken seriously – a fact unusual for a book that spoke to issues current in a very different time.

Already by 1950, when the United States stood atop the world, American social critics, as if in unison, voiced concern that their society was losing the national character that, as the belief went, allowed them to overcome economic miseries and defeat powerful global enemies in World War II. By 1950, a generation of Americans had struggled with the consequences of the economic collapse of 1929 and the world war that followed. After these were in the past, there was a sense of relief and the promise of a better life. In the few years just after 1945, only America, untouched by war at home, enjoyed the false pleasures of its new affluence. For the middle class there was money enough for homes, cars, vacations, shopping, even domestic gadgets (dishwashers, air conditioners, televisions were novelties). The fear was that Americans were giving up their productive drive and individualism by conforming to the leisure-time fads of the day.

David Riesman was far from alone in expressing a version of this idea. He was, however, one of the most serious students of what he called American social character. *The Lonely Crowd* became known for his distinction between two ideal-types of social character. 'The concepts of inner-direction and other-direction . . . refer at once to social setting and social character' (Riesman, 1961: xxi). In general terms, he was more or less advancing classical sociology's foundational dichotomy of the historical tensions between the traditional past and the modern present to which he added a third historical concept meant to characterize the revolution occurring in his day; thus, tradition-directed, inner-directed, and other-directed types of social character. Riesman realized he was playing with fire when he sought to apply the types to the grand sweep of world history. He understood that ideal-types are, as others would say, analytic and never full realized in history, that 'types don't exist in reality but are a construction based on a selection of certain historical problems for investigation' (1961: 31). He grew concerned, as successive editions of the book were commented upon, that readers took inner- and other-directed as discrete phenomena. Ever since Max Weber introduced the problem of ideal-types – for which, not incidentally, traditional/modern was one of his clearest instances – social theorists have struggled, as is obvious in the methods of Parsons and Alexander, to negotiate the tensions between analytic logics and empirical evidence.

Riesman, the accidental sociologist, did astonishingly well with the dilemma. For one, he did his best to set the inner- and other-directed types in historical context by locating them in what he considered the second of two great historical revolutions. The first was the breakdown of ancient and medieval traditionalism occurring, in the West, roughly between the thirteenth and sixteenth centuries. This was the period when the tradition-directed character in which individuals have a 'well-defined functional relation to the group' gave way to an inner-directed individual whose sense of inner purpose is 'implanted early in life by the elders' after which in adult life the individual lives more or less autonomously according to well-directed goals of, in effect, her own making. The second great historical revolution was, predictably, the one from inner- to other-directed, where an individual's direction comes from those around her: friends, family, colleagues, as well the character portrayed in the mass media.

To be sure, like all analytic definitions, these are rather raw. What redeems *The Lonely Crowd* is that this very long book is replete with illustrations, historical context, and empirically-grounded arguments. Not all of these hold-up today (notably his intermittent references to the demography of population curves which are a bit old-hat given the influence of W. W. Rostow's modernization theory). Yet, what stands up very well today, in spite of the book's dated nature, is his use of popular culture illustrations from theatre, literature, mass media and the like. He had a knack for pithy characterizations of the truth of the categorical, like: 'from the bank account to the expense account.' On the one hand, this may have been the thread that made the book so accessible to the general public; on the other, it is the kind of literary form that was permitted, perhaps encouraged, at a place like the University of Chicago in the post-World War II era.

What is common to all other-directed people is that their contemporaries are the source of direction for the individual – either those known to him or those with whom he is indirectly connected, through friends and through the mass media. This source is of course 'internalized' in the sense that dependence on it for guidance in life is implanted early. The goals toward which the other-directed person strives shift with that guidance: it is only the process of striving itself and the process of paying close attention to the signals from others that remain unaltered throughout life. This mode of keeping in touch with others permits a close behavioral conformity, not through drill in behavior itself, as in the tradition-directed character, but rather through an exceptional sensitivity to the actions and wishes of others.

David Riesman (1961) *The Lonely Crowd: A study of the changing American character*, abridged version. New Haven: Yale University Press, pages 21–2.

Riesman is not generally thought of as a social theorist. Yet, even a passing review of the definition of the other-directed character demonstrates his ability to use ideas subtly without lapsing into over-strong typifications. The other-directed type is presented not as a radical shift to mere conformity but as a state in which individuals are more attuned to social 'signals' from others, near and remote. Not incidentally, even in the definition, he refers to mass media, which at the time were widely thought to be a threat to the interior critical capacities of the individual. Most famously, this view was expressed by Max Horkheimer and Theodor Adorno in their 1947 essay 'The Culture Industry: Enlightenment as Mass Deception.' (See the section on Adorno in Chapter 3, The Frankfurt School.) Riesman did not belabor the point about mass media, but he certainly took media into account which also contributed to the popularity of *The Lonely Crowd*. Early in the 1950s, the then new media, including the vast vacuity of early television programming, were making themselves felt to mind-numbing effect.

The Lonely Crowd might not present as social theory, yet Riesman was astute in organizing his claims according to precise and telling concepts.

Given that he was not trained as a sociologist, this skill may be the imprint of his background in the law. He knew how to brief a case. Thus, in the concluding section of the book Riesman deploys the comparative series: the adjusted, the anomic, and the autonomous (for which he cites the influence of Robert K. Merton's 'Social Structure and Anomie'). Of which he confesses they are, 'like the three historical types (tradition-directed, inner-directed, and other-directed) . . . constructions necessary for analytic work.' To which he adds:

> Every human being will be one of these types to some degree; but no one could be completely characterized by any one of these terms. Even the insane person is not anomic in every sphere of life; nor could an autonomous person be completely autonomous, that is, not irrationally tied in some part of his character to the cultural requirements of his existence.
>
> (1961: 243)

Like Merton, no single type of individual response to social structures is ever pure. We are all at once autonomous and insane; or conformist and deviant with respect to the prevailing norms of social character.

What is at play in Riesman's theory of the changing American social character is the question of what is to become of the Anglo-American cultural individualism. Historically, and here Riesman is to the point, when the American twentieth century settled into its post-Depression and postwar period, it had to catch up with European culture. By the time of the war of 1914, Europe had grown deeply skeptical of nineteenth-century moral individualism. To be sure, the relation of the individual to the social order was always in the deep background of modern social theory. But in America the question of *individualism* as an ethical orientation was always distinctive going back to the early nineteenth century. In 1835, Alexis de Tocqueville in *Democracy in America* gave the concept of individualism its classical definition as a decisively American category (see Elliott and Lemert, 2006). Throughout the nineteenth and early twentieth centuries in America, simple individualism was the (mostly bourgeois) desire to cut oneself off from the wider society, in Tocqueville's words: 'a calm and considered feeling which disposes each citizen to isolate himself from the mass of his fellows and withdraw into the circle of family and friends' (1969: 506). Naturally, the ideal changed as American society became more stratified; yet, the late nineteenth-century frontiersman shared a version of the early American ethical orientations of the gentleman and the early modern American shopkeeper and entrepreneur. By the 1950s, the norm began to fade as mass culture and the leisure-time activities of the relatively affluent, expanding white middle class incited a dream of a proud future. As the better-off working class aspired to the traditional middle class, many of the middle aspired to a burgeoning upper middle class. Vance Packard's *The Status Seekers* (1959) summed up the general phenomenon, as William H. Whyte's *The Organization Man* (1956) and Sloan Wilson's novel *The Man in the Grey Flannel Suit* (1955) pointed to the conformism that had already become a prerequisite for the aspiring middle and upper middle class corporate men.

Riesman's book was vastly more sophisticated and historically well-informed than most social commentaries on the decline of individualism before a new conforming social norm. The consequence of the anxiety over conformism for both popular and learned social theory was the unsettled question of just how the individual is meant to interact with others in society. In the abstract, this is an old question. In Riesman's day in America, it was a practical question of urgency. Hence, his figurative, if not literal, contribution to the interaction order.

Erving Goffman: impression management and the interaction order

It is not clear who, if anyone, coined the expression 'the interaction order.' In some ways, it is so basic to life in society that it may well have come into play on its own. But there is no doubt who gave the interaction order its theoretical and empirical heft.

Erving Goffman may well have been America's most original and literary social thinker. He has been called American sociology's Franz Kafka because his writing so captures the hidden, even nightmarish, dimension of social interaction. His view of the interaction order is that the order is not so tidy as one might hope because interactions are as much rule breaking as they are norm affirming.

Goffman was born in 1922, in Alberta, Canada, to a family of Jewish immigrants from the Ukraine. It is possible that his distinctly outsider view of social life was shaped, at least partly, by his rural, national, and ethnic origins. His university education was, first, at the University of Manitoba, then at the University of Toronto. For graduate studies he went to the University of Chicago at the high point of its status as the major American sociology program that ran counter to the dominant Harvard and Columbia schools. Goffman's outsider attitude caused him to cut against the grain even of the Chicago school. Many erroneously interpret him as purely and simply a Chicago student of the urban underground, even as a Symbolic Interactionist. Though there are similarities, Goffman always set off on his own.

Faculty in the Department at Chicago must have known what was coming from 'On Cooling the Mark Out: Some Aspects of Adaptation to Failure,' his earliest, still widely cited article, published in 1952, when he was still a graduate student. Goffman was nothing if not independent, as is evident in the opening lines of this article:

> In the argot of the criminal world, the term 'mark' refers to any individual who is a victim or prospective victim of certain forms of planned illegal exploitation. The mark is the sucker – the person who is taken in. An instance of the operation of any particular racket, taken through the full cycle of its steps or phases, is sometimes called a *play*. The persons who operate the racket and 'take' the mark are occasionally called operators.
>
> (1952: 451, emphasis added)

Here one can see an early formulation of the theory original to Goffman. The example from the criminal underworld is of a particular kind of interaction order. What Goffman made of it, in general terms, is that in normal life we are all playing a con-game in which we cool out various marks we encounter to con them into accepting the impressions we are trying to manage.

In his thesis fieldwork in the Shetland Islands, Goffman (himself a kind of con-artist in the best sense of word) essentially ignored his supervisor's advice in order to redefine his study. Instead of a more traditional and descriptive study of the community as a whole, he focused specifically on the interaction order of the Islanders. Many of his observations were based on what he saw in local pubs. The result was his justly famous book, *The Presentation of Self in Everyday Life* (1959). This is the book usually identified as the beginning of dramaturgical sociology in which the social self and social interactions are characterized as closer to a theatrical performance than to the expression of an individual's interior self. Though Goffman clearly intended to characterize social interactions as a kind of role playing found in theater, he also meant the term 'play' to include the confidence game, as is clear from the use of the word in the passage from 'Cooling the Mark Out.'

The Presentation of Self in Everyday Life is somewhat more sober than Goffman's occasional essays, still he means to dismiss the traditional idea of what he called 'ego identity' or an interior, autonomous moral self. Goffman's dramaturgical theme is well represented in his well-known distinction between front-stage (or region) and back-stage aspects of a social performance:

> A social establishment is any place surrounded by fixed barriers to perception in which a particular kind of activity regularly takes place. I have suggested that any social establishment may be studied profitably from the point of view of impression management. Within the walls of a social establishment we find a team of performers who operate to present to an audience a given definition of the situation. This will include the conception of own team and of audience and assumptions

concerning the ethos that is to be maintained by rules of politeness and decorum. We often find a division into back region, where the performance of a routine is prepared, and front region, where the performance is presented. Access to these regions is controlled in order to prevent outsiders from coming into the performance that is not addressed to them.

(1959: 238)

The apparently simple descriptive distinction between front and back regions is actually loaded with implications.

Goffman not only uses the regions to explain impression management in an interaction order, but he adds an important ingredient – information control. Goffman's theory of the dramaturgical self pictures the individual as one who controls personal information some of which *must not* leak into the front stage of a performance where it would spoil the show. Here Goffman applies the further distinction between strategic and dark secrets which, in *The Presentation of Self in Everyday Life*, are described chiefly as secrets kept among members of one's performance team.

A basic problem for many performances, then, is that of information control; the audience must not acquire destructive information about the situation that is being defined for them. In other words, a team must be able to keep its secrets and to have its secrets kept.

(1959: 141)

Thus, here, Goffman characterizes information control as a social enterprise; also, here too is an early, if indirect, sketch of his view of the interaction order.

Information control, thereby, is a key element in the ongoing interactions of social life. Individuals depend on their social teams who are necessary to one's ability to offer, or to be, a coherent self in relations with others. A team, at the least, colludes to keep or to leak his secrets. Thus a strategic secret is one that, though regulated, allows personal information into a public performance. If, for example, a student new to a social setting happens to be from a well-known family, in most colleges she is unlikely to want to open a conversation with that fact. She will, thus, depend on close friends in that setting to keep the secret. Yet, a secret of this sort can have social value, especially if the person who keeps it presents herself as, let us say, indifferent to whatever status she may bring to the situation. It is common for people with this sort of secret to manage the information indirectly – perhaps by playing the role of a regular person unaffected by her unearned status, thereby allowing her team of friends to leak the fact of the matter. This is what Goffman calls a strategic secret.

By distinction, a dark secret might be one kept by another student who covers college expenses by working as a stripper. The world being what it is, it is probable that some others, presumably friends close to her, would know of the nature of her enterprise. They would be crucial to keeping her secret. In most, but not all, settings the fact of the matter would be dark in that, especially in more religiously conservative settings, such a dark secret would negatively affect who she is thought to be. If the secret is darker still – when, let us say, the person has done time for sexual assault – he would probably try, at all costs, to avoid any setting where someone might know this fact of his life. Yet, again, things being what they are, there is always the possibility that someone who knew of it, or had happened upon the dark secret, would enter the setting, thus to put his new social identity at risk. Almost surely, the bearer of the dark secret would be forced either to flee the setting or to bribe, even if only by persuasion or seduction, the bearer to keep quiet. This would entail Goffman's third, generally benign, secret, the insider secret held by back stage team members. What makes it benign is that the dark truth must be managed by agreeable means that of course are always fragile. One misstep and the accord is broken, the secret is out and the performance ruined for the time being.

Thus, it is plain that Goffman's interaction order is vastly more complex than the more common theory of the social self as one who interacts, even if dynamically, with others to formulate and defend an interior sense of moral integrity in the world. However well-advanced social theories of the self may be (the pragmatist views of George Herbert Mead for example), most of them come down to the idea of a self to which is imputed a sense of interior coherence much similar to the pre-modern ideal of the personal soul. Not even Riesman's artful typology of the stages of change in the individual's relations to others comes close to Goffman's revolutionary reformulation of the interaction order as a thoroughly social order. For Goffman individuals are, in effect, nothing if they are unable to manage the information to be made available to, or kept from, others in their interactive worlds.

Though *The Presentation of Self in Everyday Life* aims to be robustly social in its analysis of the dramatic self, not even Goffman could ignore the evident individual aspects of a self's destiny. This is because, if nothing else, it is the individual who must bear the consequences of a failed performance. No matter how well she may recruit a series of teams to support her performance, in the end when a self fails (or, for that matter, succeeds extraordinarily well), she alone will suffer the consequences (or benefit from the successes). Team members may have to deal with embarrassment or reflected glory but what they suffer is far less severe. Being known to have been friends with a stripper or even a convict is not the same as being the one discredited by a discrediting past. Thus it is that, before and after *The Presentation of Self in Everyday Life* in 1959, Goffman took up the theoretical problems lurking on either side of his controversial statement of the individual in the interaction order.

One of the two problems is how even a well-presented self manages to maintain its sanity from setting to setting. She must, at least, bear with her a sense of who she has been, and intends to remain, as she moves on. At the least, a younger person moving away to work or study must recruit new teams of sufficient reliability to allow for a recognizable identity that makes sense to both self and others. It would be a strange, improbable sort of person who would even attempt to be someone new every time she comes into a different crowd. Even if one were to have such a project in mind, no one is free to 'be' any type of person she might, in her worst moments, want to be. Everyone must, as a minimum, speak an ordinary language, respect local customs, and present a character others are likely to respect. She may have no personal discomfort with being or having been a stripper but flaunting it in a new position as, say, assistant bank manager would simply not work.

Thus, in one of Goffman's earliest essays, 'On Face-work: An Analysis of Ritual Elements in Social Interaction' (1955), he begins with another of his ironic concepts. Face-work isolates the experience most of us have, if we are honest, of losing face – of, put simply, embarrassing ourselves by being out of character. Usually, these events are relatively slight embarrassments we can repair. When a star ball player misses a shot he may play-act the proper motion as he goes back to the bench. An actress who trips on the stairs on the way to collecting an award may make a joke of her fall, thereby demonstrating that, in addition to being a star, she has the face of one with a humorous sense of perspective.

Yet, the repair of a face must be done according to a script or, what Goffman called a good sense of acceptable ritual order. The actress might choose some other method of repair (looking back at the stair as if the problem were with the carpeting). But she would be ill-advised to pretend the trip hadn't happened. In other words, to repair a loss of face one must use an accepted and available social rule that will serve to demonstrate that the person is worthy of being restored to a proper face:

> Universal human nature is not a very human thing. By acquiring it, the person becomes a kind of construct, built up not from inner psychic propensities but from moral rules that are impressed upon him from without. These rules, when followed, determine the evaluation he will make of himself and of his fellow-participants in the encounter, the distribution of his feelings, and the kinds of practices he will employ to maintain a specified and obligatory kind of ritual equilibrium. The general capacity to be bound by moral rules may well belong to the individual, but the particular set of rules which transforms him into a

human being derives from requirements in the ritual organization of social encounters.

(1967 [1955]: 45)

Here, more than any other place, Goffman defies the common view that he was nothing more than a micro-sociologist. His interaction rituals and rules are evidently taken from Emile Durkheim's general theory of culture (a source he clearly acknowledges).

The second problem arising from Goffman's presentation theory of self raises the question of just how the individual experiences *and* manages himself in respect to the social requirements and the risks of his performances. These were the issues addressed in a 1963 book, *Stigma: Notes on the Management of Spoiled Identities*. Stigmas, he explains, are precisely those consequences for an individual when personal identity is found to be out of synch with a presented social identity.

A social identity is the social face one has composed in a setting – such as that of being an exceptionally nice person in spite of her famous family background. A given face may be carried over from one setting to another but only when there are social others who recognize the ritual by which it is formed well enough to join in its presentation. A personal identity, accordingly, comprises the actual facts of a person's biography. These could include a range of secreted factors – that in her home town she is well known to have been a snob, that she was adopted from an orphanage by parents who then regretted having her, that she was a rebel who worked as a stripper, that she had been known to have cheated on the exams that got her into her college, and so on. None of these is hard to imagine, though no one individual is likely to be beset by so great a number of 'true' facts of life, which, by the way, could very well include that back home she was known to have been a genuinely humble and 'good' person. Whichever ones, among others, apply, these are marks that cannot be gotten around just as, for example, a criminal record cannot be erased. They may include genetic or physical attributes such as deafness, which in some cases can be well disguised. When they are visible marks, like a racial nature, or a bodily handicap like the loss of a limb, the bearer of these marks must still be able to fabricate a social fact that is acceptable – whose differences do not render the person outside the norms of a social order.

Whatever the personal information behind a personal identity, it must be managed in respect to a person's social identity, which is never exactly the same. No one can create a social identity (or a face) that exposes everything about his 'true' self. This for any number of reasons – it would be too much for others to take it all in; too many personal facts do not a good social performance make; and some (being dark secrets) simply must not be made known; and so on. Thus, in *Stigma*, Goffman lends nuance to his earlier ideas on the awkward, uncertain relations between social and personal identities. When they are out of synch, one loses face and when they are terribly out of synch, one can become stigmatized, or discredited. It is one thing to trip on a gown; quite another to be exposed as a fraud.

In principle, all of us are as likely to be discredited as to lose face – even when the fear of what we might consider discrediting is way out of line with any truly stigmatizing quality. The guy who did time for sexual misconduct has something real to manage. The girl who presents as humble in spite of her background has less of a stretch. Others might even expect her to have some character flaws owing to her background. What matters, however, is how she feels about the possibility or actuality of being discredited. Some ex-convicts have learned to accept the negative opinion of others. Prison can do that to a person. They might be hardened, not as criminals, but as persons who know what others may feel and have learned not to let them- selves feel as others do. This is ego-identity for Goffman – not a quality of moral interiority but a given set of feelings when a social face is lost. Thus, the girl who pretends to be more regular than she is could well be *more* upset with being found out for being what others are likely to assume she is than the convict would be for being the stigmatized deviant he actually is.

In *Stigma* Goffman crystalizes the underlying fact of his theory of the social self as presented – namely, that there is no clear distinction between the normal and the deviant. If all must manage impressions against the threat of being discredited by a hint of some or another dark secret, then all are engaged, at least, in a practical dishonesty. We do not, according to Goffman, present ourselves fully and honestly. We cannot. Not only would it lead to practical nonsense but, even more, the attempt to be fully honest would sooner or later expose us as a fool of some hard-to-categorize kind.

Hence, the remarkable conclusion of Goffman's theory of the presented self is that the distinction between normal and deviant persons is artificial. We are all, in effect, normal deviants. In Goffman's interaction order, order itself is at once normal and deviant in the sense that interaction must always involve a play of presentations that obey social rituals and rules while at the same time breaking them in the pursuit of a socially acceptable face.

One can therefore suspect that the role of normal and the role of the stigmatized are parts of the same complex, cuts from the same standard cloth. Of course, psychiatrically oriented students have often pointed out the pathological consequence of self-derogation, just as they have argued that prejudice against a stigmatized group can be a form of sickness. These extremes, however, have not concerned us, for the patterns of response and adaptation considered in this essay seem totally understandable within a frame of normal psychology. One can only assume first that persons with different stigmas are in an appreciably similar situation and respond in an appreciably similar way. . . . And secondly, one can assume that the stigmatized and the normal have the same mental make-up and that this necessarily is the standard one in our society; he who can play one of these roles, then, has exactly the required equipment for playing out the other, and in fact in regard to one stigma or another is likely to have developed some experience in doing so. Most important of all, the very notion of *shameful* differences assumes a similarity in regard to crucial beliefs, those regarding identity. Even where an individual has quite abnormal feelings and beliefs, he is likely to have quite normal concerns and employ quite normal strategies in attempting to conceal these abnormalities from others . . .

Erving Goffman (1963) *Stigma: Notes on the Management of Spoiled Identity.* New York: Simon and Schuster, page 131.

Over the years after *Stigma* in 1963 until his death in 1982 Goffman wrote on an array of subjects – *Interaction Ritual: Essays in Face-to-Face Behavior* (1967), *Strategic Interaction* (1969), *Relations in Public: Micro-studies of the Public Order* (1971), *Frame Analysis: An Essay on the Organization of Experience* (1974), *Gender Advertisements: Studies in the Anthropology of Visual Communication* (1976; 1979), *Forms of Talk* (1981), among many other shorter writings. As this selection of titles suggests, the interaction order was always in the background, usually also in the foreground.

Naturally, there have been criticisms of his writings for various reasons – too focused on language and the symbolic, too micro-sociological, too much lacking in an explicit politics. Yet, to the extent that the complaints are plausible, in each instance he never failed to lodge his ideas in a broader frame of reference. Yes, there were strong elements of the symbolic, especially in *Frame Analysis,* but this criticism (made famous by Norman Denzin) may have neglected the ways this book was Goffman's most robust venture into a structural theory of the cultural elements in social interaction (and thus into an aspect that even his critics, including Denzin, would come to see as important to social analysis). Yes, also, even Goffman referred to his work as micro-analysis, but then too from the first he granted that the interaction order depended on interaction rituals, a theme he took from Emile Durkheim who was hardly a micro-sociologist. And yes, also, he was not overtly political even in the sense that his older contemporary, David Riesman, addressed the political order, but he was very much a cultural radical whose ideas in time had a lasting effect on the issues of postwar American culture. Nowhere is the depth and range of Goffman's social theory more in evidence than in 'The Interaction Order,' his presidential address to the American Sociology Association, a paper that sadly was not delivered in person because his terminal illness prevented him from appearing in public. Still, in it Goffman sets the terms that made the interaction order a central feature of late modern American social theory:

> Social interaction can be identified narrowly as that which uniquely transpires in social situations, that is, environments in which two or more individuals are physically in one another's response presence. (Presumably the telephone and the mails provide reduced versions of the primordial real thing.) The body to body starting point, paradoxically, assumes that a very central sociological distinction may not be initially relevant: namely, the standard contrast between village life and city life, between domestic settings and public ones, between intimate, long-standing relations and fleeting impersonal ones. After all, pedestrian traffic can be studied in crowded kitchens as well as crowded streets, interruption rights at breakfast as well as in courtrooms, endearment vocatives in supermarkets as well as in bedrooms. If there are differences along tradition lines, what they are remains an open question.
>
> (1983: 2–3)

For Goffman nothing was sacred – not the truths of a given culture, not the basic historical assumptions as to the uniqueness of modern society, nor those of sociology and social theory. He was, in his way, *sui generis*. His influence continues even now, yet, just as he did not come directly from his teachers at Chicago, he did not produce a school in his name. It was not his nature to follow or lead but to stand out against things as they were. Just the same, there are traces of his influence all across subsequent social theory in America.

Ethnomethodologies: Aaron Cicourel and Harold Garfinkel

When ethnomethodology burst into the open in the 1960s, many were irritated, some just plain confused. Even today the most brilliant people writing theory dismiss Garfinkel. He chose, said one,

> to write in gobbledy-gook, and although I do not begrudge him the enjoyment he so obviously received from this activity, I also see no

reason to wade through the results to extract arguments that were made previously and more clearly by others.

(Martin, 2011: xi)

Over the years others have said the similar, if with less edge and wit. If, thus, brilliant people dismiss a leading proponent of ethnomethodology as too confusing and little original, then why bother with it? Of course, one answer could be that they are wrong. The better answer is that there is something there that does not meet the eye. That there might be is suggested by the fact that Garfinkel's virtual co-founder of ethnomethodology, Aaron Cicourel, does not write in gobbledy-gook and, though less well known, is clear on the original elements of the theory.

Cicourel, like ethnomethodologists in general, does something that disturbs the scientific theorists. He argues that measurement is ubiquitous in social practices of all kinds, whether high science or common sense practical living. What we are doing in whatever we do (whoever we are) is measurement. By this he means that all social practices are the work of using general available interpretive procedures in order to decode, thus to measure, the local settings of our social interactions. Here ethnomethodologies bear a comparison to Goffman but with a sharp difference. Where Goffman's face work was social in nature, guided by interaction rituals, for Cicourel the work of daily life is social in the sense of relying on common procedures to interpret the variety of ordinary life situations. Thus for Cicourel explicitly, and Garfinkel implicitly, social actions proceed according to linguistic or, better, semiotic rules. Some might say that it is a little too playful to call this measurement. But Cicourel is dead serious:

> Traditional measurement seeks to assign numerals to objects and events according to some explicit set of rules or coding practices. In making such assignments researchers make use of interpretive procedures that remain an unwitting resource to them. The coding practices are unavoidably embedded in a context-restricted setting having indexical properties. Thus studying the researcher's coding practices becomes indistinguishable from studying speaker-hearer's use of interpretive procedures.

(1974: 91)

The key word in all this is 'indexical,' which is to say: a property of social settings whereby participants *point to* meanings available to interpretation. These may be gestures, silences, body postures, words, signs, almost anything in the interaction order whereby one is able to measure the meaning of what is going on.

Ethnomethodologists all put indexicality at the heart of social inter-actions, whether lay or professional, common sense or scientific. Cicourel, however, is more likely to call this approach cognitive sociology. In addi-tion, more than others, he emphasizes the linguistic or communicative features of ethnomethods. Accordingly his sources were different – Alfred Schutz and Noam Chomsky, as unlikely a theoretical pair as one could imagine. Naturally, he drew on many others, but Cicourel's juxtaposition of these two allows him to formulate a striking definition of the task of soci-ology as 'the search for and measurement of invariant properties of social action within the context of changing social order' (1974: 197). Hence, his version of the indexical concerns of social theory – how to understand the measuring of social structures in the real tensions between invariant cogni-tive procedures and variant social contexts; or, as he clearly understood, the dilemma of social structures. Thus, in general terms, social theory is the theory of measurements, both scientific and practical.

Naturally, Cicourel's cognitive sociology is inherently controversial at least to the extent that he deploys so strong a structural theory as Chomsky's deep theory of grammar. Yet, his intent is clear – to locate in the inevitable variety of social contexts the apparent, if remarkable, fact that in social interactions actors seem to create orderly arrangements more often than not. Cicourel's ethnomethodology may thus be directed at an old problem but his aggressive use of a strong theory of social grammar certainly invites an original theory of, in effect, the semiotic nature of social communication and social order.

Harold Garfinkel's version of ethnomethodology, while less formally reliant on a linguistic model, is like Cicourel's primary concern with the inherent similarity of social and practical theories. Garfinkel thus started his *Studies in Ethnomethodology* saying that

> [ethnomethodological] studies seek to treat practical activities, prac-tical circumstances, and practical reasoning as topics of empirical study, and by paying to the most commonplace activities of daily the attention usually accorded extraordinary events, seek to learn about them as phenomena in their own right.
>
> (1967: 1)

Hence, Garfinkel's idea that ethnomethodology is the study of people's methods for creating a sense of structure in their mundane worlds.

The most famous generic example of how Garfinkel professed to study the methods of ordinary people is the notorious breaching experiment, in which students and other researchers are sent into ordinary social situ-ations with the instruction to break the normal rules of the interaction setting. Thus, examples of breaching experiments would be: when at home a student might treat his mother as though she were a waitress; or in a fast food restaurant to order a Big Mac, then when the order is delivered to attempt to negotiate the well-known price; or in conversation with an acquaintance to respond to an ordinary statement by questioning the meaning of that statement. As a mother would most probably demonstrate her righteous indignation, and the server would exhibit puzzlement before calling on the manager, so in ordinary conversation a breach can reveal the ordinary measures we use to point to our meanings.

In the English language, 'How are you doing?' is a generic expression that may refer to knowledge of, say, a recent illness or the like, but just as often it invokes a general opening to conversation. When said at a bar to a stranger it can operate as a proposal for communication and much more when the stranger is of potential sexual interest. If the query is offered in the latter case, the reply could well be an abrupt; 'Fine, my boyfriend just went out for a smoke.' Thus, it is clear that, 'How are you doing?' isn't necessarily a question or, if it is, not one that requires a statement of one's health. There are many examples of the same: 'Waz up?' '*Ça va?*' 'How's it going?'

> (S)   Hi Ray. How is your girlfriend feeling?
> (E)   What do you mean, 'How is she feeling?' Do you mean physical or mental?
> (S)   I mean how is she feeling? What's the matter with you? (He looked peeved.)
> (E)   Nothing. Just explain a little clearer what do you mean?
> (S)   What's the matter with you? Are you sick?
>
> Harold Garfinkel (1967) *Studies in Ethnomethodology*. Eaglewood Cliffs: Prentice-Hall, pages 42–3.

Breaching experiments may do no more than call to attention the existence of ordinary routines. One is well advised not to hit on someone who is obviously 'in a with' (in one of Goffman's phrases). The fool who walks into a joint without studying the scene is likely to lose face unless he has a pretty good sense of who might be available and who not. On the other hand, those available for a 'How are you doing?' usually make their availability known by various means including so small a gesture as holding the slightest smile or slightly turning her face toward the other. Of course, these experiments don't say very much in themselves but they do open up a field of study in social interactions that lead to more formal study of other elements in the interactional setting.

Ethnomethodologists thus often invent their own brand of categories. One example is the function of the *et cetera principle*. Conversation like social action itself is never complete in itself. We never say everything we mean in words. Talk is usually interrupted by silences or, when the going gets rough, queries as to the progress of the talk. 'Do you get what I mean?' Likewise our routines are broken by sudden changes of expression: gestures pointing to nowhere in particular, head shakings and the like. These and much else are means by which, in the variety of social orders, we point to or indicate assumed meanings. Cicourel may be too strong in asserting that the indexicality of ordinary life relies on invariant interpretive procedures. Yet, insofar as pointing procedures do obviously carry over across different cultures, as they do, then he is not that far off. If he were, we could never find a train or buy an orange in a country where we knew none of the native languages and little of local habits.

It evident that the ethnomethodologists struck off on their own. They wrote at the same time as Goffman, with little notice of his ideas. Yet, they are engaged in something not unlike other theories of the interaction order. Most obviously, ethnomethodology takes seriously the behaviors and rules of an interaction order, much as Goffman did in his way and Riesman did in a more abstract fashion. Yet, the weak point of this range of interaction order studies is the tendency to underestimate the effect of long-enduring social structures. Obviously, this is less true of Riesman except for the fact that his working assumption that in the 1950s a major structural change was taking place is at least open to inspection. If he was right, as he may have been, the evidence he drew from narrative examples of the alleged change fell short of a robust social history of the times (which, of course, can never be written when the purported changes are taking place). Goffman and the ethnomethodologists, especially the latter, put forth theories of structures, but they did not fully realize those theories in ways that locate the way local rules and practices are strongly determined or related to larger structural forces. Goffman did little to study the interaction rituals he referred to, just as when Cicourel and Garfinkel refer to structures they are typically referring to situated structures.

Thus one can well appreciate why sociologists such as John Levi Martin are irritated by more than their language. Part of what is at issue with ethnomethodology is also what is original to it – eliminating for all intents and purposes the professional distance between social sciences and social life. Goffman never spoke this way of sociology but his ideas had much the same effect in that he wrote always from a position closer to the dramas of daily life than to any professional sociological language. His genius was that he captured the deviant elements of ordinary life because he was a deviant sociologist – always looking below its surface rules, even while claiming allegiance to the field.

the interaction order

One common error is to assume that work on questions of the interaction order is merely a version of Chicago sociology. It may well be true in that both Riesman and Goffman had certain accidental relations to Chicago as well as to sociology. It is not true of ethnomethodology. Garfinkel was informed as much by Parsons at Harvard as Cicourel was by his studies at UCLA and Cornell. Yet, the differences being acknowledged, the social study of the interaction order does bear a distinctively American aspect. For one, European Marxism and the rigorously structural and historical thinking it encourages, is little in evidence in these classic theories of the interaction order. They were largely formed in the 1950s through the early 1970s before European thinking in general, and Marxism in particular, became common grist for the American theoretical mill beyond the defining sources provided by Parsons.

It is not clear that there is a definitive lesson about American culture in this line of thought; certainly not as there is in pragmatism. It may only be that, in its foundational day, interaction order theories were affected by having been worked through in relative isolation from the true structural effects of the twentieth century's world wars. Americans won these great wars. The country was hit hard by economic depression but the second war conquered the economic crisis in America – thereby certifying the nation's idea of its special providence. Structural social theories are bred by deep social troubles of an intimate and continuing kind. That American studies of the Interaction Order were formed without a structural tradition may have led them to their greatest virtue – the study of the subterranean mysteries of human social life. All of these thinkers were serious. All looked critically and deeply at social life. Thus, all were pioneers of a kind – writers who worked in alien territory without giving in to the innocence of American postwar triumphalism.

Summary points

1 The roots of the Interactional Order concept can be found, to some degree, in the founding principles of innovation and intellectual independence at the University of Chicago, and the vibrant atmosphere of its home city at the close of the nineteenth century.
2 In his bestselling *The Lonely Crowd: A Study of the Changing American Character*, 'accidental sociologist' David Riesman distinguishes between three 'ideal types' of social character: tradition-directed, inner-directed and outer-directed.
3 Riesman argued that the rise of the affluent middle class in America during the postwar period signaled a shift towards outer-directed

social character, which entails the internalization of guidance from acquaintances and the mass media, and a heightened sensitivity to social signals.

4   Erving Goffman, an atypical Chicago School graduate, provided a framework for the Interactional Order with his dramaturgical analysis of performative social interactions. *The Presentation of Self in Everyday Life* introduced Goffman's distinction between front-stage, where impressions are carefully maintained for the benefit of an audience, and back-stage, where access is restricted to those involved in the production.

5   Face-work, another of Goffman's influential early ideas, describes the processes by which actors maintain their presentation of self, and repair potential breaches, according to socially-prescribed scripts.

6   Stigmas, one of Goffman's later concepts, occur when a rift emerges between the actor's personal biography and the social self they attempt to present. Stigmatized individuals are unable to present a normalized face, but the distinction between what is normal and stigmatized is artificial; actors possessing stigmatizing characteristics may still employ prescribed scripts to present themselves as normal.

7   Ethnomethodology takes the 'practical as empirical,' studying the interpretive procedures used to establish meaning in day-to-day social practices; it pays attention to indexical signs – gestures, movements and silences as well as words – that operate in pre-established patterns and allow participants to interpret meaning.

Further questions

1   Evaluate Riesman's argument that the postwar American character transformed from inner- to outer-directed (bearing in mind that these categories represent ideal types rather than concrete reality).

2   Thinking of a social setting, can you identify which elements are front-stage and back-stage? What would result if that separation failed?

3   What is the distinction for Goffman between what is normal and stigmatized?

4   'Universal human nature is not a very human thing. By acquiring it, the person becomes a kind of construct, built up not from inner psychic propensities but from moral rules that are impressed upon him from without.' Do you agree?

5   Can you think of a situation where you 'breached' the normal rules or patterns of behavior? How did others react?

Further reading

David Riesman

The Lonely Crowd: A Study of the Changing American Character (New Haven: Yale University Press, 1961)

Erving Goffman

The Presentation of Self in Everyday Life (New York: Doubleday Anchor, 1959)
Stigma: Notes on the Management of Spoiled Identity (New York: Simon and Schuster, 1963)
Interaction Ritual: Essays in Face-to-face Behavior (New York: Random House, 1967)

Harold Garfinkel

Studies in Ethnomethodology (Englewood Cliffs, NJ: Prentice-Hall, 1967)

Aaron Cicourel

Cognitive Sociology (New York: Macmillan, 1974)

chapter 9

Theories of Structuration

Contents

In the dreamy routines of daily life, we seldom think of ourselves as accomplished individuals using various skills to negotiate the social things about us. We seldom think of ourselves in this way partly because most of us, most of the time, adopt a 'natural attitude' to the world and to others around us, and partly because daily life does indeed exhibit various dream-like qualities. To say that daily life is oftentimes dreamy is to say that much of what we do, as well as why we do what we do, is *mysterious*. One of the mysteries of our daily or habitual behaviors is that our skills or accomplishments seem to be governed by forces out of the immediate reach of consciousness. Perhaps nowhere is this dreamy not-quite-consciousness of everyday life better dramatized than in the routines we all follow first thing in the morning, after rising from our dream-filled slumbers.

Like every household throughout cities of the West, my own family has developed its own internal rhythms – a richly crafted tapestry of routines – which comprise our morning happenings. If it is a weekday, I rise to skim the morning newspapers, check my email, get ready for work at university, and otherwise attend to helping my kids prepare for the day ahead at school. If my own morning routine has a degree of unremarkable consistency to it, this is easily countered by the intricate routines followed by my young children. My eldest daughter, who is in the early years of primary school, starts the day gently – requiring much encouragement to get out of bed. Breakfast is her favorite meal of the day, and she prefers to take her time, sampling from a range of breakfast cereals and other foods. My five-year-old son, by contrast, tends to scoff his breakfast – in order to get on with the demanding ritual of staging dinosaur battles. Meanwhile, my youngest daughter at only six months enjoys the attentions of her mother for an hour or so and then her routine dictates that she returns to bed for further sleep.

Routines of this kind are, as I say, unremarkable and yet run deep throughout society. Routines are very often considered by people as merely private – expressive of only individual preference. Routines are surely this – a central part of our private make-up as individuals – but they are also something else. From a sociological perspective, routines might be regarded as the 'social glue' that holds together the regular flow of daily life. How routines become established over time and well-sedimented in daily life has long attracted the attention of social theorists. From this angle, if routine emerges as a sociological concept and not simply a psychological disposition, this is because the term is fundamental to the question of the relation between the individual and society, selfhood and culture. Social theorists are thus preoccupied, among other things, with the issue of how the mundane routines of our daily life affect, and are affected by, the organization of whole societies.

Recent social theory has moved center stage the question of how our daily routines, habits and competencies serve to shape our social worlds. This chapter introduces the work of two famous social theorists – England's Anthony Giddens and France's Pierre Bourdieu.

Anthony Giddens: structuration and the practical routines of social life

Very broadly speaking, there have been two major approaches to explaining the relationship between the individual and society (see, for example, the Frankfurt School). In what we might call society-dominated accounts, a view is advanced that common culture, socialization and general social structure generates individual practices. There also exist what can be described as individual-dominated accounts, in which it is individuals who are treated as the source of broader social relations. By contrast to each of these approaches, Anthony Giddens is more concerned with coming to grasp how individual action is structured within the mundane practices of social life, while simultaneously recognizing that the structural and organizational features of contemporary societies are reproduced by individual action. This way of phrasing things may at first appear simply academic, but Giddens insists it is a fundamental advance for social theory to break from the individual/society dualism. For to continue to define the relation between the individual and society in strictly oppositional terms is to misunderstand what goes on within the intricacies of practical social life. To approach the issue differently, therefore, Giddens develops in his book *The Constitution of Society* (1984) the concept of *structuration*, by which he means to account for the production of habitual practices as simultaneously the force of systemic structures and the individual accomplishments of agents. The starting point of his analysis is not society as fixed and given, but rather the active flow of social life.

Like various structuralists, Giddens's argument is that we fashion ourselves as individuals and societies in and through language. Society, according to this view, is therefore clearly 'structured' in some sense or other by language. Yet Giddens is also very critical of structuralism and post-structuralism. He rejects, for instance, the structuralist argument that 'society is like a language;' his reasons for holding to this view will be examined in some detail later in the chapter. The point to note at the outset is that, in contrast to the structuralist standpoint, Giddens contends that social action is similar to language primarily in the sense that it is 'rule-following.' As we go about our daily activities – thinking and talking about our worlds and, thus, in some sense helping to make and remake these very worlds – we use all sorts of 'rules' to do so. These rules are sometimes explicit or formal, as when someone driving a car follows traffic rules and stops at a red light. More often than not, however, the 'rules' we draw from to do the myriad things we do in social life derive from *common sense* – the 'taken-for-granted' knowledge of a society. But the crucial point for Giddens, as we will see, is that whilst social action is rule-governed it is not preset by such rules. There are many ways of following and applying rules to social situations – many of which are appropriate, some less so. When Giddens talks of social practices as 'rule-governed,' then, he means to emphasize the creativity of human action – the capacity of actors to apply rules in transformative, perhaps even novel, ways. Rules at once serve to shape social doing and action and also contain the possibility of acting otherwise.

Action, according to Giddens, cannot be adequately sociologically understood by looking at the discrete 'acts' of individuals. Rather than dissolve action into individual particles – intentions, motivations, reasons – Giddens contends that human action is a *continuous flow*. Whereas acts are discrete segments of individual doing, action refers to the ongoing flow of social practices, as people monitor or reflect on the social world of which they are part. On a general plane, Giddens advances a 'stratification model' of the human subject comprising three levels of knowledge or motivation: *discursive consciousness, practical consciousness* and the *unconscious*. He explains this stratification model of agency in *The Constitution of Society* as follows:

> Human agents or actors – I use these terms interchangeably – have, as an inherent aspect of what they do, the capacity to understand what they do while they do it. The reflexive capacities of the human actor are characteristically involved in a continuous manner with the flow of day-to-day conduct in the contexts of social activity. But reflexivity operates only partly on a discursive level. What agents know about what they do, and why they do it – their knowledgeability *as* agents – is largely carried in practical consciousness. Practical consciousness consists of all the things which actors know tacitly about how to 'go on' in the contexts of social life without being able to give them direct discursive expression. The significance of practical consciousness is a leading theme of the book, and it has to be distinguished from both consciousness (discursive consciousness) and the unconscious.
>
> (1984: xxii–xxiii)

Discursive consciousness thus refers to what agents are able to say, both to themselves and to others, about their own action; as Giddens repeatedly emphasizes, agents are knowledgeable about what they are doing, and this awareness often has a highly discursive component. *Practical consciousness* also refers to what actors know about their own actions, beliefs and motivations, but it is practical in the sense that it cannot be expressed discursively; what cannot be put into words, Giddens says following Wittgenstein, is what has to be done. Human beings know about their activities and the world in a sense that cannot be readily articulated; such practical stocks of knowledge are central, according to Giddens, to the project of social scientific research. Finally, the *unconscious*, says Giddens, is also a crucial feature of human motivation, and is differentiated from discursive and practical consciousness by the barrier of repression.

Giddens, as I've mentioned, repeatedly emphasizes 'what people know' is important – both to social action itself and to social analysis. This underscoring of individuals as knowledgeable agents refers, in the broadest sense, to the capacity of people to explain – both to themselves and to others – why they act as they do. Discursive consciousness is the ability of people to *put things into words* – articulation of the reasons for social action. But Giddens also recognizes the limits of language: *talk* takes us so far, but it is not all. Much of what people know about the social world, and of their reasons for acting in the ways that they do, cannot be articulated. To refer to some part of our human capacities as 'preconscious' or 'practical consciousness' is simply to say there are some things we cannot put into words. Much of human conduct, in other words, is practically guided or steered.

Practical social life, especially the rules we follow (whether we know it or not) as we go about our everyday activities, might thus be recast as the terrain of *mysterious accomplishments*. Consider, for example, the morning routine of which I wrote at the beginning of this chapter. Accessing email in the morning seems a relatively straightforward affair, provided all is fine with my computer. But, if asked to recite the technical specifications of the computer to explain how I am able to retrieve email from the network, I would very quickly exhaust my working knowledge of the topic. That is to say, I can operate the computer program to a certain level of skilled accomplishment, but have next to no idea of how to explain the technical aspects of electronic communication. The same holds true, for that matter, of language – in this case, the talk I engage in with my children and wife as we conduct our morning routine. Whilst we are engaged easily in talking, I would still be hard pressed to explain the finer rules of grammar which govern our linguistic exchanges in the morning. Of course, if I were a professional linguist and not a sociologist, I would presumably be able to detail more about the grammatical rules governing our conversation. But even then that is a matter of degree and not kind, and the point is that our conscious understandings of the world around us continually fluctuate between discursive articulations and practical accomplishments.

Structure . . . refers, in social analysis, to the structuring properties allowing the 'binding' of time-space in social systems, the properties which make it possible for discernibly similar social practices to exist across varying spans of time and space and which lend them 'systemic' form. To say that structure is a 'virtual order' of transformative

But what of social structure? What of social power, political authority, common culture? The first thing to emphasize about Giddens's social theory, in this respect, is that 'social structure' is not something that exists externally. Society is certainly 'structured' or 'textured' for Giddens, but not as a result of the intrusion of 'out there' social forces such as capitalism or bureaucracy into the inner realms of our lives. Rejecting the sharp division between the individual and society in social theory, Giddens instead argues that social structure, or 'society,' is a constant product of our social activities – of our talk, our practices, our doings. Such a conception of social structure contrasts powerfully with more mainstream sociological accounts. Sociologists have tended to conceptualize structure in terms of institutional constraint, often in a quasi-hydraulical or mechanical fashion, such that structure is likened to the biological workings of the body or the girders of a building. Giddens strongly rejects functionalist, biological and empiricist analyses of structure. Following the 'linguistic turn' in twentieth century social theory, Giddens critically draws upon structuralist and post-structuralist theory, specifically the relationship posited between language and speech in linguistics. He does this, not because society is structured like a language (as structuralists have argued), but because he believes that language can be taken as exemplifying core aspects of social life. Language, according to Giddens, has a virtual existence; it 'exists' outside of time and space, and is only present in its instantiations as speech or writing. By contrast, speech presupposes a subject and exists in time/space intersections. In Giddens's reading of structural linguistics, the subject draws from the rules of language in order to produce a phrase or sentence, and in so doing contributes to the reproduction of that language as a whole. Giddens draws extensively from such a conception of the structures of language in order to account for structures of action. His theorem is that agents draw from structures in order to perform and carry out social interactions, and in so doing contribute to the reproduction of institutions and structures. This analysis leads to a very specific conception of structure and social systems. 'Structure,' writes Giddens (1984: 26), 'has no existence independent of the knowledge that agents have about what they do in their day-to-day activity.'

Giddens's theoretical approach emphasizes that structures should be conceptualized as 'rules and resources': the application of rules which comprise structure may be regarded as generating differential access to social, economic, cultural and political resources. In *The Constitution of Society* Giddens argues that the sense of 'rule' most relevant to understanding social life is that which pertains to a mathematical formulae – for instance, if the sequence is 2,4,6,8, the formula is $x = n+2$. Understanding a formula, says Giddens, enables an agent to carry on in social life in a routine manner, to apply the rule in a range of different contexts. The same is true of bureaucratic rules, traffic rules, rules of football, rules of grammar, rules of social etiquette: to know a rule does not necessarily mean that one is able to explicitly formulate the principle, but it does mean that one can use the rule 'to go on' in social life. 'The rules and resources of social action,' writes Giddens, 'are at the same time the means of systems reproduction' (1984: 19). Systems reproduction, as Giddens conceives it, is complex and contradictory, involving structures, systems, and institutions. Social systems, for Giddens, are not equivalent with structures. Social systems are regularized patterns of interaction; such systems are in turn structured by rules and resources. Institutions are understood by Giddens as involving different modalities in and through which structuration occurs. Political institutions, for example, involve the generation of commands over people in relation to issues of authorization, signification, and legitimation; economic institutions, by contrast, involve the allocation of resources through processes of signification and legitimation.

Routines and rules are different to be sure. But for Giddens they both enable and guide the practical conduct of social life. Social rules and routines, amazingly, are learned and nurtured by us in a largely semi-conscious way. We know how to apply countless rules to the conduct of our social life – we know 'how to go on,' as Giddens says – even though we may not be able to explicitly formulate those rules. Taking my kids to school, for instance, involves me in all sorts of conversational exchanges with other parents. For the most part, these exchanges are of a routine nature – mostly involving talk about our respective kids, organizing play-dates and such like. Following the school run, I then drive to university to give some lectures or seminars in my area of expertise – social theory. What is curious, when viewing this routine through the lens of Giddens's structuration theory, is that things work well enough when I apply the 'rules' of social interaction – not that I am often aware of doing so – to these practical situations. Parents talk to me at school about matters to do with my children; students talk to me at university about matters to do with social theory. But try imagining what might happen if I got mixed up in this routine, and applied the wrong rules. Talking about the social theory of 'structuration' itself in the school grounds is something unlikely to win me many friends, and certainly not the approval of my children. If I were to keep talking the abstract language of social theory in the school grounds, as opposed to the university classroom, it is likely something that would have the school headmaster contact the local authorities and report me as a nuisance. Fortunately, social rules are usually applied to the appropriate social situation. Rules, remember, form part of our practical consciousness – and that for Giddens involves knowing 'how to go on,' how to apply the right rules to particular social contexts.

The constitution of agents and structures are not two independently given sets of phenomena, a dualism, but represent a duality. According to the notion of the duality of structure, the structural properties of social systems are both medium and outcome of the practices they recursively organize. Structure is not 'external' to individuals: as memory traces, and as instantiated in social practices, it is in a certain sense more 'internal' than exterior to their activities in a Durkheimian sense. Structure is not to be equated with constraint but is always both constraining and enabling. This, of course, does not prevent the structured properties of social systems from stretching away, in time and space, beyond the control of any individual actors.

Anthony Giddens (1984) *The Constitution of Society*. Cambridge: Polity Press, page 25.

Giddens's structuration theory, which powerfully distinguishes practical from discursive consciousness, thus yokes a sociological appreciation of the generative power of structures (albeit, 'virtual') to a phenomenological conception of common-sense, taken-for-granted knowledge. When we talk about, or act on, the world, we do so by mixing together rational accounts of our actions (the discursive) and a general awareness of taken-for-granted knowledge without being aware of it at any particular moment (the practical). From this angle, practical consciousness is the capability of actors to use a range of rules and methods that are taken for granted – which means, roughly, that in our heads we are not usually conscious of them. We speak language to varying levels of grammatical proficiency, and yet for the most part are unable to detail the grammatical rules we use. Many of the practical codes governing daily life operate in a similar manner. Men may, depending on when and where they were brought up, accord priority to women in entering and exiting social gatherings – without knowing exactly why.

Another way of putting this point is to say that social theory trades equally with that which we know on the one hand, and that which we intuitively grasp (but cannot explicitly formulate) on the other. However, there are other, subterranean forces at work within people's lives – although these are not readily accessible within the language of sociology. To that end, Giddens turns to psychoanalysis in order to account for more primitive elements of human agency. Drawing from a range of psychoanalytic perspectives, and most notably from Lacan's Freud in some of his earlier writings, Giddens argues that there are some things of which we will never know – due primarily to the 'barrier of repression' which is imprinted upon the unconscious mind during childhood. This is an important insight into the emotional dimensions of our lives as human agents acting in the world, although it is not one that Giddens focuses upon in any particular detail. Rather than thinking through the repressed unconscious for an account of human action, Giddens for the most part limits the disruptive force of the unconscious to that which erupts only at crisis moments. Except for the 'critical moments' of social upheaval or political crisis, Giddens contends that unconscious anxiety is – by and large – held in check by our habitual routines. The routine, he says, brings emotional security. From this angle, he draws especially from psychoanalyst Erik Erikson's account of 'ego-identity' to understand how early childhood routines help to establish a sense of emotional security and faith in the durability of the social world.

In the last few paragraphs I have noted how Giddens approaches issues of human action, agency and subjectivity. It is important to link these more subjective aspects of his social theory back to issues of social practices and structures in order to grasp his emphasis upon duality in structuration theory. Agents, according to Giddens, draw on the rules and resources of structures, and in so doing contribute to the systemic reproduction of institutions, systems, and structures. In studying social life, says Giddens, it is important to recognize the role of 'methodological bracketing.' Giddens argues that the social sciences simultaneously pursue *institutional analysis*, in which the structural features of society are analyzed, and the *analysis of strategic conduct*, in which the manner in which actors carry on social interaction is studied. These different levels of analysis are central to social scientific research, and both are crucial to structuration theory. Connected to this, Giddens argues that the subjects of study of the social sciences are concept-using agents, individuals whose concepts enter into the manner in which their actions are constituted. He calls this intersection of the social world as constituted by lay actors on the one hand, and the metalanguages created by social scientists on the other, the 'double hermeneutic.'

Giddens on modernity and the self

None of the outline of structuration theory so far casts specific light on the sociological issue of what may be distinctively *new* to our own age of, amongst others, intensive globalization, hi-tech finance and new information technologies. It was not until the early 1990s that Giddens turned his sociological attention to consider this acceleration of social change, most notably in his books *The Consequences of Modernity* (1990) and *Modernity and Self-Identity* (1991). Here Giddens set out a powerful account of the tensions and contradictions of contemporary societies – ranging from current anxieties affecting identity and intimacy to high-intensity global risks, such as nuclear war. His basic thesis is that modernity heralds dramatic social transformations – the kind which social theory today stands unable to adequately confront. Rejecting Marx's equation of modernity with corrosive capitalism, and wary of Weber's portrait of the modern age as a bureaucratic iron cage, Giddens instead presents an image of modernity as *juggernaut*. Giddens's juggernaut is a world certainly beyond control, but one which nonetheless offers immense personal opportunities and political possibilities, even though its menacing dark side – the high-consequence risks of ecological catastrophe, political totalitarianism or nuclear destruction – threatens to bring all this undone. He argues that our experience of the modern world is one always divided – split between security and risk, intimacy and impersonality, reassuring expert knowledge and disorientating cultural relativism. As with the stress on the open-ended nature of social relations in his earlier work, Giddens sees modernity as unpredictable. 'To live in the "world" produced by high modernity,' writes Giddens (1991: 28), 'has the feeling of riding a juggernaut. It is not just that more or less continuous and profound processes of change occur; rather, change does not consistently conform either to human expectation or to human control.'

A fundamental feature of modernity for Giddens is the *reflexivity of social life*. Reflexivity, as we have seen, is regarded by Giddens as an essential aspect of all human activity. How people think about, monitor and reflect on what they do, according to Giddens, is crucial to how society constitutes itself. In our own age, however, there is a radical intensification of reflexivity, such that self-monitoring and social relations become increasingly interwoven. Giddens (1990: 38) defines this intensification thus: 'The reflexivity of modern social life consists in the fact that social practices are constantly examined and reformed in the light of incoming information about those very practices, thus constitutively altering their character'. In current times, we can see a clear acceleration in processes of social reflexivity. This is obvious, for example, in the expansion of communications media and new information technologies. Recent changes in mass media and information technology have arguably made the globe more *interconnected* than was previously the case, and this, in turn, has led to increasing reflexivity of social things happening across the world. What happens on one side of the planet can now be relayed worldwide virtually instantly thanks to advances in media technology. In this sense, our 'social eyes' have dramatically expanded. And as our 'social eyes' take in these distant happenings, so we come to incorporate such knowledge into how we talk about, and act upon, our more local worlds.

Consider, for example, what we know of the changing social landscape of marriage and divorce. Ours is a high divorce and remarriage society. Divorce statistics in the UK and across Europe indicate that over a third of marriages entered into today will end in divorce; in some states of the United States, the figures rise as high as fifty percent or more. Giddens's thesis of accelerated social reflexivity emphasizes that such statistics are not merely incidental to marriage today, but influence and reshape people's understandings of what marriage actually is. When a couple walks down the aisle in these early days of the 2000s, they do so 'knowing' (in a blend of the discursive and practical) the general chances for marriage longevity. The shift from marriage till-death-do-us-part to marriage until-further-notice is, from the vantage point of Giddens's theory of modernity, the result of people reflecting on the changing cultural norms governing identity, intimacy, marriage and divorce.

Reflexivity for Giddens means a world of self-monitoring – of our own lives, the lives of others (both proximate and distant), and wider social happenings. Reflexivity here doesn't equate with reflective control or predictability, since much of what unfolds in daily life involves reflex-like actions and knee-jerk responses. Nor is it accurate to view reflexivity as merely personal. Whilst reflexivity goes to the heart of how we perform the most basic tasks of our personal routines (such as catching a train or emailing a friend), it also is deeply inscribed in social processes and organizations in the broadest sense. Microsoft, British Petroleum and Calvin Klein are all companies with global reach, but the point is that these organizations could not operate in the global economy if not organizationally structured in reasonably reflexive ways. For this reason, Giddens distinguishes between *individual reflexivity* and *institutional reflexivity*. If the former is to do with self-monitoring and the ongoing observation and retracing of personal life, the latter is to do organizational tracking, administrative surveillance as well as broader economic and market forces. His emphasis on institutional reflexivity connects closely with science and expert knowledge too. In a world of dramatic scientific advances, for instance, there is – as a result of intensive reflexivity – a rise in the questioning of science. Paths of action and scenarios of choice are undertaken against a reflexive backdrop of a variety of other ways of doing things. Giddens offers the following overview, for example, in relation to global warming:

> Many experts consider that global warming is occurring and they may be right. The hypothesis is disputed by some, however, and it has even been suggested that the real trend, if there is one at all, is in the opposite direction, towards the cooling of the global climate. Probably the most that can be said with some surety is that we cannot be certain that global warming is *not* occurring. Yet such a conditional conclusion will yield not a precise calculation of risks but rather an array of 'scenarios' – whose plausibility will be influenced, among other things, by how many people become convinced of the thesis of global warming and take action on that basis. In the social world, where institutional reflexivity has become a central constituent, the complexity of 'scenarios' is even more marked.
>
> (1994: 59)

Written in 1994, this overview of scientific and lay opinion on global warming already looks quaint. However Giddens's reasoning remains convincing: it is because so many people across the planet have become deeply concerned about the potential risks of climate change, and have pressed their governments to take important policy initiatives in this respect, that global warming has become the debate of our times. Giddens's argument – that the complexity of 'scenarios' is central to our reflexive engagement with the wider world – speaks directly to the global pathways we face in the early twenty-first century.

The experiential character of contemporary daily life is well grasped by two of Giddens's key concepts: *trust and risk* as interwoven with *abstract systems*. For Giddens, the relation between individual subjectivity and social contexts of action is a highly mobile one; and it is something that we make sense of and utilize through 'abstract systems'. Abstract systems are institutional domains of technical and social knowledge: they include systems of expertise of all kinds, from local forms of knowledge to science, technology and mass communications. Giddens is underscoring much more than simply the impact of expertise on people's lives, far-reaching though that is. Rather, Giddens extends the notion of expertise to cover 'trust relations' – the personal and collective investment of active trust in social life. The psychological investment of trust contributes to the power of specialized, expert knowledge – indeed it lies at the bedrock of our Age of Experts – and also plays a key role in the forging of a sense of security in day-to-day social life. Trust and security are thus both a condition and an outcome of social reflexivity. Giddens sees the reflexive appropriation of expert knowledge as fundamental in a globalizing, culturally cosmopolitan society. While a key aim may be the regularization of stability and order in our identities and in society, reflexive modernity is radically experimental however, and is constantly producing new types of incalculable risk and insecurity. This means that, whether we like it or not, we must recognize the ambivalence of a social universe of expanded reflexivity: there are no preordained, or even clear, pathways for individual or social development today.

In *The Transformation of Intimacy* (1992), Giddens connects the notion of reflexivity to sexuality, gender, and intimate relationships. With modernization and the decline of tradition, says Giddens, the sexual life of the human subject becomes a 'project' that has to be managed and defined against the backdrop of new opportunities and risks – including, for example, artificial insemination, experiments in ectogenesis (the creation of human life without pregnancy), AIDS, sexual harassment, and the like. Linking gender to new technologies, Giddens argues we live in an era of 'plastic sexuality.' 'Plastic sexuality' (1992: 2), writes Giddens, 'is decentered sexuality, freed from the needs of reproduction . . . and from the rule of the phallus, from the overweening importance of male sexual experience.' Sexuality thus becomes open-ended, elaborated not through pre-given roles, but through reflexively forged relationships. The self today, as the rise of therapy testifies, is faced with profound dilemmas in respect of sexuality. 'Who am I?,' 'What do I desire?,' 'What satisfactions do I want from sexual relations?' – these are core issues for the self, according to Giddens. This does not mean that sexual experience occurs without institutional constraint, however. Giddens contends that the development of modern institutions produces a 'sequestration of experience' – sexual, existential and moral – which squeezes to the sidelines core problems relating to sexuality, intimacy, mortality and death (see Elliott 1992).

Giddens, in other words, adopts an idealist language of autonomy, stressing as he does the creativity of action and the modernist drive to absolute self-realization, while remaining suspicious of intellectual traditions that prioritize subjects over objects, or actors over structures. This comes out very clearly in his work on the changing connections between marriage, the family and self-identity. According to Giddens, individuals today actively engage with novel opportunities and dangers that arise as a consequence of dramatic transformations affecting self-identity, sexuality and intimacy. For Giddens, divorce is undeniably a personal crisis, involving significant pain, loss and grief. Yet many people, he argues, take positive steps to work through the emotional dilemmas generated by marriage breakdown. In addition to dealing with financial issues and matters affecting how children should be brought up, separation and divorce also call into play a reflexive emotional engagement with the self. Charting

theories of structuration

territory from the past (where things went wrong, missed opportunities, etc.) and for the future (alternative possibilities, chances for self-actualization, etc.) necessarily involves experimenting with a new sense of self. This can lead to emotional growth, new understandings of self, and strengthened intimacies. Against the conservative critique of marriage breakdown, Giddens sees the self opening out to constructive renewal. Remarriage and the changing nature of family life are crucial in this respect. As he develops this point:

> Many people, adults and children, now live in stepfamilies – not usually, as in previous eras, as a consequence of the death of a spouse, but because of the re-forming of marriage ties after divorce. A child in a stepfamily may have two mothers and fathers, two sets of brothers and sisters, together with other complex kin connections resulting from the multiple marriages of parents. Even the terminology is difficult: should a stepmother be called 'mother' by the child, or called by her name? Negotiating such problems might be arduous and psychologically costly for all parties; yet opportunities for novel kinds of fulfilling social relations plainly also exist. One thing we can be sure of is that the changes involved here are not just external to the individual. These new forms of extended family ties have to be established by the very persons who find themselves most directly caught up in them.
>
> (1991: 13)

Marital separation, as portrayed by Giddens, implicates the self in an open project: tracing over the past, imagining the future, dealing with complex family problems and experimenting with a new sense of identity. Further experimentation with marriage and intimate relationships will necessarily involve anxieties, risks and opportunities. But, as Giddens emphasizes, the relation between self and society is a highly fluid one, involving negotiation, change and development.

The manner in which current social practices shape future life outcomes is nowhere more in evidence than in the conjunction of divorce statistics, the reckoning of probability ratios for success or failure in intimate relationships, and the decision to get married. As Giddens rightly points out, statistics about marriage and divorce do not exist in a social vacuum; everyone, he says, is in some sense aware of how present gender uncertainties affect long-term relationships. When people marry or remarry today, according to Giddens, they do so against a societal backdrop of high divorce statistics, knowledge of which alters a person's understanding and conception of what marriage actually is. It is precisely this reflexive monitoring of relationships that, in turn, transforms expectations about, and aspirations for, marriage and intimacy. The relationship between self, society and reflexivity is thus a highly dynamic one, involving the continual overturning of traditional ways of doing things.

Criticisms of Giddens

Giddens's work is a brilliant conjuncture of social theory and modern sociology, involving a provocative account which examines the very constitution of society through recurrent social practices. It is not, however, without its difficulties. For one thing, some critics think Giddens gravely mistaken in his project to overcome the individual/society opposition. Sociologist Margaret Archer (1982, 1990) argues that not only is Giddens wrong to amalgamate agency with structure, but that he fails to grasp the necessity of treating structure and agency as analytically distinct in order to deal with both methodological and substantive problems in the social sciences. At the core of Archer's critique there lies anxiety about Giddens's strong argument that structures only exist in and through the social practices of human agents. If any society were to eliminate time in the manner that Giddens's model of virtual structures actually does, according to Archer, then it would be radically impoverished in terms of its understanding of history. That is to say, structures need to be identified historically, across time, in order for sociologists to analyze how agents have acted to both reproduce and change the structures of social life. A similar point has been made by Nicos Mouzelis (1989), who questions the applicability of structuration theory to collective actors such as social movements. According to Mouzelis, Giddens's notion of structuration is more or less appropriate to our immediate, routine lives – where agents carry out their actions without undue levels of reflection. But the model is less well suited, he argues, to situations where actors consciously and conceptually reflect on the power of structures in shaping the world. Where workers take a principled stand against unfair working conditions, or where women collectively act against entrenched forms of gender discrimination, these are situations that demand taking a highly reflective attitude to the world. They are situations, according to Mouzelis, that involve separating agency from structure – in order for actors to understand the power of structures in their lives and, subsequently, to try to change such determination. The contestation of economic or gender power, on this view, is not something that can be left to the routine actions of reflexive individuals.

Perhaps the most critical voice among commentators on Giddens has been John B. Thompson, who worked very closely with Giddens during the 1980s and 1990s at Cambridge University. Thompson clearly admires the scope and ambition of Giddens's social theory, but questions the adequacy of his notion of rules and resources for grasping social structure.

According to Thompson, Giddens's account of rules and resources is vague and misleading. The study of the rules used to speak a language, he points out, are not the same thing as the study of social structure. Linguistic and grammatical rules, says Thompson, are important forms of constraint upon human action; however, they are not the only forms of constraint in social life. Taxation laws requiring that I pay a portion of my income to the government each year are clearly more socially important than my own imposed rule that I try to exercise three times a week. Yet to grasp that importance requires some concept of social structure. Social structures are, thus, very much about the practical ways in which individuals come to reproduce, challenge, question and transform the realities of the world. In this connection, Thompson questions Giddens's account of the transformational properties of structures, and suggests there is inadequate differentiation between the structural and institutional features of social life in his approach. A worker at the Ford Motor Company, notes Thompson, might be said to contribute to the reproduction of that institution, and thus also said to contribute to the reproduction of capitalism as a structure, to the extent that the worker pursues their everyday employment activities. However it is also possible that the worker along with others might undertake activities that threaten the smooth running of Ford as an institution, but without similarly threatening to bring capitalism down.

> Every act of production and reproduction may also be a potential act of transformation, as Giddens rightly insists; but the extent to which an action transforms an institution does not coincide with the extent to which social structure is thereby transformed.
>
> (1989: 70)

Giddens is a social theorist who has done perhaps more than anyone to draw our attention to the virtual feel of structures in everyday life. Yet even in his scrupulous attention to the power of invisible structures, he always reminds us of the activities of individuals. Let us recall his formulation of structuration theory: *structures only exist in and through the social practices of human agents*. If there has been criticism of Giddens's reformulation of the concept of structure in social theory, however, there has equally been disagreement with his account of the individual or identity. The routine nature of our daily lives is a powerful sociological idea that helps account for the astonishing fact that, despite the immense complexity of social organization, there is a kind of order or regularity to the world. This may seem to be only a surface phenomenon. For whilst most of us know 'how to go on' in social situations, the actual detail of what goes on in social life is complex and contradictory. Many people are able to 'give off' the impression of things running smoothly, whilst in fact they may feel their lives to be running out of control. But even so, such personal confusion does not seem to be problematic to Giddens's social theory – at least as long as the individual is able to maintain 'role-taking' in social interaction and carry on 'business-as-usual' with the micro-situations of daily life. Certainly, Giddens makes it clear that he regards routines as essential to *both* the production of identity and society. 'Routine,' writes Giddens (1984: 60), 'is integral both to the continuity of the personality of the agent, as he or she moves along the paths of daily activities, and to the institutions of society, which *are* such only through their continued reproduction.' This is not an expression of sociological determinism (in the sense that identity is pre-programmed) or political conservatism: there is no logical reason why social reproduction demands an acceptance of *particular* habitual practices. Moreover, Giddens's more recent political writings advancing a 'third way' for social democracy plainly indicate his discontent with neo-liberalism and neo-conservativism. Rather, Giddens's stress on routinization suggests that existing, alternative and oppositional forms of life demand some sort of motivational commitment to the integration of habitual practices across space and time.

And yet it is precisely here that Giddens pushes the routinized nature of social life to breaking point – or so argue some critics. If the structured nature of social interaction is the ability of individuals to do what they do in a routine fashion, then what is it exactly that provides the sense of organizing consistency to such routines? How do the organized routines of daily life come into existence – from the imagination of individuals, or the complex social things of society? Suddenly, the duality proposed by structuration theory returns us to a familiar sociological opposition. But still there are other concerns. There is the question, for example, of how far down routines really go in private life – of whether they actually create identity through providing social consistency from situation to situation, or whether they instead provide a social framework for an already established emotional complexity of the self. And if routines are, in some sense, tied up with the making of identity, how might we come to understand the structured realities of individuals living their routine lives? What, in other words, makes for the social differences between routines in, say, China and North America? How might the notion of routine apply to the Third World? Is the term, as Giddens uses it, a sociologically neutral account of social interaction, or a normative image of Western living?

Finally, we may note that this account of the relation between society and the individual, for all its claims of transcending the dualism of subject and object, betrays a sociologically impoverished grasp of the emotional lives of people. At the center of this criticism is Giddens's use of psychoanalysis. We have seen earlier that Giddens draws on Freud's account of the unconscious to supplement his notion of practical consciousness: like practical consciousness, the unconscious is a sector of human experience that is non-discursive; unlike practical consciousness, there is much in the unconscious that cannot be brought into language due to the barrier of repression established in early infancy. The effects of the repressed unconscious, to be sure, are disabling at moments of societal stress or crisis; but there is for Giddens a certain kind of stability to the unconscious, which is regulated by the force of daily habits and routines. Predictable routines, says Giddens, keep the unconscious at bay. It is worth pausing to ask of this standpoint, however, whether the unconscious is really 'bracketed' by routines? What of the narcissistic routines promoted by consumer capitalism, in which individuals are encouraged to obsess about their bodies, or constantly measure their physical appearance against the standards of celebrity culture? Is it meaningful to speak of a routine limiting of the unconscious within these parameters of popular culture? Similarly, some critics think that Giddens closes off the radical implications of psychoanalysis for social theory through the bulk of vocabulary of self-organization – 'bracketing anxiety,' 'ontological security,' and 'emotional inoculation.' All of these terms seem to suggest an individual serenely inserted into the social order; but this is a far cry from the split and fractured individual subject of psychoanalysis.

Pierre Bourdieu: *habitus* and practical social life

Giddens's theory of structuration operates on a reasonably grand scale, revolving on such general sociological concepts as system, structure and subject, whereas the French social theorist Pierre Bourdieu is more concerned to analyze the surreptitious forms by which power inculcates itself within our personal and bodily dispositions as expressed in daily life. Like Giddens, Bourdieu is interested in the habits of whole societies – so much so that he has invented a sociological concept, *habitus*, to account for how well-practiced habits bridge individuals and the wider social things of which they are part. Also like Giddens he holds that social actors exhibit intricate complex understandings of the social conditions which influence, and are in turn influenced by, their personal decisions and private lives. It may be hard to judge the exact differences between Bourdieu and Giddens on this point – for both of them are at pains to emphasize the semi-conscious reflexiveness of social actors. Bordieu's formulation is that actors possess a 'sense of the game,' which is the basis from which people deploy a kind of semi-automatic grasp of what is appropriate to differing social situations. Where Bourdieu and Giddens certainly depart company however, and this is a point that will be examined subsequently in the chapter, concerns the extent to which power goes all the way down – for

Bourdieu, to the inculcation of bodily dispositions as well as the dramatization of personal style.

Studying how society generates particular practices in individuals is Bourdieu's way of rethinking the relation between identity and social structure in social theory. Like Giddens's blending of social structure and human action, Bourdieu wants to develop a sophisticated social theory that will neither reduce actors to mere 'supports' of social processes nor elevate them to the source of all social things. In this connection, he was attempting to steer a new direction in French intellectual culture in the early part of his career, one beyond the liberationist existentialism of philosopher Jean-Paul Sartre (arguably France's most famous public intellectual at the time) and also the equally problematic structuralism of Lévi-Strauss, Barthes and Foucault (see Chapter 5). His ambition, simply put, was the puzzle of how seemingly spontaneous individual action comes to dovetail with society's expectation that people perform appropriate practices in specific situations.

To address this puzzle, Bourdieu outlines in *Outline of a Theory of Practice* (1977) his concept of *habitus*, by which he means the molding of a set of individual dispositions interlocking with the specific cultural characteristics of the society concerned. Here is how Bourdieu develops, in his typically dense style, the concept of *habitus*:

> The structures constitutive of a particular type of environment ... produce the *habitus*, systems of durable, transposable dispositions, structured structures predisposed to function as structuring structures, that is, as principles of the generation and structuration of practices and representations which can be objectively 'regulated' and 'regular' without in any way being the product of obedience to rules, objectively adapted to their goal without presupposing the conscious orientation towards ends and the express mastery of the operations necessary to attain them and, being all that, collectively orchestrated without being the product of the organizing action of a conductor.
>
> (1977: 72)

It is because individuals inculcate particular cultural dispositions that their actions are, by and large, carried out in a fashion that appears spontaneous yet structured, unregulated yet regular. You decide you want to travel somewhere new in town, but then find yourself queueing at the railway station; you decide to express the 'inner self' by painting, but first you need to visit the local arts store to stock up on paints and brushes. It is as if the very 'spontaneity' of our daily behavior is always overwritten, as it were, with some kind of social unconscious which serves to harmonize our practices with those deeply tacit norms and values of the wider society. This is not to suggest, Bourdieu stresses, that social structures actually *determine* individual action. On the contrary, *habitus* is a flexible, open-ended structuring system, one which enables social actors to have numerous creative strategies at their disposal and thus to cope with unforeseen social structures.

As an acquired system of generative schemes, the *habitus* makes possible the free production of all the thoughts, perceptions and actions inherent in the particular conditions of its production – and only those . . . . Because the *habitus* is an infinite capacity for generating products – thoughts, perceptions, expressions and actions – whose limits are set by the historically and socially situated conditions of its production, the conditioned and conditional freedom it provides is as remote from creation of unpredictable novelty as it is from simple mechanical reproduction of the original conditionings.

Pierre Bourdieu (1990) *The Logic of Practice*. Stanford (CA): Stanford University Press, page 55.

Bourdieu developed his concept of *habitus* from his anthropological studies of the Kabyle tribespeople and, in particular, from close sociological analysis of gift exchanges in Kabyle society. Bourdieu considers that structuralism is correct in its initial diagnosis that society possesses a reality that precedes the individual. This is the point, for example, that language pre-exists us as speaking agents, and will subsequently continue as a social institution long after we have left the planet. If this is so, Bourdieu supposes, then structuralism is right to claim that language has the power to regulate, even shape, our individual speech-acts – whether we realize it or not. But where structuralism is palpably insufficient, according to Bourdieu, lies in its reduction of social action to a mechanical system of rules which imposes itself upon individuals. Studying the intricacies of gift exchange in Kabyle society, Bourdieu finds that men's sense of honor is facilitated less by an application of pre-established rules than by carrying out a whole range of practices – such as 'playing with the tempo' of response and acknowledgment of a gift. An actor's response to the receipt of a gift is not therefore socially determined by the application of mechanical rules, and nor is it a matter of mere private judgment. It rather involves the creative artistry of the recipient, experimenting within a fluid structuring structure, one marked by group norms of acceptable practice, obligation, reciprocity and honor.

Habitus, in the sense of deeply ingrained dispositions, is a structuring feature of social practices, but it is more than just that. If our practical, or habitual, behaviors have a degree of consistency to them, this is because our bodies are literally molded into certain forms that interlock with existing social arrangements. One way of thinking about how *habitus* reaches all the way down into bodily needs and dispositions is to consider the process that sociologists call 'socialization.' The notion of socialization refers, broadly speaking, to the training or regulation of children within the structure of bigger social things. The learning of good manners at home, or respect for figures of authority at school, are examples of the socialization process. Bourdieu's account of how *habitus* penetrates the body – what he calls the 'corporeal hexis' – is similar to the idea of socialization, but is much broader in scope. Socialization conveys too much the sense of active or conscious learning, and this is not how Bourdieu thinks we come to act in the world. Instead, he is interested in getting at the subtle ways in which messages are relayed to people over time, such that cultural norms become routine patterns of behavior and, thus, withdrawn from consciousness. The parent who routinely tells their son or daughter to 'sit up straight' at dinner, or who instructs to 'always say thank you' when offered food at the home of a fellow class-mate, is thus going about the business of reproducing the *habitus* of modern society. This is the sense, too, in which *habitus* bites deeply into the very bodies of individuals – structuring the ways in which people come to talk, walk, act and eat. *Habitus*, thus, is deeply interwoven with the stylization of bodies.

What has been discussed so far about social practices and bodies is central to the analysis of human action, and yet it hardly needs saying that – for regular social life to get up and running – such practices must be anchored in wider institutional contexts. Bourdieu seeks to do this by introducing the notion of 'field,' by which he means the structured space of positions in which an individual is located. For Bourdieu, there are various kinds of fields – educational, economic, cultural – which contain different kinds of social properties and characteristics. A field, says Bourdieu, pre-exists the individual. It ascribes an objective place to individuals within the broader scheme of social things, and thereby serves as a relation of force between individuals and groups engaged in struggles within certain fields. As John Thompson explains this social reach of the field in Bourdieu's work:

> A field may be seen synchronically as a structured space of positions, such that the properties of these positions depend on their location within the space and not upon the personal attributes of their occupants. However different the fields may be – whether, for example, it is a pedagogical space in which teachers transmit a form of 'knowledge' or a cultural space in which literary works are offered for consumption – there are certain general laws which commonly obtain. Thus, in every field, one may struggle between the nouveaux entrants who try to jump over the rights of entry and to alter the structure in their favor, and

those established agents or groups who try to defend their monopoly and to exclude competition.

(1984: 49)

Questions of Taste: Bourdieu's *Distinction*

Cultural tastes and social preferences are *habitus*, in Bourdieu's terminology, but they are also an outwardly expression of power and social class. In *Distinction: A Social Critique of the Judgment of Taste* (1984), Bourdieu developed a brilliant analysis of the habits and tastes of French society – which he divided into the working class, the lower middle class and the upper middle class. His argument, broadly speaking, was that whilst economics is the baseline of social order, the struggle for social distinction is played out with other forms of capital too – notably, cultural capital and symbolic capital.

In Bourdieu's view, the struggle for capital is more a matter of practices than ideas, which in turn brings us to core distinctions between poverty and affluence in the realm of culture as well as lifestyle practices. As Bourdieu (1984: 77) writes:

> If a group's lifestyle can be read off from the style it adopts in furnishing or clothing, this is not only because these properties are the object of the economic and cultural necessity which determines their selection, but also because the social relations objectified in familiar objects in their luxury or poverty, their 'distinction' or vulgarity, their 'beauty' or their 'ugliness' impress themselves through bodily experiences which may be as profoundly unconscious as the quiet caress of beige carpets or the thin clamminess of tattered garish linoleum, the harsh smell of bleach.

Culture then is the sense of fine living, manners, refinement or an elegant ease of social interaction that lies at the center of how individuals demonstrate social sophistication. Such social sophistication requires certain economic capital – for example, expensive private schools. But social struggles for distinction have a cultural dimension too: cultivation of the self is also a matter of learning, aesthetics, the arts.

Bourdieu's concept of cultural capital directs our attention to the means whereby social inequalities are generated through the classifying power of taste as expressed in the consumption of culture. Bourdieu found that the possession of specific forms of cultural capital – of intellectuals and artists, for example – is used to maintain social dominance over those who do not possess such competences. This valuable sociological perspective can also be extended to the analysis of popular culture and the media. In 'reality television,' for example, new forms of symbolic violence are arguably evident as regards the public humiliation of people and their relegation to an inferior social standing within the social order. Analyzing the UK television program *What Not To Wear* (similar format to *How Do I Look?*), media theorist Angela McRobbie has used Bourdieu's notion of cultural capital to focus on practices of symbolic violence and forms of domination. As McRobbie (2005: 147–8) writes:

> Bourdieu's writing allows us to re-examine symbolic violence as a vehicle for social reproduction .... The victim of the make-over television programme presents his or her class *habitus* for analysis and critique by the experts. The programmes comprise a series of encounters where cultural intermediaries impart guidance and advice to individuals ostensibly as a means of self-improvement .... These programmes would not work if the victim did not come forward and offer herself as someone in need of expert help. On the basis of her own subordinate class *habitus*, the individual will have a 'feel for the game,' a 'practical sense for social reality' which means in the context of the programmes, she will instinctively, and unconsciously, know her place in regard to the experts, hence the tears, the gratitude and the deference to those who know so much better than she does.

Bourdieu's ideas help us understand why people adopt certain kinds of cultural practices, and how – through *habitus* adjustment to dominant social classes – conformity with the requirements of consumer culture are maintained.

Criticisms of Bourdieu

Appropriately enough for a social theorist whose writings are arrestingly original, Bourdieu's work has been subjected to many – and sometimes vehement – criticisms. Critics have questioned, for example, the adequacy of the concept of *habitus* to address the complexity of social experience. The criticism here is that *habitus* overemphasizes the *containment* of cultural dispositions within social structures – thereby downgrading the capacity of individuals to negotiate or transform existing social systems through their creative actions. There may be some truth to this charge, but the criticism needs more precision. Bourdieu's *habitus* emerged as a theoretical innovation in the aftermath of structuralism and post-structuralism; it fitted well enough with a political and intellectual climate in which dissent was still possible, but now conceptualized in a fashion that fully broke with individualistic ways of understanding the world. Society for Bourdieu was less the outcome of individual acts and choices than a structuring, structured field of dispositions in which individuals mobilize themselves and act to exclude others on the base of relevant cultural capital. The *habitus*, in other words, refers to an objectivity ('society') that inscribes itself within identity. There is something about social production which is both enabling and coercive. What is most dynamic about *habitus* for Bourdieu is its status as the condition of sociality: the *habitus* prescribes the kinds of agency demanded by culture. Yet whilst this viewpoint was in some general sense radical, it seemed on the whole to have little of interest to say about specific issues of identity (the concrete negotiations of the self in relation to social relations), even if Bourdieu had provided a whole range of sociological enquiries, from education to aesthetics. Part of the difficulty in this respect is that Bourdieu might be said not to have broken with struc-turalism thoroughly enough, in the sense that structures in his work continue to confer on us our agency – to such a degree that we misrecog-nize our fate as our choice. In doing so, Bourdieu's *habitus* neglects the creativity of action which individuals bring to all encounters with social and cultural processes – a matter of profound significance to the question of social change. Ultimately, as Charles Lemert (1995: 146) writes, '*habitus* cannot account for change in *habitus*.'

The debate over Bourdieu's contributions to social theory has also addressed many other issues. One central criticism concerns certain *assumptions about society* Bourdieu appears to make in his various socio-logical analyses. Some critics contend, for example, that he takes the economy for granted, leaving unanalyzed the role of economic forces upon social life. Whilst Bourdieu was widely seen as sympathetic to the political left, the politics of his social theory was somewhat oblique; he certainly distanced himself from Marx and Marxism. Against this backdrop, some have argued that he elevated cultural capital over economic capital, thus tending to skirt issues of economic oppression. A more interesting line of criticism, in my view, is that his account of symbolic violence assumes a certain kind of consensus with respect to the norms and values that are central in society. This is less a matter of assuming that people openly agree with one another about societal values than a presupposition that those who exercise cultural and symbolic capital are perceived by others as 'legitimate' bearers of social authority. That is to say, Bourdieu can be criti-cized for conceptualizing social practice in terms of how social stability is sustained. Such an approach allows him to develop powerful insights into how symbolic domination is wielded in contemporary societies, and yet these insights arguably come at the sociological cost of understanding how social structures – or ways of acting with cultural capital – can be changed. In short, *habitus* might not be so overwhelmingly rigid.

Finally, it is now widely agreed that Bourdieu's commitment to the political notion of resistance led him to overestimate the constraints of social domination operating within specific power structures of advanced capitalism on the one hand, whilst underestimating the degree to which the world really had changed as a result of the impacts of globalization on the other hand. Certainly, there can be little doubt that Bourdieu's attacks on globalization and the neo-liberalism promoted by various French conservative governments were provocative. Notwithstanding his commitment to stand shoulder to shoulder with struggling workers, immigrants and others dispossessed from the contemporary French political system, however, Bourdieu failed to develop an outline of what a progressive politics might actually look like in our own time of accelerated globalization. French social theory has often turned on a contrast between some utopian moment of resistance to power as such and the contaminated terrain of reformist social policy, and Bourdieu is no exception in this respect. However, his disquisitions on resistance in general – when coupled to the sociological diagnosis of people's cultural *habitus* – can easily be misinterpreted as a form of defeatist politics. Here comparison between Bourdieu and Giddens is, once again, instructive. Notwithstanding the various criticisms of Giddens's theory of a radical center or 'third way' in contemporary politics, Giddens's work powerfully acknowledges the extent to which the political landscape of modern societies has changed in recent decades – primarily as a result of globalization and the information technology revolution. Certainly Giddens's late political writings have significantly influenced the direction of various center-left governments – in Britain, Canada, Germany, Brazil, Mexico, Argentina and even France. Bourdieu's political tracts did not exert this kind of policy impact, and it is interesting to consider why this was the case. Whereas Bourdieu pitched his political critique at the level of blue skies resistance to power in general, Giddens's 'third way' constituted a new political path, one designed in response to the realities of the global electronic economy. A dynamic economy for Giddens is essential not only to the creation of wealth but for social solidarity and social justice too. Whereas Bourdieu tended to dismiss globalization processes as intrinsically anti-democratic, Giddens recognized that globalism is a much more complex political phenomenon – one that opens out to 'depoliticized global space' and is central to the economic and political problems of our time. By contrast, globalization for Bourdieu appears as a remorseless totalization, one to which the only political counterweight is 'anti-globalization.'

theories of structuration

Summary points

1 Structuration theories seek to comprehend how individual action is organized within the mundane activities of practical social life, while simultaneously recognizing that the structural features of society are reproduced through individual action.

2 In borrowing the term 'structuration' from the French, British social theorist Anthony Giddens argues that society should be understood as a complex of recurrent practices forming institutions. The focus of Giddens's work is not society as fixed or pre-given, but rather the active flow of social life.

3 Giddens insists that the dualism of agency and structure should instead be conceived as a *duality*. On this view, social systems are at once the *medium* and *outcome* of the practices they organize.

4 Critiquing structuralist and post-structuralist thought, Giddens argues that society is not 'structured like a language,' although language does exemplify core aspects of social life. According to Giddens, human agents draw from structured 'rules and resources' in order to carry out social interactions, which in turn contribute to the reproduction of society as a whole.

5 Structures for Giddens have no independent existence of the knowledge that agents have about what they do in social life. Social structures thus exist outside of time and space, and exhibit a 'virtual' existence.

6 In Giddens's late work on the 'runaway world' of modernity, reflexivity is key to the production of personal life and the complexity of society. For Giddens, reflexivity means that social practices are continually examined and reformed in the light of ongoing information about those very practices – which thus influences the very texture of those practices.

7 There have been various criticisms made of Giddens's version of structuration theory, including that it is unhelpful to amalgamate human agency with social structure and that the notion of 'rules and resources' is limited for grasping social reproduction. Giddens's account of reflexivity has also been criticized for its individualistic bent, as well as neglect of emotional and interpersonal factors.

8 In French sociologist Pierre Bourdieu's version of structuration, the fluidity of social life is captured by the notion of *habitus* – which refers to how bodily dispositions and well-practiced habits bridge personal and social life.

9   For Bourdieu, the *habitus* of an individual or group is anchored in the institutional life of 'fields.' Fields, such as the domains of the economy or culture, refer to the structured space of positions in which individuals act.

10 Bourdieu's social theory has been criticized, among other things, for suppressing change in personal and social life, as well as over-emphasizing the rigidity of the *habitus* in which social practices are generated.

Further questions

1   Giddens distinguishes two key types of social knowledge: practical and discursive consciousness. What do you understand to be their differences?

2   How is it that our individual actions – daily habits, routines and competencies – help to 'reproduce' the structures of society?

3   Giddens says that social structures are *both* 'medium and outcome' of a social system? What he is getting at?

4   How does the modern reflexive monitoring of individual action come to alter social structures?

5   *Habitus* is both enabling and coercive. How so?

6   From clothing to musical taste, Bourdieu asserts that 'cultural capital' is at play. Make a reading of cultural capital in your own life.

Further reading

Anthony Giddens

Central Problems in Social Theory (London: Macmillan; Berkeley: University of California Press, 1979)

The Constitution of Society. Outline of the Theory of Structuration (Cambridge: Polity Press; Berkeley: University of California Press, 1984)

The Consequences of Modernity (Cambridge: Polity Press; Palo Alto: Stanford University Press, 1990)

Modernity and Self-Identity. (Cambridge: Polity Press, 1991)

The Transformation of Intimacy (Cambridge: Polity Press, 1992)

Beyond Left and Right (Cambridge: Polity Press; Palo Alto: Stanford University Press, 1994)

(with Ulrich Beck and Scott Lash) *Reflexive Modernization: Politics, Tradition and Aesthetics in the Modern Social Order* (Stanford, California: Stanford University Press, 1994)

Pierre Bourdieu

Outline of a Theory of Practice (Cambridge University Press, 1977)

Distinction (London: Routledge, 1984)

Homo Academicus (Cambridge: Polity Press, 1988)

Language and Symbolic Power (Cambridge: Polity Press, 1991)

The Field of Cultural Production (Cambridge: Polity Press, 1993)

The Rules of Art: Genesis and Structure of the Literary Field (Stanford CA: Stanford University Press, 1995)

The State Nobility: Elite Schools in the Field of Power (Cambridge: Polity Press, 1996)

Weight of the World: Social Suffering in Contemporary Society Stanford CA: Stanford University Press, 2000)

(with Priscilla Parkhurst Ferguson) *On Television* (New Press, 1999)

chapter 10

Variations on the Theory of Power and Knowledge

Contents

Joelle is in her forties. She lives with her still-young daughter. Joelle is poor. She works when she can find work in a city with few jobs, fewer each year. Work comes, when it comes at all, seasonally. Joelle and her daughter live in a tiny apartment in a shabby neighborhood. What income they have comes from a government program supporting minor children. Joelle is eligible for additional government benefits. The only catch is that she must provide the name and address of her long-separated but still not legally divorced husband.

Being poor usually means being deprived of many of life's taken-for-granted resources, including ready access to a computer and the knowledge of how to use it to search for solutions to everyday life problems, like finding a missing person. Joelle was completely at a loss as to how to do this, until a family friend offered to help. In a few minutes on the Internet, her friend located the missing man, who was in prison in a distant state. Armed with this information, Joelle returned to the government office with the address. She was then told that she had to present her case to a judge. She made the court date and offered the information but the judge dismissed the case on the grounds that there had to be a legal divorce or the man, who had been missing for a good decade, had to sign certain papers. This proved if not impossible, very, very difficult. The woman needed to use whatever money she could get to keep her house and home in good enough order for her child. At this point she gave up.

What is the problem here? Obviously, one problem is that knowledge of even the most basic of practical skills is not fairly distributed. Joelle is an intelligent woman. Her troubles in life are, at least partly, her own fault. She has had her struggles over the years and not always found a good way to overcome them. Still, one might ask, 'Why, in a society liberal enough to offer benefits for the very poor is there no government agent willing to help? And why is access to the means available for helping oneself so full of obstacles?' She and others know what rights and benefits are available. Some find a way to get them. Some get them illegitimately. But too many have a right to them and are discouraged by the system itself. Joelle is far from alone among those in her circumstances to give up.

The point to be made is that what knowledge we have (or don't have) in practical life comes up against the forces of wider society, against which even the more knowledgeable are sometimes powerless. Societies may profess generosities of various kinds but few of them make sure that what benefits there may be are provided to those in real and just need. Strange as it may sound, it is reasonable to suppose that, if a government offers support for the very poor, they might send someone – for example, a census taker – door to door to sign people up. Of course they never do except in the most extreme emergencies – floods, earthquakes, epidemics, individual health crises discovered in hospitals, and so forth. One might say that this is too much to expect. Yet governments usually keep pretty good tabs on the number of people in need. They, thus, have knowledge of the extent of a problem. Still, their knowledge does not readily lead to official action. The poor and powerless remain where they are – even in the most affluent of nations. The poor may be able to do more to help themselves, yet the exclusions of most societies are apparently the fault of the structures established to help – schools that don't educate all, health systems that don't care for all, social security programs that don't make all secure.

Somewhere between the two failures – of those in power, and of those in need – one finds the relation between knowledge and power. The poor who lack power are separated by their relative lack of knowledge from the more powerful who know their need is real but fail to act. Someone along the line of Joelle's search for help – government agents, legal aid societies, judges and others – surely knew enough to realize that she was likely to be in need. Yet none was willing or able to break through the technical barriers to help her. Sometimes a friend or two is not enough. No one with the authority and power to help was willing to use the power of their knowledge to do what they knew needed to be done. The agent knew, the court clerk knew, the judge knew – but none bothered to do enough to determine that Joelle's need was as real as it is. Power thus works hand-in-hand with knowledge; and vice versa. Power is never simply brute force. In the more modern societies it is nearly always a matter of knowledge. In the interplay of those lacking knowledge, and those with knowledge who refuse to act, lies the sad fact that, in time, the powerless come to accept their fate – which is to say, they come to think of themselves as not deserving the benefits they know very well they have the right to. Somewhere in this sad reality lies the terrible truth that power uses knowledge to encourage those with knowledge to consider their power to be as natural as they consider the fate of the powerless. Power and knowledge are never far apart.

C. Wright Mills: power as knowledge of structures

C. Wright Mills was the first American social theorist to write explicitly about knowledge's relation to power; and he did it well before the relation between the two was rediscovered and redefined in Europe. In this and other ways Mills was an American original. He read as widely as anyone among American sociologists in his day. At the same time, he has been called a radical nomad as much for the intensity of his intellectual independence as for his personal style, typified by his passion for motorcycles. He was a serious scholar but he was best known for his plain language non-fiction writings – *White Collar: The American Middle Class* (1951), *The Power Elite* (1956), *The Causes of World War Three* (1958) and *Listen Yankee: The Revolution in Cuba* (1960). It is fair to say that, with the possible exception of David Riesman, no academic sociologist was better known to the general public. Yet, Columbia University declined to promote Mills to full professor.

Among social theorists easily the best known of Mills's ideas was his definition of the sociological imagination:

> The sociological imagination enables its possessor to understand the larger historical scene in terms of its meaning for the inner life of individuals. It enables him [sic] to take into account how individuals, in the welter of their daily experience, often become falsely conscious of their social positions. Within that welter, the framework of modern society is sought, and within that framework the psychologies of a variety of men and women are formulated. By such means the personal uneasiness of individuals is focused upon explicit troubles and the indifference of publics is transformed into involvement with public issues.
>
> (1959: 5)

Mills died in 1962, aged 45, just a few years after this famous text was written. Since the mid-1950s his writings were less and less addressed to academic sociologists, and more and more to the general public. Even his idea of the sociological imagination, and the book of which it was a part, while apparently aimed at sociologists, carried a strong political message. The ideal of the sociological imagination was, in effect, a call for people (and not just sociologists) to see their personal troubles as embedded in society's structural issues – thus, to turn away from discouraging self-blame to a bold knowledge of the history of societal issues formed in the well-structured public sphere. In practical effect, Mills was setting down a manifesto to use social imagination as a means to knowledge of the wider social forces, and thus to move beyond indifference and despair to engaged political action.

Too often, academics treat the sociological imagination as a methodological device, a means to produce more imaginative data leading to wider knowledge of social things. Certainly this is one of the idea's entailments but to focus on this one alone is to miss the degree to which Mills, late in his short life, is actually turning sociology on its head by equating its narrow positivism of facts as truth with the self-same implicit positivism of liberal politics, in which facts are instruments of rhetoric without the hard edge of criticism of society at large:

> This refusal to relate isolated facts and fragmentary comment with the changing institutions of society makes it impossible to understand the structural realities which these facts might reveal; the longer-run trends of which they might be tokens. In brief, fact and idea are isolated, so the real questions are not even raised, analysis of the meanings of fact not even begun.
>
> (1960: 256)

Mills wrote these words in his important 'Letter to the New Left,' the year after he wrote *The Sociological Imagination* (1959). This text was a manifesto read by young radicals the world over and one of the inspirations for the new left movement of the 1960s. It is important to add that the New Left, along with the Civil Rights Movement, was among the forces that called into question the 1950s culture of conformity that so troubled Riesman and others.

So, for Mills, power and knowledge were part and parcel. Knowledge that reverts to claims built on isolated facts and local perceptions is powerless. The powerful use knowledge to weaken opponents; the powerless suffer it in taking on society's failures as their own. Mills, thus, called out knowledge, the sacred cow of enlightenment modernity, into the exposed truth of power itself. Mills's theory of power's relation to knowledge was not as direct as Michel Foucault's power-knowledge which was coming into its own at the same time in France. But they were kin, born of a global weariness, not just with war, but with obtuse war mongering, colonizing political powers and deadly state powers of exclusion.

Mills, it should be said, did not discover these ideas until late in life. They were always on his agenda, formed by his reading of Marx alongside academic sociology, of pragmatism alongside Parsons and Merton, of Weber alongside liberal political theory. Of his sources, Weber was, in some ways, the most striking.

Early in his scholarly career, Mills edited *From Max Weber* (1946) with Hans Gerth. At the time, in 1946, there were but a few of Weber's key texts in English. Weber's massive *Economy and Society* would not be translated and widely available until a University of California Press edition in 1978. Thus American readers without a command of German went first to *From Max Weber*, which is still, today, a reliable key to Weber's writings on science, politics and power, religion, and social structures. Of these, none was more important than Weber's *Class, Status, and Party* in which he laid out a theory of the relations among economic, cultural and political spheres. Class, of course, was then already a staple, owing to Marx. Likewise it was well understood that in modern democratic societies political parties were basic.

Weber's essay on class, party, and status was behind the most enduring of Mills's theoretical innovations; though the three were for Weber, as for Mills, interconnected phenomena, the one that lent Mills's thinking a distinctive edge was status. Naturally the importance of status rankings was already an important consideration in modern societies where, in contrast to traditional ones, status was meant to be achieved, not ascribed. When one rises through the social ranks there is the likelihood that what status one attains will be a badge of honor – hence, Weber's expression *status honor*. This, then, is the means whereby social status transforms into an element of cultural prestige. This, too, was one of the concerns of the 1950s social critics, like Riesman, who saw the preoccupation with conforming other-directedness as a dangerous cultural form. In the words of Vance Packard, status seeking is a consequence of a culture in which achieving a status requires the acquisition of the symbols and fads whereby that status is made evident. Kings inherit their crowns and domains. The new American middle class achieved their second cars, kitchen gadgets, scrubbed children, and tract homes with picture windows exposing the family's up-to-date televisions. These were all far more than family values, houses, and the tools of a new middle-class life. They were symbols exhibiting the fact that address was that of ones who merited a certain honor due to their status.

Yet, the status of most who achieve a marginal elevation over their rural or working-class origins can be real but fragile, and far from a sure thing. This is the subject of Mills's 1951 book *White Collar: The American Middle Class*. In general, the book can be viewed as a systematic historical discussion of the extent to which Marx's idea that the working proletariat (in the 1950s, the wage-earner) is the primary victim of the dominant, bourgeois owners of industry. By the 1950s in America, it could not be denied that there had emerged a new middle class of white collar workers who achieved a certain status superior to the wage-earners. Not only that, but, in a fashion Marx could not have anticipated, they were bourgeois in their ways: work was increasingly in offices, thus white collar; the new middle class earned enough to buy homes of their own; they pursued the middling values of those who aspired to something more while achieving something less than their dreams. Still, in a manner different from, but not unlike, Marx's idea of the exploited workers, the white collar worker was, and is, subject to the less overtly cruel but still arbitrary whim of the dominant managerial class. Their salaries were always modest. Their positions could be taken away in a sudden down-turn of business. They could be ordered about, even if in a more reasoned language than nineteenth-century bosses of industry may have deployed. Thus, said Mills, the new middle class suffered a constant threat of status panic. What they had was real but in an instant it could disappear and the arbitrariness of their status was the tool by which management controlled them. They sought and had status of a kind, yet they could never be certain of what they had. The American rich got richer, the American middle class remained, at first, static then, in time, many slipped back closer to the status of their wage-earning parents and grandparents. Thus it is clear that Mills's insight in *White Collar* was based on a version of Weber's theory of the interplay of class, status and party. Class, if economic, is never merely economic. Statuses are sought after because cultural prestige is important in the modern system. But when attained, they are never settled. The new rich seek more wealth; the newly middle class seek to hold on to what they have.

In 1956, in his most famous book, *The Power Elite*, Mills completed his account of the instabilities of postwar America. Here his subject is typified by the theme of the book's first chapter, 'The Higher Circles.' In particular, Mills put the emphasis on the then (and probably still) most powerful American elite sectors – the economic, the political, and the military, of which he said:

> The higher circles in and around the [economic, political, and military] command posts are often thought of in terms of what their numbers possess: they have a greater share than other people of the things and experiences that are mostly highly valued. From this point of view, the elite are simply those who have the most of what there is to have, which is generally held to include money, power, and prestige – as well as all the ways of life to which these lead.
>
> (1956: 9)

Here he offers the clearest and most systematic outline of his Weberian theory of class, status, and power. *The Power Elite* analyzes in fine detail the workings of the power elite in all these respects – as celebrities, as the corporate rich, as warlords.

Mills's exposition of the history, tastes, powers, and cultures of the power elite made the lasting contribution of being the first description of the interlocking directorate of the postwar American dominant strata. In this, Mills solved a problem that Marx left unsolved. If power, as Marx held, is from the societal top down then *how* does the dominant class do its dirty work? Mills's answer: By sharing common interests and a common elite culture, and by interacting behind the scenes in the higher circles. Ever after, sociologists, especially in America, took this notion of an interlocking directorate as a fundamental point of departure for the study of power in society. For Mills, it should be noted, their power was as much in what they know as in what they do. The elite know what their shared interests are, who their status allies might be, and how they can work their will against the much larger number of lesser folk.

What then are the lesser powers to do if they are not to assume that what they lack is their fault? To begin with, they must use their informed imagination to study the ways of the power elite and all other forms by which structural power affects and limits them.

If we took the one hundred most powerful men in America, the one hundred wealthiest, and the one hundred most celebrated away from the institutional positions they now occupy, away from their resources of men and women and money, away from the media of mass communication that are now focused upon them – then they would be powerless

Alvin W. Gouldner: the culture of critical discourse

Just more than a decade after Mills' *Sociological Imagination*, another book had an even greater impact on American social theory. Alvin W. Gouldner's *The Coming Crisis of Western Sociology* (1970) took sociology, in particular, but also a goodly portion of the general intellectual culture, by storm. As Mills had declaimed the reasoned needs for a new left, Gouldner wrote in its wake. In a sense, politics in the United States, by the 2010s, was still reeling from a rigid conservatism that was soaked in the dregs of the traditional white Southern Confederacy, which stained the very fabric of its basic values. But in the 1960s, young radicals swore by and meant to advance progressive versions of feminism, GLBT and civil rights, as well as anti-war movements. Gouldner was writing just when the full, if confused, force of late 1960s radical politics and culture was being felt. Many, especially the young, rushed to join in. Others, mostly older and white, hated the whole thing. Though May '68 in Paris was more emblematic than the American Sixties, it was America that struggled deeply with these revolutionary movements. In a sense, politics in the United States, by the 2010s, was still reeling from the rigid conservatism – rooted in the dregs of the white Southern confederacy, torn at the fabric of the very basic values – that in the 1960s, even young radicals swore by and meant to advance in its versions of feminism, civil rights, gay, and anti-war movements. Though 1968 was the year of a world revolution that sealed the end of the progressive and exploitative modern era, that revolution was experienced differently in America which had so feeble a history with deep historical changes that it had its own reasons for fearing change all the more.

Gouldner did not address his 1970 book to America as such, as Mills had in studying the American social histories after World War II, but there was little doubt that his ideas were aimed at American culture. Though *Coming Crisis* was about Western sociology, it was directed at America. Gouldner had just ended a long exile in Europe, where he founded the international journal *Theory and Society*. He brought from abroad a familiarity with European culture and ideas to challenge the vibrant but, as always, still innocent America, especially its young. *Coming Crisis* was thus almost weirdly preoccupied with destroying the hold Talcott Parsons was thought to still have on American social theory. It was no less critical of how, in his experience in Europe, he saw Marxism, especially Soviet socialism, failing to come to terms with the new world order. Reading the book more than five decades after it first appeared, it is possible to see in it Gouldner's frustrations equally with the US as with Europe – with, that is, Western social theory. Yet it was too soon for even so brilliant a social thinker as Gouldner to announce a program for political and social change. The one with which he ends *Coming Crisis* is almost pathetic. He called for 'the theorist to pull himself together' by adapting a reflexive attitude that allowed the social theorist to be aware of his own personal intrusions upon theory as much as to be the artful theorist who can stand outside the social order in which he was formed. As it turned out for Gouldner himself (the shadow subject of *Coming Crisis*), his book was a catharsis that allowed him to begin a project that would consume him for the next decade, and which turned out to be the last one of his life.

Gouldner himself was a firebrand or, as he described himself, a street fighter from the Bronx. Despite this, his most important teacher in graduate studies was Robert K. Merton, who was the most gentlemanly of souls. Yet Gouldner took to him. They remained friends until Gouldner died in 1980; this in spite of their different temperaments and differing intellectual interests. Merton's influence is evident in the most systematic of Gouldner's books, *Patterns of Industrial Bureaucracy* (1954), a classic in the field of industrial and organizational sociologies. Plus which, his many articles in major journals – gathered in *For Sociology* (1975) – were among the most widely cited works by academics in his day. Yet, his street fighter instincts drew him toward Marx and Marxism, and then to the wider world of European, radical social theories.

In the 1970s, Gouldner published a trilogy he called 'The Dark Side of the Dialectic.' The first book, *The Dialectic of Ideology and Technology* (1976), opens with the tell-tale line: 'this study is about ideologies as a form of discourse, i.e., as a culture of critical speech; i.e., as an elaborated sociolinguistic speech variant.' The hint here is that this, the first of the trilogy, and the second, *The Future of Intellectuals and the Rise of the New Class* (1979), were his important writings on culture and discourse. The third volume, *The Two Marxisms* (1980) was published a year later, the year of his death, and served as the most systematic of his critiques of Marxism in its various forms. Gouldner always thought against the grain of one or another tradition of thought, usually sociology and Marxism. This was his theoretical method – new ideas require the old from which they draw their force. 'Marxism,' he said, 'constitutes itself by developing a critique of "ideologies," by setting itself over and apart from what it calls "ideologies" ' (1976: 5). Thus it was that the single most important, if today still unappreciated, concept was the one announced in the first of these books.

Gouldner's ingenuity was to see that, by the 1980s, the emergent social form was that formed at the intersection of technology and ideology. Today some might have said technology and culture. But Gouldner, in his day, remained the post-Marxist social theorist for whom culture is basically and necessarily ideology.

Where Gouldner advances the generically Marxist idea of culture as ideology is by recognizing the decisive difference of modern culture as it had come to be clear by his time:

> What, then, may be said of the differences between older ideologies, e.g. nationalism, *laissez faire*, socialism, the supposedly modern ideology which seeks to ground the legitimacy of modern neo-capitalism, and bureaucratic socialism in the idea of a technologically guided society? How much has actually occurred, if any, and in what directions, in the transition to the technocratic ideology? . . . The new technocratic ideology . . . does not simply claim to produce something better for all, but also claims this happy administration of things is supervised by a kind of secular ministry, the scientists, who are interested in no gain for themselves, and whose work can be judged by its fruits, superior consumerism, comfort, health.
>
> (1976: 257–258)

In other words, Gouldner both recognized the changes occurring in the technological advances of the modern *and* went straight to their defects. This was the idea that he developed in the second book of the trilogy.

Few books come to mind that say more in a few pages than Gouldner's *The Future of Intellectuals and the Rise of the New Class* (1979) where he systematically advances his theory of technological culture. The new class was, already in Gouldner's day, a well-commented upon phenomenon especially in postwar America where the brilliance of the nation's scientific and managerial class was considered, rightly, the key to its triumph in war and in economic success in the postwar period. Yet, as few others did, Gouldner began, predictably, with the defects of the Marxist scenario of the new class of modern intellectuals and scientists. In effect, Gouldner appreciated, but went far beyond, Marxism's economistic interpretation of capital. Thus, he began:

> The two most important theoretical foundations needed for a general theory of the New Class will be, first, a theory of its distinctive language

behavior, its distinctive culture of discourse and, secondly, a general theory of capital within which the New Class's 'human capital' or the old class's moneyed capital will be special cases.

(1979: 5)

Gouldner's New Class comprised intellectuals and scientists, on the one hand, and the scientific administrators of corporate capitalism, on the other. On the surface, though, these would be two quite distinct groups. Yet what was clear in the postwar decades was that they shared more than would have been predicted a century earlier, in the first years of industrial capitalism, when the bourgeois capitalists were the more apparent ruling elite; hence, the expression, New Class.

As the old class stumbles into the future, the production of the New Class grows. Some of the statistics for higher education are relevant: in 1947 (even after the influx of veterans from World War II) there were only some 2.2 million college students in the United States, and they constituted only some 16% of those of college age. From 1955 to 1960 this number increased from 2.6 million to 3.6 million, about 35% of the college age youth. In the 1970s there were some 8 million college students, who were about 40% of the college age youth. . . . In 1947 the bill for higher education was about one billion dollars, in the early 1970s it was about 25 billion dollars, and is expected to rise to about 44 billion in the 1980s. The New Class is reproducing itself faster than any other class in society.

Alvin W. Gouldner (1979) *The Future of Intellectuals and the Rise of the New Class.* New York: Continuum, page 90.

Gouldner's idea was, in brief, that the modern era advanced beyond mere industrial power by its increasing reliance on new technologies that went far beyond the basic needs of industrial efficiency. In addition, technology became the cultural basis of both scientific and philosophical inquiry. In our time, in the twenty-first century, this is so obvious that one might suppose that Gouldner was saying nothing new. We know that informational technologies are, for all intents and purposes, everywhere. Academic cultures of all kinds, like scientific research generally, would be helpless without technologies for the storage and retrieval of information and sources, as well as for rapid communication. Today, astronomers work with data captured and sent out from the Hubble telescope. Their data, thus, are entirely computer based. Astronomers of distant spaces, thus, do not look through a telescope. They see what is to be seen by interpreting reconstructed visual presentations of events so distant in the long ago and far away as to be, in effect, invisible to the naked eye. In the same way, the student of ancient Greek texts might be able to go somewhere to see the remnants in the originals but more often they read transcriptions available online. Likewise, even the ordinary citizen who has access to a computer searches the world for information, as best she can. Not all of us have the technical knowledge of the advanced technologies upon which the better off depend, but all of us rely at least on the certain basic language required to use them. Today we *download* mail and data, a notion that would have made no sense in Marx's day, much less in the early postwar years. Likewise, we *search* for something or other, most often online – and (sadly) seldom in a library or bookstore.

Gouldner thus realized that even the most elementary forms of scientific or intellectual work had come to require a special kind of language – an ability, that is, to talk *about* the subject matter at issue in a critical way. It is one thing to hear others use the word 'download,' then to repeat it more or less correctly. But quite another to know what it means and, for example, which browser is the best for one's purposes. 'I've got to go home and download dinner for my kids.' Versus: 'They closed iGoogle last November but I think this was a mistake.' The former is jargon; the latter is a critical discourse. Thus, long before the full implications of his ideas were fully understood, Gouldner proposed that late modern culture was becoming a culture of critical discourse. Here he was borrowing heavily from ideas that were already much discussed in Europe, where both critical theories in general and language-based theories of social process in particular had emerged in the postwar period as tools for rethinking culture. Yet, Gouldner put his own conceptual turn on these movements by arguing, as the critical theorists in Germany did, that no social theory could afford to be less than critical and, as the French structuralists and their opponents did, that discourse was the primary surface of social and political life.

Yet, Gouldner was not a mere optimist. He considered the critical culture of the New Class of intellectuals and technocrats to be a powerful elite, yet also a deeply flawed universal class. The New Class was, thus, a new ruling class that, viewed one way, was more critical, while viewed another way just as much a ruling elite as what came before. Here it is possible to detect the giant steps that Gouldner took in the few years after C. Wright Mills. Mills was critical of the power elite. He believed they more or less knowingly operated in a culture that reinforced their sense of their own rights to power. Thus Mills thought that the new critical political actors could, by applying sociological imagination to their personal lives, become critics of the structured powers and, thereby, a new source of political change. Gouldner, by contrast, claimed that real power in the late modern world lay with all those who possessed the capacity for critical discourse; thus that the capacity to criticize power lay in the very culture that power used to rule. For Mills, power for change was with those outside the power elite; for Gouldner, power was held, and used, inside the ruling elite by virtue of its critical culture.

Hence, the dialectic of technology and ideology (in the words of Gouldner's earlier book) was the contradictory force inside the ideology of late modern culture that both led to scientific and intellectual advancements and served as an administrative tool for the managing class. Science and technology, thus, are the resources both for human enlightenment and for political authority. The culture of critical discourse was not in an external authority but in the very discourse by which the elite ruled and social criticism used. Power, thus, was becoming universal or ubiquitous (a notion similar to Foucault's micro-politics). This is a widely shared idea in our time, at least to the extent that we know very well that even the most elementary of political enemies can use information technologies to attack and wound those they hate. If power resides in the workings of this kind of discursive culture, then power is universal and the New Class is, as Gouldner put it, a flawed universal class. If, in effect, power is knowledge, then it is available to all, but, by that fact alone, power is at once liberating and corrupt.

By the time Gouldner settled on his theory of the culture of critical discourse, in Europe Foucault's idea of power-knowledge was already well known, if slow to come to the attention of American critical theorists. Gouldner, in spite of his sojourn in Europe, remained an American through and through, as he remained, in his way, loyal to his friend Robert Merton. Gouldner's theory was not, to be sure, straightforward functionalism, but it was nearly as much Weberian as it was Marxian. Gouldner drew on Marxism more than any other major figure, even more than Mills, but he was always as critical of Marxism as he was of sociology. In the end, he opened a new space between the two that illuminated the inherent contradictions and connections between power and knowledge.

Dorothy Smith: power and knowledge from the feminist standpoint

Dorothy Smith is a Canadian sociologist, now retired to British Columbia, and a feminist, a decidedly partisan one. Her enduring importance as a social theorist is that she was among the first to construe feminist theory in direct and robust criticism of sociology's not so subtle masculinist methodological attitudes. In many articles and books since the 1960s, Smith has written on suicide, the news, Virginia Woolf, mental illness, education, family life, ethnography, and power relations, among other topics. Yet, with rare exception, the range and number of her writings sooner or later turn to a central question of feminist theory, usually referred to as the question of the feminist standpoint: 'How to develop sociological inquiry from the site of the experiencing and embodied subject as a sociology from the standpoint of women?' (1990: 1)

Smith was among those feminists, early in the 1970s, who began to think through the implications of feminism as an epistemology, even a methodology, as opposed to a general set of political values. Hence, the feminist standpoint, which, more generally, led to the insight that knowledge is situated in a particular social experience. Smith herself is quite open in admitting that she and others were pushed in this direction by the early women's movement that, in the United States, grew in part from the Civil Rights Movement, and in greater part from the revolutionary 1960s as a whole. By the 1970s, many activists, including women, were returning to their intended careers in academic life. For them, the question of how a new gender sensibility could alter the traditional canons of learning and methods of research were front and center.

In 1974, Smith published two of her earliest and best-known statements of her feminist sociology: 'Women's Perspective as a Radical Critique of Sociology' (in *Sociological Inquiry*) and 'The Ideological Practice of Sociology' (in *Catalyst*). Neither appeared in what, at the time, was considered a mainstream journal. Yet, both were read carefully and passed on among the younger feminists in the academy. In the second of these, Smith said 'A feminist sociology must, it seems to me, begin with actual subjects situated as they actually are; it must be, therefore, an insider's sociology, a sociology of society as it is and must be known by people who are active in it' (1990a: 36). The striking aspect of statements like this is that, in retrospect, they may seem all too simple, even obvious. Yet, it is important to say, the very basic truth that knowledge ought to begin with an insider's perspective was, at the time, fresh if disturbing to those with a stake in traditional theories of knowledge.

From these early statements of feminist insider knowledge, Smith developed her standpoint epistemology. Roughly put, she argued that, in their daily lives, women experience a 'line of fault' between what they know and what is officially known. They live, therefore, with a 'bifurcated consciousness' (1987: 82). Official knowledge – conveyed always in texts as though they were objective – is an ally in the relations of ruling. Objectivity (the insistence on general, thus extralocal, knowledge as the standard of truth) supports ruling. Both aggressively exclude women's experience. Sociology, insofar as it traditionally insists on objectivity standards, partakes in the relations of ruling. Women, living on this line of fault between the demands of extralocal ruling/knowing and their daily experience of local particulars, possess a unique epistemological standpoint.

It is evident that, in the 1970s, Smith was severely critical of her field, sociology, and by extension other academic methods. Much has changed since she wrote these words. The academy and a good bit of public life have come to appreciate the experience of women and others formerly ignored. Many have also come to see the limitations of objectivism. Yet, the underlying point holds up. Women, and a good many others who are closely tied to the dilemmas of local lives, are even now subjected to official, objective knowledge. In the academy, all forms of experience-based knowing are still, to a regrettable extent, considered insufficiently rigorous. In public life, the poorer neighborhoods are still beset by official educational, social scientific, and governmental sources determining how their children are to be taught, how their poverty is to be relieved, and how their housing projects or districts are to be planned and administered. If you doubt this, just study the work of women and others rejected for tenure; or read a good ethnography of poor neighborhoods; or, for that matter, just ask and listen to those who live in a world where their experiences are devalued. Some things have changed for many, including a good many women, since the 1970s. Still Smith, and other standpoint theorists of so-called second-wave feminism, made an enduring contribution to advancing the importance of local experiences as a powerful source of knowledge, and hence of social theory.

One of the more important features of American social theory as it came to be in the 1970s, is that it broke the mold of inherited and all-too-traditional thinking about knowledge and, even, truth. In Europe the new theories were, in large part, a function of attempts in the postwar period to come to terms with a radically changed social environment for which Marxism, psychoanalysis, and their entailments were the principal sources of criticism. In America the postwar social and economic environments were different, as were the sources American social theorists drew upon. Dorothy Smith, for example, was influenced in some good measure by Marxism but it was a vague sort of Marxism. Even her sharpest structural idea, the relations of ruling, was recast in relation to her interest in women's experience (for which distinctively American ideas, notably ethnomethodology, were the source). And, generally speaking, there was scant reference to the economic basis for women's exclusion.

Over the years since her first writings, Smith introduced many elements of nuance to her theory and these, most often, were advanced through a good many empirical studies. Even in her earliest texts, to her credit, she seemed to understand the inherent limitations of any social theory that identified any subject experience as the source of anything like a *unique* social knowledge. Yet, when feminism, Afrocentrism, radical queer theory, or for that matter radical post-colonial theory, or any strong standpoint theory claim *superiority* for the subject experience of a given group, their

the theory of power and knowledge

foundational claims soon enough run into difficulties. It is fair enough to reject the narrow, dead-white-gentlemanly culture of the high nineteenth century. But there are problems as well. To rule out sources like, say, Shakespeare or Marx *because* they are dead white men is, in its way, just as foolish as to ignore the epistemological experience of women, blacks, gays, and others. Some early standpoint feminisms gave into this temptation or, at least, failed to clarify the limits of their theories. Thus in the decades following the first forays into standpoint theory, there emerged a vastly more subtle social theory; and again feminism led the way.

Donna Haraway and Patricia Hill Collins: the fractured matrix of power

Earlier in the 1980s a mysterious paper began to circulate among young feminists. More than a few were puzzled by it. Yet, in 1985, 'A Cyborg Manifesto: Science, Technology, and Socialist-Feminism in the Late Twentieth Century,' was published in *Socialist Review*. Even some among the editorial circles of this well-regarded leftish journal were confused by the essay – not least because it included a strong criticism of socialist feminism while proposing a daringly new kind of radical feminism.

It helps to unravel Haraway's complex ideas by understanding that, as a student, she studied science, taking her PhD from Yale in biology. Yet, even her doctoral thesis was written from the perspective of philosophy and literary criticism. The subject was the role of metaphoric thinking in experimental biology, published in 1976 as *Crystals, Fabrics, and Fields: Metaphors of Organicism in Twentieth Century Developmental Biology*. Yet, since 1984, her academic career has been based in the most important cultural left academic graduate program in the United States – the History of Consciousness Program at the University of California at Santa Cruz. Trained in science, she became a feminist social theorist.

Still, it is fair to ask what is a cyborg and what does it have to do with feminist theory? Haraway starts her famous essay with an explanation: 'Contemporary science fiction is filled with cyborgs – creatures simultaneously animal and machine, who populate worlds ambiguously natural and crafted' (1991: 149–150). She adds that they are also found in medicine where bodies are treated, diagnosed, even inhabited by various machines like heart monitors; also in plant life; and production where, in her words, the production line is governed by a combination of human worker and technologies that reduce the human to a mechanical tool. So, she continues emphasizing the science *fiction* figure of speech. 'My cyborg myth is about transgressed boundaries, potent fusions, and dangerous possibilities which progressive people might explore as one part of needed political work' (1991: 154) As the cyborg is a transgressive being, Haraway is formulating a radical politics.

One might follow her this far and still wonder if this is not just a transgressive way of stating the purposes of socialist politics. Marx himself was surely a transgressor in theory. Yet, Haraway challenges both socialist and (in effect) standpoint feminisms. As socialist politics begin with class, so radical (her word for standpoint) feminisms begin with gender. Both are, thereby, totalizing in that each assumes that a single grand category – class in the one case, gender in the other – can serve as the organizing, deductive origin of all other politics; hence, from class are race, gender, and sexual exploitations derived, as from gender are poverty, racism, and homophobia understood. Haraway's point is that neither is sufficiently partial. In life, no individual or any group of apparently similar individuals is ever identified by any one essential attribute. The idea is that we (so to speak) are all at once part gendered, part racial, part class-bound, part a sexual type, and so on almost endlessly. Thus what starts as a slightly weird way of doing little more than restating versions of political theories, turns out to be entirely serious in its myth of the cyborg – that we are all made up of unreconcilable aspects; thus by nature individuals are in a given aspect partial, always transgressing themselves and, thereby, any dominant culture that wants to reduce everyone and everything to an essence. The best known concept in 'The Cyborg Manifesto' is *fractured identities*. 'Identities seem contradictory, partial, and strategic. With the hard-won recognition of their social and historical constitution, gender, race, and class cannot provide the basis for belief in an "essential" unity.'

There are no essences; only transgressions. 'Cyborg politics is the struggle for language and the struggle against perfect communication, against the code that translates all meaning perfectly, the central dogma of phallocentrism' (1991: 176). Obviously, this is at least a feminism of a new kind, but also a socialism of an interesting kind. At the very least, Haraway is attacking both the dominant culture of the modern West and its theory of knowledge as the articulation of the laws of essences. Her attack is meant to be strategic; which is to say, political.

It is not too hard to see that Haraway is critical of strong standpoint feminisms, at least by default. The important thing to note is that her theory of feminist knowledges is of a kind of knowledge that fractures by transgressing not just essential truths but also the most basic of practical assumptions about the interior *and* social natures of human beings. There may be in this an implicit accord with standpoint theories in the apparent assumption that in this world women are more cyborgian than men. Yet this interpretation is not apparent in her writings but it is suggested by the fact that Haraway made some of the earliest and clearest statements of the idea of 'situated knowledges' – a formulation not at all at odds with Smith's idea of women's local experience. But more importantly, Haraway brought to the fore the now evident parallels among the situated knowledges of people of color, gays and lesbians, the poor, as well as women; and treated the idea of situated knowledge as an important aspect of radical identity politics (which is to say, a politics that accounts for the real differences of those who inhabit this world as it is – a social not a psychological matter). Standpoint feminisms were, by and large, sensitive to these parallels; but Haraway made them central not just to feminism theory but to social theory as such. She was not alone.

1990 was a kind of *annus mirabilis* of feminist social theory in the United States in that two of its late modern classics appeared that year: Patricia Hill Collins's *Black Feminist Thought* and Judith Butler's *Gender Trouble* (Butler's contribution to feminism is discussed further in Chapter 12). As Butler's book became a turning point in feminist queer theory, so *Black Feminist Thought* established the fundamental importance of Black women's experience as both a political and epistemological force in modern life. The miracle year, it should added, came between Gloria Anzaldùa's *Borderlands/La Frontera: The New Mestiza* (1987) and the collection of Donna Haraway's major essays in *Simians, Cyborgs, and Women: The Reinvention of Nature* (1991).

Collins's *Black Feminist Thought*, in some ways, was meant to sum up the distinctively American theories of power/knowledge, as is evident in the book's subtitle: *Knowledge, Consciousness, and the Politics of Empowerment*. As did the other books in and around 1990, Collins's came to be one of the most influential theoretical texts of the time. This is all the more remarkable because, in 1990, Collins was teaching at a relatively less well-known school, the University of Cincinnati, while also engaged in local community politics. Today she is a Distinguished University Professor at the University of Maryland, and a recent president of the American Sociological Association, and her work has become required reading in any number of fields, including, interestingly, critical race studies in law schools.

Part of the appeal of *Black Feminist Thought* is that it is surprisingly plain spoken and straightforward, while making a series of compelling theoretical points that somehow straddle the differences between standpoint and fractured feminisms. Collins's standpoint is that of African American women who in the United States embody the ways structures of race, gender and class oppress. This is an idea that had been around in the United States since the nineteenth century, but it was Collins who worked it out systematically. In effect, she holds that the African American woman occupies the standpoint of the most oppressed, which requires and allows her at once to see and understand all of the major vectors of power in society. Her knowledge, thus, is her power. Thus to the extent that Collins's theory is a standpoint feminism it works in an entirely different way from what, for better or worse, has to be called white feminism in America. This is made evident in the way the book is structured.

The major and longest section of *Black Feminist Thought* is actually a social history of the cultural and social experiences of Black women seen both in their experience in the Black community and in American culture as a whole. She identifies and analyzes the most prominent cultural images of Black women in America – among them, mammies, matriarchs, and sexualized Jezebels. Collins's method is thereby historical in that she describes the Black Woman's standpoint as the experience of a number of contradictory forces – never simply male domination, or white racism, or economic exclusion, but all and more at once. In their communities they may be matriarchs in charge of children and men, while in their work world they can be viewed as mammies. From this, it is apparent that Collins's standpoint is one of individuals whose experience is itself fractured. Here she introduces a notably new and structural idea that she came to call an *intersectional paradigm,* which she remarks 'untangles the relations between knowledge and empowerment and sheds new light on how domination is organized.' She adds at this point her most famous concept: 'The term *matrix of domination* describes this over all social organization within which intersecting oppressions originate, develop, and are contained' (2012: 398).

The important idea behind Collins's matrix theory is that it locates *all* members of a society somewhere in the scheme of domination. Thus, even white male members of the dominating class are, in their way, caught in the matrix they control. In a way they are subject to the raw but harsh innocence of a system where, in the United States, Black women (and by extension women of color in America and the world over) are forced into the more inferior social positions in society. Yet, following many thinkers, from Hegel through Du Bois, Collins asserts that those in lesser social positions possess the special knowledge of their experience of living the reality of the vectors of domination. The slave knows the master, while the master is ignorant of the slave (to paraphrase Hegel). In effect the American social system, from the point of view of race, is an especially corrupting contradiction of its high moral self-understanding. In Collins's way of thinking, the Black Woman's fractured experience is at once central to her distinctive knowledge and the foundation of her political empowerment.

The long and winding road of social theories of power and knowledge in America has been at considerable odds with the similar path in Europe where Foucault and Habermas – their sharp differences notwithstanding – worked through theories of power/knowledge (Foucault's term of course) in more direct and explicit terms. This in part is due to the fact that American social theory was slow to read and think through European ideas. But it is also due, in larger part, to the fact that America's culture of innocence combined with its post-World War II affluence (not to exclude its Red Scare, so-called) to thwart earlier honest considerations of the degree to which knowledge of all kinds is necessarily affected by power relations and implicated in them.

Summary points

1   C. Wright Mills was one of the first American sociologists formally to explore the links between knowledge and power. His influential text, *The Sociological Imagination*, emphasized the role of largely structural forces in day-to-day experience, and argued that the individual's interests are served by engagement in broader political action in the public sphere.

2   In *The Power Elite*, Mills made explicit his theory of power and knowledge. The upper echelons of American society, Mills argued, gained their position, and thus their power, through unequal consumption of resources and cultural symbols of status. The lower classes are held back by insufficient knowledge of the means of access, and by collusion between the various branches of the elite to keep this knowledge privileged.

3   After Mills, Alvin W. Gouldner examined the link in American culture, as he put it, between technology and ideology. As technological advances led to improved 'quality of life' in the West, Gouldner argued, the intellectuals and administrators jointly responsible for these changes emerged as a new social elite. With this emerging New Class came a new culture of critical discourse, a powerful tool for social change.

4   Dorothy Smith honed the broad political movement of 1970's feminism into a critique of the existing forms of sociological knowledge. Smith argued that the experience of women, previously dismissed within a masculine-oriented 'objective' sociology, represented a unique intersection of objective knowledge and everyday understanding. Smith called for an 'insider sociology' to take account of differing forms of knowledge.

5   Donna Haraway used the metaphor of the cyborg, a melding of human and machine, to critique existing forms of socialist, as well as feminist, knowledge. Haraway points out that all identities contain multiple, and conflicting, elements, that cannot be distilled into a unified essence, be it class or gender. For Haraway, new forms of knowledge must emerge that take into account the transgressive, fractured nature of everyday experience.

6   Patricia Hill Collins argues that the Black Woman is a unique inter-
     section of the structures of race, gender and class. Collins theorizes
     a 'matrix of domination' that encompasses all members of society.
     But, for Collins, the experience of living within intersecting forms of
     oppression creates unique forms of knowledge that can provide the
     basis for political empowerment.

Further questions

1   In what ways does your day-to-day experience affect the way that
     you engage with broader social issues?

2   How do you use critical discourse in everyday life? Is it empow-
     ering? Can you think of a time where another person using critical
     discourse has made you feel uncomfortable, or even powerless?

3   How can social theorists make use of insider knowledge?

4   What are the elements that make up your identity? Are there
     conflicts between them?

5   What does it mean to be located in the matrix of domination? For
     yourself? For others?

Further reading

C. Wright Mills

The Power Elite (New York: Oxford University Press, 1956)
The Sociological Imagination (New York: Oxford University Press, 1959)

Alvin W. Gouldner

*The Dialectic of Ideology and Technology: The Origins, Grammar of Future of
    Ideology* (New York: The Seabury Press, 1976)
*The Future of Intellectuals and the Rise of the New Class: a frame of
    reference, theses, conjectures, arguments, and an historical perspective
    on the role of intellectuals and intelligensia in the Modern Era* (New York:
    Continuum, 1979)

Dorothy E. Smith

The Everyday World As Problematic: A Feminist Sociology (Boston, MA: Northeastern University Press, 1987)

Texts, Facts, and Femininity: Exploring the Relations of Ruling (London: Routledge, 1990)

Donna J. Haraway

Simians, Cyborgs and Women: The Reinvention of Nature (London: Free Association Books, 1991)

Patricia Hill Collins

Black Feminist Thought: Knowledge, Consciousness and the Politics of Empowerment (New York: Routledge, 1991)

chapter 11

Contemporary Critical Theory

Contents

In early 2002, the United States Government identified Iraq, along with North Korea and Iran, as part of an 'axis of evil.' The argument put was that Iraq, under President Saddam Hussein, was a threat to America specifically and the world in general because of its stockpiling of weapons of mass destruction. In addition, the United States argued that Hussein had tyrannized his own population and politically unsettled the Middle East. At a meeting of the United Nations General Assembly in late 2002, United States resident George Bush urged the body to deal with the 'grave and gathering danger' of Iraq. A period of intensive political debate throughout the world about Iraq and the imminent threat it posed to global peace followed. The UN Security Council imposed new arms inspections on Iraq. Many observers argued that Hussein's regime was cooperating with the demands imposed by international law. But countries such as the United States, Great Britain and Spain remained unconvinced, warning that military action against Iraq may become inevitable. The political debate and dialogue continued throughout early 2003, whilst massive peace demonstrations were held in cities throughout the world. Eventually, however, the process of political debate and diplomatic dialogue came to an end – at which point talk transmuted into violence, dialogue into destruction. On 19 March 2003, the United States launched 'Operation Iraqi Freedom,' an ongoing round of coordinated air strikes against Baghdad, coupled with the invasion of troops into the country. In its invasion of Iraq, the United States had, in one stroke, embraced unilateral militarism and brought unstuck the structure of international law.

A great deal of ink has been spilt explaining the American invasion of Iraq in 2003. Defenders argued that the United States invoked its military supremacy in order to maintain world peace – an argument that became increasingly dubious in light of the subsequent evidence that Iraq did not possess weapons of mass destruction. Critics of the war attributed the invasion to an American lust for oil. Others argued that the Iraq war was a result of widespread fear of Islamic terrorism. Some others contended it was part of a neoconservative agenda to democratize the Middle East. Still others discerned the interests of turbo-capitalism at work: the high-pitched moral discourse of freedom and democracy was, it was argued, a cover for the profits reaped from the industrialization of war.

Whatever the precise mix of social forces at work, this disturbing episode in recent world history can help us to see the complex relation between democratic debate and political dialogue on the one hand, and the systemic institutional control of economic and bureaucratic logics on the other, in social and political affairs. In the approach of the world's leading critical theorist today, Jürgen Habermas, the deliberation over Iraq became systematically bent out of shape by extra-discursive forces (such as lust for oil profits, or the territorial ambitions of Empire) – at which point debate was replaced by the destruction of war. Rooted in the tradition of the Frankfurt School, Habermas's writings have been central to the revitalization of social theory and the progressive political imagination in recent decades. His ground-breaking work on how lapses of communication and social misunderstandings are rooted in the power of invasive institutional forces has become increasingly influential, and much of this chapter is devoted to reviewing and appraising Habermas's critical social theory. Later in the chapter we will turn to consider other developments in contemporary critical theory, notably Axel Honneth's theory of disrespect and recognition, as well as theories of discursive democracy.

Habermas: the democratization of society

The ideas of reason and rationality, fundamental to the tradition of classical social theory, had come under fire through the most daring social critique with the Frankfurt School. The alleged connection between reason and progressive social change was profoundly challenged in the writings of Marcuse, Fromm, Adorno and Horkheimer. The major thrust of Frankfurt School critical theory was to explore the intricate interrelations between the textures of reason and the dominance of techno-scientific rationalization, which from the outset was used to explicate the social barbarism and mass terror of the age, from the rise of Nazism and fascism in Europe to the degeneration of the Russian revolution into Stalinism and the spread of technocratic societal management. In the aftermath of the Second World War, however, new political possibilities spread throughout Europe; the world, in short, looked very different to the bleak social diagnosis presented by the Frankfurt School. For example, West Germany commenced the task of developing a liberal political culture after the Allied powers had imposed a basic legal structure that provided for democratic political institutions, a development which took place against the international backdrop of growing Western economic prosperity. During this period, as discussed in Chapter 3, Marcuse remained in the United States, penning books which catapulted him to celebrity status with the New Left. Adorno and Horkheimer resettled in West Germany, and sought to defend their social critique. Yet, in various ways, the social theory elaborated by the Frankfurt School appeared somewhat out of kilter with the postwar world, and it was to fall to a new generation of critical theorists – the most prominent of which was Jürgen Habermas – to remold the basic tenets of social theory.

If the societal backdrop to the Frankfurt School writings of Marcuse, Fromm, Adorno and Horkheimer was that of the Great Depression, Nazism and Soviet communism, the historical period in which Habermas developed his core theoretical and sociological preoccupations was very different indeed. As the nightmare of social barbarism and mass terror receded in the public mind, the world appeared to open out to different social pathways and more optimistic political possibilities. Habermas, a research assistant to Adorno in postwar Germany, developed his political sensibilities not only against the backcloth of the country's emerging preoccupation with democracy and liberal constitutionalism but also the student protests and new social movements sweeping Europe and the United States during the 1960s. Seeking to reformulate critical theory around the imperative of a radical democratization of society, Habermas believed that the basic assumptions of the Enlightenment – particularly the expansion of the spheres of freedom and solidarity – were adequate to transforming society.

Under the pragmatic presuppositions of an inclusive and non-coercive rational discourse among free and equal participants, everyone is required to take the perspective of everyone else, and thus project herself into the understandings of self and world of all others; from this interlocking of perspectives there emerges an ideally extended we-perspective from which all can test in common whether they wish to make a controversial norm the basis of their shared practice; and this should include mutual criticism of the appropriateness of the languages in terms of which situations and needs are interpreted. In the course of successfully taken abstractions, the core of generalizable interests can then emerge step by step.

Jürgen Habermas (1995) 'Reconciliation through the Public Use of Reason: Remarks on John Rawls's Political Liberalism,' *Journal of Philosophy* vol. 92, no. 3, pages 117–18.

Habermas conceived of his work from the outset as an attempt to reorientate social theory towards an interest in language in general and communication in particular. Like many other European intellectuals of the postwar years, such as Michel Foucault, Jacques Lacan and Jacques Derrida whose contributions we have examined, Habermas makes language a central preoccupation of social theory. But his analytical rigor and his interest in language is deployed to take critical social theory in a very specific direction, primarily as a means to understanding *the power of rationality in everyday life*. Language, communication and rationality are key themes of his revised social theory, and he insists that the heritage of Enlightenment reason is no mere projection of local tradition, preference or power. In this connection, his argument is that language is always orientated by and toward mutual agreement and consensus. This can be shown, he argues, in our most basic human capacities for speaking, hearing, reasoning and argumentation. In every act of speech, however shaped by power interests, validity claims are raised and reciprocally recognized: that what we say makes sense and is true, that we are sincere in saying it, and that there is a performative appropriateness to the saying of it. In reformulating critical theory in this way, Habermas projects from this conceptualization of language a radical approach to truth, defined as that which we ultimately come to rationally agree about through communicative dialogue. It is from our capacity for communicative reason that Habermas claims to discern a normative image of the political values of freedom, equality, mutuality and ethical responsibility.

The early Habermas: development and decline of the public sphere

A concern with the sociological distinction between the public sphere and private life has been fundamental to Habermas's social theory from his earliest published writings. *The Structural Transformation of the Public Sphere: An Inquiry into a Category of Bourgeois Society*, a detailed historical study which traces the emergence of a new kind of 'public opinion' to the eighteenth century, managed to combine Habermas's core interests in the public sphere and institutional structures, bourgeois society and social transformations, in its very title. In this early work, he traces the notion of the public sphere to the life of the *polis* in classical Greece. In ancient Greece, the public realm was constituted as a profoundly dialogical arena, a place where individuals came to meet to engage in a public discourse of critical reason and to debate issues of common interest, With the decline of ancient Hellenic civilization this form of critical engagement in the public sphere disappeared also It was not until the development of mercantile capitalism in the sixteenth century, however, that the meaning of 'public opinion' began to shift away from the domain of courtly life as embedded in the traditional texture of old European societies and toward the expansion of market economies and newly defined spheres of division between the state and civil society. In the societies of early or market capitalism, individuals performed a vital role in mediating between the differentiated spheres of the state and civil society through interpersonal interaction, business dealings and civic association. Habermas argues that the essential condition for the emergence of these developments was the culture of the bourgeois family. In the intimate sphere of comfortable family life, a new individual subject emerged, one who was free to think about and probe the traditional textures of hierarchical authority. This emergent, critical attitude was transferred in time to the public domain and, consequently, the institutional structure of societies was transformed.

The emergence of the bourgeois public sphere, according to Habermas, can be traced to various forums of public discussion. Of key importance in this respect was the rise of newspapers, weekly journals and clubs throughout the cities of early modern Europe. In particular, newspapers and journals were used by various educated elites when interacting to debate and question political authority and the conduct of the state. 'Newspapers,' writes Habermas, 'changed from mere institutions for the publication of news into bearers and leaders of public opinion – weapons of party politics.' At the same time, the social basis of this emergent public realm became rooted in the coffee houses, lodges and literary salons of early eighteenth-century Europe, where individuals and groups met to exchange opinions on a dizzying array of ideas and ideologies. Under these social conditions, critical debate flourished.

> The bourgeois public sphere may be conceived above all as the sphere of private people come together as a public; they soon claimed the public sphere regulated from above against the public authorities themselves, to engage them in a debate over the general rules governing relations in the basically privatized but publicly relevant sphere of commodity exchange and social labor. The medium of this political confrontation was peculiar and without historical precedent: people's public use of their reason (*öffentliches Räsonnement*). In our [German] usage this term (i.e. *Räsonnement*) unmistakably preserves the polemical nuances of both sides: simultaneously the invocation of reason and its disdainful disparagement as merely malcontent griping.
>
> Jürgen Habermas (1989 [1962]) *The Structural Transformation of the Public Sphere: An Inquiry into a Category of Bourgeois Society*. Translated by Thomas Burger with the assistance of Frederick Lawrence. Cambridge MA: MIT Press, page 27.

This then is a narrative of the bourgeois age in which unfettered public dialogue reigns supreme, and in which gentlemen come together in clubs and cafes to debate the key issues of the day. Habermas's account of the emergence of a debating public thus grants particular privilege to reason and rationality, logical thinking and consensus. Moreover, he sees in the rise of the bourgeois public sphere a direct parallel between the *polis* of classical Greek city-states and the literary salons and coffee houses of early eighteenth-century Europe, where the critical functions of dialogue and debate were celebrated as a kind of social good. This contrasts, says Habermas, very sharply with modern times. In industrially advanced mass democracies, these critical and probing aspects of the public sphere become substantially reduced. According to Habermas, the commercialization of the media begins to alter the bourgeois public sphere as a forum for the criticism of politics and public decision-making processes. In particular, there is a breakdown in the separation between the state and civil society. Under these conditions, the state comes to penetrate more and more into the economy and civil society, and as such the public sphere is compressed. The rapid expansion of capitalism, and associated intensification of cultural consumption, spells the demise of the public sphere. The public sphere is shrunken, according to Habermas, as the corrosive bureaucratizing logic of capitalist society comes to eat away at the practical and civic agencies of everyday life as well as eroding the influence of broader cultural traditions.

These developments have significance, Habermas argues, not only for the relations between public and private life but also for politics in the contemporary age. The commercialization of the media and the growth of the culture industries in our own time, Habermas concludes, has produced a degradation of genuine civic engagement and the quality of public political debate. In order to understand this distortion of politics, Habermas outlines a critique in which he suggests that individuals today encounter mass communications in essentially *privatized* terms, as isolated selves obsessed with mediated spectacles.

> In comparison with printed communications the programs sent by the new media curtail the reactions of their recipients in a peculiar way. They draw the eyes and ears of the public under their spell but at the same time, by taking away its distance, place it under 'tutelage,' which is to say they deprive it of the opportunity to say something and to disagree. . . . The sounding board of an educated stratum tutored in the public use of reason has been shattered: the public is split apart into minorities of specialists who put their reason to use nonpublicly and a great mass of consumers whose receptiveness is public but uncritical.
>
> (1989 [1962]: 170–1)

Our age of mediated conversation (TV chat shows, radio talkback) is that of politics trivialized. As Habermas concludes, 'today the conversation itself is administered'. The privatized reception of media communication is such that it may be pointless to speak of a robust public sphere at all, which in turn lies at the core of the urgency of Habermas's attempt to reconstruct critical social theory.

There are, however, various difficulties with Habermas's account of the development and decline of the public sphere. Whilst there are many more critical points raised in the general literature on Habermas, there are three significant limitations that I think are worth noting. Firstly, one important criticism is that Habermas's theory of the public sphere, through a series of progressive exclusions, ascribes significance to the *bourgeois* public sphere at the cost of displacing attention from other forms of popular culture and a variety of social movements. But this criticism demands immediate qualification. Habermas's work is not blind to the impact of various forms of popular culture as well as social movements upon the institutional character of modern states. Yet he does underestimate its significance. Recognition of the importance of popular cultural forms is not adequately taken into account in his theorization of the emergence of the public sphere, in the sense that these alternative world-views and ideologies seem in no way to significantly influence, either positively or negatively, the coffee-house debate and discourse that Habermas privileges.

Another, perhaps harsher, criticism of Habermas's early social theory is that it is premised upon a model of the rational human subject which has come under fire and today is widely discredited. In this connection, critics argue that *The Structural Transformation of the Public Sphere* is marred by a typically male and Western overestimation of 'reason' itself. In portraying gentlemen engaged in coffee-house debate as the principal bearers of public opinion in the early modern period, Habermas arguably fails to engage with the deeper political implications of the constitution of the bourgeois public sphere as a predominantly white, male preserve. Feminist, post-feminist and post-colonial social theorists have, for example, profoundly challenged the supposed universal claims of the white, male subject to rationality, and have argued that such global claims have historically been implicated in the marginalization and oppression of minority cultures. If the white, male bourgeois figure is the principal agent of the public sphere in the early modern period, it is for structural, political reasons – the exclusion of women, ethnic minorities and others was so vital to the delineation of political life in early modern Europe, to such an extent as to be fundamental to the very character of the public sphere. It is thus that Habermas's attempt to generalize the male culture of the bourgeois public sphere is questionable, as is his argument that this model of public political life can provide a basis for freedom if successfully reinstated in the contemporary period.

Finally, Habermas's arguments concerning the demise of the public sphere are questionable. The central limitations of this standpoint are twofold. The first is that, while this account is surely correct in emphasizing the commercial character of the media as a factor in explaining the trivialization of politics and depoliticization of public life, Habermas fails to adequately consider the changing nature of the relation between the media, culture and society. Some critics argue that, while Habermas's account of the socio-economic shifts which have led to an erosion of the separation between the state and civil society as well as the emergence of a depoliticized culture is substantially valid, what he nevertheless fails to do is put those shifts into context in terms of issues of media consumption and cultural reception. Few would deny, for instance, that the commercialization of the media and cultural consumption do not impinge on many aspects of our lives. And yet it is surely too simplistic to suggest that such social developments have produced in one fell swoop a systematic degradation of public political life. The second limitation here concerns Habermas's failure to seriously engage with new forms of communication and information technology. Had he considered current developments in communications and transformations of technology, he would surely have recognized the increased complexity of the public political sphere in today's media age. For the development of communications media, particularly the Internet and digital technologies, has significantly altered the relation between the public sphere and private life and – contrary to Habermas's diagnosis of the demise of the public sphere – politics is now a long way from being merely administered. Many of these developments in communication media, especially the growth of digital, decentralized technologies, might not at first sight appear to promote an extension of public political debate. But this is only the case if such developments are judged against traditional, highbrow media formats. If disconnected from anachronistic assumptions about what constitutes genuine public debate, these trends might be used to make some sense of the otherwise puzzling explosion of new voices that the contemporary media ushers into existence. For many of these new media forums and formats, from talkback and talk shows to Internet chat-rooms, are where many people engage with the public sphere, defining issues of social importance which critics have too hastily defined as apolitical or trivial. The present media age is certainly not identical with Habermas's portrait of the demise of the public sphere, and it seems evident that what social theory now requires is a framework of analysis for the public sphere that is relevant to transformations of twenty-first century social life.

Habermas on capitalism, communication and colonization

During the late 1970s and throughout the 1980s, Habermas became increasingly preoccupied with addressing the social conditions of rational decision-making and of delineating the conditions under which communicative argumentation and debate might best flourish in modern societies. In one sense, this shift away from consideration of the public sphere to the social critique of communication made his social theory more directly politically relevant. The historical reconstruction of the public sphere, its flowering and faltering, had given way to more pressing realities of social rationalization and capitalist commodification in societies of the West. Modernity was a world which combined lethal rationalization with seductive consumerism, one upshot of which for Habermas was a wholesale fragmentation of social consciousness. Against the backdrop of a dramatic rise in large corporations, as well as pervasive cultural rationalization stemming from the break-up of society into various specialized, technical processes, it was not surprising that Habermas's work from this period became more specifically sociological in orientation. If the arrival of late capitalism signaled a new phase of globalism, then so too did social theory require a new analytic with which to confront the most pressing issues of the day. In Habermas's hands, this meant a return to Grand Theory.

Habermas's Grand Theory scoops up and reconfigures conceptual traditions from Marxism to the Frankfurt School, whilst along the way managing to incorporate the traditions of Symbolic Interactionism and functionalism. As far as the relationship between rationality and communication goes, however, Habermas's key reference point in *The Theory of Communicative Action* is the work of Max Weber. For it was Weber's account of purposive-rational action, according to Habermas, that paved the way for grasping the rationalization of Western culture, from science, law and politics to art, music and literature. Yet there remain various respects in which Weber's theory of Western modernization as the upshot of a universal historical unfolding of rationalization remains inadequate for understanding the production of modern society. It is against this backdrop that Habermas reassesses Weber's critique of reason. There is a key difference, Habermas contends, between believing in reason as fundamental to the attainment of the good society on the one hand and processes of rationalization on the other. You can believe in the power of reason without being committed to the social rationalization of culture. Indeed, Habermas raises the important question of whether Weber failed to consider that capitalist modernization represents only a partial attainment of the development of reason through degraded processes of rationalization.

In one sense, rationalization is inescapable, since the functional reproduction of large-scale technical systems, such as banking or pensions, is essential to the coordination of life today as we know it. Nevertheless, the coordination of such systemic mechanisms does not take place in a social vacuum. All societal structures, no matter how seemingly technical or administrative, must be anchored in the deeper symbolic textures of society. This, to be sure, requires attention to language, communication and cultural relations. And it is against this backdrop that Habermas situates his social theory with reference to what he terms the 'lifeworld,' that everyday space of Symbolic Interaction and communicative dialogue in which individuals generate particular practices and encounter social structures that become incarnate in their daily activities. In doing so, Habermas develops in his magnum opus, *The Theory of Communicative Action* (1987), an account of the relations between rationality and communication that differs in many respects from the first generation of critical theory. While Habermas, like the Frankfurt School, retains many of the links between political domination, social pathologies and repression of the self, he refuses to accept that the idea of the 'administered society' provides an adequate characterization of late capitalist societies. According to Habermas, the fatalistic vision of reason as self-mutilating in early critical theory arises because of a specific theoretical assumption: namely, that technological rationality applies writ large in all spheres of social action. For Habermas, however, societies develop not only through technological modes of action but also through Symbolic Interaction, or what he calls 'communicative action.' If mastery of the external world is dependent upon forms of instrumental rationalization, then it is crucial to recognize that the social world is structured to its core through language, communication, and symbolic exchange. For Habermas, this analytical separation indicates there are cognitive, moral, and expressive dimensions of social life. The expansion of science, morality, and art in modern culture, in Habermas's view, suggests that rationality can be divided into 'three worlds:' our relation to the external world, our social relations with others, and an aesthetic-expressive dimension which we bring to our own 'inner nature.'

The lifeworld for Habermas refers to certain fundamental convictions and traditions, to collectively shared commitments. These commitments are not necessarily easily articulated, but they are fundamental to the way people live. To believe that it is decent to give a friendly welcome to colleagues arriving at work, to demonstrate extra caution driving a car when children are crossing the road, to offer your bus seat to someone elderly: these are basic kinds of commitments that both preserve the cultural traditions of previous generations and contribute to the reproduction of personal identity and social integration. By contrast, there are actions to do with the functional integration of society which are only partially related to the symbolic field of the lifeworld. Functional systems, then, do not pertain to the question of having value-commitments. That my bank maintains its technical support system for Internet banking is primarily an achievement of what Habermas terms 'systematically stabilized action-contexts.'

> Things are different when system integration intervenes in the very forms of social integration . . . the subjective inconspicuousness of systemic constraints that *instrumentalize* a communicatively structured lifeworld takes on the character of deception, of objectively false

consciousness. The effects of the system on the lifeworld, which change the structure of contexts of action in socially integrated groups, have to remain hidden. The reproductive constraints that instrumentalize a lifeworld without weakening the illusion of its self-sufficiency have to hide, so to speak, in the pores of communicative action. This gives rise to a *structural violence* that, without becoming manifest as such, takes hold of the forms of intersubjectivity of possible understanding. Structural violence is exercised by way of systematic restrictions on communication; distortion is anchored in the formal conditions of communicative action in such a way that the interrelation of the objective, social, and subjective worlds gets prejudged for participants in a typical fashion.

Jürgen Habermas (1987 [1981]) *The Theory of Communicative Action, vol. 2.* Translated by Thomas McCarthy. Cambridge: Polity Press, pages 186–7.

It follows from this analytical separation of system and lifeworld that one must distinguish processes of administrative and economic rationalization from distortions inflicted upon the symbolic texture of everyday life. Habermas argues that the rationalization of systems on the one hand, and that of the lifeworld on the other, follow entirely different logics. According to Habermas, the uncoupling of 'system' from the 'lifeworld' is *not* a sign of cultural domination. On the contrary, this division is intrinsic to modernity. Modern societies, in short, are highly differentiated, divided between the technical reproduction of complex systems and the communicative competence of social actors. On one side, there are system domains, specializing in the material reproduction of capitalism and the modern bureaucratic state. On the other side, there is the lifeworld, specializing in symbolic reproduction – involving communicative competence and dialogue as reproduced in processes of self-formation, socialization and cultural transmission. Now as far as the good society goes, this theory obviously carries significant implications. For one thing, Habermas stresses that any account of the freeing potential of rationality must recognize that the complex systems of modern social life are here to stay. The functional regulation of society, which necessarily entails the coordination of economic and administrative structures, is an essential part of modernity. Such intrinsic aspects of modernity must be carefully distinguished, however, from those insidious forces by which the rationalized logic of systems reproduction seeps into everyday communicative practice. In Habermas's view, the spheres of systems and communicative rationalization sometimes intersect in perversely damaging ways, one upshot of which is personal alienation, lack of societal direction and cultural crisis.

From this more differentiated account of rationalization, Habermas is able to return to the traditional concerns of critical theory: analyzing the distorted and pathological aspects of the modern era. Like Marcuse, Fromm and Adorno, Habermas agrees that modern culture has become increasingly subjected to administrative and bureaucratic control. As the modern state has become increasingly centralized and systematized, so, too, have the communicative and consensual foundations of the lifeworld been subjected to rationalization. In fact, systems integration in modernity has become rationalized to such an extent that Habermas speaks of an 'inner colonization of the lifeworld.' He summarizes this destruction of the resources of cultural tradition as follows:

> The analysis of processes of modernization begins from the general assumption that a progressively rationalized lifeworld is both uncoupled from and made dependent on formally organized action domains, such as the economy and state administration, which are always becoming more complex. This dependence, stemming from the mediazation of the lifeworld through system imperatives, assumes the social-pathological form of an *inner colonization* in so far as critical disequilibria in material reproduction (that is, steering crises accessible to system-theoretical analysis) can be avoided only at the cost of disturbances in the symbolic reproduction of the lifeworld (i.e. of 'subjectively' experienced, identity-threatening crises or pathologies).
>
> (Habermas in Thompson 1984: 291)

In modernized societies, then, functional rationalization has reached the point where it threatens the very foundations of cultural transmission, socialization, and the formation of self-identity upon which it depends for its own legitimation. Having gone beyond their facilitating roles, the economic and administrative systems of the institutional order are today producing 'pathological' effects via the rationalized penetration of the lifeworld. However, the distinction between 'system' and 'lifeworld' allows Habermas to claim that processes of rationalization are not as total in character as they might first appear. There is a deep resistance, he contends, at the core of subjectivity. The pathological effects of such cultural rationalization will often be defended against by the lifeworld. The rise of new social movements, such as ecological and anti-nuclear associations, highlights for Habermas the existence of such tendencies.

The importance of these issues becomes clear if we consider the links between the capacity to engage in social discourse and public debate and certain contemporary ideological biases which repress, privatize, and displace particular interests from the dialogic process. Nancy Fraser, in a persuasive critique of Habermas's work, argues that male dominance and female subordination is a basic element of the current gender system which profoundly delimits equal sexual access to the medium of public debate (Fraser 1985). Fraser charges Habermas's model with a gender-blindness in theorizing the conditions for free communicative practice, claiming that it represses any consideration of women's institutional incapacity to bring certain issues, thoughts, and feelings to light. As an example of women's incapacity to enter public discourse, Fraser points to the many legal jurisdictions in which marital rape is not sanctioned as a crime. If, in the legal domain, women are unable to refuse sexual relations, Fraser enquires, how can they possibly bring their deeper needs, aspirations, and desires to a dialogic process which renders their interests invalid? If women's relationship to collective autonomy is already systematically distorted in this way – 'when a woman says "no" she means "yes" ' – then surely the crucial matter of women's participation in political debate is also likely to be consistently misunderstood and devalued? The key problem, in Fraser's view, is that Habermas's model closes down consideration of the relation between the public sphere of political speech and the institutional repression of interests precisely at the point in which the most pressing problems arise.

Emotional imperialism: feminist criticism of Habermas

Our present political order in the affluent West is based upon the invasion of economic forces into relationships of intimacy, care and our emotional lives as never before. Increasingly, in both the affluent West and the developing world, we witness the invasion of economic thinking into the private realm of personal identity, interpersonal relationships, family life, sexuality and intimacy.

Consider, for example, the 'outsourcing' of care for the young, sick and elderly from rich countries to the developing world. In countries such as Sri Lanka, Thailand and the Philippines, many marginalized, poor women feel economically compelled to migrate to the West in order to obtain paid employment by providing care in contexts of affluent family life. American sociologist Arlie Hochschild terms this global trend the 'care drain,' a kind of asset-stripping of migrant labor from the developing world.

We can better conceptualize the social forces driving this care drain with reference to Habermas's ideas on the colonization of the 'lifeworld' by the 'system.' As contemporary women and men in the work-orientated West find themselves with less and less quality time available for non-work pursuits, so the private sphere and family life – traditional spaces of care and nurturance – come under the influence of invasive economic forces. This dominance arises through the importing of care from the developing world, as traditional caring roles are more and more replaced by economic relations involving cash, credit and power inequalities.

Put this way, Habermas's social theory directly engages with how globalization is restructuring fundamental aspects of our lives. However, some feminists argue that Habermas's view of modernity as involving an uncoupling of 'system' and 'lifeworld' leaves untouched the complex connections between society and gender. That is to say, Habermas's work fails to examine the arguments and evidence concerning transformations of modernity along gendered lines.

In an influential critique, Nancy Fraser (1985) contends that Habermas's thesis of a colonization of the 'lifeworld' by the 'system' is blind to current gender inequalities. Moreover, this blindness reasserts a traditional masculine view of the relation between the public and private spheres as gender-neutral. Habermas's distinction between the private realm of the lifeworld and the institutional economic system, according to Fraser,

> directs attention away from the fact that the household, like the paid workplace, is a site of labor, albeit of unremunerated and often unrecognized labor. Likewise, it does not make visible the fact that in the paid workforce, as in the household, women are assigned to, indeed ghettoized in, distinctively feminine, service-orientated, and often sexualized occupations. Finally, it fails to focalize the fact that in both spheres women are subordinated to men.
>
> (1985: 107)

This sheds light on an unexplored dimension of the social changes affecting the public-private distinction in Habermas's social theory. Fraser highlights the gendered subtext of Habermas's theory of the modern age: the private sphere of the lifeworld, she argues, is far from gender-neutral; it has fallen to women, over a long historical period, to carry out the work of domesticity and of providing the emotional labor of care, comfort and nurturance in family life. But money and power, she notes, should not be viewed as separated off from the private sphere, or as somehow only recently penetrating the world of domestic family life from the institutionalized economic system. According to Fraser, money and power have always been intricately intertwined with the internal dynamics of the family.

How convincing do you find Habermas's argument that the 'lifeworld' is under threat from invasive economic systems? Is this helpful for thinking about our current gendered world?

Habermas on globalization and post-national societies

As cultural awareness of the immense possibilities and threats of globalization accelerated throughout the 1990s, Habermas began renewed reflection on the conditions and consequences of democracy in a world where transnational forms of liberal democratic decision-making are increasingly viable and necessary. In his more recent work, he has argued that since the nation-state is poorly equipped to deal with the extraordinary political, legal and normative challenges posed by globalization, a new 'post-national constellation' is needed at the transnational level to promote democracy and human freedom. Deeply appreciative of the immediate challenges posed by globalization to traditional conceptions of democratic self-governance, political institutions, the public sphere as well as freedom, ethics and justice, he has maintained the goal of a new society based on communicative rationality, one centered upon democratic processes of collective decision-making across territorial borders.

In his discussion of globalization and the political possibilities for new transnational institutions, Habermas explores whether in the complex societies of late capitalism the nation-state is still the central driving force in institutional politics. Whilst acknowledging that proclamations about the supposed 'death of the nation-state' have been greatly exaggerated, he notes that there has been a perceptible change in public consciousness concerning the capacity of nation-states to effectively respond to, and deal with, global political problems. There are a number of persistent key themes in Habermas's late writings in this connection, and these can be summarized as follows. Firstly, he argues that the disempowering consequences of globalization for national governments are increasingly evident. He writes:

The fiscal basis for social policies has steadily dwindled, while the state has increasingly lost its capacity to steer the economy via macro-economic policy. Moreover, the integrational force of nationality as a way of life is diminishing, along with the relatively homogeneous basis of civil solidarity. As nation-states increasingly lose their capacity for action and the stability of their collective identities, they will find it more and more difficult to meet the need for self-legitimation.

(2001c: 80)

Secondly, he contends that the moral and political challenges facing the European Union cannot be met by adapting a policy of laissez-faire, much less by embracing neo-liberal or postmodern theories of globalization processes. He writes:

Under the changed conditions of the postnational constellation, the nation-state is not going to regain its old strength by retreating into its shell. Neo-nationalist protectionism cannot explain how a world society is supposed to be divided back up into pieces, unless through a global politics which, right or wrong, it insists is a chimera. A politics of self-liquidation – letting the state simply merge into postnational networks – is just as unconvincing. And postmodern neo-liberalism cannot explain how the deficits in steering competencies and legitimation that emerge at the national level can be compensated at the supranational level without new forms of political regulation.

(2001c: 81)

Thirdly, Habermas argues that the prospects for transnational political institutions are better than ever before, but also that our need to achieve global solidarity has never been greater. Again, he stresses that European Union institutions can significantly contribute to the furtherance of democratic political communication, and in this connection he questions the political claims advanced by Eurosceptics, Market Europeans and Eurofederalists. The growth of transnational or transboundary problems for national political communities can only partly be addressed by bureaucratic initiatives and market dynamics; we are compelled, says Habermas, to recognize both the intensity and extensity of globalizing forces, with all the radical challenges this presents for democratic political thought. Finally, he argues in favor of popular processes of collective will-formation at the global level. In short, he suggests that social solidarity, which has for so long been stabilized at the level of nation-states, must be shifted up a gear in order to produce a cosmopolitan sense of shared commitments and shared responsibilities. Such a radicalization of democracy, comments Habermas, is not necessarily abstract; the flowering of culturally cosmopolitan sentiments of belonging, inclusion and shared interests are already emerging from the weakening of the nation-state. In terms of the debate over Europe, Habermas wishes to speak up for a pan-European political public sphere that presupposes a European civil society, complete with interest groups, non-governmental organization, citizens' movements, and so forth. Transnational mass media can only construct this multivocal communicative context if, as is already the case in smaller countries, national education systems provide the basis of a common language – even if in most cases it is a foreign language. The normative impulses that first set these different processes in motion from their scattered national sites will themselves only come about through overlapping projects or a common political culture.

(2001c: 103)

It is perhaps not difficult to discern parallels between Habermas's call for cosmopolitan global government and his early, ground-breaking arguments concerning political transformations of publicness, as set out in *The Structural Transformation of The Public Sphere* (1962). An emphasis on the rapid expansion of political participation within the bourgeois public sphere was an essential aspect of Habermas's early social and political thought, particularly the democratic initiatives leading to new forms of public life beyond the sphere of the state. The historical emergence of a bourgeois public sphere in the eighteenth century, as represented by Habermas, signified emergent individuation, autonomy and enlightenment – even though he acknowledged the political form of such a 'public' did not last for long. It is clear, at least in the context of the arguments developed in his essay 'The Postnational Constellation and the Future of Democracy,' that Habermas still sets ultimate political value on public participation and the widest reaching democratization of decision-making processes. Only popular processes of communication and practical discourse, reflecting the impress of collective will-formation, will adequately generate forms of cosmopolitan solidarity geared to the pluralization of democracy emerging at the level of transnational or global social policies. Crucially, moreover, it is clear that Habermas views such democratization as central to the advancement of modernity, especially in terms of the development of post-conventional learning patterns in the realms of society, personality and culture. As he puts this,

The artificial conditions in which national consciousness arose argue against the defeatist assumption that a form of civic solidarity among strangers can only be generated within the confines of the nation. If this form of collective identity was due to a highly abstractive leap from the local and dynastic to national and then to democratic consciousness, why shouldn't this learning process be able to continue?

(2001c: 102)

Towards deliberative democracy

Perhaps more than any other contemporary social theorist, Habermas's recent writings on communicative discourse and ethics are responsible for an explosion of interest in the possibilities and dilemmas of democratic politics in the current age. Since the collapse of authoritarian communism in the late 1980s throughout the former Soviet Union, in East Central Europe and the Baltic countries, along with apparent shifts from dictatorship to liberalism in countries such as Brazil, Argentina and the Philippines, a global trend towards democracy has been celebrated and critiqued in equal measure by many social scientists and intellectuals indebted to Habermas. Some of the most prominent social scientists writing on contemporary politics – such as Amy Gutmann, Seyla Benhabib and Iris Young – have drawn from Habermas's recent work not only to better understand how communicative rationality and reasoned judgments shape the contours of democracy. They have also drawn from Habermas to better understand the *processes* by which reasoned decisions are collectively framed and considered. This focus on the processes of fair and transparent communication is what many social and political theorists have termed 'deliberative democracy.' The idea of deliberation, it is argued by such authors, provides for a conception of democracy that can chart the continued spread of democratic autonomy throughout the globe, as well as critique oppositions to this democratic trend – as demonstrated in the many civil wars, ethnic and national conflicts of recent years, from the Middle East to North Africa.

What is 'deliberative democracy'? The deliberative conception of democracy is firmly grounded in the collective judgment of the people. According to proponents Amy Gutmann and Dennis Thompson,

> deliberative democracy affirms the need to justify decisions made by citizens and their representatives. Both are expected to justify the laws they would impose on one another. In a democracy, leaders should therefore give reasons for their decisions, and respond to the reasons that citizens give in return.
>
> (2004: 3)

What is being underscored here is the capacity of citizens to reflect on arguments and differing points of view, the ability of individuals to deliberate on particular policy proposals and political judgments. What matters is that decisions are reached through a *process* of collective decision-making. But this should not be taken to imply that the deliberative process will always produce agreement. Disagreements between individuals and groups are an endemic feature of politics, and hence deliberative democracy must be conceived as open-ended. It may then help to view deliberation less as a particular style of politics, than as a particular open-ended process of argument and counterargument within politics.

Consider, once more, the invasion of Iraq in 2003. Prior to commencing military action against Saddam Hussein, the United States Government sought to *justify* its decision to go to war before the Congress and United Nations. Various arguments were advanced by the Bush administration concerning the exhaustion of nonmilitary options against Iraq. Secret intelligence relating to Iraq's alleged weapons of mass destruction was also cited by, among others, American, British and Australian governments as *justifying* the military decision to attack Iraq. But whilst individuals may not have had sufficient time to carefully appraise these political arguments at the time they were made, what matters from the standpoint of deliberative democracy is that individuals were subsequently able to profoundly question their original judgments. As Gutmann and Thompson argue:

> the deliberation that did occur laid the foundation for a more sustained and more informative debate after the U.S. military victory than would otherwise have taken place. Because the administration had given reasons (such as the threat of the weapons of mass destruction) for taking action, critics had more basis to continue to dispute the original decision, and to challenge the administration's judgment. The imperfect deliberation that preceded the war prepared the ground for the less imperfect deliberation that followed.
>
> (2004: 2)

How relevant do you find the deliberative conception of democracy to today's political realities? How might the idea of deliberative democracy apply in a world of 24/7 media and global information flows?

Criticisms of Habermas

Habermas's writings on communicative action, democracy and discourse ethics, as well as Europe and the post-national constellation, rank among the richest, most sophisticated contributions to contemporary critical theory. His writings have been, nevertheless, subject to a barrage of criticisms. I will concentrate upon three major weaknesses identified by critics – the first concerning his analysis of modern societies, the second concerning his model of language for social critique, and the third concerning his notion of democratic deliberation and discourse ethics.

Social theory ought to be able to provide some account of its own political positioning and historical contextualization as discourse, especially as regards the relationship between social critique and the analysis of social domination. It seems, however, that for some critics Habermas's thesis of the inner colonization of the lifeworld is simply too generalized. One complaint sometimes heard is that Habermas has replaced one top-heavy critique of the present day – that of the 'administered society' developed in early critical theory – with another top-heavy version. On this view, the thesis of the inner colonization of the lifeworld remains too indebted to the theories of social rationalization advanced by Adorno, Horkheimer and Marcuse. Society stands over and above the individual, with big social institutions ultimately controlling the actions of actors. I have already indicated that it is mistaken to see Habermas as equating processes of social rationalization with the phenomenon of administered societies traced in early critical theory. For one thing, the analytical differentiation of system and lifeworld recognizes the complexity of processes of social reproduction in a fashion that certain currents of Marxist thought cannot; for another, the interpersonal perspective deployed by Habermas for theorizing communication in the contemporary era is significantly different from the solitary, subject-centered orientation to be found in Adorno, Horkheimer and Marcuse. Another charge sometimes heard against Habermas, somewhat more plausibly, is that he has taken over too much of Weber's gloomy social diagnosis and renovated it for the contemporary era. In a striking paradox, then, Habermas's criticism that Weber confined rationalization to purposive-rationality is, in the final analysis, disowned in his theory of communicative action. While separating out the spheres of social rationalization and communicative rationality at a theoretical level, Habermas ends up concurring with Weber that a degraded form of rationality predominates in modern societies. In this, as in other ways, the legacy of classical sociology reasserts its power over modern social theory.

However the more pressing difficulty arising from Habermas's work, in my opinion, concerns not the top-heavy or gloomy account he provides of social rationalization and domination (for, as noted, Habermas is far too subtle and sophisticated a social analyst for these charges to have much force), but rather why actors do not perceive such threats more acutely. In effect, this is to raise the question of how might Habermas's theory of the inner colonization of the lifeworld round upon its own conditions of possibility as lived experience? John B. Thompson puts such concerns forcefully:

Why do members of the lifeworld not perceive that they are threatened by the uncontrolled growth of system complexity, rooted ultimately in the dynamics of capital accumulation and valorization? Why do they not resist this growth directly and demand, in an open and widespread way, the transformation of the economic system which underlies it?

(1984: page unknown)

If a traumatized lifeworld threatens to bring society undone, this would appear to be a trauma that for Habermas remains blocked to consciousness – denied, displaced, disowned. But such an assessment of modern culture is surely questionable. It may be that social practices like booking a flight online, watching a DVD or listening to talkback radio are so contaminated by the functional logic of late capitalism that people can't possibly think outside of these terms. But could the same be said for donating money to Oxfam or Save the Children, attending a community meeting on local government issues or reassessing the weekly grocery list in terms of environmental considerations? There is no easy way to understand the ideological or political differences as regards such social practices in Habermas's sociology, save for invoking the terms 'inner colonization' or 'social pathology.' Yet one might reasonably wonder how suggestive such terms are for grasping the diversity and plurality of social practices in the current age.

Secondly, Habermas's work has come in for some sharp criticism as regards his model of language and of how he ties forms of communicative rationality to the project of critical theory. There are serious reservations, for example, about the supposedly invariable, intrinsic connections between language, rationality and the counterfactual ideal speech situation which Habermas posits. In what sense, one might reasonably wonder, does the yelling of obscenities at a football match presuppose an orientation towards mutual agreement and consensus? How might one discern in the slogans of fascist organizations, such as the British National Party or the National Front, respect for the ideals of communication and community? These are indeed serious problems, and some critics have gone as far as to suggest that Habermas's model of communicative rationality is too procedural and legalistic, unable to account in all but the most abstract fashion for how people might agree on what counts as a better argument in concrete instances of political conflict. How might the impact of colonialism, post-colonialism, race, ethnicity, sexuality and gender affect participants in debates affecting their forms of life? Part of the difficulty here, according to Seyla Benhabib, is that Habermas's model is pitched so wide as to accommodate only the 'generalized other' and not the 'concrete other.' Viewed from this perspective, we can identify the political limitations of Habermas's theory of communicative rationality more precisely. In theory, Habermas's model presumes that reason permits individuals to decide on competing perspectives and that decisions or norms can be judged fair provided that all people are equally affected. But how can such a political ideal of communicative rationality be projected from a model of language to a world in which actions, decisions, debates and norms affect millions and millions of people widely scattered in space and time?

Finally, some commentators are especially critical of Habermas's reconceptualization of the normative dimension of the public sphere in terms of the theory of communicative action and deliberative democracy. For these critics, it is not easy to see how democratic ideals can be projected from the allegedly universal structures of language. The weak version of this criticism is that Habermas's deep consensus theory of truth does not sufficiently protect liberal values such as human rights or freedom of expression (see Gutmann and Thompson 2004). The stronger version of this criticism is that Habermas's overall democratic project fails to adequately account for the grip of neurotic, compulsive patterns of behavior – patterns that block the very grounds for deliberating rationally in modern societies. The argument, bluntly put, is that Habermas's notion of rational consensus is out of kilter with the plurality of moral, ethical and related evaluative standpoints that proliferate in contemporary societies. How might it be possible, for example, to provide individuals with equal chances to deliberate, let alone ever successfully disentangle the 'force of the better argument,' on the controversial political and moral issues of our times? And quite how Habermas's vision of unconstrained communication applies to our 24/7 media and entertainment culture is not immediately apparent. Other critics note that Habermas's stress on participation in rational debate cannot cope with problems arising from the exclusionary character of the public sphere – exclusions on grounds of, say, identity, gender or ethnicity (see Fraser 1985). Ultimately, all of these criticisms appear to acknowledge that democratization requires an undoing of the systematic distortion of the communicative structures of modern societies. Where these critics part company with Habermas, however, concerns the adequacy of the notion of rational consensus as a means of confronting the moral and practical issues of our times. The problem, in other words, is that Habermas's consensual, cooperative theory of social action seems to bear little relation to the kinds of politics, cultures and lifestyles that predominate in these early years of the twenty-first century.

Honneth: the struggle for recognition

One of the more influential inheritors of the tradition of critical theory in our own time is Axel Honneth. Like Adorno, Marcuse and Habermas before him, Honneth attempts to unmask pathologies of society as rooted in the fragility and fragmentation of reason. Yet whereas Habermas connects the fitful interplay of reason and irrationality to other fundamental forces, revolving on language, communication and dialogue, Honneth is more concerned to trace our daily social conflicts in terms of moral experiences of disrespect, denigration and humiliation. To do this, Honneth focuses in *Disrespect* (2007) on the notion of recognition, drawing attention to the growing political demands today of individuals and groups for public acknowledgement of particular identities, needs, emotions and more particular ways of life. According to Honneth demands for social recognition derive from relays or transmissions of negative, painful experiences of disrespect. From the psychological experience of humiliation to the political ramifications of injustice, social antagonisms and cultural conflicts are for Honneth associated with the attempted recovery of individual needs and desires for self-respect. Recognition, rather like the interpersonal, dynamic process of communication itself, is an open-ended affair which facilitates ceaseless explorations of, and reconciliations between, self-assertion and dependency, individualism and solidarity.

Social life contains different kinds of recognition, each anchored in different experiences of interpersonal interaction and moral claims. Honneth focuses on three forms of recognition in particular, which he seeks to connect to the normative or utopian aspirations of critical theory. These are (1) self-confidence; (2) self-respect; and (3) self-esteem. Confidence in continuity of the self derives from our primary emotional relationships with familial or significant others in childhood. These earliest experiences of love are, for Honneth, essential preconditions for the realization of mature ego-development. Drawing from the psychoanalytic theories of D. W. Winnicott, Honneth considers how early experiences of love contribute to the emergent individual's negotiation of social interaction – with a focus on the role of unconscious spontaneity in shaping the moral conduct of daily life. What matters in such early interactions between the infant and mother, or significant other, is not that the child learns to view itself as a fully independent being in one fell swoop; rather, a complex emotional interplay between self-assertion and attachment is established. At their emotional core, human relationships are always marked by a radical tension between connection and separation, dependence and self-assertion. And it is from this interplay that individuals develop a positive emotional relation to their own identities, as well as self-confidence for acting in the wider world.

Love, in Honneth's opinion, fulfills the role of preparing individuals for the difficult emotional work of reconciling demands, throughout life, for recognition from others, on the one hand, with the desire for self-assertion, on the other hand. Love is thus, one might claim, at the very root of both moral identity and political society. Indeed, Honneth contends that the experience of self-confidence which derives from love is 'conceptually and genetically prior' to other forms of identity recognition – such as respect and esteem. The demand for recognition knows no inner limit. It can be held in place only by intersubjective, reciprocal, moral, political and legal forms, which means that it is always in process rather than some final point of destination. This is surely one reason why all demands for recognition betray a kind of personal injury or cultural trauma at their very core. The form or kind of violation in question, according to Honneth, can be of three sorts – corresponding to the earlier typology of self-confidence, self-respect and self-esteem. Because people are routinely maltreated in familial and wider social circles, the experience of self-identity often contains some degree of emotional damage. A similar logic is at work with the modern political world in general, where exclusion from certain legal rights is insep-arable from harm to a person's sense of self-respect. In another sense, the fate of self-esteem hangs on how others react to, and engage with, the way of life a person has chosen.

Demands for recognition, then, always harbor certain experiences of disrespect, which they seek to recall and reconfigure in social and political terms. Feelings of shame, humiliation or rage are an emotional infinity, which can be interpreted as signs of injustice. Indeed, the desire for freedom is shaped to its core by experiences of social disrespect – there is an *internal link*, according to Honneth, between the sense of injustice and the demand for recognition. Such injustice, or the experience of disrespect, acts as a trigger for the launching of social antagonisms or cultural conflicts against the established political order. Only in this way, says Honneth, can the progressive movement towards more democratic public spheres be understood. Consider, for example, the women's movement and feminism. The emergence of the women's movement, and especially the heyday of feminism in the 1960s and 1970s, involved the critical examination of certain exclusions of women from the workforce in particular and the wider society in general. The whole sensibility of feminism involved a reappraisal of women's suffering away from the narrowly psychological realm and towards social life as a whole. There was a genuinely excited sense that feminism as a social movement offered a new, enlightened understanding of women's oppression. The anxiety and depression which many women suffered in the modern age had their roots not in any emotional failings or maladjustments of women themselves, but in power imbalances and gender divisions throughout society. Using the ideas of Honneth, the exclu-sion of women from the public sphere and confinement to domesticity occurred as part of a patriarchal blending of control and violence, denigra-tion and injustice. Feminism, as both social theory and social movement, thus came about as more and more people came to a new self-consciousness of these traumatic exclusions – determined as they were to initiate a societal shift from gender injustice to gender struggle.

> **F**or the victims of disrespect . . . engaging in political action has the direct function of tearing themselves out of the crippling situation of passively endured humiliation and helping them, in turn, on their way to a new, positive relation-to-self. The basis for this motivation for struggle is connected to the structure of the experience of disrespect itself. . . . Social shame is a moral emotion that expresses the diminished self-respect typically accompanying the passive endurance of humiliation and degradation. If such inhibitions on action are overcome through involvement in collective resistance, individuals uncover a form of expression with which they can indirectly convince themselves of their moral or social worth. For, given the anticipation that a future communication-community will recognize them for their present abilities, they find themselves socially respected as the persons that they cannot, under present circumstances, be recognized for being. In this sense, because engaging in political struggle publicly demonstrates the ability that was hurtfully disrespected, this participation restores a bit of the individual's lost self-respect.
>
> Axel Honneth (1995) *The Struggle for Recognition: The Moral Grammar of Social Conflicts*. Cambridge: Polity Press, page 164.

In one sense, Honneth's reorientation of contemporary critical theory away from communication and towards recognition brings social critique closer to the bone of current political conflicts. That is to say, Honneth underwrites the sociological significance of a range of new social movements, respecting their demands for political recognition and seeing in them a radical challenge to traditional ideas about class, economy and the nation-state. For Honneth, a critical theory of recognition dovetails with the new politics of identity, culture, ethnicity and difference – which runs all the way from post-feminism and the green movement to the struggles of indigenous peoples and the politics of multiculturalism. This is not to say that recognition theory is simply an index of the contemporary political climate; it is also, vitally, a normative or utopian image of how individuals and groups might navigate the troubled waters of the twenty-first century. From this angle, for example, the fight that an organization like Amnesty International has waged against state torture can be recast as part of a 'politics of self-confidence' – the unmasking of forms of bodily violation, tied to the demand for human rights.

Honneth's theory of recognition has been important for contemporary social theory. In outlining alternative strategies for engaging the new politics of identity and cultural difference, his work has scooped up and reconfigured social theory, moral theory and political philosophy. His approach has certain affinities with other theorists of the 'politics of recognition,' such as Charles Taylor and Seyla Benhabib, but arguably Honneth's is the richest in terms of social theory rather than political philosophy. For to understand social conflicts after Honneth means being able to grasp the new politics of recognition as rooted in the experience of disrespect or humiliation. From this perspective, Honneth's attempt to recover the political meanings and normative possibilities springing from displaced emotions is a return to the original Frankfurt School project of investigating the personal dimensions of social crisis and political domination. Notwithstanding this, and whilst also acknowledging that Honneth's work is still in the process of elaboration, there are difficulties worth noting. For one thing, it is not immediately obvious what needs to be done to conclusively prove Honneth's account of recognition correct. That is to say, how exactly might such an abstract account of human needs – manifesting as the desire for recognition – be tested against current global realities? Does the fact that only some groups in society demand special forms of public recognition invalidate the general sweep of Honneth's theory? What about the personal and social conditions under which people become aware of hurt feelings? Honneth seems to assume that the objective forms of disrespect – towards women of color, ethnic groups, indigenous peoples and others marginalized – are always accompanied by an awareness of hurt feelings. But is this, in fact, so? What of the consequences of cultural trauma? Is it not the case that the suffering and pain inflicted upon some victims of state violence is so brutal that individuals are unable to struggle against such injustice? Part of the difficulty here is that Honneth, whilst attentive to the emotional dimensions of human suffering, and whilst selectively engaged with psychoanalysis, fails to appreciate that the *unconscious* can block the translation of hurt feelings into the public demand for recognition.

The shift from disrespect to a struggle for recognition and justice, in other words, is only likely to come about in quite specific personal and political conditions. In our own time, the rise of globalization, multinational corporations and a wall-to-wall entertainment culture is arguably such that many individuals are incapacitated to some degree in their emotional capacities concerning the translation of private injuries into demands for political recognition. Not only is this something that Honneth is insufficiently alert to – unlike the Frankfurt School, for example, he says little about the 'culture industries' – but it leads him to overestimate the degree to which demands for recognition can actually transform social relations. In Honneth's account, the emergence of more inclusive institutional forms of recognition – which unfold through the new politics of identity and cultural difference – is intrinsically tied to the moral progress of society.

But, again, why should this be so? Why should the politics of recognition result always in the progressive moral advancement of society? How, at any rate, might we adequately judge between morally valid and invalid types of identity-politics? What of the demands for recognition from neo-nationalist movements or ethnic tribal traditions? Cornelius Castoriadis captures this political point well:

> I do not respect other's difference simply as difference and without regard to what they are and what they do. I do not respect the difference of the sadist, of Eichmann, or Beria – any more than those who cut off people's heads, or even their hands, even if they are not threatening me directly.
>
> (1997a: 398)

If it is true that recognition struggles lead to moral progress, the onus is on Honneth to demonstrate how this might tally with a world in which disrespect appears limitless. Like Habermas, Honneth focuses on morality to emphasize the learning capacities of individuals, groups and social institutions within society. This is a fundamental aspect of contemporary critical theory. But it is a dimension of both Habermas's and Honneth's work which at times pulls uneasily against the commitment to social critique elaborated in the Frankfurt School writings of Adorno, Fromm and Marcuse. For as the Frankfurt School demonstrated, moral discourse is around to help us realize the best of which we are capable; whilst it is the task of social theory to remind us of how and why, as a society, we often fall short of such lofty ambitions.

Summary points

1   Contemporary Critical Theory represents the systematic extension of ideas developed by the neo-Marxist Frankfurt School in order to analyze current global transformations. The leading representative of contemporary critical theory is Jürgen Habermas, Emeritus Professor of the University of Frankfurt and one of Europe's foremost public intellectuals.

2   Habermas's contributions to social theory span some five decades. But all of his contributions, broadly speaking, contest technocratic social policy and power politics in the name of a more rounded communicative approach to social life and morality.

3   Focusing on language in general and communication in particular, Habermas seeks to reconstruct the presuppositions of human

communication, dialogue and debate. His essential idea is that any statement about the world raises three validity claims: that the claim makes sense and is true, that the claim is sincere, and that there is a performative appropriateness to the saying of it. From this idea, Habermas derives a theory of truth defined as rational agreement through communicative dialogue.

4   In Habermas's studies of the public sphere, reason and rationality are traced as fundamental to the transformed relations between personal and social life in market capitalism. In advanced capitalism, however, bureaucracy, technology and the culture industries erode the quality of public political debate. Politics and social life, says Habermas, become *administered*.

5   Modern societies for Habermas are powerfully torn by conflicts between the 'lifeworld' and 'systems reproduction,' so much so that the latter comes to *colonize* the former. These conflicts are between communicative action in the lifeworld (the social dialogues that remain in principle open to rational debate) on the one hand, and on the other hand capitalist culture, bureaucracy and technology that have come to dominate the modern world.

6   There have been various criticisms made of Habermas's reformulations of critical theory, including that his account of the colonization of the lifeworld by large-scale technical systems is too Marxist or deterministic. A related criticism is that Habermas neglects how culture and the economy intermingle in the life of individuals; contemporary cultural processes are simply dismissed as trivializing and, thus, Habermas ignores the vital ways in which cultural creativity can be used to contest social pathologies issuing from capitalism, bureaucracy and technology.

Further questions

1   Does public debate lead to an advancement of reason and rationality?

2   What are some modern arenas for public debate?

3   Habermas argues that freedom and solidarity are universal values that should be supported. Do you agree? Should they be supported with force?

4 What kinds of contact with the public sphere have you experienced throughout your life? How does discussion and deliberation lead to a better society?

5 Do you use Internet news sources such as blogs, chat rooms, or discussion boards to engage with political developments and news?

Further reading

Jürgen Habermas

The Theory of Communicative Action (Cambridge: Polity Press, 1987)
Moral Consciousness and Communicative Action (Cambridge Mass.: MIT Press, 2001a)
The Structural Transformation of the Public Sphere (Cambridge: Polity Press, 1989)
Between Facts and Norms: Contributions to a Discourse Theory of Law and Democracy (Cambridge: Polity Press, 1996)
The Postnational Constellation: Political Essays (Cambridge: Polity Press, 2001b)

Axel Honneth

The Struggle for Recognition: The Moral Grammar of Social Conflicts (Cambridge: Polity Press, 2005)
Disrespect: The Normative Foundations of Critical Theory (Cambridge: Polity Press, 2007)

chapter 12

Feminism and Post-feminist Theory

Contents

In a university where I worked some years ago, an email exchange amongst colleagues rapidly and dramatically threatened to bring some promising academic careers undone. The precise details I have long since forgotten, but the core of the matter concerned what people then called a 'gender incident' – a matter which had arisen upon nothing more and nothing less than the hasty deployment of words (issuing from a colleague's email), and which then attached itself to powerful emotions throughout this university department. This served to divide and antagonize various members of staff. Along the way, several staff noted for their reconciliatory talents tried to intervene in the dispute. Yet each further email only seemed to make matters worse, as if dragging language away from whatever connections to social things and events it might once have had. Such was the play of emotional forces operating inside this heated exchange of language that confusion abounded, no one could agree or take up any single, consistent viewpoint in relation to the incident. Established patterns of meaning within this academic department were thrown into question. Plus which, the original parties to this dispute were going through absolute contortions in order to defend themselves against certain misunderstandings and possible transgressions of gender politics. Each email, or at least this according to memory, began: 'What I meant to say was . . .'

When, more than thirty years ago in Europe, the psychoanalytic feminist Julia Kristeva wrote so insightfully of a pattern or play of unconscious forces at work inside language, she might have had in mind experiences of this kind, even though as a literary critic the bulk of her own work has addressed the writings of poets and novelists. Kristeva, whose contribution to feminism and post-feminist theory we will examine in some detail throughout this chapter, looks to the emotionally-laden realm of the repressed unconscious – what she terms the 'semiotic' – as enabling for feminism. Like many feminist social theorists who have turned to psycho-analysis to better understand how unequal gender relations shape identities and everyday life, such as Juliet Mitchell, Nancy Chodorow, Jessica Benjamin and Judith Butler, Kristeva focuses on the repressed unconscious or 'semiotic' as a means of undermining the patriarchal sexual and social order of modern societies. Kristeva's version of feminism, as we will see, is in one sense all her own – an exotic blend of Lacan, linguistics, literary criticism and post-structuralism. In the course of this chapter, however, we will also review much other ground-breaking feminist criticism, ranging across engagements with sociology, psychology, political theory, postmodernism and queer theory. In all of these approaches, feminism and post-feminist theory provides a crucial link between embodied experience and social relations, between identity and culture, between problems of identity or sexuality and problems of social organization.

Theorizing patriarchy: 1970s feminisms

The university dispute over gender I mentioned above took place in the 1980s. This was a time in which academics, feminists and political progressives of various kinds were becoming increasingly aware of multiple differences between women, between women and men, and indeed of the powers of social diversity and cultural difference in the making of identity itself. This is perhaps why, in the university gender dispute I'm recalling, there seemed to be as many divisions between female colleagues as there were political differences between women and men. At the level of social theory, this increasing attention to both gender differences and social divisions within feminism was closely aligned with the influence of post-structuralism (see Chapter 4). Various post-structuralist emphases, from its suspicion of 'identity' to its debunking of metaphysical foundations, seemed to fit hand-in-glove with the rise of the more consumerist and individualizing 1980s. Yet deconstructing the differing styles of gender, through either post-structuralist or postmodern discursive analyses, was itself a counter-reaction to an earlier feminist sensibility. I am referring to 1970s gender theory, in which an emphasis on women's shared needs and political interests was considered key to the critique of gender.

In her classic book *The Second Sex* (1988: 295), the French feminist Simone de Beauvoir declared: 'One is not born, one becomes, a woman.' This statement prefigured the whole cast of 1970s gender theory, with its totalizing claim that gender goes all the way down, and thus organizes the very constitution and shape of 'femininity' and 'masculinity.' Human beings are born male and female, but become men and women through a process of social construction. Seeking to give some analytical precision to this gendered process of social construction, the British feminist Ann Oakley (1972) wrote of a distinction between biological 'sex' and socialized 'gender.' This was an attempt, in effect, to overwrite the naturalization of biology with the cultural learning investigated by sociology. Gender reproduction, on this view, refers to the ways in which people are socialized into distinct gender patterns of behavior. Gender roles of 'masculinity' and 'femininity' might be experienced by people in their daily lives as spontaneous dispositions, but are in fact deeply determined by the wider society and culture. Gender is bound up with cultural forces of socialization, role learning and gender stereotyping.

'Sex' is a biological term: 'gender' a psychological and cultural one. Common sense suggests that they are merely two ways of looking at the same division and that someone who belongs to, say, the female sex will automatically belong to the corresponding (feminine) gender. In reality this is not so. To be a man or a woman, a boy, or a girl, is as much a function of dress, gesture, occupation, social network and personality, as it is of possessing a particular set of genitals.

This rather surprising contention is supported by a number of facts. First, anthropologists have reported variation in the way different cultures define gender. It is true that every society uses biological sex as a criterion for the ascription of gender, but, beyond that simple starting point, no two cultures would agree completely on what distinguishes one gender from the other. Needless to say, every society believes that its own definitions of gender correspond to the biological duality of sex.

Culturally, therefore, one finds the same biological distinctions between male and female coexisting with great variations in gender roles. By contrast one also finds individual people whose culturally defined genders coexist with indeterminate sex.

Ann Oakley (1972) *Sex, Gender and Society.* Melbourne: Sun Books, page 158.

The claim that the whole of our lives are carried out within the frame of certain 'sex roles' or 'sex-role stereotyping' gave rise to the highly politically charged character of much feminist social theory throughout the 1970s. Whether studying the broader gender context of family life, education or the job market, feminist social theorists argued that gender and sexuality are key organizing forces of social relations and cultural domination. One valuable insight of feminism in the 1970s was the unearthing of the intricate connections between personal and family life, sexuality and culture. Gender stereotypes or norms were demonstrated to be indissociable from certain ideological forces – such as capitalist market relations or bureaucratic authority – and thus deeply bound up with issues of power and social control. If gender roles reflected patterns of sexual inequality, this is because we live in a social order in which men are dominant. On this reckoning, masculinity symbolizes power and prestige, with women recast by a sexist culture as subordinate and oppressed. The political task of feminism thus emerged as involving not only the critique of men's dominance in the social order but a particular form of politics, concerned with social justice and the transformation of gender relations in modern societies.

The rise of gender theory during the 1970s occurred when radical politics, especially liberationist movements and Black civil rights protests, was ascendant. Feminism, as part of a multitude of liberationist social movements, was concerned to put the whole sexual and social order of modern societies into question in the name of a transformed and emancipated social organization. For some, the ambitiousness of feminism's social critique was over-politicized; for others, the emancipatory zeal of feminism was mere utopianism. Nevertheless, the women's movement – as the political wing of feminist social theory – was stunningly successful in its impact upon both personal and political life. From the nursery to marriage, the field of gender was unmasked by feminist social theorists as social and political to its very roots. Gender was deployed in this context to refer to both the constitution of differences between men and women and the perpetuation of male domination throughout history. The upside of this political deployment of social theory is that it offered a strikingly direct account of the social dynamics of gender – with power encircling solicited gender roles at every turn. The downside of 1970s feminism, however, is that gender binaries – dominant masculinity, subordinate femininity – seemed to become entrenched. Not only were possible similarities and points of emotional connection between women and men sidestepped, but the matter of social and cultural differences between women was theoretically and politically ignored. As feminist theorist Lynne Segal observes of the limits of 1970s gender theory:

> many men have little or no purchase on the power that is supposed to be the prerogative of their sex, while a significant minority of women have access to considerable power and privilege. Gender binaries never exist in pristine form. Women and men are always already inserted in contexts of race, class, age, sexual orientation and multiple other belongings: each with their deeply entrenched connections to power and authority, or the lack of it.

> (1999: 42)

Gender theory of the 1970s is now some thirty years or so behind us. Yet the social theory of gender undertaken throughout the 1970s was not all cut of the same cloth. Whilst gender theory undoubtedly had as its prime focus issues of women's shared needs, social subordination and gender inequalities, there were countless reworkings of feminist social theory during this period. Some of the most significant theoretical breakthroughs concerned trying to understand how unequal gender relations bite deeply within the fabric of personal experience and the textures of daily life. Other innovative feminist research focused on the interplay of women's role as mothers on the one hand, and the cultural learning of gender on the other. In both approaches, gender was understood as sociologically and psychologically complex in character, and, in the ground-breaking work of feminist social theorists such as Mitchell, Dinnerstein, Chodorow and Benjamin, the field of gender was always conceptualized within the broader structures of society, culture and politics.

Juliet Mitchell on femininity and sexual difference

The publication in 1974 of Juliet Mitchell's *Psychoanalysis and Feminism* represented a path-breaking moment in feminist theory in the English-speaking world. This widely read book defended the importance of psycho-analysis to feminism and women's oppression, developed a powerful critique of the biological reductionism implicit in then influential feminist psychologies, and introduced Lacan to many English-speaking people. Like many other social theorists we have looked at in the course of this book, Mitchell made use of Lacan's approach in studying identity in order to grasp how modern societies perpetuate gender divisions. In emphasizing the importance of loss to the making of identity (see Chapter 7), Mitchell radicalizes Lacan's emphasis.

> The greater part of the feminist movement has identified Freud as the enemy. It is held that psychoanalysis claims women are inferior and that they can achieve true femininity only as wives and mothers. Psychoanalysis is seen as a justification for the status-quo, bour-geois and patriarchal, and Freud in his own person exemplifies these qualities. I would agree that popularized Freudianism must answer to this description; but the argument of this book is that a rejection of psycho-analysis and of Freud's works is fatal for feminism. However it may have been used, psychoanalysis is not a recommendation *for* a patriarchal society, but an analysis *of* one. If we are interested in understanding and challenging the oppression of women, we cannot afford to neglect it.
>
> Juliet Mitchell (1974) *Psychoanalysis and Feminism*. London: Penguin Books, page xiii.

Mitchell argues that the unconscious acquisition of patriarchy in modern societies is central to women's suffering. In Mitchell's analysis of femininity, the family and sexual politics, a Lacanian-based feminism is developed to make the following points: the positioning of the human unconscious within asymmetrical power relations as men and women; the separation between biological sex and the construction of sexual difference; and the consequent interlinking of sexuality and other forms of ideology for the replication of unequal power relations. That the account of sexual difference offered by Freud and Lacan should be read as an *analysis* of the psychic roots of patriarchal social relations, and not as a justification for patriarchy, is perhaps the main contribution of Mitchell's early work to feminism. On this view, Freud's account of the central 'marks of womanhood' – masochism, penis-envy, jealousy, a weak superego – are understood as a consequence of women's subjection to patriarchal law, and not as innate psychological attributes.

Femininity, for Mitchell as for Lacan, is defined by loss. Woman, on this view, is nothing outside of the various linguistic, psychological, social and cultural constructions in which identities are forged. Sexuality and subjectivity, intertwined in the unconscious, are constituted with entry into the symbolic order of language. (See the discussion of Lacan's Saussurian-influenced account of language in Chapter 7.) Perhaps one of the most controversial psychoanalytic claims that contemporary social theory engages with is the idea that gender identity is tied to loss – specifically, the possession or absence of the penis. When considering Lacan's theory in Chapter 7, we looked in some detail at how his 'return to Freud' involved reinterpreting certain core concepts in psychoanalysis – the Oedipus complex and castration, for example – through the lens of post-Saussurian linguistics. It is these aspects of Lacan's work on sexuality to which Mitchell is especially attentive, which now requires us to reconsider some aspects of Freud's work and its subsequent modification by Lacan. Several features of Freud's theory are relevant for understanding Mitchell's feminism. In Freud's account of the Oedipus complex, an active, masculine sexuality is attributed to children of both sexes – as Freud puts this, 'the little girl is a little man.' Biological sex difference, on this view, remains irrelevant for the child until the onset of the phallic phase, in which sexual difference becomes centered on the possession or absence of the penis. In the case of boys, said Freud, Oedipus depends upon an imagined event of the father's threat of castration; in the case of girls, castration is imagined as having already been inflicted.

Why does Freud argue that girls suffer from 'penis envy'? Many feminists reject Freudian psychoanalysis as sexist, and initially at least it is easy to see why. But Mitchell rejects this claim; she argues that Freud's claim about the little girl's 'penis envy' is, in fact, a critique of how patriarchy goes all the way down – to our emotional lives, gender and intimacy. Girls, as

Mitchell rehearses Freud, respond to the discovery of genital difference through *imagining* that castration has already taken place – both upon themselves and their similarly 'castrated' mothers. Freud makes clear this occurs at the level of *fantasy*; but nonetheless it is a fantasy that calls into question the girl's former masculine sexuality – she realizes that she lacks the penis with which to pursue her active, libidinal desires. Rejecting her mother in fury, the girl emotionally withdraws and instead turns toward her father. But this is a kind of emotional dead-end, once the girl realizes that she cannot have her father exclusively. As such, the girl turns back – unconsciously – toward the mother, and forges an identification with her feminine gender position.

It is precisely these aspects of Freud's account of gender identity – Oedipus, the castration complex and sexual difference as the result of a painful emotional division within the child – which Mitchell feels are fruitfully extended in the work of Lacan. In Lacan's theory, as discussed in Chapter 7, the child's entry into social relations occurs at the symbolic level of language. The shift from the child's imaginary unity with the maternal body into a symbolic order of social and sexual differences requires the intervention of a third person (the father), or term (language). By prohibiting the child access to the mother's body, the symbolic order (or what Lacan calls the 'Name-of-the-Father') operates to institute the threat of castration – the *power* backing this threat being symbolized by his *phallus*. The phallus both serves to wrench the child away from desire for the mother (which must be repressed) and stands for entry into the symbolic order. That is to say, the position that an individual takes up as a gendered-subject within the symbolic order is necessarily tied to a fundamental loss – the loss of the maternal body. And it is because of this loss of the maternal body that human sexuality is understood as being created within a lack, leaving the phallus to stand in for the divided and incomplete human subject at the level of sexual division.

Following Lacan, Mitchell argues that the phallus – at the level of cultural fantasy – inscribes unequal gender-relations at the heart of identity. One reason why gender relations are unequal, says Mitchell, is that social difference is *represented* by men. Children encounter difference through reference to the father, as representative of language and the symbolic world. Linking Lacan with structuralist emphases, Mitchell thus argues that female sexuality is not something with 'positive' content. Femininity only acquires meaning by way of its *difference* from masculinity. The category 'woman' operates as an idealized Other, entirely separate from particular females, that men and women fantasize as a potential site of desire, fulfillment, joy, and wholeness. Female sexuality is thus an imaginary supplement to that lack which informs the structure of subjectivity. A radical feminist politics, for Mitchell, implies interrogating and subverting those rigid masculine, phallic fantasies that are so central to our systematically unequal gender relations.

What perhaps was so striking, and ultimately so disturbing, about Mitchell's feminist engagement with psychoanalysis was its by-passing of notions of cultural learning or socialization in favor of a more complex model of both psychic experience and gender identity. This involved an in-depth feminist reading of both Freud and Lacan, and in particular grappling with the psychoanalytic claim that fathers or men – in breaking the imaginary unity of the mother and child unit – represent the core links between power and desire in the current gender order. Of course, one response within feminist social theory to Mitchell's work was simply to dismiss psychoanalysis itself as sexist. However, and as noted, Mitchell had already confronted that claim directly, refocusing psychoanalysis as a *critique* of patriarchy. More interestingly, some critics asked whether fathers or men must always stand as the representative of the symbolic order of language? For if this is so, surely it seems to suggest that a non-patriarchal symbolic order is impossible, thus undercutting the feminist political project in one stroke. Such questions were obviously vital to feminist social theory, and in time served to clarify the principal shortcomings of Mitchell's approach to gender identity. Perhaps the most widely agreed limitation is that, notwithstanding her use of very complex psychoanalytic categories and concepts, Mitchell's analysis tends to exaggerate the rigidities and uniformity of gender in the current social order. If, as Mitchell claims, women entirely repress their unconscious sexuality and become symbolically fixed in relation to the phallus as the lacking Other (that is, as men's object of desire) it is extraordinarily difficult to understand what motivates feminist strategy in the first place or how a radical politics might destabilize gender categories.

Contrary to Mitchell's exploration of gender identity, we might still ask: Is the symbolic order of language, painstakingly tracked in psychoanalytic theory and post-structuralism, really so rigid and monolithic? Can femininity only be defined as the negative pole of masculinity? These are questions to which feminist social theory returns, and develops some novel answers, throughout the 1980s and 1990s. But first we must turn to some other versions of feminist social theory, which seek to shift the emphasis away from fathers or men and towards mothers or women in the constitution of gender identity.

Dinnerstein: societal nurturing arrangements

The idea that our earliest emotional experiences of family life is fundamental to the formation of gender identity has been central to many feminist interpretations of patriarchy. Dorothy Dinnerstein is one theorist who has given particular emphasis to the impact of mothering under patriarchy in the analysis of gender inequality. In *The Mermaid and the Minotaur* (1976), Dinnerstein examines the psychic impact upon the sexes of societal nurturing arrangements. Her claim is that, given exclusive female mothering in late-capitalist societies, children of both sexes encounter a social context that violently deforms gender. Female mothering, Dinnerstein says, leads us inevitably to fear women. Both sexes fear the power that mothers wield over them as infants, a fear which leads children to betray the 'engulfing mother' by turning to the father in search of emotional security. Paternal authority offered by the father offers an escape route from ambivalence, involving infantile helplessness, rage and hate felt towards the mother. As Dinnerstein writes: 'It is as we leave infancy that the possibility of transferring dependent, submissive feeling to the second parent – whose different gender carries the promise of a new deal, a clean sweep – entices us into the trap of male domination' (1976: 186). In other words, patriarchy is the outcome of a denial of emotional ambivalence: unconscious anguish in connection to the mother is denied, coupled to an idealization of paternal authority. The psychic costs of this denial are severe. Men and women remain haunted by the memory of maternal dominance. For while infantile helplessness may have been repudiated, the return of the repressed continually threatens to outstrip masculinist culture. Significantly this situation, says Dinnerstein, is worse for women than for men. Associated with the power of mothering, women are doubly denigrated – as mother and as wife or lover – within the contemporary gender system.

Situating her analysis of the mother/child relationship within a the theoretical framework of influential child psychoanalyst, Melanie Klein, Dinnerstein contends that socially predominant ideologies of gender are marked by a failure to work through persecutory and depressive anxieties about women, especially women's role as mothers. Instead of gaining a sense of the mother as an independent agent, fantasies proliferate about women as all-powerful and thus as objects of fear. In this context, Dinnerstein locates some of the most pathological features of contemporary culture: man's need to control and humiliate women; woman's collaboration in denigrating her own sex; the domination of nature; sexual violence; and, the cultural denial of human fragility. The way forward to a transformation of gender, says Dinnerstein, is through shared parenting. 'So long as the first parent is a woman,' writes Dinnerstein, 'women will inevitably be pressed into the dual role of indispensable quasi-human supporter and deadly quasi-human enemy of the self' (1976: 111).

Dinnerstein's work offered one of the first psychoanalytic challenges to mainstream feminist accounts of gender relations. Society, for Dinnerstein, is not something external, which then 'goes to work' on people by imprinting gender power. Rather, society is a force that penetrates to the deepest emotional roots of sexual experience, engendering anti-female feelings in the very act of constituting the self. As such, her work raises important issues about the connections between sexuality, power, and culture. Significant as it is, though, Dinnerstein's critique of gender is severely limited by several major flaws. She assumes, for example, that the avoidance of psychic pain in early life connects with the devaluation of women in a universal, mechanistic way. What this overlooks, however, is that motherhood is situated in a social, political, and economic context – a *patriarchal* context which distorts the social organization of parenting and child rearing. In other words, what Dinnerstein's model cannot adequately accommodate is the impact of ideology: those complex, contradictory political forms through which society influences the feelings, thoughts and aspirations of individuals. This is a serious omission, and it is one which causes Dinnerstein to ignore the point that men, as well as women, can be idealized, envied, feared, and hated. Moreover, Dinnerstein's account of the contemporary gender system runs into a kind of theoretical brick wall since she cannot comprehend resistances to, or transformations in, gender power. Women and men are simply deemed dependent on patriarchy as a way of sidestepping their neurotic, paranoid reactions to motherhood, child-rearing and nature.

Chodorow: *The Reproduction of Mothering*

In *The Reproduction of Mothering* (1978), Nancy Chodorow argues that exclusive female mothering leads to gender oppression. In her view, women's mothering is pivotal for understanding gender development and division since it is a global feature of the sexual division of labor. Chodorow argues that, in mothering, women become primarily preoccupied with emotional and relational issues; women turn their energies to the care of their children and families. By contrast, men work in the cold and detached world of public and economic affairs. As men are less connected to their emotional lives, they develop more analytical modes of relating to others and the wider society. Chodorow says that we need to know more about this division of gender roles, and accompanying sense of self, in order to understand the cultural logic of gender hierarchy and to contest oppressive social relationships.

According to Chodorow, Freud's model of gender development – in which the mother hovers in the background – is unconvincing at best and plainly defective at worst. In situating the mother as the first emotional attachment for the child, Freudian theory opened up a fertile research area relating to the emotional consequences of maternity. Yet mothers, paradoxically, are accorded little recognition in shaping the psychology of the self in Freud's writings. Instead, the child's attachment to the mother is broken up through the intrusive impact of the father – which Freud theorized in terms of the Oedipus complex. The symbolic intervention of the father, represented by the phallus, into the mother/child dyad is fundamental to the constitution of selfhood, gender, sexuality, meaning, rationality and culture. Freud's theory is essentially father-centered; mothers do not get much recognition for their input into self or gender development. Rejecting what she sees as the patriarchal assumptions of classical Freudian theory, Chodorow turns to object-relational theories of psychoanalysis and also to theories of core gender-identity. In doing so, she develops a perspective that examines, not only the infant's needs and desires in its earliest years (as with classical Freudian theory), but also the desires for, and behavior toward, the child experienced by parents. The constitution and development of self and gender, says Chodorow, involves a two-way traffic – between parents and child.

It is Chodorow's contention that the creation of self and gender depends upon the internalization – an emotional taking in or incorporation – of imagery of the mother. In the early pre-Oedipal period, where the father does not figure as a strong emotional presence, the process of gender differentiation is set in train by the mother's mode of relating to, and interaction toward, her child. This brings us to the core of Chodorow's argument: *mothers relate to daughters in a fashion that they do not to sons.* The mother, Chodorow says, relates to her daughter as an extension of herself, as a double, as belonging to the same gender. As daughters are treated by mothers as the same, the daughter in turn finds it extremely difficult to separate from her mother, to establish a sense of personal identity and autonomy. The consequences of this are complex. Chodorow suggests that daughters are likely to grow up with a strong sense of emotional continuity with their mothers. This sense of continuity provides for intimate, relational connections throughout women's adult life, but it also results in problems of merging with others, difficulties with interpersonal boundaries, and disturbances of self and identity. All this serves to drive the daughter from the love of her mother to the security offered by her father; this subsequent and defensive identification with the father serves as an unacknowledged support for oppressive gender relations and patriarchy.

Mothers tend to experience their daughters as more like, and continuous with, themselves. Correspondingly, girls tend to remain part of the dyadic primary mother-child relationship itself. This means that a girl continues to experience herself as involved in issues of merging and separation, and in an attachment characterized by primary identification and the fusion of identification and object choice. By contrast, mothers experience their sons as a male opposite. Boys are more likely to have been pushed out of the preOedipal relationship, and to have had to curtail their primary love and sense of emphatic tie with their mother. A boy has engaged, and has been required to engage, in a more emphatic individuation and a more defensive firming of experienced ego boundaries. Issues of differentiation have become intertwined with sexual issues. This does not mean that women have 'weaker' ego boundaries than men or are more prone to psychosis. Disturbances in the early relation to a caretaker have equally profound effects on each, but these effects differ according to gender. The earliest mode of individuation, the primary construction of the ego and its inner object-world, the earliest conflicts and the earliest unconscious definitions of self, the earliest threats to individuation and the earliest anxieties which call up defences, all differ for boys and girls because of differences in the character of the early mother–child relationship for each.

Nancy Chodorow (1978) *The Reproduction of Mothering.* Berkeley: University of California Press, pages 166–7.

The sense of sameness imposed by mothers upon their daughters stands in marked contrast to the projection of difference and otherness onto sons. Boys, according to Chodorow, separate more easily than do girls because the mother treats the male child as different, as a member of the other gender. Here masculinity is constituted by maternal disengagement: the mother, because of the child's otherness, propels the boy toward differentiation and individuality. Boys must learn to deny their primary emotional attachment to the mother. By turning away from their emotional dependence on the mother, boys direct their energies to more active, and very often aggressive, forms of play and relationship. In doing so, boys, with the help of their mothers, begin to prepare for the sort of emotional detachment and analytical form of reasoning that the economic world of capitalism will demand from them in later life.

If Chodorow sometimes worries that gender identity is not as clear-cut as her theory implies – what of lesbian mothers? what influence do house-husbands wield? what impact do siblings have? – the story that emerges from her book about the emotional roots of women's mothering is forceful and compelling. Since the emotional core of feminine identity is relational – that is, there is a strong preoccupation with issues of nuturance, care, empathy and relatedness – women will tend to look for such emotional resources in other people in their adult relationships. But here women run into difficulties. Since men are very often emotionally detached and unresponsive to more reflective and caring relationships, women routinely find themselves cut off from interpersonal communication and erotic intimacy with their partners. In order to escape from this emotional deadlock, women turn instead to the prospects and challenges of motherhood. Chodorow thus suggests that the desire to mother is, in part, produced from current distortions and pathologies of gender hierarchy. Against this bleak assessment, she urges shared parenting as a means of challenging and subverting the reproduction of gender difference and hierarchy.

Chodorow's work has exercised enormous influence in feminism, sociology and social theory. Her account of core gender identity (that is, socially induced psychological constructions of femininity and masculinity) is appealing because of its potentially wide application – from public policy issues concerning parenting to differences in the moral outlooks of men and women. Her argument that there is a basic gender identity for males and females has proved attractive to many wishing to understand the persistence of patriarchy. In this respect, Chodorow's claims about female psychology are illuminating – especially her assertion that women want to have children in order to recapture the primary bond of the mother/daughter relationship. Women's lives, she says, are potentially emotionally bereft because men are cut off from sexual intimacy and interpersonal communication. From this angle, the desire to have a child is actually rooted in the distortions of the current gender system. Conversely, the abstract traits of male selfhood described by Chodorow provide a direct purchase on men's anxieties over intimacy and love. Masculinity, says Chodorow, necessarily involves the adoption of intolerance, insensitivity, and emotional coerciveness. From this angle, male sexual dominance, often involving the use of violence towards women, has its roots in the damaged, fragile, and precarious nature of masculine identity.

However Chodorow's feminism, as the reader will have gathered, is not without its problems. There is, for example, something too neat about Chodorow's claim that exclusive female mothering produces gender oppression. Chodorow presents us with a model of woman as mother, as primary caretaker, with female desire sharply constrained by this social role. Yet is mothering really so sharply constrained and constraining? For instance, what of mothers who encourage 'feminine' modes of expression in their sons? What of mothers who foster 'masculine' aims of autonomy, independence, and achievement in their daughters? What of the sharp rise of single-parent, mother-led families? The difficulty is that Chodorow tends to ignore the vast complexity of familial life in modern societies, and privileges instead a traditional style of mothering rapidly in decline today. As Lynne Segal notes:

> I have found everywhere evidence of the amazing diversity buried within the ideology of the familial: fathers who were present and caring, 'working' mothers who were strong and powerful within the home, daughters who bonded tightly with fathers or older brothers, mothers who could not love their sons, mothers who never accepted their daughters, mothers who identified with their sons, and so on.
>
> (1987: 140)

Other psychoanalytically orientated feminists have made some harsh criticisms too. Jacqueline Rose, for example, has suggested that Chodorow does not explain the psychodynamics of sexual identity and selfhood, but rather addresses the question of gender roles. For Rose, Chodorow's work displaces the core psychoanalytic concepts of fantasy and the unconscious in favor of a sociological notion of 'gender imprinting.' The psychic lives of women and men, Rose points out, are more contradictory or split than Chodorow's theory suggests. Likewise, Janet Sayers argues that Chodorow conflates femininity with motherhood.

These are legitimate criticisms, and can actually be pressed further. Chodorow assumes that the mother's manner of relating to her daughter or son is fairly more or less consistent with established gender norms; to the extent that she does, these patterns of relating will have very clear-cut emotional consequences at the level of self, sexuality and gender. But we need to be careful about assuming that children's emotional responses to significant others can be understood through reference to parental or cultural norms. We need to be careful because, as Freud himself and other social theorists after him argue, the child experiences others and the wider world through fantasy, as well as other cognitive modes of understanding. Chodorow rides roughshod over this psychoanalytic insight, and thus arguably her concept of 'core gender identity' returns us to pre-Freudian understanding of identity. That mothers perceive, on a deep psychological level, their daughters as the *same* as themselves is surely evidence of the psychological importance of sexual difference and its cultural structure; the ways in which fantasy shapes, distorts or transforms this psychological and cultural structure requires analysis.

Here Freud's theory of the Oedipus complex and Lacan's emphasis on language and symbolism are important. In Freud and Lacan, it is the father's phallus, as the mark of sexual difference, that separates the child from the maternal body and plunges her or him into the order of language and the world of symbolism. In this approach, desire is founded in language – the sexes are organized around linguistic shifters – 'femininity' and 'masculinity,' 'woman' and 'man,' 'his' and 'hers.' Chodorow, by contrast, sees the mother as playing a more central role in the establishment of gender identity, and her use of object relations theory to analyze emotional connection and separation offers a substantial correction to the father-centered perspectives of Freud and Lacan. Yet reversing the Freudian emphasis from the father to the mother is hardly a radical political gesture unless the question of sexual difference is itself raised and problematized. Chodorow, it might be said, fails to see that the psychoanalytical theory she draws from is deeply inscribed in asymmetrical gender relations.

Benjamin: the analysis of love

Jessica Benjamin, in her widely influential *The Bonds of Love* (1988), extends Chodorow's analysis by focusing on women's and men's experience of love. Like Chodorow, Benjamin sees patriarchy as devaluing motherhood, whilst underwriting the symbolic power of fatherhood with agency and power. Unlike Chodorow, however, Benjamin argues that sexual identity does not simply mirror gender asymmetry. To understand why this is so, Benjamin develops the concept of 'identificatory love,' by which she means a pre-Oedipal phase of rapprochement in which the child seeks to establish a sense of attachment *and* separation with parental figures. Emotional continuity is central here. Through identification, the small child is able to separate out a sense of self while remaining emotionally connected to others.

Reflecting upon contemporary culture, Benjamin argues that children must displace or disown their pre-Oedipal identificatory love with parents. Children of both sexes cannot maintain their identificatory love for the mother since she is devalued by current sexual ideology. This leads Benjamin to adopt a similar position to Chodorow. The core of her argument is that, while boys can identify with the father and his phallus to separate from the mother and establish autonomous individuality, the same path to psychic individuation is denied to girls. An alternate, empathic relationship with the exciting father, says Benjamin, is usually refused, the result being women's 'lack' of desire and its return as masochism in idealizations of male power. For Benjamin, what this means is that the tension between dependence and independence, which underpins healthy emotional relationships, breaks down within culture at large. Moreover, sexual relations between men and women grow diseased and deformed into master/slave patterns.

In *Like Subjects, Love Objects* (1995) and *The Shadow of the Other* (1998), Benjamin explores in more detail the range of multiple identifications that women and men forge or discover through sexual object choice as well as the negotiation of personal identity. In this interpersonal feminist psychoanalysis, Benjamin elaborates upon post-Oedipal constructions in which the self accepts multiplicity and difference, owns complementary erotic fantasies or gender ideals, and tolerates oscillating and alternating identifications. Benjamin's arguments in these works are highly complex, though she starts from the relatively uncontentious position that traditional psychoanalysis has been too father- or masculine-centered. She forcefully questions Freud's construction of gender identity along the lines of splitting and polarization – masculinity versus femininity, activity versus passivity, same versus other. Oedipal theory, says Benjamin, too neatly divides the sexes around the notion of anatomical difference, foreclosing the myriad psychic paths through which individuals identify with, as well as emotionally own, both masculine and feminine ideals within the self.

Against the Oedipal construction in which object love and identification are polarized, Benjamin focuses instead on the murky, indistinct emotional identifications with both mother and father, stressing throughout that interpersonal relationships and fantasy always coexist. Perhaps what is most important here is Benjamin's stress on the bisexual or polymorphous identifications of the most primitive stage of psychosexual development, the pre-Oedipal position. According to Benjamin, pre-Oedipal bisexuality suggests that the defensive repudiation of opposite sex identifications in the Oedipal stage depends upon a denial of bisexual identifications as well as the adoption of mutually exclusive gender positions. Such substitution of paradox for polarity, argues Benjamin, may be an accurate portrayal of dominant forms of gender relationship in masculinist culture. However, her critical point is that the recuperation of the pre-Oedipal phase can be revisited throughout life, and indeed cross-identifications of the pre-Oedipal stage, with tolerance for difference and multiplicity, inform what she terms the 'post-Oedipal' configuration, in which a more playful and creative approach is taken to identity, sexuality and gender.

Benjamin's argument carries important implications for the analysis of gender, particularly as regards the development of boys. According to her, the psychological task of replacing splitting and polarization with the sustaining of psychic tension and the ability to manage opposing emotional dispositions towards self and other results from fluid boundaries between Oedipal and post-Oedipal configurations. For the boy, inclusion of denied feelings or blocked identifications depends upon regaining contact with multiple identifications of the pre-Oedipal period, in particular experience of the mother as a creative subject.

What of the possibilities for change? Benjamin differs sharply from both Chodorow and Dinnerstein in her evaluation of gender transformation. Paternal identification, Benjamin says, can play a positive role in the achievement of autonomous female subjectivity. According to Benjamin, however, any identification with the father is likely to prove counterproductive as long as the cultural devaluation of women remains in place. In this context, an alteration of parenting arrangements – as proposed by Chodorow and Dinnerstein – is itself an insufficient basis to transform gender structures. Non-repressive gender relations, Benjamin argues, depend rather on replacing the cultural split of progressive, autonomous father against regressive mother with new sexual identifications that permit a less rigid set of sexual roles. This would involve the repudiation of defensive modes of separation – that is, the father's phallus would no longer be used as the dominant medium to beat back an engulfing mother. Instead, children might construct more fluid sexual identifications – expressing both masculine and feminine aspects of identity – in relation to a socially and sexually autonomous mother, and a more empathic, caring father. Two figures of love and idealization – mother and father – are thus located as necessary for the creation of non-patriarchal patterns of socialization.

Julia Kristeva: semiotic subversions

The writings of the French social theorist Julia Kristeva press the feminist critique of identity to a parodic extreme. Her post-Lacanian inspired reading of Freud and feminism leads her to outline an emotional realm she terms 'semiotic,' a residue of pre-Oedipal longings or drives that both structure and disrupt the operations of everyday speech. This notion of a semiotic process operating within the established meanings of ordinary language was given powerful expression in Kristeva's first book, *Revolution in Poetic Language* (1984), of which she has said:

What interested me was, by way of the semiotic, to further elaborate a level of psychic representation that for Freud remains extremely primitive and imprecise, which is the representation of affects that are psychic inscriptions, hence very primitive and very fragile: drives and affects that are in fact already psychic.

(Guberman and Kristeva: 22)

Kristeva's ambitious psychoanalytic extension of the concept of the semiotic powerfully confronted some of the central weaknesses of structuralist and post-structuralist thought, especially the theorem of the arbitrary character of the sign. Kristeva may well have formed many of her key concepts in the heyday of Parisian post-structuralism, yet the implications of her conceptual developments have not only outstripped the ideological parameters of the structuralist controversy but continue to inform the endeavors of social theorists the world over.

Kristeva's genius is evident certainly in the manner in which she questioned Saussure's model of individual and society, particularly her criticism that structuralism has no intermediate terms for connecting the affective dimensions of subjectivity, the play of signifiers at the level of subjecthood and meaning, as well as the linguistic system as a whole. Yet her supple, civilized intelligence is also evident in her style as a writer, her voice. For in attempting to show that affective pressures and primitive anxieties structure the constitution and reproduction of society, it was through her poetic and expressively crafted sentences that Kristeva uncovered how the rhythm and sound of language exerts a kind of unconscious pressure within language itself. She sees in this fluid, heterogeneous flow of affects a sort of residue of attachment to pre-Oedipal experience, specifically the ongoing impact of memory issuing from the child's contact with the mother's body. The semiotic is thus the 'other' of the symbolic, even though Kristeva insists that these two modes of signification are always intricately entwined.

[F]or me signification is a process that I call *significance*, and to recognize the dynamism of this process, I distinguish between two registers: the register of the symbolic and register of the semiotic. By symbolic, I mean the tributary signification of language, all the effects of meaning that appear from the moment linguistic signs are articulated into grammar, not only chronologically but logically as well. In other words, the symbolic is both diachronic and synchronic; it concerns both the acquisition of language and the present syntactic structure. By semiotic, on the other hand, I mean the effects of

feminism and post-feminist theory

meaning that are not reducible to language or that can operate outside language, even if language is necessary as an immediate context or as a final referent. By semiotic, I mean, for example, the child's echolalia before the appearance of language, but also the play of colors in an abstract painting or a piece of music that lacks signification but has a meaning.

Julia Kristeva (1996) 'A Conversation with Julia Kristeva' in R. M. Guberman (Ed.) *Interviews*. New York: Columbia University Press, page 21.

In her various studies of art, literary creation, motherhood, psychoanalysis and philosophy, Kristeva has time and again observed the semiotic at work in children's play and mental life, as well as in the avant-garde poet's language which she sees as highly evocative of the feminine as well as memory of the maternal body. In this linking of the semiotic so closely to the theme of femininity, Kristeva underscores the importance of her social theory to feminists in particular and the analysis of gender power in general. She explains this often-questioned connection of the semiotic to feminism thus:

> In our monotheistic-capitalist societies, 'the woman effect' entails a specific relationship to both *power* and *language*, or, if you will, to the power of language. This particular relationship is based not on appropriating power and language but on being a source of silent support, a useful backdrop, and an invisible intermediary. I have called this modality of the linguistic (and social) functioning of language the '*semiotic*.' The semiotic is heard in rhythms, intonation and children's echolalia as well as in artistic practice and in discourse that signifies less an 'object' than a *jouissance*.
>
> (Guberman and Kristeva 1996: 104)

It is as if there were a connecting path between the semiotic and the feminine that works both ways – which we will shortly examine in more detail. Silence, support, invisibility, sound, inflexion, intimation: these are the terms through which the semiotic makes the body signify.

Kristeva was only just in her early thirties when *Revolution in Poetic Language* became a major talking point amongst intellectuals on the left-bank of Paris. Her doctoral training with Roland Barthes and, in particular, the imprint of the thought of Jacques Lacan was highly evident in this mammoth undertaking. Yet what perhaps caused the real intellectual stir was her audacious blending of disciplinary concerns, ranging as the book did over Hegel, Husserl, Freud and Lévi-Strauss, whilst managing the exceptional feat of elaborating a *post-Lacanian* understanding of the complex relations between self and society.

In *Revolution*, Kristeva looks to psychoanalysis as a means of overcoming the fixed positions and binary oppositions of structural linguistics. Although her thinking was much influenced by Saussure, she is profoundly aware that the static conception of language advanced by structuralists – in which culture speaks its subjects – is 'helplessly anachronistic when faced with the contemporary mutations of subject and society.' One of these mutations that most interests Kristeva is feminism, from which during the late 1960s and early 1970s the women's movement had launched a sustained assault on the patriarchal sexual order of contemporary societies. The oppressiveness of existing sexual relations, for Kristeva as for Lacan, issues from patriarchy – symbolized by the phallus – in which subjects are accorded symbolic positions as defined by sexual difference. As we saw earlier when looking at the theories of Lacan, the evolution of Oedipal, gendered identity in the symbolic order of things provides the individual with an illusion of centeredness and stability.

For Kristeva, the merit of Lacanian psychoanalysis is that it uncovers how the constitution of the speaking subject revolves around a pre-given structure of social roles and sexual relations – the individual's painful decentering within the Symbolic order. However, Kristeva argues that Lacan's central blindness – notwithstanding the stress on the 'split subject' – is his overemphasis on the determining power of speech and language at the expense of pre-verbal experience. While language is the realm of meaning and its encounters with the rules of social interaction, the dynamism of self and society is sustained and nourished by deeper emotional forces. It is thus Kristeva's central project – psychoanalytical, social-theoretical and political – to elucidate the *pre-verbal sensations* which leave their imprint upon the life of the subject and of our lives in a wider social context.

The corporeal origins of the semiotic are traced by Kristeva back to the small infant's pre-Oedipal interaction with the mother, or primary caretaker. As a pre-Oedipal realm prior to the establishment of sexual difference, the infant does not yet have access to language and thus the place of pre-verbal experience is paramount. The mother's caresses, touching, rhythmic rocking, singing and general care of the child are vital to the foundation and function of the pre-verbal semiotic. For Kristeva, the sensory qualities of maternal care leave an indelible stamp upon the psychic life of the individual subject, all of which is constituted as a flow of affective sources and energetic drives. It is in a sense the virtue of the semiotic that it is geared towards others – and thus towards language – because the affective domain is interpersonal through and through. And this, in itself, deconstructs the rigid determinism of Lacanism, with its insistence that the child's entry into the symbolic order of language involves an overriding or limiting of the imaginary. For it is in describing the pre-verbal semiotic as a form of language, as psychic inscriptions of sensory experience operating *inside* language, that Kristeva most forcefully challenges Lacan's objectivism as well as underscores the role of affects in psychic and social life. This is not to say, however, that Kristeva positions affect over and above the symbolic order. She is insistent, for example, that there is an ineluctable closure of the semiotic process with the child's entry into the relatively stable domain of symbolization and language. This closure, however, is not complete: the criss-crossings of the semiotic and symbolic are interestingly mobile. The semiotic, Kristeva intimates, is always 'at work' within the operations of language, threatening an identity-forming break or transformation from the imposed form and structure of symbolic processes.

Another way of putting all this is to say that, for Kristeva, we are – all of us – nine-tenths ventriloquists of the culture. We simply mouth the words of others, in gestures that express an essentially passive relation to the codes of culture and society. Yet, confoundingly, every so often we say something startlingly original, something different, something unique. If the imposed symbolic order of language closes us to the genuinely new and different, the semiotic reopens the psyche to complex imaginaries and the drives and affects they bring into play. For the early Kristeva of *Revolution*, the semiotic is the sight of our imaginative attempt to contest symbolic structures in the name of desire – and one noticeable place in her account where this can be seen historically is in the poetic language of various modernist writers such as Mallarmé and Lautréamont where 'semiotic transgressions' explode traditional literary discourse. Another location where Kristeva sees the semiotic at work, at least in her subsequent writings, is in psychoanalysis itself – where the unspeakable emotion unlocked through processes of regression with an analyst bring directly into play intense modulations of primitive anxiety and affect, both pleasurable and destructive.

Kristeva conceptualizes the semiotic as intimately entwined with memory of the mother's body and thus with the feminine more generally. As we have seen, however, if the semiotic is a force operating inside discourse this is far from a language exclusive to women. Noting that the semiotic is fabricated from a pre-Oedipal phase, which itself is prior to the imposed Oedipal distinctions of gender hierarchy, the semiotic remains for Kristeva an affective force within language available to either sex. Thus in her work throughout the 1970s, the pre-verbal, destabilizing semiotic is detected at work by Kristeva in the writings of various male avant-garde poets and writers. Some feminists sharply criticized Kristeva for ignoring female writers in her studies of semiotic literary practice, arguing that the semiotic might in theory function as a mode of experience available to both sexes, but in Kristeva's literary criticism at least the supposed radicalism of this unconscious force appears to operate mostly in the hands of men. It is perhaps as a result of this critique that Kristeva subsequently conducted a multi-volume study on female genius, in the spheres of literature, philosophy and psychoanalysis.

Yet it is in Kristeva's writings on motherhood and maternity that the specific emotional contradictions of female identity are explored in detail. This work dates from the late 1970s and early 1980s, at which point Kristeva herself became a mother, and there can be little doubt that her suggestive theories of a 'maternal ethic' have served to stimulate developments in feminism and social theory. For the Kristeva of this period, in books such as *Powers of Horror* (1982) and *Tales of Love* (1987), motherhood represents 'the semiotization of the symbolic.' 'A mother,' Kristeva announces, 'has always been a permanent division, a division of the flesh itself, and consequently a division in language.' All experiences of pregnancy and maternity call into play powerful unconscious forces and primitive anxiety, reawakening the repressed division between flesh and word, imagination and representation, nature and culture.

Kristeva on motherhood and maternal ethics

In a series of provocative essays about mothering and childbirth – most importantly 'Stabat Mater' (1986), 'Motherhood According to Bellini' (1980b), and 'From One Identity to an Other' (1980a) – Kristeva analyzes both dominant cultural representations of maternity and the psychic experience of motherhood itself. These essays contain Kristeva's argument that the psychoanalytical concept of fantasy is of core importance for grasping the complexity of maternity, and especially the complex emotional dynamic between mother and child.

Kristeva suggests that dominant scientific understandings of maternity, from the cult of the Virgin in Christian theology to media images of women in popular culture, have objectified women. In conflating femininity and maternity, she argues, the mother's desire exists only in so far as it is related to her desire to have children, to reproduce the species, to fulfill her biological function in the name of patriarchy. Kristeva focuses on *fantasies* of maternity rather than *practices* of motherhood. In doing so, she makes explicit her debt to the Freudian conceptualization of the self. She suggests that, although maternity has been disfigured by patriarchy, motherhood is in fact associated with repressed desire. In developing this provocative argument, Kristeva returns to classical psychoanalysis. Freud regarded maternity as a return of the repressed, a return of the daughter's buried wish to bear a child for her own father. Fundamental to Freud's view is the presumption that women's desire exists only in so far as it is directed towards the phallus – that is to say, the symbolic father of the Oedipus complex. According to Kristeva, Freud constructed maternity in wholly patriarchal terms. But this association of motherhood with the masculine logic of Oedipus prevents the woman from voicing her own desire, her own enjoyment, her own ambivalent fantasy of maternity. For Kristeva, motherhood must be approached differently, in a fashion other than that emphasized in philosophical, literary and psychoanalytic traditions, with their stress upon biological and social reproduction.

In 'Stabat Mater,' a title that refers to the anguish of the Virgin Mary at the Crucifixion, Kristeva reflects on her own experience of pregnancy and birth. Dividing the essay into two discourses, she writes on one side of the page of the mythical language of Christian theology and the rationality of science, while on the other side she develops a more private and autobiographical account of motherhood. In dividing the narrative of her essay in this way, Kristeva seeks to underscore the split or hiatus between the ideal and actuality of maternity. Most importantly, she argues that splitting itself defines maternal experience. Maternity for Kristeva involves a state of radical paradox, of heterogeneity, of singularity and plurality, of sameness and difference. In Kristeva's words:

> A mother is a continuous separation, a division of the very flesh. And consequently a division of language – and it has always been so. Then there is this other abyss that opens up between the body and what has been its inside: there is the abyss between the mother and the child. What connection is there between myself, or even more unassumingly between my body and this internal graft and fold, which, once the umbilical cord has been severed, is an inaccessible other? . . . Trying to think through that abyss: staggering vertigo. No identity holds up.
>
> (1986: 178–9)

The passions associated with maternity, according to Kristeva, split the woman between identity and its collapse, between consciousness of self and its erasure.

The mother's experience of transformations occurring in her own body during pregnancy reorient her away from the narrow confines of masculine logic and patriarchy. Whereas Freud sees maternity as an expression of repressed paternal longings, in Kristeva's eyes the desire to have children is itself a sublimated desire to recover the maternal body. That is to say, Kristeva suggests there is a homosexual component implicit in women's desire to mother, or at least this is so in fantasy at any rate. 'By giving birth,' writes Kristeva, 'the woman enters into contact with her mother; she becomes, she is her own mother' (1980: 239). In underscoring this homosexual facet of motherhood, Kristeva rewrites psychoanalysis away from the father and the Oedipus complex and toward the (imaginary) relation between women, a relation that persists over time and across generations.

Kristeva connects the complexity and heterogeneity of maternal experience not only to women, but also to the emotional development of children. She emphasizes the importance of maternity in shaping and regulating the emerging self prior to entry into the Oedipus complex – in which the acquisition of language, rationality and sexual subjectivity occurs. This is a very important aspect of Kristeva's argument, an aspect that directly challenges the claim advanced by Freud and Lacan that it is the father alone that propels the child into an order of language and symbolism. By contrast, Kristeva argues that the mother imposes a sense of regulation and order upon the child's psychic world. Before 'the Law of the Father' (Lacan), the child constantly encounters various maternal regulations, what Kristeva terms 'the law before the law.' Whereas Freudians and Lacanians view the regulation of the self in terms of rationality or structure, Kristeva emphasizes the importance of the body to the constitution of the self. The mother, says Kristeva, regulates what goes into, and also what is evacuated from, the child's body. This maternal regulation and control of the infant's traffic with both nourishment and love provides a foundation for the emotional dealings of the self with itself, other people, and the wider society.

Appraisal of Kristeva

Kristeva's suggestive work based on gender, has made a considerable impact on recent social theory, especially in feminism, no doubt in part since it is reflective of profound personal, cultural and political changes occurring in contemporary societies. Kristeva is among those public intellectuals who have contributed to a revised understanding of the relations between self and society, linked particularly to a heightened sensitivity to the intersections of the unconscious, affect, gender, sexuality and intersubjectivity. This is an understanding that foregrounds dynamism, innovation, imagination and the new in personal and political life, and so would seem to accommodate various complex processes of social re-definition – issuing from, for example, the women's movements, gay and lesbian movements as well as other new social movements – that occurred in the final decades of the twentieth century as well as at the beginnings of the twenty-first. Particularly as the 1970s and 1980s gave way to the postmodern 1990s, and as the globalization of commerce, communication and culture became increasingly evident to all, Kristeva's powerful mapping of the emotional dynamism of the individual subject seemed suited to grappling with the social conditions of women and men in which self-reflexivity was increasingly prized and economic flexibility increasingly demanded. This was perhaps nowhere more evident than in gender relations where sexual norms, which engage some of the deepest emotional dimensions of social life, have been powerfully transformed.

Viewed against the backcloth of Lacanian psychoanalysis, the theory of the semiotic developed by Kristeva may be seen as a means of calling into question the individual's subjection to symbolic norms. An over-emphasis on the discursive remains, in the eyes of Kristeva, a fundamental weakness of contemporary theory and is thus at the core of the inability of Lacan and his followers to grasp how language encodes unrepresentable emotion. Notwithstanding the importance of this recovery of the role of emotion and affect in the context of childhood, maternity, the family and the private and public spheres, however, much criticism of Kristeva's work has been directed against her whole attempt to develop a theory of pre-verbal signs, in which the distribution of unconscious forces, energies and drives structure and transform processes of signification. Thus some feminists have criticized as illusory and reactionary the search for semiotic signs which might somehow function as an *alternative* to impose symbolic forms of identity or patriarchal sexual orientation. The results of such general theoretical criticism have lead, in turn, to more specific concerns as regards the analysis of gender power. Some feminists, for example, criticize Kristeva for eliding the semiotic with motherhood.

Not all feminist sociology has been as critical of Kristeva as this, and many have pointed out that her project involves rethinking the basic categories of gender in ways that mainstream social science has tended to ignore. Her examination of maternity in terms of the semiotic as a kind of internal limit to gender power does not then involve essentialism, and it is important to keep in mind that she is not proposing the semiotic as an emancipatory alternative to the symbolic order of language. Kristeva, a practicing psychoanalyst, is certainly well aware that rejection of the symbolic order can only spell emotional catastrophe – namely in the form of psychosis. Yet she is rightly insistent that the symbolic order of language is not a monolithic structure. Rather, symbolic order provides an illusion of stability; social power and symbolic order are fluid and contestable, and from this angle the semiotic is at the core of our imaginative attempts to battle with, and subvert, dominant frames of reference.

Kristeva may thus be said to have fashioned a post-Lacanian approach to subjectivity, society and history that cuts through traditional opposition between the unconscious and the symbolic, desire and the social, the inner world and the external one. Yet however insightful her observations are regarding the semiotic as an affective source within language and public political discourse, there remain important difficulties with her account of how such primitive emotional processes relate to society as well as processes of social transformation. For one thing, it is not clear how the semiotic process – centered on the individual – might be methodologically applicable to broader social structures, particularly the workings of social power and political domination. For another, the semiotic too often appears in Kristeva's work as a kind of mini-agent, operating within or behind the back of an individual. Yet how, exactly, do individuals reflect on – become aware of – semiotic displacement of symbolic power? Are these primarily revolutions in poetic language (and thus the preserve of the critic), or are these wide disruptions to daily life? And how, in any event, are such internal transformations threaded to the power networks and technical processes of contemporary society?

Notwithstanding these criticisms, it is clear that Kristeva's influence on contemporary research into identity and culture within social theory is immense. Her reading of Freud and Lacan is bold and productive and, in an astonishingly radical interpretative stroke, locates the 'subject-in-process' in the imaginative substratum of historical life, in its exquisite creativity and pure open-endedness.

Irigaray: the feminine imaginary

Luce Irigaray, a French philosopher who trained as a psychoanalyst with Lacan, controversially argues that the feminine cannot be adequately symbolized – in discourse or in theory – under patriarchy, as femininity is the repressed or hidden support structure upon which phallocentric social relations depend. Irigaray, taking her cue from Lacan, proposes the feminine as permanently excluded from language in the symbolic order. She writes of the corrosive personal consequences for women of the process of 'specularization'; women, she says, reflect back to men particular phallocentric ideals concerning masculinity, such that the feminine is defined not in its own terms, but always as mirror, reflection, or object. From maternal devotion to sexual masquerade, the seductive presence of the feminine frames the illusions of masculine desire.

More concretely, Irigaray argues that the pre-Oedipal mother/daughter relationship remains on the 'outside' of symbolic boundaries – an outside that leaves women in a state of 'dereliction,' undifferentiated from maternal space. As she puts this,

> there is no possibility whatsoever, within the current logic of socio-cultural operations, for a daughter to situate herself with respect to her mother: because, strictly speaking, they make neither one nor two, neither has a name, meaning, sex of her own, neither can be 'identified with respect to the other.'
>
> (1985: 143)

In contrast to Lacan, however, Irigaray contends that the idea of woman as outside and Other always threatens subversion, thus transforming the dominant masculinist social order. The feminine, says Irigaray, threatens subversion to patriarchal language and culture. Here Irigaray's position has affinities with Kristeva's notion of the semiotic. However, Irigaray goes further than Kristeva as regards the disruptive impact of female sexuality, proposing a direct link between women, feminine sexuality, and the body. In line with other feminists of the 'écriture féminine' movement, such as Hélène Cixous, Irigaray grounds the feminine in women's experience of sexuality and the body, an experience which is plural, dispersed and multiple. Women, says Irigaray, need to establish a different relationship to feminine sexuality, affecting a range of displacements to patriarchy through writing as a cultural practice. Speaking the feminine, says Irigaray, can transform the constricted and constricting sexed identities of patriarchy. In her more recent work, from *An Ethics of Sexual Difference* (1993) to *To Be Two* (2000), Irigaray locates the renegotiation of identities in the frame of ethical practice, specifically the recognition of the otherness of the other sex. An ethics of sexual difference, she argues, would respect the Other in her or his own right, with regard or sensitivity to finitude, mortality, creation and the divine.

Irigaray's writings have been sharply criticized as biologically essentialist. Here it is suggested that Irigaray's direct appeal to feminine specificity or the material female body assumes that there is an unchanging, transhistorical female sexuality subversive of all social contexts. This critique of Irigaray's essentialism has been forcefully developed by both Moi and Segal. Other feminists have questioned this essentialist critique, and have instead argued that Irigaray's work seeks to theorize the reproduction and transformation of feminine specificity in terms of the broader cultural force of sexual difference. While Irigaray is certainly concerned to trace the impact of distorting socio-symbolic forces upon the pre-Oedipal mother/daughter relationship, it does seem that her appeal to feminine specificity is problematic, to say the least. Juliet Mitchell sums up the difficulty with this position:

> You cannot choose the imaginary, the semiotic, the carnival as an alternative to the symbolic, as an alternative to the law. It is set up by the law precisely as its own lurid space, its own area of imaginary alternative, but not as a symbolic alternative. So that politically speaking, it is only the symbolic, a new symbolism, a new law, that can challenge the dominant law.
>
> (1984: 291)

Judith Butler: scripts of gender performance

To see language as encoding powerful emotional, semiotic forces is a critical advance on viewing it as simply the 'neutral' expression of rational intentions. For if the pre-verbal residue of the semiotic can be seen as a form of language, this means there are always at work powerful undercurrents of affects and anxieties in our daily social contact, and perhaps nowhere more evidently so than when we negotiate social practices of gender. Let us go back for a moment to the 'gender incident' I outlined at the beginning of the chapter, where former university colleagues of mine were caught up in a heated exchange of words over the politics of gender. I implied that much of this political heat stemmed from the issue of career advancement – that for many of my colleagues the matter of promotion was, so to speak, an outcrop of gender politics itself. Everyone, it seemed, had a view about this. And even if they didn't, colleagues were quickly accorded a 'position' in the debate: siding with the traditionalists, speaking with the liberals, or adopting the pose of radicalism. Attention to the semiotic modalities of these exchanges, at least according to Kristeva's way of viewing things, would no doubt reveal all sorts of complex unconscious forces and drives in what people actually said to each other. Such an emphasis on the disruptive power of repressed desires and primitive anxieties may indeed well account for why many of my colleagues had difficulty resuming everyday dialogues well after the incident had passed – in fact, some still don't talk!

To say that interpersonal communication is routinely outstripped by powerful unconscious forces is not, however, the only way one might try to figure out what is going on here. Indeed, notwithstanding that emotional life has become a central topic in much recent sociology, there are many social theorists and feminists who would contest Kristeva's idea of the semiotic as a force inside language. Asking about the emotional dispositions as linked to gender identities in the situation I've been outlining, some would argue that the idea of sexual hierarchy as enforcing deep divisions in university affairs is itself an illusion created by *repeated gender performances*. In other words, the 'taking up' of gender positions amongst my former colleagues was a learned, situational performance whose dramatic consequence was the production of inner feelings and disposition – the latter of which might only then be labeled disruptive or subversive of everyday life.

The notion that gender is constituted through 'repeated performance' – the 'doing' of gender roles – has been advanced by Judith Butler, one of the most influential critics within debates over sexuality and feminism in our own time. In her *Gender Trouble* (1990), Butler not only boldly questioned the ways in which feminism has invoked an identity-based theory which unintentionally serves to reinforce the binary gender hierarchy it opposes, she outlined a provocatively original theory which emphasizes the performative nature of identity and gender. *Gender Trouble* had an almost instant massive impact in feminism, sexuality studies and the formation of queer theory, and Butler's work since has continued to be at the cutting edge of developments in social theory. Part of the reason Butler's *Gender Trouble* was so influential was due to timing: the 1990s inaugurated a shift from the era of post-structuralism to the reign of post-modernism, and Butler's work represented a critical and stylish blend of the perspective of the French historian Michel Foucault, the psychoanalytic theory of Lacan, plus the deconstructive operations of postmodern feminism.

Language or discourse is Butler's central theme in *Gender Trouble*, and in particular the post-structuralist insight that the sign is always a matter of difference. Butler will have nothing of the search for attributes of a core gender identity. Rather, her critique of *The History of Sexuality* is derived more or less directly from an exploration of the consequences of the idea of identity as a 'discursive effect' – first as drawn from the writings of Foucault, and then as reformulated with reference to Lacanian psychoanalysis. Butler seeks to understand the relational character of identity positioning in the context of post-structuralist philosophy. In the same fashion that the subject is constituted in the structuring of language through difference, so speech situates us as women or men by connecting discourse with a binary gender order. Thus, for example, identity is not immediately *present* in a sign: it is by learning to use language situationally – which is itself a matter of linguistic differences and cultural conventions – that subjects project themselves into gender roles as women or men.

So far this account of the construction of gender identity might sound like little more than a feminist reworking of post-structuralism, and there is some merit to seeing Butler's work in this way. But Butler's appropriation of post-structuralism themes is neither straightforward nor uncritical. What emerges from her radical feminist systemization of Foucauldianism is a new emphasis on how language or discourse compels our attention to inner or emotional aspects of subjectivity itself; gender performance, anchored in ordinary speech, constitutes and sediments the possible range of identities, congealing over time to create illusions of self as interiority, emotions, desires. As Butler puts this, there is 'no doer behind the deed.' Questioning the dualisms of outside and inside, externality and internality, Butler argues that people only come to see themselves as the authors of their own inner lives through a set of repeated gender performances. Such performances are regulated with reference to constraining cultural representations of masculinity and femininity, as well as the narrative scripts of gender that are told and retold within the culture at large.

If there is something right in Beauvoir's claim that one is not born, but rather *becomes* a woman, it follows that *woman* itself is a term in process, a becoming, a construction that cannot be rightfully said to originate or to end. As an ongoing discursive practice, it is open to intervention and resignification. Even when gender seems to congeal into the most reified forms, the 'congealing' is itself an insistent and insidious practice, sustained and regulated by various social means. It is, for Beauvoir, never possible finally to become a woman, as if there were a *telos* that governs the process of acculturation and construction. Gender is the repeated stylization of the body, a set of repeated acts within a highly rigid regulatory frame that congeal over time to produce the appearance of substance, of a natural sort of being. A political genealogy of gender ontologies, if it is successful, will deconstruct the substantive appearance of gender into its constitutive acts and locate and account for those acts within compulsory frames set by the various forces that police the social appearance of gender.

Judith Butler (1990) *Gender Trouble: Feminism and the Subversion of Identity*. London: Routledge, page 33.

feminism and post-feminist theory

Another way of putting this point is to say that gender performances are always copies, imitations fashioned out of fantasies or idealization of dominant cultural representations of femininity or masculinity. Performance for Butler has a minimum of agency or voluntarism – the 'formed' nature of gender identity conceals social and political forces that constitute individuals as set subjects – and this in itself suggests that gender is a determining structure. Yet Butler shrewdly insists that constraint is the condition of possibility of sexuality and gender. In linking gender performance with a post-structuralist treatment of language and power, Butler is out to show how sexualities, bodies, and desires are rendered coherent and continuous within the symbolic field and yet are also implicated in disruptions to the reproduction of gender itself. For despite the constrained and constraining aspects of dominant heterosexual norms, Butler does not consider people as 'cultural dopes.' All gender performance, she argues, involves an open process of repetition. And repetition, for Butler as for Freud, opens to possibilities of change. As Butler contends,

> If every performance repeats itself to institute the effect of identity, then every repetition requires an interval between the acts, as it were, in which risk and excess threaten to disrupt the identity being consti-tuted. The unconscious is this excess that enables and contests every performance, and which never fully appears within the performance itself.
>
> (1990: 137)

Repetition of everyday social practices and gender norms thus secures the regularized aspects of identity formation. Yet because repetition itself oper-ates through a temporalized reiteration of the performative, there is an *intrinsic instability* at the heart of dominant gender relations. Every perform-ance of identity, for Butler, is at once self-reproducing of symbolic norms and potentially transgressive of those norms. The performative process of gender resignification is always potentially disruptive and disturbing, and it is against this analytical backcloth that Butler attempts to specify the expli-citly political consequences of her feminist analysis. According to Butler, the parodic planes with homosexual identities evident, for example, in queer practices and politics highlight the complex ways in which sexualities, bodies and desires are reproduced and destabilized in the course of their reiteration. A transgressive edge is accorded in particular to 'drag' and 'gender bending.' Butler writes,

> In imitating gender, drag implicitly reveals the imitative structure of gender itself – as well as its contingency. Indeed, part of the pleasure,

the giddiness of the performance is in the recognition of a radical contingency in the relation between sex and gender in the face of cultural configurations of causal unities that are regularly assumed to be natural and necessary.

(1990: 137)

Appraisal of Butler

There are several important reasons why Butler's work has been especially well received in sexuality studies, feminism and social theory. First, it provides a powerful theoretical account of various disjunctions between sex, gender and identity that chimes with key transformations of intimacy occurring in society at large. It has primarily been questioned over the fracturing of cultural and sexual identities, rooted in the actual political conditions of Western societies, which highlights the limitations of mainstream identity politics. Butler is among the first feminists to call attention to the dynamics of social life as a challenging mixture of identities, sexuality and reality; deconstructing 'women' as a category of identity, the political aim has been to demonstrate that people are not simply 'masculine,' 'feminine,' 'straight,' 'lesbian,' 'queer' or any one identity. The feminist, postmodern and post-structuralist preoccupations with the performative and reiterated aspects of identity, with subverting constructions of gender and sexuality, were responses to the cultural mood of the 1990s, and the sense of identity especially cannot be reduced to any defining essence.

Second, Butler's view of gender as enacted in repeated cultural performances has proved attractive to intellectuals and activists dismissive of traditional political strategies for combating experiences of exclusion and domination. Postmodernists especially have welcomed Butler's refusal of identity politics, finding in her stress on the performative a means to contextualize a series of profound social changes in the relation of globalization, media, information technology, identity, culture and representation. Some have appropriated Butler to subvert the liberal politics of contesting social exclusion in the name of fairer participation in institutional life, pointing out that such single-interest politics is a thing of the past. The world can no longer be adequately understood according to traditional notions of representation in politics and the public sphere; in conditions of globalization, it is the logics of performance which are most appropriate for grasping disjoinings of sex and gender, the private and public spheres, as played out in mass media. Others have drawn upon Butler to argue for new social alliances and forms of political contestation, as have sociologists associated with cultural studies, critical race theory and post-colonial theory.

However there are various problems with Butler's work, both in terms of social theory and as a model of gender critique. Many of Butler's critics worry about the notion of 'performance,' claiming that it seems to suggest a voluntarist process of choosing a gender at will. This criticism involves in my view an inaccurate reading of *Gender Trouble*, and indeed Butler herself has empathized that gender performativity involves not so much choice as it does a forced repetition of the sexual norm. If anything, she stresses the structuring rather than the agency of the human subject. Gender identities for Butler take on what stability and coherence they have through the performative reiteration of discourses, all of which she locates at the structural level of the 'heterosexual matrix.' Seen in this light, Butler's theory of the subject is perhaps best recast as one of *involuntary performance*. Even so, however, it is not clear that such a perspective can avoid reproducing the deterministic emphasis of Foucault, insofar as Butler privileges the moment of constraint in her account of repeated gender performances. What is arguably missing from Butler's theoretical framework is, among other things, a reflexive notion of agency – particularly as this pertains to the relation between gender identity and social structure.

Related to this is the considerable criticism and debate which have followed from Butler's account of dissident sexual performances which makes trouble for established gender categories. Butler's theory of gender trouble emphasizes, as we have seen, the potentially disruptive power of marginalized or non-normative sexualities, an undoing of the heterosexual matrix which secures sexual binaries and gender hierarchy. From lipstick lesbians to drag queens, every performance of gender bending may potentially weaken, disrupt or transgress normative gender framing. However, Butler's invoking of the transgressive theatrics in perverse or queer gender performances gains its rhetorical force primarily in relation to routine or mainstream enactments of gender identity. In the final analysis, some critics find this division of performativity into mainstream and transgressive unduly restrictive. As Lynne Segal notes:

> Icons of mass culture, from Mae West to Madonna, Valentino to Michael Jackson, have always thrived on forms of sexual ambiguity which suggest the seductive appeal of a transgressive or perverse dynamic at the very heart of heterosexist culture. But with drag and queer display as popular (or unpopular) with reactionary as with radical audiences, its ability to unsettle and subvert normal structures of gender and sexuality seems no more powerful than its ability to mirror and to legitimate them.
>
> (1999: 61)

Ultimately, the criticism of Butler's underwriting of drag or gender bending is that this represents a trivial response to the complexities of fashioning alternative sexed, sexualized and gendered forms of identity in the contemporary age.

Queer theory

The affirmation of self-identity can sometimes be as much limiting as it can be freeing. Controversies over the personal and cultural problems involved in identity politics, especially in respect of asserting a common identity and community, have frequently plagued those committed to progressive sexual politics. The dilemma is primarily one of how to redress social exclusion and political oppression by creating a new sense of self, solidarity and community while avoiding the confinement of fixed identities and categories. Most of us, most of the time, make sense of identity by telling stories about our experience, shared understanding, sense of communal belonging, and so forth. We want the interrelationship between personal and cultural life to be open-ended in this complex and pluralistic world; we seek to avoid simple generalizations about our identity, and none of us want our experience coded as stereotype. A preoccupation with the relation between personal identity and social difference has been increasingly central to sexual politics over the last few decades, especially as developed by the lesbian and gay movement and also in queer theory and politics. The core challenge for the self, as defined by such standpoints, is to find some balance between the need for identity and the recognition of cultural diversity and social difference. In the remainder of this chapter, I shall chart some of these changes in the intimate texture of social life, paying special attention to conceptions of the self that have arisen from contemporary sexual politics. Contemporary feminist and gay studies, in particular, have developed powerful ideas about the historical formation of sexual identities, with the social impact of the science of sexuality a key theme. This research represents, in many respects, an alternative history of the self and sexual identity, and it is worth briefly noting some of the more salient aspects of such perspectives on sexual identity and the self.

There are various ways of denoting sexual orientation. At various historical points, in various cultures, the terms 'homosexual,' 'gay,' 'lesbian' and 'queer' have been deployed to refer to same-sex sexual desires and practices. The etymological evolution of 'homosexual' is especially interesting in this context. The word 'homosexual' was coined in 1868 by the sex reformer Karl Kertbeny; it was taken up by the Swiss medical practitioner, Karoly Maria Benkert, the following year. Yet it was not until the end of the nineteenth century that the word became commonly used in English, and indeed a public culture involving core distinctions between homosexuality and heterosexuality as distinctive identities did not fully emerge until some point in the 1920s or 1930s. Prior to this, homosexuality was – for the most part – thought of as a particular kind of behavior; the law punished illegal activity (sodomy), not deviant identity. The slow filtering through of the medical/expert term 'homosexual' into public discourse and common culture changed all this, and is a good example of the intrusion of expert knowledge into the fabric of daily life that I have emphasized in preceding chapters. For it was in and through this invasion of social-scientific knowledge that homosexuality came, in time, to be established as a unique identity, a specific psychological disposition, a particular sense of self, and thus as separated or marked off from the heterosexual main-stream. This in turn opened a path to the coercive idea that psychological health depends upon a normalized sense of personal identity, something to which homosexuality was from the beginning excluded in the view of the medical establishment. For homosexuality, in the majority of medical discourses, was treated as a pathology. But it also opened a path for the ongoing interrogation of identity – in this context, a problematization of the idea that homosexuals have a specific sexual nature and sense of self. *Coming Out* (1977), by gay studies theorist Jeffrey Weeks, accounts for homosexual identity as just such a cross between social and historical event on the one hand and the absorption of social-scientific ideas governing sexuality by the wider public on the other. In charting the role of science, especially sexology, in the historical making of a specific homo-sexual identity, Weeks tells a compelling story of how these historical forces have shaped identity-based gay liberation in both progressive and constraining ways.

Throughout the 1960s and 1970s, the rise of gay liberation in many Western countries was closely associated with an ongoing interrogation of dominant conceptions of sexuality, self and identity. Some gay writers argued that homosexuality was psychologically and socially the equal of heterosexuality; this standpoint, in one stroke, embraced all in the main-stream who viewed the homosexual as a distinct type of person, but with the crucial inversion that homosexuality was now cast as just as morally worthy as heterosexuality. According to this approach, which in one version or another was extensively adopted in the gay movement, the notion of a distinctive sense of personal and sexual identity should be deployed to defend gays against the homophobia of the wider culture, and thus to advance gay rights.

There are a number of important criticisms of the political radicalism of gay liberation. I shall only note in passing those that directly relate to the topic of the self. It is sometimes argued, particularly by postmodern sexual theorists, that gay liberation rode roughshod over race, ethnic and class differences. There is some accuracy to this charge, since the desire to legislate an affirmative gay identity was often pursued at the cost of awareness of wider social issues – especially ignorance of the emotional damage that other social and historical forces have had upon the self. However this argument can be overstressed; there is always a danger of oversimplification when discussing the gay movement as a unified entity, and in fact many gay activists shared a strong political commitment to other issues of discrimination (such as the Black and union movements). Perhaps more importantly, and no doubt ironically, the gay liberation movement has been criticized by many for reinforcing the divide between homosexual and heterosexual cultures, positing essentialist identities, and carving the world into majority and minority experience.

In time, the identity framework of the gay movement gave way to a different sort of politics concerned with sexual identities, preferences and activities, one connected with the new social theories of post-structuralism and postmodernism. In the late 1980s and 1990s, the term 'queer' was used by theorists and activists alike to attack identity politics, to interrogate sexuality and decenter the self, and to construct alternative political geographies for the heterosexual/homosexual divide that shapes our communities and cultures. Queer theory represents a sexual politics sensitive to our new era of transnational capital, globalized technology and postmodern culture. The social and historical forces influencing the shift from identity to queer politics are located in the fragmentation of social identities and political alignments associated with globalization. Queer politics is pluralistic, multidimensional, and open-ended, especially at the level of addressing experience of the self and sexuality.

The writings of Diana Fuss are important in this context. Reflecting upon the widespread discontent with identity politics in the 1980s, Fuss developed an influential critique of the ways in which gay and lesbian liberation discourses unwittingly reinforced heterosexual norms; her critique, in turn, shaped the politics of subversion advocated by queer theorists. Describing configurations of sex, gender and sexuality in terms of our culture's obsession with notions of sameness and difference, Fuss contended that the opposition between homosexuality and heterosexuality reinforced the social imperative to divide the world between norm and pathology, inclusion and exclusion, identity and otherness. The hetero/homosexual logic of identity is one premised on difference. Such forms of sexual orientation, however, are in fact constantly crossing into each other. It is only through psychological exclusion and repression that homosexuality is rendered subordinate to heterosexuality. Part of the problem here, according to Fuss, is that we are lost in identity, its logic and categories. Questioning identity categories, Fuss asks:

Is politics based on identity, or is identity based on politics? Is identity a natural, political, historical, psychical, or linguistic construct? What implications does the deconstruction of 'identity' have for those who espouse an identity politics? Can feminist, gay, or lesbian subjects afford to dispense with the notion of unified, stable identities or must we begin to base our politics on something other than identity? What, in other words, is the politics of 'identity politics'?

(1989: 100)

Fuss asks us, in effect, to consider what our lives might be like without the anxious grip of identity categories. She questions what the self can do without, a challenge taken up and developed in queer theory and politics in the 1990s.

The best known and most influential author associated with the queer critique of feminist theorizing is Eve Kosofsky Sedgwick, routinely described as 'the mother of queer theory.' A professor of English with an uncanny gift for grappling with the sexual politics of language, Sedgwick stresses the experiential significance of discourses on homosexuality not only for the self and identity, but for the production and distribution of knowledge in the wider society. In her most important book, *The Epistemology of the Closet* (1990), Sedgwick describes the hetero/homosexual opposition as our culture's 'master term,' a term that structures not only self, identity and sexuality, but also social conventions, modes of thought, and cultural knowledge to its core. The normative regulations and sanctions governing homosexuality have never applied, and never will, to gays and lesbians alone; rather they cut to the heart of heterosexual identity, which maintains itself in opposition to homosexual experience. But what is repressed returns. Heterosexuality and homosexuality are intimately, hysterically intertwined; homosexual identifications, for Sedgwick as for Butler, are contained within heterosexual relationships, just as heterosexuality is gathered up and transfigured in gay and lesbian relationships.

Sedgwick has perhaps done more to interrogate the political limits of self, identity and sexuality than any other scholar associated with contemporary gay and lesbian studies. Her version of queer theory is out to demonstrate that homosexuality is integral to the culture of heterosexuality which hysterically repudiates same-sex desire. Not surprisingly, given her predilection for language as at the center of social life, Sedgwick worries away at the cluster of key words that betray the dreads of heterosexist culture. Thus 'the closet' turns out to ground knowledge of sexuality and gender in ways that pathologize. Bluntly put, Sedgwick argues that 'the closet' – as representation, metaphor, desire, fantasy – is installed at the heart of both homosexual and heterosexual identity, experience and definition. Consider, for example, the experience of coming-out. Coming-out stories have long been a common part of gay experience. 'It's OK to be gay': this is one of the better known slogans promoted by the gay and lesbian movement to assist young people negotiate the difficulties of coming to terms with their homosexuality. Yet for the most part, asserts Sedgwick, coming-out stories have the capacity to disturb and damage dominant conceptions of sexuality. Because of the erotic energy and anxious fear associated with the closet and coming-out, we can never know the truth about the self, sexuality, or gender. The closet is the underside of 'normal sexuality,' always threatening to open or be opened.

The apparent floating-free from its gay origins of that phrase 'coming out of the closet' in recent usage might suggest that the trope of the closet is so close to the heart of some modern preoccupations that it could be, or has been, evacuated of its historical gay specificity. But I hypothesize that exactly the opposite is true. I think that a whole cluster of the most crucial sites for the contestation of meaning in twentieth-century Western culture are consequentially and quite indelibly marked with the historical specificity of homosocial/homosexual definition, notably but not exclusively male, from around the turn of the century. Among these sites are, as I have indicated, the pairings secrecy/disclosure and private/public. Along with and sometimes through these epistemologically charged pairings, condensed in the figures of 'the closet' and 'coming out,' this very specific crisis of definition has then ineffaceably marked other pairings as basic to modern cultural organization as masculine/feminine, majority/minority, innocence/initiation, natural/artificial, new/old, growth/decadence, urbane/provincial, health/illness, same/different, cognition/paranoia, art/kitsch, sincerity/sentimentality, and voluntarily/addiction. So permeative has the suffusing stain of homo/heterosexual crisis been to that to discuss any of these indices in any context, in the absence of an antihomophobic analysis, must perhaps be to perpetuate unknowingly compulsions implicit in each.

Eve Kosofsky Sedgwick (1990) *The Epistemology of the Closet.* Berkeley: University of California Press, pages 72–3.

The political implications of such an assault on identity categories, in the recent history of queer theory at least, are highly ambiguous. In the work of Fuss, Sedgwick and others, legitimating forms of cultural identity as something coherent, unified or fixed are progressively called into question by a subversive critique that interrogates the oppressive fusing of sex, gender and sexuality at the level of the self. As a kind of anti-identity politics then, queer theory advocates and celebrates a coalition of alternative, subversive and transgressive sexual identities. Queer politics embrace not only lesbian, gay and bisexual identities, but also fetishists, sadists, drag queens, transsexuals, butches and gender benders. The mobilization of identities as queer is potentially indeterminate, as the assessment of queerness depends on a self-identification with forms of sexuality that question or subvert 'the normal' within patriarchal power relations. Like much post-modernist culture, queer theory and politics is unashamedly open-ended, plural and multiple; the transgression of sexual norms is the key that defines queerness. But how transgression constitutes a progressive politics is not altogether clear. Jeffrey Weeks makes this criticism well:

> In the long perspectives of history, queer politics may well prove an ephemeral ripple rather than a refreshing wave. Queer politics has all the defects of a transgressive style, elevating confrontation over the content of alternatives. Although it seeks to deconstruct old rigidities, it creates new boundaries; although it is deliberately transgressive, it enacts dissidence through the adoption of a descriptive label which many lesbians and gays find offensive, often seeking enemies within as much as enemies without.
>
> (1995: 115)

Much like Butler's notion of subversive performance, the slant towards transgression in queer theory is perhaps geared more towards fashion than the fine detail of concrete political transformation.

It is against this backdrop that some commentators have suggested that queer theory is unable to provide a progressive basis for politics. The emphasis upon literary deconstruction in queer theorizing is, for some critics, intellectually interesting but politically shallow; the whole style of queer theory, with its relentless droning of sexual transgression, is said to be apolitical, with little analytical concern for the realities of social institutions, economic development or the policies of government. In post-modern culture, the language of transgression is sometimes only an inch away from anti-political irrationalism – or so some argue. Others, however, welcome queer theory's dismantling of social science and literary criticism as distinct fields of study, and see in the queer critique of identity a radical revaluation not only of self-experience and social relationships, but also of knowledge and politics. Indeed, as Patricia Clough has argued, the style of queer theoretical interrogations of the self, identity and sexuality suggest that style itself is political, always over determined with cultural assumptions and sexual ideologies. In particular, the style of mainstream social science, with its patriarchal longing for certitude, structure and order, is rendered dubious in this respect.

Similar doubts hang over the question of the self in queer theory. Is queer theory's ongoing interrogation of selfhood radical or reactionary? Certainly the focus of queer theory upon, say, transvestite performance or gender-corrective surgery dramatizes the incoherence of our culture's obsession with stable selves, identities, sexualities and genders. But it is far from obvious that, in its relentless debunking of the self and identity politics, queer theory can provide any psychological analysis of self. It is one thing to decenter or deconstruct the autonomous, rational, masculinist self of Enlightenment culture; yet it is quite another to imagine that self as a category can be conveniently done away with altogether. The critique of identity I have described in the foregoing pages, from Butler to Sedgwick, does not, in my opinion, attempt to transcend the realm of individuality and the self in such a manner. It remains the case, however, that the exuberance and idealism of queer theory, however intellectually invigorating the call to sexual transgression might be, does underestimate the considerable personal and emotional difficulties involved in cultural change and political transformation.

Summary points

1   Feminism views the relation between gender and identity as a core political issue. In 1970s gender theory, the fundamental distinction is that between biological 'sex' (viewed as innate) and socialized gender (viewed as constructed socially). In the 1970s and early 1980s, gender theory was eclipsed by a feminist interest in the complexity of women's role as mothers as well as the psychodynamic intricacies of femininities and masculinities.

2   The psychoanalytic theories of Freud and Lacan, according to feminists such as Juliet Mitchell, offer crucial critiques of how unequal gender relations come to be emotionally experienced by women and men. According to Mitchell, it is through language that the child is subjected to the law of the Name-of-the-Father, which operates to institute repression, sexual difference and gender identity by the threat of castration.

3   Mitchell's feminism has been widely criticized for exaggerating the rigidities and uniformities of gender hierarchy.

4   Exclusive female mothering, according to feminist Nancy Chodorow, is central to gender asymmetry in modern societies. It produces social relations split between connected, empathic female identities on the one hand, and isolated, instrumental male identities on the other. Masculine identity is built on a denial of primary maternal

identification resulting in a fragile sense of self, defensively structured by an abstract attitude to the world. Feminine identity is
grounded in a strong sense of gender, but is limited in capacity for
autonomy and individuality. The only viable route out of contemporary gender asymmetries, says Chodorow, is through shared
parenting.

5   In various French feminisms, there is an engagement with Freud and
    Lacan to critique the patriarchal sexual order of contemporary soci-
    eties. In Kristeva, this is represented through the notion of the
    'semiotic' – a pre-Oedipal realm of intense affect associated with
    the imprint of the mother's body. In Irigaray, the subversive 'femi-
    nine' is grounded in relation to women's plural, multiple experience
    of sexuality and the body.

6   For Judith Butler, gender identity is a 'discursive effect.' Sexuality is
    shot through with psychological and cultural illusions created by the
    repeated performance of gender.

7   The term 'queer' has been used by social theorists from the late
    1980s and 1990s to critically interrogate sexualities and the
    decentering of identity. Queer theory is a politics affirming the
    plural, multidimensional and ambivalent.

Further questions

1   In the light of this chapter's discussion of feminism and post-
    feminism, what do you understand the sex–gender distinction to
    denote?

2   In what ways do you think psychoanalysis has either enhanced or
    constrained the feminist critique of unequal gender relations?

3   Has feminism been eclipsed by the advent of a post-feminist
    sensibility?

4   How might the repressed 'feminine' be politically mapped in con-
    temporary masculinist society?

5   What are some of the political ramifications of the queering of
    sexualities?

Further reading

Juliet Mitchell

Psychoanalysis and Feminism (London: Penguin Books, 1974)
Mad Men and Medusas (New York: Basic Books, 2001)

Nancy Chodorow

The Reproduction of Mothering (Berkeley: University of California Press, 1978)
Feminism and Psychoanalytic Theory (London: Polity Press, 1989)
Femininities, Masculinities, Sexualities: Freud and Beyond (Lexington: University Press of Kentucky, 1994)

Jessica Benjamin

The Bonds of Love: Psychoanalysis, Feminism, and the Problem of Domination (New York: Pantheon Books, 1988)
Like Subjects, Love Objects: Essays on Recognition and Sexual Difference (New Haven: Yale University Press, 1995)
Shadow of the Other: Intersubjectivity and Gender in Psychoanalysis (New York: Routledge, 1998)

Julia Kristeva

Powers of Horror: An Essay on Abjection (New York: Columbia University Press, 1982)
Revolutions in Poetic Language (New York: Columbia University Press, 1984)
Tales of Love (New York: Columbia University Press, 1987)
Strangers to Ourselves (London: Harvester Wheatsheaf, 1991)
Black Sun: Depression and Melancholia (New York: Columbia University Press, 1989)

Judith Butler

Gender Trouble: Feminism and the Subversion of Identity (London and New York: Routledge, 1990)
Bodies that Matter: On the Discursive Limits of Sex (London and New York: Routledge, 1993)
The Psychic Life of Power: Theories in Subjection (Stanford, California: Stanford University Press, 1997)

Eve Kosofsky Sedgwick

Between Men: English Literature and Male Homosocial Desire (New York: Columbia University Press, 1985)
The Epistemology of the Closet (Berkeley: University of California Press, 1990)
Tendencies (Durham: Duke University Press, 1993)

feminism and post-feminist theory

Postmodernity

Contents

In the course of this book so far we have examined a number of perspectives and problems in contemporary social theory. The theoretical perspectives surveyed – post-Marxism, structuralism, feminism – have been considered in terms of their different preoccupations in approaching the critique of society. And yet all of these social theories have been united by their concern to put into question a whole form of social life in order to entertain possible alternative futures. That is, the social theories reviewed in previous chapters display a certain totalizing bent, indebted as they are to the modernist assumption that the whole definition, constitution and transformation of society can be comprehensively mapped at the level of theory. The Frankfurt School (see Chapter 3) had revealed that the culture industries are intricately interwoven with the organizing logics of advanced capitalism, manipulating personal life in terms of surplus repression and reorganizing public life in terms of intensified consumerism. Structuralism (see Chapter 5) had shown that the signs and structures that frame personal and social life, popular and high culture, are governed by the systemic processes of language. Feminism (see Chapter 12) had probed the interlocking of sex and gender, and made its appeal to emancipation in the form of autonomous identity unencumbered by the oppressive weight of patriarchy.

For those social critics that found themselves less than impressed with the programmatic, synoptic ambitions of modernist social science, one way out from these conceptual conundrums and political deadlocks lay in displacing and decentering the operations of social theory as a whole. Why go on trying, the skeptics asked, to locate single drivers of social reproduction and political domination – capitalism, language, gender – when it is more and more obvious that we live today in a multidimensional world that continually escapes the powers of theory? Why continue with the act of conceptual house-tidying, dividing the world into neatly segmented sub-systems, micro-processes and deterministic identities, when it is evident that theory practiced in this fashion is a form of repressive political closure? In short, why scratch where it does not itch? Dispense with the totalizing ambitions of social theory – which are, in any event, ill-conceived, a hangover from the Enlightenment – and grasp what most people today intuitively recognize: that human experience is multiple, dispersed, fragmented, complex, contradictory. In the announcement of this novel cultural mood, we have entered the troubled waters of postmodernism.

Postmodernism was a response in the 1980s to the waning of radical politics and of theory, the outsourcing of manufacturing from the West to various Second and Third World countries, the spread of a seemingly unstoppable universal consumerism, the development of new information technologies as well as the emergence of new forms of identity-politics.

There are already several accomplished surveys of the history of the term 'postmodernism' in the critical literature (Anderson, 1998), which readers may wish to consult. More interesting than its conceptual history, however, is the speed with which the term 'postmodern' has entered the lexicon of popular culture. Everything from MTV, Madonna and mobile phones to irony, information culture and iPods has attracted the label 'postmodern.' In this sense, postmodernism – as suggestive of a fresh cultural mood and novel aesthetic styles – scandalizes identity, society and politics, with its leveling of hierarchies, its interpretative polyvalence, its dislocating subversion of ideological closure, its self-reflexive pluralism.

In introducing the main parameters of postmodern social theory in this chapter, I shall concentrate on the central ideas developed by various social theorists in their visions of postmodernity. These visions might be labeled, for our purposes at any rate, as follows: (1) postmodernity as schizoid desire; (2) postmodernity as simulated media culture; (3) postmodernity as global capitalist transformations; and, (4) postmodernity as liquid sociality. In describing postmodernity in these ways, I have in mind the work of Gilles Deleuze, Félix Guattari and Jean-François Lyotard as belonging to the first category; the French sociologist Jean Baudrillard to the second category; the American cultural theorist Fredric Jameson to the third category; and, the European sociologist Zygmunt Bauman to the final category. The writings of Deleuze, Guattari, Lyotard, Baudrillard, Jameson and Bauman are of crucial significance for any sustained critical reflection upon postmodernity. Each of these authors has developed an immensely powerful aesthetic, cultural or sociological understanding of the conditions and consequences of postmodernity. Yet each author has also expressed reservations about the very notion of the postmodern, and each in their own way has attempted to keep some distance from the so-called 'postmodern turn' in social theory. This makes their respective ideas of key importance for appraising the characteristics of postmodernity, and throughout the chapter I shall interweave other important studies on postmodern transformations of identity, culture and society.

Deleuze and Guatarri: postmodernity as schizoid desire

The work of Gilles Deleuze and Félix Guattari emerged in the context of post-1968 libertarian left politics in France. Deleuze, a philosopher who committed suicide in 1995, and Guatarri, a psychoanalyst who was very active in the anti-psychiatry movement of the 1960s, worked together to produce some arrestingly original books expounding what they termed 'the philosophy of desire.'

In their celebrated work *Anti-Oedipus* (1983), a book widely hailed in postmodern and radical political circles, Deleuze and Guattari detailed a vision of schizophrenic desire as the basis for an account of social transformation. *Anti-Oedipus*, which scandalized French psychoanalysis and the academy, developed a postmodern vision of desire from two main perspectives. Firstly, Deleuze and Guattari use psychoanalytic theory against itself, launching a polemical assault against the tenets of classical Freudianism. Secondly, they outline a multiple, depersonalized account of desire, which they term 'schizoanalysis.' Deleuze and Guattari invoke schizophrenia as a model for understanding the nature of desire in contemporary times – that is, the emerging social landscape of postmodernity. They propose a celebration of the fluid and multiple intensities of schizophrenic desire, primarily in order to oppose the repressive functioning of social norms under capitalism. To this end, they develop the notion of a 'subjectless machine,' a kind of schizophrenic overflowing of desire that produces and reproduces itself in aimless circulation. Against the Oedipalizing logic of capitalist discourse, where desire is channeled into prescribed pathways under the sign of the commodity form, Deleuze and Guattari speak up for the impersonalized flows of schizoid desire, a productive network of libidinal articulations which potentially short-circuits capitalism.

In this view of postmodern social transformations, the world is seen as a mix of libidinal and symbolic forms that continuously displace one another. The historical development of capitalist production is interpreted by Deleuze and Guattari in terms of the injurious traumas of repression. In its early stages, capitalism is said to have severed the economic realm from symbolic forms such as kinship systems, customs, religious beliefs and the like. Capitalist production, at this historical point, was embedded in a form of collectivism, with pre-given social roles and identities. The emergence of monopoly capitalism, however, radically transformed the social world: it swept away traditional social forms, as economic forces bite deeply into the symbolic textures of society itself. The creation of an international capitalist system and of world markets, it might be said, breaks down the symbolic framework of the local community and of tradition. Deleuze and Guattari refer to this process as the 'deterritorialization' of social codes. Capitalism ruthlessly dismantles bourgeois cultural forms and moral codes, replacing these with the exchangeability and anonymity of commodities. Deleuze and Guattari argue that the logic of capitalist economic relations is deeply interwoven with the discontinuities of schizophrenic desire. Like the indifference of the commodity itself, schizophrenia knows no symbolic limit, no constraint of reality, no high-minded guilt born of the superego. Instead, schizoid desire produces itself in fragments of pleasure, slicing capitalist temporality into the fluidity of the moment. 'The order of desire,' write Deleuze and Guattari, 'is the order of *production*; all production is at once desiring production and social production' (1983 [1977]: 296).

Capitalism, however, not only 'deterritorializes' but constantly 'reterritorializes' in radically new ways. Against capitalism's dismantling of pre-existing social boundaries, Deleuze and Guattari point to a proto-fascist, paranoiac tendency at the heart of modernity, a tendency that restructures schizoid flows into oppressive norms and which thus functions as ingrained pathologies. What is being emphasized here is the oppressive nature of late capitalist society, its recoding of desire into the ordered, conventional world of international banking, stock markets, and insurance companies. Schizophrenic and paranoid desire are both forms of production to be found at work within the social system. Global capitalism produces a profound deterritorialization of social forms into schizoid flows on the one hand, while simultaneously recoding these flows into the symbolic circuit of culture on the other. From iPods to the International Monetary Fund, the schizophrenic signals of desire are endlessly recoded to support the economic logics of capitalism.

> The decoding of flows and the deterritorialization of the socius thus constitutes the most characteristic and the most important tendency of capitalism. It continually draws near to its limit, which is a genuinely schizophrenic limit. It tends, with all the strength at its command, to produce the schizo as the subject of the decoded flows on the body without organs – more capitalist than the capitalist and more proletarian than the proletariat. This tendency is being carried further and further, to the point that capitalism with all its flows may dispatch itself straight to the moon: we really haven't seen anything yet! When we say that schizophrenia is our characteristic malady, the malady of our era, we do not merely mean to say that modern life drives people mad. It is not a question of a way of life, but of a process of production. Nor is it merely the failure of codes, such a parallelism is a much more precise formulation of the relationship between, for example, the phenomena of the shifting of meaning in the case of schizophrenics and the mechanisms of ever-increasing disharmony and discord at every level of industrial society.
>
> Gilles Deleuze and Félix Guattari (1983) *Anti-Oedipus: Capitalism and Schizophrenia*. Translated by Robert Hurley, Mark Seem, and Helen R. Lane. Minneapolis: University of Minnesota Press, page 34.

As with the creative destruction of capitalism, similar contradictions are at work within psychoanalysis itself. Desire prior to Oedipus, Deleuze and Guattari contend, is multidimensional, discontinuous and shifting. Desire just *is* the production of 'machine parts,' spilling out across libidinal surfaces, pluralized in its operations through contact with other human 'machines.' 'The breast,' they write, 'is a machine that produces milk, and the mouth a machine coupled to it' (1983 [1977]: 1). Desire is schizoid to its roots, subjectless through and through, an impersonal force of production. Not so, however, after the impact of Oedipalization. The impersonal force of schizoid desire, according to Deleuze and Guattari, is repressively codified through Oedipus. For Deleuze and Guattari, the Oedipus complex works to *personalize desire*, referring all unconscious productions to the incestuous sexual realm of family life. Oedipus, then, is a prime instance of the capitalist recoding of desire. Deleuze and Guattari argue that psychoanalysis functions as a repressive force which projects desire into the personalized, neurotic structures of 'daddy-mummy-me.'

The process of capitalist reterritorialization is in this view paranoid to its roots; such social pathologies, whilst deeply entrenched however, do not go all the way down. For Deleuze and Guatarri, the schizoid nature of desire constantly *escapes* the well-ordered structures of capitalist production. The schizoid tribulations of desire, argue Deleuze and Guattari, are transgressive, polymorphous, fragmenting. In its anarchic, heterogeneous lines of libidinal intensity, schizophrenic desire offers, paradoxically, to outstrip the centralized, unified organization of capitalist production in which it is encoded. 'Schizophrenia,' write Deleuze and Guattari, 'is desiring production at the limit of social production' (1983 [1977]: 35). Like the Surrealist avant-garde, then, Deleuze and Guattari are fascinated by the idea of transgression, the breaking of limits and undoing of rules. Smashing through the boundaries of ordinary life, schizoid desire is pure production: desire turning back upon itself to further the production of desire.

Deleuze and Guattari's celebration of the transgressive edge of desire lies in stark contrast to the Lacanian model of the unconscious, as discussed in Chapter 7. Whereas Lacan ties the unconscious to loss, Deleuze and Guattari conceive of schizoid desire as pure affirmation. Moreover, they view Lacan's Freud as essentially conservative in political orientation. Psychoanalysis, both traditional and Lacanian, constructs desire as loss for the purpose of adapting human subjects to the social order. From this angle, psychoanalysis deciphers and re-inscribes Oedipal compulsions for identification which are essential to the ego-centered, neurotic structures of subjecthood in late capitalism. In this manner, the signs of power constitute us as individual subjects through and through. In contrast, Deleuze and Guattari emphasize the multiple paths of desire – schizoid proliferations, openings, zigzags and flows. To designate this, they propose 'schizoanalysis,' which interprets unconscious desire hydraulically as a desiring machine; unconscious flows of libidinal energy at once anchor and destabilize the social process. For Deleuze and Guattari, schizophrenia is revolutionary since it defies identification, categorization, and differentiation. According to this view, unconscious desire represents nothing, neither representation nor the sign. Desire simply *is*. Desire floats in the social field as indeterminate, impersonal production. Hence the factory metaphor, 'desiring machines.'

Deleuze and Guatarri's arguments have provoked a barrage of critical responses. Some critics lampoon the suggestion that schizophrenia is naturally rebellious and subversive. In celebrating the mind-shattering flux of schizoid desire, so critics argue, Deleuze and Guatarri sidestep the issue of how personal change and social change interweave. Clinical portraits of schizophrenia are said by various critics to belie the celebratory gloss provided by Deleuze and Guattari. What clinical studies reveal is a world, not of euphoric celebration, but of disintegration, fragmentation, terror and emotional devastation. Some defenders of Deleuze and Guatarri have argued that to anticipate how the world might be radically altered from the standpoint of the schizophrenic *process* is not the same as promoting schizophrenia itself. Yet as regards social theory, it certainly seems doubtful that schizoid processes offer a fruitful basis for the rethinking of social organization. Even if it is granted that schizoid processes break apart received social meanings in potentially productive ways, who would seriously put forward such a case for social change given the pain, emptiness and terror of schizoid experience? Perhaps most limiting of all, however, is the failure of Deleuze and Guattari to distinguish between different forms of social organization. In defending the 'schizo' against the repressions of modernity, Deleuze and Guattari appear to slide into an indiscriminate rejection of politics as such. All social systems become, in effect, 'terroristic' irrespective of their modalities of power. But what of the vital political differences between liberal democracy and fascism? What about the impact of ideologies, such as religious fundamentalism, nationalism, and political militancy? In lamenting the 'terror of norms,' Deleuze and Guattari are left without any secure footing to elucidate the revolutionary political agency to which they attach key importance. Instead, Deleuze and Guattari are left with a romantic, idealized fantasy of the 'schizoid hero.'

The postmodern condition: Lyotard

Alongside the work of Deleuze and Guatarri, the social theorist whose name is most closely associated with postmodernism is the French philosopher, Jean-François Lyotard. Like Deleuze and Guattari, Lyotard wishes to speak up for a postmodernism with strong political commitment. Abandoning the claims of the Enlightenment and universal theories of knowledge, Lyotard offers an original analysis of today's transformed connections between libidinal desire and social differences.

Whereas Deleuze and Guattari interpret society in terms of schizoid desire against repressive desire, revolutionary against fascist desire, Lyotard in *Libidinal Economy* (1974) sees the social as itself secretly libidinal, with sociality inscribed on the 'inside' of desire. Society, though dependent on a repression of desire, is traversed by 'libidinal intensities.' Yet interestingly, Lyotard rejects the libertarian view that transgression is inherently good, repression bad. All societies, he argues, are complex networks of discourse and desire. Instead of prioritizing desire over signification, as in Deleuze and Guattari's *Anti-Oedipus*, Lyotard highlights different modalities of desire and the structures of their production. Highlighting ambivalences in Freud's account of the unconscious, Lyotard discerns two aspects of desire: desire-as-wish (fantasy) and desire-as-force (libido). Desire-as-wish, the figural component of the unconscious, is the representational form impressed upon lost objects. Here the individual subject fantasizes images of the self, of others, and of the world as a compensation for various lacks or exclusions. In this regime, desire operates under the sign of lack, absence and negativity. By contrast, desire-as-force, the energetic component of the unconscious, is pure energy, libido and primary process. In this regime, desire functions through the act of its own production, endlessly reproducing itself in some transcendental process of repetition.

Lyotard wishes to claim desire-as-force as inherently positive and affirmative. He advocates, in Nietzschean fashion, a celebration of libidinal intensities. Libidinal intensities consist of a flux of desire, energy in a state of continuous nonlinear movement. Lyotard refers to a rotation of a 'libidinal band' that constantly disrupts all intersections of self and other, of internal and external, of the differentiation of 'this' from 'not-this.' The whole notion is somewhat like the 'action painting' of Jackson Pollock, in which figural lines interweave without end. For Lyotard, libidinal intensities are an unconscious force prior to representation and conscious knowledge.

If the libidinal intensities of which Lyotard writes constitute symbolic representation, however, it is not his political aim to oppose the libidinal to the social. Rejecting as politically naive proclamations about the 'truth of desire,' Lyotard turns instead to the dissolution of symbolic representation as a *medium* of the libidinal band itself. The dominant ideological forms of the Enlightenment, including doctrines of truth and freedom, self-determination, reason and universality, are thus recast as inseparable from a libidinal poetics. Knowledge itself is just one mode of libidinal intensity among others. Here we reach the core of Lyotard's political analysis in *Libidinal Economy*: contemporary social theory must reject the view that desire does not flow freely enough in contemporary society – as Deleuze and Guattari contend. For Lyotard, by contrast, desire circulates endlessly around objects, surfaces, and bodies. In this connection, late capitalism is an immense desiring system. He describes late capitalist society as a culture swamped with flashy commodities and signs, in which all social forms are colonized by the economic logic of exchange. Yet the implications of this for radical politics are not necessarily bad news. According to Lyotard, the exchangeability and anonymity of contemporary capitalist processes parallels the aimless flux of the libidinal band itself. He advocates embracing the fragmentation of desire as a way of intensifying the lived experiences of postmodern culture. The challenging and exhilarating task for postmodernism is to recognize that desire is always already realized, to extract pleasure from the fragments and surfaces in which identities are constituted.

In *The Postmodern Condition*, the work for which Lyotard is most widely celebrated and which helped ignite the debate over postmodernism, the distinction between modern and postmodern models of knowledge is examined. Lyotard views the defining features of the postmodern condition as involving a rejection of the 'grand narratives' of the Enlightenment, such as Truth, Freedom, Justice and Reason. Modernity, for Lyotard as for some other postmodern theorists, is characterized by the grounding of knowledge and science in appeals to 'master or metanarratives.' The seductive, rhetorical force of epic narratives, such as the Enlightenment's story of human progress or the Marxist story of the coming of socialist utopia, has helped legitimate oppressive social hierarchies and political domination. For example, the political terror unleashed in the former Soviet Union under Stalin throughout the 1940s and 1950s was made possible with ongoing reference to the epic narrative of Marxism. This was not necessarily the result of any in-built fault of Marx's work itself, something which Lyotard – a former socialist militant – is at pains to emphasize. But Marxism, just like all political ideologies, has involved a synthesizing of its world-view with various epic

Enlightenment narratives, which in turn have given rise to the tragic consequence of a terroristic Reason. Grand narratives for Lyotard are intrinsic to the social repression and political domination of modernity.

But not so the postmodern condition, which finds a novel way of contextualizing knowledge. 'I define postmodern,' announces Lyotard, 'as incredulity towards metanarratives.' In conditions of postmodernity, knowledge is fragmented into multiple disciplines, diverse sites and particular paradigms. Following the philosopher Wittgenstein, Lyotard posits that knowledge today is more and more 'grounded' in contextualized 'language games,' with each game conducted within a locally agreed, tentative specificity. Abandoning the universal categories of modernist science, the postmodern universe of knowledge is perspectival and incomplete in its self-ruling singularity. From Einsteinian relativity theory and quantum mechanics to paralogical science and black holes, the purity of perspectival, provisional knowledge is key. Social conflict, symbolic violence and political injustice occur in postmodern societies when one language game is ruthlessly imposed upon another.

Lyotard's vision of the postmodern condition has had a considerable impact upon social theory. At the center of his postmodernism lies a political concern with grasping the development of knowledge and science in the era of new information technologies, and specifically with highlighting the decentering of society in non-essentialistic ways. Any understanding of society which reduces knowledge multiplicity into unity, or which freezes identities and cultural meanings with reference toward an epic narrative, is no longer credible according to Lyotard. What becomes of science and knowledge in conditions of postmodernity is a turning back upon their own linguistic practice and self-legitimating language games. Struggles over knowledge always take place in singular spheres which are dispersed, fragmented and heterogeneous. One important upshot of Lyotard's standpoint, therefore, is that any attempt to fix, close or stabilize the meanings we attach to, say, identity, sexuality, gender, ethnicity or social class is unjust and politically dangerous.

There are, however, problems with Lyotard's account of the postmodern condition – of which two will be briefly mentioned here. The first is the criticism that Lyotard celebrates pluralism as good in itself, without any broader political content. Multiplication of small, singular language games: this is, in short, Lyotard's rallying cry for a postmodern politics. Yet there are difficulties in assuming that small revolts against large authorities are always politically progressive. What of the resurgence of neo-fascism in Europe? What of the British National Party? Fortunately, the number of members of fascist political parties remains gratifying small in the West, but the point is such social practices surely constitute a 'small language game' in Lyotard's terms. It seems doubtful that the affirming of a pluralism purged of political substance can promote social differences, especially the recovery of rights for marginalized and excluded groups, in the manner desired by Lyotard.

The second problem arising from Lyotard's account is that some have criticized his dismissal of the link between rational knowledge on the one hand and a meta-view of society on the other. According to critics, Lyotard fails to appreciate that all language games – no matter how provisional and tentative in formulation – implicate assumptions about the shape of society. Ecological discourses, for example, proceed from an awareness of, and desire to transcend, the environmental ills of industrial production. To that extent, such discourses certainly adopt elements of a 'meta-view' of society, and necessarily so in order to engage with and confront the risks of global environmental degradation.

What do you see as the gains and losses of Lyotard's postmodern perspective on knowledge? Is Lyotard's approach to contemporary living more or less convincing than that offered by Deleuze and Guattari?

Baudrillard: postmodernity as simulated media culture

To see culture in terms of signs and spectacles, not as symptom of deeper economic contradictions but as a productive constituent of daily life, is to cast the postmodern as a dehistoricized affair, depthless, decathected and disfiguring – for which, as Jean Baudrillard has argued, 'simulations' are all that exist. In his early works such as *The System of Objects* (1968), *The Consumer Society* (1972), *For a Critique of the Political Economy of the Sign* (1972) and *The Mirror of Production* (1973), Baudrillard appeared as a semiological structuralist, analyzing the signifying systems of mass media, advertising, packaging and fashion with effortless theoretical panache. In reinterpreting Marx's theory of capitalist exchange-value through a Freudian lens that emphasized the fetishizing of commodities, he sought to demonstrate how objects are encoded within a system of symbolic exchange that is fast transforming consumer societies of the West. The early Baudrillard's social semiotics, while not in any sense postmodernist, nonetheless drew from an extended array of other theories – including his sociology teacher Henri Lefebvre's 'critique of everyday life,' the work of Guy Debord and the Situationists, Jacques Lacan's reading of Freudian psychoanalysis and George Bataille's theory of expenditure and symbolic exchange. Indeed, the stylish, playful, satiric prose of Baudrillard's sociology even at this relatively early juncture entered into conflict with the scientific rigors of structuralist semiotics, and in a sense already prefigured the mature Baudrillard's characteristic blend of post-structuralism and postmodernism – what he subsequently termed 'fatal theory.'

Signs and symbols are Baudrillard's key themes, and in particular his early work draws from both Saussure's structural linguistics and Roland Barthes's semiological analysis of signifying systems. (See Chapter 3 for a discussion of the structuralism of Saussure and Barthes). He was deeply influenced by the structuralist emphasis on the arbitrary character of the sign, with its problematization of the relations between images and things, language and reality. Signs, for Baudrillard as for Saussure, are primarily constituted through differences within the structures and rules of signification of any given society. Yet the radical impulse behind his early work lies in his attempts to situate the arbitrary character of signifiers and what they signify both critically and historically. In Baudrillard's view, advanced capitalism inaugurates a new structure of signs, one in which the forces of consumption outstrip the logic of production that organized industrial societies. 'The social logic of consumption,' writes Baudrillard, 'is not at all that of the individual appropriation of the value of goods and services. . . . It is a logic of the production and manipulation of social signifiers' (1998 [1972]: 60). For Baudrillard, the 'signifier' is less a particular seductive message or enticing representation which manipulates the masses into unthinking or unwanted acts of consumption, than a kind of super-object that defies all attempts at classification, an erasure and overcoming of the product simply by mediating it, and in turn structuring the consumer's fascination with the signifier as central to the process of consumption. In this sense, the signifier is the 'real of desire.' Whether through the purchase of a Mercedes, an Apple iPod or Nike trainers, individuals make their identities through the signs they consume and display to others. In the ideological code of consumerism, identities are fashioned primarily through the exchange of symbolic differences.

From the vantage point of Marxism as well as Baudrillard's association with the French political Left throughout the 1960s, this was an unsettling perspective. In placing economic productivism at the core of social life, says Baudrillard, Marxism had functioned as a mirror to bourgeois society. The early semiological Baudrillard rejects the Marxist critique of commodities in terms of exchange value as economistic; it is *sign value*, as he comments, that shapes expressions of style, power and prestige in the age of consumer society. Moreover, he trusts to the possibility of a semiological critique of society's structured code, suggesting the critic might establish a sufficient analytical distance from the capitalist order of symbolic exchange in order to play a role in its dismantling and reconstruction. Yet, as Baudrillard came to recognize in *Simulacra and Simulation* (1994), the world of culture and critique is constituted to its roots in the depthless, fragmented surfaces of postmodernist society, and thus the idea that critical discourse can be cut loose from the play of signs that constitutes media and consumer societies is itself just metaphysical nostalgia.

This led Baudrillard to pay much more attention to transformations in media culture, particularly the role that communication media play in shaping the world in which we live. The era of hi-tech capitalism, as he explains, transmutes social reality to a mediascape of floating signifiers and codes, as images and spectacles proliferate endlessly. Baudrillard is genuinely fascinated by these details of global information culture, and considers it essential to craft a self-parodying, scrupulously stylized language capable of addressing the sublimely promiscuous and polymorphous terrain of popular entertainment, information and communication technologies. In *Simulacra and Simulation*, he addresses the issue of communicative exchange in a world dominated by the media. Unlike many major postmodernist theorists, for whom modernity is a discredited project of political domination and oppression, Baudrillard isolates the critical rigor of classical social theory as concerned with both the powers and limits of that social order's production and consumption of commodities. Such analytical attention towards commodity production and political economy, however, has now been rendered outmoded he contends, as postmodern societies are organized increasingly through the production of signs, images and codes. As postmodern culture develops, the more and more people come to define their identities based on media images and signs.

Indeed, Baudrillard's *Simulacra and Simulation* is at its most subversive and scandalous in its critique of 'hyperreality,' a kind of outstripping of reality by the logic of media simulations. Media simulations, thanks to their brilliant hallucinogenic excesses, are the ruin of all structured realities, bringing low modernist distinctions between object and representation, original and copy, thing and idea. Hyperreality is itself self-referential, a free-floating world of signs in which transgression, self-expansiveness and implosion are central. The scandal of postmodernity for Baudrillard lies in its conversion of codes, models and signs into seductive excess, a rendering up of radically ambiguous simulations that at once cut to the core of common experience and yet somehow remain aesthetically distant from everyday life. Reality is thus made foreign, perverse, uncanny. Yet in a strange reversal, what is produced out of this non-reality, or hyperreality, is one of the most imaginative forms of cultural production of the current era.

For simulacra, in Baudrillard's eyes, have no grounding in any 'reality' except their own production. TV news creates information streams only to narrate them, sex is out-fantasized in pornography and politics is raised to the second power in terrorism. From this angle, postmodernism is less a microcosm of societal forces than a world which operates independently of the culture it draws upon and transfigures.

> In this passage to a space whose curvature is no longer that of the real, nor of truth, the age of simulation thus begins with a liquidation of all referentials – worse: by their artificial resurrection in systems of signs, which are a more ductile material than meaning, in that they lend themselves to all systems of equivalence, all binary oppositions and all combinatory algebra. It is no longer a question of imitation, nor of reduplication, nor even of parody. It is rather a question of substituting signs of the real for the real itself; that is, an operation to deter every real process by its operational double, a metastable, programmatic, perfect descriptive machine which provides all the signs of the real and short-circuits all its vicissitudes. Never again will the real have to be produced: this is the vital function of the model in a system of death, or rather of anticipated resurrection which no longer leaves any chance even in the event of death. A hyperreal henceforth sheltered from the imaginary, and from any distinction between the real and the imaginary, leaving room only for the orbital recurrence of models and the simulated generation of difference.
>
> Jean Baudrillard (1994 [1981]) *Simulacra and Simulation*. Ann Arbor (MI): University of Michigan Press, page 167.

In the age of the satellite and digital technology it is a mistake to imagine that what occurs on the surface is merely the level of the super-ficial. On the contrary, postmodern culture glitters at the edge of its surfaces, in media simulations, computational signs and globalized codes, and such surfaces for Baudrillard encode particular forms of political power. Baudrillard's vision in this connection might be described as Nietzschean, in that he holds to the view that there is nothing but surface. *Pace* modernity, with its hidden organizing logics and surreptitious systematic forces, postmodern society does not lend itself easily to interpretation or critique by inherited modernist traditions. This leads Baudrillard to launch a full-blooded assault on the hermeneutics of suspi-cion in *Seduction*, where Marxism, structuralism and psychoanalysis come under attack for their metaphysical rationalizations and intellectual deceptions. The modernist notion that the manifest operations of bourgeois society can be critiqued in terms of latent functions or hidden structures is dismissed as deterministic. Postmodernism itself expresses no hidden, determining essence. The condition of postmodernity is itself just fleeting appearance, the transient moment, sensuous surface. Baudrillard's strategy for confronting this autonomy of the postmodern, a world cut loose from all relationship to modernity, lies with mapping the terrain of symbolic exchange, today's ever proliferating network of images, signs and codes. In *Seduction* he urges the importance of hallucination, self-referentiality, simulation. Contemporary society, he says, is dominated by the logic of the sensuous surface – in a play of seduction which he sees as the very lifeblood of the postmodern.

It is evident that Baudrillard's position, at the period of *Simulacra and Simulation* and *Seduction*, underscores the misalliances between self and world, the individual and social, in contemporary social conditions. Indeed, Baudrillard explicitly states that postmodern consumer society positions the individual in a state of fragmented multiplicity, denoting a psychic frame of never-ending seduction and mesmerization, such that the contemporary self is increasingly unable to differentiate itself from the informational blizzard of global media culture. In his subsequent writings, this objectivist strand of post-structuralist theory about the fate of subjectivity feeds further into his postmodernism. In *Fatal Strategies*, in which the contours of 'fatal theory' are contrasted to critical theory, Baudrillard contends that the self-constituting, self-authorizing subject of modern philosophical thought no longer provides an adequate reference point for interpreting the world; indeed, in the aftermath of the 'death of the subject,' the object is to be privileged *over* subjects, such is the limitless control that the world of things now exerts over our senses. It is the object – specifically the hyperreal object, the simulated object – which for Baudrillard produces postmodern 'ecstasy' and an aesthetic hallucination of culture. What fascinates Baudrillard is the incessant productivity which lies at the core of hyperreal objects, the sense of euphoria, seduction and ecstasy which is instilled in subjects, and the endless multiplication and proliferation of images, messages and codes as reproduced through media spectaculars and the transnational culture industry.

Baudrillard, like many other major postmodernists, likens postmodern mentalities to schizophrenic fragmentation. A schizoid incapacity to distinguish between inside and outside, surface and depth, becomes culturally common. Here the postmodern subject, according to Baudrillard, lives in

a state of terror which is characteristic of the schizophrenic, an overproximity of all things, a foul promiscuity of all things which beleaguer and penetrate him, meeting with no resistance, and no halo, no aura, not even the aura of his own body protects him. In spite of himself the schizophrenic is open to everything and lives in the most extreme confusion.

(1988: 27)

In a culture of virtualization, hallucination and seduction, the most one can do is channel-hop, surf the Net or absorb the inanities of American-dominated popular culture, such is the overloading of images and information upon the human mind. Baudrillard thus casts the postmodern subject in a wilderness of hyperreal mirrors; the subject is 'a pure screen, a pure absorption and resorption surface of the influence networks' (1988: 27).

Baudrillard's non-event: 'The Gulf War did not take place'

The arrival of the 1990s witnessed one the largest deployments of military arsenal by the United States in the history of warfare. The target was Iraq and its President Saddam Hussein. War was in the air: mass media were predicting it was only a matter of time until President Bush gave the green light for air strikes and a ground offensive. Meanwhile, on 4 January 1991, the French newspaper *Liberation* ran an article by Jean Baudrillard, 'The Gulf War will not take place.' On 16 January, America launched air strikes against Iraq. In February, this was followed by a three-day ground offensive. Astonishingly, however, Baudrillard stuck firm to his line. On 29 March 1991, he penned another article for *Liberation*, 'The Gulf War did not take place.'

Baudrillard's claim unleashed massive controversy. Many inside and outside of academia were offended by these articles. Critics lampooned the 'absurdity' of Baudrillard's postmodernism, finding abhorrent his alleged denial of human suffering on a massive scale. But forgotten in all the intellectual anxiety over Baudrillard's claims was his underscoring of our hi-tech media world, of televisual wars and of moral indifference generated through virtual violence. For what Baudrillard did – notably in focusing on the 'place' of war in this technological programming of military violence at the Gulf – was to question our cultural assumptions about what it means for an event to 'take place' and to suggest, scandalously, that simulation drains reality from the world. Baudrillard thus sees the spectacular visibility of the Gulf War as a dubious non-event, or pseudo-event, of uncertain remainders by virtue of its instant transformation into the media and their hyperreal appropriation. There are two key aspects to this analysis. Firstly, the culture of militarism; and secondly, the media's hyperrealization of reality as 'truer than true.'

For Baudrillard, the Gulf War was a non-event in the sense that combat was written out of the military scripting in advance. What happened in the Gulf was rather a military simulation of war – prescripted, programed and produced by the US administration. Baudrillard's 'The Gulf War did not take place' is filled with technical discussion of how a non-event materializes its signs and excludes anything not scripted for the program, but the core political points can be well-enough summarized: US military processing meant that the enemy appeared only as a computerized target, with little or no possibility of reaction; the deployment of America's superior military hardware meant the enemy was, in effect, already dead in advance; the programming of precision bombing at a distance from the site of conflict effectively excluded any exchange of munitions and arms, thus guaranteeing a one-sided war. This for Baudrillard was not war but the theatre of war.

The military scripting of the war, premised upon the coalition's technological superiority, was in turn intensified by the media's production of the conflict as a TV event. The media produced a virtualization of war through its 24/7 coverage, endless commentary, consultation with experts and ongoing speculation. Paradoxically, such attempts to represent the war in real-time transformed it into its opposite, into a whirl of pure information – simulacral distancing. 'War,' says Baudrillard, 'implodes in real-time' (1995: 49).

Baudrillard's claims offer a novel perspective on the illusions of war. To the extent that his articles were published to astonished condemnation in Paris, and in time to global denunciation, this reminds us that Baudrillard's arguments must be viewed in the wider context of his social theory of simulation. There are, of course, many limitations to Baudrillard's social theory and, in the context of his articles on the Gulf War, critics are certainly right to be concerned about his often excessive claims as to how media simulation outstrips the force and power of reality in our daily lives. But whatever the precise import of such criticisms, Baudrillard's claims concerning the Gulf War should not be seen as a denial of human suffering. It has been estimated that over 100,000 Iraqis lost their lives in the conflict, with many more seriously injured and wounded. This was but one of the terrible social costs of the West engaging the third world in a first world war. But if Baudrillard is right, then ultimately the terror of the war was even more evil than this – since, in the end, the conflict was processed, produced and packaged as deathly simulation in advance.

Do you agree with Baudrillard's thesis regarding the virtual construction of wars? Is simulation the face of new wars for the coming century?

Jameson: postmodernity as global capitalist transformations

One of the main attractions of the theory of postmodernity as simulated media culture, associated especially with the work of Baudrillard, is its specific delineation of new social processes that no longer operate according to the laws of industrial capitalism. Since Baudrillard's main preoccupation is with signs and their impact upon the rest of society, there is a sense in which materialism dissolves into the background in this version of postmodernist culture. If this is indeed the case, we are now in a new era dominated by symbolic reproduction, from information processing to digital high tech. In Baudrillard's eyes, the postmodern spells the 'end of political economy.'

There might, nevertheless, be some way of working across from – or cross-referencing – the information society or spectacles of consumerism to money markets and the incessant flows of speculative finance. It is just this kind of project that has been taken up by Fredric Jameson, the doyen of American cultural theorists, who argues the case for a full-blooded, systematic materialist conceptualization of postmodernity as part of a new stage of multinational capitalism. His magisterial *Postmodernism: or, The Cultural Logic of Late Capitalism* is a sprawling, interdisciplinary book, which gives particular emphasis to the discontinuity between modernity and postmodernity and manages to link postmodernism, culture and capitalism in its very title. What Jameson calls theories of 'postmodernism in culture' have displayed a repressed historical periodization as well as an implicit or explicit political stance on the conditions of advanced capitalism. In an age which has fetishized culture, Jameson develops his theory of global capitalist transformations in conscious contrast to accounts of the postmodern that displace or bury the movements of capitalism itself or alternatively render the postmodern as merely a kind of incipient materialism.

Jameson is critical of those authors who have sought to coin new terms, like postindustrial society or consumer society and the rest, for explicating contemporary cultural transformations. According to him, rather than terminological innovation it is necessary to look again at the nature of capitalist modernity itself, particularly the ways in which the consequences of capitalism are becoming both more global and abstract in scope. Rather than entering a period beyond political economy, Jameson stresses that we can perceive the contours of a new and 'higher' stage of capitalism. In advancing this position, he draws from the economist Ernest Mandel's periodization of 'long waves' of capital expansion, as set out in Mandel's benchmark book *Late Capitalism* (1975), for grasping the disorienting consequences of new forms of social organization. As Jameson puts this,

> there have been three fundamental moments in capitalism, each one marking a dialectical expansion over the previous stage. These are market capitalism, the monopoly stage or the stage of imperialism, and our own, wrongly called postindustrial, but what might be termed multinational, capital. . . . Mandel's intervention in the postindustrial debate involves the proposition that late or multinational or consumer capitalism, far from being inconsistent with Marx's great nineteenth-century analysis, constitutes, on the contrary, the purest form of capital yet to have emerged, a prodigious expansion of capital into hitherto uncommodified areas.
>
> (1991: 35–6)

For Jameson, this purest form of capital, witnessed in the global spiraling of multinational capitalism, has dramatically compacted both space and time with its instant electronic communications and digital flows, thereby ushering in the first genuine global cultural ideology. Understood in this way, postmodernism represents a new ideological form of capitalism, a 'cultural dominant' truly worldwide in scope.

Jameson is a pluralistic theorist in many senses, drawing from (and reconfiguring in the process) the discourses of structuralism, post-structuralism, phenomenology, hermeneutics and psychoanalysis. If his theoretical comprehensiveness can sometimes appear too accommodating of competing idioms, it is partly because he is so insistent that intellectual discourses and political ideologies must be situated within the broader economic and structural conditions of the current historical moment. Certainly, the Jameson of *The Political Unconscious* (1981) establishes just such a placement of contemporary social theory within the broader dynamics of the economy and society at large, insisting as he does that post-structuralism and deconstruction must be contextualized within the Marxian conceptualization of History. In his writings on postmodernism and late capitalism, Jameson similarly argues that the ascendancy of the category of space over time and hence our contemporary experience of cultural fragmentation and dispersal intimates that there are now profound transformations occurring at the level of personal identity and psychic structure. Indeed, as we will see, such are the spatiotemporal dispersions and liquidizations of postmodernity and its cultural logic that human subjects can only but barely struggle to hold their inner and outer worlds together, as the imaginary has become almost entirely subordinated to signifiers of the global.

In a remarkably probing analysis of this lifting of global technologies into the operations of the mind itself, Jameson proposes a detailed check-list of the pervasive emotional climate of postmodern culture. These include 'The Waning of Affect,' 'Euphoria and Self-Annihilation,' 'Loss of the Radical Past,' 'The Breakdown of the Signifying Chain' and 'The Abolition of Critical Distance.' Such is the intensification of reification – primarily under the operations of the service, finance and communications sectors – that postmodern living becomes a kind of cynical parody of modernist manners and orientations, flowing from a Deleuze-like readiness to abandon Enlightenment rationalities as a false path and instead savor the delicious sensuousness of erotic intensities.

Conventionally postmodernism denotes a transmutation of the aesthetic, detected by critics principally in the fields of literature, architecture, the plastic arts and philosophy. Much the same is true of Jameson's analysis of the transition from modernism to postmodernism in the arts, humanities and culture at large. Yet from Jameson's own Marxist standpoint, it is critical to connect the terrain of postmodern culture to structural transformations occurring within the economic operations of capitalism itself. This is a vital conceptual and political move, as we will see, allowing Jameson to open the debate over postmodernism beyond the spectrum of the arts to the domains of both the economy and society. The postmodern for Jameson is totalizing, discontinuous, expansive – a new world economic system. At the center of this radical transformation from modernity to postmodernity lies the revolution in electronics and the societal impact of new information technologies. Here Jameson points to the vastly expanding role of the communications sector in capitalist innovation and profit.

As the force-field of globalization came to restructure international flows of trade, investment and culture during the 1980s and 1990s, so the entire capitalist system was to extend its operational hold over whole regions, communities and continents. For Jameson, this was nowhere more evident than in the organizational dominance of transnational corporations and their outsourcing of manufacturing to cheap-wage locations in the developing world. Meanwhile, in the polished, expensive cities of the West, speculative finance moved away from industrial manufacture and toward the service and communication sectors. Media conglomerates such as Time Warner and News Corporation, now wielding unprecedented power across national borders, altered the connections and relations between peoples and communities. With communications revolutionized – largely due to the increasing use of digital methods of information processing – the economy became cultural as never before, ever more dependent on image and information.

Cultural sensibility is one of Jameson's principal themes, and in particular he reworks the Marxist proposition that social experience is, in the end, a matter of multiple economic and historical determinations. In Jameson's hands this is much more than an attempt to relate post-Marxism to the subtleties of post-structuralism, and nor is it simply a matter of relating culture to the economy. Rather, there is a complex interplay for Jameson between the social and economic fields. What exactly are the cultural consequences of postmodernity, he asks, for the experience of subjectivity? As the countercultural 1960s and 70s gave way to a profound sense of political defeatism in the 80s and 90s, a new depthlessness came to afflict individuals at an emotional level. Among the characteristics of this postmodernization of subjectivity, in Jameson's view, is the collapse of any active sense of historical memory, in the sense of enabling either pasts or oppressive traditions. It is one of the functions of history to give 'narrative shape' to social experience, to link past, present and future. Yet with the waning of history, narrative and memory, the psychic experience of identity becomes disconnected and empty – locked on the images, codes and messages of digital media and the information superhighway.

Late capitalism for Jameson is saturated to such a degree with signifiers, codes and messages – rooted in a multi-billion-dollar culture industry and media spectaculars – that what is unfolding is 'a new and historically original penetration and colonization of Nature and the Unconscious' (1991: 36). This lifting of the logics of commodification into the psychic texture of experience is, for Jameson, akin to the fragmentation of schizophrenia. This dislocating, dispersed flux of unconscious intensities disrupts modernist relations between self and others, desire and discourse; it also leads to a breakdown of the signifying chain itself, to structures of meaning. Such an image of subjecthood is one in which the imaginary is regulated by the symbolic as never before, with individuals taking their cultural cues from media messages whilst mindlessly surfing TV channels. More than another Marxist cultural lament over the powers of commodification, however, Jameson impressively extends his analysis of the postmodern to encompass the insights of Lacanian psychoanalysis, and in particular Lacan's theorization of schizoid fragmentation as deeply interwoven with a derailment of the Symbolic order of language. Following Lacan, Jameson argues that the depthlessness of postmodern media culture produces a snapping of the signifying chain, a 'schizophrenia in the form of a rubble of distinct and unrelated signifiers' (1991: 26). In the age of mass consumption and transnational corporations, it is specifically the euphoria of the subject that captures Jameson's analytical attention. And perhaps not surprisingly for a Marxist theoretician, it is the libidinal pleasures of consumerism – 'the commodity rush' – that Jameson isolates as pivotal to the reproduction of postmodernity.

Consumerism is nowadays the duty of the newly affluent professionals and yuppies who emerge as a result of the take-off of the service and communication sectors of the economy, and personal freedom is increasingly defined in terms of access to markets and the shopping mall. Yet how to assess the possibilities of autonomy when postmodernization of the subject involves both the spread of consumerism and the rise of pseudo-individualism? For Jameson, the problem is only compounded by the vast networks of corporate power and production, whose high tech operations criss-cross the globe and wreak havoc upon both the cognitive and emotional capacities of human subjects to grasp the links and disjunctions of the new global capitalism. As a radical, Jameson believes that change remains possible and contends that the task of the Marxist project is to critically trace the intermediate forms linking experiential or subjective responses to the postmodern on the one hand and regional, national and global institutional developments on the other. This he terms, borrowing from the urban studies of Kevin Lynch, the postmodern aesthetic of 'cognitive mapping.' Grasping the multinational system of postmodernism from within, cognitive mapping involves for Jameson a re-imagination of the relations between identity and culture; it unfolds, as he explains, through sustained, systematic reflection upon the intertwining of the local and global, identity and non-identity, the present and the past. Cognitive mapping is thus presented as an emancipatory principle necessary to confront the disorder of global capitalism, a kind of counter to postmodern forms of fragmentation, dispersal and dislocation.

Bauman: postmodernity as modernity subtract illusions

The story of what this wholesale aestheticization of culture will do to society in more general terms, as contemporary women and men find themselves increasingly seduced by the fetish of surface and style as well as the cult of hedonism and libidinal intensities as promoted by late capitalism, belongs to a more properly sociological critique of postmodernity. For it is the sociology of postmodernity, rather than the elaboration of a postmodern sociology, which seeks to understand the global transformations that have shaped the society in which we live today – and it is just this project which acclaimed sociologist Zygmunt Bauman takes up and develops to brilliant effect. It is hard to imagine an analyst of the postmodern condition more theoretically sophisticated and consistently innovative than Bauman. His is a voice cautioning that our new globalized world is one of uncertainty, unpredictability and ambivalence. In his view, postmodernization creates radical new patterns of power and inequality, from which fresh opportunities and risks arise for everyone. During the last twenty or so years, Bauman has published an astonishing series of books that offer a trenchant sociological critique of postmodernity, from his highly acclaimed study *Legislators and Interpreters* (1987) to his more recent visionary arguments detailed in *Liquid Modernity* (2000) and *Liquid Love* (2003). Certainly the great strength of this research is his tenacity in pursuing the idea of the postmodern through its every shifting guise and mutation, from the economy to entertainment. He tracks cultural pressures, emotional torments and political dilemmas with a uniquely agile understanding, helping us to glimpse, if not the solutions, then at least the complexities of global postmodern transformations.

Bauman's interest in postmodernity and global culture has come increasingly to the fore, but he was a leader of the cultural turn in sociology as far back as the 1970s. His first book published in English, *Between Class and Elite* (1972), took the British labor movement as its field of investigation. In the following years, in books such as *Culture as Praxis* (1973), *Socialism: The Active Utopia* (1976) and *Memories of Class* (1982), he established himself as a dazzlingly erudite analyst of the interconnections between class and culture. Bauman's fame, however, rests upon his more recent writings on modernity and postmodernization. *Modernity and the Holocaust* (1989), his masterwork, is a dark, dramatic study of the deathly consequences of Enlightenment reason. Auschwitz, in Bauman's eyes, was a result of the 'civilizing' mission of modernity; the Final Solution was not a dysfunction of modern rationality but its shocking product. The Holocaust, according to Bauman, is unthinkable outside the twin forces of bureaucracy and technology. In subsequent work, including *Modernity and Ambivalence* (1991) and *Postmodernity and Its Discontents* (1997), Bauman moved from a concern with the historical fortunes of the Jews as victims of modernity to an analysis of the complex ways in which postmodern culture cultivates all of us as outsiders, strangers, others.

Bauman's analysis of postmodernity stresses its characteristic ambivalence and ambiguity, on the one hand, while on the other being thoroughly suspicious of its implications. Sociologically speaking, his work analyses the fissures between modernist cultural practices one the one hand and postmodern global transformations on the other, with particular emphasis on the deregulation and privatization of all things social. Any compressed reconstruction of the main arguments of Bauman's sociology of post-modernity cannot possibly do justice to it as a whole, such is its sheer imaginative sweep and intellectual breadth of concerns. These include a liquid mode of experience – experience of the self and others, of space and time, of life's possibilities and risks – that is shared by women and men the world over; the separation of power and sovereignty from the politics of the territorial nation-state; the collapse of 'society' as a bounded complex, or set of structures, and thus the eradication of sociology's disciplinary self-evident client; and the outsourcing of public political functions to non-political, deregulated market forces. This last is a central theme, and gives his work a highly radical political edge. Privatization and deregulation, according to Bauman, become a vital preoccupation of the postmodern age for a whole host of reasons. In the neo-liberal epoch, the drastically shrinking world of public political space may seem (and in various respects is) an upshot of transnational capitalism. Yet at the same time, privatiza-tion of life-experience and life-politics is pretty much policed and regulated by culturalist and sub-political processes that follow a kind of Weberian logic all their own, an institutional development which the discipline of sociology has been too slow to recognize. As Bauman develops this:

> Governments are today no less, if not more, busy and active than ever before in modern history. But they are busy in the TV Big Brother's style: letting the subjects play their own games and blame themselves in the event that the results are not up to their dreams. Governments are busy hammering home the 'there is no alternative' message, the 'security is dependency' and the 'state protection is disempowering' messages, and enjoining subjects to be more flexible and to love the risks (read: erratic and unpredictable) life-settings is fraught with.
>
> (2002: 68)

(For an influential critique of Bauman's interpretation of bureaucracy, consult Paul du Gay, *In Praise of Bureaucracy*, London: Sage, 2002.)

Notwithstanding his suspicion of traditional institutional politics, Bauman is in various senses a collectivist thinker, the product of his training in the Polish sociological tradition with its affinities to Weberian-Marxism. What is striking about Bauman's sociology from the earliest texts is the scrupulous exactness with which he maps not just class power or social hierarchy, but social oppression and political domination in general. There were after all no ruling capitalists throughout central Europe after the Second World War, and this is undoubtedly one reason why Bauman became so peculiarly attuned to various modes of 'ordering action' and forms of repression. Socialism, in the postindividualist sense of affective solidarity, can be seen as the collective unconscious motivating resistance to capitalism, a kind of 'counterculture of modernity,' as he puts it in *Socialism – The Active Utopia* (1976).

Modernity is an obsessive project, marked by desire for constant change. Whatever is seen as old must be replaced by the new – always, and in itself, a sign of progress. Science and its technological offshoots are the central drivers of assigning an object, event or person to ever-new systems of rational classification; and in this way rationalization and science consequently merge in curious ways to further modernity's obsessive urge to control. Modernity is thus a high-brow, abstract affair, concerned above all with constant rationalizing and the logics of classification, at once distant and dismissive of the messiness and unpredictableness of the everyday. In fact, if modernity takes an interest in the dynamics of everyday life, this is primarily driven out of its obsessive quest for order, stability and consistency. If modernity and modernism in their various guises are interested by the everyday details of human ambivalence and ambiguity, the point of this interest is to strengthen the impulse for order. To keep things neat and tidy, with all glimmerings of ambivalence safely disowned, is key.

Bauman himself demonstrates something of an obsession with ambivalence, from *Modernity and Ambivalence* (1991) to *Wasted Lives* (2004), but he is able to connect this contemporary cult of the unpredictable to radical political ends. For Bauman, as for Sigmund Freud, ambivalence is essential to human subjectivity, at once enriching the affective texture of interpersonal experience and multiplying the complexity of social life itself. The more we become aware of ambivalence, undecidability and uncertainty as intrinsic to human life and forms of association, the more dense networks of social dependencies become. And yet modernity is the moment at which ambivalence becomes prohibited, constructed as both aberrant and abject. The modernist impulse to order is a regime governed by intolerance, inflexibility and symbolic violence, with regulating patterns of classificatory inclusion and exclusion serving less as a transparent rational medium than as a surreptitiously hegemonic form of repression.

There is a sense in which Bauman initiates a postmodern recasting of the ordering ambitions of modernity, preferring to cobble together fragments of various modernist and postmodernist mentalities, orientations, dispositions and world-views. He is certainly no enthusiast of post-structuralist or postmodernist versions of postmodernity, of what he terms 'the preachers and enthusiasts of the postmodern bliss' (2000: 339). 'It is simply,' he says, 'a salutary decision to speak of postmodernity, rather than late modernity, without necessarily accepting every rubbish written in the name of postmodern theory' (2001: 20). For him, everything postmodern is fashioned out of something modern. There is no definitive line of separation between the modern and the postmodern, as postmodernity is itself 'a self-conscious stage in the development of modernity' (2001: 20). In the end, Bauman rejects pronouncements of the 'end of modernity' and yet – retaining the enthusiasm of some postmodernists – declares the postmodern a 'chance of modernity,' a chance for tolerance, solidarity and autonomy. This sense of potential transfiguration, deriving from reflexive self-consciousness of the temporal and spatial flux of contemporary life, is what gives Bauman's portrait of the postmodern age its sociological distinctiveness.

This tension in Bauman's writing – between embracing and rejecting certain elements of the discourse of postmodernism – is the sign of a familiar sociological dilemma. If the postmodern is a cultural phase beyond modernity, it is granted a peculiar stamp of autonomy which is somehow free of ambivalence; if postmodernity represents a break with the modern, it displaces the modernist surgical ambition of social engineering but – in pluralizing the social and cultural pursuit of order – runs the risk of 'anything goes.' It is for this reason that Bauman resists the widespread tendency to historically periodize the modern and postmodern, and indeed the point of his sociology is to have it both ways: modernity and postmodernity mix, and necessarily so in various overlappings and criss-crossings. Bauman writes,

> Postmodernity is modernity that has admitted the non-feasibility of its original project. Postmodernity is modernity reconciled to its own impossibility – and determined, for better or worse, to live with it. Modern practice continues – now, however, devoid of the objective that once triggered it off.
>
> (1991: 98)

It is in this way that Bauman can simultaneously proclaim the energizing dimensions of the postmodern, opening a space for the imaginative plural-ization of structures of meaning, and critique the cultural consequences of modernity. Contemporary women and men aspire to power, to modernist dreams of certitude, order and structure; yet they equally seek to live without guarantees, trading yesterday's road-maps for the sudden lurches of mood generated by today's hi-tech blend of lifeworlds and experiences. We are neither one nor another, but potentially both, modern and postmodern.

If for Jameson postmodernism is a cultural dominant, tendentially global in scope, it is for Bauman a more unstable affair, often on the brink of bringing itself undone. Indeed the postmodern, which for Bauman repre-sents not transcendence but a societal turning back on the consequences of modernity, is everywhere evident (especially in popular culture, the plastic arts and new communication technologies) but nowhere supreme – such is the ruthless colonizing logic of modernist desires for homo-geneity, control, order and certitude. At once akin and estranged, both inside and outside each other's culturalist or ideological range, modernity and postmodernity share in common the crisis of identity that afflicts life in the contemporary West. Yet if the postmodern world-view – permeated with a sense of the ambivalence of existence – is premised upon a compact with reflexivity, it is also involves a thorough-going dismantling of the normative force of standards, ideals and truths. This, one might immediately hasten to add, is not necessarily bad news – as the following passage from Bauman regarding postmodern wisdom plainly indicates:

What the postmodern mind is aware of is that there are problems ... with no good solutions, twisted trajectories that cannot be straightened up, ambivalences that are more than linguistic blunders yelling to be corrected, doubts which cannot be legislated out of existence, moral agonies which no reason-dictated recipes can soothe, let alone cure. The postmodern mind does not expect any more to find the all-embracing, total and ultimate formula of life without ambiguity, risk, danger and error, and is deeply suspicious of any voice that promises otherwise. The postmodern mind is aware that each local, specialized and focused treatment, effective or not when measured by its ostensive target spoils as much as, if not more than, it repairs. The postmodern mind is reconciled to the idea that the messiness of the human predicament is here to stay. This is, in the broadest outlines, what can be called postmodern wisdom.

Zygmunt Bauman (1993) *Postmodern Ethics*. Oxford: Blackwell, page 245.

Bauman's postmodernism here is close to a celebratory affair, but in a manner that sociologically delineates between postmodern world views (seen as potentially subversive) and postmodernity (a mix of opportunity and risk). There is, at any rate, a force at work in the postmodern habitat making for autonomy, even if, sociologically speaking, this movement towards autonomy is necessarily to collide with the more oppressive features of postmodernity as a social system.

Beyond the postmodern: Bauman's theory of liquid modernity

By the late 1990s, the label 'postmodern' had everywhere – from academia to popular culture – become co-terminous with a form of cultivated relativism in which 'everything goes.' It was, ironically, this very flattened and generalized view of the postmodern that Bauman wished to distance himself from with his new idea – outlined in the early 2000s – of 'liquidity.'

Liquids, says Bauman, do not keep any shape for long and are constantly prone to alteration. Liquids, unlike solids, undergo continuous changes of shape. Liquids make salient the fractured, brittle nature of human bonds today: there are compelling reasons, writes Bauman (2000: 2), 'to consider "fluidity" and "liquidity" as fitting metaphors when we wish to grasp the nature of the present, in many ways *novel*, phase in the history of modernity.' What is important in the social dimension of liquidity is not its specific gravity but rather the looseness fluids possess.

This focus on liquidization provides a conceptual plank from which Bauman reformulates some of the central preoccupations of social theory, particularly accounts which focus on the production and reproduction of modernization. Many key features associated with modernization and industrialization are recast as instances of what he calls, provocatively and poignantly, 'heavy modernity.' Modernity as 'heavy' assumes a dominant role with the development of industrialization and the intensification of modernization throughout the West. Vast machinery, huge factories, massive workforces: economic success defined in terms of size, and symbolic power defined in terms of volume, are central to the contours of heavy modernity.

'Heavy capitalism,' writes Bauman (2000: 58), 'was obsessed with bulk and size, and, for that reason, also with boundaries, with making them tight and impenetrable.'

The heavy version of modernity appears, in the view of Bauman, as a certain type of society subsumed to a specific organization of space and time. The conquering of space was fundamental to the ordering ambitions of heavy modernity: spatial expansion was deeply interwoven with the logic of social control and the logic of symbolic power. Space was to be tamed, colonized, domesticated – indeed, devoured. The 'Fordist factory,' the gigantic plant that contained all the workers and plant machinery needed for production, was heavy modernity's ideal model of engineered rationality. 'Fordism,' writes Bauman (2000: 57) 'was the self-consciousness of modern society in its "heavy," "bulky," or "immobile" and "rooted," "solid" phase.' This socially engineered delineation of space existed, argues Bauman, through a concomitant regularization of time: 'It was the routinization of time that held the place whole, compact and subject to homogeneous logic. . . . In the conquest of space, time had to be pliant and malleable' (Bauman, 2000: 115). This space/time binding of heavy modernity produced, in turn, the immobilization of labor and capital. 'The frozen time of factory routine, together with the bricks and mortar of factory walls,' writes Bauman (2000: 116), 'immobilized capital as effectively as it bound the labor it employed.'

The era of heavy modernity for Bauman was slowly but steadily undermined by an intrinsic contradiction: the social ordering ambitions, ethical ideals and economic and political goals of heavy modernity were presented as foundational, transcendent and eternal, but were in fact counter-productive and corrosive. This spelt the beginning of the end for heavy modernity. Bauman consequently introduces the notions of 'light modernity' and 'software capitalism' as superseding those of 'heavy modernity' and 'hardware capitalism': he refers to the unprecedented power of *liquidization* in objective alterations of the private and public domains of contemporary societies. Among others, Bauman points to the rise of multinational conglomerates, the outsourcing of manufacturing to the 'developing world,' and the shifts in investment towards the communications, finance and service sectors. These developments, according to Bauman, have produced a new 'weightlessness of capital' and concomitant 'liquidization of life' – in business cycles, employment patterns, family relationships, communal fates, political horizons.

'Light modernity' signifies a 'new irrelevance of space' and the killing off of time. Bauman writes,

> In the software universe of light-speed travel space may be traversed, literally, in 'no time'; the difference between 'far away' and 'down here' is cancelled. Space no more sets limits to action and its effects, and counts little, or does not count at all.
>
> (2000: 117)

Liquidization assumes different forms across the space/time zonings of contemporary institutional life, from twenty-four hour finance markets to media-ridden culture. Yet liquidity for Bauman can be said to be culturally dominant to the extent that social life is organized in and through the 'insubstantial, instantaneous time of the software world' (2000: 118).

Liquid modernity not only reshapes social institutions; it also penetrates to the core of the self and the fabric of everyday life. These are issues that Bauman addresses directly in a number of recent works, including *Liquid Love* (2003), *Identity* (2004) and *Liquid Life* (2005). Life and identity in conditions of liquid modernity are for Bauman increasingly fluid, fractured, flexible and frail. As he develops this perspective:

> Liquid life is a precarious life, lived under conditions of constant uncertainty. The most acute and stubborn worries that haunt such a life are the fears of being caught napping, of failing to catch up with fast-moving events, of being left behind, of overlooking 'use by' dates, of being saddled with possessions that are no longer desirable, of missing the moment that calls for a change of tack before crossing the point of no return. Liquid life is a succession of new beginnings – yet precisely for that reason it is the swift and painless endings . . . that tend to be its most challenging moments and most upsetting headaches. Among the arts of liquid modern living and the skills needed to practice them, getting rid of things takes precedence over their acquisition.
>
> (2005: 2)

Small wonder that in such circumstances the newly constituted terrain of 'privatized identity' comes to bear a heavy burden of expectations, hopes and fears in a world where traditional social bonds are loosening their choke-hold.

Bauman's recent social theory has the outstanding merit of highlighting the political significance of the demise of the 'long term,' now recast as liquidization or liquefaction, in contemporary social processes. There are, however, various problems with Bauman's social theory. One criticism most forcefully made against Bauman's account concerns the *adequacy* of his sociological diagnosis of liquid modern times. There are both *strong* and *weak* versions of this critique, which I discuss in more detail in Elliott (2007b). The strong version of this criticism rests upon the misgiving that a liquidization of human bonds cannot provide a generalizable model for the sociological analysis of global institutional change, as well as forms of sociality in contemporary societies. The weak version of this criticism is that, by focusing attention on the liquidization of the self, social relations and everyday life in a globalized world, Bauman tends to neglect the ongoing significance of more structured, solid forms of sociality: what Bauman possibly neglects are the many ways in which liquid modern societies still depend on traditions, world-views, regimes of discourse, modes of power as well as structures of feeling that are characteristic of organized or 'hardware' modernity.

Liquidized forms of experience and identity, with their emphasis on short-termism and relentless self-transformation, are undoubtedly characteristic of large areas of contemporary cultural life – particularly through the world of commodified images in the media and new information technologies. However, due to the generality and sweep of the theory of liquid modernity, what threatens to recede into the shadows is the point that all of us have multiple identities, some overlapping, some contradictory, and that at any moment these identities are interacting with – incorporating, resisting and transforming – broader social values and cultural differences, shaping and being shaped by contemporary societies.

Criticisms of postmodernism

Postmodernism no longer enjoys the cultural and political cachet it once did. Indeed, the postmodern celebratory cult of endings – of history, meaning, ideology and identity – may itself now be outdated. The pioneering work of the leading figures ordinarily associated with postmodernism, such as Lyotard, Baudrillard and Deleuze, is already many years past. Such is also the case for the debate that raged in social theory over modernity and postmodernity in the writings of Jürgen Habermas, Anthony Giddens, David Harvey, Fredric Jameson, Seyla Benhabib and Zygmunt Bauman. This passing of time since the postmodern constellation first took off on the radar screens of social theory in the mid-1980s has served to highlight not only that the so-called radical credentials of postmodernist thought are highly ambiguous, but that postmodernism occurred in the context of a specific social history. For one of the central claims of this book is that a social theory alert to social differences and cultural ambivalences cannot simply be limited to a concern with the exhaustion of Enlightenment reason – sweeping though the epistemological issues to be addressed may be in this connection – but has to investigate a range of personal and political dynamics which are increasingly reconfigured through transformations associated with modernity, globalism and postmodernization.

The powers and limits of postmodernism in both political and sociological terms is by now well-trodden terrain. Intellectual assessments of the adventures of postmodernity as a concept have been launched from almost every conceivable perspective, from critical theory to psychoanalysis, feminism to post-colonialism. For many, principally the hard-core devotees of Baudrillard or Lyotard, postmodernism could do no wrong. Media theorist Arthur Kroker celebrated digital culture and technology as the exemplar of postmodernism, reveling particularly in its unleashing of commercial flows and libidinal intensities, while the post-structuralist historian Mark Poster raised some interesting sounding questions about the status of historical truth in an age that has almost altogether sidelined discourses of Truth, Freedom and Meaning. For others critical of this wholesale aestheticization of culture and critique, postmodernism was much more politically troubling. At one end of the spectrum, luminary critical theorist, Jürgen Habermas, criticized postmodernism as an element of neoconservative cultural criticism. The other end of the spectrum witnessed more diverse responses, with Marxist sociologist Alex Callinicos offering the platitude that postmodernity was only a 'theoretical construct' (and one which he felt, obviously enough for a Marxist, lacked comprehension of the economic operations of capitalism) and Sara Ahmed lamenting that an ascendant postmodernism now dictated the contemporary feminist agenda. On an altogether different register, others penned – at astonishing speed and in suitably postmodern style – introductory primers on the lexicon of postmodernism – with titles from the straight-laced *Introducing Postmodernism* to the DIY-styled *Teach Yourself Postmodernism*. In between much of this academic noise, there was the occasional genuine critical insight – such as Terry Eagleton's *The Illusions of Postmodernism* (1996) or Perry Anderson's *The Origins of Postmodernity* (1998).

The four versions of the postmodern examined in this chapter are not easily separable, though each contains quite distinct preoccupations and concerns. If postmodernity as simulated media culture is to be exact about the organizing logics of contemporary social experience, it must identify an epochal rupture with modernity, one which bids farewell to productivism and political economy and embraces instead ever-expanding and spiraling cycles of signs and codes. By disconnecting the modern and postmodern in this way, advocates of postmodernity as simulated media culture can euphorically celebrate the play of signs, spectacles and simulacra, cut loose communication technologies, entertainment and information from any relation to an external 'outside,' and dissolve the concepts of the political and society as mere metaphysical nostalgia. Baudrillard, as we have seen, has more than a touch of Nietzschean nihilism about him, as when he speculates about 'fatal strategies' of melancholy, passivity, silence. In giving priority to the depthless, fragmented surfaces of postmodernist culture in this way, Baudrillard's suggestion is that critics must learn to view silence, apathy and passivity as signs of a potentially productive vitality of social life against its drive for seductive domination in an age of simulation and virtuality. For followers of Baudrillard's account of postmodernity as simulated media culture, there is nothing but pure surface.

Postmodernity as global capitalist transformations takes something from this emphasis on simulations and hyperreality, but mixes it with analytical attention to the worldwide economy, finance capital and new structural forces generating exploitation, repression and the like. From postmodern aesthetics, this critique adopts an emphasis on blendings of high and mass cultures, the dissolution of art into everyday life and the acceleration of schizoid or fragmentary elements of self-constitution as such, but crosses this with a modernist impulse to unearth generalized structures of socioeconomic domination as well as the search for political justice and human autonomy. This response to the global crisis of postmodernization, as we have seen, is crystallized in Jameson's notion of 'cognitive mapping' – the working through for a resourceful critique of the subject's inability to mentally represent or locate themselves in the global postmodern, with a view to rewriting possible intermediate forms of connection between the conditions of identity on the one hand and the global economy on the other. In an age of image, information and identity, Jameson's breathtakingly audacious project is to refloat the question of the postmodern so that it may be considered as a historical-ontological condition from which deeper structural antinomies can be assembled, critiqued and transfigured.

Alternatively, rather than posit some intolerable conflict between modernity and postmodernity, it is possible to establish a two-way traffic between these two modalities of culture and critique. In bracketing off the issue of historical periodization, what is at stake here – under a response to the crisis of postmodernity as generalized social systems – is nothing less than the pluralization or liquidization of human ambivalence. What links modern and postmodern orders for Bauman is that for both, though in very distinct ways, ambivalence is key to social life and its reproduction. Modernity is no longer a description of a particular historical period than a kind of social practice seeking the erasure or prohibition of ambivalence by rationalizing classifications, an essentially permanent cultural possibility within which hegemonic patterns of compulsory inclusion and exclusion are rehearsed daily by women and men. The postmodern here is the reverse lining of modernity and takes the other way out as regards ambivalence. If ambivalence is here to stay then the postmodern response seeks to fully acknowledge this, embracing ambiguity, difference and otherness as the basis for, or any result of, human creativity. Postmodernity is thus symptomatic of a ruthless and episodic existence, one in which thick global flows of cash and credit unleash staggering new possibilities and risks, novel forms of polarization between rich and poor and the globalization of a whole way of life in which structures of reflexivity and self-experimentation become increasingly dominant.

My own inclination is to argue for a more complex relation between modernity and postmodernity than has been grasped in the social sciences hitherto, and to focus on the importance of such concepts as human agency and societal complexity as well as transformations of emotion in contemporary global affairs. Since the postmodern – aesthetic, cultural and political – is always, and in advance of, an approach to human affairs from the perspective of the post-contemporary or post-traditional, it is not easy to imagine what a stage beyond the postmodern would look like exactly. That said, the transformation of global affairs today presents social theory with fresh challenges, opening personal and political alternatives to the postmodern orthodoxy. Notwithstanding the emancipatory promise of fractured, fluid and multiple perspectives as developed in much postmodernist theory, such standpoints have failed to adequately engage with a range of vital new political issues concerning the multiple ways in which a sense of personal identity is constituted in contemporary societies, as well as the growing sense many of us live with of our mutual interconnectedness and vulnerability in the changing structure of the global order. Of course, this is not to say that these issues do not bear upon postmodernism, nor that postmodernism cannot be deployed to think about such developments in interesting and fruitful ways. The contribution of postmodernism to social theory – with its leveling of hierarchies, its interpretative polyvalence, its dislocating subversion of ideological closure, its self-reflexive pluralism – is of immense value. And yet since the attack on the World Trade Center and the Pentagon of 9/11, and the follow-up war against Iraq in 2003, there is undeniably a growing societal sense that crises in contemporary culture are so deep and so pervasive that they demand new forms of political thinking, indeed a wholly fresh approach. It is in this sense that we might speak of the current generation as coming *after postmodernism*, most specifically as concerns the formulation of a new political agenda for tackling today's most pressing global problems.

Summary points

1   Postmodernism represents, for some social theorists at least, the end of modernity. The postmodern, at a sociological level, consists in profound social transformations associated with the transcendence of the modern. From the rise of transnational corporations to identity-politics, from the 24/7 dominance of media culture to a new cultural aesthetic of pastiche and parody: postmodern virtual reality portrays a world that is doubtfully real.

2   The postmodern confounds modernist hierarchies – with its dislocating subversion of ideological closure, its interpretative polyvalence, its self-reflexive pluralism.

3   In postmodern social theory, there is a marked focus on the deconstruction and fragmentation of the human subject. In Deleuze and Guatarri, this dispersal is theorized in terms of 'desiring machines.' In Lyotard, it is part of the logics of libidinal intensities. In Lyotard, it consists of a series of inquiries into 'hyperreality.'

4   For Fredric Jameson, postmodernity represents the cultural logic of late capitalism. This is the idea that the postmodern ushers into existence such spatial dispersion and temporal liquidization that human subjects can no longer effectively map their place within the social system.

5   Contrasting the sociology of postmodernity with a postmodern sociology, Zygmunt Bauman argues that the postmodern is modernity reconciled to its own limitations.

6   Bauman's recent works have shifted their focus from postmodernity, seeing society instead as continuously and irreparably fluid or liquid in its essential social coordinates. The world of heavy modernity – of heavy industry and massive workforces – has been displaced by light or liquid modernity, based around economic deregulation and the instant global transfer of capital.

Further questions

1   Postmodernism has been explained as involving fragmentation, dislocation and dispersal. How do you see the postmodern reflected in popular culture?

2   From iPods to cars, it seems that we are always desiring some new product. How is it that capitalism interacts with our desiring processes and how might this be overcome according to Deleuze and Guattari?

3   What does Baudrillard mean by hyperreality? Evaluate the claim that media representations are more seductive, powerful, and 'real' than reality.

4   Is your life more liquid than that of your parents? How so? What is the significance of this?

5   How does postmodernism represent a new form of capitalism? What are some tangible examples of the new economy?

6   How might the ambivalence of postmodernism open up new moral questions?

Further reading

Gilles Deleuze and Félix Guattari

Anti-Oedipus: Capitalism and Schizophrenia (Minneapolis, MN: University of Minnesota Press, 1983)

A Thousand Plateaus: Capitalism and Schizophrenia (Minneapolis, MN: University of Minnesota Press, 1987)

On the Line (New York: Semiotext(e), 1983)

Jean-François Lyotard

The Postmodern Condition: A Report on Knowledge (Minneapolis, MN: University of Minnesota Press, 1984)

Jean Baudrillard

The Mirror of Production (St Louis, MO: Telos, 1975)
For a Critique of the Political Economy of the Sign (St Louis, MO: Telos, 1981)
Simulacra and Simulation (New York: Semiotext(e), 1983)
In the Shadow of the Silent Majority (New York: Semiotext(e), 1983)
America (London: Verso, 1988)
The Ecstasy of Communication (New York: Semiotext(e), 1988)
Seduction (London: Macmillan, 1990)
Fatal Strategies (London: Pluto, 1990)
The Transparency of Evil (London: Verso, 1993)
The Illusion of the End (Cambridge: Polity, 1994)
The Gulf War Did Not Take Place (Sydney: Tower Press, 1995)

Fredric Jameson

The Political Unconscious (Cornell University Press, 1982)
Postmodernism, or, The Cultural Logic of Late Capitalism (Duke University Press, 1991)

Zygmunt Bauman
Modernity and Ambivalence (Cambridge: Polity Press, 1991)
Intimations of Postmodernity (London: Routledge, 1992)
Postmodern Ethics (Oxford: Blackwell, 1993)
Life in Fragments (Oxford: Blackwell, 1995)
Liquid Modernity (Cambridge: Polity Press, 2000)
The Individualized Society (Cambridge: Polity Press, 2001b)
Society under Siege (Cambridge: Polity Press, 2002)
Liquid Love (Cambridge: Polity Press, 2003)
Wasted Lives: Modernity and Its Outcasts (Cambridge: Polity Press, 2004)

chapter 14

Social Movements, States and the Modern World-system

Contents

When they were boys they formed a gentle gang of strong ties. They were growing up after a great war that had affected all in their nation and many millions around their world. Children in their country did not directly experience the horrors of war as had children the world over. Yet, spared the worst pain, they suffered the second worse. These boys were too young to have known much of their fathers before they left for war.

Those fathers who survived to come home were changed; or so boys were told by mothers, aunts or grandmothers. Some were better somehow. Tom's father became a successful business man. Dave's returned broken by a lingering affliction of some kind. He died. Chaz's father was good enough in his career but he was given to rants and rages that frightened the other boys who were understanding enough to include Chaz in the gang activities so long as they didn't have to deal with his weird father. Chris's father bought a gas station and settled into a life of noble if modest economic success. Bruce's father was a minister, exempt from the war. Yet, the gang was kind to him, and occasionally invited Bruce to join in most things except the afterschool basketball game when, they knew, he always had chores at home. As they grew older, Bruce was one who did not join their experiments with cigarettes and cheap beer.

In high school they played sports at the high school, did reasonably well at school, learned to drive and wasted evenings hanging out at a local Big Boy burger joint. Summers, they would drive over the border to Indiana to chase girls on the beach of a state park. Winters, after school dances, they double dated which usually meant finding a dark street to park and make out in the muting noise of the car heater. It was exciting to touch and be touched while hearing the shared symphony of the pantings and groans of young love making, all of it coitally innocent, or so they assumed. The fun carried on until high school ended.

They went off to colleges near and far. For the first few years away, they made an effort to reknit the gang when home for holidays. But soon enough they brought home college pals who, in time, frayed the local ties. The bonds slackened, then in time fell away. A few kept in touch. All had some word where the others were. Eventually the news slowed to a trickle, until the occasional class reunions generated but a ripple from the few who bothered to attend. The gang vanished into the ether of adult life in deep post-war America.

Decades later, after some had died and all had grown gray and worn, Facebook made it easier for some to find others. One of Chaz's flames from school days, Stephanie, was living in California. She made it her business to keep track of classmates as best she could. She would send around what addresses and phone numbers she could gather. Tom, it turned out, had retired to Vermont. Dave was still an active physician in Wisconsin. Chris and Bruce had disappeared into whatever lives they invented. Chaz retired to Connecticut. He was the one who called Tom in Vermont. In his older years, Tom did not sound like the ebullient gang leader who, when they were young, organized the after-school basketball games and weekend trips out on the Ohio River on his dad's power boat. Tom seemed oddly withdrawn. He and his wife, another classmate, had some news of others. He shared what he knew, diffidently. When Chaz asked if he'd welcome a visit. Tom did not quite say no. But it was clear what was meant by his comeback: 'We don't see people much.' Chaz was taken aback by the rebuke. There had been so much, he thought, to talk about. Some months later, he sent an email to Dave who called one summer afternoon. They talked with excitement and promised to keep in touch. But that never happened. And that was the end of the gang. Years more passed. They started to die, as had their fathers. Time passed on. Post-war America gave way to television, Vietnam, cell phones, other wars – none like the one they had been born into. The world was changed but Stephanie kept up her Facebook postings.

The death of the gang is the way of the world. In America in the 1950s, that way was different from what it was with boys in Japan, China, Finland, or everywhere else for that matter. National cultures lend texture to the way lives are lived and understood. It seems to be human nature to ask what happened to youth, to the past, to the world as we knew it. Even when the worlds of our lives seem frozen in time, they are not. The mixture of local values with eternal truths always affects any given story. This being so, social theories must have something to say about the stories a people tell, about their histories and the social movements that changed them; then about the dominant powers whether empires or states, and ultimately about the world systems in which all else is lodged for better or worse.

American social theory, thus, took its time coming to terms with these grand issues of the post-World War II period. Most other places in the West and Far East, certainly the Southern tier, had suffered long and hard with all sorts of human invasions and intrusions, all of them deadly and bloody. From this they, at least, knew that the world changed according to various sorts of movements and powers. To be sure, many suffered throughout America's history, most of all those native to the land and those pressed onto it from Africa. Yet, as a national culture, America was relatively inno-cent, perhaps until as late as 9/11. Still, whenever the false magic of American self-pride was finally broken, it started to yield in the 1960s. Revolutions were not new to Europeans; counter-cultural movements were not new to Africa and other southern cultures; the raw failure of states to assure anything like human freedoms was not new to most of the world. When the world revolutions of the late 1960s came to America there followed, hard upon the vain hopes of the young, the crude regressions of the older and entrenched.

Among social theorists, the result of American culture coming straight up against the world, as it had long been, was new and original theories of social movements, states and revolutions, and the modern world system. It hardly needs to be said that the 1960s had perturbing effects on social theories in Europe and, consequently, the world over. Yet, if one were to consider the three principal European sources of social theory – Germany,

France, and the UK – it is possible to observe that each had its own distinctive theoretical culture. In Germany, critical theories remained the dominant form. Habermas, still today, even as there have been a good number of German critics, continues to pursue a revision of what, before the war, Adorno and Horkheimer, in particular, called the project of Enlightenment. How, he still asks, can anything like a universal principle of emancipation resolve the failures of the Enlightenment culture? Hitler remained Germany's ghost. In France, the preoccupying question was how to salvage a radical theory of social structures without lapsing into either subjectivism or objectivism, as Bourdieu put it. Thus from Lévi-Strauss to Foucault and Derrida, then to Bourdieu in France, varieties of discursive practices were the central themes. The silence of the Occupation haunted France. And in the UK, the question was how to revise a theory of what Giddens called structuration against the uncertainty of subjective meanings and the objective reality of hard-won national triumph. Though the British, with the Americans, were the triumphant powers in war, Britain had to deal with the reality that it was so threatened by war in the Atlantic that it essentially ceded what partly remained of its global empire to the Americans as the stake that saved the nation. Great Britain thinks in the shadows of its lost colonial empire.

America lost many in the war but came out of it a rich global power. American social theorists from Merton and Parsons to Mills and Gouldner and Smith, faced the Sixties with little real sense of what the nation had to lose – its abiding innocence. Thus, American social theories, as is apparent in Gouldner and radical feminists and, even, in an odd way, Goffman and Garfinkel – had to reinvent *ex nihilo* the idea of what it meant to be seriously critical of political and global processes. Thus by the late 1960s American social theories were a riot of phenomenologies, theory constructionisms, feminisms, interactionisms, and vaguely Marxist reconstructions. From this, there emerged in the late 1970s and the following period three enduring social theories of serious political moment – resource mobilization theories, new theories of State, and world-systems analysis. All three continue down to the present time as vital forces in social theory.

Charles Tilly: contentious social movements

In the most productive years of Charles Tilly's career from the early 1970s until his death in 2008, no one was more serious in defining and advancing social scientific history. Among his many works in this vein were *The Contentious French* (1986) and *Popular Contention in Great Britain, 1758–1834* (1995). He was, in works like these, an intensely disciplined historian, yet always a social historian – by which he meant an historian whose research took its organizing clues from analytically evident social structural issues. As these two titles suggest, one of his preoccupying theoretical concerns was the role of contention and conflict in the political history of modern societies.

Tilly typically resisted writing in a plainly theoretical manner. Yet he sometimes did, notably in what may be his best known work of social theory, *From Mobilization to Revolution* (1978). It was here that he set forth his understanding of resource mobilization theory – the question of how social movements seized upon and organized the resources required to contend with other social groups for control of political structures. But, even here, his specific theoretical ideas were set against the historical work he and others had done. Few who took his ideas seriously failed to appreciate their relations to the long history of political contention in the modern West. Thus, instead of anything like a grand theory of *social movements* as such, he substituted the historically more complex idea of *contenders*. His point in this was rooted in historical reality that, to take the most famous revolution in the early modern era, the French Revolution did not issue from a particular social movement but from a variety of contending groups. Together they threatened the power of the throne. Even Marx realized this, though he begs off by focusing on the revolutionary potential of the early industrial period. Yet it is well known that the late eighteenth and nineteenth centuries were unstable, as a growing bourgeois elite contended with small shop keepers, peasants, new working classes, the very poor, and others. Thus, though Tilly is known for his contributions to the study of social movements, he set specific movements in the broader polity of actors who, together, create the conditions for collective action as the interplay of contenders for political power.

It helps, thus, to consider Tilly's plain-spoken enumeration of the elements necessary, in his view, for the study of collective action:

> The analysis of collective action has five big components: interest, organization, mobilization, opportunity, and collective action itself. The *interests* which concern us most are the gains and losses resulting from a group's interaction with other groups. . . . The *organization* which concerns us most is that aspect of a group's structure which most directly affects its capacity to act on its interests. . . . *Mobilization* is the process by which a group acquires collective control over the resources needed for action. . . . *Opportunity* concerns the relationship between a group and the world around it. Changes in the relationship sometimes threaten the group's interests. They sometimes provide new chances to act on those interests. . . . *Collective Action* consists of people acting together in pursuit of common interests.
>
> (1978: 7)

This apparently neat model is more complex than one might assume. For one thing, it is an abstract model, thus an analytic check list of conditions and aspects of collective action. For another, viewed from another angle, there are quite a number of relations. In the background are *populations* within which groups and movements subsist and *beliefs* that are deep elements defining the interests of a group as well as its mobilizing principles. Then, too, there are *actions* which are never simply the action of a group but of all the groups, including the organizing political structures within and against which action occurs. At the same time, viewed from still another angle, there are the dynamic relations between groups and events, among which social movements win or lose whatever interests a group seeks to attain.

One of the underlying assumptions Tilly held throughout his career is, put bluntly, that when it comes to social movements there are no sure bets. Groups may have strong beliefs as to their interests, events may be trending in favor of those beliefs, but still a movement does not come to pass. Additionally, even when a movement comes together, brought along by the action of its constituting groups, there is no assurance that its interests will be attained, nor that a revolution will transpire. Tilly was quite clear that the subject of his theoretical and empirical work was collective actions that may or may not lead anywhere satisfying to the groups involved.

Social movement theories in general and theories of collective action, like Tilly's, have been a staple of American social theory since the 1960s, as the movements themselves have been prominent in American (and global) public life. An obvious illustration is one that others, if not Tilly, studied closely in the following years. Of the actions and events of that period, none is more paradigmatic than the Civil Rights Movement. None better illustrates the problems and promises of collective action.

The American Civil Rights Movement began in earnest in December 1955, in Montgomery, Alabama. This was the year after the *Brown v. Board of Education* Supreme Court decision outlawing segregated schools, which opened the opportunity structure for the long-ready civil rights movements in the American South. The decision lent an important institutional indication that the nascent civil rights actions in the South might succeed were they to launch a collective movement in pursuit of long-denied interests in full political participation. Not since Reconstruction after the American Civil War, nearly a century before, had there been so decisive a federal government action, opening the way for African-American groups. The Supreme Court decision in 1954 was, thus, an opening in the opportunity structures that allowed a movement to begin, then, in this case, to take off. In effect, while the decision did not assure protection to Blacks in the South seeking new freedoms, including desegregation, it did weaken the hold of white, racist political authorities on local black citizens.

Yet a break in an opportunity structure does not assure a movement. A group must be in a position to mobilize the resources necessary for collective action. These are many: a sufficient network, connecting actors; a clear sense of which interests are to be pursued in a given action; sufficient financial resources to support the action; places to which actors can retreat in order to rest, regroup and exchange news of events as they are taking place; a cadre of agreed-upon leaders; and more, depending on the situation.

In Montgomery, Alabama, as in other communities in the South, many of these resources were in place. African-American churches and local organizations like the NAACP (National Association for the Advancement of Colored People) were able, to a point, to fund various actions, to provide meeting places, to support networks, and even usually to provide leaders. Rosa Parks had long been active in the NAACP. In addition, a good many ministers sheltered those who in the past sought to take action against the segregated bus company. Dexter Avenue Baptist church was centrally located in the heart of the city and had just hired a young minister, just twenty-seven years old, Martin Luther King, Jr.

Once Rosa Parks refused to give up her seat on 1 December 1955, meetings were called and word circulated in the black community. The Women's Political Council led the way; then came the Dexter church, a leading middle-class institution in the Black community. The decision was taken to initiate a boycott by which Blacks refused to use the public bus system. They would walk or car pool to work. The movement took as its name the Montgomery Improvement Association which quickly elected King its leader. He, of course, provided a crucial resource – the ability to articulate interests and goals and, as the movement took shape, to represent those interests to the wider world.

No one expected the movement to survive. But day after day for, it turned out, a year, Montgomery's Blacks boycotted the buses and brought the system to the verge of bankruptcy. Still the whites held firm for segregation. Eventually a federal judge ruled bus segregation illegal. The city appealed. Finally, the Supreme Court upheld the lower court ruling. Though the whites held on, eventually the federal order to disband the segregated bus system was sent down. The political grip of the whites was broken. The interests of early Civil Rights Movement were met. The Montgomery action was the first decisive break in the white racist power structure. The opportunity structure opened. The wider Civil Rights Movement gained force as groups in other Southern cities took action. When the white powers used violence against civil rights activists, images of the brutalities spread around the world. Whites from the North moved quickly to join blacks in their struggle. Money flowed from around the nation. The movement grew, through pain and suffering, over a decade, culminating in the last successful Civil Rights Movement. The final most important success took place where it began. The 1965 march from Selma to Montgomery created political pressure on the Congress to pass the 1965 Voting Rights Act, signed by President Lyndon Johnson. After, the Black movement splintered as the Black Power movement demanded a more general social and economic reform.

Tilly himself did not write extensively on the American Civil Rights Movement, but others did, notably Doug McAdam, currently at Stanford. Still, as an example of Tilly's theory of contention and social movements, it illustrates well his key ideas. Social movements are never singular and unidirectional. They hardly ever result in a revolution, strictly understood. Yet, they are part of a democratic society's best nature – the encouragement of contention among rival interest groups seeking their own advantages, gaining when they can some measure of success until the conflict and contention is renewed. Tilly was far from alone in revitalizing a radical theory of political action, but he was one of its clearest proponents.

Theda Skocpol: *States and Social Revolutions*

States and Social Revolutions: A Comparative Analysis of France, Russia, and China (1979) was Theda Skocpol's first great book, published at the beginning of her career at Harvard when she was barely thirty years old. It was immediately recognized by younger social scientists and theorists for what it now is – a classic in contemporary American social theory. Just the same, Harvard denied her tenure. Skocpol was then offered positions at virtually every prestigious university in the country, any one of which would have been, at the time, more desirable than Harvard's sociology program. Skocpol, however, fought Harvard's decision and won. This little story is important mainly because it illustrates a certain political tough-mindedness that she, and many of her generation, had learned from the political turmoil of the 1960s.

Today Skocpol is among the most influential intellectuals in the United States. This, in part, because of her many books subsequent to *States and Social Revolutions*, but also because, as an academic leader and a public intellectual, she firmly pursues what Americans often call, somewhat awkwardly, left-political values. Of these latter, the most remarkable is Scholars Strategy Network (SSN) which she founded and directs. She and others involved are persistent in seeking ways that left-inclined scholars are able to make their *research* known through any and all media and other public events. SSN is not, important to say, about 'making social science relevant' but about persuasively altering public policy based on hard-won scientific knowledge. This may seem, as it is, a long way from Skocpol's first book as a younger scholar, but it is possible to identify the connections between her academic career and her work as a politically alert and engaged intellectual.

The important contribution of Skocpol's *States and Social Revolutions* to American social theory was to introduce a rigorously structural method, demonstrated in respect to convincing empirical evidence illuminating the importance of the State in revolutionary events.

> We shall analyze the causes and processes of social revolutions from a nonvoluntaristic, structural perspective, attending to international and world-historical, as well as intranational, structures and processes. An important theoretical concomitant will be to move states – understood as potentially autonomous organizations located at the interface of class structures and international situations – to the very center of attention.
>
> (1979: 33)

Granted, this is a mouthful. That would have been all it would be, had this jam-packed statement not appeared at the end of one of the better introductions to a scholarly work one can find. The chapter, 'Explaining Social Revolutions,' puts radical political action forward as the defining theme of the book.

The state, in short, is fundamentally Janus-faced, with an intrinsically dual-anchorage in class-divided socioeconomic structures and an international system of states. If our aim is to understand the breakdown and building-up of state organizations in revolutions, we must look not only at the activities of social groups. We must also focus upon the points of intersection between international conditions and pressures, on the one hand, and class-structured economies and politically organized interests, on the other hand. State executives and their followers will be found maneuvering to extract resources and build administrative and coercive organizations precisely at this intersection. Here, consequently, is the place to look for the political contradictions that help launch social revolutions. Here, also, will be found the forces that shape the rebuilding of state organizations within social-revolutionary crises.

Theda Skocpol (1979) *States and Social Revolutions: A Comparative Analysis of France, Russia and China.* Cambridge, UK: Cambridge University Press, page 32.

What makes Skocpol's *States and Social Revolutions* such an important text in American social theory is that she combines a clear and original statement of her theoretical position, then applies it astutely to three historical cases where social revolutions decisively transformed state power – the French revolution in the late eighteenth century and the Russian and Chinese revolutions in the twentieth. The French revolution is often considered the classical type of a modern revolution that transformed traditional authority organized around the throne into a modern, more-or-less democratic regime. The Russian revolution did similarly by deposing the reign of the Czars but eventuated in a socialist regime. The Chinese revolution was prolonged, from the Nationalist Party under Sun Yat Sen after 1911 to nationalism's decisive defeat by Mao's socialist state in 1949. Each of the three revolutions was complex in a different way. Each resulted in different state forms, constituted through struggles of varying lengths of time, from the relatively brief period in Russia from 1917 to 1921, then France from 1787 to 1800, to China from 1911 to 1949. Yet, even these dates represent ongoing social and political struggles that had roots in earlier events, and they continued for many years to alter the revolutionary states. France did not become a stable democratic polity until after 1871. Russia's state socialism went through numerous iterations until the collapse of the Soviet system in 1991. China's Communist Party is ruling well into the twenty-first century but in a manner threatened by the introduction of global capitalism made possible with the death of Mao in 1976 and later the Deng reforms after 1978.

Skocpol's theory, thus, was not founded on the similarities among these revolutions. On the contrary, they were among the salient revolutions of the modern era *and* they differed in important ways while together illustrating her basic rule for a revolution. 'Social revolutions are rapid, basic transformations of a society's state and class structures; and they are accompanied and in part carried through by class-based revolts from below' (1979: 4). From this short declarative definition it is apparent that she drew on Marx's classical statement while distinguishing herself from it, and from a good many other theories of revolutions. Her purpose was to emphasize a strong theory of state structures. To this end, she was distinguishing her argument from others then current, late in the 1970s, that had been influenced by the public events of the 1960s, among whom were at least two major figures in American political and social science. One was Ted Robert Gurr who, in *Why Men Rebel* (1970), emphasized the role of a shared sense of relative deprivation as the originating impulse for political conflict. Another was Chalmers Johnson who, in *Revolutionary Change* (1966), emphasized the role of a society's functional need to adjust its system of core values to include dissenting parties.

Oddly, Skocpol placed Charles Tilly together with Gurr because of their parallel emphasis on collective action and political conflict. It is far from clear that this is fair to Tilly who did, after all, emphasize the importance of change in the politics of sovereignty, thus in state power. Skocpol was, nonetheless, setting forth her own distinctive theory – a task that encourages a degree of overstatement. In this case she sought to emphasize the total transformation in state structures as she sought to isolate social revolutions as distinctive from collective actions that may or may not be revolutionary. Similarly, she accused Immanuel Wallerstein's world-systems analysis approach of being narrowly economistic when in fact he clearly identified the importance of a new, modern geoculture. Just the same, whatever the flaws, one sees in Skocpol's theory the analytic risk of attempting to formulate general theory in relation to specific empirical cases. A good but specific theory requires a degree of precision and, in Skocpol's case, she sought to account for collective action in respect to changes in state and class structures, while also allowing for the influence of international forces on the revolutionary situation.

The strengths of her theory are, thus, to be judged in how she evaluated her three cases. For simplicity's sake, take the somewhat more familiar case of the French revolution, which is one of Skocpol's most striking cases. The French revolution is all too often taken simply as a revolution from below, in which the rebelling classes are moved by their sense of exclusion and deprivation (an attitude consistent with Gurr's). This is a popular misconception, owing to a wide variety of fictions, music, and cinema that view all revolutions as a kind of 14th of July effusion of radical feeling and action in the fashion of *Les Misérables*. It was that to an extent, but Bastille Day was but one moment in a prolonged struggle involving many different political actors and forces at all levels of French society. Surely, as a more functional theory (like Johnson's) would have it, France was struggling to establish a new liberal polity based on shared democratic values. In the end it more or less did, but only after a good century of successes and failures. It was not until the defeat of the revolution of 1848 that liberal republican values dominated; then, after the defeat of the Paris Commune of 1871, that Napoleon III and the string of imperial restorations were put in the past and the way was opened for more democratic polities.

When applied specifically to the events issuing from 1789, Skocpol's theory is rigorously structural, as she stated in the introduction of *States and Social Revolutions*. In France, as in her other two cases, she identified social revolutions as the decisive outcome of collective actions embroiled in historical events that involve multiple contending groups, with sufficient opportunity, to undercut pre-existing state forms (the absolutist monarchy of Louis XVI in France, the last vestiges of Czarist power in Russia, the already feeble Ming Dynasty in China). In France, the contending groups (to use Tilly's term) were many – initially the aristocrats before 1789; then the workers, peasants, and shopkeepers; then, too, the developing bourgeois class of industrial owners and cultural leaders descendent from the French Enlightenment. The emergent events in the years after 1798, including the Reign of Terror, led to another round of political violence and contention eventuating in Napoleon's rise to power in 1800, and the Empire in 1804. Napoleon's power derived in part from his military genius and his will to advance French expansionism, but also had its base in the revolutionary movement begun in the 1780s. In the American Revolution after 1776, France had, of course, backed the colonies against the British but at a debilitating cost to its treasury. Thus its early revolutionary history was framed by France's fiscal vulnerability owing to changing international events. Thus, even before 1789, the aristocracy was emboldened to challenge the throne, a challenge made possible by debt and taxation policies required by the State's overreach in the Americas. Likewise, more than a decade after 1789 France's internal turmoil created a vulnerability to international force, which gave an opening to Napoleon's aggressive role in defending France against rival powers in Europe, his overreach led to the defeat of his Imperial reign.

Skocpol's book, thus, introduced a new wave of radical structural theory into the American debate. This she achieved by not fearing to set herself in a relation to Marxist thinking, while also criticizing the limiting elements of then prominent American thinking about political action. First, she de-emphasized non-voluntary actors in order to focus instead on masses moved by feelings of relative depredation. Then second, she called scholarly attention to the determining role of state formation as a post-revolution process, while rejecting the functionalist idea that a revolution led naturally to a fresh bond of cultural and political values. And, third, she insisted that, in addition to state transformation, there must also be a robust change in the class structure. These were her principal theoretical points. Together they were sufficient to provoke a major rethinking in American social theory of both the specific elements in politically aroused social change and the importance of a structural theory in social research.

To be sure, Skocpol seems to have overstated her theoretical case in respect to Tilly. His ideas on the mobilization of action at a moment of opportunity in the prevailing sovereign polity are not wildly inconsistent with Skocpol's theory; hers is a more sternly structural theory of states while Tilly's emphasized contending movements. Skocpol may also have made her theoretical task somewhat easier by examining instances where revolutions already met her stipulated definition of a revolution. Tilly's thinking was more restrained. He thought that contention and political violence may lead to change of certain kinds but seldom to full-scale revolutions – a point Skocpol would have been hard put to deny. It is a matter of doing the same or similar kind of thinking applied to related but different forms of political history. Yet, Skocpol achieved something unique in American sociology – a subtle, well defined, sharply informed, historical theory of the structural importance of the state alongside the class structures.

Skocpol's other books suggest just how steadily she maintained a commitment to the structural study of social and political life; among them: *Protecting Soldiers and Mothers: The Political Origins of Social Policy in the United States* (1992), *Social Policy in the United States: Future Possibilities in Historical Perspective* (1995) and *The Missing Middle: Working Families and the Future of American Social Policy* (2000). Her work over the years since *States and Social Revolutions* could be viewed as a change of mind from a prominent social theoretical effort to a more empirically informed policy histories. Yet, it is far better to see that first great work as a sort of clearing of the decks by setting structural social theory as the ballast for a distinctively American sociology of public policy – distinctive in the sense that the Americans were, and still are, always more keenly empirical than European theorists; to a fault, one might add. Skocpol's work as a whole demonstrates that rigorous empirical work not only can be, but must be, well settled on a strong, structural course.

Immanuel Wallerstein and analysis of world-systems

Since 1974, when Immanuel Wallerstein published the first of four volumes in his magisterial, socio-historical study of the modern world-system, he has insisted that his work should be identified as modern world-systems *analysis*, as distinct from a theory of the modern system. This insistence is likely due to his own graduate studies in Columbia University Department of Sociology in the 1950s, when the Merton-Lazarsfeld tradition lent the idea of theory a very particular and systematic relation to empirical research – as that is always, as some put, theory *and* methods. Wallerstein means to distinguish his approach from any such prevailing American idea of social research. One might say, even if he would not, that analysis is his term for a kind of theory that is not so much articulated in relation to research methods, as itself a method whereby social theory is unrelentingly based on historical facts.

Wallerstein's world-systems analysis serves as a rebuke of much of what has kept American social theory in the social sciences from being as robust as social theories have been in Europe. To found a theory on evidence is unquestionably a good thing. But to insist on a certain narrow range of evidences, derived from rather specifically social forms of research like demography and survey research, is not necessarily a good thing.

Whether world-systems *analysis* is a theory or not, it remains a powerful social scientific method based on abundant historical facts.

For one thing, whereas many *social* theories are decidedly vague as to what they mean by 'social' (and others aim to be concrete by taking the just as vague idea of *society* as their topic), Wallerstein is at once clear and broad-minded in defining the unit of his social theory as the world-system. In this he is making both an analytic claim and asserting a historical judgment. There is no such thing as a singular and isolated society, in that all states organized in reference to a state are historically embedded in an inter-state system. This has been the case since, if not before, the Treaty of Westphalia in 1648, when an odd mixture of polities from smaller kingdoms to the Holy Roman Empire signed an agreement to respect state boundaries. Thus began, in principle, the modern state. But Wallerstein notes, rightly, that if this is when the modern state began, it began as part of an inter-state system of considerable scope.

Hence, by extension, Wallerstein's world-system, no less than the common idea of the state, comprises a complex set of systematic aspects:

A world-system is a social system, one that has boundaries, structures, member groups, rules of legitimation, and coherence. Its life is made up of the conflicting forces which hold it together by tension, and tear it apart as each group seeks eternally to remold it to its advantage. It has the characteristics of an organism, in that it has a life-span over which its characteristics change in some respects and remain stable in others. One can define its structures as being at times strong or weak in terms of the internal logic of its functioning.

(2011 [1974]: 347)

Wallerstein's definition of the world-system is notable in a number of ways. Like other American social theorists of the 1970s (notably Tilly and Skocpol), Wallerstein's idea is seriously structural; unlike them his unit is, as we say today, global as distinct from specific to states like France. Like functional theories of the 1950s, there is a kind of organic figure of speech at play; but unlike structural functionalists Wallerstein insists that a world-system has its own life course, marked by tensions, periods of strength and weakness, and a definite life-span at the end of which they come to their end. This latter aspect is important, though there is surely a kind of functionalism at work in the scheme. Before Wallerstein's world-systems analysis is a theory, it is a history.

Though quick-witted in all ways, Wallerstein is also a hedgehog. He is willing and able to plow through any literature that applies to the issue at hand. As a younger scholar, Wallerstein was an Africanist. In the years before his first great work in 1974 he had focused, as he says, on Eastern Europe, then Latin America. Then, too, he has always been a Europeanist.

world-systems analysis

Behind Wallerstein's method is the work of the great French historian, Fernand Braudel, whose classic study, *The Mediterranean and the Mediterranean World in the Age of Philippe II* (1949), is the principal source of such concepts as long-enduring time – the idea that history is never simply a matter of time-specific events but of all long-enduring times, including those of nature, climate, the seas and the mountains. Wallerstein worked closely with Braudel, after whom he named his research center at The University of Binghamton. To this day, Wallerstein visits Paris each winter to do research for his books on the history of the modern world-system. Among other influences, Braudel's thinking is what distinguishes Wallerstein from American functionalists, even though he used some of their language. For Wallerstein, social research must begin with the longest enduring social forms – their economic, social, and geographic aspects. In the modern world, thus, there was one such system – the one that began in the sixteenth century when European states began to build their systems of global colonies until, in his view, roughly 1990 when the Cold War system collapsed making way for a less well ordered system of multiple centers – Europe, the US, and China, at the least.

The first of Wallerstein's as of now four volume history in 1974, is thus the history of the beginnings of the European world-economy, as its subtitle indicates: *The Modern World-System I: Capitalist Agriculture and the Origins of the European World-Economy in the World-System*. This book, and the others in the project, are richly historical in the sense that Wallerstein seems to have read and deployed every major historical study at issue in this and other of the subsequent periods in the modern system. Thus, first, he begins with the idea of a global unit of analysis, in respect to which he studies the historical record, from which he derives his famous conceptual scheme:

> World-economies are divided into *core-states* and *peripheral areas* of the world-economy. I do not say peripheral 'states' because one character-istic of a peripheral area is that the indigenous state is weak, ranging from its nonexistence (that is, a colonial situation) to one of a low-degree of autonomy (that is, a neocolonial situation). . . . There are also *semi-peripheral areas* which are in between the core and the periphery on a series of dimensions, such as the complexity of economic activities, strength of the state machinery, cultural integrity, etc. Some of these areas had been core-areas of earlier versions of a given world-economy. Some had been peripheral areas that were later promoted, so to speak, as a result of the changing geopolitics of an expanding world-economy.
>
> (2011 [1974]: 349)

The analytic terms – core, periphery, semi-periphery – turned out over the years to yield a powerful explanatory history of the modern world-system which, from the first, he noted, was capitalist. Herein lies one of his important historical claims – that a world-system is different from an empire in that the latter engages in force to expand their territorial and economic reach, while a capitalist system (no stranger, of course, to violence) primarily relies on rational methods for the accumulation of capital.

[E]mpires] were a constant feature of the world scene for 5,000 years. There were continuously several such empires in various parts of the world at any given point of time. The political centralization of an empire was at one and the same time its strength and its weakness. Its strength lay in the fact that it guaranteed economic flows from the periphery to the center by force (tribute and taxation) and by monopolistic advantages in trade. Its weakness lay in the fact that the bureaucracy made necessary by the political structure tended to absorb too much of the profit, especially as repression and exploitation bred revolt which increased military expenditures.

[. . .]

In a capitalist world-economy, political energy is used to secure monopoly rights (or as near to it as can be achieved). The state becomes less the central economic enterprise than the means of assuring certain terms of trade in other economic transactions. In this way, the operation of the market (not the *free* operation but nonetheless its operation) creates incentives to increased productivity and all the consequent accompaniment of modern economic development. The world-economy is the arena within which these processes occur.

Immanuel Wallerstein (2011 [1974]) *The Modern World-System I: Capitalist Agriculture and the Origins of the European World-Economy in the World-System,* page 16.

Thus the modern system began with the late medieval period of proto-capitalist agricultural efficiencies that, over time, permitted a capital surplus beyond the needs of a population and its ruling classes. Among other effects, this surplus led, in the sixteenth century, to the ability of the Iberian powers to control the Atlantic, to the end of exploring then settling in the Americas from which it extracted further fungible capital wealth. The Iberian powers were thus the early core that, in effect, emerged before the system of modern

world-systems analysis

rational states. In the earliest period, Hispanic America and Eastern Europe were the peripheral regions from which resources were extracted and converted into capital that further supported the growing world-economy.

At the first, the Netherlands and Britain were semi-peripheral areas that, in due course, became core states as their own global economies developed in East and South Asia, the Pacific, as well as North America. By the mid-twentieth century, the British core was eclipsed by its former peripheral colony, the United States, as Great Britain, France, and much of Western Europe settled back into semi-peripheral states, notably after Germany's defeat in 1945. Then, too, after World War II (and as a result of its key role in the defeat of Hitler), the Soviet Union emerged as a world power that, throughout the Cold War, posed a military, if not economic, threat to the United States.

When the Soviet Union collapsed in 1991, according to Wallerstein, the five-century-old, modern world-system fell into a period of uncertainty. The United States remained the world's dominant military power and the largest economy by volume. But, as Russia relapsed into a normal semi-peripheral state, China and the European Union emerged as economic forces upon which the American economy depends. The Americans borrow from China, which in turn provides a market for its goods, while Europe, also a world banker, is both a producer of goods and a consumer. Thus a one-time core (Europe) and a former peripheral region (China) rose to occupy, in effect, a core-like power in the system in which, early in the twenty-first century, former peripheral areas like India and Brazil are rapidly rising to a comparable status. The current situation is one in which the modern system has fallen into a state of bifurcation, in which the system is torn among forces that are at once interdependent and competitive.

The present situation still early in the twenty-first century is, thus, one of at least uncertainty, at worse chaos. The system remains in the sense that there are global powers and, clearly, peripheral regions in Africa and parts of Asia as well as Siberia and the Arctic from which the powers extract resources. Yet, the line between core and semi-periphery is blurred to the point that one cannot speak of a core as such.

> The modern world-system in which we are living, which is that of a capitalist world-economy, is in precisely such a crisis. . . . The crisis may go on for another twenty-five to fifty years. Since one central feature of such a transitional period is that we face wild oscillations of all those structures and processes we have come to know as an inherent part of the existing world-system, we find that our short-term expectations are necessarily quite unstable. This instability can lead to considerable anxiety and therefore violence as people try to preserve acquired privileges and hierarchical rank in a very unstable situation.
>
> (2004: 77)

Many say that a good theory is one that is able to predict outcomes. Wallerstein's diagnosis of this end, or transformation, in the modern world-system may not be a prediction but it is a rarity among social theories – a clear-headed, well-informed and persuasive analysis of the world as it is.

American social theory has lagged behind Europe's. This is often said to be due to its unnatural pragmatic inclination to attend to the empirical facts as they can be discerned. Yet, American social theorists like Tilly, Skocpol and Wallerstein – each differently indebted to Europe – have opened American social theory's flank to powerful theories based on close empirical evidence of social movements, the State, and the world-system. Though many other American theorists of pragmatist, culturalist, and critical orientations have done both important theory and serious research, the structuralist shift late in the 1970s has lent a special authority and rigor to social theory in America, to join scientific values to sound, even radical, theoretical principles.

Summary points

1   American social theory in the late 60s and 70s struggled to engage with the unforeseen cultural conflicts and crises occurring in that period. Three theories of political movement – Tilly's Resource Mobilization, Skocpol's understanding of the State, and Wallerstein's World-Systems Analysis – emerged as serious tools of social critique, and remain influential to this day.

2   Charles Tilly brought historical rigor to the analysis of social contention and conflict. He argued that social movements involve often disparate parties with separate interests, who must organize and mobilize resources. Crucially, Tilly adds, even with these factors in place, the opportunity for change must be present in existing social structures.

3   Theda Skocpol's analysis of revolutions in France, Russia and China led her to a radical revision of the state structure, taking into account both the international pressures and internal, class-based conflicts that lead to social revolution.

4   Immanuel Wallerstein's world-systems analysis takes as its unit of study the complex interconnected system of states and economic entities that make up the capitalist world-economy. Wallerstein's world-system is made up of dominant core-states, politically weak peripheral areas, and semi-peripheral areas that provide a buffer between the two poles. This system has remained stable for the last 500 years of world history, through periods of growth and changes

in core and periphery status. But the collapse of the Cold War stalemate has brought on a period of uncertainty in the world-system, with no single dominant core-state.

Further questions

1   Think of some of the recent international political upheavals that you have seen in the news. Can you identify the contending groups within these social movements?

2   Taking the example from above, were there any international developments that influenced the revolution? What were the internal class structures involved?

3   Which states are currently in the core of Wallerstein's world-system? Do you see one of them becoming dominant, or is the system likely to change?

Further reading

Charles Tilly

From Mobilization to Revolution (Boston, MA: Addison-Wesley Publishing, 1978)

Theda Skocpol

States and Social Revolutions: A Comparative Analysis of France, Russia and China (Cambridge, UK: Cambridge University Press, 1979)

Immanuel Wallerstein

World-Systems Analysis: An Introduction, (Durham, NC: Duke University Press, 2004)
The Modern World-System I: Capitalist Agriculture and the Origins of the European World-Economy in the World-System, (Berkeley, CA: University of California Press, 2011)

chapter 15

Globalization

Contents

Jenny reclines on a couch at home, alongside members of her family, watching satellite television. Surfing the channels, she wanders from an American soap to a British documentary to a Japanese music video. As her family tires of her incessant channel hopping, Jenny relinquishes the remote control and turns her attention to her mobile phone and incoming text message. Opening the inbox, she reads a message from her friend, Carmel. Jenny got to know Carmel at university in London, before the latter embarked on a gap year in Australia. The text tells of Carmel's good news: she's been accepted into a doctoral program at an ivy-league university in the USA. Jenny responds to Carmel's text immediately, and is drawn into an intimate exchange of ongoing texts with her friend on the other side of the world. Her family, meanwhile, still sitting in the same room as Jenny, now drift into the emotional background.

Another typical evening for a prosperous London family enjoying the technological paraphernalia – satellite TV, mobiles, texting – of contemporary life in the West? Perhaps. What can be said with some confidence is that communication networks are at the center of this episode from modern family life. As noted in previous chapters, we now live in a world in which much of practical social life, not to mention the operations of business and organizations, is conducted through email and the Net. There is more going on here, however, than simply the endless spinning communications of new information technologies. For the information networks and communication systems that Jenny and her friend Carmel deploy in their texting 'bite' deeply into the fabric of personal and emotional life. For one thing, this texting is clearly of sufficient emotional gravity that it brings Jenny into closer contact with her friend Carmel (who, remember, is on the other side of the world to her) than with those sitting in the same room – namely, her family. For another, it re-orientates and restructures perceptions of social space, as well as of time, in the flow of daily life. As if by magic, what is on the 'other side' of the world – in this case, Australia – is now brought centrally within Jenny's world in London. Such a redrafted, spinning world is referred to in sociology as the world of globalization – the main theme of this chapter.

Globalization has become one of the key buzzwords of our times. One needs to be careful assessing arguments about the consequences of globalization, however, as what people call 'globalization' has many different meanings – not all of them coherent, few reconcilable. One central part of what globalization means for many critics is advanced capitalism in its broadest sense, and thus by implication the term has come to revolve around Americanization. This is the view that globalization is a central driver in the export of American commerce and culture, of the vast spread of mass consumerism, of the unleashing of US controlled turbo-capitalism. Others view globalization through the lens of a much longer historical perspective, beginning with the age of discovery and the migrations from the Old to the New World.

We will consider these differing accounts of globalization throughout this chapter, focusing especially on the main theories of globalism which have come to dominate social theory, the social sciences and public debate in recent years. It is perhaps worth noting at the outset, though, that communications media and new information technologies play a vitally significant role in many accounts of the conditions and consequences of globalization. Indeed, it is probably fair to say that recent transformations in communications are uppermost in people's minds when talking about what is truly new about globalization. Political theorist, David Held, captures this point well when he contends:

> What is new about the modern global system is the chronic intensification of patterns of interconnectedness mediated by such phenomena as the modern communications industry and new information technology and the spread of globalization in and through new dimensions of interconnectedness: technological, organizational, administrative and legal, among others, each with their own logic and dynamic of change.
>
> (1991: 206)

Certainly the notion of globalization, many agree, captures something about the ways the world in which we live is now continuously changing. Hence, the preoccupation in globalization theory with, amongst others, forces of multilayered political governance, shifting patterns of post-industrial production, global financial flows and exchange rates. Each of these clusters is a subject of intense debate in academic circles, and it is telling that such debates are played out globally or at least throughout the contemporary West, in universities and government think-tanks from San Francisco to Sydney. Yet globalization as a concept involves considerably more than academic debate alone. Reference is made here not only to the globalized protest strategies of anti-globalizers in Seattle, Genoa, Porto Alegre and elsewhere but also the myriad ways in which the forces of globalism impact upon both the personal and social aspects of everyday life. Today, there is good reason to think that the world really has changed, and profoundly. For anyone wanting to understand these changes, it is necessary to get to grips with what globalization is, with what it is doing to our societies, and with the profound consequences it carries for our personal and emotional lives.

The globalization debate

In recent years, the term 'globalization' has fast become a central organizing category in academic disciplines from economics to international relations, from cultural studies to sociology. Some argue that the globalization debate is maddeningly abstract, with all its talk of 'borderless worlds,' 'turbo capitalism' and 'transgovernmental networks'. Others contend that globalization is now invoked to describe so many things – from the spread of AIDS to the war on terrorism – that it is in danger of losing all meaning. One of the amazing facts about globalization, though rarely commented upon, is just how quickly it has come to dominate academic and public debate. Twenty or so years ago, the preferred terms for analyzing worldwide change were those of 'internationalism' or 'internationalization.' Today, by contrast, and in that relatively short period of time, the term 'globalization' has pretty much gone global. The term is now everywhere – in the newspapers, business magazines, radio and television, and throughout our universities.

In order to contextualize this debate, we will now turn to examine three influential accounts of globalization. These three theoretical approaches to globalization turn on distinct interpretations of the changing nature of organizations, economics, society, the nation-state and personal life. Later in the chapter we will consider criticisms of the globalization debate, as well as ways in which this debate has influenced contemporary sociology and the social sciences.

Global skeptics

When various public intellectuals and academics during the 1990s pointed to the term 'globalization' to explain the major social changes going on around us, many reacted in a skeptical fashion. The skeptics in the globalization debate questioned the idea that we were witnessing an overall shift towards world integration. Pointing to trade and investment statistics from the late nineteenth century, they argued that worldwide economic flows had intensified as regards interaction between nations during the course of the twentieth century – but that, otherwise, the world was not particularly different from the recent past. Arguing against proponents of the globalization thesis (see below), the skeptics contended there is not much new to the world.

An especially interesting version of the case put by global skeptics was that of Paul Hirst (1999). What, Hirst asked, was actually 'global' about globalization? His answer, disarmingly direct, was 'very little.' In this connection, Hirst rejected nearly every claim associated with the globalization thesis. Whilst acknowledging that there is today more cultural and communicational contact between nations than in previous periods, Hirst and his colleagues contended that such contact did not amount to a truly globalized economy. Studying the period from 1890 to 1914, for example, they argued that trade and investment flows were higher for that period than for today, that national borders were not as restricted and that, consequently, there were higher levels of transnational immigration. In a related fashion, Hirst and his colleagues questioned the scope of one of the key institutional emblems of globalization: the multinational corporation. So-called global transnational corporations (TNCs) were not really 'global' at all, they said; they were, instead, nationally based companies at the center of international networks of subsidiaries. In contrast to the notion of 'footloose capital,' in flight around the globe seeking out ever greater profits, the majority of economic activity across the international economy occurred primarily in the OECD (Organization for Economic Cooperation and Development) countries. Regionalization rather than globalization, it was said, defined the shape of the worldwide economy: because of the heavy regionalization of such trading blocs as the European Union and North America, the world economy was becoming less, not more, global. Moreover, nation-states were not becoming progressively less sovereign – on the contrary, internationalization was regarded as fundamentally dependent on the regulatory control of national governments.

The strong concept of a globalized economy . . . acts as an ideal type which we can compare to the actual trends within the inter-national economy. This globalized economy has been contrasted to the notion of an inter-national economy in the above analysis in order to distinguish its particular and novel features. The opposition of these two types for conceptual clarity conceals the possibly messy combination of the two in reality. This makes it difficult to determine major trends on the basis of the available evidence. These two types of economy are not inherently mutually exclusive: rather in certain conditions the globalized economy would encompass and subsume the inter-national economy. The globalized economy would rearticulate many of the features of the inter-national economy, transforming them as it reinforced them.

[. . .]

The opposite of a globalized economy is thus not a nationally inward-looking one, but an open world market based on trading nations and regulated to a greater or lesser degree by both the public policies of nation-states and supranational agencies. . . . Such an economy has

Alongside the skeptics of globalization were to be found the anti-globalizers. The anti-globalization brigade, in all its manifestations from anti-capitalist protesters to policy think-tanks, put forward a list of powerful charges cataloguing the sins of globalization. Globalism was allegedly empowering multinational corporations and speculative finance, compounding inequality and eroding democracy, promoting Western imperialism and the Americanization of the world, destroying environmental standards, as well as brutalizing the public sphere and the state governmental structures through which it operates. The emergence of a planetary scale, global market with ever decreasing tariffs, ever greater international production, as well as more integrated financial markets with higher trade flows, had unleashed a turbo-charged capitalism of unprecedented forms of economic exploitation and political oppression; or so argued the anti-globalizers.

The link between global Westernization or Americanization on the one hand and turbo-capitalist exploitation on the other in the anti-globalization discourse is sometimes explicit, sometimes implicit. A neo-Marxist conviction that capitalism exhibits a pathological expansionist logic, one which now expands the geographical reach of Western corporations and markets to the nth degree, informs this argument. The imperial West, it is suggested, has carved up and re-divided the world into exclusive trade, investment and financial sectors and flows, with new institutions – such as the G8 and World Bank – exercising global surveillance and domination. As a result, globalization is seen as a top–down process, its effects uniform. The weakness of this case, however, is that it cannot adequately justify the grounds of its own social critique: if globalization were really so omnipotent, all-powerful and manipulating, how would the social theorist ever find a position from which to launch an objective critique? In any event, the assumption that the globe is always geared to perfectly integrated markets is certainly deficient. That is to say, such critics have reductively equated globalization with an economistic version of world markets. Yet, as we will see, concentrating solely on processes of economic integration, and thus neglecting current social, cultural and political transformations, leads to an impoverished understanding of how globalization is constituted, contested and shaped.

Radical globalists

Radical globalists are generally upbeat about globalization, sketching an optimistic view of the rise of free trade and open markets. The radical globalist account emphasizes the benefits to democracy and alternatives to centralized power arising from global financial markets, the growth of multinational corporations and the worldwide diffusion of popular culture. This does not mean that radical globalizers are unperturbed by current distributions of wealth and economic power, but advocates of this case do see globalization as generally beneficial and historically inevitable.

Globalization, argue radical globalists, cuts across national borders. In doing so, the forces of globalization initiate new forms of social life and world order based upon altered patterns of economic globalization, of power, and of territory. One of the best known radical globalists, the Japanese business analyst Kenichi Ohmae (1990, 1995), describes globalization as heralding a 'borderless world' – a world in which capital circulates in search of the highest investment returns irrespective of systems of national governance. According to Ohmae, the emergence of, and rapid growth in, the global economy spells the demise of the nation-state – as individual countries no longer have an effective fiscal means to control their economies. In a world where more than a trillion dollars a day is turned over on global currency markets, national governments are increasingly under strain in responding to transitional issues that cross their borders – from currency speculation to illegal immigrants to environmental risks. This challenge to sovereignty is so great that, according to Ohmae, nations are fast becoming mere 'fictions.' The fiction is that sovereignty is still vested in political leaders, but for the most part politicians have lost their capacity to shape socio-economic outcomes in our intensive age of globalization.

The global economy follows its own logic and develops its own webs of interest, which rarely duplicate the historical borders between nations. As result, national interest, as an economic, as opposed to a political, reality has lost much of its meaning. And as information about products and services becomes more universally available, consumers everywhere will be able to make better-informed choices about what they want. It will matter less and less where it all comes from. Governments – and the national boundaries they represent – become invisible in this kind of search. There is no call for them to continue to pick and choose which products can be produced or sold or to decide which are good and which bad. The economic interests to be served are those of individual consumers. Governments do not need to insulate or protect them from the offerings of multinational companies. Consumers can make their own choices. And they do.

Kenichi Ohmae (1990) *The Borderless World: Power and Strategy in the Interlinked Economy*. New York: Harper Business, page 183.

For Ohmae, it is regions rather than states that are the key drivers of globalization. The current world economy, based upon unprecedented finance and capital flows, takes its cue from new regions and economic zones with large populations. Most of the giant multinational companies focus their activities now on regions, not single countries. For example, Nestlé selected the Kansai region around Kobe and Osaka, rather than Tokyo, when moving into the Japanese market.

Global transformationalists

In contrast to the global skeptics and radical globalists, a third-way position has emerged within the globalization debate – that occupied by global transformationalists. The transformationalists argue that globalization inaugurates a 'shake-out' within the realms of economics, politics, culture and personal life. This is less the heralding of a completely new age (as argued by radical globalists), and rather an adjustment to a world that transforms previous structures, a world that shakes up distinctions between domestic and international, internal and external affairs.

One of the most sophisticated proponents of the transformationalist position is David Held, who has tackled head-on the critics, both skeptics and antiglobalizers. Held, a professor at the London School of Economics, has quickly emerged as a leading global expert on globalization. He powerfully argues that the critics are wrong on almost all the major points. Is globalization the driver of Americanization? Yes says Held (2004), the US is the major player in shaping economic markets, but globalization is not just an American phenomenon. As he points out, American companies account for around only one-fifth of world total imports, and approximately one-quarter of total exports. The compounding of inequalities? Individual income differences in the wealthiest and poorest countries are greater than ever, but perhaps the most significant development is that those living in the very poorest conditions appear to be on the decline worldwide. Global markets triumphant over national governments? In the West, government expenditure and taxation levels have generally risen. Globalization, says Held (2004: 6), 'has not simply eroded or undermined the power of states; rather it has reshaped and reconfigured it.' The globalizing of communications threatening national cultures? The diffusion of instant communication across large parts of the world cannot be doubted, but Held argues that available evidence indicates local and national cultures remain robust.

In their ground-breaking work, *Global Transformations* (1999), Held and his associates delineate, with considerable precision, what is truly 'global' about globalization. In order to say anything meaningful about patterns of contemporary globalization, and particularly of how today's world order differs from previous historical forms of globalization, Held sets out four analytical dimensions of analysis:

- the extensity of global networks
- the intensity of global interconnectedness
- the velocity of global flows
- the impact propensity of global interconnectedness.

For Held, globalization certainly involves a *stretching* of social relations. What he means to underscore with this notion of stretching or extensity is that decisions or events occurring in one part of the world come to have ramifications for people living elsewhere. From global labor markets to global warming, it is nearly impossible today not to live with the consequences of the widening reach of networks of social activity and political power. But still there is more. For globalization implies not only a stretching of activities across frontiers, but also a rapid *intensification of interconnectedness* between peoples, institutions and states. Here the networked world of high-speed telecommunications is the most obvious example. Stretching and intensity of social relations are thus key for Held; but there are also two other forces at work in the play of global things. One is velocity, by which Held seeks to underscore the *speeding up of social life*. This refers to the emergence of a 24/7 media culture, in which breaking news – from terrorist attacks to the fighting of wars – is relayed virtually instantly around the globe. But it also refers to the speeding up of transport, travel and the global communication of information. The other concerns impact, in particular the magnification of local events or decisions into issues of global import.

> **[G]** lobalization is not simply a monolithic process that brings in its wake wholly positive or negative outcomes. It is formed and constituted by complex processes with multiple impacts which need to be carefully dissected and examined. But one thing is already clear: globalization does not simply lead to the 'end of politics' or the demise of regulatory capacity. Rather, globalization is more accurately linked with the expansion of the terms of political activity, and of the range of actors involved in political life. Globalization marks the continuation of politics by new means operating at many levels.
>
> David Held (2004) *Global Covenant: The Social Democratic Alternative to the Washington Consensus*. Cambridge: Polity Press, page 10.

Such global transformations spell, in turn, major changes for the nation-state. And Held and his associates provide some dramatic statistics to prove that the growth of transnational organizations alters the dynamics of both state and civil society. At the beginning of the twentieth century there were only 37 intergovernmental organizations (IGOs) and 176 international non-government organizations (INGOs) in force. Today, in addition to the many millions of private firms doing business across state borders, there are an estimated 7,000 IGOs and some 50,000 non-governmental, not-for-profit organizations operating around the globe. These bodies – from Amnesty International and Christian Aid to the International Red Cross and Transparency International – make up a vast, multi-layered structure of global civil society. To this pattern of extensive non-governmental interconnectedness can also be added a thick web of key, global policy-making bodies, including the United Nations, IMF, G8, World Trade Organization, European Union and Asia Pacific Economic Cooperation.

Is the nation-state dying out? Not necessarily, according to Held, and in this connection he outlines a highly nuanced theoretical position – one which puts him at some distance from those radical globalists for whom the state is, more or less, finished. Held certainly recognizes that many traditional domains of state activity have been eroded. He develops this point as follows: 'individual states on their own can no longer be conceived of as the appropriate political units for either resolving key policy problems or managing effectively a broad range of public functions' (Held and McGrew 2002: 23). But he thinks it a mistake to deny the ongoing relevance of the state to world affairs – witness, for example, the ongoing power of states such as the United States and China in global politics. Globalization in this sense is less about an erosion than a reshaping of the nation-state. 'The modern state,' suggest Held and McGrew, 'is increasingly embedded in webs of regional and global interconnectedness permeated by supra-national, intergovernmental and transnational forces, and unable to determine its own fate' (2002: 23).

Manuel Castells: *The Network Society*

As is no doubt clear at this juncture, global networks play an important role in explaining globalization. In his massively influential three-volume study, *The Network Society*, Manuel Castells charts the rise of global informational networks and a network economy. He argues that the rise of information technology has unleashed networks that can process information in almost any part of the world. As a result, society has been transformed into a different kind of space – according to Castells, 'a space of flows that is made up of networked places.' Timeless flows and networked spaces: these notions, as we will see, are at the heart of Castells's social theory and are fundamental to its powerful account of social change. To Castells, the enormous advances in communications technology of recent decades – especially the Internet and the spread of mobile telephony – have unleashed decentralized networks that facilitate communications on the move and have de-sequenced social interaction at great distances from the physical places in which social actors are embedded.

The culture of virtual reality associated with an electronically integrated multimedia system . . . contributes to the transformation of time in our society in two different forms: simultaneity and timelessness.

On the one hand, instant information throughout the globe, mixed with live reporting from across the neighborhood, provides unprecedented temporal immediacy to social events and cultural expressions. To follow minute by minute in real time the collapse of the Soviet state in August 1991, with simultaneous translation of Russian political debates, introduced a new era of communication, when the making of history can be directly witnessed, provided it is deemed interesting enough by the controllers of information. Also computer-mediated communication makes possible real-time dialogue, bringing people together around their interests, in interactive, multilateral chat writing. Time-delayed answers can easily be overcome, as new communication technologies

> provide a sense of immediacy that conquers time barriers, as much as the telephone did but with greater flexibility, with the communicating parties able to lapse for a few seconds, or minutes, to bring in other information, to expand the realm of communication, without the pressure of the telephone, ill-adapted to long silences.
>
> Manuel Castells (1996, 2000, 2nd edition) *The Rise of the Network Society, The Information Age: Economy, Society and Culture*, Vol. I. Cambridge, MA; Oxford, UK: Blackwell, page 461.

The notion of network society has been among other things Castells's way of keeping social theory up-to-date, an underwriting of the period of massive social and technological change in which we are living. In some ways, especially from today's vantage point, this rewriting of social theory around networks and information technology may all seem fairly self-evident. From SMS texting to satellite television, we now live in a world that spins increasingly around the structures of communications technology. From Sydney to San Diego, Beijing to Bangkok, communication networks rule. But Castells is himself interesting not only because he was one of the first social theorists to notice these large-scale shifts from industry to information, but because he systematically analyzed the global structures through which the economy became networked. This he did by becoming a truly global social theorist, lecturing and conducting research surveys in, amongst other cities, Paris, Hong Kong, Moscow, Amsterdam, Mexico and Montreal. As the economy became networked throughout the 1980s, shifting away from industrial manufacture to the communications, service and finance sectors, Castells sought to underscore the changing dynamics of *space* in the constitution of identity, power and society.

For a long time, social theorists tended to equate space with the operations of national societies. Space was fundamental to society, and both were theorized in terms of strictly defined boundaries, borders, territories and maps. As the 1970s gave way to the 1980s, and as manufacture was 'outsourced' to cheap wage spots around the globe and the West made the transition to an informational economy, space was up-for-grabs in social theory once more. Anthony Giddens wrote of 'time-space distanciation' – the stretching of social relations across space and time. David Harvey theorized 'time/space compression' in conditions of postmodernity. And Paul Virilio spoke of the 'annihilation of space' in our age of computational speed. All of these ideas were to become highly influential in social theory. And yet to define space in purely virtual terms – stretching it all the way to the point of the death of distance – meant that social theory ran the risk of ignoring those functional logics and social contexts in and through which spatialized social relations are organized. Castells, highly attuned to these dilemmas, instead defined *space as flows*, and insisted in his own way on the interwovenness of identity and power, the personal and the political. To grasp today's space of flows in our networked societies, Castells argues, means identifying the 'purposeful, repetitive, programmable sequences of exchange and interaction between physically disjointed positions held by social actors.' Purpose, repetition, programs, sequenced interaction and disjointed identities: this is roughly Castells's position on transformations of space induced by the network society. We cannot describe what is going on in the world today, says Castells, as we fail to factor in the impacts of 'timeless time' and 'placeless space.' In the network society, identities, organizations and cultural life – whether in marketing, technology, biomedicine or higher education – are increasingly restructured by an accelerated space of flows, particularly in the major metropolitan centers.

There are three core features that comprise Castells's account of the space of flows. The first is the *informational circuits and communication infrastructures* that permit individuals and organizations to connect with each other in real time on a global scale. Castells devotes considerable sociological attention to the technological infrastructure of networks, underscoring that such circuits or conduits always operate from certain locations (and thus are territorially anchored) – even though such infrastructure organizes a global space of flows (that is, social practices without geographic contiguity). Technological infrastructure is therefore the hardware of global networks, an indispensable medium organizing the cables, computers, airports and automobilities which connect people, places, goods and information in the space of flows. In this network paradigm, enterprises and corporations fundamentally rely on instantaneous digital information to coordinate the linking of demand and supply. Through the sharing of electronic information, networked organizations are able – and now at the touch of a button – to track inventory, check budgets, contact customers, recruit staff, extend product development and revise project management. Through the computational loading, updating and integration of system software programs, firms and large-scale organizations schedule the supply of goods and services to customers. To do this, networked corporations rely on high-speed transportation links through land, sea and air.

The second feature of Castells's account focuses on the *nodes* in and through which networks are organized. Nodes facilitate the growth of network relations through the efficient processing of information, permitting communication connections between people and organizations across large distances. Nodes are thus shorthand for the uprooting of human action and social relations from local contexts and cultures when organizations become interwoven with information and communication technologies. For example, multinational corporations, in breaking up the local organization of their production processes, have reorganized production chains through nodal links in many different countries throughout the world. Nodes thus come to be identified with specific places – although these anchored locations remain fluid and depend largely on the cost advantages to specific companies and organizations. Interlocking nodes of computational, administrative and financial services thus create forms of de-localization – the shifting of social activities away from local contexts and cultures and reconstituting them within distant networks. For example, manufacturing nodes throughout the 1990s and early 2000s have been increasingly located in China and Malaysia, customer support in India and the Philippines, engineering in Russia and the US, design in Taiwan, and on and on. In a networked world, multiproduct companies use interconnected nodes in order to outsource, offshore and generally expand the supply-chain of their operations.

The timeless and placeless logic of nodes equates with a trend towards decentralized networks. This, again, differentiates the network society from industrial society. For Castells, we have left the industrial world of solid structures – hierarchical, formal and centered – well and truly behind. Network enterprises in which information, communication and people move freely within and across nodes is now fundamental to social life. Networks, says Castells, decenter power – transforming it as diffuse, shifting, and spatially fluid. Castells writes,

> By definition, a network has no center. It works on a binary logic: inclusion/exclusion. All there is in the network is useful and necessary for the existence of the network. What is not in the network does not exist from the network's perspective, and thus must be either ignored (if it is not relevant to the network's task), or eliminated (if it is competing in goals or in performance). If a node in a network ceases to perform a useful function it is phased out from the network, and the network rearranges itself – as cells do in biological processes. . . . Thus, the relevance, and relative weight of nodes does not come from their specific features, but from their ability to be trusted by the network with an extra-share of information. In this sense, the main nodes are not centers, but switchers, following a networking logic rather than a command logic, in their function vis-à-vis the overall structure.
>
> (2000: 15–16)

But how, exactly, does trust operate in the network society? This brings us to the third feature of Castells's account, which focuses on *people* dispersed and interconnected within networks. Here Castells's principal concern is the managerial elite. This is an emergent global force of gold collar class professionals – cosmopolitans who roam the planet feeling 'at home' in all the major cities. They may work for major corporations, live in gated communities, travel business or first class, belong to exclusive social clubs and eat at the most expensive restaurants. These are individuals with a sharp sense of the centrality of information and communications technology to the expanding reach of business today. What is important about this elite, for Castells, is not simply the vast sums of money they earn – which sharply marks them off from the 'network have-nots.' It is rather, as winners from the revolution in communications, that such individuals inhabit an *exclusive shared culture*. This is a culture that transcends both time and geographic location. For these are generally people who have attended the 'right' schools, gone to top universities (such as Harvard or Cambridge), are fluent in several languages, shop in designer stores (Gucci, Prada, Armani) and on and on. For Castells, this cosmopolitan global elite is sociologically significant to the network society because their shared culture supersedes the specific geographic environments in which such individuals live. That is to say, managerial elites make decisions and process information about networks from a global perspective.

To speak, therefore, of a network society is to speak of high-speed infrastructures of communications and mobilities, of nodes clustered in specific cities or regions for the advanced processing of information and production, and of professional elites that make decisions and reproduce the culture of advanced network societies. But if networks, nodes and nomadic lifestyles are in one sense identical for Castells, they are not in another. Networked enterprises for Castells do not produce a trend towards social uniformity. For one thing, networks do not result in global sameness. Castells is wary, for example, of Marshall McLuhan's much celebrated announcement during the 1960s that modern communications have rendered the world a 'Global Village.' Because networks impose both a forced globalization and individualization, Castells rejects outright the idea of a global village. By enabling people and organizations that are geographically scattered throughout the world to interact through new communication technologies and automobilities, networks instead suggest to Castells the image of a 'global network of individual cottages.' For another thing, Castells specifically warns that it is a fundamental mistake to view network societies as framed upon one economic or cultural model. All the facets of economic networks today – the infrastructure, nodal size and complexity, as well as the interconnections of the movements of information, people and goods across the globe – are enormously different as one moves from country to country. He quotes as an example the case of Russia. Some aspects of Russian society have very highly developed information networks and are globally connected to world markets. But much of the Russian economy is disconnected. Indeed, Castells views countries such as Russia as characterized by the predominance of disconnection over connection from global networks.

Nonetheless, if networks are internally tied to globalization processes, then they will tend to exert a dominant force over the relations between identity and society in general. This, no doubt, is what Castells seeks to underscore when he describes the global network economy as an 'automaton.' Global networks for him are now a medium of domination, and thus threaten to uproot the world from human control. Castells writes

> Humankind's nightmare of seeing our machines taking control of our world seems on the edge of becoming reality – not in the form of robots that eliminate jobs or government computers that police our lives, but as an electronically based system of financial transactions.
>
> (2000: 56)

This is Castells in apocalyptic mode, in which the global network economy – apparently beyond the reach of social actors – appears to run on autopilot.

Criticisms of Castells

Notwithstanding its brilliant insights, however, Castells's social theory is not without its difficulties. One major concern is that the role of 'networked communications' in social life is unduly inflated. Castells claims that the network society is constituted by the knowledge-based information of new technologies and the communications revolution. In saying this, he is surely correct. The new global economy is *networked*. And networks do, in various senses, re-constitute the social relations in which we live. Still, we might question Castells's obsession with networked communications. The ubiquity of networks can be profitably questioned because, when expanded in the manner of Castells, they appear to become co-terminous with lived experience itself. But are identities and social relations really as fully permeated by networks as Castells suggests? What, for example, is the social difference between someone who only occasionally uses the Internet at the local library, and someone (like Gemma) who spends much of their working life online? If working in finance involves wall-to-wall networks, then what of the local fish shop or second-hand fashions outlet? The idea that they might all be described as networked is surely dubious. As Urry develops this criticism:

> The term 'network' is expected to do too much theoretical work in the argument. Almost all phenomena are seen through the single and

undifferentiated prism of 'network.' This concept glosses over very different networked phenomena. They can range from hierarchical networks such as McDonald's to heterarchic extremely inchoate 'road protest movements,' from spatially contiguous networks meeting every day to those organized around imagined 'cultures at a distance,' from those based upon strong ties to those based on very important and extensive 'weak ties,' and from those that are pretty well purely 'social' to those that are fundamentally 'materially' structured. These are all networks, but they are exceptionally different in their functioning from one to the other.

(2003: 11–12)

The point is that, notwithstanding the occasional acknowledgment that networks vary across cultures, Castells expands the notion of 'networked communications' to breaking point. The concept thus loses sociological precision, and Castells is unable to adequately capture the complex interplay between more traditional, bureaucratic structures on the one hand, and those contemporary fluid and diffuse processes on the other that comprise networked identities and organizations today.

A related concern is that, whilst Castells presents a general theory of networks with universal application, the approach is arguably a highly specific account of certain informational transformations affecting life in the expensive, technologically sophisticated cities of the West. One way of expressing this criticism is to argue that Castells's social theory of networks is at its most relevant to those who inhabit the techno-worlds of Microsoft, Apple or Google, whilst it seems to struggle grasping the poverty and suffering of those in the Third – or, what some now call the Fourth – World. This criticism raises complex issues about some of the unexamined assumptions in Castells's social theory. Being blithe about the ubiquity of networks can quickly become a way of neglecting the many millions who are disconnected from our age of informationalism. This may not, however, be a wholly accurate charge against Castells: he notes in various aspects of his writings that network societies produce new forms of social exclusion and cultural polarization. That said, he has welcomed the communications revolution as heralding a culture of networked consciousness – at least among the cosmopolitan cultural elite. How far down in society this ethos of the global network economy penetrates remains an open question, however. Why do the immediate images that spring to mind for the network society consist of investment bankers on Wall Street or software innovators in Silicon Valley? By contrast to Castells's undifferentiated account of new times, it can be plausibly argued that we have transcended neither modernist nor industrial-age power hierarchies, although their ideologies have undeniably been subject to considerable upheavals as a result of information technology and the spread of flexible networks. But the critical point is that global networks produce both discontinuities and continuities with earlier social practices, and this in turn raises questions about the adequacy of Castells's theorization of identity.

Globalization since 9/11

The debate over globalization, according to many, was irrevocably transformed on 11 September 2001 – the day the planes brought down the Twin Towers in New York. This was the day the world changed forever – or, at least, this was how the globe was represented by the mass media in the days, weeks and months following the New York terror attacks. The 9/11 terrorist attack on the World Trade Center and the Pentagon revealed, in a most shocking and disturbing way, the new global power of networks (as discussed earlier in this chapter). From one angle, 9/11 showed us the ultimate interconnections and conflicts of our lives in an age of globalization. 9/11 and its aftermath certainly spelt terror, but it was also inextricably bound up with media, communications, information, signs and spectacles. It was, in short, a *global media event*, with all that entails as concerns communications networks. As Douglas Kellner writes,

> 9/11 could only be a mega-event in a global media world, a society of the spectacle, where the whole world is watching and participates in what Marshall McLuhan called a global village. The 9/11 terror spectacle was obviously constructed as a media event to circulate terror and to demonstrate to the world the vulnerability of the epicenter of global capitalism and American power.
>
> (2003: 41)

The technological terror of 9/11, to be sure, involved the reuse of airlines and buildings as instruments of mass destruction, but the deployment of such technologies of mass destruction only became truly global through the mediatization of 9/11.

From another angle, there was an even deeper affinity between networks and globalization issuing from the 9/11 attacks. If networks were vital to the spread of communication in which people around the globe watched 9/11 and its aftermath unfold on TV screens, radio and the Internet, they were also essential to the very orchestration of the attacks, since the use of global networks was part and parcel of the strategy and methods of Al-Qaeda. Indeed, from fund-raising to new technological bomb-detonation, Al-Qaeda emerges as a kind of 'global network of networks.' Robert J. Holton explains these links between globalization and terrorist networks thus:

Al-Qaeda is a truly transnational global network. Its leaders and key personnel have been drawn from a range of societies including Saudi Arabia (bin Laden), Egypt (al-Zawahiri) and Jordan (al-Zarqawi), but are also strikingly mobile across a range of societies. . . . The appeal of Al-Qaeda is global and trans-contextual. This is linked ideologically with the outreach of Islam, and organizationally through the idea of a decentralized network of networks. These networks are differentiated according to key functions such as planning or training, and involve key figures such as al-Zawahiri and al-Zarqawi, each of whom brought key associates into the network of networks. They are also decentralized not so much to particular localities as to translocal spheres of operation. The Al-Qaeda presence in each country is not limited to locals, and draws on those from other countries.

(2008: 189)

Global terrorist networks such as Al-Qaeda are formidably hard to track for the reasons Holton identifies – their organizational base is transnational, their activities cut across national boundaries, and their terror is obscenely excessive in its indiscrimination between combatants and civilians. By and large, global terrorism is also unlike traditional forms of terrorism in that targets are transnational and beyond the locale of grievance. The World Trade Center was attacked because it was a global icon of American economic power.

What political forms of globalization, then, do such terrorist networks represent? And how, exactly, have our everyday understandings of globalization changed since the terror attacks of 9/11? Social theorists have undertaken considerable study of terrorist networks and the changing contours of globalization since 9/11, though curiously some of the major conceptual reference points for debate predate the attacks. One such work is Samuel Huntington's polemical *The Clash of Civilizations and the Remaking of World Order* (1996), which grabbed the attention of various neo-conservative Republicans within the Bush administration. According to Huntington, global conflict in the post-Cold War era becomes increasingly motivated by religion and takes place between 'civilizations.' The modern political order for Huntington is a cross between different cultures and religions, with the latter outstripping and reorganizing the former and thereby mobilizing potential conflicts between civilizations. The potential conflicts in an age of globalization are multipolar, and include Islam, China, Africa, Russia, Asia and the West. But the real challenge in Huntington's eyes remains Islam, and the argument soon shifts from multi-polar conflict to the issue of the supremacy of Western modernity and the maintenance of its military-industrial complex. Thus the future shape of politics, says Huntington, is likely to involve ongoing clashes between 'the West and the Rest.' A similar line of analysis is developed in Benjamin Barber's influential book *Jihad vs. McWorld* (1996). Barber sees the world as radically split, between a globalizing West geared towards ceaseless modernization as driven by multinational corporations on the one hand, and premodern tribalism and religious fundamentalism opposed to the modernist idea of progress on the other. This fundamental cleavage is the only global conflict which really counts.

In the emerging world, the relations between states and groups from different civilizations will not be close and will often be antagonistic. Yet some intercivilization relations are more conflict-prone than others. At the micro level, the most violent fault lines are between Islam and its Orthodox, Hindu, African and Western Christian neighbors. At the macro level, the dominant division is between 'the West and the rest,' with the most intense conflicts occurring between Muslim and Asian societies on the one hand, and the West on the other. The dangerous clashes of the future are likely to arise from the interaction of Western arrogance, Islamic intolerance, and Sinic assertiveness.

Alone among civilizations the West has had a major and at times devastating impact on every other civilization. The relation between the power and culture of the West and the power of the cultures of other civilizations is, as a result, the most pervasive characteristic of the world of civilizations. As the relative power increases, the appeal of Western culture fades and non-Western peoples have increasing confidence in and commitment to their indigenous cultures. The central problem in the relations between the West and the rest is, consequently, the discordance between the West's – particularly America's – efforts to promote a universal Western culture and its declining ability to do so.

Samuel Huntington (1996) *The Clash of Civilizations and the Remaking of the World Order*. London: Simon and Schuster, page 183.

The advent of global terrorism has undoubtedly cast a shadow over previous polarizations of globalization, particularly the debate of those 'for' and 'against' – that is, 'radical globalists' against 'global skeptics.' Against this backdrop, recent social theory has sought to engage more critically with the consequences of globalism in terms of such issues as democracy, cosmopolitanism, social justice, militarism and terrorism. Among other attempts to analyze and critique contemporary globalism is Dennis Smith's *Globalization: The Hidden Agenda* (2006). Smith seeks to redefine the political stakes of globalization away from the struggle between the West and terrorism, and instead towards the possible catastrophic consequences of countries at war with each other *within* the West. In our own time of network terrorism, writes Smith, globalization is one name for the traumatic, shattering, excessive and uncontainable forces of multinational capitalism that dissolve traditional society and shake identities and communities to their roots. Whilst terror and the problem of evil moves center stage throughout the world in the wake of 9/11, it is for Smith the shapeless immensity of socio-economic contradictions within the West that remain of utmost significance. As Smith writes,

> On one side, there are supporters of decent democracy, delivering substantial benefits, such as dignity, freedom and fair treatment, to all citizens; on the other, proponents of liberated capitalism, enforced by the domineering state, excluding many from its benefits. The outcome of this struggle will shape the world for the rest of the twenty-first century.
>
> (2006: 1)

From the collapse of communism to 9/11, Smith asserts that the world as we know it is disintegrating. Yet if the world is really coming apart, and in particular if America's global dominance has now entered into terminal decline, what political shape will the globe now take? Smith advances the following points on the 'hidden agenda' of globalization: the emerging collapse of the US as global monarch; a massive build-up of Europe's military strength to match its pervasive economic powers; the rise of China and India as 'global super-powers'; and, a sociological vision of increasing millions throughout the globe subjected to social exclusion, poverty and humiliation. It is around this last theme that Smith argues globalization *wounds*. A 'dynamics of humiliation' is part and parcel, he says, of the expansionist logic of globalization.

If the West abandons decent democracy as a genuine option, if it abandons the duty of care, if it says the market will cure all ills, what will happen then? Who then will make the case for embedding decent democracy and human rights in the working practices of strong global-regional and global institutions of governance? Probably no one.

In that case, our global city-dwellers will be left with the choice between liberated capitalism and the domineering state, each offered to them by a different set of local politicians. They are likely to favor the latter. It

However provocative this account might appear, there are good reasons to be cautious of such far-reaching political claims. It seems unlikely, for example, that the EU will seek to replace the US as the world's moral guardian via a massive build-up of its military strength. As Anthony Giddens (2006) has argued, the EU is not an emergent superpower but, rather, an elastic regional community. Or, as Timothy Garton Ash (2004) has argued, Europe is the world's Not-America. Similarly, whilst China has now surpassed Japan as the world's second largest economy, it will not necessarily seek to become the next global monarch. Indeed, the whole notion of a world as structured by a single dominating power has been eclipsed; global power floats away from centers, dispersed throughout overlapping regions. For what the controversy over globalization demonstrates is that patterns of social relation, power and identity are breaking down into forms that are increasingly fluid, irregular, even liquid.

Ulrich Beck: organized lives in a world of risk

In order to understand how danger is assessed, scholars of globalization have found it useful to consult the work of Ulrich Beck; in particular, his work on risk society has been especially influential. Beck has traced in detail the many, inescapable ways in which risk both presses in on our lives and reorganizes the ways in which we live as a result. He has developed powerful analyses of the ways in which the rise of what he calls 'risk society' is transforming societies, nature and the environment, sexuality and intimate relationships, politics and democracy. Whether one actively embraces or defensively repudiates the dangers, hazards and terrors of the world today, Beck's central claim is that *the notion of risk is increasingly fundamental to global social life*. For Beck, modernity is a world that introduces global risk parameters that previous generations have not had to face. Precisely because of the failure of industrial society to control the risks it has generated, such as the ecological crisis, risk today rebounds as a largely defensive attempt to avoid new problems and dangers.

Beck is careful to introduce some key sociological distinctions into his analyses of risk society, and it is important to keep these in mind when thinking about his claim that risk today qualitatively changes our experience of the world. In this connection, Beck contends that it is necessary to separate the notion of risk from that of hazard or danger. The hazards of pre-industrial society – famines, plagues, natural disasters – may or may not come close to the destructive potential of techno-science in the contemporary era. Yet for Beck this is not in any event key, since he does not wish to suggest that daily life in today's risk society is intrinsically more hazardous than in the premodern world. What he does suggest, by contrast, is that no notion of risk is to be found in traditional culture: preindustrial hazards or dangers, no matter how potentially catastrophic, were experienced as *pre-given*. They came from some 'other' – gods, nature or demons. With the arrival of the modern age and scientific designs of social control, particularly with the idea of steering towards a future of predictable security, the consequences of risk become a political issue. This last point is crucial. It is societal intervention – in the form of decision-making – that transforms incalculable hazards into calculable risks. 'Risks,' writes Beck (1997: 30), 'always depend on decisions – that is, they presuppose decisions.' The idea of 'risk society' is thus bound up with the development of instrumental rational control, which the process of modernization promotes in all spheres of life – from individual risk of accidents and illnesses to export risks and risks of war.

The historically unprecedented possibility, brought about by our own decisions, of the destruction of all life on this planet . . . distinguishes our epoch not only from the early phase of the Industrial Revolution but also from all other cultures and social forms, no matter how diverse and contradictory. If a fire breaks out; the fire brigade comes; if a traffic accident occurs, the insurance pays. This interplay between before and after, between security in the here-and-now and security in the future because one took precautions even for the worst imaginable case, has been revoked in the age of nuclear, chemical and genetic technology. In their brilliant perfection, nuclear power plants have suspended the principle of insurance not only in the economic but also in the medical, psychological, cultural, and religious sense. The 'residual risk society' is an uninsured society, in which protection, paradoxically, decreases as the threat increases.

Ulrich Beck (1991) *Ecological Enlightenment: Essays on the Politics of the Risk Society*. Amherst (NY): Prometheus Books, pages 22–3.

In support of the contention that protection from danger decreases as the threat increases in the contemporary era, Beck (1994) discusses, among many other examples, the case of a lead crystal factory in the Federal Republic. The factory in question – Altenstadt in the Upper Palatinate – was prosecuted in the 1980s for polluting the atmosphere. Many residents in the area had, for some considerable time, suffered from skin rashes, nausea and headaches, and blame was squarely attributed to the white dust emitted from the factory's smokestacks. Due to the visibility of the pollution, the case for damages against the factory was imagined, by many people, to be watertight. However, because there were three other glass factories in the area the presiding judge offered to drop the charges in return for a nominal fine on the grounds that individual liability for emitting dangerous pollutants and toxins could not be established. 'Welcome to the real-life travesty of the hazard technocracy!' writes Beck, underlining the denial of risks within our cultural and political structures. Such denial for Beck is deeply layered within institutions, and he calls this 'organized irresponsibility' – a concept to which we will return.

The age of nuclear, chemical and genetic technology, according to Beck, unleashes a destruction of the calculus of risks by which modern societies have developed a consensus on progress. Insurance has been the key to sustaining this consensus, functioning as a kind of security pact against industrially produced dangers and hazards. (Beck draws substantially from the work of François Ewald in developing the idea that society as a whole comes to be understood as a risk environment in insurers' terms. (See Ewald 1986, 1993)) In particular, two kinds of insurance are associated with modernization: the private insurance company and public insurance, linked above all with the welfare state. Yet the changing nature of risk in an age of globalization, argues Beck, fractures the calculating of risks for purposes of insurance. Individually and collectively, we do not fully know or understand many of the risks that we currently face, let alone can we attempt to calculate them accurately in terms of probability, compensation and accountability. In this connection, Beck emphasizes the following:

- risks today threaten irreparable global damage which cannot be limited, and thus the notion of monetary compensation is rendered obsolescent;
- in the case of the worst possible nuclear or chemical accident, any security monitoring of damages fails;
- accidents, now reconstituted as 'events' without beginning or end, break apart delimitations in space and time;
- notions of accountability collapse.

Criticisms of Beck

The relevance of Beck's ideas on risk to social theory is clearly evident on a global scale. Even so, there are problems with Beck's social theory, both in itself and as a sociological critique of risk. It is not clear, for example, that Beck's approach can withstand historical scrutiny as to the parameters and depth of death-dealing risks that wiped out entire populations in previous eras. The sociological focus of Beck's analysis, as he says, depends on contrasting the contemporary risks of the global era with the hazards and dangers of pre-modern societies; but Bryan S. Turner (1994) has shown that such a distinction might well be merely scholastic. From bubonic plagues and epidemics of syphilis to environmental and political catastrophes of earlier civilizations, such human devastation involved mixtures of impersonal, unobservable, democratic and global risk. That is to say, these were dangers and risks which functioned in much the same manner as Beck claims for today's supposedly 'new' risk phenomena. It is true that Beck does distinguish first-order hazards and second-order risks – that is, between traditional and modern societies – and it might be conceded that his analysis of risk society is thus best read as a provocative political engagement with the current era of advanced techno-science and globalization. But it is surely questionable to upgrade 'risk' as a social category to the point where it becomes the exclusive worry in the plight of contemporary women and men. Are we all really so worried about risk? And, whether we know it or not, are we all really making the kinds of cost/benefit calculations about risk that Beck claims? More disturbingly, is the means–end rationality of risk spreading into personal and intimate spheres of life (such as marriage, friendship and child-rearing) in the unified ways that Beck contends? Does the concept of risk actually capture what is new and different in the contemporary social condition?

To see the relation between risk and society in the means–end, instrumentally rational fashion as described by Beck is to adopt a strongly objectivist account of how social relations are reproduced – this is not the naïve structuralist notion that structures operate behind the backs of actors, but it is one that ascribes a *dominant rationality* to contemporary women and men. To that extent, it might be argued that Beck's otherwise provocative social theory displays a lack of curiosity in how people perceive, engage or disengage with the risks they encounter in daily life. It is from this angle that the American sociologist Jeffrey C. Alexander (1996: 135) criticizes Beck for outlining an 'unproblematic understanding of the perception of risk' – one that is utilitarian, objectivist and emotionally shallow. The criticism is, in effect, that risk may be the new catch-cry of contemporary political life, but that Beck's rendition of it was too simplistic, even reductive. It is perhaps ironic that Beck should make such a great deal out of risk, given that he ignores the aesthetic and emotional dimensions of embodied experience from which contemporary women and men deal with risk (see Lash and Urry 1994; Elliott 2004; Hollway and Jefferson 1997). Beck has also been criticized for divorcing the cultural politics of risk assessment from its interpersonal contexts.

'Risk' is of course a fluid term, which can be either personal or global, and arguably both. And this, in fact, is one important reason why it is crucial for social theorists to attend to the complex, myriad ways that people figure out and reflect on risk. But such explorations require consideration too of the socio-political contexts in which it is evaluated, managed and calculated. The anthropologist Mary Douglas (1986, 1992), for example, argues that advanced industrial risks are primarily constructed through the rhetoric of purity and pollution. For Douglas, what is most pressing in the social-theoretic analysis of risk is an understanding of how human agents ignore many of the potential threats of daily life and instead concentrate only on selected aspects. Interestingly, Beck fails to discuss in any detail Douglas's anthropology of risk. Where Beck comments on Douglas, the concentration is typically upon the schism in sociology between the analysis of traditional-agrarian and modern-industrial societies. (see Beck 1997: 57–8, 87). This would seem peculiar not only since Douglas's groundbreaking analyses of risk appear to have laid much of the thematic groundwork for Beck's sociological theory, but also because her work is highly relevant to the critique of contemporary ideologies of risk – that is, the social forms in which risk and uncertainty are differentiated across and within social formations, as well as peculiarly individuated.

Beck's theory of risk has also come under heavy criticism for its narrow or unproblematic understanding of power and domination (see Elliott 2001). According to Beck, risk society combats many of the distinctive characteristics of power, turning set social divisions into active negotiated relationships. Traditional political conflicts – centered around class, race and gender – are apparently superseded by new, globalized risk conflicts. 'Risks,' writes Beck (1992: 35), 'display an equalizing effect.' Everyone is now threatened by risk of global proportions and repercussions; not even the rich and powerful can escape the new dangers and hazards of, say, global warming or terrorism. Equally so, risk today erodes class consciousness (personal difficulties and grievances no longer culminate in group or collective causes) and also, to some considerable degree, class-in-itself (contemporary social problems are increasingly suffered alone). In short, class as a community of fate or destiny declines steeply. However, while it might be the case that developments associated with the risk society are affecting social inequalities, it is surely implausible to suggest, as Beck does, that this involves the transfiguration of class as such. What Beck fails to adequately consider is that both risk and individualization (while undoubtedly facilitating unprecedented forms of personal and social experimentation) may directly contribute to, and advance the proliferation of, class inequalities and economic exclusions. That is to say, Beck fails to give sufficient sociological weight to the possibility that individualization may actually embody systematically asymmetrical relations of class power.

Criticisms of the globalization debate

The debate over globalization, as we have seen, ranges over many issues. From the globalization of finance and the economy to the shopping mall and consumerism, and from the environment, pollution and global warming to civil society and the emergence of new global forms of cosmopolitanism, it appears there is no aspect of the structure of social life that globalization does not reach. That said, and while global skeptics may have lost much intellectual and political ground to radical globalists, a number of forceful criticisms have been made of the globalization debate. There is the question, for example, of how far down these global networks, flows and processes really go – of whether they are actually 'global,' or whether they are for the most part Western. Whilst globalization denotes a number of socio-economic and technological developments in cities such as Sydney and Singapore, it is arguably a more open question as to what globalization actually means in Sofia, Skopje or Sana'a? How might globalization apply to societies of the Third World? Is the term a culturally neutral description of geo-political realities in the twenty-first century, or a normative image of a certain form of life?

Globalization, work and the new economy

Notwithstanding the foregoing criticisms of the globalization debate, there has been a widespread appreciation – in both the social sciences and public political debate – that the economy, employment market and our working lives have undergone significant changes in recent years due to the impacts of globalization. The transnational activities of multinational corporations, able to export industrial production to low-wage spots around the globe, and to restructure investment in the West away from manufacture to the finance, service and communications sectors, has in particular spelt major changes in the ways people live their lives, how they approach work, as well as how they position themselves within the employment marketplace. Whilst employment has become much more complex than in previous periods as a result of the acceleration of globalization, one key institutional fact redefining the contemporary condition has been the rapid decline of life-time employment. The end of a job-for-life, or of a career developed within a single organization, has been interpreted by some critics as heralding the arrival of a 'new economy' – flexible, mobile, networked.

If downsizing, flexibility and job insecurity have become the mark of our times, how might these changes affect people's working lives? How do such economic changes impinge upon people's sense of identity? And how can long-term personal goals – that is, the self as an ongoing project – be pursued in a world devoted to the short-term? Richard Sennett, an American sociologist, has shown just how difficult the imperatives of flexibility and risk-taking can be in our new, globalized world of work. He has also shown how damaging an economy without long-term commitments or larger meaning can be for self-identity and the self. Sennett's argument, bluntly put, is that we have moved from a work world of rigid, hierarchical organizations, in which self-discipline shaped the durability of the self, to a brave new economy of corporate re-engineering, innovation and risk, in which the fragmented or dislocated nature of self-experience moves to the fore.

In *The Corrosion of Character* (1998), a book that has had a significant impact upon the debate over work in the era of globalization, Sennett contends that a

> change in modern institutional structure has accompanied short-term, contract, or episodic labor. Corporations have sought to remove layers of bureaucracy, to become flatter and more flexible organizations. In place of organizations as pyramids, management wants now to think of organizations as networks. . . . This means that promotions and dismissals tend not to be based on clear, fixed rules, nor are work tasks crisply defined; the network is constantly redefining its structure.
>
> (1998: 23)

For Sennett, the rise of flexible capitalism, however much flexibility and risk-taking are said to give people more freedom to shape the direction of their lives, actually leads to crushing new burdens and oppressions. Flexible capitalism is 'flexible' in as far as its workers and consumers accept the dictates of a post-hierarchical world, accept that it is they and they alone who must strive to be ever-more flexible, and accept the abandonment of traditional models of work as well as standard definitions of success.

'Who needs me?' is a question of character which suffers a radical challenge in modern capitalism. The system radiates indifference. It does so in terms of the outcomes of human striving, as in winner-take-all markets, where there is little connection between risk and reward. It radiates indifference in the organization of absence and trust, where there is no reason to be needed. And it does so through reengineering of institutions in which people are treated as disposable. Such practices obviously and brutally diminish the sense of mattering as a person, of being necessary to others.

It could be said that capitalism was always thus. But not in the same way. The indifference of the old class-bound capitalism was starkly material; the indifference which radiates out of flexible capitalism is more personal because the system itself is less starkly etched, less legible in form.

Richard Sennett (1998) *The Corrosion of Character: the Personal Consequences of Work in the New Capitalism*. New York: Norton, page 146.

The flexibility demanded of workers by multinational corporations, according to Sennett, promotes a dominant conception of individuals as dispensable and disposable. It is against this sociological backdrop that he cites statistics indicating that the average American college student graduating today can expect to hold twelve positions or jobs in their lifetime, plus which they will be required to change their skills base at least three times. From this viewpoint, yesteryear's job-for-life is replaced today by short-term contract work. No wonder flexible capitalism has its discontents, who find to their dismay that the alleged benefits of free markets are less and less apparent. In a subsequent work, *The Culture of The New Capitalism* (2006), Sennett spells out the deeper emotional consequences of such big organizational changes thus: 'people fear being displaced, sidelined, or underused. The institutional model of the future does not furnish them a life narrative at work, or the promise of much security in the public realm' (page 132). Today's corporate culture of short-termism is producing a thorough-going erosion of the loyalty and trust that employees vest in their workplaces. 'Work identities,' writes Sennett, 'get used up, they become exhausted, when institutions themselves are continually reinvented' (141). In a corporate world where people are always thinking about their next career move, or preparing for major change, it is very difficult to remain loyal to any one company or organization.

Sennett's sociology speaks directly to the practical difficulties of living in a globally interconnected world. He is especially attentive to the personal dimensions of global change, and uses much biographical material in his work to chart the impacts of globalization upon the lives of working people. At the heart of his book, *The Corrosion of Character*, for example, is the story of Rico – a materially successful businessman with a very high income, who nonetheless feels a sense of discontent with his high-pressured life-style. What most surprises Sennett about Rico is the degree to which his personal sense of identity is shaped by the dictates of work. For, after grad-uating from university and marrying a fellow student, Rico changed jobs four times since reaching the top of his profession – with each move carrying complicated emotional disturbances for himself and his family. Rico works in the hi-tech electronics industry; it is a world that involves him in continual networking, on-line short communications, flexible contracts and the like. In discussion with Sennett, Rico confesses to feeling emotion-ally adrift and vulnerable; he worries that his highly demanding job leads him to neglect his wife and children; he worries about the weak ties that define his few friendships; he worries, above all, about a lack of ethical discipline, fearing the superficial morality that defines his life. Prosperous as he is, Rico is a man whose life is dominated by the imperatives of the money market; the more he tries to adjust to the dynamic pressures of the global market, the more he feels he is losing control of his purpose in life and his sense of self.

When people are inserted into a world of detachment and superficial cooperativeness, of weak ties and interchangeable relationships, and when all this is shaped by the pursuit of risk-taking and self-reinvention, the power of traditional social norms and cultural traditions begins to diminish. This can be potentially liberating: the self finds the potential to define itself anew and create fluid and innovative social relationships. But there is also something deeply unsettling. For a self that is constituted entirely through episodes and fragments has little to hold itself together in emotional terms; it is this drift of character, of corrosion of the self, that Sennett fixes his attention firmly upon. According to Sennett, as the coherent life narrative breaks down, so does the symbolic texture of the self. In contemporary social conditions, durable selfhood is replaced by a kind of supermarket identity – an assemblage of scraps, random desires, chance encounters, the accidental and the fleeting. Moreover, as Sennett notes (1998: 133), this suits the requirements of dynamic global capitalism: 'A pliant self, a collage of fragments unceasing in its becoming, ever open to the new experience – these are just the psychological conditions suited to the short-term work experience, flexible institutions, and constant risk-taking.' According to Sennett, the flexible regime of the new capitalism – with its instant global transfers of money, its hi-tech cultural production, and its radical restruc-turing of the labor market – begets a character structure geared towards the superficial, the fleeting and the fragmented. 'In the flexible, fragmented present,' writes Sennett (1998: 135), 'it may seem possible only to create coherent narratives about what has been, and no longer possible to create predictive narratives about what will be.'

Globalization, communication and culture

Thanks to today's vast global flows of information, imagery and identity, the icons of popular culture are legion. McDonald's, Coke, Nokia, Apple, Gucci, Nike: these are just a few of the transnational companies advancing global products and brands in and through which people's identities are remade and transformed in the context of an intensive consumer culture. Sociological studies have devoted much attention to the rise of electronic media globalization in terms of addressing the huge expansion in information diffusion and advertising of consumer goods and other cultural products. In these diverse studies, people's identities and experience of everyday life are understood as marked irrevocably by the emergence of global communication networks and new information technologies. The sheer scale, intensity and speed of mass communication and media technology emerges, in this viewpoint, as an unprecedented feature of global society. In historical terms, it is of course the case that people have, by and large, lived out their daily lives in a web of local cultures – consisting largely of set routines and local interactions structured along national and territorial lines. In an age of so-called global mass culture, however, such cultural fixity well and truly fragments; the more the global spread of communication networks and telecommunication systems occurs, the denser and more complex become patterns of cultural life and layers of identity. Or, as we will see, so say some sociology authors.

In the past few decades, major transformations have occurred within the media industries. The spread of communication infrastructures – radio, television, the Internet, satellite and digital technologies – has made instant communication across the globe a daily reality for many. Such transformations in communication stem from the early 1970s, when the first telecommunications satellites were positioned in geosynchronous orbits, thus allowing for the emergence of virtually instantaneous electronic communication between individuals, institutions, societies and cultures. These and related new technologies have, in turn, spelt a shift away from national controls over media information and towards a global market in which information cuts through and across geo-political boundaries. Also striking about today's media globalization is that it is largely driven by corporate interests: the producers and distributors of contemporary global media encompass about twenty multinational corporations, from Time Warner to Rupert Murdoch's News International.

For many critics, the rise of global communication systems has gone hand in hand with the erosion of national culture. The massive cultural flows of electronic media globalization, on this view, fragment the power of national identity and territorial axes of identity more generally. There are various political anxieties at work here. Some critics worry about the threat that unrestricted global media poses to the workings of democracy. Edward Herman and Robert McChesney (1997), for example, point to the dangers of a commercialized media dominated by global corporations in which entertainment triumphs over political debate and civic participation. Other critics, whilst still concerned with commercialization and the power of trans-national corporations, are more concerned with the structural changes associated with media globalization. According to these critics, the global media are little more than the purveyors of a new cultural uniformity. This is, in short, the thesis of *global cultural imperialism* – in which the media function to implant American values and ideologies in less developed countries.

> [M]edia globalization effects, while still hard to sort out, are dominated by commercialization and its impact on the public sphere. For smaller and less economically developed countries, there is a further force of economies of scale and technical and promotional sophistication that greatly facilitates media and cultural penetration by the great powers.
>
> There is a strong tendency in the globalizing process for advertiser pref-erences for light fare to prevail, giving zero weight to the positive exter-nalities of public service programming, and at the same time giving full play to audience-attracting programs featuring sex and violence, all in accord with market logic. Put otherwise, the globalizing media treat audiences as consumers, not as citizens, and they are most attentive to those with high incomes.
>
> Edward Herman and Robert McChesney (2004 [1997]) *The Global Media: The New Missionaries of Corporate Capitalism*. London: Continuum, page 188.

As we have seen throughout this book, however, we need to be especially careful when such comprehensive claims are made about the future direction of society. Whilst many worry about the Westernization or Americanization of communication networks today, there is considerable sociological evidence to suggest that the picture remains more complex, perhaps even puzzling. According to critics of the cultural imperialism thesis, for example, the globalization of communication does not, in fact, spell the globalization of culture. Globalization, it is argued, does not have any one, single consequence. Notwithstanding the growing corporate control of communication networks today, as social theorist John B. Thompson argues in his book *The Media and Modernity* (1995), media messages are continually interpreted in novel ways by national audiences. Whether watching American serials like *The Sopranos* or *Six Feet Under* in Asia, listening to hip-hop in China, or surfing the Net in Lagos, there is a multiplicity of background assumptions, discourses, norms, values and ideologies through which people make sense of media messages and products. This, according to Thompson, would suggest that cultural diversification is hardly at an end with the advent of globalization. According to another study by media theorist John Tomlinson (1991), imported media products are always locally interpreted and transformed in the process of such local readings. This is not to deny that cultural imperialism poses significant risks to various local cultures. It is rather to assert that new global communication systems create 'hybrid cultures'; electronic media globalization, as Stuart Hall has suggested, can have a 'pluralizing impact' on identities. The emphasis here is on the word *can*; the task of future social theory is to critically probe and interrogate the social conditions through which global media can both enhance and undermine national cultures and national identities.

The undeniably high profile of the mass media in contemporary cultural practices set against the evidence that people bring other cultural resources to their dealings with it, suggests that we can view the relationship between media and culture as a subtle *interplay of mediations*. Thus we may think of the media as the dominant *representational* aspect of modern culture. But the 'lived experience' of culture may also include the discursive interaction of families and friends and the material-existence of routine life: eating, working, being well or unwell, sexuality, the sense of the passage of time and so on.

John Tomlinson (1991) *Cultural Imperialism: A Critical Introduction*. London: Pinter, page 61.

Globalization and the new individualism

Globalization, to repeat the argument of this chapter, reshapes not only institutions and organizations but also the very fabric of identity and personal life. In some of my own recent writings with the American sociologist Charles Lemert, notably *The New Individualism: The Emotional Costs of Globalization* (2006), we have sought to broaden the debate over globalization by examining how individuals react to, and cope with, corporate and networking pressures at the level of self-identity. The argument, broadly speaking, is that throughout the polished, expensive cities of the West there is an emergent 'new individualism' centered on continual self-actualization and instant self-reinvention. What are the broader social forces sustaining this new individualism? Briefly put, there are four central 'drivers' to the new individualism thesis: (1) reinvention; (2) instant change; (3) speed; and (4) short-termism.

First, the new individualism is marked by a relentless emphasis on self-reinvention. This is the claim that a 'reinvention craze' – which involves continual self-reconstruction and self-recalibration – is now integral to contemporary living, and represents a kind of 'tipping point' for various contemporary addictions, obsessions and compulsions. An example of the reinvention craze is the pressure consumerism puts on individuals to 'transform' and 'improve' every aspect of their lives: not just homes and gardens, but also careers, eating habits, sex lives, minds and bodies. The dynamics of reinvention can be profitably explored with reference to the shifting boundaries of private and public life. The emergence of a reinvention compulsion is evident in re-framings of public and private life – in everything from TV talk shows such as Oprah, Ricki Lake and Geraldo to confessional autobiographies such as Elizabeth Wurtzel's *Prozac Nation*, from life-coaching to web-based technologies of self-reconstruction. Throughout, reinvention is continually under-scored. Self-help manuals, 12-step therapy programs, personal counseling, memory recovery experts, addiction-management gurus, phone and cybertherapy, peer counselors, Internet analysts: the self in conditions of advanced globalization becomes a life-project geared to reinvention.

Second, the new individualism encodes an endless hunger for instant change. This individualist trend is discernible throughout various sectors of contemporary social life, not only in the rise of plastic surgery and the instant identity makeovers of reality TV, but also in compulsive consumerism, speed-dating and therapy culture. There are various market-directed, consumer culture solutions – from self-help to therapy culture, from instant identity makeovers to plastic surgery – tailored to instant transformation, and reduced to a purchase mentality.

In Elliott's *Making The Cut* (2008), a study of cosmetic surgical culture and the makeover industries, the social logics of instant change are explored in depth. From Botox and collagen fillers to liposuction and mini-facelifts, the message peddled through cosmetic surgery is one of instant change. 'Instant change' has become a corporate message that the self can be changed however the individual so desires; literally, identity knows no limit. The study highlights the degree to which many cosmetic surgical procedures are anything but swift; the sociological focus is squarely on the industry's 'promise' that various liquids, compounds, threads, treatments and operations will instantly transform the body. Today's surgical culture promotes a fantasy of the body's infinite plasticity. The message from the makeover industry is that there is nothing to stop you reinventing yourself however you choose; but, for the same reason, your surgically enhanced body is unlikely to make you happy for long. For today's reshapings of the body are only fashioned with the short term in mind – until 'the next procedure.' Even so, cosmetic surgical culture combines brilliant technology with dramatic self-fashioning, medical advances with a narcissistic understanding of the self as a work of art. The current cultural fascination with cosmetic surgery represents the struggle of fantasy against reality, the pyrrhic victory of society over biology.

Third, the new individualism is fundamentally tied to transformations associated with speed. There is now an extensive literature documenting the rise of social acceleration, speed, dynamism and accelerated change as regards the self. But while speed is most obviously associated with the communications revolution and the arrival of digital culture, it also presses in deeply upon the self. Life in the 'new individualist' fast lane is certainly one of rapid acceleration – full of thrills and spills. We live, as Milan Kundera brilliantly put it, in a culture of 'pure speed' – in which lines of flight from person to person, organization to organization, at once proliferate and intensify. Consider, once more, the spread of self-help literature as illustrative of this tendency. The genre of self-help is not new, but it has in recent years witnessed key changes as regards the time-frame of its much sought-after delivery of personal change. The time/space architecture of self-help literature is driven more and more by pure speed. 'The 4 Hour Body,' '34 Instant Stress Busters,' 'Instant Self-Confidence,' 'Fast Road to Happiness': these are just some of the books currently available to women and men seeking to refashion, restructure and rebuild their personal lives.

Finally, the new individualism is shaped in and through a preoccupation with short-termism, or episodicity. There are important new links between, on the one hand, the advent of the global electronic economy and socio-economic logics of intensive globalism and, on the other, the popular explosion of interest in re-invention or makeover industries and short-term identity reconstruction. In this connection, the impact of multinational corporations, able to export industrial production to low-wage spots around the globe and to restructure investment in the West away from manufacture to the finance, service and communications sectors, has spelt major changes in the ways in which people live their lives, how they approach work, as well as how they position themselves within the employment marketplace. While employment has become much more complex than in previous periods as a result of the acceleration of globalization, one key institutional fact redefining the contemporary condition has been the rapid decline of lifetime employment.

The theory of new individualism has, in recent years, become increasingly influential in contemporary sociology and social theory. In particular, the thesis of new individualism has been utilized in sociologies of the self and sexuality studies – deployed by a range of sociologists from Jeffrey Weeks to Stephanie Lawler. The notion of new individualism has also been commended in sociological circles for extending the study of emotions into the realm of globalization. New individualist theory has also been prominent in recent discussions of the self in film and cinema studies, American studies, political theory, and cultural studies. In retrieving what individualization theory pushed to the margins – namely, the emotional costs of globalization – the theory of new individualism has been applauded by many critics for underscoring the significance of the emotions, affects and desires in contemporary redraftings of the self. Even so, the new individualism thesis has also been criticized for a range of reasons – among others, for sidelining counter-trends to speed and seductive sexualities at the level of self-reinvention.

Life on the move: Elliott and Urry

In *Mobile Lives* (2010), Anthony Elliott and John Urry investigate what it means to live a 'mobile life' at the start of the twenty-first century. Their research contributes to the growing field of study which probes what is unique about the contemporary social world through the prism of 'mobilities.' Elliott and Urry's main goal is to demonstrate that the development of various mobility systems has bearing on the way in which the self is constituted and transformed. By conducting analysis of mobilities at this more intimate and personal level, the authors avoid depicting mobility as an 'out there' phenomenon, far removed from the individual – an approach that recalls Anthony Giddens's view of globalization (1999: 12).

In order to grasp how complex mobility processes profoundly structure – and are restructured by – people's ordinary lives, Elliott and Urry put forth a number of interrelated propositions. First, an individual's engagement with hugely complex, contested mobility systems (from automobilities to aeromobilities) is not simply about the 'use' of particular forms of movement. Rather, the rise of an intensively mobile society reshapes the self – its everyday activities, interpersonal relations with others, as well as connections with the wider world. In this age of advanced globalization, we witness portable personhood. Identity becomes not merely 'bent' towards novel forms of transportation and travel, but fundamentally recast in terms of capacities for movement. Put another way, the globalization of mobility extends into the core of the self. Mobility of the self is an increasingly prized asset in the global electronic economy. Immobility of self, by contrast, comes to represent a kind of symbolic death.

Second, the trend towards individualized mobility routinely implicates personal life in a complex web of social, cultural and economic networks that can span the globe, or at least certain nodes across parts of the globe. Elliott and Urry can find a starting point for this phenomenon in the familiar experience that people have of finding 'connections' in common, either professionally or personally. This is the 'small world thesis,' the idea that people's networks do in fact overlap through a short chain of acquaintances. As many business analysts have pointed out, networking practices are central to organizational redefinitions of the self. In our own time of the Internet, digital media and wireless communications, however, there has been a further 'shrinkage' of the degrees of separation of the world's population. On this view, the self is continually redefined and reorganized through globally connected networks of information and communication.

Third, life 'on the move' is the kind of life in which the capacity to be 'elsewhere,' at a different time from others, is central. Due to the trans-national spread of various fast 'mobility systems' (from the car system to air travel, from networked computers to mobile phones), people seem to define aspects of their self-identity, as well as schedules of self and life strategies, through reference to de-synchronized, post-traditional or 'de-traditionalized' social settings, where such schedules are rarely shared. Such mobile lives demand flexibility, adaptability, reflexivity – to be ready for the unexpected, to embrace novelty, as even one's signifi-cant others are doing different things and at different times. Such mobile lives are based on forms of self-choosing, among and between options. If self-choosing is central to the rise of mobile lives, however, there are many millions of others for whom mobility is enforced: refugees, asylum seekers and the veritable explosion of forced migrants in the twenty-first century arising from regional and transnational political conflicts.

Fourth, the onset of new mobilities opens up enticing opportunities, as well as unsettling challenges. On the one hand, access to some mobile technologies and systems allows people to move from place to place, network to network, in ways not previously possible. But, on the other hand, this movement may involve the uncertainties of delayed and unpredictable journeys and the regular separation from family and neighbors. There are of course various virtual mobilities (mobile telephony, email and so on) to repair the journeys or to keep in touch; but these are only so good as long as they work, which quite often they do not.

Fifth, mobile lives are marked by a certain amount of social division, as mobilities typically presuppose the immobilization of some lifestyles. For every jet-setting professional, for example, there are also baggage handlers, check-in clerks, aircraft and hotel room cleaners, and transit security officers. The movement of some, in other words, is facilitated by the 'immobilization' of others. Mobile lives are, in other words, intricately interwoven with regimes of immobilization.

Sixth, the self is today increasingly implicated in and generated through the deployment of what Elliott and Urry have termed miniaturized mobilities – mobile phones, laptop computers, wireless connections. The concept of miniaturized mobilities seeks to capture both essential elements of communications 'on the move' and, specifically, how digital technologies are corporeally interwoven with self in the production of mobile lives. Miniaturized systems, often carried directly on the body and thus increasingly central to the organization of self, are software-based and serve to inform various aspects of the self's communication with itself, others and the wider world. Techno-systems such as electronic address books, hand-held iPhoto libraries, iTunes music collections and digital video libraries usher in worlds that are information-rich, of considerable sensory and auditory complexity, and easily transportable.

Seventh, Elliott and Urry present a picture of 'miniaturized mobilities' that departs from the conventional view that people mainly use such information technologies to transmit information from sender to receiver – the communications model of 'inputs' and 'outputs.' The social impact of these mobile technologies can only be fully grasped if we can recognize how the use of various miniaturized mobilities involves trans-formations in self-experience. When people use miniaturized mobile devices, communication is not only cognitive; it also occurs on an emotional plane, and people store and retrieve affects, moods and dispositions in these very objects. This storage and retrieval of affects and emotions is what generates new modes of identity that are less tied to fixed localities, regular patterns or dwelt-in cultural traditions.

Finally, it is argued that there are traces associated with living a life 'on the move.' These traces are often deposited in space and time when one traverses across a mobility system like the air system or the Internet. These traces can, in principle, be retrieved for review or regulation or disciplining at a moment's notice, as there is a range of institutions that routinely gather and report information about the self in movement. Thus, for a life 'on the move,' privacy may be increasingly difficult to come by. The mobile self is thus bound up with various regimes of surveillance and securitization.

Through these eight propositions, Urry and Elliott have sought to demonstrate how people's lives are being reorganized as selves of mobility. From this vantage point, mobility is not only central to the ongoing effort of social scientists to understand the social world – its institutions, processes and socialities – but also to the daunting task of engaging with the texture and composition of people's everyday lives.

Summary points

1 Globalization refers to the chronic intensification of patterns of interconnectedness (economic, technological, organizational, administrative, among others) generating transnational or interregional flows of activity and networks of interaction.
2 Globalization impacts on all aspects of current social life, from the rise of multinational companies to global warming.
3 Some critics equate globalization with Americanization or Westernization. Others focus on the historical dimensions of globalization, tracing its conditions to the 'age of discovery.'
4 There are three core social theories of globalization. *Global skeptics* question an overall shift towards world integration. *Radical globalists* see globalization as heralding new forms of social life based on free trade and open markets. *Global transformationalists* see less the dawning of an entirely new age than a transformation of previous structures.
5 In Castells's approach, networks are open structures, defined as center-less and as decentering established forms of power. In the new network society, power is transformed as diffuse, shifting and spatially fluid.

6　Today's world of global interconnectedness permeated by supra-national, intergovernmental and transnational forces gives rise to novel possibilities for the spread of cosmopolitanism and global governance.

7　Global networks are also intricately interwoven with the emergence of new political threats and risks, such as hi-tech terrorism. Some critics view transnational terror networks – such as Al-Qaeda – as threatening the fabric of the world as we know it.

8　In Beck's social theory, the contention is that humanity faces risks of a global scale and magnitude that previous generations have never faced. Risk today threatens devastating global consequences (for instance, ecological catastrophe or nuclear disaster) which cannot be limited in time and space and in which notions of individual or organizational accountability collapse.

9　The routine corporate downsizing, and associated job insecurity, associated with the global electronic economy has profound conse-quences for people's working lives. Globalization, in the view of sociologist Richard Sennett, is producing a 'corrosion of character.'

10　There is much sociological debate over the consequences of global-ization as regards culture and everyday life. Some critics equate globalization with the erosion of national culture. Such new patterns of social uniformity are the result of *global cultural imperi-alism*. But other critics doubt that globalization produces any single, one consequence. There is considerable sociological evidence which demonstrates, on the contrary, that global media are producing 'hybrid cultures' and pluralized social identities.

11　Globalization is said to be tied to the emergence of new forms of individualism. The *new individualism* is fixated on instant change and short-term living.

Further questions

1　To what extent is the world globalized? Is the 'global turn' merely partial to the West, or is it now wall-to-wall across all societies?

2　It is easy to grasp the economic forces of globalization, but harder to understand the globalization of culture and personal life. Discuss.

3　When did globalization arise?

4   How does globalization give rise to new job insecurities?

5   Given today's global risks, what are your own ways of coping?
     How do these coping mechanisms fit with the wider society?

Further reading

Ulrich Beck

Risk Society: Towards a New Modernity (London: Sage, 1992)
The Reinvention of Politics (Cambridge: Polity, 1997)
Democracy and Its Enemies (Cambridge: Polity, 1998)

Manuel Castells

The Rise of the Network Society, The Information Age: Economy, Society and Culture, Vol. I. (Cambridge, MA; Oxford, UK: Blackwell, 1996, 2000, 2nd edition)
'Communication, Power and Counter-power in the Network Society' (*International Journal of Communication* 1, 2007: pages 238–66)

David Held et al.

Global Transformations (Cambridge: Polity Press, 1999)

Anthony Giddens

Runaway World: How Globalization is Reshaping Our Lives (London: Profile Books, 2002)

Robert Holton

Global Networks (London: Palgrave, 2008)

Afterword: Social Theory Today and Towards 2025

From Giorgio Agamben to Manuel DeLanda

In the course of this book we have critically considered a number of key perspectives in contemporary social theory. From the Frankfurt School to globalization theories, we have looked at the profound troubles arising from the whole language and culture of modernity. Social theory, we have seen, is vitally engaged with the repression, oppression and indignity of unequal social relations: it is a deeply political, sometimes melancholic, but profoundly humane critique of the structural forces which underlay the self-destructive pathologies of contemporary societies. Indeed, so serious is the damage done to human life today that much social theory insists it is only by confronting the worst and most painful aspects of current global realities that we might hope to develop plausible alternative social and institutional possibilities. Hence the surprising innovations of recent years – post-feminist, queer, postmodern, risk and liquidity theories – which address anew why modernity leaves so large a number of the world's population unsatisfied, displaced and outcast.

When social theory does the excavating work of digging behind cultural illusions, it engages most directly with the public sphere and the whole issue of the future direction of political society. Yet some critics claim that social theory is merely obscurantist jargon. The criticism, in brief, is that social theory inserts arid abstractions which have little to do with the concrete realities of politics. Still more, the charge is made that social theory is near powerless in changing how we think about politics and social things.

Against the backdrop of such criticism, let us in conclusion briefly consider some recent public interventions by social theorists – both for what they have to tell us about the political nature of social theory and also its capacity to impact upon our worlds. In a series of articles over recent years, published in the Opinion columns of such newspapers as *International Herald Tribune* and *The Guardian*, Anthony Giddens has addressed the massive disconnect between the high-consequence risks of globalization on the one hand, and the lifestyle changes necessary to combat these worldwide risks on the other. He has argued, in a provocative and polemical fashion, that the big issues of our time do not reduce to traditional divisions in politics between left and right. From climate change, to energy security, to coping with international crime, today's major political problems transcend nation-state boundaries, as well as traditional national categories of thought used for so many years to frame nation-state politics. The core changes arising from the global electronic economy help to create, says Giddens, a new agenda for politics – at least in terms of policy thinking. The political challenge today – on global economic crises, transnational terrorism, global warming – is for nations to find new ways of working together, cooperating through transnational forums and processes and inter-governmentalism to develop novel models of 'global governance.' This is, in effect, the quantum leap for politics in the early twenty-first century: shifting from nation-state politics to globally cosmopolitan politics.

Giddens's call for a more cosmopolitan approach to politics in our age of globalization is born partly out of his social theory of reflexivity and structuration – discussed in detail in Chapter 9. This, to be sure, is not necessarily easy to spot or to substantiate. In the large bulk of his newspaper articles, for example, Giddens does not use the more difficult social-theoretical terminology of 'structuration,' 'time-space distantiation' or 'reflexivity.' To the extent that he shies away from such specialist discourse, his political interventions might be likened to, say, a pediatrician or computer scientist commenting in plain language on some aspect of their research competence. There is thus something of a divide between the conceptual analysis informing Giddens's recent political contributions and his media framing of them. But the point is that social theory is at the core of this analysis, at least for anyone who cares to look. Giddens's arguments in favor of 'positive welfare,' for instance, derive from his social theory – which holds that globalization ushers into existence an increasingly reflexive citizenry. In the shift to post-traditional or post-industrial society, the old social stratification has gradually been replaced by a new pattern of 'individualization' – where people are much more involved in the self-design of their lifestyles. This necessitates for Giddens a transformation from the traditional welfare state of support and dependency to novel forms of enabling welfare.

It is one thing to write opinion articles, and yet another to actually influence the shape of contemporary politics. But it is just that which Giddens has done, giving the slip in the process to the charge that social theory is removed from concrete politics. For Giddens, as noted in Chapter 9, developed the notion of 'the third way' in political thinking, first as an advisor to UK Prime Minister Tony Blair (where he also played a role in Blair's dialogues with US President Bill Clinton from 1997 onwards), and second as a member of the House of Lords in the British Parliament. The level at which Giddens has moved in British political circles clearly represents an extraordinary contribution to civic and public life. But the power of Giddens's social and political theory does not end there, as both his account of 'third way' politics as well as his broader social theory penetrates well beyond the UK and US to encompass Europe, Asia, Latin America and Australia. At work on projects as diverse as the future of the European social model on the one hand, and the obesity epidemic and associated lifestyle issues on the other, Giddens has become the most sought-after social theorist – by political leaders, think-tanks and universities – in the world today.

Compare Giddens's political interventions as a social theorist with those of Manuel Castells. In 2008, Castells appeared as part of the 'Big Thinker' lecture series sponsored by Yahoo! Research. Acknowledging that for too long social theory had sidelined the social implications of communications technology, Castells reappraised the relationship between society and the Internet. Social theory may have been silent on the socially beneficial aspects of new information technologies, but so at the same time had been nearly everyone. The media was especially to blame in this connection. 'Media sensationalism,' argued Castells (2008), 'is responsible because it always picks up on bad news.' Yet there are many ways in which the Internet extends and reshapes social relations, and Castells is particularly attentive to how such technology might be harnessed to create a more autonomous society. 'The Internet,' says Castells, 'does not isolate users, nor does it depress or alienate. The more you use the Internet, the more social you are offline. The Internet adds, rather than subtracts, sociability.' Elsewhere, Castells details statistics on blogs and the Internet thus: of the 60 million blogs worldwide, one is created every second and 55 percent of new bloggers remain active after two months of Internet use. Whilst only 9 percent of blogs are directly political in scope, Castells points out 'still, that's a lot of blogging.' In the end, says Castells, the Internet in general increases political interests and activities.

But, as it happens, there is no need to rehearse the exceptional contributions of Giddens and Castells as somehow unique in terms of the import of social theory for public political debate. In fact, the bulk of luminary social theorists reviewed in the course of this book have not only contributed to the public sphere and politics, but have found ways of extending and enriching it. The pioneering contributions of Herbert Marcuse, Theodor Adorno, Roland Barthes, Michel Foucault and Jacques Derrida have been of lasting value to debates on both repression and freedom in contemporary politics. Jürgen Habermas, Zygmunt Bauman, Ulrich Beck, Judith Butler, Slavoj Žižek, Fredric Jameson, Homi Bhabha, Julia Kristeva: these too are social theorists who have spent their lives not only studying the social world and its struggles, but as politically engaged public intellectuals. Their contribution has been, among other things, an engagement with fundamental questions about power, domination, repression, identity, sexuality and intimacy in contemporary social processes. And it has been through consideration of these matters – in outlining social theories which are, admittedly, sometimes dense or difficult, but for the most part arrestingly original – that these authors have had a great deal to say about contemporary politics, culture and society.

There remain some key questions which as yet have not been raised. What is the future of social theory? Do recent developments in society, culture and politics give us any indication of where social theory might be headed over, say, the next five to ten years? And will social theory continue to promote the general good of society? Will social theory still engage sizeable publics in 2025? These questions cannot be answered in a simple fashion, partly given the complexity of social theory as an interdisciplinary enterprise and partly because social theory is not really in the business of seeking to predict the future. Yet there is another reason, too, why it is not easy to speculate about the future of social theory. The review of contemporary developments in social theory provided in the course of this book suggests that the prevailing violence, risks and dangers facing the planet are coming closer and closer to crashing the established social structures of modern life. This is perhaps but another way of saying we may be facing the end of the world as we know it – although whether new, more dynamic types of societies and spaces are likely to emerge remains, as some post-structuralists are fond of saying, 'undecidable.' But what surely is self-evident – at the levels of both professional and practical social theory – concerns those radical transformations in social institutions with which intellectuals, political activists and policy makers, as well as ordinary people, have long traded. I refer to core transformations in the very institutional units of society, from identity and sexuality, to the family and work, to the nation and politics. These institutional units are both eroding and recombining right before our eyes in these early years of the twenty-first century, and in the remainder of what follows I want to briefly examine some of the more interesting attempts in social theory to develop, if not exactly the answers, at least some interesting sounding questions about our possible global futures.

Contemporary social theory, I have suggested, began with the German school of Frankfurt critique. In the works of Adorno, Marcuse and Fromm, there was a powerful attempt to understand the pain of those who suffered under Hitler – as well as the wider society living under conditions of 'the administered society' – in both emotional and historical terms. Social theory following the Frankfurt School, right through to the present-day, has continued to be shaped by forms of political and ideological turmoil occurring in contemporary societies. In more recent social theory, for example, Zygmunt Bauman has also discussed political themes like violence, suffering and death, and how they apply to our increasingly global world. For Bauman, the killing of six million Jewish people by the Nazis cannot be explained as a simple reversion from civilized modernity to pre-Enlightenment barbarism. The Holocaust, says Bauman, could only happen because of modernity's twin combination of bureaucracy and technology. Along with gas chambers and other modern technologies facilitating mass murder, the hold of bureaucratic rationality in Hitler's Germany created the social conditions in which moral responsibility evaporated. Similarly the keynote to life lived in today's so-called global cosmopolitan society, at least according to several leading European social theorists, remains that of the *concentration camp*. In the relatively short historical march from Auschwitz to Guantanamo Bay, says the Italian social theorist Giorgio Agamben, a 'state of emergency' has been turned into the norm for constitutional political power in Western democracies. Whilst legal systems may make provisions for intermissions of various kinds, there is a wider change of governance across the world – or so Agamben argues – in which the rule of law is routinely displaced by the 'state of exception,' understood as the platform through which extra-judicial state violence is inflicted upon citizens.

Agamben understands the political emergence of permanent states of exception largely in terms of Foucault's critique of biopolitics, of which the United States response under the Bush presidency to the terror attacks of 11 September 2001 is surely a signal example. The political irony of post-9/11 biopower politics, for a critic such as Agamben, is that the state of emergency that was the 'war on terror' was meant to protect the general population from terrorism – whereas it resulted, arguably, in a weakening of the freedoms of democratic society. What Agamben calls 'bare life' is precisely an attempt to think through the violence, degradation and suffering of extra-judicial violence inflicted upon the bodies of individuals today, from camp inmates to terror hostages. Agamben's 'bare life,' in the words of Malcolm Bull, 'provides the perfect metaphor for the naked and humiliated prisoners on Abu Ghraib' – the notorious prison in postwar Iraq, where U.S. soldiers brutalized Iraqi prisoners.

One newly emerging task of social theory, broadly conceived, consists in the dissection of the political conditions under which the planet is shared – probing the structured violence underpinning mass death, diseases and malnutrition, and ever-rising levels of poverty. From this vantage point, over half the world's population might be said to live the hell of 'bare life.' As David Held summarizes one of the most pressing global issues of our times,

> [e]ach year some 18 million die prematurely from poverty-related causes. This is one third of all human deaths – 50,000 every day, including 29,000 children under the age of five. And, yet, the gap between rich and poor countries continues to rise and there is evidence that the bottom 10% of the world's population has become even poorer since the beginning of the 1990s.
>
> (2008)

Held's summary of the global challenges to be faced reflects not only the extensive and intensive reach of 'bare life' today, but perhaps also the possibility that such a truly shocking reality might just one day erupt unpredictably on the political scene, transforming the very structured violence which maintains modernity's self-destructiveness. Any such possible eruption is what the leading French philosopher Alain Badiou (2007) calls an 'Event,' some exceptional break with the status quo or political consensus. According to Badiou, whose work has influenced Agamben, an Event can erupt on the edges of the very coordinates of social reality, at that point or void where meaning threatens to dissolve into non-meaning. As a result, new truths can be expanded, to the extent that individuals and groups are genuinely committed to the radical implications of such an Event. There is, no doubt, a good deal of French philosophical idealism about this notion, but it is worth noting that Badiou's thinking has inspired various new directions in social theory for confronting some of the most pressing global issues of our times.

If Badiou's work has pursued the philosophical possibilities for the break up, symbolic ruin and broader transformation of received political meanings, other social theorists have been concerned to map the restructuring of the very coordinates of social reality. Whilst the motive driving society has been interpreted by Marxists and post-Marxists as economic or materialist, and by Freudians and Lacanians as unconscious or affective, there is an emerging consensus that today's social coordinates are being rewritten around the politics of survival itself. In *High Noon: Twenty Global Problems, Twenty Years to Solve Them* (2002), Jean-François Rischard sets out core global challenges ranging from water and energy deficits to global warming, from toxic waste disposal to nuclear proliferation of weapons of mass destruction. But given the complexity of global social processes, it is far from settled or secure whether it is still possible to speak of a 'we' for confronting the variety of political challenges faced today. In *The Sense of The World* (1997), Jean-Luc Nancy reflects on what it means to say we live in 'the world.' Worlds, rather than world, is for Nancy a better way to grasp our 'being-with' others – including all the others separated from us in space and in time that we are unlikely to ever meet, but to whom we have a 'radical responsibility.' What Nancy calls 'naked existence' represents our increasing exposure today to a post-traditional world – one in which the meaning and destination of life is far from fixed or pre-determined. The global challenge, according to Nancy, is living within a plurality of worlds without guarantees. The challenge lies in embracing human contingency.

We have seen that a particular version of post-structuralism, sometimes transmuted as postmodernism, was the essential relay by which the whole notion of contingency entered the terrain of radical politics in the late 1980s and throughout the 1990s. In our own time, there has been a further inflation of the value of the 'contingent' in radical social theory. In a number of works bridging complexity theory with Deleuzian philosophy, Manuel DeLanda firmly rejects the kind of determinism of classical physics – which rendered the past as given and treated the future as preset – and instead faces head-on the radical implications for society of indeterminacy, multidirectionality and the 'politics of becoming.' In *New Philosophy of Society* (2006), DeLanda considers the disabling gap between subject and object, between past and future, pointing out that there is in fact no given order in social reality at all. Behind this Nietzschean approach to theorizing social space and time lies DeLanda's attempt to conceptualize history without a determinate beginning or end. Speaking up for the contingent, the indeterminate and ambivalent, DeLanda is out to capture multiple times, plural spaces and divergent social possibilities. Such a heady decentering of causality has a certain undeniable euphoric quality, in the sense that there may be nothing more life-affirming than to say 'we can become whoever we wish to be.' (This may be the point to note that, whilst born in Mexico, DeLanda now resides in the United States.) But if this can-do philosophy is uplifting at the level of considering possible alternative worlds, it may be less than useful for grasping why my credit card statement arrives at the beginning of every month without fail or why the rent is due at the month's end. In other words, this is a social theory that makes more of the world's future possibilities than adequately theorizing much of the social control exerted over cultural affairs that we take for granted.

Whatever we might make of these political limitations, DeLanda is much preoccupied with *creation*, but refers this issue to certain frames of reference derived from biology and 'matter.' What DeLanda calls 'morphogenesis' refers to particular states of 'becoming' (both at the levels of identity and society) which are organized intensively – involving differentiation, profusion, excess. The creativity of society for DeLanda is plastic, the future is radically open-ended, and the shaping of self and society involves a shaping of plural temporalities and spaces and a multiplicity of values. A similar sense of the unpredictable, but nonetheless ordered or contained, emerges as central to complexity theory dealing with the intricate interrelations between the physical and the social worlds (see, for example, Fritjof Capra's *The Web of Life*, 1996).

The notion of 'creation' suggests, finally, the writings of the late European social theorist Cornelius Castoriadis. Whilst I have not introduced the work of Castoriadis in previous chapters, there is a sense in which much of the argument of this book would not be possible without his contribution. For what has come about with the later development of global capitalism, so Castoriadis argues, is a progressive hollowing out of the radical imagination of individuals, social relations and the resources of cultural tradition. Such radical imagination, bound up as it is with selfhood and the Freudian unconscious, lies at the core of *human creation* in the strongest sense of the term. It is this creative dimension of both identity and society to which the large bulk of Castoriadis's writings is devoted. What he wishes to capture for social theory is the creation of an imaginary which is radically new, multidimensional and invented, literally, out of thin air. In the broadest sense of the term, he writes of imagination as an unconscious eruption, of creation *ex nihilo* – meaning 'out of nothing.' The flip side of such imaginative creativity is the personal and emotional straightjackets resulting from a socio-cultural system based on bureaucratic know-how and capitalistic greed – both of which enfeeble the depth and power of human creativity.

In *The Imaginary Institution of Society* (1987), Castoriadis argues that the creativity of the psyche is a site of multiple, fractured and contradictory *representations* of the individual in relation to self, to other people and to society and history. He argues that the psyche is continually elaborating representations, fantasies, affects; as the flow of representations are produced, so new positionings of self and other are defined, which in turn leads to newer forms of fantasy, identification and cultural process. There is, for Castoriadis, a delicious indeterminacy at the heart of the Freudian unconscious, such that the regulative hierarchies of self, sexuality, gender and power are constantly rearranged and sometimes transformed, at least partially as a consequence of this ceaseless psychic flux.

At its simplest, Castoriadis's emphasis on the creative nature of the imagination underscores the permutation of fantasies and identifications that selves produce endlessly in relation to society and history. We insert ourselves, through the psychic flux of imagination, at one and the same moment as both creator and created, self and other, identity and difference; we draw on existing social institutions and cultural conventions to produce new images of self and society, which in turn feed back into the cycle of representations. In all this, Castoriadis's central theme is creativity – of the individual self and the broader society. Underlining creativity, his theoretical position is a far cry from the insipid, commercially constructed notion of the 'ever-new' in popular culture. What distinguishes his position from popular understandings of creativity is his stress on the open-ended and ambivalent nature of psychic representation and cultural production, and it is this stress which necessarily involves reflecting on the more distressing aspects of violence, aggression and destruction in contemporary culture. 'Creation,' writes Castoriadis (1991: 3–4), 'does not necessarily – nor even generally – signify "good" creation or the creation of "positive values." Auschwitz and the Gulag are creations just as much as the Parthenon and the *Principia Mathematica*.' It is hard – says Castoriadis – to grasp, and harder to understand, that socio-political paths or fields of imagination stretch all the way from progressive politics to fanaticism and fascism. But the search for alternative futures, and the search for autonomy and justice, are both among the creations in Western history that people value highly and judge positively; the practice of critique, of putting things into question, forms a common starting point for a radical challenge to received social and political meanings.

Agamben, Badiou, Nancy, DeLanda, Castoriadis: these are just some of the ground-breaking social theorists of recent years. Will their originality and political ambitiousness be discussed and debated in 2025? Possibly. But the point is that no one can say with any degree of confidence what the future for social theory holds. Social theories derive from the serious attempts of women and men to make sense out of the unthinkable social things that harm, constrain, repress or damage life; social theories are of value when they most directly engage, and seek to transform, the political and ideological turmoil out of which they were born, and in the process offer alternative visions of how our personal and social lives could be lived otherwise. In terms of the important writers I have been discussing, it is clear that the themes of human creation, imagination, our 'being-with' others, and the question of autonomy present social theory with fresh challenges. In other words, what social theory requires are multi-perspectival approaches through which it can at once critique the failure of human life to flourish under specific social conditions on the one hand, and defend human needs and desires for alternative forms of life concerned with pleasure, creativity and autonomy on the other. Undeniably, the global challenges we face demand global solutions, and ones that are both future-regarding and geared to the actual needs and desires of others.

Further reading

On the political contribution and impact of social theorists, any regular glance at good quality broadsheets should reveal a great deal. As discussed in this Afterword, current social theorists contributing on a regular basis to the media include Anthony Giddens, Ulrich Beck, Jürgen Habermas, Manuel Castells, Slavoj Žižek, David Held, Julia Kristeva, and many others.

For Giddens's recent contributions, see his article 'This Time It's Personal,' *The Guardian*, 2 January 2008. The Castells lecture to Yahoo! Research is available at www.research.yahoo.com/node/2189

The best place to start reading Agamben is *State of Exception*, Chicago University Press, 2005. Also see Giorgio Agamben, *Homo Sacer: Sovereign Power and Bare Life*, Stanford University Press, 1998. For starting Alain Badiou, see his *Being and Event*, London: Continuum, 2007. For Jean-Luc Nancy, see his collection *Corpus*, London: Continuum, 2008. For Manuel DeLanda, try *A Thousand Years of Nonlinear History*, Zone Books, 2000. And for Cornelius Castoriadis, read his classic *The Imaginary Institution of Society*, Cambridge: Polity Press, 1987.

References

Addams, J. (2002) 'A Modern Lear,' in Elshtain, J. B. (editor) *The Jane Addams Reader*, New York: Basic Books.

Adorno, T. (1950) *The Authoritarian Personality*, New York: Harper.

Adorno, T. (1973) *Negative Dialectics*, London: Routledge.

Adorno, T. (1974) *Minima Moralia: Reflections from Damaged Life*, London: New Left Books.

Adorno, T. (1991 [1951]) 'Freudian Theory and the Pattern of Fascist Propaganda,' in Bernstein, J. M. (editor) *The Culture Industry: Selected Essays on Mass Culture*. London: Routledge.

Adorno, T. (1994) *The Stars Down to Earth: And Other Essays on the Irrational Culture*, London: Routledge.

Adorno, T. (2001) *The Culture Industry*, London: Routledge.

Agamben, G. (1998) *Homo Sacer: Sovereign Power and Bare Life*, Stanford: Stanford University Press.

Agamben, G. (2005) *State of Exception*, Chicago (IL): University of Chicago Press.

Alexander, J. C. (1982) *Theoretical Logic in Sociology*, California: University of California Press.

Alexander, J. C. (1996) 'Critical Reflections on "Reflexive Modernization",' *Theory, Culture and Society*, Vol. 13, No. 4, pp. 133–8.

Alexander, J. C. (1998) *Neofunctionalism and After*, Malden, MA: Blackwell Publishers.

Alexander, J. C. (2006) *The Civil Sphere*, New York: Oxford University Press.

Alexander, J. C. (2010) 'The "Marxism Project" in The History of Its Times,' *Thesis Eleven*, Vol. 100, No. 81, pp. 81–83.

Alexander, J. C. (2011a) *Performative Revolution in Egypt: An Essay in Cultural Power*, New York: Bloomsbury Publishing.

Alexander, J. C. (2011b) *Performance and Power*, Cambridge, UK: Polity Press.

Alexander, J. C. and Smith, P. (2003) 'The Strong Program in Cultural Sociology,' *The Meanings of Social Life: A Cultural Sociology*, New York: Oxford University Press.

Althusser, L. (1971) 'Ideology and Ideological State Apparatuses,' *Lenin and Philosophy and Other Essays*. London: New Left Books.

Anderson, P. (1998) *The Origins of Postmodernity*, London: Verso Press.

Arato, A. and Gebhardt, E. (editors) (1985) *Essential Frankfurt School Reader*, New York, Continuum.

Archer, M. (1982) 'Morphogenesis Versus Structuration: On Combining Structure and Action', *The British Journal of Sociology*, Vol. 33, No. 4, pp. 455–83.

Archer, M. (1990) 'Human Agency and Social Structure: A Critique of Giddens,' in Clark, J., Modgil, C. and Modgil, S. (editors) *Anthony Giddens: Consensus & Controversy*. London: Falmer Press.

Badoiu, A. (2007) *Being and Event*, London: Continuum.

Barber, B. (1996) *Jihad vs. McWorld*, New York.

Barthes, R. (1967 [1964]) *Elements of Semiology*, London: J. Cape.

Barthes, R. (1972 [1957]) *Mythologies*, London: J. Cape.

Barthes, R. (1983 [1967]) *The Fashion System*, New York: Hill and Wang.

Baudrillard, J. (1975 [1973]) *The Mirror of Production*, St. Louis (MO): Telos Press.

Baudrillard, J. (1981 [1972]) *For a Critique of the Political Economy of the Sign*, St. Louis (MO): Telos Press.

Baudrillard, J. (1988) *America*, London: Verso.

Baudrillard, J. (1990a) *Fatal Strategies*, New York: Semiotext(e).

Baudrillard, J. (1990b) *Seduction*, Basingstoke: Macmillan Education.

Baudrillard, J. (1994 [1981]) *Simulacra and Simulation*, Ann Arbor (MI): University of Michigan Press.

Baudrillard, J. (1995) *The Gulf War Did Not Take Place*, Sydney: Power Publications.

Baudrillard, J. (1996 [1968]) *The System of Objects*, New York: Verso Press.

Baudrillard, J. (1998 [1972]) *The Consumer Society: Myths and Structures*, London: Sage Publications.

Baudry, J.-L. (1970) 'The Ideological Effects of the Cinematographic Apparatus,' in Rosen, P. (editor) *Narrative, Apparatus, Ideology: A Film Reader*. New York: Columbia University Press.

Bauman, Z. (1972) *Between Class and Elite*, Manchester: Manchester University Press.

Bauman, Z. (1973) *Culture as Praxis*, London: Routledge.

Bauman, Z. (1976) *Socialism: The Active Utopia*, London: Allen & Unwin.

Bauman, Z. (1982) *Memories of Class*, London: Routledge.

Bauman, Z. (1987) *Legislators and Interpreters: On Modernity, Post-modernity, and Intellectuals*, Ithaca (NY): Cornell University Press.

Bauman, Z. (1989) *Modernity and the Holocaust*, Cambridge: Polity Press.

Bauman, Z. (1991) *Modernity and Ambivalence*, Ithaca (NY): Cornell University Press.

Bauman, Z. (1993) *Postmodern Ethics*, Oxford: Blackwell.

Bauman, Z. (1995) *Life in Fragments: Essays in Postmodern Morality*, Oxford: Blackwell.

Bauman, Z. (1997) *Postmodernity and Its Discontents*, Cambridge: Polity Press.

Bauman, Z. (2000) *Liquid Modernity*, Cambridge: Polity Press.

Bauman, Z. (2001) *The Individualized Society*, Cambridge: Polity Press.

Bauman, Z. (2002) *Society Under Siege*, Cambridge: Polity Press.

Bauman, Z. (2003) *Liquid Love: On the Frailty of Human Bonds*, Cambridge: Polity Press.

Bauman, Z. (2004) *Wasted Lives: Modernity and Its Outcasts*, Oxford: Polity Press.

Bauman, Z. (2005) *Liquid Life*, Cambridge: Polity Press.

Bauman, Z. (2011) *Collateral Damage: Social Inequalities in a Global Age*, Cambridge: Polity Press.

Bauman, Z. and Vecchi, B. (2004) *Identity: Conversations with Benedetto Vecchi*, Cambridge: Polity Press.

Bauman, Z., Cantell, T. and Pederson, P. P. (2001) 'The Telos Interview,' in Beilharz, P. (editor) *The Bauman Reader*. Oxford: Blackwell.

Beauvoir, S. de (1988 [1949]) *The Second Sex*, London: Picador Classics.

Beck, U. (1991) *Ecological Enlightenment: Essays on the Politics of the Risk Society*, Amherst (NY): Prometheus Books.

Beck, U. (1992) *Risk Society: Towards a New Modernity*, London: Sage Publishing.

Beck, U. (1997) *The Reinvention of Politics: Rethinking Modernity in the Global Social Order*, Cambridge: Polity Press.

Beck, U. (1998) *Democracy and Its Enemies*, Cambridge: Polity Press.

Beck, U., Giddens, A. and Lash, S. (1994) *Reflexive Modernization: Politics, Tradition and Aesthetics in the Modern Social Order*, Stanford: Stanford University Press.

Benjamin, J. (1988) *The Bonds of Love: Psychoanalysis, Feminism, and the Problem of Domination*, New York: Pantheon Books.

Benjamin, J. (1995) *Like Subjects, Love Objects: Essays on Recognition and Sexual Difference*, New Haven (CT): Yale University Press.

Benjamin, J. (1998) *Shadow of the Other: Intersubjectivity and Gender in Psychoanalysis*, New York: Routledge.

Benveniste, E. (1971) *Problems in General Linguistics*, Coral Gables (FL): University of Miami Press.

Berman, M. (1983) *All That is Solid Melts Into Air: The Experience of Modernity*, London: Verso.

Bhabha, H. (1994) *The Location of Culture*, London: Routledge.

Blumer, H. (1969) *Symbolic Interactionism: Perspective and Method*, New Jersey: Prentice-Hall Inc.

Bottomore, T. (1984) *The Frankfurt School*, New York: Tavistock.

Bourdieu, P. (1977 [1972]) *Outline of a Theory of Practice*, Cambridge: Cambridge University Press.

Bourdieu, P. (1984) *Distinction: A Social Critique of the Judgment of Taste*, London: Routledge & Kegan Paul.

Bourdieu, P. (1988 [1984]) *Homo Academicus*, Cambridge: Polity Press.

Bourdieu, P. (1990) *The Logic of Practice*, Stanford (CA): Stanford University Press.

Bourdieu, P. (1991) *Language and Symbolic Power*, Cambridge: Polity Press.

Bourdieu, P. (1993) *The Field of Cultural Production*, Cambridge: Polity Press.

Bourdieu, P. (1995) *The Rules of Art: Genesis and Structure of the Literary Field*, Stanford: Stanford University Press.

Bourdieu, P. (1996a) *On Television and Journalism*, London: Pluto Press.

Bourdieu, P. (1996b) *The State Nobility: Elite Schools in the Field of Power*, Cambridge: Polity Press.

Bourdieu, P. (2000) *Weight of the World: Social Suffering in Contemporary Society*, Stanford: Stanford University Press.

Bowie, M. (1991) *Lacan*, London: Fontana.

Branaman, A. (2000) *Self and Society*, Cambridge (MA): Blackwell.

Branaman, A. and Lemert, C. (editors) (1997) *The Goffman Reader*, Cambridge (MA), Blackwell.

Braun, D. (1991) *The Rich Get Richer*, Chicago (IL): Nelson Hall.

Butler, J. (1990) *Gender Trouble: Feminism and the Subversion of Identity*, London: Routledge.

Butler, J. (1993) *Bodies that Matter: On the Discursive Limits of Sex*, London: Routledge.

Butler, J. (1997) *The Psychic Life of Power: Theories in Subjection*, Stanford: Stanford University Press.

Capra, F. (1996) *The Web of Life: A New Synthesis of Mind and Matter*, London: HarperCollins.

Castells, M. (2000) *The Rise of the Network Society, The Information Age: Economy, Society and Culture*, Cambridge (MA): Blackwell.

Castells, M. (2007) 'Communication, Power and Counter-power in the Network Society,' *International Journal of Communication*, Vol. 1, No. 1, pp. 238–66.

Castoriadis, C. (1987) *The Imaginary Institution of Society*, Cambridge: Polity Press.

Castoriadis, C. (1991) *Philosophy, Politics, Autonomy*, New York: Oxford University Press.

Castoriadis, C. (1997a) 'Done and to be Done,' in Curtis, D. A. (editor) *The Castoriadis Reader*, Oxford: Blackwell.

Castoriadis, C. (1997b) *World in Fragments: Writings on Politics, Society, Psychoanalysis and the Imagination*, Stanford: Stanford University Press.

Chesneaux, J. (1992) *Brave Modern World: The Prospects for Survival*, London: Thames and Hudson.

Chodorow, N. (1978) *The Reproduction of Mothering*, Berkeley: University of California Press.

Chodorow, N. (1989) *Feminism and Psychoanalytic Theory*, London: Polity Press.

Chodorow, N. (1994) *Femininities, Masculinities, Sexualities: Freud and Beyond*, Lexington (KY): University Press of Kentucky.

Ciroucel, A. (1974) *Cognitive Sociology*, New York: Macmillan.

Clarke, S. and Moran, A. (2003) 'The Uncanny Stranger: Haunting the Australian Settler Imagination,' *Free Associations*, Vol. 10B, pp. 165–89.

Cohen, G. A. (1978) *Karl Marx's Theory of History: A Defence*, Princeton (NJ): Princeton University Press.

Cohen, S. (2001) *States of Denial: Knowing About Atrocities and Suffering*, Cambridge, UK: Polity Press.

Collins, P. H. (2012) 'Black Feminist Thought,' in Longhofer W. and Winchester D. (editors) *Social Theory Re-wired: New Connections to Classical and Contemporary Perspectives*, New York: Routledge, pp. 395–414.

Cooley, J. (1902) *Human Nature and the Social Order*, New York: C. Scribner's Sons.

Cossu, A. (2012) *It Ain't Me Babe: Bob Dylan and the Performance of Authenticity*, Boulder, CA: Paradigm Publishers.

Crompton, R. (1996) 'The Fragmentation of Class Analysis,' *The British Journal of Sociology*, Vol. 47, No. 1, pp. 56–67.

DeLanda, M. (2000) *A Thousand Years of Nonlinear History*, New York: Zone Books.

DeLanda, M. (2006) *A New Philosophy of Society: Assemblage Theory and Social Complexity*, London: Continuum.

Deleuze, G. and Guattari, F. (1983 [1977]) *Anti-Oedipus: Capitalism and Schizophrenia*, Minneapolis (MN): University of Minnesota Press.

Deleuze, G. and Guattari, F. (1987) *A Thousand Plateaus: Capitalism and Schizophrenia*, Minneapolis (MN): University of Minnesota Press.

Derrida, J. (1973) *Speech and Phenomena, and Other Essays on Husserl's Theory of Signs*, Evanston (IL): Northwestern University Press.

Derrida, J. (1976) *Of Grammatology*, Baltimore (MD): Johns Hopkins University Press.

Derrida, J. (1978) *Writing and Difference*, London: Routledge.

Derrida, J. (1981a [1972]) *Positions*, Chicago: University of Chicago Press.

Derrida, J. (1981b) *Dissemination*, London: Athlone Press.

Derrida, J. (1982) *Margins of Philosophy*, Brighton: Harvester Wheatsheaf.

Derrida, J. (1998) *Resistances of Psychoanalysis*, Stanford: Stanford University Press.

De Tocqueville, A. (1969) *Democracy in America*, Garden City: Doubleday Anchor.

Dewey, J. (1916) *Democracy and Education*, New York: The Macmillan Company.

Dinnerstein, D. (1976) *Mermaid and the Minotaur: Sexual Arrangements and Human Malaise*, New York: Harper & Row.

Douglas, M. (1986) *Risk Acceptability According to the Social Sciences*, London: Routledge.

Douglas, M. (1992) *Risk and Blame: Essays in Cultural Theory*, London: Routledge.

Du Gay, P. (2002) *In Praise of Bureacracy*, London: Sage Publishing.

Du Gay, P. and Hall, S. (editors) (1996) *Questions of Cultural Identity*, London, Sage Publishing.

Durkheim, E. (1965 [1912]) *The Elementary Forms of the Religious Life*, New York: The Free Press.

Eagleton, T. (1990) *The Ideology of the Aesthetic*, Cambridge: Basil Blackwell.

Eagleton, T. (1996) *The Illusions of Postmodernism*, Oxford: Blackwell.

Eagleton, T. (2003a) *After Theory*, London: Allen Lane.

Eagleton, T. (2003b) *Sweet Violence: The Idea of the Tragic*, Oxford: Blackwell.

Eagleton, T. (2008) *Literary Theory: An Introduction*, Minneapolis (MN): University of Minnesota Press.

Elliott, A. (1992) *Social Theory and Psychoanalysis in Transition: Self and Society from Freud to Kristeva*, Oxford: Blackwell.

Elliott, A. (2003) *Critical Visions: New Directions in Social Theory*, Oxford: Rowman & Littlefield.

Elliott, A. (2004) *Subject To Ourselves*, 2nd edition, Boulder (CO): Paradigm Publishers.

Elliott, A. (2007a) *Concepts of the Self*, 2nd edition, Cambridge: Polity Press.

Elliott, A. (2007b) 'The Theory of Liquid Modernity: A Critique of Bauman's Recent Sociology,' in Elliott, A. (editor) *The Contemporary Bauman*. London: Routledge.

Elliott, A. and Lemert, C. (2006) *The New Individualism: The Emotional Costs of Globalization*, London: Routledge.

Ewald, F. (1986) *L'Etat Providence*, Paris: B. Grasset.

Ewald, F. (1993) 'Two Infinities of Risk,' in Massumi, B. (editor) *The Politics of Everyday Fear*. Minneapolis: University of Minnesota Press.

Foucault, M. (1970 [1966]) *The Order of Things: An Archaeology of the Human Sciences*, London: Tavistock Publications.

Foucault, M. (1972 [1969]) *The Archaeology of Knowledge*, London: Tavistock Publications.

Foucault, M. (1973 [1963]) *The Birth of the Clinic: An Archaeology of Medical Perception*, London: Tavistock Publications.

Foucault, M. (1978) *The History of Sexuality*, London: Allen Lane.

Foucault, M. (1979) *Discipline and Punish: The Birth of the Prison*, New York: Vintage Books.

Foucault, M. (1980) 'Two Lectures,' in Gordin, C. (editor) *Power/Knowledge: Selected Interviews and Other Writings, 1972–1977*. New York: Pantheon Books.

Foucault, M. (1982) 'The Social Triumph of the Sexual Will,' *Christopher Street*, Vol. 64, May, pp. 36–41.

Foucault, M. (1985) *The Use of Pleasure: The History of Sexuality, Vol. II*, New York: Pantheon Books.

Foucault, M. (1986) *The Care of the Self: The History of Sexuality, Vol. III*, New York: Pantheon Books.

Foucault, M. (1988) 'Technologies of the Self,' in Martin, L. and Gutman, H. (editors) *Technologies of the Self: A Seminar with Michel Foucault*, Amherst (MA): University of Massachusetts Press.

Foucault, M. (1991) 'Governmentality,' in Burchell, G., Gordon, C. and Miller, P. (editors) *The Foucault Effect*, Chicago (IL): University of Chicago Press.

Fraser, N. (1985) 'What's Critical about Critical Theory? The Case of Habermas and Gender,' *New German Critique*, Vol. 35, pp. 97–131.

Fraser, N. (1989) *Unruly Practices: Power, Discourse and Gender in Contemporary Social Theory*, Minneapolis (MN): University of Minnesota Press.

Freud, S. (1961 [1900]) 'The Interpretation of Dreams,' in Strachey, J. (editor) *The Standard Edition of the Complete Psychological Works of Sigmund Freud, Vol. 4*. London: Hogarth Press.

Freud, S. (1973 [1930]) *Civilization and Its Discontents*, London: Hogarth Press.

Fromm, E. (1941) *Escape from Freedom*, New York: Farrar & Rinehart.

Fromm, E. (1955) *The Sane Society*, New York: Holt, Rinehart and Winston.

Fromm, E. (1957) *The Art of Loving*, London: Allen & Unwin.

Fromm, E. (1973) *The Anatomy of Human Destructiveness*, New York: Holt, Rinehart and Winston.

Fromm, E. (1985 [1932]) 'The Method and Function of an Analytical Social Psychology,' in Arato, A. and Gebhardt, E. (editors) *The Essential Frankfurt School Reader*, New York: Continuum.

Fuss, D. (1989) *Essentially Speaking: Feminism, Nature & Difference*, New York: Routledge.

Garfinkel, H. (1967) *Studies in Ethnomethodology*, Englewood Cliffs (NJ): Prentice-Hall.

Garton-Ash, T. (2004) *Free World: America, Europe, and the Surprising Future of the West*, New York: Random House.

Geertz, C. (1973a) 'Religion as a Cultural System,' *The Interpretation of Cultures*, New York: Basic Books.

Geertz, C. (1973b) 'Thick Description,' *The Interpretation of Cultures*, New York: Basic Books.

Giddens, A. (1971) *Capitalism and Modern Social Theory: An Analysis of the Writings of Marx, Weber and Durkheim*, Cambridge: Cambridge University Press.

Giddens, A. (1979) *Central Problems in Social Theory: Action, Structure, and Contradiction in Social Analysis*, London: Macmillan.

Giddens, A. (1984) *The Constitution of Society*, Cambridge: Polity Press.

Giddens, A. (1990) *The Consequences of Modernity*, Stanford: Stanford University Press.

Giddens, A. (1991) *Modernity and Self-Identity: Self and Society in the Late Modern Age*, Stanford: Stanford University Press.

Giddens, A. (1992) *The Transformation of Intimacy: Sexuality, Love, and Eroticism in Modern Societies*, Stanford: Stanford University Press.

Giddens, A. (1994) *Beyond Left and Right: The Future of Radical Politics*, Cambridge: Polity Press.

Giddens, A. (1999a) *Runaway World: How Globalisation is Reshaping Our Lives*, London: Profile.

Giddens, A. (1999b) *The Third Way: The Renewal of Social Democracy*, Cambridge: Polity Press.

Giddens, A. (2006) *Europe in the Global Age*, Cambridge: Polity Press.

Giddens, A. (2008) 'This Time It's Personal,' *The Guardian* (UK).

Giddens, A. (2009) *The Politics of Climate Change*, Cambridge: Polity Press.

Goffman, E. (1952) 'On Cooling the Mark Out: Some Aspects of Adaptation to Failure,' *Psychiatry*, Vol. 15, No. 4, pp. 451–463.

Goffman, E. (1959) *The Presentation of Self in Everyday Life*, New York: Doubleday Anchor.

Goffman, E. (1963) *Stigma: Notes on the Management of Spoiled Identity*, New York: Simon and Schuster.

Goffman, E. (1967 [1955]) 'On Face-Work: An Analysis of the Ritual Elements of Social Interaction,' *Interaction Ritual: Essays in Face-to-face Behavior*, New York: Random House.

Goffman, E. (1983) 'The Interaction Order: American Sociological Association, 1982 Presidential Address,' *American Sociological Review*, Vol. 48, No. 1, pp. 1–17.

Gore, A. (2006) *The Planetary Emergency of Global Warming and What We Can Do About It*, Stroud: Bloomsbury Publishing.

Gouldner, A. W. (1976) *The Dialectic of Ideology and Technology: The Origins, Grammar of Future of Ideology*, New York: The Seabury Press.

Gouldner, A. W. (1979) *The Future of Intellectuals and the Rise of the New Class: a frame of reference, theses, conjectures, arguments, and an historical perspective on the role of intellectuals and intelligentsia in the Modern Era*, New York: Continuum.

Gross, N. (2005) 'The Detraditionalization of Intimacy Reconsidered,' *Sociological Theory*, Vol. 23, No. 3, pp. 286–311.

Gutmann, A. and Thompson, D. (2004) *Why Deliberative Democracy?*, Princeton (NJ): Princeton University Press.

Habermas, J. (1987 [1981]) *The Theory of Communicative Action, Vol. 1*, Boston: Beacon Press.

Habermas, J. (1987 [1981]) *The Theory of Communicative Action, Vol. 2*, Boston: Beacon Press.

Habermas, J. (1989 [1962]) *The Structural Transformation of the Public Sphere: An Inquiry into a Category of Bourgeois Society*, Cambridge (MA): MIT Press.

Habermas, J. (1989 [1981]) *The Theory of Communicative Action, Vol. II*, Boston: Beacon Press.

Habermas, J. (1995) 'Reconciliation through the Public Use of Reason: Remarks on John Rawls's Political Liberalism,' *Journal of Philosophy*, Vol. 92, No. 3, pp. 109–31.

Habermas, J. (1996) *Between Facts and Norms: Contributions to a Discourse Theory of Law and Democracy*, Cambridge: Polity Press.

Habermas, J. (2001a) *The Liberating Power of Symbols: Philosophical Essays*, Cambridge: Polity Press.

Habermas, J. (2001b) *Moral Consciousness and Communicative Action*, Cambridge (MA): MIT Press.

Habermas, J. (2001c) *The Postnational Constellation: Political Essays*, Cambridge: Polity Press.

Han, S. (2011) *Web 2.0*, Oxon, UK: Routledge.

Haraway, D. J. (1991) *Simians, Cyborgs and Women: The Reinvention of Nature*, London: Free Association Books.

Harker, R., Maher, C. and Wilkes, C. (1990) *Introduction to the Work of Pierre Bourdieu*, London: Macmillan.

Held, D. (1991) 'Democracy, the Nation-State and the Global System,' in Held, D. (editor) *Political Theory Today*, Cambridge: Polity Press.

Held, D. (2004) *Global Covenant: The Social Democratic Alternative to the Washington Consensus*, Cambridge: Polity Press.

Held, D. (2008) 'Global Challenges: Accountability and Effectiveness.' Open Democracy. Available online at www.opendemocracy.net/article/global_challenges_accountability_and_effectiveness

Held, D. and McGrew, A. (2002) *Globalization/Anti-Globalization*, Cambridge: Polity Press.

Held, D., McGrew, A., Goldblatt, D. and Perraton, J. (1999) *Global Transformations: Politics, Economics and Culture*, Cambridge: Polity Press.

Herman, E. and McChesney, R. (2004 [1997]) *The Global Media: The Missionaries of Global Capitalism*, London: Continuum.

Hirst, P. and Thompson, G. (1999) *Globalization in Question: The International Economy and the Possibilities of Governance*, Cambridge: Polity Press.

Hochschild, A. (2003) 'Love and Gold', in Hochschild, A. and Ehrenreich, B. (editors) *Global Woman: Nannies, Maids and Sex Workers in the New Economy*, New York: Metropolitan Books.

Hollway, W. and Jefferson, T. (1997) 'The Risk Society in an Age of Anxiety: Situating Fear and Crime,' *The British Journal of Sociology*, Vol. 48, No. 2, pp. 254–266.

Holton, R. J. (2008) *Global Networks*, New York: Palgrave Macmillan.

Honneth, A. (1995) *The Struggle for Recognition: The Moral Grammar of Social Conflicts*, Cambridge: Polity Press.

Honneth, A. (2007) *Disrespect: The Normative Foundations of Critical Theory*, Cambridge: Polity Press.

hooks, b. (1984) *Feminist Theory from Margin to Center*, Boston (MA): South End Press.

Horkheimer, M. and Adorno, T. (2002 [1944]) *Dialectic of Enlightenment: Philosophical Fragments*, Stanford: Stanford University Press.

Huntington, S. P. (1996) *The Clash of Civilizations and the Remaking of the World Order*, London: Simon and Schuster.

Irigaray, L. (1985) *This Sex Which Is Not One*, Ithaca (NY): Cornell University Press.

Irigaray, L. (1993) *An Ethics of Sexual Difference*, Ithaca (NY): Cornell University Press.

Irigaray, L. (2000) *To Be Two*, London: Athlone.

James, W. (1907) *Pragmatism: A New Name for Some Old Ways of Thinking*, Oxford: Longmans.

James, W. (1981 [1890]) *Principles of Psychology*, Cambridge (MA): Harvard University Press.

James, W. (1982 [1902]) *Varieties of Religious Experience*, New York: Penguin Books.

James, W. (2000 [1907]) *Pragmatism: A New Name for Some Old Ways of Thinking*, New York: Penguin Books.

Jameson, F. (1981) *The Political Unconscious: Narrative as a Socially Symbolic Act*, London: Methuen.

Jameson, F. (1991) *Postmodernism: or, The Cultural Logic of Late Capitalism*, Durham (NC): Duke University Press.

Jay, M. (1984) *Marxism and Totality: The Adventures of a Concept from Lukacs to Habermas*, Cambridge: Polity Press.

Jay, M. (1996) *The Dialectical Imagination: A History of the Frankfurt School 1923–1950*, Berkeley: University of California Press.

Kellner, D. (1989) *Critical Theory, Marxism and Modernity*, Cambridge: Polity Press.

Kellner, D. (2003) *From 9/11 to Terror War: The Dangers of the Bush Legacy*, New York: Rowman & Littlefield Publishers.

Kristeva, J. (1980) *Desire in Language: A Semiotic Approach to Literature and Art*, New York: Columbia University Press.

Kristeva, J. (1982) *Powers of Horror: An Essay on Abjection*, New York: Columbia University Press.

Kristeva, J. (1984 [1974]) *Revolution in Poetic Language*, New York: Columbia University Press.

Kristeva, J. (1987) *Tales of Love*, New York: Columbia University Press.

Kristeva, J. (1989) *Black Sun: Depression and Melancholia*, New York: Columbia University Press.

Kristeva, J. (1991) *Strangers to Ourselves*, New York: Columbia University Press.

Kristeva, J. (1996) 'A Conversation with Julia Kristeva,' in Guberman, R. M. (editor) *Interviews*. New York: Columbia University Press.

Kuhn, T. S. (1962) *The Structure of Scientific Revolutions* Chicago: University of Chicago Press.

Lacan, J. (1977 [1949]) 'The Mirror Stage as Formative of the Function of the I', in Miller, J.-A. (editor) *Ecrits: A Selection*, London: Tavistock Press.

Lacan, J. (1977 [1953]) 'The Field and Function of Speech and Language in Psycho-analysis,' in Miller, J.-A. (editor) *Ecrits: A Selection*, London: Tavistock Press.

Lacan, J. (1977 [1957]) 'The Agency of the Letter in the Unconscious or Reason since Freud,' in Miller, J.-A. (editor) *Ecrits: A Selection*, London: Tavistock Press.

Lacan, J. (1979) *The Four Fundamental Concepts of Psychoanalysis*, Harmondsworth: Penguin.

Lacan, J. (1988) *The Seminar of Jacques Lacan, Vol. 1: Freud's Paper on Technique 1953–54*, Cambridge: Cambridge University Press.

Lacan, J. (1992) *The Ethics of Psychoanalysis 1959–60: The Seminar of Jacques Lacan*, London: Routledge.

Lacan, J. (1998a) *The Seminar of Jacques Lacan, Vol. 2: The Ego in Freud's Theory and in the Technique of Psychoanalysis 1954–5*, Cambridge: Cambridge University Press.

Lacan, J. (1998b) *The Seminar, Book XX: Encore, On Feminine Sexuality, The Limits of Love and Knowledge*, London: Tavistock Press.

Lash, S. and Urry, J. (1994) *Economies of Signs and Space*, London: Sage Publishing.

Leach, E. (1970) *Claude Lévi-Strauss*, London: Fontana.

Lemert, C. (1995) *Sociology after the Crisis*, Boulder (CO): Westview Press.

Lemert, C. (2005) *Social Things: An Introduction to the Sociological Life*, 3rd edition, Lanham (MD): Rowman & Littlefield Publishers.

Lemert, C. (2007) *Thinking the Unthinkable: The Riddles of Classical Social Theories*, Boulder (CO): Paradigm Publishers.

Lévi-Strauss, C. (1969) *The Elementary Structures of Kinship*, Boston: Beacon Press.

Lévi-Strauss, C. (1970 [1964]) *The Raw and The Cooked: Introduction to a Science of Mythology*, London: J. Cape.

Lyotard, J. F. O. (1984 [1979]) *The Postmodern Condition: A Report on Knowledge*, Minneapolis: University of Minnesota Press.

Lyotard, J. F. O. (1993 [1974]) *Libidinal Economy*, Bloomington: Indiana University Press.

Mandel, E. (1975) *Late Capitalism*, London: Humanities Press.

Marcuse, H. (1955 [1941]) *Reason and Revolution*, London: Routledge.

Marcuse, H. (1956) *Eros and Civilization*, New York: Vintage Books.

Marcuse, H. (1964) *One-Dimensional Man*, Boston (MA): Beacon Press.

Martin, J. L. (2011) *The Explanation of Social Action*, New York: Oxford University Press.

Marx, K. (1911) *A Contribution to the Critique of Political Economy*, Chicago: Charles H. Kerr & Co.

Marx, K. and Engels, F. (2008) *The Manifesto of the Communist Party*, London: Pluto Press.

McRobbie, A. (2005) *The Uses of Cultural Studies: A Textbook*, London: Sage.

Mead, G. H. (1903) 'The Definition of the Psychical,' *The Decennial Publications of the University of Chicago Vol. III*, Chicago: University of Chicago Press.

Mead, G. H. (1934) *Mind, Self and Society*, Chicago: University of Chicago Press.

Menand, L. (2001) *The Metaphysical Club*, New York: Farrar, Strauss and Giroux.

Merton, R. K. (1938) 'Social Structure and Anomie,' *American Sociological Review*, Vol. 3, No. 5, pp. 672–682.

Merton, R. K. (1957) *Social Theory and Social Structure*, New York: Free Press.

Merton, R. K. (1970) *Science, Technology and Society in Seventeenth Century England*, New York: H. Fertig.

Mills, C. W. (1956) *The Power Elite*, New York: Oxford University Press.

Mills, C. W. (1959) *The Sociological Imagination*, Oxford: Oxford University Press.

Mills, C. W. (2008 [1960]) 'Letter to the New Left,' in Summers, J. H. (editor) *The Politics of Truth: Selected Writings of C. Wright Mills*, Oxford: Oxford University Press.

Mitchell, J. (1974) *Psychoanalysis and Feminism*, London: Penguin Books.

Mitchell, J. (1984) *Women: The Longest Revolution*, New York Pantheon Books.

Mitchell, J. (2001) *Mad Men and Medusas*, New York: Basic Books.

Mouzelis, N. (1989) 'Restructuring Structuration Theory,' *Sociological Review*, Vol. 37, pp. 613–35.

Nancy, J.-L. (1997) *The Sense of the World*, Minneapolis (MN): University of Minnesota Press.

Nancy, J.-L. (2008) *Corpus*, London: Continuum.

Oakley, A. (1972) *Sex, Gender and Society*, Melbourne: Sun Books.

Ohmae, K. (1990) *The Borderless World: Power and Strategy in the Interlinked Economy*, New York: Harper Business.

Ohmae, K. (1995) *The End of the Nation State: The Rise of Regional Economies*, New York: Free Press.

Packard, V. (1959) *The Status Seekers: An Exploration of Class Behavior in America and the Hidden Barriers that Affect You, Your Community, Your Future*, Philadelphia, PA: David McKay.

Paolini, A. (1999) *Navigating Modernity: Postcolonialism, Identity, and International Relations*, Boulder (CO): L. Rienner Publishers.

Parsons, T. (1937) *The Structure of Social Action*, New York: The McGraw-Hill Book Company.

Parsons, T. (1951) *The Social System*, London: Routledge and Kegan Paul Ltd.

Parsons, T. (1971) *The System of Modern Societies*, Englewood Cliffs (NJ): Prentice-Hall.

Parsons, T. and Shils, E. (editors) (1951) *Toward a General Theory of Action*, Cambridge (MA): Harvard University Press.

Parsons, T., Shils, E., Naegele, K. D. and Pitts, J. (editors) (1961) *Theories of Society: Foundations of Modern Sociological Theory*, New York, Free Press of Glencoe.

Paterson, M. (2006) *Consumption and Everyday Life*, New York: Routledge.

Peirce, C. S. (1878a) 'The Fixation of Beliefs', Vol. 12, pp. 1–15.

Peirce, C. S. (1878b) 'How To Make Our Ideas Clear,' *Popular Science*, Vol. Jan 1878, pp. 286–302.

Peirce, C. S. (1892) 'Man's Glassy Essence,' *The Monist*, Vol. 3, No. 1, pp. 1–22.

Peirce, C. S. (1960a) *Collected Papers of Charles Sanders Peirce Vol II: Elements of Logic*, Cambridge (MA): The Belknap Press of Harvard University Press.

Peirce, C. S. (1960b) *Collected Papers of Charles Sanders Peirce Vol V: Pragmatism and Pragmaticism*, Cambridge, (MA): The Belknap Press of Harvard University Press.

Putnam, R. (2000) *Bowling Alone: The Collapse and Revival of American Community*, New York: Simon & Schuster.

Ragland-Sullivan, E. (1986) *Jacques Lacan and the Philosophy of Psychoanalysis*, Urbana (IL): University of Illinois Press.

Ray, L. (2007) 'Bauman's Irony,' in Elliott, A. (editor) *The Contemporary Bauman*, London: Routledge.

Reich, W. (1972 [1933]) *Character Analysis*, New York: Farrar, Straus and Giroux.

Richardson, R. D. (1995) *Emerson: The Mind on Fire*, Berkeley (CA): University of California Press.

Ricoeur, P. (1970) *Freud and Philosophy: An Essay on Interpretation*, New Haven: Yale University Press.

Riesman, D. (1961) *The Lonely Crowd: A Study of the Changing American Character*, New Haven: Yale University Press.

Rischard, J.-F. (2002) *High Noon: Twenty Global Problems, Twenty Years to Solve Them*, New York: Basic Books.

Ritzer, G. (1993) *The McDonaldization of Society: An Investigation into the Changing Character of Contemporary Social Life*, Thousand Oaks: Pine Forge Press.

Rorty, R. (1989) *Contingency, Irony and Solidarity*, Cambridge: Cambridge University Press.

Rose, N. S. (1996) *Inventing Our Selves: Psychology, Power, and Personhood*, Cambridge: Cambridge University Press.

Rose, N. S. (1999a) *Powers of Freedom*, Cambridge: Cambridge University Press.

Rose, N. S. (1999b) *Governing the Soul: The Shaping of the Private Self*, 2nd edition, London: Free Association Books.

Rylance, R. (1994) *Roland Barthes*, New York: Harvester Wheatsheaf.

Saussure, F. D. (1974 [1916]) *Course in General Linguistics*, London: Fontana.

Sayers, J. (2007) 'Liquid Love: Psychoanalysing Mania,' in Elliott, A. (editor) *The Contemporary Bauman*, London: Routledge.

Sedgwick, E. K. (1985) *Between Men: English Literature and Male Homosocial Desire*, New York: Columbia University Press.

Sedgwick, E. K. (1990) *The Epistemology of the Closet*, Berkeley: University of California Press.

Sedgwick, E. K. (1993) *Tendencies*, Durham (NC): Duke University Press.

Segal, L. (1987) *Is the Future Female? Troubled Thoughts on Contemporary Feminism*, London: Virago.

Segal, L. (1999) *Why Feminism?*, New York: Columbia University Press.

Sennett, R. (1998) *The Corrosion of Character: the Personal Consequences of Work in the New Capitalism*, New York: Norton.

Sennett, R. (2006) *The Culture of the New Capitalism*, New Haven (CT): Yale University Press.

Skocpol, T. (1979) *States and Social Revolutions: A Comparative Analysis of France, Russia and China*, Cambridge: Cambridge University Press.

Smart, C. and Shipman, B. (2004) 'Visions in monochrome: families, marriage and the individualization thesis,' *British Journal of Sociology*, Vol. 55, No. 4, pp. 491–509.

Smith, D. (2006) *Globalization: The Hidden Agenda*, Cambridge: Polity Press.

Smith, D. E. (1987) *The Everyday World As Problematic: A Feminist Sociology*, Boston (MA): Northeastern University Press.

Smith, D. E. (1990a) *The Conceptual Practices of Power: A Feminist Sociology of Knowledge*, Boston, MA: Northeastern University Press.

Smith, D. E. (1990b) *Texts, Facts, and Femininity: Exploring the Relations of Ruling*, London: Routledge.

Thompson, E. P. (1978) *The Poverty of Theory and Other Essays*, London: Merlin Press.

Thompson, J. B. (1984) *Studies in the Theory of Ideology*, Cambridge: Polity Press.

Thompson, J. B. (1989) *Social Theory of Modern Societies: Anthony Giddens and His Critics*, Cambridge: Cambridge University Press.

Thompson, J. B. (1995) *The Media and Modernity: A Social Theory of the Media*, Cambridge: Polity Press.

Tilly, C. (1978) *From Mobilization to Revolution*, Boston (MA): Addison-Wesley Publishing.

Tomlinson, J. (1991) *Cultural Imperialism: A Critical Introduction*, London: Pinter.

Turner, B. S. (1982) 'The Government of the Body: Medical Regimes and the Rationalization of Diet', *British Journal of Sociology*, Vol. 33, pp. 254–69.

Turner, B. S. (1984) *The Body and Society: Explorations in Social Theory*, Oxford: B. Blackwell.

Turner, B. S. (1992) *Regulating Bodies: Essays in Medical Sociology*, London: Routledge.

Turner, B. S. (1994) *Orientalism, Postmodernism and Globalism*, London: Routledge.

Urry, J. (2003) *Global Complexity*, Cambridge: Polity Press.

Urry, J. (2007) *Mobilities*, Cambridge: Polity Press.

Wallerstein, I. (2004) *World-Systems Analysis: An Introduction*, Durham (NC): Duke University Press.

Wallerstein, I. (2011 [1974]) *The Modern World-System I: Capitalist Agriculture and the Origins of the European World-Economy in the World-System*, Berkeley (CA): University of California Press.

Weber, M. (1978) *Economy and Society; An Outline of Interpretive Sociology*, Berkeley (CA): University of California Press.

Weeks, J. (1977) *Coming Out: Homosexual Politics in Britain from the Nineteenth Century to the Present*, London: Quartet Books.

Weeks, J. (1995) *Invented Moralities: Sexual Values in an Age of Uncertainty*, Cambridge: Polity Press.

Westergaard, J. (1995) *Who Gets What?*, Cambridge: Polity Press.

White, H. (1992) *Identity and Control: A Structural Theory of Social Action*, Princeton (NJ): Princeton University Press.

Whyte, W. H. (1956) *The Organizational Man*, New York: Simon and Schuster.

Wiggerhaus, R. (1994) *The Frankfurt School: Its History, Theories, and Political Significance*, Cambridge (MA): MIT Press.

Wilson, S. (1955) *The Man in the Grey Flannel Suit*, New York: Simon and Schuster.

Winnicott, D. W. (1976 [1960]) 'Ego Distortion in Terms of True and False Self,' *The Maturational Process and the Facilitating Environment: Studies in the Theory of Emotional Development*, London: Hogarth and the Institute of Psycho-analysis.

Žižek, S. (1989) *The Sublime Object of Ideology*, London: Verso.

Index

men: as fathers 53, 295, 297, 298,
    299, 300, 301, 308; as sons 295,
    296, 298, 299, 301
Menand, Louis 82
Mermaid and the Minotaur, The
    (Dinnerstein) 293–4
Merton, Robert K. 140–4, 149, 151,
    187, 240, 244, 366, 375
metanarratives 335, 336
Metaphysical Club 70
middle class 237
middle range theory 141
militarization 25
Mills, C. Wright 234–9, 243, 244, 251,
    366
mimicry 177
Mind, Self and Society (Mead)
    85–8
miniaturized mobilities 419
Minima Moralia (Adorno) 46, 54
mirror stage 158–9
mirroring 158
misrecognition 159, 163, 168
Mitchell, Juliet 285, 289–92, 324
Mobile Lives (Elliott and Urry)
    417–20
mobilities 417–20
modernity 20–1, 263; and
    Giddens 213–18; heavy 354–5;
    light 355; and Lyotard 335;
    and postmodernity 351–2,
    358, 359, 360, 361; 'reflexive
    modernization' 7; and tragedy 33
Modernity and the Holocaust
    (Bauman) 349
Modernity and Self-Identity
    (Giddens) 213
Montgomery, Alabama 368, 369, 370
moral bonds 27–8, 29, 31, 32
moral panics 35
morphogenesis 430
Morrison, Toni 177
motherhood: and Chodorow 294–9,
    324; and Dinnerstein 293–4; and
    Irigaray 311–12; and Kristeva
    306–8, 309
Mouzelis, Nicos 218
multiculturalism 177, 279
multinational capitalism 344–5, 402
multinational corporations 280, 355,
    386, 387, 388, 389, 395, 408, 410,
    412, 416, *see also* transnational
    corporations
Mythologies (Barthes) 110–12, 113
myths 43–4, 112–13, 131

NAACP 369
name-of-the-father 161, 291, 308,
    324
naming 174
Nancy, Jean-Luc 429, 431
narcissism 48, 49, 158, 162, 163, 164,
    167, 168, 170, 179
nation-states 3–4; and globalization
    269, 270, 386, 388–9, 391–2, 424,
    see also states
nature, and culture 107, 108
Nazism 42, 43, 44, 54, 256
neo-liberalism 228
Netherlands 379
networks 7; and globalization
    390, 392–9, 418, 420, 421; and
    terrorism 399–401, 427
Neuwirth, Robert 3
New Class 241–2, 243, 244
'new economy' 408–11
*New Individualism, The: The
    Emotional Costs of Globalization*
    (Elliott and Lemert) 414–17
new left movement 236
New Philosophy of Society (DeLanda)
    429
nodes 394–5
nom-de-pére (name-of-the-father)
    161, 291, 308, 324
non-governmental organizations
    (NGOs) 391

Oakley, Ann 286–7
object, the 78–9
Oedipus complex 52–3, 59, 161,
    175, 290–1, 295, 298, 300–1, 305,
    307–8, 311–12, 331, 332
Ohmae, Kenichi 8, 388–9
'On Face-work: An Analysis of Ritual
    Elements in Social Interaction'
    (Goffman) 192–3, 202
One-Dimensional Man (Marcuse) 60,
    63
one-dimensional society 42, 60–1,
    62, 65
online shopping 41, 42

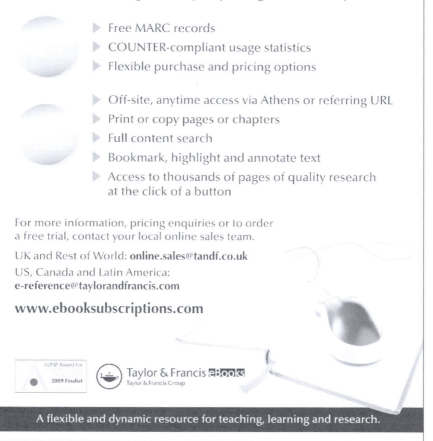